The Development of
Anthropological Ideas

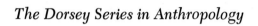
The Dorsey Series in Anthropology

The Development of Anthropological Ideas

JOHN J. HONIGMANN
The University of North Carolina
at Chapel Hill

 1976

THE DORSEY PRESS Homewood, Illinois 60430
Irwin-Dorsey International Arundel, Sussex BN18 9AB
Irwin-Dorsey Limited Georgetown, Ontario L7G 4B3

First Printing, April 1976

ISBN 0-256-01803-0
Library of Congress Catalog Card No. 75–35107

Printed in the United States of America

Preface

In this book ANTHROPOLOGY means cultural anthropology; more specifically, ideas pertinent to ethnology, social anthropology, and the theoretical foundations of archeology. Not all such ideas, however. Within cultural anthropology I have made further selections. I concentrate on fairly general ideas about human society and culture, giving only an occasional look at ideas about specific societies. Research methods are little noticed, although the reader's attention is drawn to underlying assumptions and theoretical issues connected with certain methods. Emphasis is put on naturalistic ideas; supernaturalistic explanations of social phenomena receive no serious consideration. I have, however, included concepts that bear on the proper development of human nature or the good life and that call attention to desirable and undesirable cultural arrangements.

Ideas have been included when they resemble concepts appearing in recent anthropology. Relying on this criterion of relevance, I suppose, makes me guilty of the Whig Interpretation of history. Although I remain aware of differences in the context and purposes with which each age approached the study of society and culture, generally I minimize historical context. My aim has not been to write a history of anthropological thought but to reinterpret past ideas in order to bring out instances where they are continuous with recent concepts. Judging past ideas by their resemblance to more recent concepts is worthwhile because it exposes the long roots—going back perhaps to early folk beliefs—of a number of anthropology's best known notions, such as the progressive development of culture. Once we realize the constant recurrence of certain concepts or sudden recurrence after an interval, we can ask why they recur. Historical research may succeed in discovering the route whereby, say, Aristotle's ideas about social reciprocity reached Marcel Mauss, or may indicate the recurrences to be independent of one another. Little historical research has been done on anthropological ideas; hence I cannot as often as I would like trace concepts directly from later to earlier writers. The Appendix, titled "Further Readings," provides for each chapter a comprehensive bibliography of works dealing with the development of anthropological topics during the period to which the chapter is devoted.

Generally the following pages subordinate individuals to ideas, though in the case of important figures in anthropological history, footnotes guide the reader to biographical sources. Birth and death dates will be found in the name index.

Readers may find the book too uncritical, especially with respect to recent theory about which a considerable degree of dissensus reigns. The only defense I can offer—apart from pointing out that occasionally critical appraisals are made—is to say that my eclectic outlook and philosophy of science allow me to see value in many diverse points of view.

Two dates of publication are cited in footnotes when a work originally appeared more than ten years before the edition or printing being referred to. An exception to this rule occurs in the case of works originally issued prior to the beginning of printing.

Without the benefit of J. S. Slotkin's *Readings in Early Anthropology*, published in 1965, I doubt if I would ever have been moved to start this book. Slotkin was an influential teacher, though personally I knew him only slightly. I have taken advantage of a number of suggestions made by Ward Goodenough and Victor Barnouw when, as publisher's readers, they read the manuscript of my book. I acknowledge, too, the invaluable, manifold assistance I have received from Irma Honigmann in preparing the book; the skillful typing, mostly by Dorothy Yarbrough; research assistance from Alan McGinigle and Jon Anderson; and the patience of the publisher who waited nine years for the manuscript.

March 1976   JOHN J. HONIGMANN

Contents

Anthropology: *Complete Objectivity Impossible.* A Momentous Period: *Cultural Process.*

*Little Traditions. Advice for Technical Assistance. The Process Itself.
Kinship: Social Equalizers and Differentials. Kin Terms in Evolutionary
Perspective. Kinship Behavior.* Descent Groups and Kindreds: *Clarifying
Descent Groups.* Family and Marriage: *Conceptual Clarification. Phylo-
genetic Origins of the Incest Rule. Alliance through Women.* Magic,
Ritual, and Belief: *Instrumental and Expressive. Need Satisfier or Tran-
quilizer? Projections of Hostility, Hope, and Desire.* Critical Anthropology:
*Culture, Empirical and Nonempirical. A Nonobjective Science. Abetting
Imperialism.* New and Old Concepts: *Discovering Dynamics.*

1

Anthropological Ideas

The Continuity of Anthropological Thought

Ideas and Contexts

Anthropological thought began whenever it was that people first began to reflect about the nature of society and the customs they or their neighbors followed. Practically speaking, our ability to discover early evidence of such thought is confined to times or places where written records were kept and have survived. Within that limitation, in the Western world the earliest anthropological ideas come from ancient Greece. No doubt earlier or equally early beliefs about society and culture could also be recovered from ancient Egyptian, Mesopotamian,[1] Indian, and Chinese written sources, but in the following pages I will not venture east of the Aegean coast.

Before the latter half of the 19th century when anthropology became a discipline, ideas about human society and culture were put forward by historians, philosophers, theologians, essayists, antiquarians, and political economists. Their concepts are anthropological because they resemble or anticipate ideas that later came to interest ethnologists and social anthropologists. Though a number of such ideas have frequently recurred from classical antiquity to the present—for example, the function of incest rules in creating alliances, religion as a source of intellectual satisfaction in the face of otherwise inexplicable events, and the interdependence of culture

---

Notes to this chapter are on page 10.

and personality—the contexts in which those ideas occurred differ greatly from one period to another. The Greek philosophers studied society out of a concern with the conditions that make men virtuous or evil; the Fathers of the early Christian Church did so to show God's plan at work; and 16th- and 17th-century scholars, in a spirit of newly released curiosity and emboldened independent reason. What Thomas Aquinas has to say about kinship and incest rules is related to his primary purpose of justifying the Church's marriage laws, whereas Claude Lévi-Strauss and David Schneider regard those subjects, or problems they perceive in them, as significant wholly in their own right. Terminology also changed with time —more fully than the following pages acknowledge because my aim has been to reinterpret early ideas in terms of later interests, and for that purpose modern terms are quite apt.

Early ideas resemble later anthropological concepts when they treat society and customs naturalistically. That is, they eschew supernatural explanations; treat familiar customs with some degree of distanciation, at least enough to regard them with curiosity; look for nonobvious meaning in acts and beliefs; and describe the processes whereby society and culture arose, change, and persist. But because recent anthropologists have also dealt with cultural achievements evaluatively, continuity in anthropological thought is likewise manifested by earlier writers who critically appraised their own and other societies' social arrangements.[2] Recent anthropology has also felt the need to appraise epistemologically the character of its knowledge, but even that was anticipated; for example, by 18th-century writers who became aware of the fallacy of using living cultures to reconstruct culture history, and by Giambattista Vico's observation that people are inclined to judge exotic or distant things by what is familiar and close at hand.

Orienting Concepts and Theories

The anthropological ideas traced in this book are of two types: orienting concepts and theories. Orienting concepts, such as the pair I am now introducing, shape experience, guide perception and cognition, and discriminate between types of events. They specify the subjects of inquiry. Without orienting concepts there is little we can know and nothing we can study or reflect upon. As anthropology developed, its stock of orienting concepts increased, and individual concepts became more sharply defined, more discriminatory. Suitably defined, terms like "savagery," "magic," "religion," "convention," and "custom" refer to specific ideas that have for many centuries oriented observers to aspects of the world deemed worthy of attention. Other orienting ideas consist of very general theoretical propositions which state basic assumptions, such as that culture traits are distributed in space, that cultures develop through time, that some cultures are more primitive than others in their social structure and technology. Around these and other orienting ideas, anthropology drew its boundaries when it became a discipline.

Theories are compounded out of orienting concepts. A theory consists of one or more propositions—statements capable of being true or false—that state how things or events referred to by the orienting concepts are related to each other. Strictly speaking, theories refer only to propositions that explain how events are brought about, how they predictably occur, or can be produced. But anthropologists are accustomed to using a broader concept of theory and apply the word to certain other propositions as well, and even to the stock of orienting concepts with which the discipline is furnished.

Anthropological theories have been constructed about features of social life universally present in society and culture, present in only certain types of society and culture (or at certain levels of development), and present in particular societies that have been ethnographically studied. Theories also differ in comprehensiveness, in the generality with which they grasp events. At a high level of comprehensiveness, for instance, we have the postulate that diffusion has been the major process operating in culture history. Below that level are propositions of more restricted scope, each specifying a condition under which cultural traits are likely to diffuse from one culture into another.

At every level of comprehensiveness, the greater part of anthropological theory—whether presented in the pages of classical philosophy written over 2,000 years ago or in a recent issue of the *American Anthropologist*—offers dynamic, or synchronic, explanations of social and cultural phenomena; provides historical, or diachronic, explanations of them; or makes the phenomena more understandable by exploring their meaning or motivation. In other words, the greater part of anthropological theory consists of three kinds of propositions. First, explanatory propositions corresponding to the form "if this, then. . . ." Such statements specify the conditions that predictably give rise to particular cultural phenomena—for example, the family, division of labor, or deviant behavior—or trace their consequences (functions). Second, anthropological theory consists of general propositions tracing unique changes that have taken place in society and culture through time, outlining, for example, the transition from savagery to barbarism and barbarism to civil society or the development of color terminology. By the strict definition of theory, such historical propositions, regardless of their relative generality, would not be considered theoretical, because they do not specify conditions under which given consequences are predictably likely to occur. Third, we have propositions exposing the meaning or motives of social phenomena, including myths, sacrifice and other ritual acts, deities, and nonreligious symbols. Well-known research in cultural symbolism has been done by Sigmund Freud and other psychoanalysts, but they were not pioneers in this type of theory. Propositions of this third type also don't accord with the strict definition of theory.

These three major kinds of theoretical propositions do not exhaust anthropological theory. Another important class of theory, which has increased greatly since anthropology became a discipline, does not refer directly to society or its customs, but is about procedures followed in studying social and cultural phenomena. It consists of methodological and metatheoretical propositions defending the importance of studying something, justifying, for instance, why certain methods of investigation or viewpoints are preferable to others, or explaining how information about culture is acquired.

Viewpoints in Cultural Anthropology

Orienting concepts and theories are always applied from a perspective, or combination of several perspectives, which a writer chooses as desirable for his purpose. From time to time in the following pages I will refer to the fairly small number of viewpoints that recur from the period of ancient Greece to the present. At least some of these viewpoints can also be detected in the folk ethnologies of primitive and civilized societies whence, no doubt, they passed into the sources I will mention.

By a viewpoint in cultural anthropology I mean a vantage point, orientation, or perspective adopted for thinking about ethnological, social anthropological, or archeological phenomena. One popular viewpoint, the historical, looks at the processes whereby cultural elements originate, come to acquire their present distribution in space, and alter their forms, perhaps as a result of evolution or ecological adaptation. It conceives of culture as a product of the past, as the precipitate of historical events which it seeks to recover. Underlying the historical perspective is the theoretical, or metatheoretical, assumption that the past, even though it be beyond direct inspection, can be known from evidential traces—archeological, documentary, and others less direct—it has left and which can be studied in the present. The contents of a prehistoric site are the plainest and least inferential of such traces, although excavated artifacts require a considerable degree of inference when they are used to reconstruct behavior. More debatable are the ingenious means devised by preanthropologists and anthropologists for using simply the spatial distribution of culture traits to discover what happened in the past. Sometimes the investigators were trying to emulate the success with which philologists, lacking the benefit of written records, reconstructed the history of languages by reasoning back from the contemporarily spoken forms of those languages. The historical viewpoint is not limited to long stretches of time, but may be applied to short intervals, too; for example, in studying the recent acculturation of a society or the socialization of individuals.

Another viewpoint, the developmental, also works with time and frequently adopts the techniques of prehistory and history. It finds direction in the cultural record of the past and refers to historical processes, like diffusion, evolution, or acculturation, as factors governing the direction followed in the development of culture traits. Developmentalists have identified various directions in culture history. During the 18th century it was progress, defined as the improved quality of life and the growing hegemony of reason in the place of superstition. More recently, the direction has been greater cultural or social complexity, higher levels of sociocultural organization, or increased utilization of natural energy for work. Such trends are progressive, i.e., they move toward a goal, but ostensibly they do not imply that the goal is good or nets greater individual happiness. The end-state visualized by developmentalists has also been degressive, involving cultural degeneration or deculturation, though anthropologists have found no evidence for such goals in culture, generally, but only in particular societies which were struck by war, natural catastrophy, or acculturation.

The historical and developmental perspectives, often conjointly employed, have been the most consistently used standpoints for studying society and culture since ancient classical times. Often another orientation, the viewpoint I call integration, has been combined with them. The integational approach has as its premise that parts of culture are interrelated, either causally—in the relationship between forms of marriage and kinship terminology, for example—or noncausally. Parts of culture are noncausally related when they share a common quality, when they correlate in measurable characteristics, or when they exist in some kind of conceptual opposition, whether it be noted by the members of a society or only by an observer. The contradictions in a society which, according to the theory of historical materialism, dialectically promote change, refer to the integrated nature of culture at the same time that they describe a process whereby historical change occurs.

One more long-current orientation in cultural anthropology conceives of society and customs are having utilitarian value. The instrumental viewpoint is best known from Malinowski's very general theoretical proposition, which states culture to be a vast instrumental apparatus serving individual and social survival. However, instrumentalism was not created with the functionalism of Bronislaw Malinowski or the equally famous brand professed by his contemporary, A. R. Radcliffe-Brown. Long before them, other writers tracing the origin and early development of culture gave emphasis to the practical value of certain culture traits. Later, when Darwinian evolutionary theory was adopted by cultural anthropology it, too, incorporated a utilitarian outlook as it studied how traits adapted to the social or natural environment contribute to a group's survival and growth.

Unlike the frequently employed historical, developmental, integrational, and instrumental viewpoints, the configurational perspective, best known from the work of Ruth Benedict, is rarely encountered. Closely related to integration, configurationalism reaches beyond relationships linking specific parts of culture. It regards cultures or societies as total systems, oriented toward goals or, like personalities, possessing overall distinctive qualities that pervade all the parts. Studying cultures and social systems as wholes—the underlying assumption in configurationalism maintains—can produce information beyond anything that could be learned by concentrating on the component parts; for the whole is greater than the sum of the parts.

The last three orientations I will review have also been employed since the earliest period. They assume relationships between culture and the biological or psychological makeup of individuals, or between culture and the geographical environment.

The biological viewpoint—revealed, for example, in the idea, first advanced in Renaissance times, that the family is grounded in the physiological fact of the human child's helplessness—has, until the recent advent of ethology in cultural anthropology, never served as a major point of departure. The usual premises underlying biologism in cultural anthropology maintain that cultural forms, including social organization, are influenced by the construction and physiological functioning of the human organism. Sometimes the complementary position has been taken, the morphological condition of the individual or his physiological functioning, most notably illness, being seen as influenced by the cultural factors. As these positions indicate, the biological viewpoint deals with ideas lying in the boundary zone between cultural and physical, or biological, anthropology.

The psychological perspective has enjoyed much more popularity than the biological, especially since the 17th century, in the form of postulating motives, thought processes, emotional complexes, and other mentalistic dispositions by means of which cultural phenomena become understandable. In the 20th century a number of theories came into use, mostly under the influence of psychoanalysis, that perceives the sources of psychological traits to lie partly in cultural factors, often those associated with child-rearing. To close the circuit, the social inputs entering the individual's personality are then traced as they express themselves in culture traits or as they contribute instrumentally to the survival of the social system.

Theorists who adopt a geographical orientation assume a continuous interplay between social phenomena and features of the natural environment. Frequently attention has been given to geographical factors, especially climate, exerting an influence on society and culture, perhaps through the medium of the people's physiological condition. This position has had its ups and downs since it was vigorously set forth in the Hippocratic texts. Recent ecological ideas in cultural anthropology usually omit any implication of direct environmental determinism as they examine the cultural adaptations societies make with respect to resources and limitations in the environments they occupy.

Obviously the eight viewpoints are only analytically disinct. A writer's work, we will have many occasions to see, can easily accommodate several simultaneously and, in a given instance, it may be difficult to decide, without knowing the writer's intention, if a particular statement was written from one perspective or another.

Themes and Issues

In addition to viewpoints, I will call attention to a small number of persistent themes and issues, propositional in nature, around which anthropological thought has revolved and which have sometimes been vigorously debated. Not even the notion of man's basic unity—morphological, physiological, as well as motivational and cognitive, or psychic—has been free of controversy. The assumption was used consistently since ancient classical times but was departed from in the controversy over the nature of the American Indians, sparked in the Renaissance by the discovery of the New World; in overdone travelers' tales of human beings with tails; in allegations that some societies think prelogically; and in 19th-century racist theories about inferior brains or innate intellectual limitations affecting certain categories of mankind. Such controversies, however, gained little foothold in anthropology after it became a discipline.

Equally old is the theme of cultural relativity, the idea that every way of life is to some extent incommensurate with any other. Sometimes the idea has been heuristically held; for example, in the claim that another culture cannot be correctly understood unless it is approached in its own terms. The investigator entertaining this idea will adopt, as far as possible, the society's own meanings and standards of value. More general philosophical relativism asserts that there can be no universal standard for deciding between culturally different standards of the true, good, or beautiful; all designs for living are equally valid in the eyes of their followers, and beyond that anything is meaningless.

Every theme has its opposite. Irresoluble controversy ensues when the two positions are treated as if they were mutually incompatible, or contradictory, rather than complementary. Recent social science illustrates such intransigence in the issue over the primacy of the individual or the collectivity (society) for producing and changing culture. Those who stress the importance of the individual see little value in investigating collective processes, except as epiphenomena, although of course the individual is always part of a society. Those who stress the collectivity dismiss the opposite point of view as unproductive reductionism, despite the fact that social phenomena are ultimately derived from individuals.

Another theme asserts the power of society and culture in patterning individual behavior in its intellectual, emotional, and motor aspects. In contrast, nativism assumes certain potentialities for behavior to be innate; looks to inherent drives and instincts as the source of institutions; or, in the modern form of nativism represented by the cultural ethologists, assumes behavioral proclivities—including a proclivity for culture itself—to have been built into the human species through evolution.

No serious disagreement has broken out around the distinction between nature and culture, which has been recognized since classical times and, according to Lévi-Strauss, is universally present in the folk ethnology of primitive societies. However, not everyone has drawn an equally sharp distinction between the two realms. Even writers unattracted by theories of instincts or other innate bases for social behavior have accounted for culture by naturally provided human needs or by culture-building resources present in the natural environment. Methodologists who favor studying society and culture with procedures paralleling as much as possible those followed in the natural sciences by implication minimize the distinction between nature and culture, whereas those opting for special methods suited to cultural phenomena tend to emphasize it.

Cumulative and Additive Development

Although in the title of this book I speak of ideas developing, the development I describe is more often additive or substitutive than cumulative. In cumulative development, one generation validates and otherwise improves the viable discoveries of its predecessors. Orienting concepts become more precise, boundaries between phenomena are more sharply demarcated, and phenomena with different antecedents or consequences are conceptually distinguished. Careful observation, reasoning, and experimentation are resorted to in order to select between theoretical propositions.

Some cumulative development has taken place in anthropology, most conspicuously in the theory of kinship terminology introduced by Lewis Henry Morgan a hundred years ago. Other topics, though pursued much longer, have not seen equal refinement of orienting concepts or validation of theory.

Instead of being cumulative, the development of anthropology has been largely additive and substitutive. Loosely articulated orienting concepts and propositions, even contradictory theories, have accumulated, persisting alongside each other with little attempt being made to devise empirical procedures for choosing between them. Additive development also is conspicuous in the increased number of topics and interests launched for investigation, and in the variety of methods proposed for studying the topics. At times, in the case of national character research, for example, concepts were abandoned in response to unfavorable logical criticism, with hardly any attempt being made to cumulatively develop theory and methods by meeting the critics' valid objections.

Summary

Since ancient classical times Western philosophers, historians, theologians, explorers, and other preanthropologists have coined ideas about society and culture that resemble ideas later put forward when anthropology became a discipline. Anthropological ideas include orienting concepts specifying the subjects into which the field inquires, as well as synchronic or diachronic theoretical propositions that state the sources or conditions controlling social phenomena, trace changes in society and culture, elucidate the meaning and motivations of culture, or are concerned with the character of the method followed in inquiry.

Eight pervasive analytical perspectives have been taken through the centuries in studying society and culture: the historical viewpoint perceives events in time and studies the present as a product of the past; the developmental looks for direction in the way cultural phenomena have changed through time; and a third viewpoint, routinely conjoined with the other two, assumes causal and noncausal relationships to exist between cultural phenomena. The instrumental perspective, also frequently combined with a historical or developmental outlook, directs its attention to the utilitarian value of cultural traits or social institutions. Compared to these four orientations, the configurational viewpoint has been only rarely employed. It goes beyond searching for relationships between discrete parts of culture, instead studying cultures and societies as total systems, greater than the sums of their parts. Ideas embodying the remaining three viewpoints—the biological, psychological, and geographical—associate data belonging to the realm of society or culture with features of individuals or the natural environment.

In addition to adopting these viewpoints, anthropological thought has also persistently revolved around a few general themes or issues, including psychic unity, cultural relativity, cultural patterning, the importance of invention and diffusion, and the distinction between nature and culture.

The development of anthropological ideas has more typically been additive than cumulative. Loosely articulated concepts and theories have accumulated in the discipline, with little attention being given to devising empirical means for choosing between theories. The result has been an increase of diverse ideas, topics, interests, and methods, which often bear no relationship to one another except that they pertain to society and culture.

Notes

1. Sumerians, for example, apparently conceived of human society as evolving in stages, from hunting to pastoralism to grain agriculture. See Henry F. Lutz, "The Sumerian and Anthropology," *American Anthropologist*, vol. 29 (1927): 202–209.

2. In its humanistic concerns, anthropology overlaps with philosophical anthropology; for the latter, see Georges Paul Gusdorf, "Anthropology, Philosophical," in *Encyclopaedia Britannica* (1974), *Macropaedia*, vol. 1.

2
Greek and Roman Writers

Greek Anthropological Thought

Prosperous, Intellectually Fertile, and Conservative

The story of anthropological ideas in the Western world begins in the generally prosperous, intellectually fertile, and far from peaceful civilization of the Greek mainland, the islands of the Aegean Sea, and the coastal strip of Asia Minor. Here the rational tradition to which early Christian, medieval, and Renaissance philosophers owe the bases of their thinking had developed, mostly the by the third century before the Christian Era, and doubtlessly on foundations the Greeks owed to other civilizations further east in Egypt, the Near East, and India.

The earliest decipherable documentary knowledge about ancient Greek interests—useless for our purpose because they reveal no inkling of generalized ideas about the course and nature of social life—resides in terse administrative memoranda recovered from the second millennium ruins of Mycenae. Classical Greek literature, comparatively far richer in anthropological ideas, for our purpose ends with the informative multiple volume works written by Strabo and Plutarch during the time of the Roman Empire in the first two centuries of our era. The Greek Dark Ages, following the collapse of Mycenae and extending from 1100 to 800 B.C., are impenetrable to inquirers after ideas. So, largely, is the succeeding period of political instability, when power in the city-states passed from kings to

---

Notes to this chapter begin on page 39.

ambitious nobles and then to tyrants, although to this time belong the epics of Homer and Hesiod. The latter's eighth-century lament about the social disintegration of his world, we will see, contains a poetic vision of human history having progressed morally downward. Only in the fifth century does the intellectual and artistic activity we inevitably associate with classical Greece burst out, accompanying the Persian invasion and the destructive 27-year-long Peloponnesian War between Athens and Sparta for the domination of Greece. Around the time of the Peloponnesian War (431–404 B.C.), Aristophanes and Euripides composed their poetic dramas; Herodotus and Thucydides, their histories; Plato, the dialogues incorporating what he had learned from Socrates; and in the next century, Aristotle wrote his treatises on ethics, politics, psychology, and other subjects. In scouring the fragmentary writings of the very early pre-Socratic philosophers and the surviving historical and philosophical works of later times, anthropological ideas of the kind we seek show up delightfully unexpectedly as whole, well-formed shells among the fragments on a beach.

Until the Macedonian conqueror Philip unified Greece in the fourth century, the country was politically divided into independent city-states, each dominating a small area beyond the city walls. Yet the Greeks felt united in possessing a common ethnicity, language, and culture, including a single religion with a pantheon of male and female deities ruled by Zeus. Though different gods were honored in various cities, famous shrines and oracles connected with them attracted believers from afar. The cities maintained a high degree of specialization: in Athens there were merchants, wholesale and retail, specializing in different products; persons engaged in transportation; customs officials; bankers; many specialized manufacturers, including toy makers; and persons engaged in serving others, including cooks, barbers, physicians, and entertainers. Labor, however, the Greeks considered somewhat degrading; they left it as much as possible to slaves, many of whom were imported from the outer world of Asia. Beyond Greece lived barbarians, people following a brutish and backward way of life but not necessarily with a simple culture, for the militarily accomplished Persians ruling a great empire were barbarians in the estimation of the Greeks. Athenians attending the theatre heard about barbarians who lacked any education, law, or restraint, compared to whom the worst-reared Greek was a paragon of virtue.[1]

Reading Greek social personality from fifth-century literary sources reveals an ethnocentric people who, for all the intellectual activity of the philosophers, tended to be conservative in their attitude to tradition, especially in the fields of law and religion. The Greeks valued individual autonomy (except for slaves) as well as personal honor and fame. They possessed a pronounced streak of competitiveness. The upper classes in tolerating male homosexuality carried male bonding to its fullest expression, though the society never accepted physical intimacy between males as wholly proper. Earthly life counted higher than the next for the Greeks, so they tended to justify the necessity of morality on rational grounds, rather than by warnings of supernatural punishment. They were an intellectually curious people about the principles of conduct as much as about the structure of nature and the conditions of the social order, and in the fruits of their curiosity we find their contribution to anthropology.

Society as a System

Although the discipline of history—by which I mean perceiving human events in chronological order and in naturalistic terms, without much reference to gods or mythological heroes—began with the Greeks, the historical perspective does not predominate in their anthropological thought. Greek thinking about society and culture is not as engrossed with the past or with problems of social development in bygone centuries as was anthropological thought in the 18th and 19th centuries. Diachronic concerns, of course, turn up in what the Greeks wrote, but in keeping with their own predominant interest I will postpone those concerns and begin my account with the observations the philosophers, starting in pre-Socratic times, made about the bases of social order.

As early as the sixth century B.C., Pythagoras and his followers recognized the ordered nature of society.[2] Pythagoras, a refugee from the Ionian coast, the region on the fringe of Asia where physics originated, migrated to a Greek colony in southern Italy where he gathered a band of disciples. These men mixed in politics in ways that proved so unpopular that some were killed and Pythagoras had to flee. Nothing he himself wrote survives; we know what he taught only from writings dating to the fifth century left by his followers.

In their writings Pythagoreans describe the city, or as it is advisable to say, society, metaphorically, calling it a cosmos. They identify society as a system of diverse elements, meaning people, fitting together so harmoniously that the system is admirable to behold. Order in a social system does not occur automatically, as it would were all the elements of the system similar in nature and rank. Because the human elements are diverse they must be brought into harmony and maintained in orderly relationships to one another. These results are achieved through individual self-restraint as well as through social pressure exerted by individuals on each other. Harmony in the city is also maintained, Pythagoras is supposed to have said, through friendship and as a result of people holding possessions in common. Using words from later times, Pythagoreanism stressed the importance of division of labor, reciprocity, and complementary diversity in the things members of a society do or believe in producing social integration. The philosophy dwells on social integration more than on the integration of cultural ideas and activities, and hence is more social anthropological than ethnological, using the distinction advanced in the 1920s by A. R. Radcliffe-Brown. He and his students in Great Britain and elsewhere, studying how social systems persist, pursued an interest very similar to that of the Pythagoreans.

A fuller acknowledgment of the advantages accruing from division of labor appears in *The Republic,* written about a century after Pythagoras, where Plato interprets society as an instrumental organization for meeting human needs and insuring survival.[3] Plato was the son of a distinguished Athenian family. When he was 24 years old he experienced the defeat of his city in the Peloponnesian War, and five years later the shock of his revered teacher's forced death during the tyranny that followed the defeat. In *The Republic,* as well as in other dialogues, Socrates is the wise mouthpiece for Plato's ideas, some of which are Pythagorean in origin. We will fasten on one small part of the book, the point in the dialogue when Socrates obtains consent to digress from a discussion of justice to examine the basis of social organization. Here Plato explains social organization as springing from human needs. Social organization arises because individuals have many more needs than each can supply alone, and so need the help of others if they are to survive. They turn to one another, in this early version of contract theory, in order to meet their requirements, and thereby form groups and devote themselves to different specialized tasks. Some cultivate food, others rear the animals needed for plowing, while others manufacture housing, clothing, and other things. Each specialist parts with what he produces and in exchange receives necessary things made by others. Merchants and seamen contribute their services, thereby allowing locally unavailable goods to be imported. The present tense indicates Plato is thinking of ever-present dynamic sources maintaining social organization as an organized system founded on diversities. But a diachronic outlook takes over in his thinking when he also ascribes the ultimate origin of society to the organization of differences along technological lines.

Social diversity, as the Pythagoreans understood, includes more than the division of labor in technological and commercial activities to which Plato restricted himself. Plato distrusted diversity and tended to exaggerate the importance of consensus for the maintenance of social order.[4] Not so Aristotle, the son of a Macedonian court physician who had studied with Plato in Athens until the latter's death in 347 B.C. Aristotle frankly recognized that without considerable diversity society would be impossible, for society arises only because differences between people draw them into interaction with one another.[5] In *The Ethics,* a philosophical inquiry into the kinds of life desirable for people endowed with different qualities of virtue, he implicitly conceives of society as a system of social relations, or "friendships," for he uses the same word as the Pythagoreans. The differences which bring people into relationships must be complementary, or mutually desirable. A relationship will not spring up if what one party offers another diverges too greatly from what the other has been accustomed to, or something in which the second party sees no value. Aristotle illustrates with a simple example. In the political sphere a ruler by his intelligence is able to plan; slaves by virtue of their bodily strength are endowed to work; both are drawn into relationship with one another by common interests, of which Aristotle specifies only safety. So far Aristotle has been talking about differences related to reciprocity, about social relations rationally calculated for the benefits they promise to provide. Society, he recognizes, is also based on another kind of social tie, one based on the moral feeling each party has for the other, in which no thought intrudes of what will be gained or lost through continuing the relationship. This type of friendship he illustrates with the example of a parent's and child's feelings of mutual obligation. In the modern language deriving from Emile Durkheim, clear-cut reciprocities, best illustrated in the division of labor, create organic solidarity in society. What Durkheim calls mechanical solidarity, the bond resulting from a strong sense of attachment to the group and other sentiments held in common by members of the group, is not as clearly revealed in Aristotle's second type of friendship, but the parallel with Durkheim's concept seems reasonably close.

When Aristotle in his treatise on politics writes about the state, we can frequently read him as referring to society, conceived of now as an organized aggregate of people, rather than as a system of social relations.[6] He, too, describing the state as a pact or alliance contracted between its members for the sake of certain ends, resorts to contract theory in order to express the nature of social order. But he recoils from taking a purely utilitarian view of society. To regard organized social life only from an instrumental perspective, as existing entirely for the material benefits it provides to the contracting parties, fails to recognize society's moral responsibility for the development of its members. Furthermore, since individuals cannot exist without society, they cannot be considered as voluntarily bringing it into existence. Aristotle, of course, is not thinking of specific political orders which citizens can redesign to suit their wishes, but of society as a universal phenomenon constantly found together with mankind. His famous aphorism, man is a political animal, makes his meaning clear: human beings are by nature intended for society and achieve their humanity in organized association with other human beings. Society, achieved through culture, is not entirely a product of convention; like later anthropologists who saw human society to be continuous with, and therefore a development from, animal society, Aristotle perceives the social order to derive partly from nature and consequently to be in some degree necessary, rather than the outcome of choice.

Unlike Aristotle, Epicurus, who began to teach in 310 B.C., a decade after the former philosopher's death, could not seriously entertain the idea of society existing for a reason other than the gratifications it provides to its members.[7] A severe skeptic of other men's philosophies and a firm believer in the pleasure principle as the proper source of human behavior, Epicurus considered society to be a purely instrumental organization. The social order is designed to provide protection against fellow members of the society, to allay fear of external enemies, and to promote the enjoyment of life. The social order is entirely a matter of convention, and the laws through which order is maintained are rationally arrived at by agreement as being expedient in preventing one person from harming another and to prevent himself from being harmed. The question of whether a law is just or unjust depends on whether it serves any useful purpose in regulating social intercourse under given conditions. Even if laws serve such a purpose and therefore are just, if conditions change making the laws inexpedient, then they also cease to be just. The cultural relativism in Epicurus's theory of law is plain. His position with regard to the conventional nature of law is close to the popular contract theories of society advanced in the 17th century, and to the utilitarian doctrine of the next century calling for social arrangements that will promote the greatest good for the greatest number of people.

Law and Deviant Behavior

Theories of law, its nature and function, began before Epicurus. The harmony of the social cosmos, the Pythagoreans pointed out, does not occur automatically, and in the punitive sanctions imposed by law, Protagoras and Democritus in the fifth century, almost 200 years before Epicurus, perceived one of the ways in which order in society is maintained.

Protagoras, a Thracian from the land between the Aegean and the Black Sea, adopted a radical way of thinking about legal punishment. Traditionally, punitive sanctions had been regarded as retribution; Protagoras conceived them as a social force for deterring and correcting persons whose behavior gets out of line.[8] His contemporary, Democritus, also from Thrace, famous for his theory of atomism, saw law as a cultural means of checking selfish inclinations in people, thereby to insure that everyone enjoys a sense of security.[9] Both writers, via an instrumental understanding of law, approach the notion of socialization whereby culture shapes human nature to make it fit the demands of the social order. Democritus, to explain why legal norms sometime fail to restrain misconduct, offers a theory of deviant behavior with a surprisingly modern ring. Immoderate envy of those who are well off drives an individual continually to try new ways of improving his well-being, even ways of behavior forbidden by law. Private distress, according to Democritus, is easier to bear than general distress, in which the sufferers perceive no shred of hope of relief. He doesn't follow through, as sociologists studying deviant behavior have, or as anthropologists studying crisis cults have, reasoning that when a whole population is in the grip of misery its members will be especially prone to try new ways of enhancing their well-being, including sometimes deviant ones.

The conventional, or cultural, nature of law was indicated by Antiphon, another contemporary of Protagoras, whom the Athenians executed for treason during the last stages of the war with Sparta.[10] Antiphon draws attention to differences between natural and man-made laws. One cannot avoid the penalty of breaking a natural law, but someone who escapes detection in breaking a man-made law incurs no punishment. Furthermore, laws established through convention may flatly contradict natural laws—society forbidding what nature allows or requires. Plato has the legendary Callicles give an instance of society altering the natural state of affairs.[11] Conquerors have always acted on the natural principle, revealed as being natural from the way animals behave, that it is right for the strong to possess more than the weak and to rule over the weak. Society, however, through laws made by the majority, who are weak, harnesses the minority of strong men. Or society, through education, takes the strong while they are still children and enslaves them to laws that harness them unhappily. Regardless of whether Callicles is correct in his generalization concerning animal behavior, he unmistakably intimates the relativistic doctrine, which Michel de Montaigne and other Renaissance philosophers would delight in or see as perplexing problems, that society has the power to make anything right.

Socialization and Personality

The Greeks' theories of law, as I have pointed out, lead straight into the idea that socialization plays an important role in maintaining the social order. Nobody made the general observation more plainly than Protagoras, himself a renowned teacher. Education, he says, endows children with the values they are supposed to possess when they become adult members of society.[12] By various kinds of instruction, including training in music—which works on the soul to give self-control—parents, nurses, and teachers impart the instruction they perceive to be necessary for good conduct. When school is finished, the laws begin to play their inescapable educational role for sound citizenship.

The same basic conception of education fitting individuals for society appears in Plato's remarkable theory, written when he was about 60 years old, tracing relationships between early socialization, personality, and social structure.[13] It is remarkable not only because it anticipates much later work in psychological anthropology, but for the way it utilizes a simple paradigm to systematically explain how psychological factors govern the rise and decline of several types of political structures commonly recognized by the Greeks. Plato, however, has no intention of presenting a dispassionate comparison of political systems, but rather a justification of his own utopian vision of a society ruled by philosophers. Hence he defines the political types according to his own values.

Political systems, he aphorizes, do not grow out of stones but are products of men's (and he really does seem to mean males) minds and manners, which in turn are forged by social conditions, especially those present in childhood. In other words, the political organization of society grows out of social personality, and Plato shows that as types of personality in a society change by adopting new ambitions and shedding old ones, the political structure also becomes transformed. He starts with aristocracy, the ideal political system as he defines it, which depends on individuals dedicated to the virtues of moderation and respect for tradition. These are the basic values the aristocratic educational system implants. After aristocracy, all types of political structure represent pathological departures from the ideal.

Plato begins to show the causal influence of personality on social structure and the role of socialization in forming personality, when he explains how aristocracy degenerates into timocracy, by which he means a society founded on ambition. The seed out of which timocracy grows is implanted in aristocrats' sons who regularly hear their fathers belittled for showing too little drive and acquisitiveness. In fact, anyone given to moderation is scorned, and in an aristocracy that must include the vast majority. Sons learn values at variance from those of their fathers and become self-willed, avaricious, competitive, and ambitious for office.

As ambition hypertrophies and gaining wealth becomes a dominant motivation, the rich rise in social esteem and the political system changes from a timocracy to an oligarchy. Oligarchies are products of profit-oriented, miserly men who, although not wholly conscienceless, will take a chance at being dishonest if the possibility of escaping detection looks good. The personality bearing those traits is formed with the help of ambitious fathers whose whole being is fixed on earning money.

Oligarchy turns into democracy as the citizens increase their desire for indolence, pleasure, and luxury, rewards that money can buy; and the lack of restraint, developed in pursuing money, generalizes to produce a personality disinclined to practice restraint in anything. The democratic personality recognizes no distinction between necessary and unnecessary needs: both are equally compelling. It regards all pleasures as equal, the way all people are regarded equal in a democratic society. The democratic personality also values freedom highly and is rife with the desire to emulate. Men develop these qualities through growing up under ineffectual fathers who are unable to control their sons, leaving the youths open to the influence of peers.

In time, tyranny takes over in society as the love of liberty hypertrophies in the democratic personality type and the last restraints vanish. For security, people look to a strong leader, but he, as soon as he achieves office, puts down every sign of opposition and becomes a despot and plunders the rich. Tyrannies are products of a personality type in which the desire for gratification absolutely predominates. It is formed in the company of peers who condone complete license, as well as by other social influences that make it easy for a young man to behave lawlessly.

Plato offers no historical evidence to support the theory that hypertrophying appetites for wealth, luxury, and freedom transform one type of social structure into another. It is essentially a parable. No doubt it mattered little to him that he could not find a psychological explanation for the transformation of aristocracy into timocracy, but resorted to an ad hoc biological theory, inconsistent with his paradigm, claiming copulation at the wrong time produces ungifted children unsuited for an ideal state. One can understand the difficulty that drew him into nativistic thinking, for an aristocracy based on respect for tradition and controlled by wise leaders would hardly allow variant ambitions to develop. So he had to go outside of his theory for the factor capable of undermining an ideal society.

Plato constructed his parable of the transformation of political systems out of a deeply held belief, shared by many other classical writers, in a connection between what people are and what their society is. Society arises not out of material conditions but from conditions associated with individual values and conduct, factors we call psychological. Plato limited himself to those aspects of individuality which possess moral significance. No more than political systems do the moral qualities of individuals grow out of nature. They are inculcated, sometimes far from consciously, through factors we recognize as cultural. Plato returns to the same theory in *The Laws*, a later dialogue, where he engages in a bit of psychohistory concerning Persia.[14] The judicious blend of liberty and subjection formerly found in Persia, he explains, came to an end because Cyrus, abandoning the former pattern of child-rearing, put his sons in charge of women who, never thwarting the boys in anything, effectively if unintentionally deprived them of opportunities to learn self-discipline.

A broader conception of socialization emerges in two metaphors for education employed by the essayist Plutarch 400 years after Plato.[15] One, calling attention to the critical importance of childhood for learning, compares a child's mind to soft wax that easily takes an impression. The other metaphor compares education to agriculture. Untrained human nature is the soil, the teacher corresponds to the farmer, instruction is the seed, and the results produced by teaching are comparable to the crop secured by cultivation. Both metaphors have endured for a long time in popular and scholarly Western thought.

Cultural Origins and Development

Greek thought about society and culture was not exclusively preoccupied with social anthropological interests paralleling those later emerging in the works of Charles de Secondat de Montesquieu, Durkheim, Radcliffe-Brown, and the British sociological anthropologists. A second stream of classical thought, concentrating on the origin and early development of culture and on other cultural processes, broached topics subsequently appearing in the ideas of James Burnett, Adam Ferguson, Edward B. Tylor, Fritz Graebner, and Franz Boas.

Adhering strictly to my definition of anthropological ideas, Hesiod's poetic account in *Works and Days* of the progressive degeneration of mankind could easily be excluded on account of its undiluted supernaturalism.[16] Nevertheless I include it, partly because the poem does reveal a retrospective interest in mankind's development and partly because it goes back at least as far as the eighth century, that murky period of Greek history when monarchical power in the city-states was settling into the hands of ambitious nobles. Hesiod deplores the trends of the times, quite possibly because corruption in the courts had lost him his share of his father's inheritance. In poetic images he depicts humanity growing almost constantly morally worse and increasingly unhappy since its idyllic beginning as a race good as gold. The first people created by the gods were themselves as gods, free of pain and misery, untroubled by war, their bodies never tiring from work. They survive as spiritual helpers of mankind, guardians of fortune. The breed of mankind next divinely fashioned was as inferior to the first as silver is to gold. These people were unable to control themselves, they injured one another, lived brief and anguished lives, and refused to serve the gods. When Zeus removed them he converted them into spirits of the underworld. The third race made by Zeus was worse, and in quality equivalent to bronze, the metal from which its weapons were made. These men made war a way of life and as a result killed themselves off, despite their strong bronze weapons. Just before Hesiod's time a fourth, for once nobler, godlike race appeared, a company of heroes created by the divinities who brought a short respite to the course of progressive degeneration. Some of the heroes, Hesiod's poetic fancy believes, still survive, living gloriously in remote corners of the earth. With the disappearance of the others, however, Zeus made another race, common as iron, to which Hesiod wishes he did not belong. For with it came times in which work and suffering never end, children dishonor their parents, the rich oppress the poor, oaths are violated, and right depends solely on might. Nothing current is admirable, and Hesiod longs for the day when men will be allowed to quit the earth to join the gods in heaven.

Hesiod's mythological account of a vanished golden age deeply influenced European literature, but the course he traced of mankind's development gained hardly a toehold in anthropological thought, where an image of progressive cultural competence has tended to be the rule.

Such a positive image is available in a thoroughly naturalistic narrative of cultural development attributed to the fifth-century B.C. atomist, Democritus.[17] He begins by describing the earliest people as undisciplined; living singly as animals do; lacking clothing, shelter, and fire; without knowledge of agriculture; and making no attempt to store food. Social life arose when, to protect themselves against attacks by wild beasts, human beings gathered together in groups where they could furnish each other aid. Social life in turn gave rise to language, whose origin Democritus derives from random speech sounds. A group's members agreed amongst themselves to assign specific meanings quite arbitrarily to particular combinations of sounds. Different languages arose in parallel fashion in the isolated groups among which mankind was distributed. Gradually the early groups learned to find shelter by holing up in caves, to build fire, store food, and master other practical arts, some copied from what they saw animals do. Once basic needs were satisfied, music and means of augmenting happiness were invented. Human beings would never have acquired these arts or managed to survive, Democritus points out, were it not for prehensile hands, an ability to reason, and a capacity for language, through which knowledge discovered by one person could quickly be transmitted to other people for their benefit.

As if reading a moral in the story of cultural development, Democritus thought people did not sufficiently appreciate the resources they possess as human beings. He deplored their reliance on supernaturalism when they have it within their own power to win resources from nature and to control their own follies, not the least of which is an immoderate desire for material possessions.

Democritus stands as a towering figure in early anthropological thought for more reasons than because he replaced Hesiod's image of mankind's moral degeneration with a more modern image of growing human resourcefulness. It is to his credit that he grounds culture in biological attributes of the human species, namely, prehensility and the capacities for rational thought and language. More by implication than direct statement he traces relationships between earlier and later phenomena. Social life made language possible, and once both were established they accelerated the spread of culture. He dwells on the utility of cultural forms: group life gave protection, caves furnished shelter, and language permitted knowledge to be quickly shared to further survival. There is even a suggestion that cultural development occurred through people discovering better means for adapting to the environment, an idea most directly borne out in his explanation of group life arising as protection against wild animals. Other themes familiar in recent anthropology show up. When he says every group arbitrarily created its own language, he is looking at an aspect of culture relativistically. He opts for independent invention occurring along parallel lines in different groups. Finally, he recognizes the opposition between nature and culture and the emergence of culture from the natural world, including the activities of animals from which men learned.

Plato in the dialogue titled "Protagoras," gives a résumé of early cultural development corresponding closely to Democritus's narrative except for ascribing the origin of reverence and justice to direct supernatural intervention in human affairs.[18] In *The Laws* he takes up a somewhat different approach as he describes the reconstitution of society following a mythical deluge survived by only a few hill shepherds.[19] The hill people came through the flood without metals or other amenities to which Plato's contemporaries were accustomed, but did manage to rescue clothing, containers, and a few domesticated animals. What is most significant is the admiration with which Plato regards the simple life of those days and the mutual good will spontaneously pervading the social systems of the small rustic populations. Gathered in small family groups, people had no need of law. Whatever government they required resided in the father who shared authority with his wife. Each isolated group of postdiluvial folk invented different customs, and through education stamped them on their children. However, as the groups grew in size and expanded into tribes, the uncoordinated diversity of culture among these groups became a problem, one which people very reasonably solved by appointing arbiters to evaluate different customs and to recommend those best suited for preservation. The arbiters announced their selections to assemblies of tribal chiefs who declared them law. In what is really another parable, he imagines wise rulers—equivalent to a philosopher-king— benevolently but firmly ordaining the cultural norms of the ideal society.

The derivation of larger bases of social organization and more embracive levels of sociocultural integration from patriarchal family groups remained in favor for a long time. Rarely, however, are early writers able to explain how the members of those groups were led to invent true forms of government, except by referring to the useful and important functions they serve. Aristotle refined Plato's sequence by distinguishing three levels of social organization, starting with the patriarchal household formed when a man takes a wife and owns slaves.[20] Then came the village, an organization comprising a number of houses occupied by sons and grandsons of the ancestral patriarch, and finally the association of a few villages into a city or a state. Along with his three stages of social development, Aristotle recognizes three primary modes of human subsistence: nomadic pastoralism, the easiest to practice; hunting and fishing; and agriculture. He doesn't correlate the subsistence patterns with the stages of social organization; in fact, there is but the barest suggestion that he intends his sequence to be the order in which subsistence developed historically.

Kinship itself, while acknowledged to antedate the state as a basis of social organization, in Greek sources receives none of the attention that was to be lavished on it in the 19th century by Lewis Henry Morgan and his successors. Only in Aristotle's *Ethics* do we come across a brief, tantalizing notion of the basis of kinship reckoning.[21] Aristotle, taking what has become known in recent anthropology as the extensionist theory of kinship, shows the recognition of kin growing out of the parent-child tie. Thus the affectionate bond between siblings results from brothers and sisters being born of the same parents, while ties to cousins and other collateral relatives grow out of bonds linking parents and their siblings.

Needless to say, all early reconstructions of remote cultural origins and development are based on no archeological or other direct evidence of the past. They were rationalistically conceived, rather than empirically based. The philosophers reasoned out how it must have been, sometimes; for example, Democritus referring to the significance of prehensility, drawing highly plausible deductions which we are still inclined to accept. In a similar manner, the author of a treatise titled "Of Ancient Medicine"— it is usually attributed to the fifth-century physician Hippocrates—deduces how medicine and food preparation must have been invented.[22] Medicine, the writer points out, is based on the fact that indispositions of the organism can be overcome with treatment. He implies that if humans were constituted differently than they are, the art of medicine would have to be different, too, or it might not exist at all. The same reasoning is easier to follow when applied to the invention of food preparation. Milling, baking, and other culinary techniques were invented because mankind, unlike animals, is unsuited to survive on raw food. Before people understood the need to prepare foodstuffs for consumption, many persons died at an early age. Cultural development, through finding means for better adaptation, is again implicitly alluded to. Without the adaptation of cooking, the author reasons, humans could not have survived as well as they have.

Cultural Processes

The long-range viewpoint attending to directions taken by culture in its development complements another orientation that looks at the processes whereby cultural elements originate, come to acquire their present distribution in space—for example, through migration of people or cultural diffusion—and alter their forms under certain circumstances. Although the developmental and historical viewpoints are consistent with one another, the processes of culture history were little noted in Greek anthropology. The famous fifth-century historians, Herodotus and Thucydides, mostly took account of political events. Although their books report historical facts of migration and instances of cultural diffusion, they only incidentally or implicitly take heed of the abstract processes represented by particular historical events. Thucydides deals with migration abstractly, as a general process, when he theorizes that migrations were easily undertaken in olden times because people had few possessions to anchor them, and the enjoyment of those they possessed was highly insecure.[23] Aristotle to some degree perceives culture contact in general terms, or at least the ill effects he fears can come from it. Thus he postulates that in city-states exposed to many foreigners, exposure to many different norms of conduct will undermine the social order.[24] The geographer Strabo toward the first century A.D. acknowledged culture contact indirectly when he remarks about the knowledge and admiration Greek writers in earlier times had of Scythian nomads who were known to live frugal, orderly lives and to hold property in common, and who remain uncontacted by outsiders simply because they had nothing to be conquered for.[25] The description of these people, incidentally, is an exception to the tendency of the Greeks to portray barbarians in disparaging terms. These examples indicate that the Greeks possessed a very clear concept of diffusion as a process and, of course, an equally clear idea of variability in the spatial distribution of languages and other cultural traits. Strabo felt called upon to emphasize that culture trait distributions are matters of accident and chance, not the result of design.[26] Herodotus reveals a perplexed awareness of the problem of proving a theory of cultural diffusion, the same problem that became so important among the German and British diffusionists.[27] Greek Dionysian rites, he suspected, had originated in Egypt, where he observed similar rites being practiced. But how without historical evidence could one be sure that they had not originated in Greece? Herodotus did what later ethnologists have done when faced with similar problems under identical circumstances: he propped up his surmise with deductive reasoning. Had the rites originated in Greece, he reasons, they would be more Greek in character than they are. His unstated premise, easily inferred, holds that with time customs become infected, or patterned, by other parts of the culture which they join. As a result, traits borrowed recently will not have had time to become highly patterned, and will consequently show up as atypical. Obviously, the validity of such proof depends on the validity of the premise, which must either be self-evident or supported by good, independent ethnological evidence. Herodotus offers no independent evidence supporting his premise, that traits do with time become increasingly assimilated to the cultural pattern.

Through his *Histories*, Herodotus won lasting fame for his detailed ethnographic descriptions of foreign customs, some of which he himself noted during his 17 years of intermittent travel in eastern Asia, Egypt, the Aegean islands, and the Greek mainland. Other customs he learned about from informants, not always realizing when he was being deceived. *The Histories* is a highly particularistic book—Herodotus, as Jean Jacques Rousseau observed, presenting manners more through narrative than by comment.[28] Behind the ethnographic particularities lies a definite cultural schema, a fairly clear-cut idea of the universal culture pattern likely to be present in every society. How explicitly Herodotus held the idea of a universal culture pattern we don't know. Unlike later writers, he doesn't mention an outline of cultural materials useful for making observations in foreign cultures, and he follows no regular order in presenting details of people's dress, crops, farming, etiquette, transportation, sacrifice, rituals, forms of divination, sex role, sex practices, and other customs. Yet the fact that he selected those things for observation indicates he had in mind a schema defining certain cultural phenomena making them worthy of note. Interspersed in his descriptions is evidence that he knew the power that culture wields over individuals, constraining their range of choice and values, and that he was aware of the unequal receptivity of societies to cultural diffusion.

Another historian, Xenophon, writing in about 355 B.C., shows the results cultural patterning can achieve in traits when they have not, like the Greek Dionysian rites in Herodotus's opinion, been lately acquired.[29] Describing Sparta at its almost mythical period 400 years previously, he shows how pregnancy customs, education, and sports bear the impress of that culture's highly specialized values and goals. Practically everything contributes to producing strong, hardy, vigorous, and obedient citizens capable of maintaining a powerful military unshaken by internal conflict. Cultural integration is well-nigh complete in his account, Spartan culture forming a highly self-consistent, goal-oriented configuration.

Thucydides' observations of old cultural elements persisting at the margin of the Greek world, long after they had disappeared from Athens, contains evidence of another historical process, tarriance.[30] Implicitly, the historian recognizes the tendency of older traits in a culture area to be found in marginal geographical locations, where they have had time to diffuse, and to persist there while the rest of the area changes. Tarriance is the process underlying the principle, known as the age-area hypothesis, whereby the relative age of cultural elements is judged from the spatial range across which those elements are distributed. That is what Thucydides does as he identifies customs known to have at one time belonged to the Hellenes and be still followed by foreigners, and points them out as survivals of a remote past.

Nobody showed greater consciousness of culture history than the essayist Plutarch, using myths for the origins of Roman ceremonial observances and other customs practiced in the first two centuries of the Christian Era.[31] He understood the ease with which customs shift their meaning far from what it was originally, and points out a number of secondary interpretations. Sometimes his reconstructions are quite as fanciful as those advanced in the 19th century by scholars explaining that a country is called "motherland" because originally women were rulers, or accounting for the extension of the kin term "mother" to the mother's sisters by an early custom of sibling marriage. Why, Plutarch asks, do Romans prohibit a newly married woman from stepping over the threshold when she enters her new home? Perhaps because in former times men used to carry home abducted brides. We find an alternative explanation he offers more acceptable: possibly the custom symbolizes the woman's reluctance to enter a place where she will lose her virginity. Here Plutarch implies that the Roman custom symbolically enacts the reluctance the bride is supposed to feel when she approaches sexual relations with her husband. Often he gives more than one cause for a custom without attempting to choose between them, and several times his explanations are synchronic, rather than historical, and point up the underlying symbolism. Thus he explains why Romans avoid marrying in May, saying May is the month when expiatory sacrifices are made in which male images are cast from a bridge. Nuptials, he seems to imply, would be inappropriate in temporal conjunction with rites whose symbolism reflects opposition between men and women.

One of his questions, the answer to which is wholly synchronic as well as functional, broaches the topic of incest rules, destined to receive much attention in centuries to come. Why don't Romans marry women who are near kin? Because they want to create a large network of relationships between consanguineally unrelated families. Another reason, less clearly written, suggests that disagreements are likely to arise in marriages between near kin because affinal obligations create conflict with natural rights. I believe Plutarch is implying that marriage between a brother and sister or a father and daughter would lead to conflict between the consanguineal roles played by those relatives and the spouse roles created through marriage. If I am right, he not only proposed the alliance theory of incest rules, one of the major functional explanations advanced in anthropological history, but also a second major functional concept: incest rules regarded as devices for avoiding conflict between the contradictory role demands that would be created by marriage between consanguineal kin. Context indicates that Plutarch did not advance either explanation as the historical cause of incest rules. He avoided the fallacy others have committed when they treated the function of a custom as equivalent to the custom's origin.

Dynamic Sources of Religion

Plutarch was a priest, which may be related to the considerable interest he took in ritual symbolism. For example, in an extensive analysis of

Egyptian religion he notes divergent opinions over why Egyptian priests cut off their hair and wore linen rather than woolen garments.[32] According to his reasoning, hair and wool are refuse and therefore impure. The priests, required to be pure for their rites, symbolized purity by shedding impurities. They also avoided eating sheep flesh and pork, because those animals produce much surplus fat, which is impure, and they avoided salt, which is impure because small creatures are caught and die when salt crystallizes. Plutarch ascribes veneration of the sheep and cow in Egyptian religion to their usefulness in everyday life, of the scarab beetle to the remarkable behavior it manifests, and of the dog to both its utility and remarkable behavior.

By the relatively late date in Greek history when Plutarch was active, Greece possessed a long tradition of studying religion naturalistically. As far as evidence tells, the anthropological study of religion in that country goes back to the sixth century with Xenophanes, who belonged to the philosophically fertile land of Ionia where Greek materialism originated. Only fragments of his writings survive, and in them he makes the generalization that every people casts its gods in its own image.[33] Ethiopians picture theirs as black, with broad flaring nostrils; Thracians give theirs gray eyes and red hair. A simile leaves no doubt about his meaning. If oxen, horses, and lions could create gods, each would endow theirs with bodies similar to their own. The conventional nature of culture and the relativity of religious conceptions could not be more plainly stated. Yet, Xenophanes implies, there are limits to inventiveness. The imagination is not wholly free to create religious ideas but is governed by a tendency to project onto the supernatural plane familiar phenomena from everyday life. The idea that societies cast their supernaturals in the mold of familiar experiences persisted in European thought until it appears in 20th-century psychoanalytic formulations and social anthropological interpretations relating religion and social structure.

About a century after Xenophanes, the fifth-century B.C. writer and public figure Critias gave a developmental account of religion full of naturalistic observations.[34] Like his nephew Plato, Critias studied with Socrates, but what he learned from that teacher did not prevent him from becoming a bloodthirsty and unscrupulous politician. After the victory of Sparta, he became a member of the council of tyrants ruling Athens, and was killed in a battle with the forces restoring democracy to the city. The origin of religion he places in a period preceding the invention of law, when might alone ruled and evil remained unpunished. Religion was adaptive in such a society, as some wise man perceived when he hit upon fear of the gods as a means for restraining abusive conduct. The same clever person placed the residence of the gods in the sky, the source of terrifying thunder and lightning as well as of the useful rain. There people, moved by fear or thanksgiving, learned to direct their worship. Democritus at about the same time held a similar idea concerning the emotional basis of supernatural beliefs, but he suggests the origin of religion to have been a gradual process, and makes no allusion to a single inventor.[35] Human beings are led to the idea of god by astonishing events. Thunder, lightning, eclipses, and the collision of stars frightened early man because to his unenlightened mind they constituted the works of the gods.

Also in the fifth century B.C., Prodicus added to naturalistic concepts of religion by holding the gods to be anthropomorphic symbols standing for the sun, springs, and other material things furthering human life and welfare.[36] The symbols are created as people take to reverencing wine, fire, bread, and other useful substances.

By the fourth century B.C. the major theories concerning the dynamic sources of religious conceptions, which would continue to appear in anthropological thought during the next 2,000 years, had been formulated. They are: the concept of gods as symbols; the idea that supernatural beings aid in social control; the origin of religion in fear and awe; and the intellectualistic notion that deities explain remarkable events for which a people cannot otherwise account. Aristotle in the fourth century contributed to demystifying religion by contending that dreams cannot be divinely inspired, since animals dream, and, among human beings, dreams are not limited to men noted for wisdom and divine inspiration.[37] He also throws doubt on the prophetic power of dreams, holding their concurrence with the events they picture could well be a matter of chance or fancy.

Geography and Culture

The line of thought appearing in the fifth century B.C., connecting social behavior with geographical influences, has failed to win the general agreement of European scholars that they accorded to naturalistic theories of religion. Already at the beginning of the Christian Era empirical evidence intimated that the influence of geographical factors on culture was not as great as was claimed. Even earlier, we see from our modern vantage point, the theory of geographical determinism was contradicted by certain then current ideas, including the social patterning of human behavior and the conventional nature of culture.

Abundant evidence of geographical determinism in early Greek anthropological thought can be found in a group of medical treatises appearing in the fifth century.[38] The earliest of these writings are generally credited to the Father of Medicine, the physician Hippocrates, who came to the Greek mainland from an Aegean island off the Asian coast. One thesis, "On Airs, Waters, and Places," as the title implies, considers a variety of geographical factors capable of influencing behavioral dispositions. The work pays close attention to climate, and for many centuries afterwards climatic influences were mostly referred to in geographical explanations of social phenomena.

The author's general position is stated at the outset, when he says that whoever wants to investigate medicine should in the first place pay attention to the various seasons, wind, temperature, quality of water, and general geographical situation for their effects on human beings. The climatic environment in which a population lives exerts an effect on the form of the body; on physiological processes, including disease and resistance to disease; and on behavioral dispositions. The people of Asia and Europe act differently because the parts of the earth they inhabit vary in wind, temperature, and rainfall. Generally speaking, Asia is a mild land where things grow in abundance; therefore, its inhabitants are also mild, affectionate, unwarlike, even cowardly. But in parts of Europe where temperatures go to extremes of heat and cold, the human temper is greatly upset and the emotions are aroused. Here people are courageous and pusillanimous. Aristotle applied the climatic principles given in "On Airs, Waters, and Places" to the Greeks.[39] Just as Greece occupies a middle position between the cold and hot regions of Europe and Asia, respectively, Greeks are endowed with a combination of both courage and mildness. Their endowment, he thinks, explains why they have the best political institutions.

The geographer Strabo, living into the first century A.D., was too widely traveled and familiar with the world of his day to find his colleagues' geographical explanations of behavioral dispositions and cultural differences acceptable.[40] He points to differences, often noted by many Greek writers, between the characters of the Athenians and Spartans. How can geographical influences explain those differences when both groups share the same climate? "As regards the various arts and faculties and institutions of mankind, most of them, when once men have made a beginning, flourish in any latitude whatsoever."

A geographical perspective is capable of taking in more than climatic determinism or more comprehensive theories of environmental determinism; but the ancient Greeks, although developing geography as a science, only incidentally noted geographical factors, other than climate relating culture to the natural environment. Aristotle does so in *The Politics* when, after referring to the importance of communication by sea for cities dependent on trade, he wonders whether the good order of commercial cities visited by many kinds of foreigners is not likely to be undermined by the diverse norms of conduct that the foreign visitors spread.[41] Strabo, surveying world geography, comments on many particular observations in ways that reveal assumptions about the relationship between geography and culture. For example, he ascribes brigandage and savagery among the mountain folk of Corsica to the land's poor economic possibilities, and he explains the commercial character of Cumae, a western Greek colony, by the right proportion of lime in the sand, which makes it easy to build jetties into the sea, thus creating bays in the open sea where ships may safely moor.[42]

Roman Writers

Culture and Genius

Roman anthropology is small beer after the neat wine of the Greeks. Also, knowledge of Roman anthropology comes from a much shorter span of history. Practically all the authors I am going to cite were born or wrote in the two centuries immediately preceding or just starting the Christian Era, centuries in which the experiment with a republic ended (27 B.C.) and a new form of government, rule by an emperor, began. These were years when cultural influence radiated over Europe from the capital on the Tiber —but the Roman writers frequently thought with ideas derived from Greek sources. They did little to develop those ideas through refinement and testing. Nor were they exceptional in failing to do so; anthropology, I have said, has consistently been more additive than cumulatively developmental. The Romans, however, failed even to add a significant number of new orienting concepts or theoretical ideas.

There were exceptions, one being Lucretius in the first century B.C., who is notable for the way he uses imagination to enrich the picture of primeval society and to explain how mankind took the first steps into culture.[43] In his philosophical poem "On the Nature of the Universe," he ascribes all human behavior, basically, to the aims of securing gratification and maintaining life, an assumption he adopted from Epicurus, the philosopher who held the goals of pleasure and avoidance of pain to be the chief human motives. So broad a principle is almost sufficient to explain everything that happened in culture history in a book intended by Lucretius to popularize natural science. Here and there, however, he adduces more specific factors to account for particular human achievements.

The narrative opens familiarly with the first human beings described as living like wild beasts. Early man knew nothing of fire, clothing, houses, or farming. The stones and clubs employed for hunting proved inadequate to calm his fears of predatory beasts. People gave no thought to morals or laws; they mated promiscuously, whenever desire stirred, and they captured women through bribes and violence. See how closely Lucretius follows Democritus while adding details, like primitive promiscuity, from his imagination. If life in early times seems primitive, the poet observes trying to see things from the vantage point of early man but unable to raise far above the worries and values of his own time, at least the first human beings didn't have to worry about war or shipwreck and remained unspoiled by affluence.

Comforts, which cost mankind its original hardness, began as people learned to make huts and skin clothing and to capture fire from a blaze naturally set by lightning. Marriage preceded material amenities, but Lucretius doesn't describe how it happened to be instituted. Other innovations he explains by the model provided by Democritus: man learned from nature. The sun's heat taught cooking, fallen berries and acorns growing into seedlings revealed the secret of sowing, bird songs suggested music with which to soothe the mind once the body was cared for, and metalworking was derived from observing how forest fires smelted ores in the baked ground. Lucretius could not conceive that everyone was capable of making these discoveries and applying them in practical ways. In his version, only persons of outstanding mental ability—geniuses—benefited from natural instruction; they were the anonymous heroes who brought culture into existence. In time mankind improved on nature. Metalworkers, for example, learned to make molds and to hammer soft metal—Lucretius believed copper was the first metal because it is easy to work—into the shape of tools.

Lucretius employs what became a well-known technique of historical reconstruction in anthropological culture history when, using deductive reasoning, he dates certain inventions relative to others. Thus, the use of copper came before harder metals, and plaiting probably preceded weaving because the latter is a more complex technique. Weaving must have followed iron because the manufacture of looms requires iron tools.

The Roman poet ignores Democritus's view of language as a series of conventions that arose by chance. He could not imagine language being invented, not even by a genius; for how could someone have created language and been understood by others? By such reasoning Lucretius was led to adopt the nativistic thesis of an innate basis to language. Language grew out of natural sounds, such as animals make, whose meaning was innately given to mankind.

In a faint but nevertheless striking intimation of the 19th century theory of primitive animism, Lucretius traces religion back to dreams and visions in which figures of unsurpassing beauty made an appearance. People accepted such apparitions as real and credited them with omnipotence and immortality. The deities thus created were invested with the duties of severely sanctioning departures from morality, religion thereby adding a new kind of fear to the fears already besetting mankind.

Cicero, the statesman and writer, added a few other details to the natural foundations of culture pointed out by Democritus.[44] Nature gives us the organs of speech: the lungs and parts of the mouth by which speech sounds are created. Nature furnishes the prehensile hand so indispensable for useful crafts, as well as for sculpture, painting, and music. It also endows us with the senses through which experiences are led to the mind to be fashioned by thought into inventions. These are then realized by the craftsman's hand. And nature provides us with reason, the gift exceeding all the others. How marvelously everything in the world is ordered for man's safety and comfort!

Two Roman poets, Virgil and Ovid, also in the last century B.C., likewise write about prehistoric cultural development, but add nothing original to what had been said earlier. Virgil, after describing how humanity learned to till, make tools, and practice crafts, appraises those achievements with a cynicism akin to Lucretius's view of religion, blaming them for the perpetual hard work and the wants that climb unceasingly—the wants with which society is plagued.[45] Ovid visualizes two periods of culture building.[46] One, paralleling Hesiod, led to the destruction of the world by Jove, whereupon the god renewed man who thereupon set out on the course leading to contemporary civilization. Ovid also wrote a folkloristic work, *Fasti,* or Calendar, in which, somewhat like Plutarch, he adopts a historical perspective and uses myths to uncover the meaning of the names of the months and days.

Inability to Comprehend Causes

In the same century when Lucretius composed "On the Nature of the Universe," Cicero wrote "Nature of the Gods," a dialogue in the style of Plato summarizing as much as Cicero knew about Greek religion.[47] He wrote the work partly to enlighten Latin readers about those "darkest and most difficult" of all questions, the nature of the gods, and partly to cure his depression brought about by the death of his daughter in 45 B.C. Cicero was 60 years old at the time and but two years away from his own death. The theological systems he covers in this comprehensive review of comparative religion themselves lack the character of anthropological ideas. Only the pertinent comments and theoretical generalizations furnished by the three speakers, representing different philosophical positions, are of anthropological interest, and they are mostly already familiar. For example, one member of the group calls the gods fictions invented in the interest of the state. The fiction of supernatural beings allows people's behavior, uncontrollable through reason, to be checked by fear. The gods are also represented as symbols personifying inanimate forces, believed in by the ignorant—but the wise know that the true locus of divine power lies in the forces themselves. The distinction between two levels of belief, one occupied by the common folk and the other by the enlightened, recurs constantly in succeeding periods of European thought, and in recent anthropology can be recognized in the concepts of a Great and a Little Tradition.

Cicero includes the notion that fear and awe inspired by meteorological phenomena may have given rise to belief in spiritual beings; he points out how visions, hallucinations, and modes of divination may provide some people with phenomenal evidence of the gods' existence, and repeats a theory, deriving from Greece, according to which some gods represent persons who, in former times, performed great deeds or produced important inventions. In some instances the inventions themselves have become personified and deified.

For all of Cicero's wide reading in philosophy and his eagerness as a writer to enlighten the public, he was strongly conservative toward change. Perhaps we should expect as much in a Roman sympathetic to the wisdom of the philosophical Greeks. Like Aristotle, he deplored the cultural heterogeneity of commerical maritime states because of its threat to traditional institutions.[48] Such states grow wealthy, but their prosperity encourages extravagance and indolence. Soon, with the substitution of trade for soldiering and farming, the state falls into ruin.

Despite refuting some naturalistic theories of religion, Cicero no place indicates the doctrine he himself espoused. Lucretius, however, made his position quite clear. He hoped his poem would undermine supernaturalism by spreading true knowledge about natural phenomena. To help reach those goals he puts forward several ideas which, applied to magic and religion, became popular from the 17th century onwards. Religion is a fabrication filling in with supposed knowledge those areas where ignorance is rife. He blames designing priests for deliberately arousing people's anxieties by bloodcurdling prophecies, terrifying phantoms, and threats of eternal punishment in the afterlife. People's inability to comprehend the causes and troubles that beset them is what gives priests their power to deceive and terrify. Only knowledge sounder than that provided by supernaturalism will emancipate mankind from the fear and ignorance on which false beliefs thrive.

Peaks and Clusters in Culture History

Processes of cultural history interested Roman authors living in a country that as both the host and donor of culture was fully acquainted with diffusion. But convincing evidence of the pathways taken long ago by diffusion was as hard for Romans to find in the absence of written records or other surviving evidence as it has continued to be in recent anthropology. Pliny, a naturalist belonging to the first century A.D., is consequently often unconvincing as he summarizes available information concerning the origin and diffusion of notable traits, like monarchical government, the alphabet, and barbering. Nevertheless he reveals a strong interest in such problems of culture history.[49]

Several works from the last century B.C. and first century of our era refer to the dynamics of diffusion. Vitruvius, well-known for his treatise on architecture, town planning, and building construction, after surmising that mankind's earliest mud-and-wattle dwellings must have copied swallows' nests, observes that subsequent improvements in housing have not diffused evenly.[50] Barbarians in Gaul, Spain, and Portugal still follow construction practices of formerly much wider provenience, while innovations of comparatively recent origin have a more restricted distribution. He is positing the age-area hypothesis more explicitly than it occurs in Thucydides. Why better culture traits spread at all Vitruvius explains in highly general psychological terms, grounding the process of diffusion in the human capacity for learning and an inclination for competition that makes people eager to possess comforts and advantages they see others enjoying.

Vitruvius accepted the principle of geographical determinism.[51] A town should be built away from exposure to extremes of hot and cold, he advises, because variations in temperature are harmful to people. He regards the inhabitants of Italy most perfectly constituted, physically and mentally, quite in conformity to the country's middle position between the cold northern regions of Europe and the hotter southern climes. Culture, he notes, and specifically architecture, can be applied to compensate for climatic disadvantages; in northern climates houses should be roofed entirely and sheltered as much as possible, while in the south they should be sited more in the open and exposed to cool northerly winds. Vitruvius also traced the history of the Doric, Corinthian, and Ionic architectural styles, paying close attention to their constituent elements. We might expect such fine detail to cultural form from an architect, but it is also a prerequisite for ethnological analysis.

Reinterpretation, the process whereby borrowed cultural elements are patterned to fit into the cultural framework of the host society, to which Herodotus called attention, was applied knowledge among the Romans. Faced with the importation of pagan ceremonies ill-suited to traditional cultural values, they saw to it that the rituals were stripped of incongruent features and altered to acquire a Roman cultural imprint.[52]

Whereas Vitruvius noted the uneven spread of culture in space, the historian-soldier Velleius Paterculus in the first century A.D. observed the tendency for outstanding achievements in drama, philosophy, painting, or sculpture to peak and then decline in time.[53] The most eminent men in those arts and intellectual activities, among Romans as well as Greeks, have tended to belong to relatively brief periods of history. Like a species of domesticated animals grouping together, minds capable of great creativity have formed assemblages, each specializing in different forms of expression. To explain florescences in these fields Velleius, too, resorted to psychology, and even to a motive similar to competition, though he was not wholly satisfied with his theory. Emulation, he suggests, drives men to excel and to become geniuses in their chosen fields. Sometimes emulation is born of envy, at other times of admiration. Soon every art zealously pursued by gifted men reaches a height of excellence. Standing still at the peak is difficult, and so is further progress. Only recession is left, and it occurs as the ardor to overtake the masters changes to despair at not surpassing or only emulating them. As zeal flags, the attention turns to some new artistic or intellectual field where a chance to achieve eminence seems possible. Nineteen hundred years later another cultural historian, Alfred L. Kroeber, was unable to suggest a better explanation as he exhaustively documented the phenomena that Velleius Paterculus had intuitively perceived.

Another historian of the first century A.D., Tacitus, shared Herodotus's sharp eye for ethnographic detail. The strategy Tacitus follows in his book on the German tribes, as he grapples with the problem of classifying marginal cultural groups in the area, shows his grasp of the culture-area concept.[54] His task was to decide whether to include certain tribal groups bordering on the Germans with the Germans or with neighboring people. Largely on the basis of language, mode of settlement, house form, weapon type, and social habits, he decided the ambiguous tribes were German. No better strategy for culture-area classification has ever been found, and it is something of an anticlimax to have to report that Tacitus wasn't the first to have followed it. A century earlier Dionysius of Halicarnassus, a Greek historian from Asia Minor who settled in Rome, made up his mind, contrary to other opinion, that the Etruscans could not be related to the Lydians because they neither spoke the same language, worshipped the same gods, nor used the same laws and institutions.[55] But Dionysius probably had the easier problem, with Etruria being in Italy and Lydia at the eastern end of the Mediterranean.

In the manner of Plutarch, Tacitus perceived the ability of the incest rule to create alliances, though he expresses the idea quite differently, saying that a man's influence in old age is proportionate to the number of relatives he has acquired through marriage.[56] The Roman also appreciated the utility of wergild for stopping uncontrolled feuding, and he hints at a concept of ecological time, similar to the concept E. E. Evans-Pritchard observed among the Nuer, when he says that the German calendar recognizes only three seasons, a harvest season being absent because the Germans pursue agriculture only casually.

The concept of barbarian continued to carry disparaging overtones, in Roman times, never more so than in Lucan's epic poem, "Pharsalia," composed in the first century A.D., for which no historical accuracy is claimed.[57] He alludes to the rulers of Near Eastern barbarians mating with sisters and mothers and possessing enough sexual potency to copulate many times in a night with women belonging to their enormous harems. Apparently this image of Near Eastern potentates was common in imperial Rome.

Topics in Classical Anthropology

Summary of Greek and Roman Thought

The ideas we have sampled from Greek and Roman sources range across a surprisingly large number of topics that have continued to interest ethnologists and social anthropologists in recent times. The authors' object was often normative, to advance reasons why people should conduct themselves virtuously, but their minds remained open to nondirective knowledge about the constitution and processes of society and culture. Yet, although the anthropological thought of the classical philosophers, historians, geographers, and essayists—especially the Greek—is frequently astute, insightful, and in conformity with knowledge still accepted as true, for the most part the writers carried out no purposeful field work, a generalization from which Herodotus and Tacitus are notable exceptions. Mostly they obtained their facts through reading other men's manuscripts or, it would appear, from observation practiced only incidentally in their own society. Thereby familiar experiences, such as the division of labor among specialists, the practice of law, and the rearing of children, were, as Cicero puts it, led to the mind where they were fashioned by thought into inventions —in this instance, inventions consisting of ideas about society and culture. Sometimes the conclusions reached rested on very few hard data, but derived mostly from speculation and myth; for instance, in the reconstructions of cultural origins by Democritus and Lucretius or the reasons for certain Roman customs given by Plutarch. Such knowledge, however, sufficed in those times to satisfy an intellectual curiosity that must have been widely shared among the citizens whom the scholars wrote for or taught.

Foremostly, Greek and Roman thinkers noted the significance of diversity in social life, society as a system, social relations founded on practical reciprocities as contrasted with those based on nonutilitarian sentiments, the conventional nature of culture, the alliance-making function of the incest rule and perhaps its function in preventing role conflict among kinsmen, the naturalistic bases of religion, the ubiquity of diffusion, the process whereby traits acquired by diffusion become assimilated to patterns in the host culture, and the tendency of achievements in artistic and intellectual fields to peak and then decline in the course of time. Writers followed several ways of relative dating, including use of the age-area hypothesis. They recognized an isomorphy between personality and social structure, the power of custom to shape individual behavior, and the existence of something like a universal culture pattern. They perceived the nature of ritual to be a system of symbols, and generally agreed that language was a matter of agreement.

Recognizing these distinctions, relationships, and methodological principles, especially those explicitly stated, implies ability and skill in making abstractions from the materials of history. To be sure, the theories those rationalists formulated remained purely rational; the authors failed to take the next step, seeing if the relationships held up when critically exposed to new experiences. Anthropological thought has tended to follow the same pattern during the succeeding centuries—remaining much more fecund in producing theories and hypotheses than in finding ways to test the propositions experimentally.

Well before the first century A.D., all the viewpoints still current in recent anthropology had been utilized. Developmentalism shows up in Democritus's long-range view of culture and the details and motivations Lucretius added to that account. Although the type of directional thinking these men represent is sometimes called "evolution," it no more resembles modern evolutionary theory than Greek atomism resembles modern atomic theory. A historical orientation is revealed in those Greek and Roman writers who traced specific customs back in time and who reflected on the role of genius in invention, the reasons for diffusion, the uneven production of intellectual and artistic achievements from one period to another, the tendency for the meanings of cultural elements to alter while form remains constant, and other historical processes.

With the integrational viewpoint, observers perceived causal and noncausal linkages between cultural phenomena, noting, for example, that things useful in everyday life are apt to become sacralized in religion, that child-rearing produces a society's social personality which in turn forms the basis of the society's structural order, and that fear and awe are sources of supernatural belief. Instrumentalism in classical anthropological thought appears where writers point up purposes and unintended functions of culture, as they do in intellectualistic theories of religion, in holding fear of the gods to assist in social control, and in finding advantages connected with exogamy. We should also be aware that the Greeks debated whether functional explanations for institutions are adequate to account for the institutions' origins, and they wondered whether everything in culture has a use.[58] Greek and Roman authors employ the biological perspective when they ground cultural practices in natural human features like prehensility and an inclination to suffer from eating uncooked food. They take a psychological viewpoint when they find motives with which to explain diffusion, cultural development, cultural achievements or degeneration, as well as when they trace the social personality to antecedent social conditions. We have only briefly acknowledged the considerable attention classical sources pay to society regarded as an instrument for making people virtuous, a topic in itself not strictly anthropological by the criteria I follow but one closely related to the importance attributed to cultural patterning.

Finally, the environmental orientation is utilized when climate is seen as directly determining behavior and culture, in delineating more indirect relationships between geographical location and what happens in a society, and, as in Vitruvius's architectural treatise, noting how cultural traits may be designed to compensate for environmental disadvantages.

Summarizing the viewpoints has touched on a number of themes in Greek and Roman thought that have persisted and been debated in subsequent anthropology; for instance, the profound influence over the individual that is attributed to society and culture, which contrasts with the importance attached to individual geniuses as the source of culture. The literary sources admit an opposition between culture, or convention, and nature, but also recognize the role of nature in providing the materials for culture and the human attributes of reason, prehensility, and other biological features that make culture possible.

The writers, taken collectively, show ambivalence concerning cultural relativity. Of course they perceive tremendous—but not unlimited—variation between norms and customs from one group to another, within a common cultural schema. Beyond such commonplace knowledge, relativism went further, especially in Pyrrho, who belonged to the Greek Skeptics of the fourth century B.C. and who argued that since not a single good or bad obtains among all people there is no point in talking about things being good or bad by nature.[59] Everything in society exists only by convention and—getting dangerously close to the edge of a precipice down which his own logic might take him—nothing is more important than anything else. Recoiling from such extreme relativism, Aristotle warned against overemphasizing the significance of convention and man-made rules.[60] Natural standards of justice, he insists, can be discovered through the use of reason, and it matters little whether particular societies apply them differently. Among the Romans, Cicero accepted justice as a matter of convention, hence different from natural things which remain the same everywhere,[61] but he does not take his relativism as far as Pyrrho. The contradictory laws and customs of various societies cannot all be just, even though each people vouch for theirs alone being right. Like Aristotle he visualizes fixed standards of justice existing in nature, and with them, aided by reason, it is possible to judge the comparative morality of different norms and customs.

Aristotle and Cicero illustrate the importance the ancients generally attached to reason, the power that philosophers trusted for guiding societies to wise and useful cultural arrangements. During succeeding centuries the Western intellectual tradition continued to assign a major guiding role to reason: the 18th-century leaders of the Enlightenment extolling it as a means of overcoming outworn institutions, and 19th-century evolutionists finding it a rational basis for the progress that had occurred in social development.

Notes

1. Plato, *Protagoras*, 327, trans. B. Jowett, in *The Dialogues of Plato* (3d ed.; 5 vols.; London: Oxford University Press, n.d.), vol. 1.

2. John Mansley Robinson, *An Introduction to Early Greek Philosophy* (Boston: Houghton Mifflin Co., 1968), pp. 78–81.

3. Plato, *The Republic*, trans. H. D. P. Lee (Harmondsworth: Penguin Books, 1955), II.369–375.

4. Alvin W. Gouldner, *Enter Plato* (Harper Torchbooks ed.; New York: Harper & Row, 1971), pp. 42–45.

5. Aristotle, *The Ethics of Aristotle*, trans. J. A. K. Thomson (Harmondsworth: Penguin Books, 1955), III.3; V.5, 7; VIII.7, 9, 11; IX.1–3. See also Aristotle, *The Politics*, trans. T. A. Sinclair (Harmondsworth: Penguin Books, 1962), I.2, 8.

6. Aristotle, *Politics*, III.9.

7. Diogenes Laertius, "On Epicurus and the Epicureans," trans. D. J. Hicks, in T. V. Smith, ed., *Philosophers Speak for Themselves* (Chicago: University of Chicago Press, 1934), pp. 548–549.

8. Robinson, *Early Greek Philosophy*, p. 244. See also Werner Jaeger, *Paideia: The Ideals of Greek Culture*, trans. Gilbert Highet (2nd ed.; 3 vols.; New York: Oxford University Press, 1945), vol. 1, p. 309.

9. Robinson, *Early Greek Philosophy*, pp. 231–236.

10. Robinson, *Early Greek Philosophy*, pp. 250–251.

11. Plato, *Gorgias*, trans. W. Hamilton (Harmondsworth: Penguin Books, 1960), pp. 482–485, 491–492.

12. Robinson, *Early Greek Philosophy*, pp. 243–244; Jaeger, *Paideia*, vol. 1, pp. 312–313.

13. Plato, *The Republic*, IX.545–576.

14. Plato, *The Laws*, trans. T. J. Saunders (Harmondsworth: Penguin Books, 1970), III.694–696.

15. Plutarch, "The Education of Children," trans. Frank Cole Babbitt, in *Plutarch's Moralia* (Loeb Classical Library ed.; 15 vols.; Cambridge: Harvard University Press, 1936), vol. 1; Jaeger, *Paideia*, vol. 1, pp. 312–313.

16. Hesiod, *Works and Days*, trans. Dorothea Wender, in *Hesiod and Theognis* (Harmondsworth: Penguin Books, 1973), pp. 62–67. Also see J. G. Griffiths, "Archaeology and Hesiod's Five Ages," *Journal of the History of Ideas*, vol. 17 (1956): 109–119.

17. Robinson, *Early Greek Philosophy*, pp. 217–219.

18. Plato, *Protagoras*, 322.

19. Plato, *The Laws*, III.676–681.

20. Aristotle, *Politics*, I.1–2, 8; III.4, 9.

21. Aristotle, *Ethics*, VIII.12.

22. Hippocrates, *On Ancient Medicine*, trans. Francis Adams, in *Hippocratic Writings* (Chicago: Encyclopaedia Britannica, Inc., 1952), pp. 1–2.

23. Thucydides, *The Peloponnesian War*, trans. Rex Warner (Harmondsworth: Penguin Books, 1954), pp. 15–16. Other editions I.ii.

24. Aristotle, *Politics*, VII.6.

25. Strabo, *The Geography of Strabo*, trans. Horace L. Jones (Loeb Classical Library ed.; 8 vols.; New York: G. P. Putnam's Sons, 1917–1932), 7.3.9.

26. Strabo, *Geography*, 2.3.7.

27. Herodotus, *The Histories*, trans. Aubrey de Selincourt (Harmondsworth: Penguin Books, 1954), p. 122. Other editions II.49.

28. Jean Jacques Rousseau, *Émile*, trans. Barbara Foxley (Everyman's Library ed.; London: J. M. Dent & Sons, 1911), p. 416. See also Margaret T. Hodgen, *Early Anthropology in the Sixteenth and Seventeenth Centuries* (Philadelphia: University of Pennsylvania Press, 1964), pp. 22–24.

29. Xenophon, *Constitution of the Lacedaemonians*, in Xenophon, *Scripta Minora*, trans. E. C. Marchant (Loeb Classical Library ed.; London: William Heinemann, 1925). Plato's *Laws* (I.625–626, 629, 634) has a Spartan describe the institutions of Sparta as being oriented to warfare.

30. Thucydides, *Peloponnesian War*, pp. 15–16. Other editions, I.vi.

31. Plutarch, "The Roman Questions," trans. Frank Cole Babbitt, in *Plutarch's Moralia*, vol. 4; for marriage, see questions 29 and 86 (also 32); for incest rules, 108.

32. Plutarch, *De Iside et Osiride*, trans. J. Gwyn Griffiths ([Cardiff:] University of Wales Press, 1970), pp. 123–125, 235–237.

33. Robinson, *Early Greek Philosophy*, p. 52.

34. Klaus E. Müller, *Geschichte der antiken Ethnographie und ethnologischen Theoriebildung* (Wiesbaden: Franz Steiner Verlag, 1972), pp. 163–164.

35. Müller, *Geschichte*, p. 182.

36. Robinson, *Early Greek Philosophy*, p. 269.

37. Aristotle, *Aristotle's Psychology*, trans. William Alexander Hammond (London: Swan Sonnenschein, 1902), V.1–2.

38. Hippocrates, *On Airs, Waters, and Places*, trans. Francis Adams, in *Hippocratic Writings*.

39. Aristotle, *Politics*, VII.7.

40. Strabo, *Geography*, 2.3.7.

41. Aristotle, *Politics*, VII.6.

42. Strabo, *Geography*, 5.2.7 and 5.4.6.

43. Lucretius, *On the Nature of the Universe*, trans. R. E. Latham (Harmondsworth: Penguin Books, 1951), I.93, V.

44. Cicero, *The Nature of the Gods*, trans. Horace C. P. McGregor (Harmondsworth: Penguin Books, 1972), II. 147–151.

45. Virgil, *Georgics*, trans. H. Rushton Fairclough (Loeb Classical Library revised ed.; Cambridge: Harvard University Press, 1967), I.

46. Ovid, *The Metamorphoses*, trans. Horace Gregory (New York: Viking Press, 1958), I.

47. Cicero, *Nature of the Gods*, I.36–41, 82; II.7–15, 61–72, 163–167; III. 10–13, 36–40, 211.

48. Cicero, *The Republic*, in Cicero, *De Re Publica* and *De Legibus*, trans. Clinton Walker Keyes (Loeb Classical Library ed.; Cambridge: Harvard University Press, 1970), II.4.

49. Caius Plinius Secundus, *The Natural History of Pliny*, trans. John Bostock and H. T. Riley (London: Henry G. Bohn, 1855), VI.

50. Marcus Vitruvius Pollio, *The Ten Books on Architecture*, trans. Morris Hicky Morgan (Cambridge: Harvard University Press, 1914), II.1.

51. Vitruvius, *Architecture*, I.4; III; IV; VI.1.

52. R. H. Barrow, *The Romans* (Harmondsworth: Penguin Books, 1949), pp. 145–147.

53. Velleius Paterculus, *Remains of His Compendium of the History of Rome*, trans. John Selby Watson, in *Sallust, Florus, and Velleius Paterculus* (New York: Harper and Brothers, 1855), I.16.

54. Cornelius Tacitus, *On Britain and Germany*, trans. H. Mattingly (Harmondsworth: Penguin Books, 1948), ch. 46.

55. Dionysius of Halicarnassus, *The Roman Antiquities of Dionysius of Halicarnassus* (Loeb Classical Library ed.; 7 vols.; Cambridge: Harvard University Press, 1937), vol. 1, I.30.

56. Tacitus, *Britain and Germany*, chs. 20, 21, 26.

57. Marcus Annaeus Lucanus, *Pharsalia*, trans. Robert Graves (Harmondsworth: Penguin Books, 1956), VIII.394–413.

58. Theophrastus, *Metaphysics*, trans. W. D. Ross and F. H. Fobes (Hildesheim: Georg Olms Verlagsbuchhandlung, 1967), pp. 31–33.

59. Cited in T. V. Smith, *Philosophers Speak for Themselves*, pp. 571, 577.

60. Aristotle, *Ethics*, V.7.

61. Cicero, *The Republic*, III.8–11; Cicero, *The Laws*, in Cicero, *De Re Publica* and *De Legibus*, I.8–9, 14–18.

3

From the Church Fathers to the 17th Century

The Patristic Age

Tension between Faith and Reason

Between the third and the 17th centuries in Europe—the fifteen-hundred-year interval covered in this chapter—anthropological thought came almost to a halt before it was resuscitated and stimulated by the impact of classical learning, in which interest revived, and by discoveries made in the New World and other parts of the globe. Hence the literature belonging to the early centuries, when Christianity was institutionalized in the Roman Empire, contains little to hold us.

Naturalistic inquiry into society, culture, and other topics declined in early Christian times, not because of religion per se, but because of the new mode of thinking that came to dominate.[1] Knowledge came to be sought by directing reason to God's word as it lay revealed in the Scriptures. Christians tended to neglect the kind of philosophizing the Greeks had practiced in which reason is directed to experience, sometimes experience deliberately sought through directed observation. Confidence in reason based on experience as a source of knowledge never wholly disappeared. Through its lingering presence a rising tension set in between revelation, or supernaturalism (I mean the latter word nonpejoratively), and naturalistic inquiry. An aggravating opposition took form which reason itself, wielded by medieval philosophers like St. Thomas Aquinas, whose

---

Notes to this chapter begin on page 74.

first allegiance was to revelation, sought to mediate. In the long run, the compromises suggested by Christian philosophers failed to convince those scholars irresistibly drawn to naturalistic inquiry. More and more between the 13th and the 17th centuries the proponents of reason, pursued independently of theological assumptions, asserted their claims, their insistence bringing about the Age of Reason. The 16th-century Reformation and the bursting forth of natural science are products of the reassertion of independent reason; so is the renewal of anthropological thinking, which made supernaturalism itself an object of naturalistic inquiry.

God's Plan for the World

The Patriarchs who guided the early Christians lived in an economically and politically deteriorating society in which the keystone of the Western world, the Roman Empire, was disintegrating. Writing to encourage converts, combat pagan criticism of the Church, expose errors in pagan thought, and interpret the Bible, especially the Old Testament in the light of the New, the Church Fathers knew they were helping to lay the ideological foundations of a new civilization. Their break with the past, however, was far from complete, for these educated men incorporated a large part of the heritage of classical learning. Origen, for example, had studied the works of the Pythagoreans, Plato, and other Greek writers, and St. Augustine mastered the Latin classics and knew Greek philosophy from reading it in Latin translation. The Fathers thought with many of the same ideas as Aristotle and Cicero, selecting those they found useful or noncontroversial, and reinterpreting others to make them conform to knowledge derived from Scripture. A theological element prevails in their works. Yet the early Christians did not all scorn philosophy, though some did, saying now that we have Jesus Christ, away with Plato, Aristotle, and everything resting solely on human opinion. "Had the Middle Ages produced men of this type only," the Catholic philosopher Etienne Gilson says, "the period would deserve the title of Dark Ages." Throughout the Middle Ages and beyond, too, the word philosophy retained its comprehensive meaning of wisdom or knowledge, excluding theology and medicine. (In the Renaissance it even came for a time to include natural science.) What the Fathers philosophized about society and culture, however, was incidental to their religious aims, and therefore the anthropological ideas they offer are always found embedded in theological concepts. Extracted from the setting, the churchmen's anthropology often seems more naturalistic than it does in context.

The Patriarchs' fundamental premise holds social behavior, including history and the origin of culture, to be the realization of God's plan for the world. Hence to understand the social world one must know God's plan as it is revealed in the Scriptures. The ideas theologically interpreted by this premise are familiar. Origen, writing in the third century A.D., relates nature and culture and fuses the instrumental and biological viewpoint as he derives the technological aspects of culture from human biological needs.[2] According to this Alexandrian theologian, whom a synod condemned for teaching objectionable knowledge and for castrating himself to overcome sexual distraction, God created human beings with needs and also provided them with a rational mind to exercise in satisfying the needs. Human achievements—to which a millennium later the term culture would be applied—proceed as a consequence of reason and learning. Society and culture result from reason being successfully applied to invent husbandry, spinning, weaving, carpentry, and other arts for meeting human needs. Bees and other animals also form societies, build shelters; they even have sovereigns, but their achievements differ from those of human beings in being the purely mechanical outcomes of an irrational nature.

Differences in achievements among human societies Origen attributed simply to God's will. But a century later St. Jerome (also known as Hieronymus) related some of the diversity in culture to the varying use that societies make of the resources provided by nature, and to the limitations imposed by environmental settings.[3] Those animal and vegetable products that thrive in a region become staple foods, while things rarely or never found locally tend to be scorned as proper nourishment.

Another familiar idea recognized the power of custom for regulating individual conduct. St. John Chrysostom recognized how forcefully custom operates, usually below people's level of awareness, when he warned fourth-century catechumens to remain alert lest they be drawn into traditional pagan ways. Remaining aware of the compelling influence of custom increases a person's ability to resist evil and to adhere to the teachings of Jesus Christ.[4] Surely he was advocating a kind of applied anthropology. The most famous of the Church Fathers, St. Augustine, illustrates the force of cultural pattern in the instance of a judge dutifully playing his role.[5] The magistrate feels no guilt when in the line of duty he uses torture on people who may be innocent, or condemns an accused person to death without knowing the condemned person's conscience. Knowing the risks a judge must take, will a wise man accept a seat on the court bench? He will, "for the claims of human society constrain him and draw him to this duty; it is unthinkable to him that he should shirk it."

Augustine was born in North Africa, in what is now Algeria, of mixed Christian and pagan parentage. He remained estranged from religion until, in Milan where he had gone to teach rhetoric (literature), he managed to shake himself free from the sweet burden of worldly pleasures obsessing him and was converted to Christianity. The book from which I have quoted, *City of God,* a work almost as well known as his *Confessions,* is a philosophical study of history. History has brought mankind from a time when it pursued only worldly goals to the realization that the sole worthwhile good is God; in Augustine's metaphors, humanity has left the earthly city and stands at the doors of the Heavenly City, through which Christians will pass after death. The book reveals its date: Augustine wrote it in the fifth century after Rome had been captured and sacked by northern barbarians.[6] As the author looks back to the greatest days of the Roman Empire, seeing it as an opportunity for Romans to fulfill God's plan for the world, he sounds like those functionalists who show social roles harmoniously satisfying personality needs while meeting important social needs. The Romans who built the magnificent Empire were motivated by desire for glory, honor, and liberty; they did not realize that in satisfying those needs they were also furthering God's plan for checking the wickedness prevailing in the nations where Rome conquered.

Magic and divination are forms of wickedness which the Roman Empire didn't check, but which the Church sternly reprimanded. Augustine alludes to them in severe normative terms. He brands all such practices as fraudulent rites because they involve demons controlled by Satan. The identification of a class of behavior, including magic, as fraudulent or illicit and vain, is important for the later development of the concept of anthropology, as I will explain when I return to the topic in connection with the writings of Aquinas.

Augustine has relatively little to say about more remote periods of cultural history, or about the origin of society. On scriptural grounds, he believes that before the biblical flood occurred human beings reached a gigantic stature and lived to a great age. His interpretation of the flood and other Old Testament events as prefiguring the mission of Christ and the Church can be regarded as equivalent to the symbolic analysis of myth, though obviously the saint didn't consider the Bible a myth, and the interpretations he made possessed a transcendental significance. He recognizes the importance of diffusion in culture history and traces civilization from the East, where it is older, to the West, the region God decided should surpass the ancient East in grandeur. Incest avoidance is another anthropological topic he touches on. He repeats the alliance-making function of the incest rule, specifically in the nuclear family, saying that exogamy disperses affection beyond the family and knits social bonds over a wide area. No doubt the creation of social bonds by marriage was useful for the early Christians, and in that context we can understand Pope Gregory I, a century later, warning against marriage between close consanguineal relatives because such unions are unfruitful.[7] Augustine regards incest as unlikely to occur, first, because of a natural aversion for sexual relations between close relatives, and second, because of an inherent sense of decency which, speaking from the male's standpoint, makes sexual relations inappropriate with a kinswoman whom he respects.

The Middle Ages

Pragmatic and Expressive Rites

More devastation followed the sack of Rome. From the fifth to the ninth centuries European life rocked under a succession of onslaughts as the Vandals, Goths, Norsemen, and Saracens conquered, invaded, or pillaged. Throughout this turmoil Christianity diffused steadily northward and westward, monasteries serving as fortresses of learning in which the classical intellectual heritage was kept alive. Yet, before the Middle Ages were over and the Renaissance began, Europe managed to restore a measure of stability. Aided by technical inventions locally made or borrowed through diffusion, the economy recovered. Although writers during this long period rarely lost sight of God's purpose in human events, they frequently took His controlling role for granted. In tracing cultural development, for example, once having in some way acknowledged the biblical story of creation, they went on to freely speculate what happened, without troubling to ground their conclusions in scriptural revelation. They repeated many ideas familiar in the writers of antiquity. For example, Pope Gregory, like the ancient Romans, perceived the value of religious syncretism.[8] "It is impossible to cut off all things from . . . rough minds," the pope wrote to Augustine of Canterbury, his emissary to the Irish, referring to resistant converts in the western isles. He urged the missionary to graft saints' birthday celebrations onto the Britons' pagan solemnities, and to convert their animal sacrifices into thanksgiving feasts.

The romantic image of early society as happy and peaceful in its simplicity and isolation was picked up by the unfortunate Roman scholar Boethius, who had hoped to translate into Latin all the works of Aristotle but was executed for treason by his patron, the Goth king Theodoric.[9] In his *Consolation of Philosophy,* written early in the sixth century while he was in prison, Boethius refers, as had Plato and Lucretius, to human beings of an early day who were contented with what their fields produced or with acorns easily gathered, and who were not yet corrupted by affluence, knew no alcohol, and lived free of war. Would we could get rid of greed, born from the discovery of gold, Boethius sighs. Blaming greed on gold was not original with Boethius; Lucretius did, too, and added property as an additional cause of the misfortunes that came to plague mankind. The theme of cultural relativity helps Boethius to combat vanity and express the idea of fame being transitory: since the manners and customs of different societies agree so little with one another, what is considered praiseworthy among one people elsewhere might lead to punishment; a man famous in one land might be better off concealing his name in another.

Different traditions of religious belief coexisting in the same society, a concept briefly alluded to by Cicero, received fuller attention from the

Spanish Muslim theologian and philosopher Averroës.[10] He wrote many books, including commentaries on Aristotle, whose work he regarded as the height of human intellectual achievement—plainly an indication of the esteem Averroës placed on independent reason. Although he trusted divine revelation as it is embodied in the Muslim Scripture, he hoped to reconcile it with reason. In the course of doing so, he points out that there are different ways of comprehending religious truths corresponding to different classes of people in society. The mass of common people gain understanding by imagination and feeling, as every good preacher knows when he sanctions behavior by picturing an afterworld filled with pleasant sensuous expectations for the good, and with bodily punishment for the wicked. Other people, however, are unconvinced by such images. They accept something as true only when persuaded by argument or reason. For them faith, or revelation, must be made rationally probable and may not be at variance with empirical knowledge.

In the 12th century, Otto of Freising, a German historian and bishop, reiterated Augustine's view of Western civilization as having diffused from the East.[11] Otto was among the first postclassical humanists to see history as progressive, an interpretation that captured the imagination and dominates the anthropology of the 18th and 19th centuries. Even the Greeks lacked a clear-cut progressive view of cultural development, but held a cyclical view of history, according to which each rising curve of progress runs down after reaching its crest and then begins again. Otto, concerned with human achievements that developed after the biblical flood, credits culture to human abilities, specifically to the capacity for reason and to wisely designed laws.

Without spending time on environmental explanations advanced in the late Middle Ages for the biological and cultural differences dividing mankind,[12] I pass on to anthropological topics considered by the towering philosopher of the early Middle Ages, St. Thomas Aquinas, the "Angelic Doctor," who studied in Naples and Paris and taught in universities of those and other cities. Thomas parallels Averroës in his admiration for Aristotle—"the Philosopher," as he and others in the Middle Ages titled the Greek thinker—thereby revealing *his* esteem for reason based on experience as a source of knowledge. Naturalistic ideas concerned with society and culture occupy only a small place in the saint's philosophical output, and some of those are taken almost directly from Greek sources.[13] For example, he identifies a natural substratum of culture located in human reason: ability to learn, and inability to singly master all that is needed to maintain life. He points out the importance of language for social organization and as a means of disseminating newly discovered knowledge among the members of a social group. He continues with the instrumental view of social structure, holding the function of government to be the maintenance of social order and thereby insuring individual survival. More significant is the conceptual distinction Thomas draws between pragmatic and expressive rites, because it is leading directly to the anthropological conception of magic and the separation of magic from religion.[14] Rites releasing power to effect certain ends—wearing amulets for protection or addressing charms and making invocations to things, as if they were persons, and other practices anthropologists later put into the category of magic—Thomas contrasts with rites whose purpose is to honor or thank God and to show religious devotion. His identification of magical practices follows Christian tradition, and also links Thomas with the later conception of magic in Edward B. Tylor, James G. Frazer, and other anthropologists. Magic consists in signs which themselves lack the power to cause anything. Yet he indicates his belief that such signs sometimes work as the magician intends them to. Out of curiosity we will follow his supernatural line of inquiry as he explains the source of the power which sometimes makes charms and invocations efficacious. Like any sign, these can only derive their potency from another intellect. Since magical arts are often performed to further murder, theft, and other malefices, the intellect through which they work cannot be good but must be an intellect disposed to evil. Therefore magic must be due to demons, beings whose intention is to do evil.

It is quite proper for faithful Christians to wear saintly relics or to carry sacred words for protection, Thomas believes, if the power is not ascribed to the act itself but to God, or if the motive is to honor God by whom the results are controlled. Then the practices, in Frazer's words, are religious rather than magical or, as Mary Douglas would say, they avoid crossing the delicate line separating expressive form efficacious ritual.

Although techniques and beliefs that we recognize as magical are often referred to in ancient Greek and Roman writings as quite credible, I did not introduce the topic in the earlier chapter because an essential feature of the concept of magic was lacking: the naturalistic attitude as it appears in recent anthropology. The anthropological concept of magic arose gradually in Europe, starting when Christians set apart certain modes of coping, because they seemed unreasonable or illicit, and continuing in the Renaissance as philosophers, who were quite tolerant toward magic, speculated on the abstract principles whereby magical practices work.

In his discussion of incest rules, Thomas tends to be normative rather than to provide a generalized description of their functioning.[15] He accepts the idea that consanguineal kinship is simultaneously based on blood and descent. Thus "a father by procreation may be said to descend to his son" and so on in a "line." At the head of the line as a "common ancestor" stands the original procreator. Thomas explicitly identifies procreation with descent, a point I emphasize because later anthropology will insist on a distinction between descent and kinship. Then he turns to marriage, one end of which is to extend kinship ties by binding together more members of mankind or, following Aristotle's terminology, to extend "friendship" beyond the circle of close kin. Because marriage between consanguineal and affinal kin would hinder the extension of friendship, it was forbidden between near relatives in olden times and still constitutes a valid reason for forbidding marriage between persons related within certain degrees of kinship or affinity. But that is not the only argument against marriage to consanguineals, or even the most important. The primary end of marriage is the production of good offspring, and since, as Pope Gregory pointed out, marriage with close relatives hinders the good development of children, incest is wrong. Furthermore (here Thomas cites Jewish law), lust would be encouraged if the members of a household were allowed to intermarry. Thomas foresees the same prospect were affines permitted to regard one another as prospective mates. The curbing of lust, he assumes, is another end sought in marriage, and therefore a ground for prohibiting the marriage of close kin. Thomas hints, like Plutarch, that marriage within the nuclear family would encourage role conflict, though he believes such mating occurs among barbarians. Unions between children and parents are derogatory to the reverence due to parents and at variance with the lasting solicitude that a parent owes to a child. Avoidance of role conflict, he suggests, also lies behind the common custom of freeing a slave woman taken in marriage. She cannot be a slave and a spouse at the same time, he reasons. These ideas and instrumentalist explanations concerning kinship and incest rules assume much that we would like to see more explicitly developed; Thomas's purpose, however, was not to treat the subjects naturalistically but to justify, rationally, rules based on Scripture and Church law.

Bedouin and Sedentary Cultures

By the 13th century, during which Aquinas wrote, the European Renaissance was stirring. Scholars were taking a renewed interest in ancient philosophy and medicine. In the Arab world no renewal was necessary, for there classical knowledge passed directly into indigenous scholarship, where it became tinctured with Islamic concepts. In that form, ancient knowledge diffused across North Africa and in the eighth century entered Spain, where we already met one representative of western Islamic thought, Averroës. In Ibn Khaldun we meet another, though he was more at home in North Africa than in Europe, having lived in Spain for only a few years. He was enough of a Westerner to include, especially since he carried the naturalistic approach to society and culture to a height we have not heretofore seen—and will not see again until the 18th century.

After an insecure political career in the service of Muslim rulers, Ibn Khaldun with his family settled in a fortress village in Oran, an Algerian province, where he began to write a multivolume universal history. The full work has never been translated into English, although the *Muqaddimah,* or introduction, has been—itself a work in several volumes, completed in 1377. (But not into any European language, until a French version came out in the middle of the 19th century; the delay probably limited its influence on European anthropological thought.) The *Muqaddimah* must be counted as the first major work in cultural anthropology.[16]

Naturally, as Ibn Khaldun, combining several viewpoints, sketches an instrumental theory of culture, many ideas familiar from the literature of antiquity show up. He, like Origen, warns against making an exact parallel between human and animal behavior or institutions. Even if sovereignty exists among the bees, it does so as a natural disposition, not as the result of thought or other distinctive human faculties. Thinking, i.e., reason, forms the basis of the human sciences and crafts. Thought transforms the basic biological needs of human nature into concerns and routines for maintaining life. Being unequipped to survive singly as individuals, people form social aggregates wherein, through cooperation, including specialization, they satisfy their requirements. Food-getting is the basis of life and it depends on a variety of crafts and technical operations, which in society become allocated to different specialists. The same is true of defense. Along with cooperation, human survival also requires some means of restraining aggression and preventing injustice, two evils to which human nature is prone. Those ends, vital for society, are realized through forceful rulers exercising power.

Cultural materialism pervades the *Muqaddimah,* with its implicit assumption that ecology influences many areas of social life and shapes the social personality. Ibn Khaldun applies the assumption in an extensive, though repetitious, comparison of two cultural types, Bedouin and sedentary. Touching on many domains of behavior, he depicts each as a configuration suffused in distinctive values and each possessing its own ethos. Without question, he recognizes the integrated character of culture.

Bedouin culture is practiced by desert-dwelling pastoralists (including the nomadic Berbers, Arabs, Kurds, and Turks), who are restricted to the bare necessities in food, cuisine, clothing, shelter, and other amenities. Pastoral activities force them to move around for pasture, and to penetrate deep into the hills. In their lack of superfluous conveniences and luxuries, as well as in their savage habits, they resemble wild beasts. To defend themselves, men always carry weapons and constantly watch out for danger, trusting nobody but themselves. Strenuous activities make them strong and hence easily able to gain control over others; but being savages, they conquer merely to plunder. Lineage organization intensifies group feeling among the desert pastoralists, and inspires enormous self-confidence, which helps them to overpower other groups. Zealously they guard their freedom from externally imposed laws, thereby protecting their personal strength from being weakened through outside pressure and authority. The religious laws demand inner control, but also carry seeds of weakness, for when the desert people come under the influence of religious teachers and learn self-restraint, they also begin to acknowledge the legitimacy of external control imposed by leaders. These leaders grow into kings who, seeking to promote tranquility, stability, comfort, and ease for the society, estrange the Bedouin from the toughness the Bedouins formerly possessed. Gradually they are transformed into sedentary people.

Sedentary societies, located in cities, survive through agriculture. Their larger size, compared to Bedouin groups, provides them with an abundant supply of labor, which permits a high degree of specialization, resulting in a high level of affluence and comfort, because more wealth can be produced by division of labor. In sedentary societies, solidarity no longer rests on lineage organization and the group feeling that lineage inspires, but solidarity rests on mutual need, specialization, and profit making. Bedouins who enter sedentary life become weakened as a result of expanding their needs and learning to enjoy ease, refinement, elegance, and luxury. Cities built for protection also obviate the necessity of group feeling for defense. Consequently, the people's former vigor and savagery vanish just as happens in wild animals once they become domesticated. Illness increases due to the incautious way urban people eat amidst plenty, to the putrid vapors that fill the air of crowded cities, and to the lack of exercise. The city's biggest toll, however, is taken on the soul as its inhabitants more and more think only of making profit by any means, regardless of ethical considerations. Eventually, the city, teaming with competition, vice, illness, and unsavory characters, collapses into ruin.

Sedentary culture develops from Bedouin culture. Historically and logically, Bedouin culture is prior; because men, naturally, first try to obtain bare necessities before pursuing luxuries and extra conveniences. The Muslim scholar underpins his materialistic outlook with a psychogenic reason for the course taken by social development. The major force changing Bedouin into sedentary culture is the human tendency always to seek a better standard of living.

Judged by its starkness, desert culture is inferior to civilization; but in terms of such moral values as bravery, religiousness, and stamina, which thrive where life is simple and privation common, Bedouin existence is clearly superior. No doubt Ibn Khaldun also saw Bedouin culture as superior in its basis of solidarity. More explicitly than Aristotle, he delineates a distinction between a society based on mechanical solidarity, as the Bedouin are with their strong group feeling arising from lineage organization, and a society founded on organic solidarity created through intense division of labor. Urban life illustrates not only organic solidarity but, with its lack of group feeling, individualistic profit-seeking, and normlessness, also portrays the social condition that Emile Durkheim called anomie and, like Ibn Khaldun, associated with organic solidarity.

Ibn Khaldun claims the *Muqaddimah* to be the foundation of a new discipline. It is not the last time we will hear such a claim; Vico, Auguste Comte, and A. R. Radcliffe-Brown also make it. In Ibn Khaldun's case, the new discipline mixes ecology with geographical determinism and with a number of modern-sounding propositions about the influence of demographic factors in culture and culture history. The ecology we have already seen in the configurated picture of Bedouin life. Environmental determinism shows up in the proposition that people behave more like dumb animals in hot climates and develop their human capacities to the fullest in temperate zones. The importance of demography is easier for us to accept, though everyone may not agree with the causal chain Ibn Khaldun lays down between population size, economic productivity, and cultural growth. As numbers of people increase so does the demand for luxuries, together with the labor wherewith to provide the number of craftsmen necessary to produce a large supply and range of satisfiers. The power and grandeur of royal dynasties is also controlled by population expansion and the prosperity that follows. The latter principle explains the colossal size of the Egyptian pyramids and other prehistoric monuments, which were not built by a vanished race of giants, as folk belief had it, but reflect the power of the dynasty that built them.

The new discipline somewhat neglects diffusion as a factor in culture growth, although Ibn Khaldun mentions conquest as a means of spreading customs, but only the victor's. Dominated people, he says, imitate their conquerors as children imitate their fathers. He recognizes, more synchronically than diachronically, the unfavorable consequences of geographical marginality for cultural development, remarking that even large cities stagnate and remain predominantly Bedouin if they are situated in remote parts of the realm. For one reason, the centrally located government spends little money on far-off places, thereby leaving their commercial life sluggish.

Whatever the discipline represented by the *Muqaddimmah* is called, it puts great stress on cultural patterning as an influence on human nature. Bedouins become very different in personality once they leave off nomadic living and take up the sedentary life of cities. Even writing and arithmetic exert an influence on human nature; the first bestows a habit of intellection on the mind and promotes intelligence, while calculating with written numerals encourages deductive reasoning. The book may not contain the first comparison of cultural systems, but it is more comprehensive, and closer to empirical facts than anything done by Plato and Aristotle, and more systematic and generalized than comparisons done by Greek and Roman geographers. Ibn Khaldun fits even clothing into the comparison, relating tailored clothing to sedentary cultures and untailored garments to desert people, who must be content with simply draping material over the body. The avoidance of tailored garments during the pilgrimage Muslims make to Mecca he explains by the garments' symbolic significance, saying they represent luxury; therefore, their use is forbidden at a time when all indications of wordly attachment must be discarded. The analysis recalls the interpretation of Egyptian ritual customs by Plutarch.

The Renaissance

A New World Picture

In Europe not until the 15th century do a few Christian scholars show an inclination to examine society and its customs—most notably political institutions—in a manner as forthright and naturalistic as Ibn Khaldun. Their efforts, far less comprehensive in scope than the *Muqaddimah*, form part of the Renaissance, the period in the European history of ideas when a broadened conception of the world began to emerge and philosophers proceeded once again, in the style of the classical authors they devoured, to reason about things never mentioned in the Bible as well as about things that are. As the level of intellectual curiosity rose during the 14th and 15th centuries when the Renaissance flourished, people felt freer to ask novel questions, to reason independently upon experience, and to offer naturalistic explanations. See how naturalistic concepts dissolve a little the mystical sanctity associated with exalted rulers as a German cardinal, Nicholas of Cusa, early in the 15th century calls attention to ceremonial regalia and rite of anointing as the means whereby those personages' visibility is enhanced and they are proclaimed worthy of reverence.[17] The effect of his reasoning is equivalent to substituting dynastic power over labor for belief in prehistoric giants as the explanation for the pyramids.

The rapid growth of knowledge, and the New World picture to which it contributed, stimulated the idea of progress already detected in Otto of Freising. Where previous scholars regarded ancient wisdom as surpassing anything in their own day, the view now develops—although not yet stated as vociferously as it would be in another 200 years—that contemporary times represent an improvement on the past and improvement will continue. Renaissance humanists reached high for metaphors to describe human resourcefulness and ingenuity.[18] The marvelous inventions of mankind, according to Giordano Bruno, a victim of the Roman Inquisition, have lifted man out of his bestial nature and brought him closer to the status of a divine being.

The stirring discovery of America, occurring at the close of the Renaissance, boded still more intellectual ferment, and would have a stronger impact on anthropological ideas than the renewal of interest in classical scholarship. But the impact only began to register in the 16th century.

Biological Basis of the Family

The Renaissance in Italy flourished in the 14th and 15th centuries. There two scholars advanced psychological and biological explanations for social institutions, most originally for the family.

The first of the pair, Marsilius, citizen of Padua and for some time rector of the University of Paris, is best known for breaking with the principle that declares the Church and the pope superior to the state and secular rulers. Much to the pleasure of the king of Bavaria, to whose court Marsilius fled in 1326 when the pope accused him of heresy, Marsilius asserted the subordination of the Church to the secular ruler in political affairs. I include Marsilius for a contribution less bold or historically memorable, for a theory similar to Ibn Khaldun's, namely that society is precariously based on two antagonistic elements present by nature in human beings.[19] One causes people to be attracted to each other: it induces dependence, makes possible what Aristotle calls friendship, and lies at the root of cooperation and division of labor. The opposite element acts to maximize selfish interests in individuals—if need be, at the expense of the interests pursued by others. It lies at the root of disputes and conflicts that would destroy society, were it not for the countervailing pressure instituted through law and political power.

The second Renaissance Italian, Leon Battista Alberti of Venice, in a manuscript completed in 1434, hit upon a more viable explanation concerning the early development of the family.[20] A true Renaissance man, who combined painting, poetry, music, philosophy, and architecture, Alberti detects the root of family structure in the helplessness afflicting a newborn human infant. In consequence of that helplessness, a caretaking role devolved on the mother to insure the child's survival, and women became confined to the home, unable to range afield to procure their own subsistence. Thereupon men, by nature more energetic and industrious than women, assumed the specialized role of foodgetters. The monogamous family originated as individual women who had borne a child found security with single male providers. Alberti is logically certain that monogamy was original because, in the remote past a man, no matter how industriously he might work, could not possibly procure enough subsistence to support more than a single wife and their offspring. He offers a near contract theory of social organization, and seemingly builds on the Aristotelian concept of social relations being a system of reciprocities. All that is missing is some recognition of what a man obtains in return for working for his wife and their offspring, and that will come when the exchange value of the woman's sexuality is perceived. Given the state of ethnographic knowledge in the early 15th century, Alberti could not know the various types of families created through human ingenuity, or the substitutes that have been found for replacing the mother in caring for young children.

Impact of Acculturation

Cultural Origins before and after Adam

Authors writing in the first part of the 16th century still reveal nothing of the impact on thought produced by the transatlantic voyages that started in the 1490s. The character of their ideas, for example in the developmental accounts written by Juan Luis Vives and Johann Boemus, is closer to the pattern of the late Middle Ages or Renaissance than to the unhackneyed ideas of Michel de Montaigne, whose essays began to appear in 1580.

The Spanish-born philosopher and pedagogue, Juan Luis Vives, who postulates an instinct for self-preservation to explain why humanity devised culture, recalls Lucretius's view that the preservation of life is the basic aim behind human behavior.[21] And like Lucretius, Vives also found it useful to postulate additional motives—curiosity, for example—to account for the quest for knowledge, the goal to which his own career as university professor and writer was dedicated. Again like his Roman predecessor, he starts the prehistory of human social organization with a period of promiscuity, but fails to explain why or how marriage and family life came about. The influence of Aristotle shows through Vives's account of families agglomerating in a locality, thereby giving rise to villages whose original leaders were patriarchs. Acting as fathers do in the family, the old men settled complaints arising in the village community. However, people soon learned that white hair and wrinkles do not constitute unfailing signs of wisdom; so they began to choose leaders on other bases than age (and kinship?) and to devise laws to control in-group contumacy.

After people had provided for the necessities of life, they turned to innovating conveniences and pleasures to delight themselves with. Curiosity spurred them to investigate nature, at first with strictly practical knowledge as their goal. Discrete discoveries led to the generalization of universal laws, upon which future generations constantly improved as knowledge increased. People took pride in learning. A discovery produced as much joy as a military victory and caused the discoverer to be admired. Spurred by these incentives, which closely resemble the motives Velleius gave for the rising curve of excellence in artistic and intellectual fields, some people devoted themselves wholly to investigation. At this point, Vives drops his optimistic view of intellectual progress and wonders whether knowledge is really desirable when we consider all its consequences. We pursue ideas which we hope will benefit us, but opinions about what is beneficial vary, and nobody can know all the consequences of a discovery originally thought of as beneficial. Rather than leading mankind to established truths having practical value, the growth of knowledge has produced contradictions, conflict, and confusion. Vives longs for certainty and an end to the unsatisfactory subjectivity and relativity that characterize human knowledge.

One of the most radical features of Vives's narrative of cultural development is its beginning set in pre-Adamic times. Apparently the humanist did not fear the Church authorities' displeasure for going beyond the time of the biblical creation.

The renown of Johann Boemus, a German Hebraist, rests more on his ethnographic compilation of customs garnered from the then-known world than on his hackneyed ideas of early cultural development.[22] The cultural schema he implicitly had in mind while writing his compilation, for which he acknowledges Herodotus and the first-century Roman naturalist Pliny as predecessors, called his attention to housing, dress, diet, medicine, religious beliefs and observances, trade, coinage, and the status of women.

He opens his account of cultural development after the exile from the Garden, during a period when human beings lived dispersed over the land, ignorant of money, without trade, and owning lands in common. People dressed in bark, leaves, or fur, slept in the open without fear, and were content with little. Only with the appearance of discontent, disquiet, and fear did they form communities, choose leaders, draw up laws for safety, and fix boundaries around their lands. Handicrafts, agriculture, viniculture, animal domestication, animal traction, and riding also resulted from discontent as mankind grew unwilling to accept only what nature directly made available.

Far more acute observation and original thinking, as well as familiar concepts and old reasoning, turn up in the books of Jean Bodin, who wrote after the middle of the 16th century.[23] A modernist who held the present to outrank the past, Bodin also held the advanced idea that the power in a monarchical government should be balanced between parliament and the king. Yet this French jurist gave his authority freely to help crush doubt about the reality of witches. A number of his anthropological ideas are familiar, such as the theory that human beings are by nature endowed with opposing tendencies, one making for social cooperation and the other for conflict. Society tries to cultivate the first while suppressing the second. Also familiar is his perception that the incest rule creates useful affinal relationships between families, and his recognition of how greatly social life depends on the plasticity of human nature, whereby the behavior of individuals can be shaped. His environmentalism, deriving real or fancied differences in customs and social personality between European regions from climate, is also basically unoriginal. But it is tempered; the molding force of education, laws, and customs, he allows, is strong enough to offset to some extent the influence exercised by climate. Germans and other northern people, he finds, eat and drink heavily because the conditions in which they live demand intense inner heat and this creates a mighty thirst and appetite. More interested in political structure than in physical appetites, he thought that in northern climates governments rule by force, in southern ones they rely on religion, and, in the middle, work through laws to establish a just mean.

Bodin creatively combines the concepts of geographical determinism and cultural patterning to explain differences in mental illness between societies located in different climatic zones. In northern climes, the insane dance, laugh, and leap around foolishly, which is in keeping with the vigorous disposition of people in those lands; but in the south, where human nature is more disposed to use its intellect, the mentally ill experience visions or possession and speak gibberish. Even if he fails to give adequate reasons for the differences, he has drawn attention to how deeply the patterning process reaches into human behavior. His insight extends the generalization, entertained by Herodotus, of traits conforming to the culture pattern.

His social anthropological approach to culture history discloses similar originality as he describes the progressive growth of communities in size and in extent of diversification, meaning not simply increased division of labor but something new: the multiplication of each individual's social relationships. The network in which reciprocity occurs has grown. Today we say many of an individual's social relations in a large-scale society are particularized, entered into for specific purposes; whereas in a primitive society, where the same persons interact for many purposes, they are generalized. Bodin also differentiates between law and custom, by quite explicit, totally empirical criteria. A law can be instantly created by a sovereign and enforced through sanctions, whereas a custom requires no sovereign to become effective and carries neither a promise of reward nor of punishment. And instead of arising instantaneously, the way laws come into force, customs spread gradually from an innovator to more and more people, in the course of time acquiring a compelling power through general consent.

Spectacles, Rituals, and Religion

Bodin stands in the company of Nicholas of Cusa and of more contemporary political philosophers who attended to the expressive nature and social functions of ritual, religion, and other enactments couched in what Clifford Geertz calls "a vocabulary of sentiment." Bodin held the by no means original view that ceremonial eating and drinking possess the capacity to promote friendship and unity among the commensalists.[24] A year after his death, Giovanni Botero, in a manual of practical politics intended for rulers, credited the Olympic games and other spectacles with the psychological functions of satisfying people's need for variety and providing a harmless way of releasing intense feelings, thereby promoting the social function of political stability.[25] His reasoning shows, as others before him also showed, an awareness of the psychological process of displacement. Religion he recommended to princes because it insures good conduct and peaceableness in society, an opinion he supports by citing a chain of predecessors going back to Aristotle. Botero notices the alliance-creating power of exogamy in a unique way. He points out how marriage between conquerors and the subject people promotes unity where none existed before.

A more famous political philosopher and adviser of princes, Niccolo Machiavelli, compared the pagan religions of antiquity with Christianity and found that each influences personality differently.[26] The faiths of antiquity set great store on worldly honor, so much that they raised persons who attained worldly glory to the status of sacred beings. Thereby, pagan religions provided an incentive for bold actions and inculcated a love of freedom, in contrast to Christianity, which extols the humble, contemplative man and disparages worldly glory.

The Concept of Savagery

Late in the 16th century, books written by the French essayist Michel de Montaigne finally showed the reading public the meaning of the discovery of the New World and other hitherto unknown lands. His ideas presage the effect the discoveries would have on European humanism and the course of anthropological thinking.

Montaigne's essays tell us that he had read Plato, Xenophon, Lucretius, and Virgil, among other classical authors, but the ethnographic sources from which his thinking was more originally stimulated, including an account of Columbus's voyages, were entirely secondary. However, he did possess one direct link with savage society: the opportunity to observe and question an Indian from Brazil who was visiting France. Personally he never traveled further from Bordeaux, where he was at home, than to Italy, visiting Switzerland and Germany enroute. Several times on the journey he made a deliberate effort to adopt the cuisine and other customs of the country he was passing through, even writing his journal in Italian when he was in Italy. But such a journey could never by itself have been responsible for the intense appreciation of cultural diversity and cultural relativity one encounters in his essays.[27]

His ideas of cultural relativity go beyond merely recognizing that manners and beliefs differ between peoples. With Pyrrho, the Greek skeptic, he doubts whether absolute standards can possibly be applied in intercultural relations. Relativistically, Montaigne insists on the morality of exotic customs even when they run counter to one's own moral code. The human being's lack of built-in behavior patterns, he recognizes, allows people in society to follow whatever line of conduct reason reveals to be good, to endorse as meritorious even the most horrible acts, such as eating one's dead father out of piety and affection. The relativist's tolerance balks only at customs belonging to his own culture when he perceives them running counter to reason, to which, in keeping with the spirit of the times, he accords a seemingly absolute character. Among practices running contrary to reason he includes astrology and other means of prognostication, reliance upon which continues because people forget the times the predictions fail.

Refreshing as his cultural relativism may be, it is not particularly original or half as significant as the concept of savagery, with which his relativism is fully compatible. When he finishes developing the concept in the essay "Of Cannibals," we realize we have been introduced to the idea of the primitive as it got fashioned in later anthropology. First Montaigne rejects the pejorative, ethnocentrically disparaging meaning of the words "savage" and "barbaric," which they commonly possessed in previous writers. Speaking of the American Indians, he finds savages "savage" only in that their customs are different from his own. Thus for Montaigne "savage" becomes a term for describing people whose lifeways depart from familiar conventions. Second, he picks an alternate meaning of the term. Savages are wild (*sauvage*) in the same way fruits are wild when produced by nature, rather than through the artifices of domestication. Having been little fashioned by the artifices invented by the human mind, savage customs retain their naturalness, a trait Montaigne approves of, and in which he claims contemporary savage societies surpass societies living in the poetic Golden Age. Here is the concept of cultural simplicity, or lack of complexity, applied by later anthropologists to primitive society. The positive evaluation of savagery that enters this second meaning of the term was not always readily admitted into the later concept of primitivity, but Montaigne is quite certain about it. Savage lifeways, he assured his public, are more authentic than the ways of civilization. Barbarous nations are still close to their original simplicity, still governed by natural laws, and still uncorrupted by the conventions of civilized society. Montaigne illustrates the cultural simplicity of savage societies by listing European culture traits they supposedly lack: commerce, writing, mathematics, agriculture, metals, wine, wars of conquest, political hierarchy, the habit of service, economic stratification, and inheritance. He also mentions a few traits diagnostic of savagery, including abundant leisure and the use of classificatory kinship terminology.

Undoubtedly Montaigne drew too sharp a distinction between the customs of small-scale and civilized societies, but the fault is trifling compared with the enormity of the vision he shared with his audience: of a strikingly different world following strange conventions that nevertheless possess a morality and a logic of their own. The primitive world is not without its faults, but on these Montaigne refuses to dwell, as if there had been enough of that attitude toward barbarians, and it was now time to take another perspective.

The Impact of Acculturation

The character of Montaigne's ideas about society and culture is an early token of the changes that took place in western Europe, especially in France and England, after the society expanded its scale following the impact of acculturation. The revitalized study of the authors of Greek and Roman antiquity constituted a kind of culture contact in 14th- and 15th-century Europe, causing the boundaries of the society to expand backward in time. In the latter part of the 16th century, close and firsthand contact—as the definition of acculturation puts it—with hitherto unknown parts of the world, most notably America, increased scale still further, causing the boundaries of European society to expand in geographical space. Printing, invented in Europe only a hundred years earlier, allowed explorers' reports about newly discovered cultures to gain quick wide circulation and contributed to the new world picture.

A tough intellectual problem, that of the position of the American Indians and their cultures in the scheme of mankind and in the stream of culture history,[28] was solved in the 16th century. No matter how the answer had gone, it would have affected the future course of anthropology. Were the Indians subhuman, or fully human and rational like Europeans? Were they perhaps representative of those remnant human beings Plato describes, survivors of a society destroyed by a deluge with nearly all its cultural resources? In Cotton Mather's phrase, "the veriest ruins of mankind"; and now were they in the act of recreating civilization?[29] Or—exciting possibility—could their ways of life represent the same early horizons of human culture which Lucretius describes and to which all mankind once belonged but from which Europe had progressed? The stone tools reported from America strongly indicated the latter possibility, since similar objects, believed to have belonged to a premetallic age, had also been unearthed in Europe.[30] The latter answer, of course, came to prevail.

Once it did, ethnographic accounts of the American Indians could be used as sources of information to fill in more details about human society in its beginning when, in John Locke's words, "all the world was America."

The intellectual impact of the discovery of America and its inhabitants was not exhausted by learning where to place the Indians in regard to humanity or history. Their discovery and the discoveries of other primitive societies heightened Europeans' consciousness of their own culture, as Montaigne illustrates,[31] making them aware of much they had taken for granted. Confronted by other possibilities of living, and almost simultaneously freed from the constraints which had, to some extent, fettered independent reason, philosophers began to ask critical questions about the wisdom or "naturalness" of certain civilized customs compared to similar practices in primitive societies, thereby setting up a trend that carries on into the Enlightenment.

Moral history is the name that was given to the comparative study of mores, or customs, which we call ethnology. Joseph de Acosta, the Spanish historian, counterposes moral history to natural history, pointing out that whereas the latter treats "the heavens, the temperature . . . mettals, plants, and beasts," moral history deals with customs, fashions, religious beliefs, forms of worship, disposal of the dead, time reckoning, social stratification, government, warfare, and artifacts.[32] The word "history," standing for more than a narrative of past events, meant systematic description, as it still does today when we speak of natural history. "Moral" for the next 200 years continued to be occasionally employed in the sense of customary. Moral history, therefore, means the systematic description of customs, social structure, and artifacts, a task to which great importance came to be attached. For a well-organized voyage of discovery, like Sir Walter Raleigh's in 1585, explicit observation guides, or questionnaires, were written to guide professional observers and artists who accompanied the mariners in making observations of culture.[33]

The 17th Century

No Sin to Scrutinize Nature

Times are not drastically altered because the number by which a century is known changes. Far more significant is the claim made by people who remember the past that they are now living in very different times. That is how writers in the 17th century saw their period. According to an observant English biographer and antiquarian,[34] "Until about the yeare 1649 when Experimental Philosophy was first cultivated by a Club at Oxford, 'twas held a strange presumption for a Man to attempt an Innovation in Learnings; and not to be good Manners, to be more knowing than his Neighbours and Forefathers; even to attempt an improvement in Husbandry (though it succeeded with profit) was look'd upon with an ill Eie. Their Neighbours did scorne to follow it, though not to doe it, was to their own Detriment. 'Twas held a Sin to make a Scrutinie into the Waies of Nature. . . ."

Scholars had become increasingly curious and venturesome. They reasoned independently not only upon experience produced in everyday life, but upon observations deliberately contrived through "philosophical experiments" conducted in chemistry, physics, anatomy, and other fields of study represented in England's newly founded Royal Society, the "Club at Oxford"[35] Religion was still of intense concern to most people, but observations about it, done in a naturalistic and critical spirit, were undertaken more readily than in previous centuries. (Not that they were more naturalistic than the classical Greek philosophers' writings on religion.) In the natural sciences as well as in social thought, 17th-century thinkers repudiated the authority of Aristotle and condemned medieval philosophy as deficient in its too great concern with words rather than observation and experimentation. No longer did Aristotle carry the title of philosopher preeminent; in his place Francis Bacon became the primate of the intellectuals. The scholars writing on nature, politics, morals, and other aspects of society still called themselves philosophers, signifying their dedication to finding basic principles and causes. Where that goal was manifestly being achieved, in chemistry, physics, and mechanics, they spoke of "science," meaning certain knowledge.

Psychogenesists and Empiricists

Not everything in 17th-century anthropology is original. The philosophers we will meet reiterate many old ideas whose importance they rediscovered in the new social context wherein they wrote. Writers also advance some new ideas and shift certain viewpoints. For example, geographical determinism receives severe competition from psychological explanations for social structure and other aspects of culture, a tendency we saw beginning in the Renaissance. Authors frequently refer to drives, reason, imagination, emotion, and other aspects of cognition and feeling, including intolerance of ambiguity and ignorance, to explain psychogenically the origin of customs or the course taken in the development of social institutions.

Explanations couched in such terms created their own problems. For one thing, those doing the explaining didn't always agree on what particular psychogenic factors operated in a certain social phenomenon, or how they worked, and since there was no way such rival theories could be tested, contradictions between theorists stayed unresolved. Furthermore, whereas in theory at least geographical determinism could explain differences in culture or social personality by differences in environment, the universal attributes of human nature to which the 17th-century psychogenesists refer can only account for universal features of social life. They leave the impressive variability of cultural forms between societies and their historical mutability unaccounted for. For more than 200 years this limitation would affect the character of anthropological knowledge by encouraging theories of parallelism and diffusion. For if the psychological bases of culture are everywhere the same, then societies should indeed originate similar customs independently, or readily adopt them if diffusion presents the opportunity for doing so. Under the persuasive grip of parallelism and diffusion, anthropology paid comparatively little attention to dynamic theories capable of explaining cultural forms, whether locally invented or borrowed through diffusion, by relating them to contemporary cultural conditions. Not until the 19th century, in Lewis Henry Morgan and Emile Durkheim, do strong hands begin to design theories of sociogenic determinism.

At the same time that philosophers dwelt on universal attributes of cognition and feeling as explanations of society and culture, the empiricists led by John Locke were preparing the way for a new use of the psychological viewpoint. They maintained that the contents of cognition are themselves largely determined by social experience, in effect predicting that if experience is varied, different sorts of human nature would result. Of course Plato and Ibn Khaldun realized as much, but without attaching the theoretical significance to their knowledge that the empiricists did. Notwithstanding the popularity immediately accorded to empiricism, the position was challenged by the nativistic thesis, most prominently associated with Baron Gottfried von Leibnitz, who asserted that the mind by itself supplies the categories of thought which, acting like organs of the body, digest or code experience. For 250 years empiricism has dominated psychology, increasingly influencing the use made of the psychological viewpoint in anthropology, as researchers became more interested in the cultural patterning of human nature. Yet still in our day, psychological nativism survives; for instance, in the structuralism propounded by Claude Lévi-Strauss.

When All the World Was America

More than pure curiosity lay behind the intense interest which Thomas Hobbes and Jock Locke took in the ancient question of how the state originated. The question was directly relevant to their time, a period when the king's absolutism was being challenged and the rights of the individual affirmed. Each wrote to defend a political position: Hobbes, submission to authority; Locke, individual freedom.

Within a few pages I will make clear that the anthropological signifi-

cance of Thomas Hobbes lies not in the parable of the original compact—
the idea of society, or the state, being based on contract—but in his
concepts of magic and ritual. Nevertheless, something should be said
about his model of the conditions prompting people to create the state.[36]
Political structure, he holds, originated to resolve the insecurity of life
created through the presence of selfish trends in human nature. Given the
individual's fundamentally antisocial tendencies, people could never feel
safe or be content while living in their original, natural state. Driven by
self-interest, each would incessantly despoil, rob, or take revenge on his
fellows, and employ the human gift of speech to malign others or sow
confusion by representing evil as good. Being also reasonable, persons
living in the state of nature devised government as a means of preserving
themselves from the unpleasant consequences of their own natures or,
positively speaking, to guarantee a secure, contented life. The invention
was successful. Hence people continue to confer their collective power
and strength on one man, or on an assembly of men, on whom they rely
to prevent the injuries they are individually prone to inflict on each other.

Hobbes, it is said, loved contemplation much more than reading, which
may explain why he doesn't mention the tendency for social affiliation in
human nature to which his predecessors called attention. A German jurist,
Samuel von Pufendorf, soon corrected Hobbes's oversight, pointing out
that in mankind there is a potentiality for sociality—in fact, a necessity,
because without sociality no one would survive beyond infancy—as well as
a proclivity to injure others.[37] But like Hobbes, he too concludes that
people realizing the mischief the evil in them could do chose the security
even the most primitive kind of social order could provide.

Something of greater anthropological significance emerges in Pufendorf.
He relates antisocial conduct to human beings' omnipresent sexuality and
their tendency to multiply wants in excess of necessity. These powerful
"talents" are hard to restrain, and for their satisfaction individuals will
commit all manner of evil.

Pufendorf felt he had to offer some kind of logical justification for the
purely rationalistic method he followed in reconstructing prehistory. Nothing, he says, prevents us "from being able to reason out the origin of a
thing, despite the fact there remain no written records upon them."
Though his reasoning amounts to little, his defensiveness suggests a
heightened critical sense and a concern for evidence not hitherto conspicuous.

Forty years after Hobbes, John Locke presented yet another model of
mankind's original condition, this time documented with ethnographic
evidence from the New World.[38] For "in the beginning all the world was
America"; everyone lived as the American Indians still do, in a state where
nobody has greater power than another and nobody is subordinated to
anyone else, except on account of age or special quality. In those days,

everyone being equal and holding things in common led people to take a warm, reciprocal interest in each other's welfare and to extend aid when it was required. Reason told them not to injure one another, unless it be in punishment for an offense. In this happy state of affairs, political organization could hardly have arisen to control violence or other unsociable behavior. It appeared not to restrain conduct but to preserve human freedom and to enlarge opportunities for man's social nature to display itself.

Despite his well-stocked library, which included many works of travel, Locke also possessed enough critical sense to realize he was short of evidence to support his model of the origin of the state. But, as his use of ethnographic data indicates, unlike Hobbes or Pufendorf he did not rely solely on rational argument. His selective use of such data began a trend which would be followed for more than 200 years by writers seeking to complete, as far as possible, the prehistoric record of cultural development by taking details of social behavior from accounts of societies living in contemporary or near contemporary times.

Locke follows Aristotle in explaining how the idea of political organization came about. He visualizes early governance as an outgrowth of paternal authority, which accustomed people to rule by one man and taught them its benefits. Concerning the origin of the family, Locke reasons somewhat as Alberti did, tracing it to biological foundations; not only to children's long period of dependence, but also to the frequency with which women become pregnant. Under those circumstances, the survival of women and children would have been grievously imperiled without the dependable presence of one or—Locke grants the possibility of early polygyny—more men to provide for their support.

It depends entirely on the cogency of the argument whether we believe Locke, Hobbes, or neither, or a contemporary, William Temple, who bypasses the ultimate origin of the state and traces political compacts to conquest.[39] Government based on contract, he maintains, resolves conflicts over the rightful basis of authority in compound societies, which arise when one group conquers another.

The Transformation of Magic

Ideas even more original than an awareness that reconstructions of prehistory in the absence of empirical evidence needed to be justified were published in the 17th century. Two long-lasting contributions to anthropology made at this time, the concept of magic and a dynamic theory of how magic arises or is maintained, have only recently been superseded.

Magic perceived in the context of early European history belongs to a wider category of customs, including astrology, dream interpretation, divination, and belief in witches and enchantment.[40] Whatever the ultimate age of those customs may be, in Europe they passed without a break from pre-Christian times into the Christian era, where they managed to survive despite the opposition of the Church. In the late Middle Ages, as the Church began to lose dominance, ideas we call magic—such as the capacity of things to influence each other though they never come into contact—to some extent even penetrated the intellectual great tradition, becoming allied with philosophy and involved in experimentation, i.e., with incipient science. As late as the 16th century, scholars still acknowledged occult science. They distinguished between black magic, or sorcery, which works by virtue of the Devil, and white, or good, magic, which follows the laws of nature and, like everything in nature, obeys God's will. Even a materialist like Pietro Pomponazzi, who lived into the 16th century, believed in magic, dropping only the supernaturalistic element that allies it with supernatural agencies and insisting that magic, as well as miracles, works naturally.[41] He regarded magic and miracles as steps, inexplicable and strange but natural nevertheless, in a sequence of transformations that things inevitably undergo without any intervention by spiritual beings.

Such ideas, even when, as in Pomponazzi, they treat magic naturalistically, differ from the anthropological concept of magic as it was shaped by James Frazer and other disbelievers in the late 19th and early 20th centuries. But in two respects the European concept of magic as it was explicitly conceived by philosophers in the centuries immediately before the 17th is directly continuous with the view inherited by Frazer. According to the early conception, some things in nature possess an inherent tendency to be attracted to things resembling them, and to repel their opposites. Acting on this premise, someone could take an object perceived to possess a subjectively desirable property—say longevity or boldness—and logically use it in a manner calculated to reproduce the same property in himself or others. Turning to particulars, a root shaped like the male genital was believed capable of restoring a man's virility, and eating animal brains would nourish intelligence. A related premise, in the late medieval, the Renaissance, and the 16th-century conception of magic, regarded inherent properties in things as capable of being transmitted through contact or proximity. Acting on that premise, and entertaining the fancy that a whore is lecherous and impudent, someone could logically believe that a prostitute's dress would transmit the same qualities to a person who dons it. Frazer based his definition of magic on these premises, referring to them as the principles of similarity and contagion (or, collectively, as the principle of sympathy); like the Church he, too, held them to be empirically false.

Frazer, and before him Tylor, generalized that magic, wherever it is used, can be distinguished from religion by its independence from spiritual beings. In the eyes of its practitioners, magic works routinely, naturally, like a mechanical causal sequence. This is the second respect in which the anthropological concept of magic was continuous with the earlier conception. Not only Pomponazzi, but other philosophers who treated magic as a part of nature, claimed much the same thing, even though they acknowledged that ultimately all nature depends on God.

As the 16th century ended, magic and science were disengaged from each other, and by the 17th century the uncoupling was complete. What happened in the process of disengagement repeated the Church's disparagement of magic. But the philosophers did so in a different context. Churchmen regarded magic as antithetical to the Christian faith; 17th-century thinkers held it to be contrary to good reason and observation. They denied that amulets and techniques based on similarity and contagion and designed to bring about useful ends possessed the effectiveness ascribed to them. If they sometimes worked, it could only be by accident.

We find the new conception of magic in Francis Bacon's works dating from the first quarter of the 17th century.[42] Bacon, who is reported to have taken a large drink of strong beer before going to bed lest his thinking keep him awake, held several high political appointments in the English government before being accused of corruption. But he never held a university post. His attitude to the relevance of revelation for knowledge may be judged from his praise of Democritus, and of other ancient Greek physicists, for having removed God and mind from the structure of things; and also from his statement that if Adam's fall cost mankind dominion over the created world, a subordinate form of command was still available, namely, scientific knowledge. By pointing out the biases leading to false interpretations of experimental results, and by providing rules for sound induction, he sought to improve the scientific route to command over nature. Hence we understand why he had no use for explanations couched in terms of similarity and contagion, and why he dismisses the possibility of achieving ordinary, useful ends through easy means based on "vaporous imagination." Significant accomplishments can never be attained by utilizing token amounts of ingredients in which powerful properties are supposed to inhere. Bacon also distinguished between magic and witchcraft; the first anyone can do, but the latter is limited to "peculiar persons" —witches.

Thomas Hobbes, a resolute materialist but a believer in God and an opponent of atheism—or so he protested, perhaps too much—went beyond exposing the fallacies of magic. In the middle of the century he sketched a theory of the conditions supporting magic.[43] Magic arises because the majority of people don't know how to ascertain the causes of things that affect them, or they fail to take the trouble to find out if an empirical connection links a presumed antecedent and consequent. Hence they are led to expect that whatever once preceded a certain occurrence will do so again. From like things past they expect like things to come. By such thinking the credulous come to attribute good or bad luck to a place or to spoken words that once happened to accompany an event. Fortune is attributed to an accidental bystander, and a place or word comes to be thought of as lucky or unlucky. Hobbes includes omens in the concept he is describing, and Tylor also did not distinguish between divination and magic. Hobbes makes magic primarily a way of thinking. His theory, similar to the intellectualistic theory of religion offered by Greek philosophers, regards magic as an attempt to supply causes without the critical thinking whereby valid causes can be separated from accidental associations.

The Natural Seeds of Religion

Hobbes also took an intellectualistic attitude toward religion, but defined his subject carefully to avoid the possibility of being persecuted for heresy. Since human beings alone among the animals have religion, Hobbes reasoned, it must be because of some peculiar quality in human nature, some "natural seeds" with which we are born. He finds those seeds, first, in man's incessant desire to know causes, especially the causes of an individual's own good or bad fortune now and in times to come. Second, religion arises because people are ill prepared to use their reason to inquire into the natural causes for events. These two factors, ignorance and fear, plus a third feature of human nature, an uncritical disposition to believe, are responsible for the invention of the supposed causes. Sometimes the suppositions arise as the result of God's direction or divine revelation, but among the Gentiles they are superstitiously come by and depict invisible awe-inspiring powers, some of which are invoked to win assistance or to alleviate distress. Religious belief systems, then, are epiphenomena generated by psychological conditions—curiosity about causes, intolerance of ambiguity, and fear. I think it is reasonable to interpret Hobbes as suggesting that the same psychological conditions accompanied by better reasoning would produce not suppositious causes but knowledge of natural causes. Isn't he, therefore, contrasting science and religion, just as anthropology would continue to do in the 18th and 19th centuries?

Interested parties hoping to profit, Hobbes goes on to say, purposely propagate superstitious beliefs, or at least fail to contradict them. Political leaders, too, urge religion on their followers in order to make them obedient, peaceable, and amenable. Or, as Pufendorf wrote, without fear of God there would be no conscience.[44]

Neither the natural seeds of religion, its psychological sources, nor its instrumental value in behalf of social control, Hobbes perceived, suffices to maintain religion. Religion also depends on having faith in a religious leader—a priest or a political authority—who labors for people's happiness and whom they believe to be wise, holy, and receptive to divine revelation. When confidence in the person's wisdom, sincerity, and connection with divinity breaks down, the beliefs he upholds will also fall under suspicion.

Such loss of confidence will occur if the leader's behavior contradicts his teachings, if he becomes exclusively concerned with his private ends, or if supernatural signs and miracles are not forthcoming through him.

Both Bacon and Hobbes had new things to say about the ceremonial side of religion, without which, someone has said, religion would be as incomplete as meat without sauce. Bacon thought ritual antecedent to belief. In ancient times, when religion had consisted chiefly of ceremonies, it remained unified because dissension breaks out more readily over beliefs than over rites.[45]

A significant concept of ritual appears as Hobbes applies the word both to divine worship and to respect directed to eminent human beings.[46] All worship has its ultimate source in the reverence persons show to other persons who are powerful or feared, and consists of verbal or other symbolic forms, including prayer, obeying, being diligent, and serving obligingly, through which inner thoughts are expressed and honor is bestowed on a target, human or divine. Note the wide range of behavior categorized as ritual, including commonplace attributes of everyday social relations, like diligence and service. Also note the implicit definition of ritual—behavior expressive of sentiments—and its similarity to the concepts Durkheim and Radcliffe-Brown later employ. And like Durkheim, Hobbes claims that it matters nothing whether ritual words and acts are feigned or sincerely motivated; in either case they constitute overt tokens of honor or submission.

In another dispassionate and essentially instrumentalist view of religion, William Petty, an Englishman primarily interested in statistics, identified noxious social consequences of supernatural belief systems.[47] While faith enables believers to bear pain and wrongs done to them, emboldens soldiers, and through fear of supernatural sanctions keeps people honest or restrains their violence, religion also requires heavy expenditures by the faithful, creates strife between rival denominations, and by the fear it creates intensifies personal distress. His balanced approach, published late in the century, could well have been written by one of the French skeptical philosophers in the Age of Enlightenment.

The Tyranny of Custom

Habituation, Montaigne wrote in the 16th century, stupefies fear. In the same period Giordano Bruno, the Italian philosopher whose life the Inquisition ended by burning him, coined a metaphor, "triumphant beast," to describe the tight grip on thinking that is maintained by socially standardized prejudices. Seventeenth-century writings are filled with similar utterances and metaphors calling attention to the force of cultural patterning. The aim, however, was not to state an ethnological principle, but to reaffirm the importance of free inquiry guided by reason, to offset thinking with the prejudices, the stereotyped beliefs, or the "idols," as Bacon called them, of tradition which frequently run contrary to reason. Our interest, however, is in the way the philosophers recognized the extent to which culture shapes individual cognition, perception, and motivation. Bacon speaks of the "tyranny of custom," whereby people feel compelled to carry out tasks of which they personally disapprove, or to perform acts, such as self-torture and suttee, which are painful or self-destructive.[48] René Descartes reads like a passage in a modern anthropology textbook when he predicts that a person would hold very different beliefs were he brought up from childhood among Frenchmen, Germans, Chinese, or cannibals.[49] He accepted the principle of psychic unity, believing that basically all human beings reason the same way, and therefore was discomfited by the seeming ease with which different societies reached quite contradictory ideas. The English churchman, Joseph Glanvill, who was quite capable of defending both science and belief in witches, likewise observes how rearing restricts our ability to think in fresh ways.[50] Due to the "prejudice of custom," people perceive what they have learned to expect, no matter how absurd it may be in the opinion of someone reared under different conditions.

The writers who were dismayed by the strong force of cultural patterning could hardly fail to notice, or to regret, the relativity of values and beliefs. Almost nothing has not sometime or someplace been held to be a god or devil.[51] Though opinions contrary to custom are hard to teach, with time custom makes all things right[52] and endows all usages with the patina of propriety.[53]

If awareness of the power of cultural patterning conflicted dismayingly with the belief that independent reason leads to truth, the intellectuals nevertheless occasionally discovered rational wisdom in the functions of exotic customs. Temple defended the ancient Britons' practice of fraternal polyandry as probably serving to reduce jealousy between brothers, to prevent adultery with a brother's wife, and to avoid the expenses associated with polygyny.[54] A group of men rearing offspring in common also eliminates the partiality parents are apt to show to particular children. Furthermore, polyandry liberates a woman, while living with a single husband confines her to his comings and goings.

The century's best known work on cultural patterning, *An Essay Concerning Human Understanding,* Locke's treatise on knowledge, carries the idea beyond anthropology into psychology and philosophy.[55] The book also makes considerable use of ethnographic data, drawing on the variety of custom to demolish the nativistic thesis that some ideas are universally held, and to support the argument that experience is the main source of belief. Customs like killing or abandoning parents without remorse and eating one's own children are cited to drive home the point that there are no universal moral principles stamped on the mind and invariably governing human conduct. Hardly a principle of morality known to Englishmen isn't somewhere violated by a whole society. Custom, a power greater than nature, causes men to believe and worship unquestioningly whatever it commands, and to accept as perfectly natural what is in truth merely conventional. Where Alexander Ross, on the basis of a worldwide survey of religion, asserted no nation exists without some religion,[56] for Locke not even the idea of God is innate.

Locke fails to amplify the statement that diversity of beliefs between societies arises from the things members of a society regularly do. Instead, he concentrates his attention on socialization, the means whereby beliefs already generated become instilled in individuals. He argues the importance of early learning on a variety of grounds, including the firmness with which people believe and their readiness at times to lay down their lives for an opinion. Three years earlier the French archbishop and educationist François Fénelon, arguing the same point, referred to a child's soft brain on which anything can be easily and deeply etched so that early learning remains vivid and strong throughout life.[57]

Gradual Change Creates Contradictions

Consciousness of change as an abstract phenomenon was quite appropriate in a period that witnessed the English civil war, made advanced inventions and discoveries in a wide variety of fields, and expected great things from the continued application of independent reason to experience. Francis Bacon, however, understood that progress does not occur equally or in the same form in every department of cultural knowledge.[58] He distinguishes between cumulative development, which moves continuously toward perfection, as it has in the mechanical arts, between additive growth, and between lack of any growth at all, which was the condition in which he found scholastic philosophy.

More pragmatically, Descartes wanted to know how culture change could be fostered by injecting new ideas into a society to replace obsolete knowledge inherited from the past.[59] Simply grafting new to old, he feared, creates contradictions. Savage societies halfway on the path to civilization, making laws on an ad hoc basis as need arises, are, in his opinion, more poorly governed than nations living under a coherent body of law proclaimed by a wise leader. Sparta flourished because its legal code was no patchwork but an integrated whole tending toward a single goal invented by one man. Yet Descartes knew it is unrealistic to think of demolishing an outworn culture and totally reconstructing it with an integrated set of norms.

Other philosophers, also with practical intent, considered the sources of revolutionary structural change, especially poverty and want, which Bacon regarded as leading to political discord, factionalism, and sedition.[60] Temple saw government threatened when a discrepancy exists in a society between wants and socially approved means for attaining them in a situation of relative deprivation.[61] Those content with what they possess, or who believe they can achieve what they desire, will try to maintain the status quo, but those who cannot escape from want will be eager to shift the cards in a new game. He understood the dynamics of relative deprivation very well; even fortunate people, he wrote, wax discontented when they see others faring still better.

More along ethnological lines, Edward Brerewood and Sir Matthew Hale, men less often mentioned than their illustrious contemporaries, have interesting things to say about diffusion and invention. Brerewood, an English astronomer living into the 17th century, who made ethnology his hobby, wrote a survey of religious customs in different societies in which he ponders the striking recurrence of circumcision.[62] Tentatively, he entertains the theory that the custom spread from the Jews to other cultures. Then, like Herodotus facing a problem for which no documentary assistance is available, he tests his theory deductively; but in this case, Brerewood uses comparative ethnographic data. He notes the ages and attendant circumstances when the operation is performed in different societies, no doubt reasoning that if the facts are the same as among the Jews then the theory is supported. But the facts aren't the same. The experiment, nonquantitative of course, leads him to discard the theory and to conclude that diffusion from a single source cannot account for all the world's circumcision customs.

Hale, a famous midcentury British jurist, who spent his spare time on history, theology, science, and collecting antiquities, regarded diffusion as a kind of migration, not of people but of the arts, promoted by trade, conquering armies, and colonization.[63] Linguistic studies convinced him that mankind's many languages stem from a single source, and he explains the world's linguistic diversity as the product of diffusion, the invention of new words, and the mingling of people following invasion and colonization.

The process of invention interested Hale greatly, and he lists many sources through which applicable new discoveries are made. They include trial and error, serendipity, analogy, and deduction of unknown from known facts. In trying to account for the factors that produced particular cultural traits, his imagination sometimes fails and his naturalism gives way to supernaturalism. The medicinal properties of herbs, he is convinced, could never have been learned directly through experience, so the knowledge must have been implanted in people's minds by God. He wonders why some societies possess only a few arts, and he offers several suggestions, including barbarism, which he doesn't clearly elucidate, and sloth, and, in certain instances, deculturation brought about by barbarians who wrecked what was once a richer culture.

From the Church Fathers to the Age of Reason

A Millennium-and-a-Half of Development

Anthropological ideas in the sources with which we started this chapter are scarce, embedded in theology, and mostly familiar from classical writings. They become increasingly profuse, naturalistic, and original as we enter the 16th and 17th centuries. During the entire fifteen-hundred-year time span, ideas about society and culture are advanced only incidentally to other purposes—religious, philosophical, political—that change from period to period with the authors' social background. The exceptions occur in the latter centuries, especially in Montaigne, Brerewood, and Hale, each of whom devoted himself primarily to ethnological topics.

The Church Fathers selected from the ancient writers the philosophical ideas they found useful or could reinterpret to be in conformity with divinely revealed knowledge. They wrote to encourage their Christian followers, to combat pagan criticism, and to expose errors in pagan thought. In cultural anthropology their fundamental premise holds society, culture, and culture history to be the realization of God's plan for the world. They understood the integration of culture, its instrumental utility, and the relationship of culture to the God-given biological and psychological capabilities of human beings. Among other subjects touched upon by the Patriarchs—as well as by writers in the later Middle Ages who, although continuing with the same fundamental premise, were less preoccupied with theology—were the origin and development of culture, the ubiquity of diffusion, the alliance function of the incest rule, and cultural relativity. To the Muslim philosopher Averroës we owe a substantial treatment of dual religious traditions coexisting in the same society, and in Thomas Aquinas we have a distinction between expressive and pragmatic ritual that outlines the future anthropological concept of magic.

During the Renaissance, when zeal for studying the authors of classical antiquity increased, Christian scholars grew more willing to deal with social and cultural topics naturalistically, but none of them surpassed the Muslim historian Ibn Khaldun. His introduction to world history, although it contains ideas carried over from the past, when taken as a whole forms a work of astonishing originality, compared with the literature of the previous thousand years. Systematically, he compares Bedouin and sedentary culture—a distinction loosely corresponding to the contrast that later anthropology drew between primitive and civilized ways of life. The comparison is mainly synchronic, although Ibn Khaldun occasionally takes a developmental standpoint; for example, when he explains how a sedentary urban culture grows out of the nomadic, desert way of life and what the consequences of the change are for the inhabitants of the city. The antagonistic factors of sociability and self-interest, which Ibn Khaldun and European Renaissance writers postulate to exist in human nature, exemplify the mode of psychogenic explanation that will rapidly increase in popularity.

Montaigne was one of the first Europeans to reveal the impact stirred up by the discovery of American Indian cultures. His extreme cultural relativism is noteworthy, but not as original as his concept of savagery, which anticipates the idea of primitive in later anthropology. For him, savages are people whose customs depart in some striking way from familiar conventions—people who, culturally speaking, are little fashioned by the artifices of civilization and therefore follow relatively simple ways of life. In the latter respect at least, Montaigne's typical savage resembles Ibn Khaldun's Bedouin.

By the end of the 17th century, acculturation—in previous centuries promoted through renewed contact with the literature of classical antiquity as well as through exploration—markedly affected anthropological thought. Once it was decided that stone-tool-using American Indian societies paralleled those early cultures that had been imaginatively reconstructed by Lucretius and other early writers, travelers' reports about the New World could be used to fill in details of life as it had been in the beginning of human society when "all the world was America." But one development in the century's anthropological thought with long-term significance owes nothing directly to geographical exploration. I refer to the conception of magic as consisting of actions based on misplaced confidence in imitation and contagion undertaken for utilitarian ends. The intellectualistic theory of magic and religion fashioned at this time is less original, except for the fact that it allies the two forms of behavior.

Most of the major anthropological viewpoints were applied during the time span we have surveyed, but none as consistently and as self-consciously as the psychological perspective. It appears both in the form of psychogenic explanations for culture and in the concept of cultural patterning, particularly in the extreme empiricism of Locke. The historical viewpoint is manifested in the attention paid to culture change and processes contributing to change, including revolution and, from a more ethnologically oriented point of view, diffusion and invention. Along with cultural patterning, cultural relativity is a theme often referred to, and the contrast between nature and culture is found in writings by the Church Fathers, as well as in those by later authors who perceived the family and other forms of social organization to be based on manifest or assumed natural human characteristics.

Notes

1. Etienne Gilson, *Reason and Revelation in the Middle Ages* (New York: Charles Scribner's Sons, 1938).

2. Origen, *Against Celsus* (*Contra Celsum*), trans. Frederick Crombie, in Alexander Roberts and James Donaldson, eds., *The Ante-Nicene Fathers*, vol. 4, *Fathers of the Third Century* (New York: Charles Scribner's Sons, 1907), bk. 6, chs. 75, 76, 78, 81.

3. Cited in George Boas, *Essays on Primitivism and Related Ideas in the Middle Ages* (Baltimore: Johns Hopkins Press, 1948), pp. 130–131. For Origen's view, see *On First Principles* (*De Principiis*), in Alexander Roberts and James Donaldson, eds., *The Ante-Nicene Fathers*, vol. 4, *Fathers of the Third Century*, bk. 2, ch. 9.

4. John Chrysostom, *Instructions to Catechumens*, trans. W. R. W. Stephens, in Philip Schaff, ed., *A Select Library of the Nicene and Post-Nicene Fathers of the Christian Church*, vol. 9, *Saint Chrysostom: On the Priesthood; Ascetic Treatises; Select Homilies and Letters; Homilies on the Statutes* (New York: Christian Literature Co., 1889), p. 164.

5. Augustine of Hippo, *Concerning the City of God Against the Pagans*, trans. David Knowles (Harmondsworth: Penguin Books, 1972), bk. 19, ch. 6.

6. What follows is from Augustine, *City of God*, bk. 5, ch. 12 and 13–19; bk. 10, ch. 9; and bk. 15, chs. 15 and 16.

7. H. F. Muller, "A Chronological Note on the Physiological Explanation of the Prohibition of Incest," *Journal of Religious Psychology*, vol. 6 (1913): 294–295.

8. In J. N. Hillgarth, ed., *The Conversion of Western Europe, 350–750* (Englewood Cliffs, N.J.: Prentice-Hall, 1969), pp. 113–114. See also M. D. W. Jeffreys, "Some Rules of Directed Culture Change Under Roman Catholicism," *American Anthropologist*, vol. 58 (1956): 721–731, 722–723. Nine or ten centuries later the Jesuits fully followed Gregory's counsel. See Peter Duignan, "Early Jesuit Missionaries: A Suggestion for Further Study," *American Anthropologist*, vol. 60 (1958): 725–732.

9. Ancius Manlius Severinus Boethius, *The Consolation of Philosophy*, trans. W. V. Cooper, in Irwin Edman, ed., *The Consolation of Philosophy* (New York: Modern Library, 1943), pp. 33, 37, 49.

10. Cited in Gilson, *Reason and Revelation*, pp. 40–45. Coexisting, different levels of belief were also referred to by the Church Fathers, as Gilson points out on pp. 108–109.

11. Otto of Freising, *The Two Cities*, trans. Charles C. Mierow (New York: Columbia University Press, 1928), pp. 95, 123–130.

12. For a good account see Clarence J. Glacken, *Traces on the Rhodian Shore* (Berkeley: University of California Press, 1967), ch. 6.

13. Thomas Aquinas, *On the Governance of Rulers*, trans. Gerald B. Phelan (London: Sheed and Ward, 1938), ch. 1.

14. Thomas Aquinas, *Summa Theologica*, trans. Fathers of the English Dominican Province (22 vols.; London; Burns Oates and Washbourne, [1916–1935]), vol. 11, chs. 95–96; Thomas Aquinas, *The Summa Contra Gentiles*, trans. English Dominican Fathers (5 vols.; London: Burns Oates and Washbourne, [1923–1929]), vol. 4, chs. 105–109.

15. Thomas Aquinas, *Summa Theologica*, vol. 19, pp. 197–224, 343.

16. Ibn Khaldun, *The Muqaddimah, An Introduction to History*, trans. Franz Rosenthal (2 vols.; Princeton: Princeton University Press, 1958). There is also an abridged edition by the same translator (London: Routledge and Kegan Paul in Association with Secker and Warburg, 1967).

17. Nicholas of Cusa, *Concordantia Catholica* [orig. 1433–4], cited in Francis William Coker, ed., *Readings in Political Philosophy* (rev. and enl. ed.; New York: Macmillan Co., 1938), pp. 265–66.

18. Marsilio Ficino, "Platonic Theology" [orig. c. 1482], trans. Josephine L. Burroughs, in Paul Oskar Kristeller, "Ficino and Pomponazzi on the Place of Man in the Universe," *Journal of the History of Ideas*, vol. 5 (1944): 227–239, pp. 233–234. Giordano Bruno, *The Expulsion of the Triumphant Beast* [orig. 1584], Arthur D. Imerti, ed. and trans. (New Brunswick, N.J.: Rutgers University Press, 1964), pp. 205–206.

19. Marsilius of Padua, *Defensor Pacis* trans. Alan Gewirth, in *Marsilius of Padua, The Defender of Peace* (2 vols.; New York: Columbia University Press, 1956), vol. 2, ch. 3.

20. Leon Battista Alberti, *The Family in Renaissance Italy*, trans. Renée Neu Watkins (Columbia, S.C.: University of South Carolina Press, 1969), pp. 54, 112.

21. Juan Luis Vives, *Vives: On Education: A Translation of the De Tradendis Disciplinis* [orig. 1531], trans. Foster Watson (Cambridge: At the University Press, 1913).

22. Johann Boemus, *The Fardle of Facions Conteining the Aunciente Maners, Custumes, and Lawes of the Peoples Enhabiting the Two Partes of the Earthe Called Affricke and Asia* [orig. 1520], trans. W. M. Waterman (3 vols.; London: E. and G. Goldsmid, 1888).

23. Jean Bodin, *Method for the Easy Comprehension of History* [orig. 1566], trans. Beatrice Reynolds (New York: Columbia University Press, 1945), pp. 145–146, 152, 212–214; Jean Bodin, *The Six Books of a Commonweale* [orig. 1576], Kenneth Douglas McRae, ed. (Cambridge: Harvard University Press, 1962), pp. 160–162, 551–554, 556, 557, 565.

24. Bodin, *The Six Books*, p. 364. In *The Laws* (I.626) Plato refers to communal meals as instituted among the Cretans and Spartans to maintain close-knit military organization.

25. Giovanni Botero, *Practical Politics* [orig. 1596], trans. George Albert Moore (Washington, D.C.: Country Dollar Press, 1949), pp. 96, 114. Botero makes no reference to Aristotle who wrote of dramatic tragedy and music effecting the catharsis of pity, fear, and other individual emotions, thus bringing about a sort of pleasurable relief; see Aristotle, *Poetics*, 1449[b], and *Politics*, 1341[b], both in D. A. Russell and M. Winterbottom, eds., *Ancient Literary Criticism* (Oxford: Clarendon Press, 1972), pp. 97, 133. Niccolo Machiavelli, *The History of Florence* [orig. 1531], bk. 7, ch. 12; bk. 8, ch. 36; for religion, pp. 86–89, 255 ff., in *Machiavelli, the Chief Works and Others*, trans. Allan Gilbert (3 vols.; Durham, N.C.: Duke University Press, 1965).

26. Niccolo Machiavelli, *Discourses on the First Decade of Titus Livius* [orig. 1531], bk. 2, ch. 2, in *Machiavelli, the Chief Works and Others*.

27. Michel de Montaigne, *The Essays* [orig. 1580 and 1588], trans. Jacob Zeitlin (2 vols.; New York: Alfred A. Knopf, 1934). See especially, "Of Prognostications," "Of Custom, and That We Should Not Easily Change a Law Received," "Of the Education of Children," "Of Cannibals," "Of Ancient Customs," and "Apology of Raymond Sebond."

28. Margaret T. Hodgen, *Early Anthropology in the Sixteenth and Seventeenth Centuries* (Philadelphia: University of Pennsylvania Press, 1964), chs. 4–10; Lewis Hanke, *Aristotle and the American Indians* (London: Hollis and Carter, 1959).

29. Antonello Gerbi, *The Dispute of the New World* [orig. 1955], trans. Jeremy Moyle (Pittsburgh: University of Pittsburgh Press, 1973), p. 61. As the title of Gerbi's book indicates, it considers intellectual problems created by the discovery of the Indians, but is most detailed for the 18th and 19th centuries.

30. Glyn E. Daniel, *A Hundred Years of Archaeology* (London: Duckworth, 1950), p. 26; Robert F. Heizer, "The Background of Thomsen's Three-Age System," *Culture and Technology*, vol. 3 (1962): 259–266, p. 260.

31. Or Jean Léry, cited in Gilbert Chinard, *L'Exotisme américain dans la litterature francaise au XVIe siècle* (Paris: Librairie Hachette et Cie., 1911), pp. 141–143.

32. Joseph de Acosta, *The Natural and Moral History of the Indies* [orig. 1590], trans. Edward Grimston, Clements Marckham, ed. (2 vols.; London: Hakluyt Society, 1880), vol. 2, p. 295. "Moral" in this usage is derived from Latin *mos*, meaning "custom."

33. For written directives see Howard F. Cline, "The Relaciones Geograficas of the Spanish Indies 1577–1586," *Hispanic American Historical Review*, vol. 44 (1964): 341–374, pp. 363–371. For Raleigh's personnel see Samuel Eliot Morison, *The European Discovery of America* (New York: Oxford University Press, 1971), p. 630. Criticism of the standards of scholarship in early travel writing is offered in Donald F. Lach, *Asia in the Making*, vol. 1, *The Century of Discovery* (Chicago: University of Chicago Press, 1965), bk. 2, p. 793.

34. John Aubrey, in manuscript notes, undated, but from about 1698, first published in *Aubrey's Brief Lives,* Oliver Lawson Dick, ed. (London: Secker and Warburg, 1949), p. xlii.

35. Joseph Glanvill, *Plus Ultra* [orig. 1668] (Gainesville, Fla.: Scholars' Facsimiles and Reprints, 1958).

36. Thomas Hobbes, *Leviathan* [orig. 1651], Michael Oakeshott, ed. (Collier Classics ed.; New York: Collier-Macmillan, 1962), ch. 17.

37. Samuel von Pufendorf, *De Officio Hominis et Civis juxta Legem Naturalem Libri Duo* [orig. 1673], trans. Frank Gardner Moore, in James Brown Scott, ed., *The Classics of International Law* (New York: Columbia University Press, 1927), bk. 2, chs. 1–3, 5–6. Also his *De Jure Naturae et Gentium* [orig. 1672], trans. C. H. and W. A. Oldfather, cited in S. J. Slotkin, ed., *Readings in Early Anthropology*, Viking Fund Publications in Anthropology, no. 40 (1965), p. 154.

38. John Locke, *The Second Treatise of Government* [orig. 1690], Thomas P. Peardon, ed. (Indianapolis: Bobbs-Merrill Co., 1952), chs. 2–8.

39. William Temple, "An Essay Upon the Original and Nature of Government" [orig. 1672], in *The Works of William Temple* (new ed.; 4 vols.; London: F. C. and J. Rivington et al., 1814), vol. 1, pp. 11–13, 18–21.

40. For the history see Kurt Seligmann, *Magic, Supernaturalism and Religion* (New York: Pantheon Books, 1948), pp. 130 ff.

41. John Herman Randall, Jr., "Pietro Pomponazzi, Introduction," in Ernst Cassirer et al., eds., *The Renaissance Philosophy of Man* (Phoenix Books ed.; Chicago: University of Chicago Press, 1963), pp. 274, 277–278, 294, 297.

42. Francis Bacon, *Of the Proficience and Advancement of Learning, Divine and Human* [orig. 1605], in *The Works of Francis Bacon* (3 vols.; Philadelphia: Carsy and Hart, 1841), vol. 1, p. 119; Francis Bacon, *The New Organon* [orig. 1620], Fulton H. Anderson, ed. (Library of Liberal Arts ed.; Indianapolis: Bobbs-Merrill Co., 1960), pp. 228, 265; Francis Bacon, "Of Unity in Religion," in Francis Bacon, *Essays or Counsels Civil and Moral* [orig. 1625] (World Classics ed.; London: Oxford University Press, 1937).

43. Hobbes, *Leviathan*, ch. 12; for religion, see ch. 45.

44. Pufendorf, *Officio Hominis*, pp. 43–55.

45. Bacon, "Of Unity in Religion."

46. Hobbes, *Leviathan*, ch. 12.

47. William Petty, "Religion" [orig. 1685], in the Marquis of Lansdowne, ed., *The Petty Papers* (2 vols.; London: Constable and Co., 1927), vol. 1, pp. 117–118.

48. Francis Bacon, "Of Custom and Education," in his *Essays;* Bacon, *Advancement of Learning*, bk. 2, p. 211.

49. René Descartes, *Discourse on Method* [orig. 1637], in René Descartes, *Discourse on Method and Other Writings*, trans. Arthur Wollaston (Harmondsworth: Penguin Books, 1960), p. 48.

50. Joseph Glanvill, *The Vanity of Dogmatizing* [orig. 1661] (Facsimile ed.; New York: Columbia University Press, 1931), pp. 118, 125–127, 130.

51. Hobbes, *Leviathan*, p. 97.

52. Temple, "Nature of Government," vol. 1, pp. 8–9. As Montaigne put it,

there is nothing custom cannot do; see his "Of Custom," in Montaigne, *The Essays.*

53. Blaise Pascal, *Pensées* [orig. 1670], trans. A. J. Krailsheimer (Harmondsworth: Penguin Books), no. 525.

54. William Temple, *An Introduction to the History of England* [orig. 1695], in *The Works of William Temple,* vol. 3, pp. 78–79.

55. John Locke, *An Essay Concerning Human Understanding* [orig. 1690], collated and annotated by Alexander Campbell Fraser (2 vols.; New York: Dover Publications, 1959), vol. 1, bk. 1, ch. 2; bk. 2, chs. 1, 33.

56. Alexander Ross, *Pansebia or a View of All Religions in the World* (3rd ed.; London: John Saywell, 1658).

57. François de Salignac de la Mothe-Fénelon, *The Education of Girls* [orig. 1687], trans. H. C. Barnard, in H. C. Barnard, *Fénelon on Edu-*

cation (Cambridge: At the University Press, 1966), pp. 15–16.

58. Bacon, *The New Organon,* p. 8.

59. Descartes, *Discourse on Method,* pp. 45–46.

60. Francis Bacon, "Of Seditions and Troubles," in his *Essays,* pp. 22–24.

61. William Temple, "Of Popular Discontents" [orig. 1701], in *The Works of William Temple,* vol. 3, pp. 34–37.

62. Edward Brerewood, *Enquiries Touching the Diversity of Languages and Religions in the Chief Parts of the World* [orig. 1614] (London: Samuel Mearne, John Martyn, and Henry Herringman, 1674).

63. Matthew Hale, *The Primitive Origination of Mankind, Considered and Examined According to the Light of Nature* (London: William Shrowsberry, 1677), pp. 151–152, 159–164.

4

Century of Enlightenment

Goal of Progress

Achievements of Man

Men like Pierre Bayle, Charles de Secondat de Montesquieu, and François Marie Voltaire speaking out to contradict traditional ways of thinking, stamped the 18th century as an Age of Enlightenment. They saw their age as a historical watershed in which new and better knowledge was displacing old, wornout beliefs. In politics and religion the Enlightenment and, more directly, the French Revolution of 1789, sought to replace established tradition by laws and customs which reason recommended as best attuned to human nature.

Rationalism continued to be the prevailing mode of thought in 18th-century social science, though philosophers displayed an increased willingness to accept the constraint of empirical observation. "Moral" or "natural philosophy" became the preferred term for designating the parcel of intellectual activity which later broke up into the separate social sciences. The philosophers—the word still stood for researchers—were impressed by the example of physical science and intended to study marriage, the family, government, ethics, esthetics, religion, and other social phenomena "anthropologically," by which Immanuel Kant meant empirically.[1] They sought the laws governing that "delightful subject," the history of manners, laws, and the arts. The concept of culture came into use to designate those

---

Notes to this chapter begin on page 104.

achievements which men created as members of society, standardized through judgment, and perpetuated from one generation to another.[2] Often the philosophers regarded social facts from a psychological point of view; that is, from the standpoint of the motives of individual actors. The customs of societies great or small corresponded basically to habits acquired by individuals through experience.[3] Culture belonged naturally to man; "natural" here signifies not innate endowment but whatever conforms to expectancy, pattern, or law. Unlike untutored human behavior fixed by nature, culture must be mastered, and is subject to progress in the individuals as well as in society.[4]

Progress had several meanings: advancement in the use of reason, technological development, growth of scientific knowledge, flight from superstition, greater happiness, and enlightenment after the darkness of the Middle Ages. Few writers of this optimistic age shared Jean Jacques Rousseau's suspicion that civilization had taken the wrong turn and, in some respects, ran counter to nature.[5] Yet they wanted some things in civilization changed, the troublesome passion for possessions and private property, for example, and senseless sexual conventions at variance with the healthier morality of savage societies, such as those of the uninhibited Polynesians. If European civilization spread to those simple, primitive folk it would sow terrible contradictions and destroy their spontaneity and happiness.

Mankind, the philosophers agreed, is one—anatomically, physiologically, and psychologically. All people, savage or civilized, possess the same faculties, natural abilities, and basic needs. In great detail writers enumerated mankind's common features: proclivities like self-interest; pain-avoidances; imitation, deliberate and unconscious; pity; and readiness to esteem the wise and the good[6] A universal culture pattern present in all societies constituted evidence of mankind's cultural unity, for without basic human similarities, would all societies have invented signs, engage in similar patterns of social relations, exchange goods with one another, possess religion, or bury the dead?[7] At a minimum, every people harbored the potential for sharing in the universal cultural ground plan. Regarding a further explanation for the universal culture pattern, some researchers vaguely ascribed it to similar ways of thinking or to equal good sense.[8] Others who cited specific attributes of human nature, such as the long period of early dependence, the reciprocal attachment developing between mother and child, longevity, lack of a hairy body cover, and flexible hands, could account for only parts of the ground plan.[9]

If mankind shares basic faculties and proclivities, why do societies differ in cultural achievements? An analogy to individual development provided one explanation.[10] In society as well as in individuals, mental capacities require cultivation and experience to develop, and the process takes time.[11] Just as mental development reaches nearly the same point in practically every adult, so the human mind follows the same course of growth and arrives at parallel cultural achievements in societies that have reached comparable stages of development.[12] In the long run, however, social science developed not by analogizing social and individual development. More satisfactory explanations for cultural differences related the social facts to be accounted for to other social facts, including motivations instilled in people by society, on which they depended or to which they were linked.

Appetite for Society

The old question, why man lives in society, continued to be asked and to receive rationalistic answers. Henry Home, however, in an uncharacteristic flight from pure rationalism, suggested empirical proof for the idea that human weakness forms the basis of sociality. In what amounted to a comparative ethological approach, he saw just those animals least able to defend themselves individually showing "an appetite for society."[13]

In typical 18th-century fashion Henry Home, or Lord Kames, succeeded in mastering several fields: farming, the law, metaphysics, and human history. Friday night meetings of the Edinburgh Select Society allowed him to air his views and to hear those of other Scottish luminaries, including David Hume, Adam Smith, and James Burnett (Lord Monboddo), with whom Home maintained an intense personal rivalry. Burnett, in a book published five years before Home's, used the comparative ethological approach to demonstrate that because some animals live socially and yet lack language, therefore language cannot be a necessary precondition for human society.[14]

In addition to ascribing sociality to individual weakness, Home, again by comparative zoology, demonstrated tribalism to be part of man's animal heritage. In no animal species do all members associate together indiscriminately. Each contains small "tribes" that remain apart. For man he additionally explains the matter psychologically and functionally. Man possesses only a limited mental capacity to form affectional bonds. Functionally speaking, limited association insures only moderately sized states which conduce to good government. Patriotism, he avers, would vanish if the whole human species associated together indiscriminately.

Several philosophers employed Aristotle's principle of interdependence, based on differentiation, to explain society.[15] If all persons were alike in mind and body, theorized the free-thinking Paul Henri Thiry, Baron d'Holbach, nobody would need anyone else, and everyone would live independently. Adam Smith extended the principle to explain the mutual dependence of town and country.[16] The country provides the town with food and raw materials for manufacturing, and the town reciprocates with goods it produces. The theme of individuals benefiting society as they simultaneously pursue their own advantages occurs in Smith's *Wealth of Nations* and in Alexander Pope's *Essay on Man*.[17] According to Smith, the individual who invests in industry for his own gain is "led by an invisible hand" to contribute to society's good, although he intends nothing of the kind. In Pope's version, the individual approves of restraints with the selfish aim of protecting his own gains, but in doing so also acts to safeguard the advantages achieved by others. Pope as well as the German philosopher Johann Gottfried Herder repeat the theory already encountered in Leon Battista Alberti, that the prolonged infancy of human beings constitutes the basis of society.[18] Infantile dependence called out parental love and nurturance, Herder suggests, thereby habituating mankind to family life, the germ of society.

Enslaved by Custom

Since mankind everywhere has the same nature, a number of 18th-century writers were led to ascribe differences from one people to another to external social factors by which people are shaped or to institutions that counteract, constrain, divert, or extinguish certain innate tendencies.[19] We become like those by whom we are reared. Human beings are virtually enslaved by what they have learned. Custom warps human nature. Yet, as Rousseau perceived, custom also provides individuals with varied opportunities to enhance human faculties that otherwise would languish.[20] Progress from the state of nature to society extended mankind's ideas, exalted human sentiments, and broadened and refined the mind. Savage life impoverishes mentality, compared to what members of civilized nations gain from their variegated surroundings. Society provides a stage on which we may expand our talents and utilize our inventive powers.[21] Just what skills a person will perfect depends on the dominant interests of the society in which he lives, and on money, fame, or other inducements by which he is motivated.[22] Historians and poets will find little scope to develop their talents where war is the primary emphasis. What the mind finds to engage its powers may vary within a single society; witness how ideas entertained by the learned diverge from the common people's.[23]

More than anything the relativity of morals continued to illustrate the force of social patterning. Muslims accept polygyny, odious though it may be to Christians. Any vice disappears once society approves it or elevates it to general practice.[24] The literary device picturing fictional visitors traveling around Europe, surprised or shocked at what they find, threw a familiar way of life into the perspective of an exotic culture being examined by curious explorers.[25] Claude Helvétius, the French encyclopedist, gave cultural relativity a theoretical basis by his theory of interests.[26] Societies as well as individuals within them are guided by diverse and at times incompatible interests. Understanding exotic behavior requires appreciating the interests which people pursue. Tolerance, the philosophers hoped, would permit cultivated persons to deal wisely with customs at variance with their own, respecting them even while lamenting their deviation from better norms.[27] Extreme relativists like Herder accepted the incommensurability of different ways of life almost without reservation and accorded equal validity to each.[28] Other writers attempted to find common values in strange customs. Ernest Hutcheson, earliest of the luminaries of the Scottish Enlightenment, detected a note of social benevolence behind the cruelties some societies practice toward their aged. Such acts are intended to protect the old against enemies or infirmities, or to spare the able-bodied from the added burden of having to maintain the aged.[29] Analogies drawn between exotic and familiar customs provided another means of intellectually bridging the familiar and the unfamiliar. Voltaire used the method when he likened the Greek and Roman customs of perfuming, adorning, and kneeling before statues to the worship carried out by Roman Catholics.[30]

Problems with Method

In 1800, a 28-year-old French philosopher, Joseph-Marie Degérando, completed a set of directives intended to enable a scientific expedition bound for Australia to properly observe savage people.[31] The topics to be covered include language and signs, clothing, family relations, extensions of kinship, condition of women, sex, marriage, divorce, polygyny, education, law, internal and external political relations, war, cannibalism, alliances, amusements, association of ideas, sensory acuity, and endurance of illness. Although the author advocates reporting what a society commonly practices, his observation guide also alerts the traveler to crimes and the extent of insanity. Further, he proffers advice on carrying out ethnography. The observer's very presence may influence savage behavior, he warns, by stimulating fear, defiance, or reserve. He counsels against culture-bound assumptions; one should not expect savages to possess the same needs or to reason as civilized men.

Sad to say, the topics of inquiry and the counsels helped the Australian expedition hardly at all. The inept ethnographer on board carried out only the most superficial observations and totally ignored the instructions of Degérando and of other experienced travelers.[32] For the Frenchman was by no means the first to prepare a checklist for foreign travelers,[33] and not alone in formulating standards of field work. Probably the advice most frequently reiterated by stay-at-home philosophers and experienced travelers recommended studying every way of life in its own terms.[34] Observers should put themselves into the exotic situation or into another age, and guard against the temptation to reinterpret the strange in familiar terms, thereby making it easier to comprehend. Objectivity is, of course, difficult to acquire. Two travelers seldom report the same fact in the same way. Each perceives it according to his personality. Hence before an observation can be properly used, one must know who made it. Difficult though it may be to capture the meaning of an exotic way of life, we are naturally furnished with means to succeed in such an enterprise simply because we are human beings and ourselves participate in a society that shares something with the one we study. Our experience equips us to know human behavior more intimately than we can ever know nonhuman events; to those we always stand as outsiders.

Discovering how mankind acted, thought, and felt in the ages following its emergence from the state of nature posed a more perplexing methodological problem. Mute archeological remains, protohistoric monuments, and even the texts of classical authors failed to satisfy the philosophers' curiosity about the past or the development of society, so they proposed a number of ingenious procedures and assumptions to augment the limited amount of direct evidence.[35] Myths were treated as records preserving early human experiences, including errors committed by the human mind in its first attempts to explain the world. Poetry personifying inanimate objects was regarded as revealing the animistic nature of early thought. The societies of the classical world were held to embody the youth of the world. But most of all, contemporary primitive societies were taken as preserving all bygone forms of barbarism.[36] The philosophers did not venture into those societies themselves, but studied reports about them written by explorers and other travelers. The reports, they usually realized, often required critical sifting of believable fact from unbelievable fantasy. Few philosophers were as credulous as James Burnett, whose naive faith in almost any traveler's account exemplified his philosophy "that every thing that possibly can exist does actually exist," even, he believed, men with tails.[37] The ubiquity of diffusion made Henry Home wonder momentarily if any living people retained anything of the original past, but the high degree of isolation from outside influence maintained by some savage tribes reassured him.[38] They, he thought, would surely have preserved some customs from very early times.

A most penetrating critic of extant methods for reconstructing the unwritten past was Adam Ferguson, a Scotsman who began in the ministry before turning to philosophy.[39] Despite lacking special preparation for philosophical speculation, his writings brought him international distinction during his lifetime and, later, recognition as one of the major precursors of sociology and anthropology. He spurned the use of myths as valid historical evidence. Even if they originated along ago, they have assimilated the character of the times through which they have passed and not the indelible stamp of a remote age.[40] He criticized those who reconstruct the past by arbitrarily selecting a few features of a living society, ignoring others not fitting the author's preconceived notions. A far better method would be to compare travelers' accounts from every part of the world. Customs about which all agree could confidently be ascribed to the original culture of mankind. Also, he dismissed the possibility of the lower classes in the populous cities of civilized nations being an image of what mankind was in its rude, uncultivated state. Early man, like contemporary savages, lacked both the values of civilization and its vices; the poor, however, know the virtues to which they should conform, but are made base and corrupted by the circumstances of their lives.

Cultural Origins and Development

Revolt of the Clients

Several thinkers strove prodigiously to supply what Henry Home as late as 1778 found to be still wanting, "a History of the Species, in its progress from the savage state to its highest civilization and improvements."[41] Since it would be repetitious and unproductive to summarize all the well-known histories of mankind written during the century, I have limited myself to those by Giambattista Vico, Adam Ferguson, and Home himself.

With his sometimes fantastic ideas Vico went further than any pre-anthropologist (or for that matter, many anthropologists) in delineating integration between customs, institutions, belief systems, and character structure (which he called human nature).[42] A Neapolitan jurist, philosopher, and professor of rhetoric, he hoped by his *New Science* to provide for human society explanations such as Newton had furnished for nature. His achievements, however, turned out to be so much more limited that today many sociologists and anthropologists do not even recognize his name. His long, prolix, and difficult book treats history as cyclical. One cycle began following the recession of the biblical flood and ended with the Fall of Rome. Following it, another cycle started with the barbarism of the Dark Ages and culminated in the civilization of the 17th century. Each cycle is divided into three periods, and every period possesses its own form of government, type of communication, religion, method of reasoning, and other elements going to make up a cultural system. Every period develops out of its predecessor, being the outcome of conditions that brought the latter to an end.

Contrary to other philosophers of his time, Vico maintains that the earliest people, who were giants, lacked reason. Endowed with a vigorous imagination, they thought in poetic images. All the universe, even the things they themselves made and did, they believed to be Jove, the father of all men, who in lightning bolts hurled himself out of the sky and who animated everything in nature. Religion suffused the life of those times.

Terrified of Jove, people gave up their endless wandering and sought shelter in the recesses of caves, mankind's original dwellings. They based even their system of jurisdiction on religion, assessing guilt or innocence by oracles, through which they entered into the divine mind. At first the giants shared women and possessions in common while enjoying full, untrammeled personal liberty. But their unrestrained lust carried the seeds of society, for to be assured of its dependable satisfaction they were led to capture wives with whom they began to live in families. Common possessions led to quarrels, in which the strong either slew the weak, or from which the weak fled to become clients of strong protectors. Clientage thereby joined the family as another element of social structure.

The magnitude of the changes following clientage led Vico to recognize the advent of a new culture, which he called the Age of Heroes. In religion, Mars became a symbol of the military virtues displayed by the aristocratic heroes, and Venus became the symbol by which the nobles represented ideals of nobility and beauty. Life and fortune no longer depended directly on Jove but hinged on fate, which the gods controlled. Language originated during the Heroic Age, but only after a time during which the nobles communicated by blazonings on their arms and with other signs. The nobles followed a Spartan regime: playing strenuous games; training their children severely, even cruelly; buying wives and acquiring clients and treating both as slaves. Harsh treatment, however, did not prevent the clients from increasing their rights, or from enacting laws without the nobles' consent, steps that brought popular government into existence. The aristocrats, to better resist their rebellious clients, banded together into kingdoms, where they instituted courts in which justice came to depend on the adroit use of words and on solemn rituals in which not a detail could be altered.

Once progressive development of human intelligence enabled the clients to see through the pretensions of aristocracy, and to perceive themselves as possessing the same human nature as the nobles, another social revolution could not be contained. Clients insisted on their rights and succeeded, after a struggle, in establishing commonwealths where all people joined in making laws for everyone's benefit. Customs came to be obeyed out of a sense of duty, not fear; reason, not religion or might, became the source of law; and legal judgments rested on the truth of carefully examined facts. Vico regarded himself as living in such a commonwealth, but he noted other societies—America, for example—still rooted in barbarism. They had not completed the cycle of development as they would have had they not become the subjects of Europeans.

How casually Vico employs ideas that later become pivots of strenuous debate or key elements of theory: primitive promiscuity; marriage by capture; complementary opposition (between the symbols of Mars and

Venus); and a dialectical explanation of change, in which social oppositions create disequilibrium, out of which a new level of social organization
or a new type of culture comes into existence.

A Capacity for Progress

In keeping with the philosophical spirit of the century, Adam Ferguson,
too, looked for pattern, law, or direction operating behind the particular
events of history.[43] His three-stage account of mankind's cultural development rings much more familiar than Vico's, especially to readers
acquainted with Lewis Henry Morgan and other 19th-century anthropologists. It is more familiar in the names he gives the stages—savagery,
barbarism, and civil society (the names predate him, however[44]), as well
as for the use he makes of contemporary primitive societies to reconstruct
the social life of early humanity. Like contemporary savages, mankind in
a rude state of culture also subsisted by hunting, fishing, and collecting
wild plants. People paid little heed to property, possessed scarcely any
government, followed a simple religion, and bore considerable, constant
turmoil. Following the lead of Father Joseph Lafitau, who in 1724 had
compared the customs of the American Indians to the lifeways of primitive
times,[45] Ferguson rounds out the picture of social relations in the property-
less state by describing the Indians' strong consciousness of equality and
high degree of independence, which admitted no degree of subordination.
Differences in behavior followed only from differences of age, talents, or
dispositions. Like the Indians, early man had not yet attained general
principles of thought, attached little importance to foresight, and from the
earliest years cultivated fortitude. Though he refers to the Indians' grovel-
ing and mean superstitions fostered by ignorance, doubt, and anxiety, he
finds much to admire in Lafitau's presentation of those societies.

Susceptibility of improvement and a capacity for progress were always
part of human nature. They are the qualities that brought society from its
savage beginnings to the civil state it possessed in Ferguson's time. Improvements in the mode of obtaining food and in the establishment of
private property, beyond its rudimentary form in savagery, ushered in
barbarism. Barbarians raise herds and recognize distinctions between rich
and poor, distinguished and undistinguished. They follow leaders whose
wealth and noble birth place them highest in the society. Unequal ownership of wealth and the subordination of one class by another promote
domestic disorder among barbarians. As a result they are preoccupied by
war, which they wage both for love of glory and for spoils. Yet frequent
warfare had its good points, Ferguson reasons. Besides developing values
like fidelity and valor, it served also to strengthen bonds of solidarity in
barbarous societies.

In describing civil society, which is the next step in social development,

Ferguson intensifies his attention to connections between social facts. The transition from barbarism came about as a consequence of increased occupational specialization and a larger portion of energy being devoted to trade. Major changes in social structure followed. The uniformity of manners found among savages gave way to extreme differentiation, as behavior came to vary by the multiple social roles people play, although some basic values agreed upon by everyone remained. The basis of social solidarity altered. The large size into which civil societies have developed makes it impossible for everyone to take part in decisions, and prevents feelings from being evenly communicated between people, as is the case in savage society. Instead, groups of specialists organize social relations narrowly around their own interests. In place of leaders securing voluntary cooperation through force of their personal qualities, leaders compete for support from the several interest groups into which society is segmented. Each collateral group holds some power, and uses it to check the excesses of others. Liberty is maintained not by general consensus, but by the opposition constantly expressed between the collateral social segments. This conception of conflict and opposition maintaining individual liberty and group boundaries resembles Niccolo Machiavelli's appreciation of the benefits that accrue from restrained political conflict. A similar idea shows up in Montesquieu, whom Ferguson read closely, who warns that a republic's misfortunes begin once its citizens cease to intrigue or take partisan sides on public issues.[46]

A Seamy Side to Progress

Henry Home also starts his history of mankind with a stage at which people subsisted on natural food secured by hunting, fishing, or collecting.[47] Then societies took to domesticating animals previously hunted, and later to cultivating the seeds they picked. They saw the grains, to which they had become accustomed, becoming scarce due to an expanding population, and so they sowed the seeds to increase the food supply. Thus, Home says, necessity pushed humanity to the final step in the development of subsistence production. Like other writers of his time, he mostly treats the developmental sequence as if it followed the same order everywhere in the world, although he thinks tropical societies passed directly from collecting to cultivating vegetable products without going through an intermediate stage of animal domestication. Early pastoralists tended to hold flocks and herds in common, and agriculturalists farmed on common land and stored the harvest communally. But those customs soon disappeared, for they were at variance with the strong sense of property inherent in human nature, and with people's corresponding disinclination to hold possessions in common.

Trade existed from the initial stage of human society when people bartered for the few needs they could not secure directly from nature. As population expanded and wants multiplied, barter proved inadequate to maintain a system of exchange, whereupon necessity once again spurred progress. Societies adopted precious metals as media, by which goods could be evaluated, bought, and sold. In mankind's original state everyone tended to his own concerns, but even food gatherers soon discovered advantages in performing some activities cooperatively, thereby promoting greater interdependence among the members of a society. Tighter social interdependence also grew out of intensified trade and from division of labor introduced into subsistence tasks.

Progress soon showed a seamy side. Mutual affection prevailed in nascent society, aided by the abundance of game, a weak sense of property, and opportunities to discharge hostility against neighbors, rather than within the group. Discord multiplied, however, once avarice, selfishness, and pride asserted themselves to the accompaniment of more assured bases of subsistence, increasing population, the growing value of land, and a hunger for luxuries. Only the plain fact that existence without society was impossible restrained individual selfishness, and induced people to develop some degree of justice, mutual solicitude, and good manners.

Although Home and other philosophers were on the whole optimistic about the progressive course of history, they recognized undesirable features in inequality, property, religion, and other human inventions. Hence they saw their age as one of reconstruction and their works as weapons to eradicate social blemishes in the heritage of civil society. Here and there an iconoclast even denied there had been any progress whatever.[48] Life was good only when people lived as the American Indians still did: free of property; without subordination to class, government, or man-made law; obedient only to the laws of nature; and troubled by no wants but those issuing from human nature.

Unlike Home and a number of writers following him who confined themselves largely to the early phase of history, Condorcet extended the narrative into civilization.[49] He notes the consequences for science in the invention of writing, and traces diffusion of the alphabet from the Middle East to Greece. He comments on the importance of the windmill, compass, printing, gunpowder, and other cultural innovations, including discovery of the true rights of man, and in the United States of America, the institution of democratic government. Basic discoveries give rise to practical inventions, which in turn have consequences ramifying far beyond their own spheres. Witness how printing, based on the alphabet, brought about a social climate where judgments could be formed independently of tradition, and helped undermine traditional authority. A participant in the French Revolution, Condorcet regarded the history of civilization as a constantly accelerating process in which competence and knowledge expand at an ever swifter rate.

Explaining Cultural Development

When it came to explaining why society had traveled from savagery to a civil state, the philosophers alternated eclectically between psychogenic and sociogenic theories. From a psychological viewpoint, they ascribed the growth of culture and social structure to seeds within human nature. People are driven by biological wants and other goals that their nature motivates them to seek; or, as the utilitarians believed, search for what best promotes happiness. Such causes, being uniform from one people and time to another, explain uniformities in cultural development. A sociogenic explanation begins with conditions present in society. The cumulative theory of development held by Condorcet and others maintains people are inspired and restricted in discovery and invention by traits already present in culture.[50] Some cultural inventories provide better conditions for takeoff than others. Such a theory is fundamentally historical, for it visualizes generations building on their predecessors' achievements. Traits grow from one another. The rule of law and a free government were held to be among the basic factors favoring social progress, for they permitted curiosity to be freely satisfied and, in the process, the arts and sciences expanded.[51] Agriculture constituted another major launching pad for progress. It tamed the savage hunter's wild, intractable character, while the economic surplus it produced allowed more leisure time in which to think.[52] Necessity and adversity, affecting either the individual or society, spur the search for ameliorative inventions.[53] Inventions themselves can create desperate conditions from which a society will strive to escape; the advent of new weapons, for example, leads to the search for innovations capable of nullifying the threats. Once division of labor enters, it promotes development by leading to increased productivity, and by favoring the invention of labor-saving techniques.[54] A pity then, the undesirable psychological and social consequences brought about through industrial specialization.

Clearly, psychological and social conditions within a particular society have not been responsible for instigating the invention of everything that its culture contains. Borrowing achievements invented in other groups is a major process contributing to progress, Ferguson observes, but it can occur only when conditions are right.[55] People won't accept something beyond their range of interests, or for which they perceive no use. Already, Ferguson felt it necessary to warn against emphasizing diffusion to the point where it obscured the capacity for invention which every society, no matter how savage, possesses. Actually, the century's theorists dwelled more on invention than diffusion, contrary to the trend a century and a half later following the decline of 19th-century cultural evolutionism.

Reading history as a record of progress, the philosophers naturally set themselves to explain social development, rather than degeneration. Nevertheless, Ferguson points out, individual nations do decline. The reasons lie partly in individuals and partly in social conditions.[56] People become weary of sustained effort. The objects exciting them change, whereupon the pulse of commerce, politics, and art wanes. Decline also follows once differentiation in a society becomes so extreme that it undermines unity. Sometimes government by overly concerning itself with preventing injustice defeats a nation's spirit; laws seeking to foster equity may check the active powers in human nature to an extent where people virtually cease to act at all. Henry Home had a keen eye for downs in the chart of mankind's history, and notes several social and psychological factors that bring about declines in the fine and useful arts.[57] Despotism, conquest resulting in enslavement, and depopulation caused by extreme luxury and voluptuousness promote cultural degeneration. Advances in the fine arts also come to a halt once masters bring them to a degree of perfection that contemporaries despair of emulating, an observation Velleius made 19 centuries earlier. Hard-to-master crafts practiced by only a few craftspeople, Home predicted, would totally vanish if the specialists died off without transmitting their skills.

Anthropological Topics

Early Matriarchy

Probing the origin and development of marriage, myth, and religion, the philosophers furthered the naturalistic and comparative study of those anthropological topics.

Opinions divided on whether the family founded in marriage formed part of mankind's earliest social condition. Henry Home argued against Lucretius's suggestion that mothers originally reared their progeny without fathers. Food gathering, Home reasoned, would not permit a woman by her own efforts to secure enough food to support numerous offspring during the many years before children become independent.[58] Calling again on the comparative zoological approach, he claimed that since all animal species in which the young suckle also live in pairs, it could not have been different with human beings. He doesn't say what he thought of Burnett's credulous faith in travelers' reports of promiscuous copulation among brutish people,[59] but we can imagine, for the two Scotsmen maintained a keen philosophical rivalry. John Millar, despite his friendship with Home, proposed a theory of primitive matriarchy.[60] Economic uncertainty in savage society, he reasons, would have prevented marriage, leaving children to be reared by the mother. They would belong to her family of orientation. From the honor accorded a woman by her mature children, she attained a degree of influence strong enough to keep male retainers under her command. However radical the difference between Millar and Home regarding the origin of marriage and the family, both agreed that early mankind prior to entering the stage of barbarism placed no value on premarital chastity.

Two functional theories of the incest rule turn up in the century: one, already familiar, stresses the advantages of affinity created through marriage with nonkin, and the other alludes to the role conflict expectable if incest were allowed between members of the nuclear family. Hutcheson refers to both but employs the latter as a causal explanation.[61] He sees marriage between parents and children eliminated by the incompatibility between the parental and marital roles. The authority habitually exercised by parents and the respect they demand of children would run contrary to the equality expected between marriage partners. There need not be a natural basis of aversion to incest; the role conflict that incestuous marriage would produce in the nuclear family quite suffices to forestall such unions. At the same time, he thought, marriage between near relatives ought to be legally prohibited. It would confine affection too narrowly; instead of families becoming "beautifully interwoven" through affinity, regular marriage between close kin would make every family "a little system by itself."

Kinship and descent, anthropological topics of great future importance, received limited theoretical attention, and then only as they touch on inheritance. Home found no single universal rule of property succession, and remarks on the rapidity with which inheritance norms change.[62] Inheritance by agnates, he is sure, predates any rights of collateral kin, the reason being the mind's tendency to view things as they occur; persons at hand would naturally be considered before those at a greater genealogical distance.

The pleasant ideal of primitive life requiring little or no government appealed strongly to the luminaries of the Enlightenment, as did the notion of custom, or tradition, taking the place of law in savage times.[63] Among those who demurred from the latter notion was William Robertson, a Scottish clergyman with philosophical inclinations.[64] Even in the earliest stage of society, he writes, chiefs and elders resolved disputes by making rules based on discretion and commonsense. As controversies multiplied, the judges found precedents to use in resolving recurrent types of conflict, and eventually property rights and succession became the subjects of deliberately made laws.

David Hume explains the origin of government by the impossibility of living in society, at least in civilized society, without political and legal institutions.[65] The social need is sufficient to establish government, and people give it their obedience because society would othrewise disintegrate. The rudiments of government, he thinks, may have arisen from fighting between societies, the authority thereby earned by the war chief in the minds of his followers enduring beyond the occasion of battle.

Symbols in Myths

Giambattista Vico, who held that myths provided the first, language-less race of mankind with its sole means of understanding and reacting to the world, set the pattern for the 18th-century's theorizing about myth.[66] He regarded mythological characters as polysemic symbols simultaneously representing duty and other virtues, as well as thunder and similar mundane phenomena. Throughout the rest of the period, philosophers continued to treat myths as more than narratives, and sought for clues to decode the ideas for which the deities and other mythological features stood. Most explanations of how myths arose were less relativistic or tolerant than Vico's.[67] Writers treated myths as prescientific explanations of nature. Ignorance and rampant imagination transformed health into Hygeia and personified the heavenly bodies. Flattery converted kings into gods. Yet, savage mythmakers did not enjoy unlimited creative freedom; the underdeveloped nature of their minds to some extent held rein on the fecundity of their imagination. Tales in different parts of the primitive world resemble each other because the savage mind, starting with the same experiences which it sought to explain, necessarily came to the same conclusions about their causes. Down the years to Sigmund Freud, Carl Jung, and Claude Lévi-Strauss similar types of psychogenic explanation continued to serve as favorite perspectives for explicating myths and other products of imagination.

Quasi-Rational but Practical

The French and English philosophers showed intense interest in exploring the psychological sources of religion and magic and the functions those institutions serve in prescientific societies. They dealt with Christianity and the natural religions of primitive people as equally amenable to naturalistic study, thereby moving a shocked English bishop to complain that Christianity was being treated as if it were fictitious.[68] The prevailing concept, conveyed by the word "superstition," regarded religious belief and magic as quasi-rational, not wholly reasonable. As long as people lack better knowledge, religion serves to explain the world and to allay the incessant fear inflicted by the lack of adequate understanding. This concept of religion would prevail for more than a century, although when it entered anthropology after the middle of the 19th century it became tempered by cultural relativity.

Consistency could hardly be expected in answers to questions about the ultimate origin of religion or its prehistoric development. Nevertheless, it would be tiresome to review the many theories propounded, some differing only in small particulars from others. Henry Home's account provides a fair example of the rationalistic character of the speculation with which the philosophers approached the problem, although his is more complex than many in the relationships it traces between theological stages and steps in the growth of intelligence. Ignoring John Locke's teaching, Home starts by assuming an inherent sense of god.[69] Upon that premise, he traces how religious and intellectual development must have proceeded. Polytheism, consistent with a period when the mind still found it impossible to draw generalizations from several particular instances of a given event, marked the first stage. The number of deities controlling events equalled the number of significant experiences people sought to account for. The deities were all malevolent, for the reason that fear emanating from man's abject helplessness pervaded all his emotions. In the second theological stage which gradually emerged, gods and spirits acquired a nature of mixed good and evil. Then, when mankind acquired the concept of pure benevolence, they became differentiated into predominantly good or mainly evil beings. Once primitive morality grew capable of discriminating between fear and gratitude, a fourth stage arose, characterized by one supreme benevolent deity and several inferior beings, some malevolent and others good. The next step occurred when humanity learned to trace the actions of causes in nature and, as a result, could conceive of nature as less inimical to man than hitherto. Only a single malevolent being was required at this stage. Finally, at a time when people learned to group all phenomena under a general law of cause and effect, a supreme being boundless in perfection came to be recognized and worshiped.

Other writers posited no inherent sense of deity, but also derived religion from fear and helplessness inspired by illness and other calamities.

> [Superstition] 'midst the light'ning's blaze, and
>   thunder's sound,
> When rock'd the mountains, and when groan'd the
>   ground,
> . . . taught the weak to bend, the proud to pray,
> To Pow'r unseen, and mightier far than they. . . .[70]

David Hume belongs among the scholars who explained the origin of religion psychogenically.[71] In his view, mankind's attempts to account for the unpredictable world, which aroused a constant sense of threat, led to concepts of combat between opposite unseen powers or to vacillation on the part of a single supernatural power.[72] Then Hume took recourse to the doctrine of innate ideas to explain, along the lines of Xenophanes, why the powers were often anthropomorphically conceived: a universal tendency exists in man to pattern all beings after his own image, to endow them with intelligence, human sentiments, and human passions. Citing sailors and gamblers as evidence, he maintains that superstition increases "in proportion as man's course of life is governed by accident." It is a readily testable proposition, applying to religion as well as omens and magic.

Hume also engaged in comparative religion, in one instance comparing superstition with another type of belief, Enthusiasm.[73] Whereas superstition grows out of terror, puzzlement, and similar emotions, Enthusiasm springs from a mind elevated by prosperity, good health, good spirits, and confidence. The enraptured worshiper finds everything mortal unworthy of attention, and attributes his exaltation to a divine being by whom he imagines himself to be favored. Though Enthusiasm is unfavorable to sound reason, its fanatic adherents claim freedom from priestly power and endorse civil liberty. Superstition, on the contrary, is the enemy of civil liberty because it renders men submissive and favors the increasing power of priests. In another typology, Hume contrasts polytheism with the belief that succeeded it, monotheism.[74] The ability of polytheism to accommodate several deities, even those belonging to other sects, encourages greater tolerance than belief confined to a single god.[75] Furthermore, monotheism, by conceiving the deity to be infinitely superior to mankind, sinks the mind into submission and abasement. Pagan religions of the polytheistic variety, however, encourage emulation of the gods and inspire magnanimity as well as love of liberty.

In his time Hume was surely the most perspicacious thinker about religion and related belief systems. Yet he pretended neither to objectivity nor neutrality. He could even be critical of his own methods, pointing out that a priori reasoning allows anything to appear able to produce anything.[76] This aphorism spots the fundamental weakness of rationalism in 18th-century social science.

Most of the authors began the development of religion with personified, supernatural beings who in the eyes of their worshipers possessed great power. Once these beings were invented, they could be appeased in an effort to avoid the dreadful events they frequently brought about.[77] However, a theory of primitive animism was also put forward in the Age of Enlightenment to account for the beginning of religion.[78] It depicted early man interpreting all of nature as animated. Trying to understand mysterious phenomena for which no natural causes could be perceived, savages imputed to inanimate things life similar to human life.

Theories of magic followed similar lines of reasoning. According to that indefatigable antireligionist, Baron d'Holbach, savages attribute the power of good or evil to animate and inanimate objects that they by chance regularly encounter at precisely those times when they succeed or fail in some enterprise, such as hunting.[79] James Beattie also had recourse to "principles of association" to explain the origin of superstitions, like the dread of churchyards or the avoidance of certain acts on particular days of the week.[80] The encyclopedist Antoine de Botens spoke for the age when he branded magical attempts to control events as pseudo-scientific excrescences, based on puerile principles of thought, whose ineffectualness is easily proven.[81]

Functions of Religion

In speculating about the origin of supernaturalism, the naturalistic students of religion also touched on the uses it served among its credulous followers. They discovered it provided psychological means of coping with threat, offered a basis for explaining the mysterious, and gave a subjective sense of assurance or control. Montesquieu dwelled more on functions than origins, and he credits religious belief in civil society with reinforcing the laws and promoting good citizenship.[82] Religion can conduce to moral goodness more strongly than law; hence, when supernatural sanctions are mild, the laws must be especially severe. More cynically, Rousseau perceives in religion a device through which a ruler can convince his followers that their best interests lie in submitting to the laws of the state.[83]

Functions for individuals and society also attach to rituals. The most original theory for its time was undoubtedly Holbach's analysis of a puberty ceremony, among some Virginia Indians, as acting to disencumber the young from strong impressions left by childhood and thereby helping them pick up adult interests.[84] Montesquieu saw value in magnificent ceremonies and temples for attaching worshipers to the religion that reinforces the laws.[85] He also distinguished between secular and sacred ceremonies. In contrast to the latter, secular rites—for example, the rites whereby the Chinese honor parents and express filial piety—are closer to law or custom than to supernatural belief. Voltaire saw pragmatic value in Arabs' avoidance of pork, because the meat transmits leprosy, and alcoholic liquors are forbidden in countries like India, he reasoned, because the intense heat in hot lands recommends cooling drinks.[86] Citing the practice of ritual bathing in India and its absence in Russia, he concludes that ceremonies respond much more readily to the natural environment than belief, and diffuse much less freely. He also probed the meaning of symbols in ritual, interpreting phallic worship as an honoring of the penis, itself a symbol of reproduction, and ritual bathing as symbolic of cleansing from evil.

A German ethnologist, Christoph Meiners, whose work stretches into the 19th century, enumerated a large number of elemental religious acts, including cleansing, sacrifice, petition, and offerings.[87] In an early stage of religion, such ceremonials were performed only at times when people felt moved by circumstances to ask the deities to bring good fortune or prevent misfortune. Later they came to be combined into festivals, those special occasions in the round of life when people forgo customary activities and devote themselves exclusively to worship. Meiners recognized two ways of studying religions.[88] One presents successive religions in chronological order, i.e., historically. But since many of the same elements recur from one to another, such treatment means endless repetition of details. Better to start with the specific traits generally present in religion and trace their distribution in both time and space. By following this method Meiners provided a schema for comparing religions, using such features as good and evil deities, devotion to images, sacrifice, prayer, purification, uncleanliness, fasting and other forms of self-imposed suffering, festivals, processions, mysteries, sin, good deeds, temples, altars, shamans, priests, magic and witchcraft, divination, mourning, and funerals.

Dual Traditions

Hume's comparative treatment of supernaturalism and Enthusiasm recognizes that sharply contrastive belief systems may coexist in the same society. But he does not connect the dual traditions with different features of the population as specifically as Burnett does when he compares popular religion with philosophical faiths.[89] The popular religion, replete with attention-getting pomp and devotion centering on material objects, he identifies with the common people, while the idea of an abstract intelligence governing the universe belongs to those whom Nathaniel Halhed, in a similar comparison, calls the learned.[90] Halhed was a servant of the British East India Company and one of the pioneers of Oriental studies. India taught him that the illiterate people interpret myths literally, just as must have been true in the dawn of religion. Learned people, however, refine myths into systems of symbols and allegories expressing fundamental beliefs. In the course of time, such refinements bring religious understandings into conformity with improvements taking place in other aspects of an intellectually developing society.

The astute Meiners perceived a difference in the meaning of magic between primitive and civilized societies.[91] Advanced people awesomely view magical practices as working through the agency of esoteric powers which miraculously interrupt the ordinary course of nature. Primitive folk, on the other hand, look on magic as commonplace and quite within the normal order of nature.

Relationships between Social Facts

Ramifying Consequences of Change

Eighteenth-century social theorists, as we have seen, gave considerable attention to the integration of cultural features, as well as to their functional value for society and the individual. Sometimes they limited conclusions to a particular society, but at other times they offered generalizations for societies of a particular type. No more than anthropologists of a later day did they always test the validity of their generalizations, and sometimes it is difficult to see their reasons for linking certain cultural features.

Since a historical outlook predominated among the philosophers, they frequently dealt with relationships between cultural facts diachronically, looking for ramifying consequences instigated by earlier innovations. Thus, some held, the shift to agriculture led to fixed boundaries, cities, an increase in the number of useful crafts and fine arts, growth of trade, enhanced respect for women, and more laws.[92] Civil society introduced several interconnected innovations in social relations, including the institution of property, social hierarchy, intensified warfare, formal political organization, and greater cultural diversity within a society.[93] As trade grew it stimulated equality in inheritance between the sexes, for commerce requires little exertion and therefore women can ply it as readily as men.[94] Pastoralism, with its ability to increase the security of life beyond what food gathering allows, encouraged the imagination to entertain ideas of love and passion, brought chastity to the fore as a virtue, and caused sexual relations to be confined to persons of equal rank.[95] Such restrictions not only heightened sexual tension but exacerbated social animosities.

When Emile Durkheim acknowledges Montesquieu as the founder of social science, he bases his claim on the way Montesquieu searched for interconnections between social facts.[96] A community's laws and their administration, the 18th-century philosopher held, are anchored in sentiments and in the form of government that particular sentiments sustain.[97] Honor, for example, the sentiment which keeps an individual faithful to his social station, sustains monarchy. Virtue, maintaining adherence to law and dedication to one's country, underlies democracy. Fear supports despotism. The form of government and its laws will change, he predicts, should a basic sentiment alter or even weaken. Observations made while traveling through Europe also led Montesquieu to conclude that every form of government has its own type of education, the task of which is to inculcate the basic sentiments in each new generation. He discovered linkages between other customs and specific types of government. In despotic countries, where superiors feel no obligation to their subjects, he finds petitioners never addressing their leaders without making them a gift, a custom democracies find odious.

The strength of moral judgments regarding crime in a particular society varies directly with the intensity of law enforcement. So Dugald Stewart, one of the later Scottish moralists, hypothesized.[98] He explains why. Where the police are weak, people become so habituated to offenses they cease to find even murder reprehensible. In another proposition, he relates the existence of property rights to the amount of labor required to produce goods in a society. If necessities and luxuries can be secured with slight effort, property rights will be looser than they will be if people must work hard for what they possess.

Turning to propositions concerned with the social functions of cultural traits, I have already mentioned Hutcheson on the incest rule preventing role conflict in the nuclear family, Montesquieu's theory of basic sentiments sustaining social structure, and his concept of religion augmenting law enforcement. More particularistically, Montesquieu examined the benefits of polyandry for Nayar society. Several men having one wife in common, he finds, diminishes the strength of each husband's attachment to the woman, and so enables the men to concentrate on their military careers.[99] Georg Forster found social advantages in the rules imposed on female members of the aristocratic Polynesian Arioi sodality who were forbidden to bear children.[100] Should a woman have a child, she was obliged to kill it. The rules, he explains, led to population control and contributed to maintaining the island societies. He points out how prestige and other rewards accruing to individual members functioned as inducements to carry out the obligations attached to Arioi membership. In effect, the personal rewards transformed social duty into personal desire.[101]

Some philosophers, imbued by the Enlightenment's firm faith in the power of human reason to create wise social arrangements, treated the beneficial consequences of customs as causes of the origin of the customs.[102] Even Hume slips into such teleological thinking, regretting only that his imagination wasn't powerful enough to find the pragmatic value of everything.[103] The English empiricist also recognized that customs could be perpetuated beyond their original utility. He illustrates. Although a wife's chastity is essential to maintain the cooperative ties between a woman and her husband on which the welfare of their children depends, why should society demand chastity once women have passed beyond the childbearing age?

Being social critics intent on exposing unreasonable, unnatural, and outworn customs, the Enlightenment thinkers readily spotted dysfunctions and disharmonies in institutions, especially those in their own societies. The value of Christianity itself came into question when Hume compared monotheism unfavorably with polytheism.[104] A double standard of sexual conduct could deprive wives of sexual gratification and tempt them into immorality.[105] Necessary as government might be, at least for civil society, it could sap the national spirit by becoming too fixed on suppressing injustice and keeping down social unrest.[106] Adam Smith found fault with division of labor in factories because, by confining laborers to a few simple operations, it makes them stupid, uninventive, devoid of generous, noble, or tender sentiments, and unable to make judgments about matters of social importance.[107] Losing all taste for uncertainty or adventure, the workers become poor material for the army. Rousseau, with his romantic image of primitivism, launched the strongest charges against civilization.[108] Life in civil society debases human nature and prevents human beings from being all they could potentially become. By instilling needs beyond what people are capable of realizing, modern society enfeebles its members. By forcing individuals into dependence on others, it deprives them of liberty. We were meant to be full-grown, independent persons, but laws and customs keep us lifelong in the bondage of infancy.

As if mocking the rationalists' search for functions and dysfunctions in customs, the English satirist, Bernard Mandeville, showed hidden benefits in what everyone—himself included—acknowledged to be antisocial.[109] Gin shops support the state through taxes, dishonesty gives work to locksmiths, and virtuous women guarding their chastity, don't they support prostitution? Conversely, we are oblivious to evil consequences lurking in what are taken to be virtues. Not everyone perceived the humor, and Mandeville aroused considerable indignation by indulging his reasoning so fancifully.

Learning and Imitation

Of National Character

The century unquestionably accepted the idea of national character. Vico saw different types of human nature appropriate to the different cultural periods.[110] Montesquieu claimed the virtues in a national character also predispose it to particular kinds of vice; thus the Chinese, who are given to prodigious activity, become dishonest through their enormous desire for gain.[111] Hume defined national character operationally: it resides in the manners of a collection of individuals.[112] The character of a nation is formed through all the circumstances working on the mind "as motives or reason [to] render a peculiar set of manners habitual." His list of formative circumstances includes government, public affairs, plenty or penury, and a nation's relationships with neighbors. Voltaire noted variation in national characters by province,[113] and Hume discerned differ-

ences in the dispositions acquired by the members of particular professions.[114] Soldiers or priests acquire different characters through the
common conditions to which they are exposed.

Hume's neglect of climate as an agent in the formation of national
character conspicuously differentiates him from Montesquieu who followed Bodin's environmentalism. Hume's formative factors are purely
social, and their action impinges directly on the individual. Other philosophers, including his Scottish contemporary Thomas Reid, singled out
imitation as the main process in socialization.[115] But imitation would not
occur, Reid observes, were it not for the child's faith in his instructors—
those persons, we would say, with whom he identifies. Claude Adrien
Helvétius, shying away from overemphasizing childhood, termed education a lifelong process.[116] It differs for every individual, for no two persons
are ever precisely in the same position to learn anything.

In place of such psychological empiricism Herder, inspired by the rising tide of nationalism, conceived of a suprasystem combining a people's
"spirit," sense of identity, language, cultural tradition, and even physical
setting.[117] Within the national spirit, or genius, lay the directive power to
which an earlier German philosopher, Baron Gottfried von Leibnitz,
ascribed the destiny of nations.[118] Both men saw the national genius
exemplified in a nation's history and culture. It guides the development
of social institutions, enters into the artistic creations of a society, and
directs every choice made by individuals belonging to the group. In contrast to French and British empirical tradition, which had the greatest
influence on the growth of social science, Central Europeans remained attached to such organismic thinking and to the idea of cultures as systems
manifesting equifinality. Both traditions have persisted into recent
anthropology.

Although predominant opinion regarded national character as learned,
Henry Home thought of it as racially fixed.[119] Character is mutable only
if the group's biological heritage changes, something that has happened
frequently in the history of every country, due to the blending of stocks
through war and commerce.

Fertile and Barren Lands

Strong doubts came to be voiced about the influence of the natural
environment, including climate, on cultural development, temperament,
and human behavior. Montesquieu is about the last eminent defender of
geographical explanations, and in his work the chain linking milieu with
social processes tends to be complex, with the influence of the milieu
often being indirect.[120] Fertile lands, he writes, are easily subjugated;
their level surface places the inhabitants at a disadvantage in repelling

conquerors who are attracted by their rich resources. The wealth such lands produce encourages a leisurely life and effeminacy, qualities which weaken the people, making their defeat and conquest easy. The harder life found in barren countries induces industriousness, hardiness, and courage, qualities whereby the inhabitants are enabled to successfully defend their liberty. Moderate government compensates the populations of barren lands for their hard life, whereas rich, fertile regions tend to be ruled by monarchs. The reason, at least for monarchy, is ecological: agriculturalists in fertile lands are too busy to guard their liberty zealously, and hence lose it to kings. Montesquieu also explains the limited nation-building potential of hunters and pastoralists ecologically: their subsistence techniques require vast territories, but can support only a small number of people. He still regards climate as directly influencing temperament and behavior.[121] In southern lands the heat, acting on the nerves and blood, induces indolence and strong sexuality, against which government, the laws, and religion come to exert countervailing restraints. They offset nature by compelling people to work hard and to remain continent. Human arrangements, however, are not perfect; irrationally, in his opinion, India developed a religion extolling inactivity when climate required quite the opposite. Rather than being due to an excess of women over men, polygyny, according to Montesquieu, occurs in hot lands as a result of the heat hastening early sexual maturation and rapid aging of women.

Ten years after Montesquieu's death, Helvétius questioned the validity of geographical theories of behavior.[122] How can North European courage and strength be due to geographical conditions when some northern Europeans lack those personal qualities? Furthermore, what appears to be courage may actually be foolhardiness springing from ignorance of danger. In hot southern climates, people are supposed to be weak and passive; nevertheless, southern nations have been successful conquerors. How is it that although the geographical situation of a country remains constant, from time to time creativity in the arts and sciences lapses and stagnation sets in? Similarly, the Scottish moralist Millar wondered why nations living under similar climates possess quite opposite national characters and political institutions.[123] Why should the manners of a country change when environment remains constant?

Herder's theory, of external and internal factors acting in combination as the organism accommodates to the limitations of environment, did not suffice to answer such questions.[124] With considerable consistency philosophers turned away from geographical influences on human behavior and looked for social or historical explanations. Groping for a nonenvironmentalist explanation of the rise and fall of scientific productivity, Helvétius ascribes variations in creativity to changes in government and to conditions in society capable of nurturing genius.

Anthropology for Enlightenment

Heightened Interest in Exotic Cultures

A number of the writers whom we encountered in this chapter wrote books directly concerned with society and culture, in contrast to the authors of earlier times who were immediately concerned with theological, political, and philosophical questions, and who treated anthropological topics only incidentally. Nevertheless, the philosophers of the Enlightenment did not pursue cultural development, religion, and other anthropological topics for themselves alone. They admit to a larger purpose. They wanted the knowledge they produced to be practical and useful. Henry Home offered his *Sketches of the History of Man* believing that the information would help persons who were concerned about their fellow creatures. Montesquieu hoped that awareness about the subjects he discusses would provide statesmen with a sound basis for intervening in existing social arrangements.

The men whose works we have sampled reasoned independently—free of traditional religious constraints—from experiences they encountered in their own society, or in ethnographic observations made by others in distant places. Nearly all the writers showed an interest in cultural development, and found the psychological perspective inviting and devised psychogenic explanations for a number of social phenomena; they also had a clear perception of the interconnectedness of social facts, and accepted the idea that culture has instrumental value. In one or two instances—here Herder especially, but Vico, too—we also catch a glimpse of the configurational viewpoint. The philosophers regarded culture as an outcome of history, and possessed some awareness of the ecological relationship linking cultures to their geographical environments. The 18th century used those viewpoints in a rationalistic manner, and mostly to attend to age-old topics, including the cultural progress achieved by mankind, the roots (especially psychogenic) of society, reasons for differences in cultural achievements between societies (invention and diffusion were cited), the tyranny of custom, incest rules, ceremonialism, and the dynamic sources of magic and religion.

New contributions to those topics are occasionally revealed in the sample of Enlightenment thought we have considered. Adam Ferguson's three stages of cultural development—from barbarism to savagery to civil society—is one instance, early matriarchy and social synergy are others. Holbach's very modern-sounding analysis of male puberty ceremonies among the Virginia Indians would count more were it not so ethnographically specific. The idea of cultural development, formerly applied only to culture as a whole, came to be applied to a specific cultural domain in Home's, Hume's, and Meiners's stages of religion. A national genius, postulated as the guiding force in a nation's culture history, was a new concept, one that survived better in political rhetoric than in anthropological theory. The existence of a highly distinctive pattern of primitive thought—the savage mind—is also original. It did not displace the assumption of worldwide psychic unity, for the savage was also credited with being fully capable of learning advanced principles of reasoning.

The level of interest in primitive and exotic culture was heightened in the 18th century, reflecting the increased knowledge of exotic societies brought to Europe by explorers whose voyages were still continuing. The philosophers applied Montaigne's concept of savage culture being closer to nature, and, since they regarded natural things as good, beautiful, simple (in a desirable way), and morally justified, they also idealized the life close to nature that they thought primitive people followed.

Often the century's luminaries dealt with only relatively new concepts; they elaborated old ideas whose anlagen can be detected in ancient Greek sources. National character, Condorcet's theory of cumulative development, and Hume's correlation of supernaturalism and situations of uncertainty, are in this category. Some of the 18th-century's versions of old ideas exerted more influence on succeeding generations than the original writings. Montesquieu's theory that sentiments sustain social structure is an illustration; it had a direct impact on social thought, whereas a similar idea in Plato is never referred to.

The Enlightenment's contribution to the history of anthropology lies not so much in specific ideas that it developed and passed on, as in the lasting impulse it gave to the naturalistic study of society and culture. The impulse came from the books and essays philosophers published about such subjects as: man (Helvétius), philosophical history (Herder), the origin and development of civil society and social structure (Ferguson, Rousseau, Millar), the interrelationship of laws, government, and education (Montesquieu), religion (Holbach, Hume), and national character (Hume).

From yet another aspect, the Age helped to develop cultural anthropology through the explicit attention writers like Vico, Ferguson, Millar, and Degérando paid to the subject of method, using the word in its broadest sense. They warned against false tracks and sources of error in reconstructing the history of society. They pointed to the value of heuristic cultural relativism, and provided explorers and others with advice and directives for studying exotic customs without committing distorting blunders in interpretation. By writing works in which social facts gained meaning from being seen in integration with other social facts, and from being explained by social facts, they called attention to a method that has become a defining feature of social science.

The Enlightenment brought the study of society and culture nearer to being an independent discipline. The famous names of this period in

England, France, Germany, and Italy made social science more visible, thereby moving cultural anthropology closer to the status of an autonomous subject, the position it won for itself in the next century.

Notes

1. Immanuel Kant, *Foundations of the Metaphysics of Morals* [orig. 1785], trans. Lewis White Beck (Library of Liberal Arts ed.; Indianapolis: Bobbs–Merrill Co., 1959), p. 5.

2. Joseph Niedermann, *Kultur* (Firenze: "Bibliopolis," Libreria Antiquaria Editrice, 1941), pp. 211–218; Paul Henri Thiry, Baron d'Holbach, *Système sociale* [orig. 1773] (three volumes in one; Hildesheim: Georg Olms, 1969), vol. 3, pp. 3–4.

3. James Burnett, Lord Monboddo, *Of the Origin and Progress of Language* [orig. 1773–1792] (6 vols.; Menston, England: The Scolar Press, 1967), vol. 1, p. 25. Reference to great and small societies is made in Claude Adrien Helvetius, *A Treatise on Man* [orig. 1773], trans. W. Hooper (2 vols.; New York: Burt Franklin, 1969), vol. 1, p. 88.

4. Burnett, *Origin and Progress*, vol. 1, pp. 2, 149, 151. Ferguson saw the mutual exclusiveness of nature and culture exaggerated; see Adam Ferguson, *An Essay on the History of Civil Society* [orig. 1767], Duncan Forbes, ed. (Edinburgh: At the University Press, 1966), p. 6.

5. Jean Jacques Rousseau, *Discourse on the Origin and Foundations of Inequality* [orig. 1755], trans. Roger D. Masters and Judith R. Masters, in Roger D. Masters, ed., *Jean Jacques Rousseau, the First and Second Discourses* (New York: St. Martin's Press, 1964); Denis Diderot, *Supplément au voyage de Bougainville* [orig. 1796], Herbert Dieckmann, ed. (Textes Littéraires Français; Genève: Librarie Droz, 1955), ch. 2.

6. Thomas Reid, *Essays on the Active Powers of the Human Mind* [orig. 1788], in William Hamilton, ed., *The Works of Thomas Reid* (2 vols.; Edinburgh: James Thin, 1895), vol. 2, pp. 548, 562, 563; Claude Adrien Helvetius, *De l'esprit, or Essays on the Mind and Its Several Faculties* [orig. 1758], trans. Anonymous (New York: Burt Franklin, 1970), p. 2.

7. Among writers who conceived of a universal culture pattern were Giambattista Vico, *The New Science of Giambattista Vico* [orig. 1725], trans. Thomas Goddard Bergin and Max Harold Fisch (Ithaca: Cornell University Press, 1968); Antoine Nicolas de Condorcet, *Sketch for a Historical Picture of the Progress of the Human Mind* [orig. 1795], trans. June Barraclough (New York: Noonday Press, 1955); and Joseph-Marie Degérando, *The Observation of Savage People* [orig. 1800], trans. F. C. T. Moore (Berkeley: University of California Press, 1969).

8. Vico, *New Science*, p. 63; Voltaire, *Essai sur les moeurs et l'esprit des nations*, in *Oeuvres completes de Voltaire* (new ed.; 52 vols.; Paris: Garnier Frères, 1878), vol. 13, p. 182; Voltaire, *The Philosophy of History* [orig. 1766] (New York: Philosophical Library, 1965), p. 21.

9. Guillaume Thomas Francois Raynal, *A Philosophical and Political History of the Settlements and Trade of the Europeans in the East and West Indies* [orig. 1770], trans. J. Justamond (3rd ed.; 5 vols.; London: T. Cadell, 1777), p. 407; Helvetius, *L'Espirit*, p. 2.

10. The naive idea of geographical determinism, advanced early in Western anthropological thought, provides of course another explanation; but as I bring out later in this chapter, it was displaced in the 18th century, due to the influence of Locke and other empiricists, by psychologically based theories involving the role of experience.

11. Paul Henri Thiry, Baron d'Holbach [M. Mirabaud, pseud.] *The System of Nature; or, The Laws of the Moral and Physical World* [orig. 1770],

trans. William Hodgson (4 vols.; London: B. Crosby et al., 1795), vol. 1, pp. 22–24, 27.

12. William Robertson, *An Historical Disquisition Concerning the Knowledge Which the Ancients Had of India* [orig. c. 1791], in *The Works of William Robertson, D.D.* (8 vols.; London: T. Cadell et al., 1827), vol. 8, pp. 326, 340. See also E. A. Hoebel, "William Robertson: an 18th Century Anthropologist-Historian," *American Anthropologist*, vol. 62 (1960): 648–655, p. 650.

13. Henry Home, Lord Kames, *Sketches of the History of Man* [orig. 1774] (4 vols.; Hildesheim: Georg Olms Verlagsbuchhandlung, 1968), vol. 2, pp. 155–164, 173–176, 186; vol. 4, p. 52.

14. Burnett, *Origin and Progress*, vol. 1, pp. 279, 300–305.

15. George Turnbull, *The Principles of Moral Philosophy* (London: John Noon, 1740), pp. 184, 187. See also Jean Jacques Rousseau, *Emile* [orig. 1762], trans. Barbara Foxley (Everyman's Library ed.; London: Dent, 1911), p. 182; Holbach, *System of Nature*, vol. 1, pp. 205 ff.

16. Adam Smith, *An Inquiry into the Nature and Causes of the Wealth of Nations* [orig. 1789], Edwin Cannan, ed. (New York: Modern Library, 1937), bk. 3, ch. 1.

17. Smith, *Wealth of Nations*, bk. 4, ch. 2; Alexander Pope, *An Essay on Man* [orig. 1734], in Maynard Mack, ed., *The Poems of Alexander Pope* (Twickenham ed.; 6 vols.; London: Methuen and Co., 1950), Epistle III, lines 125–138.

18. Johann Gottfried von Herder, *Ideas for a Philosophy of the History of Mankind* [orig. 1784–1791], in F. M. Barnard, ed. and trans., *Herder on Social and Political Culture* (Cambridge: At the University Press, 1969), pp. 269–270; also see Arthur O. Lovejoy, "Some Eighteenth Century Evolutionists. II," *Popular Science Monthly*, vol. 65 (1904): 323–340, pp. 332–333.

19. Holbach, *Système sociale*, vol. 1, pp. 13, 15, 56–57, 158–159; Holbach, *System of Nature*, vol. 1, pp. 258–

260; Bernard de Mandeville, *The Fable of the Bees* [orig. 1724], Philip Harth, ed. (Pelican Classics ed.; Harmondsworth: Penguin Books, 1970), pp. 102–103, 237, 334–335.

20. Jean Jacques Rousseau, *The Social Contract* [orig. 1762], Charles Frankel, ed. (New York: Hafner Publishing Co., 1947), p. 19.

21. James DunBar, *Essays on the History of Mankind in Rude and Cultivated Ages* (London: W. Strahan, 1780).

22. Ferguson, *History of Civil Society*, pp. 168, 176–177.

23. Herder cited in G. A. Wells, *Herder and After* ('s-Gravenhage: Mouton, 1959), p. 73. In Europe, Herder noted, the distinction is blurred compared to the Far East, cf. Nathaniel Brassey Halhed, "'The Translator's Preface' to *A Code of Gentoo Laws*" [orig. 1776] in P. J. Marshall, ed., *The British Discovery of Hinduism in the Eighteenth Century* (Cambridge: At the University Press, 1970), pp. 145–146.

24. Paul Henri Thiry, Baron d'Holbach, "Universal Morality" [orig. 1776], in Norman L. Torrey, ed. and trans., *Les Philosophes* (New York: Capricorn Books, 1960), p. 193. Unlike Pyrrho, Holbach was no moral relativist; he didn't imply that vice becomes virtue by being approved.

25. Examples of this literary genre include Charles Louis de Secondat de Montesquieu, *The Persian Letters* [orig. 1721], trans. George R. Healy (Indianapolis: Bobbs-Merrill Co., 1964); Oliver Goldsmith, *The Citizen of the World* [orig. 1762] in Arthur Friedman, ed., *Collected Works of Oliver Goldsmith* (5 vols.; Oxford: Clarendon Press, 1966), vol. 2; Voltaire, *The Huron; or, Pupil of Nature* [orig. 1767], in *The Works of Voltaire*, trans. William F. Fleming (22 vols.; New York: St. Hubert Guild, 1901), vol. 2, pt. 1, pp. 64–163.

26. Helvetius, *L'Espirit*.

27. John Zephaniah Holwell, "Chapters on 'The Religious Tenets of the Gentoos'" [orig. 1767–1768], in Marshall, *The British Discovery*, p. 49.

28. Herder cited in Isaiah Berlin, "Herder

and the Enlightenment" in Earl R. Wasserman, ed., *Aspects of the Eighteenth Century* (Baltimore: Johns Hopkins Press, 1965).

29. Francis Hutcheson, *An Inquiry into the Original of Our Ideas of Beauty and Virtue* [orig. 1725] (5th ed.; London: R. Ware et al., 1753), pp. 208–209.

30. Voltaire, *A Philosophical Dictionary* [orig. 1764], Theodore Besterman, ed. and trans. (Harmondsworth: Penguin Books, 1971), pp. 239–240.

31. Degérando, *Savage People*.

32. F. C. T. Moore, "Translator's Introduction," in Degérando, *Savage People*, pp. 28–36.

33. One was prepared for William Penn covering housing, language, religion, marriage, medicine, subsistence, recreation, demography, and abilities like swimming, shooting, and leaping. See William Petty, "Quaeries Concerning the Nature of the Natives of Pensilvania" [orig. c. 1685], in Marquis of Lansdowne, ed., *The Petty Papers* (2 vols.; London: Constable and Co., 1927), vol. 2, pp. 115–119. A questionnaire including anthropological topics was also prepared for La Perouse's voyage of 1786; see Frederica de Laguna, *Under Mount Saint Elias: The History and Culture of the Yakutat Tlingit* (Smithsonian Contributions to Anthropology, vol. 7, 1972), pt. 1, p. 114.

34. Georg Forster, *A Voyage Round the World* [orig. 1777], adapted by Robert L. Kahn, in *Georg Forster's Werke* (Berlin: Die Deutsche Akademie der Wissenschaft, 1968), pp. 13–14; Giambattista Vico cited in Isaiah Berlin, "One of the Boldest Innovators in the History of Human Thought," *The New York Times Magazine*, Nov. 23, 1969: 76–77, 79–100, p. 84; Herder cited in Berlin, "Herder," p. 55.

35. Vico, *New Science*, pp. 82–83, 88, 105–106, 305 ff.; Berlin, "Herder," pp. 178, 182, 190, 195; Reid, *The Active Powers*, vol. 1, pp. 516–517, 606; Nicolas-Antoine Boulanger cited in Arnold van Gennep, *Religions, Moeurs et Légendes* (cinquième

série; Paris: Mercure de France, 1914), p. 193; David Bidney, "Vico's New Science of Myth," in Giorgio Tagliacozzo and Hayden V. White, eds., *Giambattista Vico, An International Symposium* (Baltimore: Johns Hopkins Press, 1969).

36. Diderot, *Voyage de Bougainville*, p. 11; Anne Robert Jacques Turgot cited in Frank E. Manuel, *The Prophets of Paris* (Cambridge: Harvard University Press, 1962), p. 322; Burnett, *Origin and Progress*, vol. 1, pp. 133–134, 141, 144.

37. Burnett, *Origin and Progress*, vol. 1, pp. 235–238; James Burnett, *Antient Metaphysics* (6 vols.; London: T. Cadell, 1779–1799), vol. 3, p. 250; vol. 4, p. 45. Condorcet knew it was wise to be judicious in reading travel accounts; see Condorcet, *Progress of the Human Mind*, pp. 8–9.

38. Home, *Sketches*, vol. 1, p. 30.

39. For a biographical account see William C. Lehmann, *Adam Ferguson and the Beginnings of Modern Sociology* (New York: Columbia University Press, 1930).

40. Ferguson, *Civil Society*, pp. 2–3, 8–9, 186. Ferguson's confidence in parallels between societies as evidence of age (in essence, the age-area hypothesis) was shared by other writers; see Vico, *New Science*, p. 97; John Millar, *The Origin of the Distinction of Ranks* [orig. 1771], in William C. Lehmann ed., *John Millar of Glasgow 1735–1801* (Cambridge: At the University Press, 1960), p. 180.

41. Home, *Sketches*, vol. 1, p. 1.

42. Vico, *New Science*.

43. Ferguson, *Civil Society*, pp. 5, 8–9, 75–103, 126–128, 168–169, 174, 180–186, 188, 190.

44. Montesquieu uses the first two terms; see Charles Louis de Secondat, Baron de Montesquieu, *The Spirit of the Laws* [orig. 1748], trans. Thomas Nugent (Library of Classics ed.; New York: Hafner Publishing Co., 1949), bk. 18, sect. 11.

45. Joseph Francois Lafitau, *Moeurs, coutumes et religions des sauvages américains* (abridged ed.; 2 vols. in one; Paris: Librairie de la Société de l'Enseignement Catholique, 1839).

46. Montesquieu, *The Laws,* bk. 2, sect. 2.

47. Home, *Sketches,* vol. 1, pp. 84–131, 162–174; 184–186, 201–206, 211, 346; vol. 4, p. 130.

48. Morelly, for example, whose first name is unknown. For his ideas see F. J. C. Hearnshaw, *The Social and Political Ideas of Some Great French Thinkers of the Age of Reason* (New York: F. S. Crofts and Co., 1930), pp. 221–223. Home, *Sketches,* vol. 2, pp. 201–219; vol. 4, pp. 140, 146.

49. Condorcet, *Progress of the Human Mind;* James George Frazer, *Condorcet on the Progress of the Human Mind* (Oxford: Clarendon Press, 1933).

50. Ferguson, *Civil Society,* pp. 168–169.

51. David Hume, "Of the Rise and Progress of the Arts and Sciences," in David Hume, *Essays Moral, Political and Literary* [orig. 1741–1742] (The World's Classics ed.; London: Oxford University Press, 1963), p. 116; also Georg Forster cited in Thomas P. Saine, *Georg Forster* (Twayne World Author Series 215; New York: Twayne Publishers, 1972), p. 64.

52. Anne Robert Jacques Turgot, *Discourse at the Sorbonne* [orig. 1750], Anne Robert Jacques Turgot, *Notes on Universal History* [orig. 1750], both in W. Walker Stephens, ed., *The Life and Writings of Turgot* (London: Longmans, Green and Co., 1895), pp. 161, 177–178, 180; Burnett, *Origin and Progress,* vol. 1, pp. 259–260; Home, *Sketches,* vol. 1, pp. 112, 162, 193, 210; Antoine Yves Goguet, *The Origins of Laws, Arts, and Sciences, and Their Progress among the Most Ancient Nations* (3 vols.; Edinburgh: George Robinson, Paternoster-Row, and Alexander Donaldson, 1775), vol. 1, p. 279.

53. Home, *Sketches,* vol. 1, pp. 165–166, 190–191.

54. Ferguson, *Civil Society,* p. 180; Smith, *Wealth of Nations,* pp. 5–17.

55. Ferguson, *Civil Society,* pp. 168–169; also see Turgot, *Discourse,* p. 165. Others who recognized the process of diffusion include Bernard Le Bovier de Fontenelle, see his *De l'origine des fables* [orig. 1724], in G.-B. Depping, ed. *Oeuvres complèts* (3 vols.; Geneva: Slatkine Reprints, 1968), vol. 2, p. 17, and his "On the Ancients and Moderns" [orig. 1764], in Frederick Teggert and George Hildebrand, eds., *The Idea of Progress* (rev. ed.; Berkeley: University of California Press, 1949), p. 177; Helvetius, *L'Espirit,* p. 35; Montesquieu, *The Laws,* vol. 1, p. 302.

56. Ferguson, *Civil Society,* pp. 210–215, 220–221.

57. Home, *Sketches,* vol. 1, pp. 112, 125, 137–138, 191–192, 281–313.

58. Home, *Sketches,* vol. 2, pp. 5–30; a similar theory is held by Dugald Stewart, *The Philosophy of the Active and Moral Powers of Man* (2 vols.; Edinburgh: Adam Black, 1828), vol. 1, pp. 32–35; Dugald Stewart, *Lectures on Political Economy,* in William Hamilton, ed., *The Collected Works of Dugald Stewart* (11 vols.; Edinburgh: Thomas Constable and Co., 1854–1860), vol. 8, p. 73.

59. Burnett, *Origin and Progress,* vol. 1, pp. 225, 227, 240; references to early promiscuity also occur in Goguet, *Origin of Laws,* p. 21.

60. Millar, *Origin of Ranks,* pp. 183–186, 199–202.

61. Francis Hutcheson, *A System of Moral Philosophy* [orig. 1755], in *Collected Works of Francis Hutcheson,* (Facsimile ed.; 6 vols.; Hildesheim: Georg Olms Verlagsbuchhandlung, 1969), vol. 6, pp. 170–172. See also Montesquieu, *Laws,* bk. 26, sect. 14; Aldridge Alfred Owen, "The Meaning of Incest from Hutcheson to Gibbon," *Ethics,* vol. 61 (1950–1951): 309–313, pp. 309–310.

62. Henry Home, "Succession or Descent," in Henry Home, *Essays Upon Several Subjects Concerning British Antiquities* (3rd ed.; Edinburgh: A. Kincaid and J. Bell, 1763).

63. David Hume, *A Treatise of Human Nature* [orig. 1739–1740], Ernest C. Mossner, ed. (Pelican Classics ed.; Harmondsworth: Penguin Books, 1969), bk. 3, part 2, sect. 8; Goguet, *Origin of Laws,* vol. 1, p. 8; Montesquieu, *The Laws,* p. 276.

64. Robertson, *Historical Disquisition*, vol. 8, p. 302. See also Goguet, *Origin of Laws*, vol. 1, pp. 10–34.

65. David Hume, "Of the Original Contract," [orig. 1748], in Hume, *Essays*, pp. 454–455, 467–468.

66. Isaiah Berlin, "The Philosophical Ideas of G. Vico," in Harold Acton et al., *Art and Ideas in Eighteenth-Century Italy* (Publicazioni Dell' Istituto Italiano di Cultura di Londra, No. 4, 1960), pp. 184, 190–191; Vico, *New Science*, pp. 31–32, 74–79, 84, 85–87, 165, 218–226.

67. For example, William Jones, "On the Gods of Greece, Italy, and India" [orig. 1784] in *The Works of Sir William Jones* (13 vols.; London: John Stockdale and John Walker, 1807), pp. 320–322; or Turgot, *Universal History*, pp. 189–191.

68. Frederick Copleston, *A History of Philosophy*, vol. 5, *Hobbes to Hume* (London: Burns Oates and Washbourne, 1959), p. 165.

69. Home, *Sketches*, vol. 4, pp. 194–234. Another who claimed that man had a natural tendency to reason to the existence of deities was George Turnbull; see his *The Principles of Moral Philosophy* (London: John Noon, 1740), p. 101.

70. Pope, *Essay on Man*, Epistle III, lines 249–254.

71. David Hume, "Of Superstition and Enthusiasm," in Hume, *Essays*, pp. 74, 76, 78. Others include Holbach, *System of Nature*, vol. 3, pp. 14–16, 21, 23–24, 27; Paul Henri Thiry, Baron d'Holbach [Jean Meslier, pseudonym], *Superstition in All Ages* [orig. 1772], trans. Anna Knoop (New York: Peter Eckler, 1890), p. 161; Ferguson, *Civil Society*, p. 90; Vico, *New Science*, p. 120.

72. David Hume, *The Natural History of Religion* [orig. 1757], H. E. Root, ed. (London: Adam and Charles Black, 1956), chs. 2–3.

73. Hume, "Of Superstition."

74. Hume, *Natural History*, pp. 23, 38–39, 48–53.

75. A similar observation had been made by Montesquieu, *The Laws*, bk. 25, sect. 2.

76. Copleston, *History of Philosophy*, vol. 5, p. 316.

77. Holbach, *Superstition*, pp. 36, 38–50, 160–161, 273; Holbach, *System of Nature*, vol. 3, pp. 14–32, 74–82, see also vol. 1, pp. 135–137; N. S. Bergier, *Les Dieux du paganisme* [orig. 1767], cited in Antonius Petrus Leonardus de Cocq, *Andrew Lang: A Nineteenth Century Anthropologist* (Tilburg: Oitg. Zwijsen, 1968), p. 82. See Voltaire's articles "Idol-Idolater-Idolatry" and "Religion" in Voltaire, *A Philosophical Dictionary*, pp. 245, 351. See also Voltaire's article "Idol, Idolater, Idolatry" in Denis Diderot, *Denis Diderot's The Encyclopedia, Selections* [orig. 1751–1772], Stephen J. Gendzier, ed. and trans. (New York: Harper & Row, 1967), p. 145.

78. Reid, *The Active Powers*, vol. 2, p. 516; see also Robertson, *Historical Disquisition*, pp. 339, 340.

79. Holbach, *System of Nature*, pp. 27–29.

80. James Beattie, *Dissertations Moral and Critical* [orig. 1783], in *The Works of James Beattie* (9 vols.; Philadelphia: Hopkins and Earle, 1809), vol. 1, pp. 129–138.

81. Antoine Noe de Polier de Botens, "Magie" [orig. 1765], in *The Encyclopédie of Diderot and D'Alembert*, J. Lough, ed. (Cambridge: At the University Press, 1954), pp. 147–154.

82. Montesquieu, *The Laws*, vol. 2, pp. 29–46; see also Vico, *New Science*, p. 117; Guillaume Raynal, *A Philosophical and Political History of the Settlements and Trade of the Europeans in the East and West Indies* [orig. 1770], trans. J. Justamond (3rd ed.; 5 vols.; London: T. Cadell, 1777), vol. 5, bk. 19, p. 403; Goguet, *Origin of Laws*, vol. 1, p. 23.

83. Rousseau, *Social Contract*, pp. 36–39, 115–120.

84. Paul Henri Thiry, Baron d'Holbach, "Huscanaouiment," in *Encyclopédie ou dictionnaire raisonée des sciences, des arts et des métiers* (1765), vol. 8.

85. Montesquieu, *The Laws*, vol. 1, p. 303.

86. Voltaire, *Philosophical Dictionary*, vol. 4, pp. 196, 206–207, 296; Voltaire, *Philosophy of History*, pp. 76–77.

87. Christoph Meiners, *Allgemeine kritische Geschichte der Religion* (2 vols.; Hannover: Verlag der Helwingischen Hofs Buchhandlung, 1806), vol. 2, pp. 101, 307–308.

88. Christoph Meiners, *Grundriss der Geschichte der Menschheit*, Part II, *Grundriss der Geschichte aller Religionen* (Lemgo: Verlag der Meyerschen Buchhandlung, 1785), pp. 13–14.

89. Burnett, *Antient Metaphysics*, vol. 4, pp. 166–172, 373.

90. Halhed, *Translator's Preface*, pp. 145–146.

91. Meiners, *Allgemeine Kritische Geschichte*, pp. 589–590.

92. Goguet, *Origin of Laws*, vol. 1, pp. 17–18, 30–33; Rousseau, *Discourse on Inequality*, pp. 141 ff; Millar, *Origin of Ranks*, pp. 203–225.

93. Ferguson, *Civil Society*, pp. 96–103, 126–127, 180, 186, 218–219.

94. Home, *Sketches*, vol. 2, pp. 26, 43, 68–69, 201.

95. Millar, *Origin of Ranks*, pp. 203–204.

96. Emile Durkheim, *Montesquieu and Rousseau*, [orig. 1893], trans. Ralph Manheim (Ann Arbor: University of Michigan Press, 1960), pp. 1–2.

97. Montesquieu, *The Laws*, bk. 3, sect. 8; bks. 4, 5.

98. Stewart, *Active and Moral Powers*, vol. 1, pp. 177, 187.

99. Montesquieu, *The Laws*, bk. 16, sec. 5.

100. Forster, *Voyage*, pp. 414–415; Saine, *Georg Forster*.

101. Cf. Melford Spiro, "Social Systems, Personality, and Functional Analysis," in Bert Kaplan, ed., *Studying Personality Cross-Culturally* (Evanston, Ill.: Row, Peterson and Co., 1961), p. 104.

102. Helvetius, *L'Esprit*, pp. 101–103.

103. David Hume, *An Enquiry Concerning the Principles of Morals* [orig. 1751] (LaSalle, Ill.: Open Court, 1946), pp. 18, 41. Cf., Raynal, *Philosophical and Political History*, pp. 596, 598; Goguet, *Origin of Laws*, vol. 1, pp. 37–38.

104. Hume, *Natural History of Religion*, pp. 48, 52.

105. Helvetius, *L'Esprit*, p. 120.

106. Ferguson, *Civil Society*, pp. 205, 218, 220.

107. Smith, *Wealth of Nations*, pp. 734–735. See also Home, *Sketches*, vol. 1, p. 193.

108. Rousseau, *Discourse on Inequality*, pp. 155 ff. Rousseau, *Emile*, pp. 46 ff. See also Herder, *Ideas for a Philosophy*, bk. 7, ch. 5.

109. Bernard Mandeville, *Fable of the Bees*, pp. 119 ff.

110. Vico, *New Science*, bk. 4.

111. Montesquieu, *The Laws*, vol. 1, pp. 296, 307. Holbach is also normative in his *Système sociale*, vol. 3, pp. 45–48.

112. David Hume, "Of National Characters," in Hume, *Essays Moral, Political and Literary*, pp. 202–203.

113. Voltaire, *Philosophical Dictionary*, vol. 9, pp. 117, 134.

114. Hume, "National Characters," p. 203. See also Ferguson, *Civil Society*, p. 190.

115. Reid, *The Active Powers*, vol. 2, p. 549; Turnbull, *Moral Philosophy*, p. 101. Imitation is also mentioned in Vico, *New Science*, p. 33, Holbach, *Système sociale*, vol. 1, pp. 15, 204, and Holbach, *Superstition*, p. 62.

116. Claude Adrien Helvetius, *A Treatise on Man* [orig. 1773], trans. W. Hooper (2 vols.; New York: Burt Franklin, 1969), pp. 12 ff.

117. Wells, *Herder and After*, pp. 199–203, 204; Berlin, "Herder," pp. 74 ff.

118. Nathan Rotenstreich, "Volksgeist," in *Dictionary of the History of Ideas* (1973), vol. 4.

119. Home, *Sketches*, pp. 31–40, 57.

120. Montesquieu, *The Laws*, bks. 14–18.

121. For another work dealing with the influence of climate, see William Falconer, *Remarks on the Influence of Climate Situation, Nature of Country, Population, Nature of Food, and Way of Life on the Dis-

position and *Temper, Manners and Behaviour, Intellects, Laws and Customs, Form of Government, and Religion of Mankind* (London: C. Dilly, 1771).

122. Helvetius, *L'Esprit*, ch. 28–30, esp. pp. 342–351, 358, 361. Holbach also departs from climate theory; see his *Système sociale*, vol. 3, pp. 2–3.

123. Millar, *Origin of Ranks*, pp. 178–180; Ferguson, *Civil Society*, pp. 108–112, 118.

124. Herder, *Ideas for a Philosophy*, pp. 289–301.

5

Anthropology Becomes a Discipline

Lines of Thought

Ethnography in an Age of Colonialism

This chapter covers the development of anthropological ideas to the threshold of the modern period, that is, up to Franz Boas and his contemporaries in the United States and to A. R. Radcliffe-Brown and Bronislaw Malinowski in Great Britain. Some of the writers who will be treated can unquestionably be called anthropologists, whatever the professions whereby they earned their incomes. The titles of the books they wrote have a familiar ring—*Ancient Society, Primitive Culture, Totemism and Exogamy, Development of Marriage and Kinship, Kinship and Social Organization, Totem and Taboo*—because the words remain part of the professional argot, though often with altered meanings. Furthermore, some authors called themselves anthropologists and ethnologists, or occupied academic or government positions bearing those titles. However, since anthropological ideas more than anthropologists are my subject, I will still be referring to works of political economists, sociologists, psychologists, lawyers, and others, some of whom—Karl Marx and Sigmund Freud, to mention two—ultimately had as durable an influence on thought about culture and society as anyone.

England and Germany were the centers of anthropological activity in the 19th century. After 1890 France, too, became potent with original

---

Notes to this chapter begin on page 180.

ideas which, although commonly referred to as sociological, within a few decades sired a new brand of anthropology.

The earliest of the writers with whom the chapter deals—Lewis Henry Morgan, Marx, Herbert Spencer, Edward B. Tylor, John Wesley Powell, John Ferguson McLennan, and Julius Lippert—grew up in the first half of the 19th century, a period of rapid culture change. Although a slack period in the development of anthropological ideas, the early 1800s in western Europe and America experienced the growing tide of industrialization; cultural nationalism, evidenced in a taste for folk literature and the simple unspoiled rural life; romanticism, with its release of feeling in music, painting, and poetry; explorations of new forms of artistic expression; and, in politics, reformist liberalism, culminating in the revolutions of 1848. We gain an insight into the magnitude of the break with tradition from John Stuart Mill's poignant allusion—partly personal, no doubt—to the plight of the old who are riveted to outworn habits and principles, and of the young who have only their own experience and observation to direct them. The rudderlessness extends to those who wield worldly power; religion has lost much of its authority over rulers, and their own moral authority has become "a broken spell."[1]

During the second half of the cenutry and the first two or three decades of the next, the period when Tylor, Lippert, and James G. Frazer published their books, and when Emile Durkheim, Arnold van Gennep, Marcel Mauss, and Fritz Graebner pioneered new approaches, technological developments in the spheres of transportation and communication knit the world increasingly tightly. The poverty and urban squalor of early Victorian England became somewhat alleviated through street paving, new towns, new housing, and sewers, amenities that also encouraged the Victorian conception of progress. These were years when the concept of Darwinian evolution became increasingly acceptable and brought about wide acceptance of our link with prehuman ancestors, as well as a freshly informed conception of the importance of natural selection in historical change. For western Europe they were prosperous years, quite conforming to the poetic image of a world spinning along the grooves of change toward ever more wonderful technical miracles. They were the decades of realism and naturalism in literature, as well as of fin de siècle decadence, Marxian materialism in philosophy and social science, and in politics an emphasis on praxis rather than ideals. Britain and America nourished the ideal of progressive cultural growth, though they did not generate the idea. The theme of social development had been abroad in western Europe for a long time; now, despite the congenial spirit of the times, it would last only for a few more decades before going into eclipse.

Throughout the century colonialism, missionizing, penal exile, and continental expansion forced people of European background on Australian, African, Melanesian, American Indian, and Paleosiberian native folk. Europeans proclaimed it their duty to carry the light of Christianity into dark places, to touch the minds of natives with the ethical ideals of Europe. Anthropologists, on the whole, accepted colonialism and worked within its framework. Though ethnological societies founded in the 1830s might show concern for the welfare of aborigines, and travelers acquainted with native people wondered about their future, generally everyone accepted the inevitability of primitive cultures giving way to change. Overwhelming as the experience was morally, culturally, and physically for those who greeted the torchbearers, the ethnographic descriptions written about as yet uncivilized societies captured valuable information that within a few decades would be unobtainable. Ethnologists tended to steer clear of the fallacies of social darwinists for whom society was always in the process of excreting its unhealthy, slow, faithless, or otherwise unfit members, and for whom the civilizing mission carried out under colonialism constituted a selective factor. Social darwinists saw in it a chance of survival for those primitive groups and individuals capable of assimilating what the agents of colonial societies sought to bestow. Until near the end of the century, anthropological labors to a large extent remained divided between residents, missionaries, and others in exotic lands who wrote the descriptive accounts about primitive custom, and ethnologists back home who sifted the ethnographic facts, compared them, constructed theories, and sometimes sent out questionnaires to be sure of getting the information they wanted. To an increasing extent as time passed anthropologists also acted as their own fact collectors; Lewis Henry Morgan among the Iroquois, William McGee among the Seri, and A. C. Haddon in the Torres Strait. In 1884 they began to arrange and join expeditions organized specifically to acquire information about human behavior or artifacts for museums.[2] Anyone who tried to apprehend an exotic culture in its own terms discovered anew the difficulty of firmly bracketing one's own assumptions. Leo Frobenius, who led 12 African expeditions between 1904 and 1935 to collect museum objects, folktales, and other information, toward the end of his long career perceived that the most learned person studying a foreign culture would fail to understand it properly unless, in some measure, he could outgrow his earlier enculturation.[3] Frazer, who did no field work, likewise realized the danger of mistaking the meaning of facts belonging to another way of life.[4] He proposed making "allowance as far as possible for our individual upbringing, character, and surroundings," calculating as exactly as possible the personal equation, and correcting what we learn accordingly.

A New Discipline

Ethnological societies in Europe and America, starting in 1839,[5] and anthropologists installed in university positions showed that anthropology was becoming a discipline. The subject won academic status in England, in 1884, when Edward B. Tylor became a reader at Oxford, and four years later in the United States, when Harvard established a department of "archeology and ethnology." Lacking clear-cut identity by virtue of its comprehensive aim of studying man totally—prehistorically and contemporaneously, in his physical and cultural dimensions—the field acquired a variety of names, about which even today there is no sure consensus. In the United States, "anthropology," a word already standing for a non-empirical theological study, became a popular general name for the subject; but in the United States and elsewhere, the subject also came to be called "ethnology." The French used *ethnographie* interchangeably with *"anthropologie";* and the Germans called it "the science of culture" as well as *"Völkerkunde,"* a word which translates badly into English. In a few decades the term "ethnology," along with two new names, "social anthropology" and "sociology," came to designate strictly the study of living cultures.[6]

The comprehensive aim of cultural anthropology meant pursuing literally everything that human beings made, did, or thought about. So by the early part of the 20th century cultural anthropologists had written about games, myths, tools, clothing, cuisine, religion, magic, incest rules, marriage, kinship nomenclature, groupings ranging from sodalities to tribes, mother-right, father-right, language, art, string-figures, folklore, and more. They dealt with those topics to illustrate evolution, diffusion, environmental adaptation, and other cultural processes. Facts of exotic life attracted them; the pages of their books overrun with customs culled from every known source, from the Church Fathers' descriptions of pagan idolatry to contemporary reports by ethnographic observers. Knowledge of customs, anthropologists claimed, had practical value.[7] Knowing the limits of what is possible in society keeps us from making costly mistakes in legislation and other matters. Studying the customs of the "lower races" could also be pragmatically justified in a colonial society which had assumed responsibility for administering, educating, and legislating for people following many different ways of life.

Developmentalism Predominant

A concern with cultural development predominated during the greatest part of the 19th century. Although the theorists of the period are usually referred to collectively as evolutionists—and I too will use the word from time to time—their outlook differed little from 18th-century and earlier developmentalism. Increasingly challenged toward the end of the century because the logic of its mainstay, a version of the comparative method, had become unacceptable, developmentalism nonetheless showed much tenacity. Although, in Germany, Fritz Graebner and Wilhelm

Schmidt complained about the speculativeness inherent in the British evolutionists' approach and proposed a more empirical method of historical ethnology, in practice they too continued to view culture history in developmental terms. In France, Durkheim and his associates struggled to escape from the theoretical sterility of evolutionism by means of a primarily synchronic type of sociological analysis, yet they also occasionally succumbed to speculating about cultural origins and development.

All developmentalists did not adhere to the speculative approach followed by Morgan and Tylor. Stories of anthropology have overlooked the genuine historical method employed by Henry Sumner Maine, Numa Denis Fustel de Coulanges, and, far less rigorously, Johann Jakob Bachofen, who based their works on documentary sources. Maine's *Ancient Law* put forward a patriarchal theory of primitive, or very ancient, social structure in 1861, a good decade before Morgan's reconstruction of early society. In 1890 Maine, comparing his method with Morgan's, claimed his alone offered "a real historical theory" based on "rational evidence."[8] Consulting documentary evidence did not, of course, guarantee conclusions that would be beyond criticism. All three scholars went beyond their sources (Maine and Fustel de Coulanges far less than Bachofen, whose sources were also less useful). They were too ambitious and undisciplined to resist filling in from their imagination what the historical sources lacked, but their bad history should not be the cause of overlooking the distinctive method they followed in studying the development of society and culture.

If anything unites the writers with whom this chapter will be concerned, joining Marx, Freud, and Durkheim to the company of Morgan and Tylor, it is the concept of cultural integration. All proceeded on the age-old assumption that the parts of a culture are interrelated, though they applied the idea in very different ways. The interconnections they traced range from perceiving marriage customs as causative factors behind kinship terminologies to identifying pottery techniques and materials as governing the form taken by the finished vessel.[9] According to one theory, the way goods are produced in a society determines the ideological superstructure of culture,[10] but another theory saw influence flowing the other way in the case of magical and religious ideas influencing ship construction.[11] And without specifying any causal direction, headhunting in Melanesia was linked up with ancestor ceremonies, canoe and house construction, and funerals.[12] In primitive society the several departments of life are inextricably interwoven and interdependent, and the distinctions we make between legal, aesthetic, religious, political, and other phenomena cannot be found.[13] There an act simultaneously involves several or all such categories, and concerns not merely interacting individuals but an entire group or tribe. At times writers recognized interdependence extending from cultural facts to geographical or demographic conditions, but such comprehensive systems-thinking remained less common than the integrational viewpoint applied to culture itself.

Recourse to a psychological point of view occurs almost as often as references to integration. It is directly enunciated in the frequent identification of ethnology as the study of mental life, and in the accompanying definition of culture as an overt manifestation of thought.[14] W. H. R. Rivers saw the ultimate purpose of anthropology being to provide explanations of individual and collective behavior in terms of the ideas, beliefs, sentiments, and instinctive tendencies.[15] Psychological, too, are many specific explanations offered for cultural development. Tylor, for example, explains the differentiation of spirits and deities from an earlier undifferentiated concept of spirit as due to the human tendency to add on to a simple idea until it becomes complex.[16] The same author refers to a tendency to "analogize," whereby primitives perceive resemblances as identities. Curiosity or an intolerance of puzzlement, the motives utilized by 18th-century philosophers to explain religion, continued to be employed as explanations in the next century. Unlike speculations about origins, the operation of these psychological processes could, in theory at least, have been verified. But as Marcel Mauss observes sourly, instead of making the discovery of basic principles governing social facts the starting point of research, in the evolutionists' hands it was often the end.[17] The mechanisms were simply asserted as pat explanations. Nobody troubled to ascertain whether they do indeed act as they were supposed to act.

While the development and diffusion of culture received the overwhelming share of anthropologists' attention, some visualized anew the possibility of discovering a body of scientific generalizations concerning the controlling factors in historical progress or the conditions governing invention and diffusion, the laws of thought behind customs, factors governing kinship terminologies, and other topics.[18] Anthropology also became more conscious of methodology. I am not referring to the far-from-new comparative method which, as employed by the evolutionists, consisted of filling in a picture of early times by taking customs from different classical as well as from living or recently studied primitive cultures.[19] The customs were selected because they fit the author's supposition of how things were. Johann Jakob Bachofen and James George Frazer supported their views about women's eminent position in early society by culling such sources. The comparative method also provided data for piecing together a chronological narrative, the author selecting from contemporary cultures examples of traits that he thought had arisen at different times of human history. So Tylor traced the evolution of religion from elementary animism to monotheism. The more important methodological innovations of the latter part of the 19th century were intended to provide safeguards for the use of comparative data by putting inferences about the past on a sounder basis. Among such innovations were Tylor's doctrine for recognizing survivals of bygone, once-useful culture patterns in contemporary customs whose meaning has dwindled to zero, and several hopeful deductive systems for inferring the relative age of culture traits. Morgan, for example, in 1871, took the worldwide distribution of the same basic types of kinship terminology as proof of great age.[20] Four years later a German ethnologist, Georg Gerland, advanced the same idea in more general terms. Saying something similar to Adam Ferguson, he postulated that the near-universal distribution of a trait indicated its possession by early man.[21] Among such traits he lists circumcision, grave houses, the levirate, blood brotherhood, cannibalism, and the idea of women being impure and dangerous to men. German ethnologists followed with meticulously defined principles, whereby to judge when the cultural resemblances between regions of the world are persuasive and sufficiently numerous to indicate diffusion beyond hardly a flicker of doubt. Their failure to convince was the negative condition which inspired new departures in anthropological method by Boas, Robert Lowie, Alfred L. Kroeber, Radcliffe-Brown, and Malinowski.

Developmental Schemas

Ethnical Periods

"A period of evolutionary schematism," Robert Lowie labeled the latter half of the century. Some of the leading social thinkers of the time certainly did schematize the sequence of development followed by religion, family forms, kinship terminology, religion, and culture as a whole; mostly, they were American and English writers, for those countries were the centers of developmental, or evolutionary, thought. However long the shadow cast by Lewis Henry Morgan's seven "ethnical periods"—for classifying the tribes of mankind and reconstructing cultural evolution—all social theorists of the time were not primarily historical schematists. Lowie ignores two writers to be dealt with in this section, Karl Marx and Friedrich Engels, who took far more pains with explaining historical change in theoretical terms than with setting up stages of cultural evolution.

In 1861 when Morgan became a member of the New York state legislature, he had already done field work among the American Indians, published a book on the Iroquois League, and begun his research on kinship terminologies, a subject heretofore very little studied.[22] A lawyer by profession, Morgan practiced anthropology as an avocation and never held an academic post. His deep curiosity in kin-term systems as indices of marriage and family forms was aroused, in 1858, upon discovering among the Wisconsin Ojibwa Indians a system of names for kinsmen closely resembling the system he had found among the Iroquois. Dictionary raking showed the same system elsewhere in the world. Eager for more information about kin-terms, he wrote to government agents, missionaries, and travelers living in areas with primitive people requesting them to report, on a schedule he enclosed, kin nomenclature in use among such folk. Traveling in the western United States on business as a railroad lawyer, he himself continued to collect terminologies as well as other information from the Indians. Thirteen years after he started his research on kinship, in 1871, the Smithsonian Institution published the mammoth volume containing the results.[23] *Ancient Society*, another book by Morgan published six years later, presents the kinship data as evidence of his view that progress in forms of marriage and the family generally, but not invariably, occurred in conjunction with developments in technology, government, and the idea of property.[24]

Morgan was born in New York State where his father prospered as a farmer and, like Lewis, also won election to the state legislature. After graduating from Union College, Lewis read law and joined a literary club dedicated to assisting Indians with their problems. His membership in the Society, Morgan later wrote, awakened his interest in Indian studies. Though invited at one point in his illustrious career to teach at Cornell University, he declined, and so never held an academic post. He was, however, in 1879, two years before his death, elected president of the American Association for the Advancement of Science.

Progress in human history, as charted in Morgan's *Ancient Society*, went through three main stages, the first two divided into three periods each. Savagery, the first stage, is divided into a Lower period, belonging to the infancy of the human species when progress was yet to come; a Middle period, which culminated in the acquisition of fire; and an Upper period, noted for the invention of the bow. The second stage, Barbarism, comprises Lower Barbarism, wherein the invention of pottery took place and, in the Western Hemisphere, horticulture; Middle Barbarism, marked in the Eastern Hemisphere by animal domestication; and Upper Barbarism, found only in the Old World wherein began the use of iron tools. Following Barbarism came Civilization, identified with the use of the phonetic alphabet. Each cultural breakthrough gave human society a powerful impulse to further advancement. Almost every one of the seven ethnical periods in Morgan's schema marks a step in technological progress, and possesses its own form of marriage, family, and other social structures; like Giambattista Vico's three ages, each period constitutes, in Morgan's words, a "distinct culture."

Otherwise, very little in Morgan's account resembles Vico's accomplishment, except the unblushing conjectures when living primitive societies fail to provide the information needed about the past. So Morgan creates domestic structures, like consanguineal promiscuity and the consanguine family, entirely out of his head, because he needed them to explain kin-term usages he discovered. During Lower Savagery, he surmises, when life was wholly communistic, the consanguine family allowed indiscriminate mating between brothers, sisters, and cousins. The Malayan-type kinship terminology, still known in societies where siblings are called by the same term as cousins, and parents by terms also applied to parents' siblings, was produced by the consanguine family. An exciting and productive idea, for it opened up decades of informative research on kinship terminology, but in Morgan's phrasing it was pure imagination. Morgan's method of reconstructing the past through surviving kin terms, like Tylor's doctrine of survivals which it resembles, in the long run proved a dead end. He implicitly assumed the systematic integration of cultural traits, as well as a modicum of autonomy attached to individual traits that enabled them to persist when the original system of which they formed part—the consanguineal family, say—had dissolved. The anthropologist takes advantage of the survivals, using them as evidence to infer the other pieces of the system in which they supposedly originated. Results obtained by such methods could only be as good as the assumptions were sound. Today we realize that Morgan's were much less sound than, for instance, Herodotus's premise that with time, cultural patterning increasingly influences borrowed traits.

Continuing with Morgan's reconstruction of early society, in the still-communistic period of Middle Savagery the punaluan family succeeded the consanguineal type. The punaluan family was founded on a rule prohibiting marriage between persons categorized as siblings. In the corresponding kin-term system, one that Morgan knew well from his researches among the Iroquois and called Turanian, children of a mother's brother and father's sister (cross-cousins) are no longer classified with siblings because siblings of opposite sex no longer intermarried. The reason for the prohibition lies in the invention of the exogamous patrilineal gens. Morgan defines the group as a body of consanguineally related persons descended from a common ancestor, distinguished by a name, and enforcing a rule of exogamy that initially applied only to siblings. Within the gens people traced descent through the mother; it couldn't have been otherwise, for under indiscriminate mating an individual couldn't know his biological father, only his mother.

No further innovations in marriage or the family took place until the period of Lower Barbarism when, in the New World, horticulture and pottery-making began. Now gens exogamy came to be extended to cousins as well as siblings, causing wives to be sought from other gens through capture or purchase. The new marriage rule, Morgan believes in a rare show of biologistic reasoning, must have given a strong impulse to cultural development by introducing vigorous new stock into societies. But the change failed to produce any new system of kinship terminology, nor did any take place when, also in Lower Barbarism, the patriarchal family made its appearance. Morgan could document this type of domestic structure, with its occasional polygyny, from the Bible. He regards it as a product of newly established male dominance growing out of male-controlled wealth, which also led to substituting the idea of personal property for communism. In the patriarchal family a man could make sure of transmitting his possessions only to the children he had sired in marriage. Horticulture and animal domestication helped to bring about the greater accumulation of wealth deemed by Morgan to have been so important in instigating patriarchy. He makes an effort to connect those technological innovations with family structure, though the origin of pastoralism did not occur until Middle Barbarism.

Lastly, in the stage of Civilization, the monogamous family showed up. It did give rise to a fundamentally different type of kin-term system, one in which terms are no longer extended to many types of relatives. Instead, it designates kin by specific descriptive terms; in the most fully developed terminology of this type, the Roman, each term refers to a single genealogical link traced through the married pair. Civilization caused displacement of the gens. Earlier gentile society, societas, had been founded on kinship, the tribe being an assemblage of gentes. Now political society, civitas, arose, based on a politically organized territory. In it, an individual's rights no longer depend on his connection to a gens or tribe but on his inclusion in a given territory controlled by a state.

Even Morgan is not wholly a schematist. Interspersed through the account of cultural development in *Ancient Society* are theories of how culture is organized and how it changes. Behind the influences of social structure, technology, and the growing amount of property produced as technology becomes more efficient, lie psychogenic factors responsible for culture and cultural development. All over the world identical, logical processes innate in the human mind have predetermined within narrow limits how culture develops. Consequently, despite tribal and national differences, mankind's progress in all continents has been essentially uniform. If some primitive tribes lagged in advancing to the stage of Civilization, remaining fixed in an early period, they were hindered only by their isolation, which prevented progressive traits from reaching them via diffusion. All new forms of behavior, social structure, and tools ultimately originate in the mind as a discovery or invention. Cultural development involves unconsciously selecting those traits that promise to improve on old ones in meeting a need or solving a problem. In this respect Morgan's theory is genuinely evolutionary, in the biological sense of the term, as it also is when he ascribes selection to the existing state of a culture at a given time. Cultural conditions limit what will be adopted, and may also proactively further adaptation by allowing the value of new traits to be perceived. The process of cultural development is not merely additive but geometric, each increment of knowledge opening up further possibilities.

Adaptation leading to development brings progress, meaning it increases happiness and security.

The Materialistic Basis of Consciousness

No one read *Ancient Society* in the decade following its publication with greater interest and appreciation than two German political economists, Karl Marx and Friedrich Engels. So delighted were they at the way the capitalist lawyer reflected their own materialistic thinking that Engels published a lengthy emendation of the book.[25]

Engels, a disciple of Marx and the son of a factory owner, had given thought to the origin of culture before encountering *Ancient Society*. Writing in England, where he was permanently settled amidst the activity of Tylor, John Lubbock, and other evolutionists, he traced the history of culture to two decisive events in human biological evolution: erect posture and the emancipation of the forelimbs from locomotion.[26] Those traits spurred cultural development as well as further biological changes, including development of the organs of speech and the brain; but their fundamental importance lies in creating the capacity for labor, the source of all wealth and the primary and basic condition of human existence. Labor itself became more perfect and diversified with time as man moved from his tropical homeland to colder environments, and as new crafts appeared. Then, as law, government, religion, and other products of the mind began to dominate society, physical labor came to be devalued.

According to the materialistic conception of history associated with Marx and Engels—from which developed the basic social science theory employed in eastern European countries—law, politics, ethics, religion, philosophy, and similar aspects of the cultural superstructure are basically influenced by the way a society is organized to produce the necessities of life.[27] They are rooted in material conditions of existence, specifically in the relationships people establish with each other as they produce goods. In turn, relationships of production in a particular society are influenced by the technical resources available to augment human labor. The cause of all important historic events lies in changes taking place in the modes of production and exchange, and in the struggle of the classes with one another. Material conditions of existence do not alone determine history. Elements of the superstructure, including their interaction with each other, also affect change, sometimes to a preponderant degree. And ultimately it is individuals who are responsible for history, but only as they act in consequence of the driving forces in culture that press for change. Discovering those forces will free mankind from their dictates by enabling them to be consciously controlled, just as tools have enabled man to control the forces of nature.

Marx, who received a Ph.D. for his studies in law—his father's profession—history, and philosophy, turned to Saint-Simonian socialist ideas while still in high school. His radical views cost him any chance of a university career, leaving him to eke out a penurious living as a journalist while pursuing social criticism as well as economic and historical studies. As a social critic he indicted industrial capitalist society for the alienation it produces in the worker on whose labor the society depends.[28] The more a worker gives himself to his work, the more powerful becomes the world of objects that he creates through his labor, and the less belongs to him. And the more he appropriates from nature through his work, the less nature directly serves his existence. Work alienates a person from the objects he produces as well as from nature. Alienation fostered by work reaches its peak in industrial capitalism, where the worker has no part in directing what he does and depends on wages for his survival. Here the worker has sunk to the level of a commodity; labor itself becomes a commodity, and the objects he produces stand as a power that he doesn't recognize as his own. The proletarian worker feels himself free only in exercising his basic needs through eating, drinking, and sex.

If the early German Communists were more theoretical in their conception of cultural development than their English contemporaries, they to some degree shared the latter's interest in periodizing development, and they, too, set up a series of stages reconstructing the history of social structure.[29] The sequence begins with a despotic "Asiatic" type based on small, isolated, egalitarian village communities. The land, communally worked by the villagers, belonged to the monarch, who collected a large share of the produce in lieu of rent and taxes. Households divided the remainder. Individuals were heavily subordinated to the group, and tradition rigorously governed behavior. The next stage, called Ancient Society, was based on the city and was marked by greater individualism, division of labor, and trade. Communities are no longer egalitarian but divided into classes, the most powerful being the landowners and the lowest being the slaves. In the following period, Feudal Society, self-sufficient peasants worked land owned by feudal lords, to whom the tillers paid rent. Individualism had increased from Ancient Society and did so even more in the last stage, Capitalism, where the means of production are freely alienable, and labor can move to wherever conditions seem best. Division of labor and trade had grown enormously by this time, most of the goods produced being intended for the market.

Evolution as Progressive Differentiation

The theory of the mode of production being the key to history made no impression on the English philosopher Herbert Spencer, who had his own grand concept to account not only for historical change but for the evolution of all nature. According to him, all realms of phenomena, including the "superorganic," or social, tend to develop from a homogeneous to an increasingly heterogeneous state. In the social realm, development brings increasingly complex social systems into existence; they possess more differentiated parts, which carry out specialized activities in the interests of the systems' survival. Robert L. Carneiro, in a careful examination of Spencer's theory, corrects the impression that the philosopher conceived of social evolution as following the same course in every society.[30] As evidence that Spencer was not a unilineal evolutionist, Carneiro quotes him saying, "Social progress [is] . . . divergent and redivergent," the nature of a particular environment playing a large role in how development occurs.

In almost everything Spencer did, he originated rather than received ideas.[31] He began his career as a writer, in 1842, with a series of newspaper letters arguing that laws of nature operate without the need for human interference. Essays, reviews, and books followed in an unending stream, embodying scientific, political, and philosophical ideas, often without reference to what had previously been said about those subjects. But Spencer was well read, especially in ethnography, from which he absorbed an enormous number of facts. Through elaborate tables (without using statistics), he sought to discover associations between traits in different societies.[32] Knowledge of correlations between ethnographic facts—between a high level of militarism and a low position of women, or between despotic government and elaborate ritual in social interaction—he considered to be far more worthwhile for promoting human welfare than bits of gossip related by historians.

His writings make considerable use of terms and concepts that became familiar in 20th-century social anthropology.[33] He speaks of function, by which, however, he means activity, rather than consequence or final cause. He refers functions to the structures, or parts, of social systems. He often mentions systems, and he identifies states of equilibrium and disequilibrium in social systems or in their relationship with the environment. His concept of social evolution primarily implies progressive differentiation within a society in the interests of social survival. Evolution involves the appearance of new parts and activities, new structures and functions, enabling the society to survive in an altered environment. The process is apt to occur when constant or drastic fluctuations of environment upset the social system's equilibrium to the point where balance can no longer be restored by hitherto customary corrective activities. Either new structures and functions are introduced to cope with the imbalance, making the system more differentiated than before, or the society risks perishing. Capacity for evolutionary adaptation varies between societies; growing complexity itself increasingly limits the social system's plasticity. Due to the integrated nature of social systems, adaptive change in one area of structure will ramify into other sectors, thereby releasing a chain reaction of changes difficult to control.

Being intensely conservative, Spencer perceived danger in evolution that occurs too quickly. On the other hand, since he identifies evolution with progress, he opposed putting any barriers in its path. But inconsistently, driven by his laissez-faire conviction more than by his faith in evolution, he claims individuals have the right to resist increased social differentiation when it takes such forms as a government-imposed licensing system for physicians or a mandatory smallpox vaccination. The state should be prevented from interfering with the free play of natural selection, through which maladaptive practices in society are weeded out in competition with ones better suited for survival.

The Complex Whole Called Civilization

Spencer had already brought his concept of evolution to bear on society in 1884, the year when Edward B. Tylor, elevated to reader of anthropology at Oxford University, became the first person to occupy an academic post in the discipline.[34] For the past 23 years he had been lecturing and publishing articles and books dealing with such topics as savage religion, magic, primitive culture, ancient Mexico, archeology, language (including slang), and eunuchs, as well as letters in which he disputed with Spencer over who had first enunciated the theory of animism.[35] He contributed directions for nonprofessional ethnographers seeking information about magic, myths, customs, taboos, fetishes, and other subjects. He industriously reviewed books in English and German by Lubbock, Maine, Bastian, Spencer, Gerland, Bancroft, Ploss, and many other writers, the reading of those works undoubtedly enriching his comprehension of the new discipline he would represent in Oxford's lecture halls. But not one in the more than 250 items in his bibliography bears on the materialist conception of history—showing how the Marxian theory went unnoticed among anthropologists. Tylor's parents were both Quakers, a religion he too professed. His father operated a brass foundry where Edward started to work when he was 16 years old. However, ill health soon forced him to quit and to travel. While abroad touring Havana, he by chance became acquainted with an ethnologist, with whom he visited Mexico and there acquired his commitment to anthropology.

So much for the man. Now to the ideas for which he is famous.[36] From German ethnologists he acquired his often cited comprehensive definition of culture, or civilization, the complex whole that includes all the institutions, customs, and other capabilities, and habits acquired by man as a member of society. Except for being an explicit definition, the concept isn't different from the implicit one revealed by Herodotus, Ibn Khaldun, Vico, Henry Home, and Joseph-Marie Degérando.

Tylor delineated another heretofore implicit concept, cultural survival. He knew the weakness of selecting from primitive tribes traits supposedly old and then using the traits as evidence of early culture, so he devised a rule for recognizing truly archaic elements persisting in living cultures. True survivals are absurd or irrational customs kept up by civilized society, even though they conform poorly to other patterns in the advanced culture. A survival lacks utility and meaning, the meaning it formerly possessed having been lost. With this conceptual tool Tylor proceeded to look for survivals, often finding them in ceremonies and children's games which, for some reason, he thought, constitute repositories of cultural elements superseded in everyday life.

In looking for reliable clues to the past, Tylor also utilized myths, regarded as reliquaries of early mentality, and language. From the information that several languages contain words for counting, which also refer to small objects (as calculation refers to calculi, i.e., pebbles), he deduced an ancient pattern of using small objects in counting. Highest of all he valued archeological evidence of bygone culture, but it was too limited to help him for his purposes.

With these and other methods, on the basis of wide reading, and with a little help from speculation, Tylor prepared his evolutionary schema. It contains three familiar stages: Savagery, Barbarism (ushered in by agriculture), and Civilization, the stage beginning with writing. No period is treated in the detailed way Morgan follows. But using the same conceptual tools, Tylor wrote one of the most detailed accounts of the development of early religion ever published.[37] I will give the gist of his account, including his well-known concept of animism, when I take up theories of religion and magic.

Despite Tylor's reputation as an evolutionist, his writings bridge the older developmental approach and German historical ethnology. He explicitly distinguishes between accounts of origins or development and explanations based on migration, diffusion, and culture contact. When two societies at different levels of culture come into contact, he expects the ruder group to adopt the arts and knowledge presented to them by the more advanced. Substantial similarities between two or more world areas constitute impressive, if indirect, evidence of a historical connection between them. But he never became as firmly committed to diffusionism as his Continental contemporaries, believing it safer to credit similarities to independent invention, based on the like working of men's minds under similar conditions, unless the similarities exceed the limits of commonsense probability. True, diffusion can promote cultural development, but ultimately it, too, rests on invention. Hence, basically all culture growth stems from psychological factors.

Considering the importance of psychological factors in Tylor's thought, one might expect them to be identified in more detail than Tylor actually provides. But he is often vague, as when he relates early—i.e., primitive people's—belief systems to special premises lying at the root of savage reasoning. Yet the savage mind works in the same logical manner as the mind of civilized man. As a result, premising the objective reality of dreams and hallucinations, savages reason quite logically in postulating the continued existence of the soul after death.

In addition to historical and psychogenic explanations, Tylor sometimes explains one part of culture by other, antecedent cultural factors. Similarities between cultures, he holds, may sometimes be due to the same causes producing like effects, such as matrilocal residence giving rise to mother-in-law avoidance, or patrilocal residence to bride service. Modifying his theory of survivals, he predicts culture traits may die out when their causes disappear. Cultural traits also disappear when they become unable to compete for survival against better traits. The attenuation of animism in modern society is a case in point; as an explanatory system it was out-distanced by science.

Tylor took heuristic advantage of cultural integration in resorting to statistics as a methodological device to support the evolutionary thesis.[38] Correlations between the same traits—for example, exogamous moieties and cross-cousin marriage—in a number of societies, he reasoned, furnished proof that they originated together in the same stage of culture and have persisted as a group. (We will encounter similar reasoning in the German diffusionists.) It was an imaginative venture, only how could he be sure two concurring traits originated together?

As a publicist Tylor set himself against Victorian views of savages: as the degenerate offshoots of a former civilization, as intellectually inferior, and as incapable of advancement. Against such prejudices he employed his reputation to educate his contemporaries about the true nature of primitive people. He pictured primitive cultures as stations along the road to progress, and identified cultural primitivity as a survival of the past, not degeneration. Primitive beliefs were reasonable, or at least intelligible, if one makes an effort to understand them. Savages are not a different species of humanity. All varieties of mankind belong to a single species with a single origin. Variations between primitive and civilized thought result from different kinds of experience; they are not the products of unequal mental endowment. "Had the experience of ancient men been larger," he writes near the close of his last book, *Anthropology* (1881), "they would have seen their way to faster steps in culture."

Out of the Pursuit of Practical Ends

Despite efforts like Tylor's to present primitive cultures as reasonable designs of living, and despite more than 200 years of sympathetic commentary by John Locke, Father Joseph Lafitau, Adam Ferguson, and others about the American Indians, people in the late 19th century still thought of the Indians as living in an inchoate state of total ignorance and ceaseless bloodshed. Or at least the United States government-employed ethnologist John Wesley Powell believed such a stereotype existed and marshaled firsthand facts to demolish it.[39] All societies, he assured his audiences and readers, possess the same institutions as civilization; savage warfare is petty compared to the great deadly wars of civilization; and savage languages can quite adequately express any idea occurring to their speakers.

Powell got to know Indians well on his geological field trips in the Colorado River country of the Ute tribe, whose language, myths, and customs he studied in close detail.[40] Born in New York, he grew up and educated himself in the Midwest, developing a passion for studying rocks, plants, and other aspects of natural science. Pursuing those things through field research appealed to him much more than his first job, teaching school. On one field trip he lived for two months among the Hopi Indians of Oraibi, whom he found hospitable to the point where they permitted him to attend a kiva ceremony he much wanted to witness. The detail, however, proved too much for his recording ability. By 1879, the geologist had attained so much distinction as an ethnologist that he was put in charge of the new Bureau of American Ethnology, created to promote knowledge and understanding of the Indians.

Though an evolutionist, and truly one in the Darwinian sense (with touches of Lamarckism, however), Powell was not primarily a cultural schematist but a theorist who, like Spencer, was much attracted to the dynamics of cultural development.[41] But his theoretical writings are flawed by a vocabulary overblown with words like "autogenous" and "syngenous" (meaning similarities due to independent invention and diffusion, respectively). He distinguished between two kinds of diffusion, "acculturation" and "cognation." The former refers to one society directly learning something from another; the latter to several distinct groups having inherited a custom from a common forebear. Fundamentally, he took an instrumental view of culture, claiming it arose out of the pursuit of both practical and self-satisfying ends: survival, health, bodily welfare, social control, communication, education, and pleasure. Once culture had come into existence, human biological evolution ceased, and culture became the effective environment to which human beings had to adapt. From now on, further progress continued in the mind, through learning, and was made manifest through cultural development, the basis of which is invention. Through selection, the better technical and social innovations come to replace less effective ones, and true ideas force out errors in knowledge and religion. Instead of simple substitution, people may graft an innovation presented to them through diffusion to an old cultural form, the way monotheism is sometimes combined with previous polytheistic beliefs.

Improved inventions have a direct influence on the development of enhanced mental ability, which in turn stimulates more inventions, making for a constantly rising curve of progress.

As Powell saw it, cultural selection differs considerably from the deadly competition involved in Darwinian natural selection. For with culture, political institutions appeared to limit physical struggle, so that violent competition became a crime or, if between nations, war. Marriage removed the need for competition for mates found in nature, and standards came to be fixed by law and convention, rather than being imposed by force.

The Care for Life

No writer in the century exceeded Julius Lippert in utilizing the principle of cultural integration to tie together manifold aspects of early social development. As a psychogenesist, he posited a single basic drive, the care for life, as the ultimate source of culture; but he also recognized the influence of maintenance systems and diet on social structure, and the significance of energy for cultural development. He employs the concepts of natural selection and alliance in analyzing change, and he can be read as illustrating how new allocations of time and effort at the behest of new values and other constraints succeed in generating new forms of social structure.

Lippert grew up in Bohemia, the son of working-class parents too poor to pay for his education.[42] However, he managed to finance his schooling up to the university level, and then became a teacher, school administrator, and active student of history. At the age of 40, dissatisfied with having only spare time available for historical research, he quit his job and with his family exiled himself for three years in a forest retreat. Here he wrote what his translator calls *Evolution of Culture,* though "cultural history of mankind" would render the original German title more literally. In addition to the significance of the book itself, it deeply influenced the thinking of George Peter Murdock, who translated it. Lippert's idea of a connection between men's and women's subsistence roles and their relative social prestige holds an important place in Murdock's theoretical work, *Social Structure* (1949).

Human society, reconstructed by Lippert, began with groups of women living with their children.[43] Men joined the groups only for the purpose of finding sexual gratification. The first major impetus to change occurred when people discovered they could survive more comfortably on energy-rich meat products than on fruits and vegetables, though the latter could be more easily procured. They applied the surplus energy released by meat to improving their weapons and devising better hunting techniques, thereby still further enlarging the basis of existence. Changes in the ecological sphere had social repercussions. Men were in charge of hunting, and as animal food grew in importance, the significance of women's subsistence roles declined, which lowered their social importance and raised the authority of men. Augmenting mother's milk in young children's diets by animal milk and meat also led to reducing the nursing period, a time when women refused to engage in sexual relations. The change increased the availability of a woman for sexual gratification, and with this inducement, sexual attachments became permanent. The greater frequency of sexual activity, following the shortening of the postpartum taboo, promoted population growth, giving groups taking that progressive step a competitive advantage over others.

With equal originality Lippert conjectures the effects of other changes in subsistence activity on domestic organization. He explains how shifting from pastoralism—the stage that followed hunting—to agriculture helped produce monogamy. The agricultural duties assumed by women in the early stage of agriculture, when polygyny still prevailed, favored the emergence of a chief wife, a woman whose authority compelled the other wives to assist her in caring for the planted fields. Polygyny disappeared in time as the chief wife became the sole wife. Simultaneously, monogamy was encouraged when men, united in a connubial league—a group exchanging brides and making other prestations—renounced bride price and adopted payment of dower. Once a man offered dowry with his daughter, he could not possibly tolerate a menial position for her in the family where she married, and so he stipulated that she must become her husband's sole wife. Lippert sees proof for his theory in the tendency for monogamy to prevail where agriculture and connubial leagues coexist.

Every society did not independently originate all the innovations it adopted. Groups adopted new traits by diffusion, adapting them to conform to traditional ways of doing things. In the process, old meanings fused with new, thereby giving traditional ideas a longer lease on life. Groups showing least resistance to change and most exposed to diffusion progressed fastest and gained competitive advantages over neighbors. But Lippert wisely recognizes that successful competition by no means always indicates ethically desirable cultural traits, and therefore adaptive progress does not necessarily correspond to general improvement.

Energetics

Where Lippert makes but a short reference to the cultural significance of energy augmented through a change in diet, Wilhelm Ostwald, a German chemist writing between 1903 and 1913, made energy the major independent variable in cultural development. The potential contribution of his ideas to culture theory remained unrecognized for a quarter of a century until they were discovered, or rediscovered, by Leslie White.[44]

"Energetics," Ostwald called his theory of cultural ecology. Social progress, the theory maintains, depends on the ability of a society to utilize
for human purposes the free energy it extracts and transforms from nature.
Tools, agriculture, and other techniques represent cultural forms for the
purposive transformation of energy. Like Spencer in the principle of differentiation, Ostwald furnishes a single criterion of energy use by which
to judge progress in organisms as well as in social systems. The system
capable of most efficiently transforming the energy at its disposal into
energy consumed for survival is the more perfect. Cultural evolution has
consisted in people finding improved methods for seizing and utilizing
natural energy. In terms of results, the evolution of culture can be objectively measured: by gauging the amount of energy successively controlled
by human beings, and by the efficiency of the tools, machines, and techniques through which the energy is put to use.

Kinship Terms

Morgan's Achievements

We have not finished with Lewis Henry Morgan, to whom belongs the
honor of having discovered that differences among kinship terminologies
arise from differences in other social institutions. Morgan and his immediate followers applied the theory with the standards of 19th-century
anthropology, which permitted them to deduce freely from assumptions
unsupported by data. The results proved to be difficult to confirm in a
convincing or objective way. Applied more cautiously, however, the theory
led to highly consistent and well-supported knowledge and made kinship
studies one of the most productive areas of anthropological scholarship.
Morgan and his followers found in kinship terminologies new proof of the
conventional nature of culture. How people trace relationships turned out
to be another socially defined matter, and not necessarily dependent on the
actual facts of biological connection.

On objective grounds Morgan accurately distinguished three main types
of kinship reckoning—for which I will use his terms Malayan, Turanian,
and Aryan—each of which he regarded as far too complex to have originated more than once.[45] Their worldwide distribution, he thought, constituted evidence of their great age. Certain features of the Malayan and
Turanian types, he found, could be deductively explained by congruent
forms of now-vanished marriage and family types, which his imagination
provided. The Aryan type, he assumed, had developed relatively recently
out of monogamous marriage. Hence the first two must be older, and by
similar reasoning he decided that the Malayan predates the Turanian.

Although Morgan reconstructed five successive forms of the family, each the product of a different system of marriage, only three family types proved influential enough to give rise to distinct kin-term systems. The consanguine family, comprising brothers and sisters either true or collateral (by collateral he means cousins who were regarded as siblings), produced the Malayan system. In Malayan terminology (today called generational) all blood relatives, no matter how remote, fall into five categories: "grandparents," "parents," "children," "brothers," and "sisters." The relationships indicated by these five terms, Morgan claims, are precisely those expected in a family created through the marriage of siblings. Under such a system, it is logical for a person to call the offspring of siblings "children" for siblings may be spouses. An individual calls parents and parents' siblings by the same term ("mother" or "father," according to Morgan), which duly recognizes the fact that in the consanguine family they are mates. The parents of the "fathers" and "mothers" are logically, if not always genealogically, "grandparents."

In the Turanian (or bifurcate merging) type system, a man still calls his brothers' children by the term used for his own offspring, because—to give Morgan's explanation—in the punaluan family where the system arose, his brother's wife is his wife as well, making the brother's son his own son. But his sisters' sons are terminologically classed as "nephew" or "niece," because gens exogamy has been instituted and hence a man's true sisters, and eventually collateral as well, ceased to be eligible wives. Consistently, a woman calls her brothers' children "nephew" and "niece," but designates her sisters' offspring as "son" or "daughter," because under the rules of punaluan marriage those women's husbands are also her husbands. How a child regards his parents' siblings under the Turanian system follows logically from the marriage customs. Fathers' brothers are "fathers" but the father's sister is an "aunt," and mother's sisters are "mothers" while mother's brothers are "uncles."

TABLE 1
Morgan's Ethnical Periods, Stages of the Family, and Associated Kin-Term Systems

Ethnical Period	Stage of the Family	Kin-Term System
Lower Savagery	Consanguine	Malayan
Middle Savagery	Punaluan	Turanian*
Upper Savagery	Punaluan	Turanian
Lower Barbarism	Syndyasmian	Turanian
Middle Barbarism	Syndyasmian	Turanian
Upper Barbarism	Patriarchal	Turanian
Civilized	Monogamian	Aryan, Semitic, and Uralian

* In places Morgan also calls the Turanian system Ganowanian.

The Aryan-type system (akin to the Semitic) arose when the family founded on monogamous marriage became established in society, allowing persons to be certain of the paternity of their children. With discrete Aryan-type kin terms, an individual can specify the precise connection between himself and mother's and father's relatives, something impossible to do in the other systems. Each term in a fully developed Aryan-type system, like the Roman, specifies a particular kinsman connected to the speaker by a particular genealogical or affinal link. Particular words designate parents by sex and distinguish them from parents' siblings, and so on.

Morgan further classified the three types of terminologies into two major classes, defining each by whether it extends primary kinship terms to secondary and more remote relatives. The Malayan and Turanian systems do so quite widely; hence he put them into the same class and called them classificatory. The Aryan, which limits primary terms to primary relatives, he labeled descriptive.

Kinship Becomes a Major Topic

Almost immediately after Morgan published his *Systems of Consanguinity*, in 1871, kinship blossomed into a major topic of discussion. One of the first reactions came from John Ferguson McLennan, a Scot jurist who, in 1865, had formulated his own version of early promiscuous human hordes, in which brides were taken by force.[46] Later, when the hordes took to capturing wives from one another, filiation became recognized, but exclusively through females. McLennan rejected out of hand Morgan's idea that primary kinship terms are extended to more remote relatives with any thought of blood relationship being present.[47] He also denied that reciprocal rights and duties are implied by kinship terms. Classificatory kin terms, he insisted, were mere courtesy titles, or greetings such as a minister gives when he calls a member of the congregation "brother" or "sister." On that interpretation McLennan was quickly contradicted by Alfred W. Howitt, whose name is inseparably linked with Lorimer Fison's. Both were English immigrants in Australia, where Fison became a missionary and Howitt a cowboy and explorer.[48] Howitt, priding himself on his firsthand knowledge of Australian native customs, retrodicted that McLennan would never have claimed kinship terms to be merely forms of ceremonial address had he personally been well acquainted with savages.[49]

Despite his lack of experience with primitive societies, McLennan supplied a more important correction to Morgan's notion of how people understood classificatory kin terms. Extending words like "mother" or "son" to secondary relatives, he maintained, should not be taken to imply ignorance of actual biological relationships. People who extend kinship terms beyond the family can tell their own mothers and know their own children from other individuals designated by the same words.

Morgan's reply to McLennan, contained in a long note appended to Part II of *Ancient Society*, makes a most significant point. Challenging McLennan's notion that human hordes once traced kinship only through females, he maintains that both the Malayan and Turanian kin-term systems plainly and conclusively recognize kinship through both sexes. To speak of kinship traced exclusively through females can only mean "descent in the female line, which is . . . a rule of a gens and nothing more." By these words Morgan reveals his recognition of a distinction between descent and filiation, the latter a custom found in all societies linking a child with parents through whom other kinship connections are then traced.

The next important step in developing Morgan's theory came a dozen years later when Tylor applied an early version of the hologeistic method to Morgan's proposition that exclusion of marriage between collateral "siblings" follows from the rule of gens exogamy. His test, made with a small sample of world cultures, showed a statistical "adhesion" between moiety organization and a rule prohibiting marriage between parallel cousins who, it happens, are often designated by sibling terms.[50] What is significant, however, is not Tylor's understanding of the correlation as evidence of how the custom had been brought about historically, but the way he used statistics to prove a synchronic relationship between kin terms and unilinear descent rules. Kinship terminology and other forms of social structure are interrelated, just as Morgan asserted, though not for the reasons he gave.

Causality in Kinship Terminology

Despite Tylor's statistical test, the idea of causality implied by Morgan's theory aroused fresh criticism when, shortly after the turn of the century, Alfred L. Kroeber questioned the whole postulate of causality in culture. His criticism was directed against William Halsey Rivers Rivers, the next major figure in kinship research after Morgan and Tylor.

W. H. R. Rivers was only three years old when an uncle gave him the first volume of *Anthropologie der Naturvölker* (1859), in German, a popular book written by the psychologist Theodor Waitz.[51] But not till 33 years later did Rivers direct his career into anthropology. In the meantime, he took medical and psychological training in England and Germany and joined the faculty of Cambridge University as a lecturer in psychology. In 1898, his expertness in perception brought him an invitation from his colleagues to join an expedition to the Torres Strait, in the course of which he investigated the sensory acuity of the natives and acquired an interest in ethnology. Subsequently, he returned to Melanesia for field work and also studied the Toda of South India. Rivers began anthropology as a social evolutionist in the tradition of Morgan and Tylor, but by 1911, the ideas of the German historical ethnologists turned him into a diffusionist. Like them, he conceived of a culture as a series of temporally super-imposed strata that could be peeled away successively to reconstruct the history of the society. Impressed by G. Elliot Smith's views he, too, thought that early Egyptian and Mesopotamian seafarers had spread many cultural traits among the world's primitive people. Rivers' influence in anthropol-ogy, and on innovative students like Radcliffe-Brown, derived neither from his psychological research nor his theories of diffusion and culture strata, but from his work on kinship and other aspects of social structure. More than anyone in this period since Morgan, he helped make kinship for anthropology what, as Robin Fox puts it, the nude is for art. Among his achievements is a conception of kinship that, unlike Morgan's, does not confine it to biological facts of procreation as socially perceived. He de-fined kinship as determined by relationships traced by means of genealo-gies, which then fix the related individuals' privileges and duties; but the relationships so traced need not always correspond to actual facts of birth or consanguineal relationship. A society may regard some social acts as creating genealogical relationships where, in fact, no ties of procreation exist; so that the man who, following a birth, pays the midwife or per-forms a ceremony acquires all the privileges and duties of a father, regardless of whether he is the child's genitor or not, and his relatives assume corresponding obligations.

Agreeing that marriage and other social structural arrangements influ-ence classificatory kinship terminology, Rivers sought to explain how they do so without bringing in unsupportable assumptions about consanguine marriage between a group of true or collateral siblings.[52] Any social insti-tution, including marriage and unilineal descent, has the power to affect kinship terminologies if it prescribes special "social functions" for persons in certain relationships. By the words in quotation marks he meant specific duties, privileges, or restrictions (such as the rule that prescribed cross-cousin marriage, exogamy, the customs of levirate and sororate, and other moral or jural norms). In the Banks Islands, he reported from his own field notes, a man calls his mother's brother's children by the same term he applies to his own children; they address him by the word they employ for their own father. This occurs, Rivers explains, because under the terms of the levirate a man might marry his mother's brother's wife if her hus-band dies.[53] (At least this was customary before the advent of Christian-ity). These peculiarities of kinship nomenclature are exactly what would be brought about in social relationships if the marriage took place: the mother's brother's children would jurally become the new husband's own children. Or take rules prohibiting incest; for example, the rule forbidding a man to have sexual relations with his wife's sister or his brother's wife. With the existence of such a rule, those relatives are found to be classed as siblings. Why or how does this happen? Because, Rivers claims, a social need exists to emphasize the gross impropriety of sex relations with those relatives. Calling the women "sister" satisfies the need.

Neither Tylor's method of statistical testing nor Rivers' logical analysis can prove a causal connection to exist between marriage customs or other social forms and kin-term systems. Yet both methods consistently yielded results that accorded with the guiding theoretical principle and created no grounds for doubting or abandoning it.

Kroeber did doubt the theory but furnished little evidence flatly in contradiction to it. He questioned the assumption that specific causes of cultural phenomena can be found, and proposed a substitute approach, one concerned not with finding independent antecedents behind kinship terminologies but with exposing the meaning of kinship terms. His argument against seeking causes proved unproductive in the subsequent history of anthropology, but the meaning underlying kinship terminologies continued to be researched, most systematically in the 1960s by the componential analysts.

In 1909, when Kroeber dissented from sociological theory of relationship terms, he had already begun what was to be a very long career at the University of California in Berkeley.[54] Thirty-three years old, he had received the Ph.D. from Columbia University eight years earlier, carried out considerable field work with North American Indians, and published over 50 papers on their art, archeology, folklore, language, religion, and other subjects. Now, in "Classificatory Systems of Relationship," he used American Indian linguistic data to maintain that kinship terms are properly understood as reflecting the psychological distinctions people perceive among relatives.[55] Relationship terms "are determined primarily by language and can be utilized for sociological inferences only with extreme caution." More specifically speaking, kin terms are linguistic forms through which a society distinguishes among a pool of kinsmen by selecting a limited number of features according to which types of relatives are categorized. He listed eight categorical features: the generation to which a relative belongs; difference of age in a generation; sex of the relative; sex of the speaker in relation to that of the relative; sex of the person through whom the relationship is traced; whether the relationship is due to a blood tie or to marriage; and whether the person through whom the relationship is traced is alive or dead. Kin-term systems are logical systems which, by means of a few features like these, enable a large number of specific kin to be reduced to a small number of kin types, usually between 12 and 60. Some languages use a comparatively small number of the distinctive features, English only four, whereas others utilize many. Since all kin-term systems categorize, the distinction between classificatory and descriptive kinship terminologies breaks down; every set of terms is to some degree classificatory, in that it puts several degrees of relationship under a single category.

The paper provoked an unsympathetic response, expectedly, from Rivers as well as from Kroeber's colleague at Berkeley, Robert Lowie, who sided with the social determinists. Kroeber adhered to his views, maintaining that causal explanations of detached cultural phenomena can rarely be satisfactorily established.[56] A survey of California Indian tribes provided him with few indications of any association between kinship terminology and marriage, descent, or other social institutions. Even when social institutions agree perfectly with kin terms, one needs independent corroboration showing the former produced the latter. Yet, in 1917, he himself admitted that the Zuni clan exerted some influence on cross-cousin terminology in Zuni kinship terminology, and, in 1952, expressed regret at having so intransigently insisted on psychological not sociological factors being behind kin terms.[57] He now thought it would have been wiser had he restricted himself to noting the unsoundness of using kin terms as if they were uncontaminated reflectors of past or present social customs. And he wished he had been wise enough to say that kin terms, as part of language, "reflect unconscious logic and conceptual patterning *as well as* social institutions." More deeply than the question of kinship, he recognized retrospectively, a deeper issue divided him from Rivers who, coming from a laboratory discipline into anthropology, wanted to make social science a true science. He, Kroeber, with a background in humanistic literature, distrusted causal explanations of culture and was quite content to search for meanings, and to delineate patterns in the phenomena he studied.

The Category Problem

Rivers and Kroeber and most other anthropologists, in the following decades of kinship research, persisted in regarding classificatory kin terms as extending to more distant relatives the meanings associated with the primary relatives to whom the words referred. Thus field workers writing in English glossed the terms with words like "mother," "father," "son," and so forth. In effect, they reasoned that if the same term applies to the mother and mother's sister, it nevertheless means "mother," although (as the quotation marks signify), from the speaker's and observer's points of view, someone other than the real mother is being designated. For a long time those who disagreed with this extensionist way of interpreting kin terms were hardly listened to. Durkheim, in 1897, offered a nonextensionist interpretation of classificatory kin terms.[58] A common term covering the mother and other women, he wrote, does so because all the women belong to the same exogamous group—the group where the father obtained his wife. The terms are not specifications of genealogical position, or based on distinctive features of relationship, but name categories of people each possessing certain duties toward the speaker. Hocart, in 1937, would make a similar point; but even in the 1950s, as we will see, when the argument was more forcibly resuscitated by Edmund Leach and others, a number of American students of kinship stuck to the position that whatever other meaning extended kin terms may possess, they initially derive a portion of their semantic content from the nearer relatives they designate.

Domestic and Descent Groups

Marriage and the Family Are Grounded in Nature

W. H. R. Rivers, we saw, abandoned the unprovable hypothesis of an ancient consanguineal family. Behind his decision lay a number of vigorous arguments offered against the notion that, in some remote period of cultural development, human beings practiced wholly free promiscuity or group marriage involving siblings. Sometimes the arguments simply cited ethnographic data from what were taken to be the simplest living primitive societies showing the existence of paired marriage and monogamous families there.[59] Australian tribes had been particularly favored for the honor of representing the oldest and most primitive forms of social structure, and had been regarded as furnishing evidence of earlier group marriage; but now new ways were learned for analyzing Australian native institutions, and they ceased to offer any support for the thesis.[60] Often the logically based arguments were more complex. Given the destructive nature of sexual jealousy, Charles Darwin suggested, would not free sexual intercourse have led to the extinction of the small hordes practicing so maladaptive a custom?[61] The Danish philologist Carl Nicolai Starcke took a different position.[62] Fanciful ideas about original promiscuity, he pointed out, present a picture of early man as more concerned with obtaining sexual gratification than with other purposes served by marriage and family life. All known societies, he maintained, distinguish between sexual relations and marriage. If people only sought sexual gratification through marriage, why would marriage occur in societies where premarital sexual intercourse is permitted? Starcke also brought the role-conflict theory of incest rules to bear against the assumption of early promiscuity. Sexual relations among primary relatives would promote complete confusion of rights and responsibilities. Maternal authority would be controverted if a man were simultaneously son and mate to his mother. Marriage between brother and sister would interject sexual interests into a relationship that societies frequently surround by conventions of shyness and modesty. Contemporary customs in primitive societies suggestive of free sexual relations or reporting wife-lending, instead of being taken as surviving evidence of early free mating systems, should be analyzed synchronically for the particular significance they possess in the contexts where they occur. By way of illustration, some societies may permit royalty to marry siblings because they perceive royal and commoner statuses as too diverse for intermarriage.

C. Staniland Wake, a quickly forgotten English amateur anthropologist who made his living as a solicitor, contributed a zoological observation: even animals rarely mate in completely promiscuous fashion; hence it is unlikely that early humans did so.[63] He dismissed the possibility of sexual relations occurring regularly between siblings because it runs contrary to the natural disinclination of people who grew up together to experience sexual feelings for one another. As a result of such natural antipathy, the incest rule of the nuclear family would in the very earliest times have ruled out the kind of early family Morgan imagined, as well as the promiscuous mating supposedly preceding the consanguineal family. Wake does not entirely reject the possibility of early group marriage, but insists that rules have always governed human mating customs. Comparative zoological evidence also allowed Edward Westermarck to deny the possibility of early promiscuity or group marriage. The custom of single pairs living together and rearing young exists widely among nonhuman species, including most of the higher subhuman primates, and therefore it very likely also existed among early human beings.[64] The Finnish philosopher Westermarck, who eventually acquired a post in sociology at the University of London where he became one of Malinowski's teachers,[65] offered other reasons supporting the antiquity of the paired family. Like a modern ethologist taking an evolutionary view, he credited the pairing instinct with adaptive value for the young; natural selection, therefore, fixed it in human society, where jural norms transformed it into a jural institution. Wake derived marriage—or at least the legitimization of sexual relations, which is one of the functions marriage secures—from a natural aversion to incest with primary relatives. Westermarck also grounded a cultural institution in nature, in the process of natural selection. Like Darwin, he believed destructive male jealousy would have prevented the full enjoyment of original promiscuity. As if not to leave any possible argument unused, he also held sexual interest to be naturally averted among close companions. Such aversion brought the incest rule of the nuclear family into existence at the very earliest stage of human society.

Offering a Daughter or Sister for a Wife

Cross-cousin marriage systems, a topic to which much future attention would be devoted, were broached by anthropologists in the late 19th and early 20th centuries. The Russian ethnographer L. Shternberg, in 1893, described asymmetrical cross-cousin marriage as it operated among the Gilyak. Every generation, males belonging to a specific sib received a bride from another specific wife-giving group to whom, however, the first sib did not return a daughter in the next generation.[66] James George Frazer based an explanation for reciprocal exchange, as carried out in preferential cross-cousin marriage, by noting its frequent occurrence in societies where marriages involve the exchange of sisters.[67] Guided by an already largely abandoned paradigm, he pursued the origin of the custom back to savage times when a man's most important possession was his wife. Too poor to purchase her, the man offered a daughter or sister instead of property. In the next generation, the two men who had married each other's sisters arranged for their children, who would be cross-cousins, to marry. Among the Arabs, Frazer saw an economic motive also operating in parallel cousin marriage, for the custom allows a daughter to inherit wealth in the patrilineage to which she belongs.

Agnatic Ties

Before Lewis Henry Morgan wrote *Ancient Society,* Johann Bachofen, Henry Maine, and Fustel de Coulanges had inquired into the origin or early development of domestic institutions and kinship. Following a method different from Morgan's, one using documentary material from early historical times, they did not refer primarily to primitive societies as Morgan did. Each recognized that the bilateral filiation contemporarily found in European society had sometimes been accompanied by another kind of genealogical linkage, namely, unilineal descent.

Back in the 18th century we saw British philosophers debating whether matricentric families might have been the original form of the family. This possibility came to be more widely entertained after Johann Jakob Bachofen, a Swiss-German student of philology and ancient law, in 1861, published a book called *Das Mutterrecht* ("Mother Right" or, more literally, "Maternal Authority"), which was subtitled "an investigation concerning gynocracy in the ancient world based on religious and legal institutions." Judging from the classical writers he cites, Bachofen found more pleasure in studying the literary works of antiquity than its legal institutions. References in Herodotus and Strabo to gynocratic societies started him on the thesis that early society was organized by a strict principle of matrilateral filiation, a thesis he documents with myths and symbols that he interprets.[68]

Maternal authority appeared in human history, according to Bachofen, following the innovation of grain agriculture and after women, with amazonian fierceness, had liberated themselves from the debased thralldom under which they lived during a time when unregulated promiscuity prevailed. Having liberated themselves, women came to dominate the family and the state, and also assumed key roles in religious ritual. During this period a child acquired its status and name from the mother, the only partner involved in conception whose biological connection to the child could be indubitably recognized by virtue of the empirical facts of gestation and birth. "Mother country," used to express devotion to one's natal land, and similar surviving traces of mother right are the best contemporary evidence Bachofen could find to support his thesis. Unlike Morgan—who appreciated the German's combing of the classical evidence —Bachofen didn't avail himself of contemporary ethnographic accounts of societies with matrilineal descent, perhaps partly because none describes the ideal gynocracy he imagined.

Morgan was heartened by the results of Bachofen's survey of evidence, interpretable as indicative of ancient gynocracy, but he felt the German scholar had missed something—matrilineal descent groups.[69] Morgan also approved of another book, *Ancient Law,* published in the same year as Bachofen's, in which Henry Sumner Maine pictured early social structure as being dominated by male authority.[70] Morgan called Maine's research brilliant, but observed that if the patriarchal system Maine describes is indeed the oldest knowable from history, then history goes only as far back as Upper Barbarism and therefore cannot document matrilineal descent, which flourished earlier.

As a recent writer points out, Maine patterned his work after comparative philology, the aim of which was to use historical evidence about one language to shed light on the history of another language for which no direct evidence could be obtained.[71] Following the philologists' method, he undertook to reconstruct the legal system of Indo-European societies by studying their historically documented legal codes and social organization. "Ancient" and "primitive" in his usage refer not to very early societies but to early representatives of the Indo-European linguistic family, in all of which he found signs of an agnatic system of relationships replaced in time by a cognatic system. Maine began life under humble circumstances but managed to complete a university education, which familiarized him with classical languages and institutions. After teaching civil law at Cambridge University, he joined the government of India and spent seven years on the South Asia subcontinent helping to codify Indian law. Thereupon he returned to academic life and historical writing.

Ancient Law delineates a system of enduring kin groups, whose members traced kinship through agnates to a single male ancestor, and recognized patriarchal authority and patrilineal succession. Society comprised an aggregate of patrilineally related families, each headed by the eldest male. The agnates owned land and other property communally and constituted corporations, which continued without break from generation to generation. Death of a family head and transmission of his rights and duties to a male successor caused a crisis within the family, for the shift in leadership momentarily threatened the group's continuity. Rituals on those occasions symbolically affirmed the unity and sacredness of the agnatic group. Thus Maine constructs a model of a culturally integrated social system, comprising a dogma of agnatic genealogical connection, joint property, patrilineal inheritance and other jural norms, patriarchal headship, and compatible religious rituals. His historical scholarship, however, has been criticized, most importantly for overlooking evidence that western Aryan societies traced kinship and inheritance rights through maternal as well as paternal relatives.

Like other authors before and after him, Maine visualized human history as following a direction toward greater individualism and personal autonomy. In ancient society, his evidence led him to believe, a person's rights and duties were rigidly ascribed through kinship. In time, however, a new social type emerged, civil society, where persons gained freedom to determine their own statuses through contractual relationships independently entered into.

In France, three years after *Ancient Law,* Fustel de Coulanges also used historical materials to describe early social systems in Greece, Rome, and India based on agnatic descent.[72] The coherence of those societies he ascribed to religion, a force more powerful than birth or filial affection in creating social solidarity. The original beliefs of a religious nature, historical evidence suggested, conceived of souls surviving after death and intervening powerfully in the affairs of the living. Out of this germinal concept arose rules of conduct requiring worship of the dead to offset their malignancy—the family altar being the center of worship—as well as rules compelling marriage and censuring celibacy, thereby insuring the production of sons to maintain the family line and carry out the religious duties. By vesting priestly duties solely in males, religion led people to define filiation solely in patrilateral terms. Matrilateral filiation counted for nothing, and women consequently possessed a low social rank. Religion, the author says, did not create the family but caused it to form a single body, and gave the body its distinctive unilateral norms and dogma. Religion, likewise, prescribed patrilineal norms of inheritance; sons, after all, needed to be provided with means to carry out their ritual obligations.

From the patrilateral family more embracive kin-based forms of social structure emerged—the patrilineal clan, alliances of clans, and the city state —each with its own system of ancestor worship to provide the foundation of social solidarity. Eventually ancient society transcended kinship organization and developed increasing individualism. As it did, religious institutions changed in a compatible manner, becoming less particularistic, more universalistic, and more abstract. The deity was no longer the ancestor of a particular domestic group or clan, but an immense universal being who protected the interests of the whole human species.

Kinship and Descent

Debate over the relative priority of matriliny or patriliny in society continued unquenchably for some time, and became enmeshed in another problem, the antiquity of sibs compared to the family. Morgan, it will be recalled, derived the matrilineal gens from the consanguine family and dated it as prior to the inception of paired marriage. In 1905, a paper by the American ethnologist James R. Swanton convincingly demolished the case for the priority of descent groups, also called sibs.[73] Using comparative ethnographic data, he graded a number of American Indian cultures by their relative complexity and found the simplest to lack descent groups of any kind. So it must have been with the stark simplicity of protoculture. Sibs become proportionately more common among tribes with agriculture and other traits indicative of complexity, suggesting that descent groups belong to later horizons of cultural development.

The question of which unilinear descent rule came first ceased to hold any interest as the impossibility of establishing any priorities became plain. Ethnologists discovered how easily patrilineal descent could be established through diffusion in societies where matrilineal descent had never gained a foothold.[74] Cases of matrilineal changing to patrilineal descent came to light, but no unequivocal indication of the opposite.[75] Growing amounts of heritable wealth in ancient society, Morgan believed, caused a shift from tracing descent through women to descent through males; but ethnographic accounts showed inheritance could occur independently of unilinear descent.[76] Furthermore, field reports demonstrated, matriliny does not imply female authority, or matriarchy. Societies with matrilineal descent groups often vest considerable authority in the mother's brother, with inheritance passing from him to another male, his sister's son. Apparently a number of factors, including marital residence, act as determinants of descent groups, or can influence changes in rules of descent, including the greater security given to a local group constituted as a strong solidary group of patrilineally related males.[77] Ethnography also revealed societies with both matrilineal and patrilineal descent rules; individuals, in those cases, simultaneously belonging to two sibs.

Bachofen, Maine, and Fustel de Coulanges never clearly distinguished between bilateral kinship ties emanating from an individual's two parents and the genealogical links more selectively recognized in assigning someone to membership in a descent group. Morgan, though not entirely free of the same confusion, as I have already stated, clarified matters by specifying that descent applies to rights and privileges conferred by membership in unilinear descent groups. Such groups, he wrote, consist of consanguineally related persons having a common ancestor and tracing their connection through males or females. Descent traced through only one parent, however, does not entirely rule out social recognition of the other. G. Staniland Wake made the same point forcefully by his sharp distinction between kinship and descent,[78] though without using those words. Descent, he argued, refers to special relationships between individuals, while kinship designates more diffuse ones. Rivers, too, made the distinction.[79] Descent regulates membership in groups, which restrict membership by some unilateral affiliation, such as the clan, the moiety, classes, and families, the latter word being best understood as referring to certain members of the family of orientation of the parent through whom descent is traced. It makes no sense, he wrote, to speak of descent in bilateral groups, such as the kindred, where both the father's and mother's kin hold membership. In contrast with descent, kinship designates relationships that depend on the family, although being socially determined it does not always correspond to the biological facts of birth and genealogical connection.

Marry Out or Be Killed Out

Since classical times, writers proposed causal and functional explanations to account for the nearly universal prohibition of incest in the nuclear family. After the middle of the 19th century, exogamy in groups larger than the family also became a problem calling for explanation. McLennan ascribed the origin of exogamy to a scarcity of women in primitive tribes, because of female infanticide. Scarcity led to capturing brides from hostile neighbors and, in time, to men's deep reluctance to espouse women belonging to their own tribe.[80]

The utility of the nuclear family incest taboo—for creating wider bases of social solidarity through marriage—had long been recognized in Western thought; hence it is no surprise that descent group exogamy should have been similarly analyzed. Tylor, after surveying the literature on the alliance-making consequences of exogamy as far back as Plutarch, postulated this function of exogamy for groups larger than the family, and in the process, identified function with cause.[81] Exogamy arose because small tribes realized they had only two alternatives: marry out or be killed out. Functionally speaking, exogamy practiced between sibs in a growing tribe maintains tribal cohesion, and preserves the community's ability to make a concerted stand against enemies. Between bands or villages, it creates alliances that lead to greater defensive strength. Although alliances may not prevent all strife, they help to keep down feuds and heal breaches when they arise.

James J. Atkinson's plot-filled and admittedly conjectural account of the origin of the incest rule explains exogamy and the marital alliances it brings about by the principle of natural selection.[82] Led by Darwin's statement that unregulated jealousy could destroy communities, Atkinson pictured the threat to survival faced by a small protohominid horde dominated by an autocratic, powerful male who monopolized all the women in the group. At first the tyrant protected his monopoly by exiling grown sons, but the mothers out of love for their sons persuaded him to allow the youths to remain. He consented, with a condition: the youths must acknowledge his sole right to sexual intercourse with the females of the horde. Thereby the "primal rule" came into force. Keeping sons at home strengthened the horde and enabled the youths to capture females from hordes weaker because they had not adopted the new customs. In a group of brothers, the wives so secured also came under the incest rule, thus preventing jealousy and hostility from disrupting relations between the males and conferring a further selective advantage on the horde. Eventually, the Cyclopean parent himself gave up his rights to the daughters, thereby opening the way for unrelated males to peacefully secure wives from the group. The marital alliances that resulted from exogamy created a basis of social solidarity in the emerging tribe. Atkinson, an Indian-born Scottish barrister, was not only influenced by Darwinian ideas of natural selection, he also cites comparative primate data to support his conjecture of a powerful male dominating early protohominid hordes. Freud, in adopting Atkinson's imaginative speculation for the psychoanalytical theory of how the Oedipus complex and incest taboo originated, would add psychodynamic elements to the story.

Not all theorists dealt with descent group exogamy in terms of its value for creating alliances. Morgan conceived its chief function in biological terms. By bringing unrelated persons into breeding groups, exogamy created more vigorous stocks, physically and mentally, and thereby contributed to cultural progress.[83] Frazer, writing nearly 40 years after Morgan's *Systems of Consanguinity,* continued to entertain the possibility of sibling marriage in ancient times.[84] Exogamous moieties, he says, originated as a device to bar incestuous marriage; thereafter, instead of marrying their sisters, men exchanged them for the sisters of men in the other moiety, thus reinforcing the already extant custom of cross-cousin marriage.

Starcke and Westermarck explained group exogamy by the same concepts they employed for the incest rule of the nuclear family. In his theory of incest regulations forestalling role conflicts between primary relatives, Starcke reasoned that sibs confer jural obligations on members.[85] Fulfillment of these obligations would be threatened if an individual simultaneously needed to act toward a member of the sib both as sibmate and marriage mate. Only individuals owing no previous obligation to one another can freely marry.

With Westermarck, we come to a psychological idea deeply buried in Atkinson's story of the primal horde and barely detectable in Starcke's theory: descent-group exogamy represents a generalization, or extension, of the nuclear family incest rule.[86] Having assumed a disinclination for sexual relations to be natural between persons who have lived together intimately since childhood, Westermarck assumes such a "peculiarity of the sexual instinct" would, through association, be extended to more re- mote relatives and to unrelated persons who live together closely, and even to those who did not live together at all. Extensionist thinking also appears in Frazer's theory of how ceremonial avoidances, functioning to control incest, come to extended to persons of the same sex.[87] Between affinal kin, as between genealogical kin, such avoidances, no matter what supernatural danger they are believed to forestall, help to prevent sexual intercourse between persons prohibited from marrying. Like other super- stitions, in Frazer's opinion, they provide a "crutch to morality." But be- tween persons of the same sex, the avoidances serve no function. They have "spread" irrationally, due simply to the deeply rooted fear of the fatal effects of illicit sexual relations bound up with the avoidances in other contexts. Extensionist thinking, usually implying the psychological principle of generalization, would become increasingly popular for analyz- ing kinship terms and other aspects of social organization, especially in the work of Malinowski and Murdock.

Totemism and Exogamy

While clarification of the meaning of kinship, marriage, and descent advanced steadily and relatively quickly, totemism remained an unclear concept marked by little consensus. Tylor, for instance, perceived its func- tion in regulating descent-group exogamy, but because it also occurs in cultures lacking descent groups, he assumed it originated prior to exogamy and had its source in animal worship.[88] In speculating about its religious origins, Tylor essentially repeats what McLennan wrote in 1868.[89] The ruder races, the Scotsman had claimed, venerate animal, vegetable, and other objects from which groups take their name. Emblems associated with Scottish clans, and other groups in civilized societies, derive from such primitive worship. Andrew Lang, English essayist, folklorist, and dilettante in anthropological research, regarded totemism in the same vein.[90] Long ago, small groups named each other after plants and animals. They thought of the animals (Lang forgets about plants) as possessing humanlike personalities, and as more gifted or powerful than human be- ings. Myths of descent from and blood relationship with animals de- veloped from the germinal idea of groups being named after powerful creatures. Then people acquired the idea of animal guardians, for whom they devised ritual observances to express reverence and respect. Lastly came firm jural rules against marriage between persons descended from the same totemic forebear. By the time Lang's theory appeared, in 1903, scholars had little tolerance for such unsupported developmental se- quences, and his work was poorly received.[91] Frazer rejected an early unity between totemism and religion, but only because he believed totemism to be rooted in magic which in his sequence antedated religion.[92] His reading of Australian ethnography led him to dissociate the origin of totemism from exogamy and trace it to a belief, entertained when primitive man was ignorant of the role of the genitor in conception, according to which conception occurs when the spirit of a natural species enters the mother's womb, whence it is born as a human child.

Other writers who conceived of totemism as a religious phenomenon included Freud and Durkheim. The author of psychoanalysis derived totemism, exogamy, and incest rules from the remorse and guilt provoked in Atkinson's imaginary horde when—as Freud tells the story—the sons rose up and slew the father in order to gain sexual possession of their mothers and sisters.[93] In an emotional reaction to the crime of patricide, the sons took to worshipping the father in the symbol of a totem. Here lies the origin of religion. Whatever the women felt about the slaying, Freud mentions nothing they contributed to the phylogenesis of culture. Durkheim's theory of totemism, although cast in developmental terms, is more complicated. As we will see in taking up his theory of religion, for him a totem or any deity symbolizes a social group and provides people with a tangible means for thinking about certain experiences they have as members of the group.[94] Rituals directed to the symbol express sentiments the group feels about itself, and serve to perpetuate those sentiments in the members' consciousness. Why do primitive societies choose a plant or animal as a totemic symbol? Because, Durkheim believed, those are the life-supporting objects with which primitive people most frequently come into contact.

Religion and Magic

Savage Postulations

While the study of kinship terminology, descent, and the family was opening up productive new avenues of anthropological inquiry, religion and magic continued to be explored along old lines until Emile Durkheim's work in 1912. Successive writers reiterated accounts of origins and developmental sequences similar to those of their predecessors, without providing any more convincing empirical evidence, simply offering more rationalistically based arguments. Yet accompanying this rather fruitless activity another approach—primarily concerned with the integration of religion and social structures, and deriving from Montesquieu—was being forged, particularly in France. Starting with Saint-Simon and going on in the work of Fustel de Coulanges, it culminated in the contributions of Durkheim and his group ridding itself more and more of developmental thinking.

Claude Henri Saint-Simon was not wholly original when, early in the 19th century, he advanced a theory of development in religion from fetishism through polytheism to monotheism, in which each new religious belief was congruent with the degree of social organization achieved in society and with the extent to which people had succeeded in organizing knowledge.[95] In the earliest period, when fetishists deified nature in its manifold forms without perceiving any link between themselves and the numerous separate deities they recognized, society was similarly fragmented. Social ties hardly extended beyond the confines of individual families, and knowledge consisted of isolated, unconnected facts. Polytheism introduced more general abstractions about the world, but still without organizing them through an all-embracive abstraction of high generality. It reflected a society in which people lived in small political units (city-states), and a system of knowledge consisting of independent clusters of facts frequently in conflict. Monotheism, however, established a general link between the several spiritual beings of polytheism by relating them to a single spiritual principle external to the universe, doing so at a time when society achieved political centralization and when science succeeded in bringing all observable facts under a few highly comprehensive laws. The French nobleman who advanced this concept of cultural integration is more often remembered for his vision of an empirical social science, a vision that inspired Auguste Comte, who bestowed the name "sociology" on the fledgling discipline.

Fustel de Coulanges, confining himself to the classical world of Greece and Rome, also related changes in religious rites and symbols to the development of civil institutions, starting with the family.[96] Using functional theory, he provides a better, evolutionarily grounded, explanation than Saint-Simon of why the changes in religion occurred. As ever larger forms of social structure developed in ancient society, including the clan, tribe, and city-state, each came to develop its own system of worship through which the stability of the group was insured. Worship of the dead proved inadequate to serve the adaptive needs of the city-state, and so other forms of worship were devised. These centered around more comprehensive deities, and offered kings and other high officials the opportunity to play priestly roles. Eventually, as society expanded further, new values inherent in the growth of reason, individualism, and secularism clashed with the religious system of the city-state, and at this point a new religious system, Christianity, appeared. With its more abstract sentiments and more generalized images, it enabled men to transcend allegiance to a particular city and to form more comprehensive groups. The new system possessed definite advantages for a large-scale, pluralistic social system such as had taken shape. In Christianity the deity, instead of being a family-based ancestor belonging to a specific genealogical kin group, or symbolically identified with a particular clan or city-state, became an immense universal being who protects the interests of the whole human species. Religion, being no longer of the earth, interfered little in terrestrial affairs, with the result that politics stood apart from religion and individuals achieved greater personal freedom.

A hint of the compensatory functions of religion appears in the work of Pierre-Joseph Proudhon, a French political philosopher. He regarded religious symbols as reflecting society and thereby as justifying—albeit in a distorted manner—unjust conditions such as hierarchy and inequality.[97] Somewhat similarly, Friedrich Nietzsche, the son of a minister, regarded Christians as revering in their God the wealth, power, and other virtues through which their society thrives and manages to prevail over enemies.[98] The worshipers enlist God as a partner in existence, a patron of the status quo.

When anthropologists today recount the century's varied speculations regarding the sources and forms of religion, they rarely mention Saint-Simon, Proudon, or Nietzsche. But they never skip Tylor, for whom the essence of religion was animism, or belief in spiritual beings.[99] Tylor sets himself to investigate the origin and "natural evolution" of animism to its climax in monotheism, and then its subsequent decay to something like its original form. Religion, he claims, began in elementary animism— the belief in the soul—and gradually progressed to the idea of individual spirits ranging "upward" to deities who control the world. Elementary animism originated in early man's puzzlement about the nature of sleep, dreams, trance, visions, and the difference between a live and a dead body. To explain those things, the "savage philosopher" postulated an element of the body—the soul—on which life depended. Some primitive societies, Tylor noted, still conceive of the soul temporarily quitting the body to travel elsewhere (hence dreams, which in ethnotheory represent the experiences of the errant soul) and returning, until it finally quits the body with death. Through generalization, or what Tylor called man's readiness to personify, the idea of a human soul gave rise to the belief that an individual has more than one soul, that plants, animals, and inanimate objects also possess souls; and it led to many more elaborate beliefs, including life after death, transmigration of souls between human beings and animals or plants, and to ideas concerning purely spiritual beings, out of which the concept of monotheism developed. We are back with Xenophanes when Tylor refers to people modeling spiritual beings after conceptions of the human soul. Direct sensory evidence, Tylor avers, constantly suggests and maintains animistic doctrines among believers; also, the appearance of spiritual beings in dreams and visions confirms their existence. Cicero reported a similar basis for religious conviction.

By his time, Tylor thought, the progressive development of animism had slowed down, being outdone by the rival explanatory powers of science. Having outlived its former usefulness, it has become a survival, a shrunken vestige of the status it still holds in primitive societies. In civilized nations it has returned to its pristine elementary form, being relegated chiefly to religious doctrines of the soul and future life.

The rage for spiritualism sweeping England in late Victorian times may explain why Herbert Spencer simultaneously adopted nearly the same theory of religious origins.[100] For him the source lies in primitive man's failure to differentiate animate and inanimate things, an error through which early man sank lower than other creatures that do distinguish between living and nonliving entities. It proved to be a fateful error, because from it developed the fundamental conception of religion: the body contains an independent spiritual substance which, upon death, becomes a ghost. Out of this germinal notion, which Spencer called manism, other ideas developed. Spiritual counterparts came to be attributed to animals and plants; good and bad spiritual entities were conceived, and ghosts came to be credited with power to control the order of nature and intervene in the ways of men. With such powers ascribed to ghosts, would it not be wise for the believers to try to procure their good will? Out of such reasoning came rituals to please friendly spirits, and to placate, evade, drive away, or defy dangerous ones. Spencer regarded religion—or, rather, fear of the dead—as the first regulative device making organized social life possible. From it, through differentiation, developed forms of political control.

Feasting on the Totem

However highly Tylor's contemporaries respected his abilities, they disputed his theory of animism as the source of religion. Given the license of the times for imaginative reconstructions of origins, as well as fecund thinkers who relished the 18th-century game of delving speculatively into the mind of early man, 19th-century anthropology soon accumulated an embarrassing richness of incompatible accounts about the sources and development of primitive religion. Andrew Lang completely reversed Tylor's sequence by putting belief in a supreme being at the very beginning of religion, in support citing the widespreadness of such belief among the "lowest races."[101] Even the fact that in some societies where the belief occurs, the supreme being is comparatively otiose, Lang sees as supporting his theory. If people believe in God but nevertheless credit more power to magic or spirits than to him, Lang reasons, it must be because over a long period the latter beliefs overwhelmed the earlier concept of a supreme being.

Far more influential was the theory of the Scottish scholar William Robertson Smith, who gained fame not only for offending the Scottish church with his unorthodox ideas of biblical history, so that he lost his post as a university teacher, but also for grounding religion in totemism.[102]

Though Smith never did field work, he traveled extensively in the Middle East observing local customs and studying the Semitic languages and their literature. When his prolix *Lectures on the Religion of the Semites* came out, in 1889, Frazer distrusted Smith's deductions because they were too simple and obvious. Later Frazer became Smith's disciple and hailed his master as a great comparative historian of religion.

According to Smith's theory of totemism, early man felt himself allied with other animals and with inanimate nature, so that humankind blended continuously into nonhuman nature.[103] Religion originated from the holiness attached to the totemic allies, each sacred totemic object being set apart and surrounded with restrictions, including a rule forbidding people to eat totems except on special occasions. The ceremonial meals, taken in a group, acquired a rich, complex significance. Eating the holy objects made the diners themselves holy and endowed them with a feeling of renewed life. From the multiplicity of totems existing in early times, all of them regarded as kinsmen and addressed as "brother," particular species were selected as gods. Thereupon the ceremonial meal developed into nothing less than communion with god, accomplished through eating the divine person himself. The fraternal relationship with the totemic species changed, people now conceiving of themselves as children living under the protection of a divine father who supervised their morality. At first each deity possessed jurisdiction only over one of the small kin groups into which early society was divided, but as the kin groups fused to form larger communities the area of divine jurisdiction also expanded; the gods became kings and were addressed as "lord," no longer by kinship terms. Smith's views concerning the integration of religious belief systems and social structure resemble those already advanced by Durkheim's teacher, Fustel de Coulanges, in *Ancient City,* and before that by Saint-Simon.

Unlike Tylor and other contemporaries who emphasized the central place of belief in religion, Smith stressed ritual. The totemic feast at which the community consumed an animal especially slain for the occasion represents the original form of sacrifice. Out of it grew private sacrifice, which cements the individual, not the group, to god, and of which bloodletting and circumcision are versions. The religious significance of the latter lies not in pain but in what is offered to the deity through them. Other offerings made in lieu of animals include bits of cloth tied to a pole at sanctuaries, first fruits brought to temples, and cannibalistic feasts offering humans captured from alien tribes. As morality developed, and people learned to feel guilty for offenses committed against gods, piacular rites arose that allowed the offenders to atone for their sins.

Among those influenced by William Robertson Smith's account of early religion was Sigmund Freud, a physician who read widely in 19th-century anthropological theory.[104] Born in what is now Czechoslovakia, the son of a wool merchant, Freud lived most of his life in Vienna until, threatened by the Nazi menace because of his Jewish ancestry, he went into exile in London.[105] As a physician strongly inclined to research, he ventured to treat neuroses by inviting the patient to talk out the circumstances under which the problem had first appeared. This treatment became the basis of psychoanalytic therapy, out of which, after the turn of the century, developed a number of psychoanalytic theories for explaining not only individual behavior but culture as well.

In *Totem and Taboo,* Freud begins his reconstruction of the genesis of religion by describing the clinical picture associated with animal phobias. He interprets these neuroses as fear of the individual's father displaced on an animal, and ontogenetically ascribes the fear to rivalry between child and father for the mother's favors. Inspired by this clinical theory, Freud identifies totems as symbols of the father. Then he conjectures on the phylogenetic origins of such symbolization in some early human horde, where the dominant father monopolized all the females until his sons, sexually frustrated, attacked and killed him. Stricken with guilt and remorse for their act, they sought to undo those emotions by ruling against any sexual contact with the mothers and sisters they had liberated. Respect paid to the symbols of the father, i.e., to totems, further assuaged their guilt and, as I have already said, instituted religion. All subsequent religions continue to work at undoing the primal crime, which mankind has never succeeded in totally obliterating from his conscience. All gods are modeled on the father, and relationships with them mirror the worshipers' ambivalent relationships with their physical fathers.

The totemic theory of elementary religion also struck Emile Durkheim as extremely plausible, for reasons he gives in *Elementary Forms of the Religious Life,* another notable book published in the same year, 1912, as *Totem and Taboo.* Though both books utilize the developmental paradigm in reaching theories about the current sources of religious feeling, they differ profoundly in how they identify the source. Freud, in the manner of Tylor, explains religion psychogenically, whereas Durkheim's explanation is sociogenic. In place of guilt, remorse, and the desire to undo evil, he makes the sense of constraint and feeling of elation experienced by belonging to a group the source of religious feeling. He explicitly rejected Edward Tylor's attempt to ground a social phenomenon like religion in individual psychological states.[106] No erroneous fantasy like elementary animism, he affirms, could have been the origin of the profound power that religious sentiments exert in human life.

Born in France, in 1858, Durkheim descended from a line of rabbis, an ancestry that nevertheless allowed him to become an agnostic.[107] After a brilliant career as a secondary school student, he prepared to be a teacher but was turned off by the emphasis normal school put on ancient languages and graduated without honors. He was, however, much impressed with one of his teachers, Fustel de Coulanges, whose work moved Durkheim to consider the influence of social factors in thought and belief. After teaching philosophy in provincial lycées and completing a doctral thesis, "On the Division of Labor in Society" (1893), he became a professor of sociology and education and, his creative talents noted, eventually received a call to the Sorbonne.

Religion, for Durkheim, consists of beliefs and rites, both revolving around sacred things. The rites grow out of collectively held beliefs, and the beliefs justify the ritual practices. Impressed by the opinion of Frazer and others that Australian aboriginal culture preserves a record of the earliest way of human life, he turned to ethnographic literature from that continent for details of Australian religion, especially the people's totemic attitudes and rituals. Religion, he concludes, originated out of the feeling of group dependence, elation, and sense of enhanced vitality experienced when people interacted as members of a prototypical group, the clan, in the presence of the totem, the symbol of the group. Unprepared to refer such experiences to their true source, society, they explained their feelings as induced by the totem, whereupon the totem became sacred. All religions, with their diverse gods, spirits, and sacred symbols, have a similar social basis and are founded on real social sentiments of the kind underlying totemic religion.

Rites, Positive and Negative

The French sociologists, Durkheim included, systematically and non-developmentally studied the forms, types, and meanings of ritual, including those whose performance may have little to do with deities. Over a decade before publication of *Elementary Forms of the Religious Life,* two of Durkheim's closest associates, Henri Hubert and Marcel Mauss, completed the earliest of such studies.[108] Devoted to sacrificial ritual, their study obviously owes a great deal to what the French authors call William Robertson Smith's initial "reasoned explanation" of sacrifice. They define a sacrifice as a communication between the profane and sacred realms, contact being established through an intermediary, the victim. During the course of the sacrifice the victim becomes sacred, removed from its customary profane associations, and thereby the offering acquires the powers ascribed to sacred things for fulfilling a variety of religious purposes. By touching the victim, eating of it, or being sprinkled with its blood, everyone present at the ritual also participates in the sacred realm. Exit rites close the sacrifice; they desacralize the participants, and usher them back to the profane world fortified by their encounter with sacred things and therefore better endowed to carry out their social role. From the standpoint of the actors in the rite, sacrifice is justified by belief in the existence of the sacred things that demand a victim. People expect to gain strength and assurance from those things, and to win other benefits through the ritual. The beliefs and the sacrifice are social not individual matters, and the act of abnegation recalls to the actors the presence of collective forces of society at the same time that it renews their beliefs.

Hubert and Mauss were each 27 years old when *Sacrifice* appeared, in 1898. Hubert, who never achieved his colleague's fame, served as professor of sociology in Paris, with interest in the history of religions and in Celtic archeology. Mauss, like Durkheim, stemmed from an orthodox Jewish background against which he reacted. After studying philosophy under Durkheim, he took up the history of religion and then moved into ethnology and comparative ethnography.[109] Although he did no field work, he drew much from ethnographic sources for his studies of magic, primitive classification, and gift exchange. He saw value in those sources because they reveal social phenomena unobservable in more complex societies, not because they preserve the past. This attitude, exemplified in *Sacrifice* reappears in a much later work by Mauss, *The Gift*.[110] His object in that book is to study prestations which, while theoretically voluntary, spontaneous, and in purpose noninstrumental, are in fact obligatory, self-interested, and demand a return on penalty of shame. Forms of expressive prestations vary greatly between societies. They include entertainments, ritual and military cooperation, the exchange of women, giving children in adoption, and the circulation of wealth. Whatever the form, such transactions in primitive and archaic societies are not purely utilitarian but possess manifold aspects: economic, jural, religious, and aesthetic. Therefore, Mauss calls prestations "total," a term he derived from Durkheim, signifying the interlocking of several social domains in a single act.[111]

Another highly original work of the period deals with passage rites. Despite the lasting significance of Arnold van Gennep's *Rites of Passage*, the Flemish author during most of his active life remained marginal to professional interests. His appointment as professor of ethnography at Neuchâtel, Switzerland, was brief; the rest of his life he was a civil servant, translator, and chicken farmer. Perhaps his isolation from university circles gave him the detachment needed to write a satirical work on the absurdities of ethnographers, linguists, and other academics infatuated with research techniques.[112]

Passage rites, according to van Gennep, have to do with the individual's constant shifts between the religious and profane spheres of life, shifts that, especially in small-scale societies, disturb society as much as they disrupt the actors' lives.[113] The function of the rituals is to reduce such disturbances. Three phases comprise a rite of passage: separation, in which the participants are removed from their previous state; transition or liminality; and incorporation, in which the participants are absorbed into a new condition. No single ceremony shows equal development of every phase, but often all are clearly evidenced and symbolize the passage which the actor is undergoing. One or another phase may predominate in a particular ritual, expressing the meaning of the occasion. Thus separation looms large in funerals, transition in initiation, and incorporation in marriage. Each phase has its appropriate symbols: separation utilizes washing, haircutting, farewells, and mutilation to represent being sundered from a previous state; transition employs acts of submission, special clothing, license, and food avoidances; incorporation makes use of greetings, token eating, binding together, sitting together, and naming.

Durkheim also gave attention to how rituals function.[114] Many rites, including sacrifice, pageants commemorating the mythological past, and piacular rituals centering around calamities, mobilize resources to protect survival. Whether the sentiments expressed be joy or dejection, the rites succeed in bringing about a meeting of minds; they draw people together more intimately and promote feelings of well-being. They raise the individual above himself, and join him to the collective consciousness, through which he is able to lead a life superior to what he would lead if he followed only his own individual whims. The periodicity with which ceremonies are performed Durkheim explains as due to society's constant need to revivify the social sentiments, whereby individuals become aware of the collective consciousness. It makes no difference, from Durkheim's functional viewpoint (or from the view of symbols taken by Thomas Hobbes[115]), whether people sincerely believe in the sentiments they ritually express. The point is, they act as if they experience the sentiments they are supposed to feel and thereby assure the revivification of the collective consciousness.

Compared to Continental scholars, British anthropologists took less interest in ritual.[116] Herbert Spencer, from an instrumental perspective, groups ceremonial behavior with social control and sees it contributing to social integration.[117] From an evolutionary perspective, he dates it prior to more differentiated forms of social regulation, such as religion and government. In fact, rites occur even among subhuman creatures, a reference to display behavior, which some ethologists also refer to as "ritual." Spencer illustrates ceremonial behavior with examples of manners, courtesies exchanged between friends and strangers, and obeisances expressing reverence for or subordination to superiors, including deities. Not since Hobbes am I aware of anyone employing so embracive a concept of ritual. Strong sanctions sometimes compel ritual performance, Spencer notes, indicating that ceremoniousness is no empty gesture.

In Germany, Julius Lippert observed how the rise of economic prosperity in the development of society was accompanied by discontinuing costly or burdensome rituals and performing them in mere token fashion.[118] William Robertson Smith had observed the same trend but ascribed it to weakened faith in deities.[119]

Religion as Defense and Compensation

By following the link between the totemic theory of William Robertson Smith and the theories of Freud and Durkheim, and then taking up the topic of ritual broached by the French sociologists, we lost track of the psychogenic tradition as it developed after Edward Tylor among British writers. None entertained it more firmly than Ernest Crawley, self-styled anthropologist and an enthusiast for all manner of sports, including revolver-shooting. The son of a minister, he studied at Cambridge and wrote a number of popular, strikingly titled books never taken seriously by anthropologists. He defines religion as a tone of life manifested toward death, birth, the strange, and, above all, relations between the sexes.[120] For many societies all these circumstances are loaded with contagious "hylo-idealistic" danger, against which precautions must be taken. Crawley describes how rituals of avoidance enable people to defend themselves against the danger, and how other rituals obviate, to a degree, the necessity for such defense. The marriage ceremony, for example, in all cultures allows a man and woman to live in intimate contact without risking the full onslaught of pollution believed to be inherent in male-female relationships. Crawley's broad—one might say "total"—conception of religion, applicable to all grades of society, suggests it is not only in savage society, as Frazer thought, that religion saturates life and fuses with many other domains of social life, but in civilized society as well.[121]

Tylor's successor at Oxford, Robert Ranulph Marett, wrote in a more conventional way and differed with his friend Tylor in rejecting elementary animism as the origin of religion. Nor did he adopt William Robertson Smith's totemic theory. Perhaps it was his early training as a classicist that led him to follow Stoic doctrine and derive religion from mysterious, spectacular natural events: thunderstorms, volcanic eruptions, eclipses, death, or the sight of an inert corpse.[122] Marett names awe as the fundamental religious feeling. From it stems a powerful impulse to objectify or personify the mysterious event, but without attributing to it soul or spirit. By means of this impulse—animatism, Marett calls it—a person comes to grips with the awesome experience and gains a sense of control over it. Animatism predates animism; it took time for the awesome happenings to be ascribed to spirits or ghosts.

Apparently not fully convinced by his own animatistic theory, Marett became converted to a conception of religion akin to the French sociologists'. Religion concerns the sacred, or whatever people hold to be widely separated from everyday affairs.[123] He lists the manifold ways of employing ritual to handle the sacred: through acts and abstinences participants acquire sacredness; by piling ceremony on ceremony they concentrate the sacred; sacrifice induces sacredness; and terminal rites following a ritual carefully demit the sacred quality accumulated in the ceremony.

Although a prolific writer, Marett in the long run played his most significant role in training some of the first teachers of anthropology in English-speaking lands, including Wilson Wallis and two men who have left their mark on Canadian anthropology, Diamond Jenness and Marius Barbeau.[124] He knew personally practically all of the anthropologists living in the early 20th century in Western Europe, North America, and the British Empire. Could his "awe theory" of religion owe anything to his shock at age eight when he found himself trapped in his room with the house afire and his parents away? In his autobiography, he traces a mild pyrophobia to the experience. His entry into anthropology occurred when as a young Oxford don he decided to enter a prize contest in philosophy, which he won with his essay on the assigned topic, "Ethics of Savage Races." In preparation for the contest, judged by Tylor among others, he immersed himself for three years in ethnographies. Marett engaged in no field work. Anthropology, he thought, was not exclusively devoted to studying primitive societies but dealt with man universally. The sympathetic bond he felt with the French sociologists when he learned of their work grew because he perceived them holding the same broad conception.

The continental psychogenesist, Freud, never renounced his version of the primal horde where exogamy, totemism, and religion originated, but in the 14 years following publication of *Totem and Taboo* he elaborated his theory of the compensatory role that religion plays in individual and social life.[125] He conceives of culture as constantly confronting people with difficult, even impossible, tasks and social life—despite its many satisfactions—as inevitably demanding sacrifice, causing suffering, and blocking freedom. Ultimately culture, with all the benefits it brings, exists only by virtue of people being persuaded to renounce spontaneous gratification of impulses, especially in the spheres of sex and aggression. Such renunciation is difficult, and the frustration it produces generates additional aggression that must also be renounced. Unable to gain release, human hostility is turned against the self in the form of conscience, that in-built sanction by which the individual is restrained when he feels tempted to release illicit impulses. Further aggravating the human dilemma is the fact that human beings are constitutionally impelled to seek pleasure and avoid pain and confinement as much as possible. Yet conscience and the necessity of culture restrict pleasure-seeking. Here religion and other ideologies—illusions, Freud calls them—step in to divert people from the conflict between pressure to quickly gratify impulses and pressures within and outside the person opposing such gratification. Religion provides an ideal view of existence, where the gods enjoy what human beings cannot attain on earth. By promising people that they, too, will someday enjoy complete bliss, provided they presently renounce illicit pleasure, religion adds another pressure. At the same time it assures people that pain and frustration are temporary. Freud sees religion as having been created out of the need to make man's helplessness tolerable. It functions to adjust the defects and evils in social arrangements, to relieve human suffering, and to insure that repressive cultural obligations are fulfilled no matter how bitter they may be.

Control through Imitation and Contagion

Edward Tylor and a number of other writers of the period dealt with magic separately from religion. According to Tylor, the distinction between the two rests on the fact that whereas religion is primarily animistic, magic (in which he includes omens and other forms of divination) need not involve the agency of spirits, ghosts, or gods.[126] Being based on mistaken associations between causes and effects, magic can be performed simply by acting on something that once belonged to the intended victim. Should spiritual beings and magic occasionally concur, there is no thought that the former control the outcome of the magical act. Tylor reveals scarcely a breadth of tolerance for, or understanding of, the such futile procedures. He felt impelled to explain how such systems of error manage to persist, when in fact they cannot accomplish the ends for which they are employed. To explain the survival of faith in magic he provides several hypotheses, including the magician's conviction that his craft is efficacious. Chance, too, contributes to perpetuation, for occasionally an omen is bound to be true or a magical act to succeed. Those occasions are readily recalled in support of the magic, while failures are forgotten.

Tylor perceived a resemblance between magic and science inasmuch as both deal with cause and effect and are based on an expectation that one can dependably predict from a prior event to the subsequent event which it controls.[127] The savage, however, lacking techniques for eliminating antecedents which do not regularly accompany an outcome, cannot test such predictions scientifically.

Contrary to Tylor, William Robertson Smith believed magic and supernatural beings to be closely associated. For him the distinction lies in the aims they serve. Whereas religion links man with friendly powers, serves the welfare of the group, and endows man with courage and confidence, magic is used out of fear to counteract hostile powers. It serves the private needs of individuals; for example, warding off pollution. Magic is older than religion, and as long as it prevailed, its close alliance with fear limited moral and social progress. The idea of magic antedating religion achieved wide circulation after it became a key element in James Frazer's theory, but both Smith and Frazer could have found it in Georg Wilhelm Hegel, who stated it 60 years before Smith's book appeared.[128]

The parallel between magic and science drawn by Tylor was greatly elaborated by Frazer, whose concept of magic, perhaps his most lasting contribution to anthropology, could for many years be found in anthropology textbooks. Although he was one of the best-known scholars of his day, enjoying the same kind of widespread popularity later won by Bronislaw Malinowski and Margaret Mead, Frazer never held an active teaching post through which he could influence students. He gained renown through his writings, and his appeal owed as much to his attractive prose as to the engrossing topics he wrote about: magic, religion, and mythology. His father worked as an apothecary and justice of peace; his mother came from a merchant family.[129] The family was devout, engaging in daily worship, and James remained a churchgoer all his life. Devotion however, did not inhibit him from drawing bold parallels between Christian and pagan deities. Although the parallels shocked some readers, he managed to win a knighthood as well as many other honors. Trained, like Marett, in classics, he became converted to anthropology by Tylor's *Primitive Culture* and through a close friendship with William Robertson Smith. After the conversion, his scholarship continued to depend on books, rather than field research. "God forbid!" he is supposed to have exclaimed at the idea of ever having had direct contact with primitive people. In an autobiographical poem he describes himself perpetually steeped in myths, the "dreamland world of fancy" his "own true home," oblivious to the world around him.[130]

> Still, still I con old pages
>   And through great volumes wade,
> While life's brief summer passes,
>   And youth's brief roses fade.

But library scholarship brings its own rewards:

> . . . A glimmering vista opes,
> Where fairer flowers are blowing
> Than bloom on earthly slopes.

Much magic, according to Frazer, follows quite logically from the premise that any effect may be "sympathetically" produced by imitating it; for example, using objects whose qualities are analogous to the desired effect, or avoiding an act with attributes opposite to the outcome being sought.[131] Other magical thought premises a close sympathetic bond existing between persons closely related, such as friends or kinsmen. Therefore, at critical times, an individual takes elaborate precautions designed to benefit a close associate. In later editions of *The Golden Bough,* Frazer takes these two patterns of magical thought, which correspond to metaphor and metonomy, respectively, and uses them to distinguish two kinds of magic. Homeopathic (also called imitative) magic is based on the association of ideas by similarity, while contagious magic relies on association by contiguity. Both forms rest on the assumption, which Frazer calls the principle of sympathy, that events can be influenced from a distance.

Magic, Frazer agrees with Tylor, need not involve supernatural agents. If the latter are invoked, then they are regarded as under the control of the magician who coerces them to do his will. Religion originated later than magic, after people's growing knowledge taught them the vastness of nature and the depth of human helplessness. Moved by this knowledge, they abandoned hope of directing the course of nature solely through magic and turned to prayer and sacrifice to enlist supernatural support. Magic became relegated to a secondary position, sometimes even being regarded as an impious encroachment of the gods' domain. Eventually, man also withdrew his confidence from religion and deposited it in science, thereby, Frazer thought, reverting in some measure to the attitude represented by magic, for like science it also postulates an invariable order in natural events.[132] His concept of science obviously antedates the modern notion of probability.

Magical customs which we regard as senseless and illogical, Frazer observes, in early times served the cause of progress.[133] By attempting to control nature, magic directed attention to linkages between natural phenomena, with which science also deals. Taboos prohibiting contact with things, regardless of the purposes for which they were observed, fostered conceptions of property rights. In the same relativistic spirit, Andrew Lang maintained that taboos still may have practical consequences—such as conserving the supply of game—of which the actors may be unaware.[134]

Freud followed Frazer's concept of magic when he explained psychoanalytically how people come to apply the principles of metaphor and metonomy in seeking control over nature.[135] He attributes magic to supreme confidence in human powers, to an excessive evaluation of the power inherent in thought. Magic corresponds perfectly to the narcissism with which a child or neurotic patient deems himself capable of accomplishing anything he wishes. Omnipotence of thought operates not only in magic but in prayer and other expressions of animism wherein, however, the person partly transfers power from himself to spiritual beings. Magic and religion declined when the ego emancipated itself from its narcissistic fixation on itself and learned to recognize the objective demands of reality.

Popular as it became, Frazer's idea of magic failed to impress Emile Durkheim, who preferred William Robertson Smith's concept of magic serving predominantly individual needs, while religion is primarily social in its orientation.[136] It was Durkheim's colleague Mauss who brought about the next major advance in the theory of magic and sought to rescue it from the derogatory position it occupies in the writings of Bacon, Botens, Tylor, Frazer, and others.[137] If we regard magic from the actors' standpoint, Mauss argued, we would not ascribe it to errors made in associating cause and effect. The crucial element in magic is the idea of an illimitable, nonmechanical force that for believers is as true as scientific knowledge is for ourselves. Magical techniques are understood to work through that force with automatic efficacy. Like all collective ideas, belief in magical power is an obligatory idea established in individual minds by society, which confirms its validity.

Robert Marett also struggled to find some rational basis that would enable his society to understand why, in many parts of the world, magic is consistently employed for ends which, objectively speaking, it can rarely attain.[138] The practitioners of magic, he suggested, are quite aware of a distinction between magical and other, more direct, modes of action. The magician, realizing his techniques lack the direct efficacy ascribed to them, in a sense playacts, but does so with his whole being. Magic is a more or less clearly recognized pretending, to which people are committed because everyone—even the victim of sorcery—shares the conventional belief that magic works. Marett, contrary to his British contemporaries, who regarded early man as a prescientific inquirer into the nature of experience, and more in line with the views of Marcel Mauss and other French sociologists, refused to identify magic with science. He regarded magic as primarily emotional, not intellectual, in nature.

Toward a Psychological Anthropology

The Mind Writ Large

The rise of psychology as a discipline probably had little to do with the prominence of a psychological viewpoint in anthropology. The psychogenic explanations of cultural development, which Edward Tylor, Herbert Spencer, Robert Marett, Sigmund Freud, and others advanced, differ little from the mode of thought current in the previous century. The doctrine of psychic unity and its role in culture history also wasn't new. According to the doctrine, parallels in culture result independently in different societies, as a result of uniform mental processes inherent in human thought. Adolf Bastian—in his convoluted, often baffling, literary style —went farthest in elaborating this explanation of cultural similarities.[139] Beneath resemblances lay the operation of similar *Völkergedanken*, world views, which have developed from identical *Elementargedanken*, elementary ideas, which he compares to chemical atoms or single cells. The human species' stock of elementary ideas is limited. Throughout history, under the influence of different geographical conditions, the elementary ideas grew into diverse world views which, in turn, diffused into other cultures where they met and blended with other world views. Bastian, the son of a Bremen merchant, studied law, medicine, and natural science.[140] Then he began his extensive travels, first as a ship's doctor and later as a museum curator. Instead of making detailed ethnographic observations on his own account in the places he visited, he carried out field work by interviewing people of foreign origin who had, for some time, been living among indigenous populations. Bastian ended his long career in the field, alone. A single mourner accompanied a mule cart carrying his body to a cemetery in Trinidad, where it was interred without ceremony.

Some theorists strong opposed explaining social phenomena in psychological terms.[141] They regarded society and its institutions as a system external to and independent of the individuals responsible for its existence. Social phenomena belong to a distinct realm, in which events follow their own laws. The problem to which they addressed themselves was exactly the reverse of what the psychogenecists studied; namely, how does the social realm, whose existence is independent of any particular individual, act on persons to shape their thoughts, feelings, and overt behavior? In *Primitive Classification,* Durkheim and Mauss regard the division of Australian society into clans as the sociogenic basis according to which the society's members categorize phenomena in nature.[142] One clan classes together smoke, honeysuckle, and certain trees; another clan puts dogs, fire, frost, and certain other trees into a single category. Obviously, the terms in any particular conceptual category possess no perceivable qualities in common. The groupings are matters of convention—related to the way the Australians group themselves. They are socially imposed and emotionally influenced—especially by religious emotion—not rationally devised.[143]

Also writing from a sociogenic perspective, Spencer holds that social evolution remolded human nature. Some behavioral tendencies vital for adaptation in early stages of culture have, he believes, lasted to contemporary times.[144] Specifically, he mentions the aggression mustered in early times for hunting and in defense against wild animals: an enduring aggressive character in the human species derives from then. But psychogenic overtones also appear in his evolutionary theory, as they occasionally do in the thinking of other sociogenecists, too. For a society to evolve, he maintains, people must develop both the requisite intelligence to devise new ways and a readiness to master new ways. They must overcome maladapted personality traits, such as the desire to live by hunting and adventure and, for the sake of future rewards, they must renounce inclinations to indulge in immediate gratification.

Primitive Mentality

The idea that society influences what or how people think is not incompatible with the period's prevailing belief in progressive cultural development, or with the accompanying methodological assumption that early stages of social development persist among primitive people. Thought depends on the level of cultural development a people have reached.[145] Though primitive folk may possess the same psychological makeup as civilized folk, being culturally backward their mentality also remains comparatively undeveloped. They tend irrationally to confuse symbol and reality, names and what they stand for, thought and effect. Inability to take a critical view of what exists, and to compare it with ideal standards, deters primitive societies from making improvements in their conditions. Childlike animism and a proclivity for myth-making confine primitive man to the error of personifying impersonal objects. His experience restricts him in learning causal sequences revealed in the regularities of nature; as a result, some primitive societies are sometimes even unaware of physiological paternity. Collective ideas, often influenced by religion, saturate the individual, leaving him little scope for individual reflective thinking. Only as primitive homogeneity gives way to the differentiation characteristic of civilization, does society's hold over the ideas of its members slacken, allowing individuals to categorize experience as their reason dictates. In such growing individualism, science has its roots.

How much more dramatic these inferences from ethnographic data sound than the more prosaic experimental findings obtained by psychologists and anthropologists who cooperated in the Cambridge Expedition to Torres Straits in 1898.[146] Measurements of Papuans' auditory and visual acuity, reaction to visual illusions, and other capacities revealed no gross inferiority compared to European subjects. At times Papuan measurements exceeded European norms, and sometimes they fell short of them.

Lucien Lévy-Bruhl's theory of two mentalities, one prelogical, belonging to primitive man, the other logical, and revealed in civilization, made no use of experimental findings nor did the author engage in any field work. Born in Paris, in 1875, Lévy-Bruhl studied psychopathology as well as philosophy, which he later taught.[147] Though friendly with Durkheim, he never belonged to Durkheim's circle. Nevertheless, his conception of primitive society maintaining a strong grip on primitive thinking closely resembles Durkheim's view of the collective consciousness.

The ideas of primitive society, Lévy-Bruhl held, are thoroughly mystical and governed by the principle of participation.[148] According to this principle, all phenomena in the universe are intimately interrelated, despite the absence of any discernible empirical connection between them.

Hence it is possible for a primitive society to claim that grain growing in the field can be affected by what people do a great distance away. The principle of participation allows objects, beings, or any other phenomenon to be simultaneously what it evidently is and something else. Such thinking is prelogical; it has failed to evolve to the point of recognizing that a phenomenon cannot logically be one thing and another thing at the same time.

Challenging the concept of a distinctive primitive mentality, critics observed that the kind of thinking held to be characteristic of primitive societies, by Lévy-Bruhl as well as others, also occurs in civilized societies.[149] W. H. R. Rivers, who had been on the Torres Strait expedition, questioned whether primitive ideas were usually contradictory or illogical.[150] Such labels are tempting when we encounter beliefs we do not fully understand, but they distract anthropologists from their fundamental duty; namely, to discover how exotic societies conceive of experience. Lévy-Bruhl absorbed such criticism, and in time he conceded that the beliefs of small-scale societies do not automatically violate the logical principle of contradiction.[151]

Cultural Semiotics

Another approach to patterns of exotic thought concentrated on the symbols and categories it produced. James Frazer documents how the Egyptians identified the goddess Isis with grain, bread, beer (brewed from grain), abundance, and human fecundity.[152] Psychoanalytic theory enabled Freud to discover less documentable symbolism in the custom of ritual defloration. When a bride is deflowered by an older man or a chief, he represents her father, and unconsciously the ritual symbolizes incestuous gratification.[153] Primitive people engage in such frank enactments of forbidden things, Freud explains, because among them repression is weaker than in civilized society. Durkheim interprets structurally the opposition between primitive conceptions of the family and sexuality.[154] Symbolically, the family stands for duty and possesses a sacred connotation; sexuality, however, has a profane significance and stands for spontaneous behavior carried out for pleasure, not duty.

The widespread symbolism attached to the right and left sides attracted the attention of Robert Hertz, a pupil of Durkheim and an early victim of the First World War.[155] Invariably, where right and left symbolism is found, Hertz reports, the right side tends to signify a sacred quality while the left symbolizes the profane, illicit, or unworldly. An insignificant biological tendency of the human body toward asymmetry, favoring the right hand over the left, lies at the root of symbolic opposition, but cannot completely account for it. The symbolism arose in early society and, like other concepts of primitive society, originated in religion. Once adopted, the idea resulted in constraints being placed on use of the right and left hands for certain purposes. These constraints, thanks to the plasticity of the human body, have encouraged the right hand to grow stronger and more dexterous than the left.

Cultural Psychology

By the turn of the century, books and articles were advocating the direct psychological study of primitive people and their socialization. A German writer, in a book that is patronizing because of its stress on the childlikeness of the members of small-scale societies, visualized the practical value likely to accrue from such research.[156] It would help white settlers deal with native people in colonial territories, and at the same time spare the natives from injuries caused by the settlers' mistakes. Without claiming pragmatic justification, Daniel Brinton in the United States advocated a "psychical anthropology."[157] Of Quaker background, he belonged to the generation of self-trained anthropologists. An industrious library scholar and imaginative thinker with very wide interests, he held a professionship in anthropology and linguistics at the University of Pennsylania.[158] Adhering partly to Durkheim's conception of the hold that primitive societies maintain over the individual, Brinton thought socialization in those societies occurs automatically. Only in "more cultured" societies do individuals examine and approve of what tradition offers, and then voluntarily adopt it. The French sociologist Gabriel Tarde knew better.[159] No place do people passively absorb what society offers; everywhere they learn their culture only insofar as they choose to internalize certain ideas.

Historical Ethnology

A Paradigm Is Shaken

If Thomas Kuhn's concept of paradigmatic shifts in science can be applied validly to the development of anthropological thought, then in the demise of classic evolutionism around the turn of the century we see a paradigm yielding.[160] For over 200 years the paradigm of cultural development had remained fundamentally unchallenged. Few features of history or culture could not be dealt with by being assimilated to the vast process of progressive social development. Following what they called the comparative method, evolutionists had accounted for the body of available ethnographic and archeological facts satisfactorily, given the prevailing standards of validity and reliability. Moreover, until the appearance Emile Durkheim's sociology and historical ethnology, late in the 19th century, no clear alternative to developmentalism existed for scholars interested in pursuing the study of society or culture. Those dissatisfied with the paradigm might defect by shifting to other disciplines, but doing so failed to create the dialectical tension within a closely related community of scholars on which the end of a paradigm hinges.

As the century drew to a close in the United States and Europe, all was by no means going well for evolutionism. The theory allowed no way of choosing between contradictory, or at least divergent, accounts of the origin and development of the family, religion, magic, and other institutions. Truly historical-minded scholars objected to the unilinear, orthogenetic orientation of the evolutionists, because it rested on highly subjective judgments regarding what is earlier or later in social life. The historians in anthropology also pointed to evolutionism's failure to study individual cultures to see if development in a particular case was due to internal processes or to diffusion and contact. Contemporary colonial history revealed plainly that no lengthy series of stages was required for primitive people to reach the threshold of civilization. The theory that psychogenic factors guided cultural development along the same path and through the same stages in all societies was confronted by another theory more compatible with biological evolution; namely, that situational factors control history.[161] Consequently, culture change is adventitious and unpredictable. Those who recognized the importance of diffusion in culture history had already reached a similar conclusion, and were forcing the evolutionists to reconsider their conception of stages following upon each other lawfully and necessarily in all parts of the world.[162] Since diffusion had been operating for millennia, how could contemporary primitive societies be regarded as fossilized relics of the past?[163] Why couldn't so-called survivals have been what Edward Tylor said they became once civilized societies inherited them; namely, symbolic acts without much utilitarian significance?[164] Marcel Mauss was still a young man, in 1898, when he complained about the British anthropologists' use of comparison.[165] They start and end with similarities. Because differences interest them only secondarily, they fail to note concomitant variation between a trait they study and other phenomena. The evolutionists, Mauss observed, are further prevented from making significant discoveries by their too-great readiness to explain by reference to psychological factors. Why indeed search for explanations when everything can be facilely accounted for as issuing from some human proclivity? Van Gennep asked whether primitive life is as simple as the developmentalists take it to be when they compare it to civilization?[166] Isn't it rather the mirror image of ours, considerably more complex below the surface in the extensive rules and codes of etiquette that people are required to follow? We have reduced such observances to a minimum.

In an effort to somewhat reduce sheer speculation about when and in what context particular social institutions originated, and how they developed in complexity, three British sociologists, with great labor, adopted Tylor's method of statistical correlation.[167] From the storehouse of ethnographic literature they chose a sample of 400 societies representing all parts of the world. First, they deduced a defined series of economic stages, from hunting to agriculture to pastoralism, representing the order in which human culture had probably developed. Each stage in their system represents a type of ecological adaptation; for example, higher hunters differ from two lower, and presumably earlier, stages of hunting by possessing permanent dwellings, the dog, spinning and weaving techniques, pottery, and good canoes. Higher agriculturalists contrast with the two lower levels of plant domestication by use of the plow, irrigation, manuring, use of metals, knowledge of textiles, and regular trade. So much the authors took for granted. They now looked to see how each stage correlates with the presence or absence of certain social institutions (the family, government, formal justice, social stratification, war, and so forth). The authors expected that social institutions correlating with a particular mode of adaptation would indicate the relative age (i.e., stage) when the institutions first appeared. The test failed to produce the neat results the sociologists hoped for, but some correspondences did show up. With progress in economic life, government and the formal administration of justice become more common in the societies being studied. Offering some kind of consideration for a bride (bride wealth, gifts, service, or another woman in exchange) increases markedly as economic culture advances. Monogamy, however, contrary to what Lewis Henry Morgan would have predicted, turns out to be distributed randomly among all economic stages, though it is rare among pastoral societies.

Statistical correlations, as a means of reconstructing the past, carry the same defect Durkheim had pointed out in other evolutionary methods where contemporary primitive societies are used for evidence of history.[168] They provide no historical understanding, he argued; they fail to get at the conditions under which social institutions originated, and ignore circumstances under which traits became modified.

The Diffusionists

Two new conceptual approaches, historical ethnology and what, for want of a better name, I call French sociology, helped drive evolutionism to the margins of anthropological thought, where it remained for the first three or four decades of the 20th century. Early historical ethnology, which I take up first, was a mixed bag of techniques and concepts directed to the problem of reconstructing the histories of preliterate cultures. Its representatives at this time were German-speaking and British ethnologists, who became known as diffusionists because they concentrated on unraveling the streams of diffusion and migration whereby the world's primitive culture areas acquired their ethnographic content. Diffusionism began in Germany, a country where evolutionism had never gained a strong hold, whence it spread to England and America, where we will pick it up in Chapter 6 with Franz Boas, Alfred Kroeber, Roland Burrage Dixon, and other figures of the American Historical Tradition.

Nineteenth-century writers had generally dealt with similarities between cultures as if they represented independent parallel developments. Although recognizing diffusion, they relegated the process to a minor role, except for a few writers like the English philosopher Patrick Edward Dove who, in 1850, held a society's unrestricted intercourse with strangers to be one of the most important sources of social change.[169] Challenging the thesis of parallel development, Friedrich Ratzel, Leo Frobenius, Fritz Graebner, and other historical ethnologists of the time placed major emphasis on migration, diffusion (or acculturation, as some called it), and, later in England, culture contact. Their approach continued the diachronic and developmental outlook prevailing up to this time, but they made little attempt to account for the developmental trend. For historical ethnologists, cultural development was an epiphenomenon produced by the processes at work in culture history. Except for a little help received from a growing body of paleolithic archeological data,[170] they faced a familiar problem: what evidence to use in lieu of direct historical testimony? To a large extent they found their evidence of the past in contemporary spatial distributions of cultures and culture traits. They mapped distributions and invented principles—assumptions really—with which to deduce temporal order, or historical succession, from the synchronous distributions the maps revealed. They wanted desperately to avoid the speculativeness inherent in the methods they repudiated. Their methods, they hoped, would be as empirical as those inductive history uses with written records. In the end, however, they failed to muster the degree of credibility necessary to convince critics.

Another difference between the evolutionists and historical ethnologists lay in the greater single-mindedness with which the latter studied primitive culture. Evolutionists had rarely lost sight of the institutions of civilization, one of their aims being to discover the roots of those institutions; but the diffusionists made primitive cultures almost their sole business.

Culture Circles

In 1891, a German geographer and zoologist, Friedrich Ratzel, who also pursued ethnology, called attention to a surprising similarity between the form of bows found in Africa and New Guinea.[171] His explanation of the resemblance as indicative of a historical connection between the Negroid inhabitants of the two regions epitomizes the substance of historical ethnology. Though Ratzel further accounted for the resemblance in bows as due to common psychological features shared by the two populations, he felt no sympathy with psychogenic evolutionism, especially with the version found in Adolf Bastian's concept of elementary ideas, because it could not support its claims with acceptable evidence. Perpetual waves of migration in human history, Ratzel maintained, probably constituted the single greatest factor responsible for the development of culture in any given area. By carrying stronger people into the lands of weaker neighbors, migrations transplanted cultures, stimulated change, promoted cultural divergence, and hastened specialization of labor where little or none existed before. Working in a country where the discipline of anthropology was closely allied with geography, he proposed a distinctive geographical method for ethnology. It called for mapping the world's culture areas and then tracing the routes between them over which cultures had spread, thereby inductively deriving world culture history.

Ratzel did not originate the idea of culture being regionally distributed. Bastian had recognized as much when he maintained that parts of the globe with generally similar environments constitute cultural areas with more or less similar *Völkergedanke*. Adjacent areas, he granted, could influence one another, and influence could reach even beyond the next region. But quite the opposite of Ratzel, Bastian warned against relying on such influences, i.e., on diffusion, to explain cultural similarities which, he thought, could usually be better explained as products of elementary ideas.

Maps showing culture areas (*Kulturkreise*, literally culture circles) were soon being drawn by a self-trained German ethnologist, Leo Frobenius, whose interest had been aroused by cultural parallels between distant places. In many instances, he noted, the parallels involve not isolated traits but many items: boats, musical instruments, and the like.[172] So many resemblances could not possibly be fortuitous, but indicated diffusion of entire cultural configurations. Ethnology faced the problem of discovering the chronological order in which such distributions had been laid down in different places.

Frobenius's conception of cultural configurations led him to deliberately ignore different uses to which similar cultural traits are put in different places. Emphasis on use can only mislead in looking for cultural origins, he advises, because it distracts attention from the primary fact of similarity. Instead of heeding use, one should attend to the meaning cultural traits derive from the pervasive property—the cultural paideuma—dominating the configuration in which they were embedded.

Self-taught by apprenticeships to museums and journeys of exploration in Africa, Frobenius had once submitted a doctoral thesis to a German university only to have it rejected. Thereupon he turned his back on universities almost for good, except for an honorary appointment at Frankfort late in life.[173] In time he abandoned research on diffusion but retained a lively interest in cultural configurationalism.[174] Applied to Africa, where he made expeditions, the concept of cultural wholes led him to discover two basic, opposed world views, each present in different degrees in particular societies. One, the Hamitic, is magical and is given to creating rigid social structures, to dealing with detailed empirical facts, and to idealizing women. The other, the Ethiopian, is mystical and tends to create fluid social structures, to experience reality as a whole, and to idealize men. Though Frobenius has been largely forgotten in recent anthropology, except in the German theory of cultural morphology, he has been praised by some leaders of Negritude for the inspiration his ideas gave the movement.[175]

In German-speaking countries, chiefly two persons, Fritz Graebner and Wilhelm Schmidt, built on the foundations Ratzel and Frobenius had laid down. Graebner mainly sought to develop quasi-historiographic principles for recognizing diffusion in the areal distribution of cultural traits, while Schmidt schematically ordered the whole world's primitive cultures in a temporal sequence.

Graebner was born in Berlin and devoted his university years to history, geography, and philology. He joined the staff of the city's ethnological museum where he and a colleague, Bernhard Ankermann, worked on the culture histories of Oceania and Africa. Frobenius sat in the audience, in 1904, when they presented early results of their work.[176] In 1911, Graebner published a manual of principles and methods for carrying out ethnological research. The outbreak of World War I caught him in Australia, where the British authorities detained him for five years as an enemy alien.

His manual contains rules applying the injunctions of historiography to test the validity not of historical documents, but of the ethnographic accounts on which historical ethnologists must rely in drawing information about culture areas.[177] More significant are the book's criteria for inferring from the geographical distributions of traits the order in which they originated and spread. Cultural resemblances between two areas, Graebner postulates, are probably due to diffusion when they cannot be explained by their relationship to use, or by the nature of the material out of which they are manufactured. The probability of diffusion increases the greater the number of similarities between two cultures or areas, and is still more enhanced if the similar traits are found continuously distributed between the places under study. In place of the evolutionists' unilinear concept of cultural development, Graebner comes closer to the Darwinian model of hundreds of separate divergent species. But the analogy fails, because diverging cultures continue to influence one another. As a particular culture that developed in one place spreads, it intersects with other cultures, influencing them, and thereby producing the enormous heterogeneity we observe in world culture. Thus migration and diffusion are responsible for the distribution of culture traits, or rather complexes, for Graebner, too, believed that bundles of closely related traits are more likely to spread than single cultural elements.

For Wilhelm Schmidt the clue to culture history lay in reconstructing the prehistoric spread of total cultural types, not mere complexes. In his youth in Germany, Schmidt resolved to be a missionary working in foreign lands.[178] Instead, after his ordination as a Catholic priest, in 1892, he studied Oriental languages, and became a teacher of linguistics in a seminary near Vienna. Here he acquired an interest in ethnology, to which he largely devoted his career as a scholar.

In line with its integrated quality, Schmidt theorized, culture sometimes diffuses in large clusters, each of which embraces all the major aspects of life: material culture, subsistence patterns, social structure, religion, and even language.[179] Any such cluster, or culture circle, will be found among many widely distributed tribes, the worldwide distribution of the circles indicating they are very old. To reconstruct the original culture in a region, one must peel away elements acquired from other, later types of culture entering the place.

The chief value of ethnography, he thought, lies in providing data with which to reconstruct the succession of cultures. Schmidt recognized four major culture circles, some with subdivisions. The oldest, the Primitive Culture Circle, belongs to the world's living food gatherers, people like the African Pygmies and the Fuegians. With his theological background it is not surprising that Schmidt looked with great interest at the belief in a personal Supreme Being, which he found extant in this culture circle because it indicated the origin of religion in monotheism.

Cultivation of plants and animals began in cultures belonging to the succeeding Primary Culture Circle, where recognition of unilinear descent also appears. Patrilineal descent resulted from animal husbandry, which gave preponderance to men in economic activity, matrilineal descent from horticulture where the role of women is emphasized. The increased confidence people began to feel in their own powers at this stage, Schmidt believes, caused them to shift their faith from God to reliance on magic. Thence we come to the Secondary Culture Circle, produced by crossings of Primary subtypes and Primitive infiltrations. It is characterized by more intensive agriculture and deified kings, who join a plethora of spiritual beings in whose pantheon the Supreme Being is absorbed. There his distinctive qualities—omniscience, omnipotence, and concern with morality—go unrecognized. Cultures of the Tertiary Circle are blends of Secondary types and correspond to the protohistoric civilizations of Europe, Asia, and America.

The spirit of German diffusionism, if not precisely its methods, spread to England where G. Elliot Smith and, later, W. J. Perry pinpointed Egyptian civilization as a center of cultural innovation.[180] The idea of Egypt as a potent stimulus in cultural development everywhere occurred to Elliot Smith, an anatomist by training, in 1907, while he was in Egypt salvaging burials from a site to be flooded by a dam. He wasn't original; James Burnett, in 1784, had also named Egypt as a source of civilization.[181] Food-gatherers, Elliot Smith believed, lived practically like apes before diffusion from the Nile Valley brought them crafts, arts, social structure, and religion. As evidence for his thesis of Egyptian diffusion, he points to clusters of culture traits lacking any inherent relationship with each other; yet found in several parts of the world, and resembling Egyptian cultural forms. The traits include megalithic constructions, especially pyramids; sun worship; tattooing; dual organization; and circumcision. The frequent distribution of the clusters along coastlines struck him as particularly significant.

Elliot Smith's historical theory fared no better than Burnett's, or, for that matter, than Schmidt's concept of worldwide culture circles and the other methodological paraphernalia from which the early historical ethnologists in their despair with classic evolutionism expected so much.[182] One particular hypothesis originating among the Germans did last, the possibility of transpacific connections between America and the South Seas or Asian mainland, and became the subject of much research among later generations of historical ethnologists. For historical ethnology did not cease. Shorn of extreme diffusionism it diffused to the United States around the turn of the century and metamorphosed into the American Historical Tradition.

Toward a Theory of Culture Change

While the diffusionists were reconstructing culture history, they and other ethnologists were also polishing concepts of culture change and persistence, including convergence—the process of parallels developing in different places, due to the operation of similar natural, cultural, or psychological conditions.[183] A German sociologist, Alfred Vierkandt, wrote a detailed book on the dynamics of persistence in culture change, in which he ascribes persistence partly to the quality of inertia in human nature.[184] He perceives individual differences in the strength of adherence to tradition, and sees it varying inversely with amount of formal education. Yet even educated people will continue a custom if experience shows it to possess value. Thus cultural traits themselves differ in their likelihood to continue. Among the most apt to be clung to, Vierkandt puts those which contribute to a group's identity or serve as its boundary markers. From a purely cultural standpoint, persistence is inevitable simply because new cultural forms always incorporate some elements of older forms and consequently perpetuate them; no cultural phenomenon, regardless how great the mind of the genius who produced it, is ever wholly original.

Vierkandt's book gives considerable attention to acculturation, by which he means changes in a society following directly or indirectly from diffusion. In doing so, he specifies conditions and types of cultural borrowing. Some traits can be taken over quickly; others, however, require a long period of contact between people before they can be fully mastered. Certain borrowings have manifold consequences, while others have much less repercussion in the host culture. Obviously, contact between societies promotes cultural similarity. A distinctive culture is possible only if the society has been isolated for a long time. Vierkandt traces a connection between the spatial distribution of culture traits and their survival chances: those restricted face the peril of disappearing through population fluctuation, war, and migration, while widespread traits are more likely to survive. Here again is the age-area hypothesis.

In France another sociologist, Gabriel Tarde, interpreted invention in the idiom of Darwinian biology.[185] He regards technical inventions as analogous to biological adaptation, because they enable humans to meet the demands of changing environments. Whether he meant to include the social realm in his concept of environment isn't clear, but he does mention intellectual dilemmas stimulating a search for resolution through cultural innovation. For an invention to be accepted by a society, he holds, it must be compatible with existing cultural conditions, otherwise it will generate ideas in opposition to each other and thereby promote social conflict.

Across the English Channel, W. H. R. Rivers put forward a number of theoretical propositions concerning the stability of culture and diffusion, some of them closely resembling Vierkandt's, though Rivers was working on a different problem. He had begun anthropology "under the sway of the old evolutionary standpoint," but under Graebner's influence he ended up, as he judged it, about midway between evolutionism and culture history.[186] Unlike the diffusionists, he acknowledged fully the interest in developmentalism he carried over from evolutionism. Following the Germans, he sought for evidence of contacts between people bearing different cultural traditions who were responsible for the contemporary cultural picture of Melanesia.[187] Like the German culture-historians, Rivers felt that valid general principles about what happens in culture contact would help him to correctly interpret the relative age of present-day culture traits and to reconstruct history in the absence of written records. He paid special attention to diffusion and other factors, such as disease, war, and other catastrophies, capable of promoting the loss of culture traits and thereby destroying historical evidence. Linkage between traits can cause borrowings in one sector of a culture to displace traits in other sectors, and it can also create a need for additional new elements after diffusion has once begun. The more highly organized or developed a culture, the less its receptivity to influence from others. The amount of cultural material borrowed is also likely to be proportionate to the relative superiority attached to an intrusive way of life; the higher the evaluation, the fewer the agents needed to disseminate new traits. Borrowed cultural traits may become so thoroughly assimilated to the host culture, to the psychological characteristics of the host society, or to the geographical milieu into which the traits have moved that a culture historian can no longer detect their original cultural home. Social structure and language, Rivers thought, are the most stable parts of culture, changing only under the most intimate blending of ethnic groups. Therefore, they provide valuable clues to the intensity of former contacts. Material culture, however, alters quickly, especially when newly introduced objects are perceived to be superior to traditional items. Hence it is of little help in reconstructing prehistoric contacts.

Such principles state a theory of culture change. Their validity for retrodiction remains untested, because Rivers seldom argues explicitly from given principles when he assigns a given trait of Melanesian culture to the indigenous period or to succeeding immigrant waves of kava drinkers and betel chewers.

Invention and Adaptation

The greater concern with invention rather than diffusion in American ethnology is seen in two anthropologists, W J McGee and Otis T. Mason. Both also recognized the importance of technology for adaptation to the natural environment, and the significance of change in the adaptation process. Human beings, McGee observed, adapt to the environment not through biological modifications but by inventing techniques and tools suited to the physical milieu.[188] Otis Tufton Mason, one of the early curators of the U.S. National Museum, defined invention to include innovations in language, institutions, creeds, and other nonmaterial features of culture.[189] Calling the inventive process indigenous to human nature, he described technological inventions as responsible for bringing human beings from a level of existence where they used only natural objects as tools to the point where they drastically modify nature in order to secure new sources of energy and laborsaving devices. Could he have read any of the early publications on "energetics" written by Wilhelm Ostwald? Originally, Mason wrote, innovations by better serving the inventor's need, benefited only the person who produced them. Currently, however, inventions may bring advantages to entire nations or to all mankind, as in the case of the telephone, an innovation with which Mason was greatly impressed.

Destructive Effects

Colonalism and the expansion of national frontiers presented anthropology with a dilemma.[190] The belief that isolation had caused primitive people to stagnate suited optimistic faith in the power of introduced schools, agriculture, and other kinds of culture change to promote progress. But people who had visited native societies knew that the end of isolation sometimes spelled disaster. It also boded the end of primitive culture in places where it had not yet been studied ethnologically.

In Oceania, where old customs were dying out, observers witnessed once healthy, warlike tribes reduced to disease and dispirited apathy, their populations decimated. A United States government ethnologist noted several outbreaks of messianism, at times accompanied by violence, among American Indians helplessly confronting white encroachment on their territories. Yet in India much of the traditional cultural heritage survived despite two centuries of Western influence, suggesting to Rivers that societies with high cultures could withstand the destructive effects of culture contact better than primitive societies. Because the transition to civilization demands greater changes from men than women, Mason saw culture contact racking men's minds and bodies while leaving women unaffected.[191] Women holding traditional ideas can maintain their former occupations, sometimes even practicing them with the aid of improved appliances.

Anthropologists decided change itself wasn't necessarily detrimental, but sudden and unregulated change was. Hence they urged a policy of gradualism. Wherever possible, administrators should act to preserve old interests, morale-producing customs, and customs connected with fertility, like polygyny.

French Sociology

The Authoritative Collective Consciousness

While in Germany historical ethnologists were struggling with inferring history from spatial distributions, in France another way of studying social phenomena was getting underway among a small group of scholars gathered around Emile Durkheim, now a professor at the Sorbonne. The company, including Henri Hubert, Marcel Mauss, and Robert Hertz, looked at social events synchronically and at the social conditions under which they occur. Calling themselves sociologists did not prevent those men from utilizing worldwide ethnographic data along with material from French society. The French sociologists, who are also called the L'Année group from a journal they published, thought systematically with a severely delimited set of basic concepts. The most important of these concepts were concerned with the powerful role society plays in generating the reality people perceive and respond to. With the theoretical concepts went methodological injunctions specifying the appropriate procedure to follow in studying social phenomena. Religion, law, and customs, Durkheim advises, should be regarded as social things, "things" meaning they are capable of being known as empirically as phenomena connected with the physical world.[192] Since social phenomena possess an objective, thing-like, or factual reality, they should be studied independently of the behavior of individuals. Social things being collective cannot be wholly explained as arising out of individual decisions or psychological states. Understanding of social facts comes from explaining them either by antecedent social facts or in terms of the functions they fulfill for the social organism. Durkheim preferred the term "function" to "purpose," because the relationship of a social fact to the needs of a society may exist whether it is intentional or not. Anyhow, intentions are too subjective to be treated scientifically.

Social phenomena in a society are interdependent, hence they must always be studied in definite types of social systems, not torn from different social contexts and mixed together, as the British evolutionists did. What is normal or pathological in social phenomena can only be determined with reference to the system to which particular phenomena belong.

Not every event performed by a member of society is a *social* fact, but only those events and accompanying sentiments occurring when individuals fulfill obligations in society. People experience the obligations as constraints, and quite correctly locate the source of the constraints external to themselves. The obligations that individuals fulfill have a collective character, deriving from their joint authorship by many individuals acting as a group. Social obligations and sentiments belong to the group's collective consciousness, a concept long misunderstood by anthropologists critical of Durkheim's thought. The collective consciousness represents a synthesis of individual ideas and sentiments whose locus is in the group, where it can be investigated as an empirical phenomenon.

Though the collective consciousness constrains thought and action, individuals sometimes commit acts at variance with the normative ideas and sentiments. Though society may claim that such deeds endanger society, often they aren't as dangerous as people make them out to be. The acts are regarded as socially dangerous primarily because they are at variance with the collective consciousness.

There is no use asking the ordinary person about the cause of a social phenomenon in which he happens to be involved. Social causes independent of human purposes operate in the internal constitution of a society or its component groupings below people's level of awareness. Take division of labor, brought about when social life, instead of being carried out in many small, independent homogeneous social segments, becomes generalized.[193] The process which follows is not controlled by human purpose. As division of labor grows, "distance" between individuals diminishes, making social relations denser, more concentrated. The social segments become incapable of maintaining themselves independently, as they did in a segmentary society; everyone's needs depend on the contributions of others. The population becomes concentrated, instead of being widely distributed, as it is when subsistence depends solely on food gathering; cities develop; and communication and transportation become more efficient.

Observe the overtones of developmentalism in Durkheim's theory of the division of labor. The distinction he draws between segmentary and generalized social systems corresponds to the difference between primitive and civilized societies, and his explanation of what division of labor brings about describes what happens as civilization develops from primitivity.

Durkheim continues his comparison of primitive and civilized society as he examines the functions of division of labor. The conclusion he comes to has been familiar since the writings of Ibn Khaldun, Aristotle, and Plato. The most remarkable consequence, he finds, lies not simply in increasing the number of tasks performed in a society by specialists, but in those tasks becoming a new basis of social solidarity. The people who perform complementary activities in society seek and require each other (just as spouses do in the family), and their needs bring them into frequent contact. The social integration produced by division of labor he calls organic solidarity.

In the course of marshaling evidence in support of this functional thesis, Durkheim draws other comparisons between primitive and civilized society. The former also possesses solidarity, but of a type founded on strict conformity brought about by a collective consciousness (whose main agency is religion) that completely envelops the person, suppressing individuality to the utmost. Mechanical solidarity, as he calls this type, rests on likenesses between individuals and between groups, as well as on the people's affection for one another. The more primitive a society, the more do individual members resemble one another physically and mentally. The greater the social homogeneity. Although civilization also promotes similarities, the organic solidarity on which it is founded presumes differences. In a civilized society, the collective consciousness exerts a weaker hold on persons; hence individuals remain diverse, and individual types are highly developed.

Whereas German historical ethnology quickly diffused to the United States to help dislodge the last vestiges of classic evolutionism, French sociology found little welcome in that country. Durkheim's ideas did, however, make a considerable impact in England where, with the advent of A. R. Radcliffe-Brown, they had a major effect on anthropological thought.

Anthropology in the 19th and early 20th Centuries

Rival Positions, New Topics, and Controversy

The future of anthropology was shaped by four developments that took place during the 19th and early 20th centuries. First, cultural anthropology separated from sociology, though the two subjects continued to share interests and topics, including interest in primitive culture. As a distinct subject, anthropology came to be primarily identified with research on primitive societies, and by that identity it was soon well known, in England at least, to a large, nonprofessional reading public. Second, professional societies were organized to further the aims of anthropology, and men professing the subject found jobs in universities or museums; anthropology thus became a discipline. Third, anthropology became an ethically and morally neutral discipline, one ostensibly value-free though of course deeply committed to methodological and theoretical values. It no longer idealized primitive cultures as the 18th-century philosophers had done, but tried, not always successfully, to view those cultures with unprejudiced naturalistic detachment. Fourth, for the first time several quite distinct theoretical or methodological positions for studying society and culture existed simultaneously, to some extent, or at least potentially, in competition with one another: so-called evolutionism in England, which was on its way out; historical ethnology in Germany, spreading to England as developmentalism there lost ground; and French sociology, destined to cross the Channel when historical ethnology in England gave way, but that didn't happen until after the First World War.

Within developmentalism several quite unrelated theoretical systems were formulated to explain how cultural development occurs; the most influential, it turned out, having been the materialistic interpretation of history authored by Karl Marx and Friedrich Engels. Herbert Spencer explained how society and everything within it becomes more differentiated as it evolves, and succeeded in saying it much more clearly than John Wesley Powell, who also essayed a theory of evolution. Julius Lippert suggested mainsprings of cultural development, but with little originality; his ideas sound like an echo of the 17th and 18th centuries, if not Lucretius. Yet, revised by George Peter Murdock, some of Lippert's suggestions concerning sexual division of labor explain quite logically the bases of domestic social structure. Early in the 20th century energetics made a little-noticed appearance; not until several decades later did Leslie White demonstrate its potential for explaining cultural development.

As in the previous century, anthropologists and other writers published books that were exclusively devoted to society and culture, not to theology or philosophy; but no longer were such works regularly issued with the declared intention of contributing to social reform or guiding the hands of statesmen. The chief object of *Ancient Law*, says Henry Sumner Maine, is to indicate some of the earliest ideas of mankind and to point out their relationship to modern thought. Lewis Henry Morgan offered *Ancient Society* simply because "It is both a natural and proper desire to learn, if possible, how all the ages upon ages of past time have been expended by mankind," and how society has advanced since the time when savagery prevailed. C. Staniland Wake presented *Development of Marriage and Kinship* partly to refute certain theories of John Ferguson McLennan and Morgan. If here and there a 19th-century anthropologist promises social value to reside in his researches, the manner in which he presents his work and the debates in which he engages with his colleagues reveal him to be pursuing subjects primarily because they are inherently problematical or interesting, not because they are relevant to contemporary social issues.

Greater methodological self-consciousness characterizes the period. It reaches a high point in the principles hopefully premised by the German diffusionists for objectively reconstructing culture history, and in the rules Emile Durkheim set out in his aptly titled book, *Rules of Sociological Method*. Concern with method is also revealed in the sharp and relentless criticism of the use made of ethnographic data by the developmentalists for describing early forms of the family, religion, kinship terminology, and other aspects of culture. Similar concern is equally disclosed in the devices that evolutionists invented to escape from their embarrassing lack of direct evidence about the past. I have in mind Edward B. Tylor's concept of survival and the application of statistics to discover, as they thought, elements associated together in the past. Methodological acumen is likewise revealed in the definition of the culture concept, intimations of which were of course present since antiquity, by which cultural anthropology now embracingly defined itself. Other equally or more powerful orienting concepts were coined, many of which remain in our present-day textbooks little altered, for discriminating "capabilities and habits acquired by man as a member of society."

The general pattern of additive growth, indicated by the competing approaches, methodological innovations, several theories of development, and expanding number of orienting concepts, is further illustrated by the new topics and interests added to anthropology. The study of kinship terminology almost immediately experienced cumulative development as ideas underwent critical examination. In time, McLennan's and Alfred L. Kroeber's ideas were rejected, as was even Morgan's interpretation of kin terms being survivals of ancient forms of social structure; but the gist of his theory survived, namely, that a predictable relationship links kin terms to social structure. Other new or partly new topics attracting the students of culture include marriage, cross-cousin marriage, descent and descent groups, totemism, passage rites, technology, material artifacts, games, culture change, and the destructive effects of European contact on the cultures of primitive people, the latter being one of the few instances where ethical overtones intrude on the dispassionate tone with which cultural research is conducted. Anthropologists did morphological analyses of cere- monies, and took new leads into cultural semiotics, as did psychoanalysts who had an interest in culture. Older topics and theories continued to be discussed: intellectualistic and emotionalistic theories of religion and magic; the functional value of the incest rule for avoiding role conflict, now extended to descent groups; and religious ritual, with some tendency (in Durkheim's work) to generalize the concept of ritual as Thomas Hobbes had done to include other ceremonialism. Diffusion—how and when it occurs—became a topic of major importance, in conformance to the paramount significance attached to the process itself as a factor in culture building.

Controversy enlivened a number of topics, in the exchanges between McLennan and Morgan and between Krober and W. H. R. Rivers, with advantage to their cumulative development. The presumption of early promiscuity and group marriage, the origin and development of incest rules, totemism, descent groups, religion, and magic, and the methods of the classical evolutionists were all vigorously debated.

All the viewpoints and themes make an appearance during the period, though naturally not in equal measure. Along with general acceptance of psychic unity, the psychological viewpoint remained popular. We meet it especially in the psychogenic explanations freely coined by developmen- talists, as well as by diffusionists and by the psychoanalyst Sigmund Freud. Nor did the French sociologists wholly escape the temptation to seek easy knowledge by inventing mental factors, though as the name implies, and as Durkheim advocated, the French students of society preferred socio- genic explanations. French sociology and historical materialism both stress the collectivity over the individual; and so, with less programmatic fanfare, does Morgan's and Rivers's theory of kinship terminology, in contrast to Kroeber's theory—edged out by the former—that the terms express psycho- logical distinctions. The historical viewpoint, aided by archeological dis- coveries, was more zealously taken up than before in anthropological thought, but with different emphases in Tylor's diffusionist interests, in the well-worked-out methodology of the German diffusionists, and in the small group of scholars—Maine, Marx, Johann Bachofen, and Fustel de Coulanges—who relied on historical materials to reconstruct features of ancient social structure. Everyone agreed on the integration of culture, and many writers noted particular examples of the utilitarian value of culture. Almost alone, Leo Frobenius leaned toward a configurational perspective. Though the significance of cultural context for discovering relative mean- ing was now and then appreciated, especially by the diffusionists, philo- sophical relativism remained muted. On the whole, the tendency was to treat society or culture as a realm qualitatively different from the realm of physical nature and as possessing its own laws or principles. Nature, however, plays a role in social life—even a psychogenesist like Adolf Bastian admitted it, and the kinship researchers recognized it, too, since every system of kinship terminology bears some relationship to the facts of procreation.

In retrospect, as far as the development of anthropological ideas is concerned, the late 19th and early 20th centuries appear as an unstable period, marked more by agreed-upon dissatisfaction with the past than by consensus on what would be a sounder method of research or better concepts for grasping the experiences of man in society. Even if the methods and concepts put forward in the period didn't satisfy everyone, the more notable contributions—historical materialism, psychoanalysis, French sociology, kin-term theory, and concern for adequate historical documentation—still prevail in anthropology.

Notes

1. John Stuart Mill, *The Spirit of the Age* [orig. 1831] (Chicago: University of Chicago Press, 1942), pp. 72–92.

2. Robert H. Lowie, *The History of Ethnological Theory* (New York: Rinehart and Co., 1937), pp. 88–89; Marvin Harris, *The Rise of Anthropological Theory* (New York: Thomas Y. Crowell Co., 1968), pp. 169–170.

3. Leo Frobenius, "Die Weltanschauung der Naturvölker" [orig. 1898], in Leo Frobenius, *Ausfahrt von der Völkerkunde zum Kulturproblem* (Frankfurt a. Main: Frankfurter Societäts-Druckerei G. M. B. H., 1925).

4. James G. Frazer, "Fison and Howitt" [orig. 1909], in James G. Frazer, *The Gorgon's Head* (London: Macmillan & Co., 1927), p. 302.

5. Sol Tax, "The Integration of Anthropology," in William L. Thomas, Jr., ed., *Yearbook of Anthropology—1955* (New York: Wenner-Gren Foundation for Anthropological Research, 1955).

6. Frazer coined "social anthropology" in 1908; see his "The Scope of Social Anthropology," in James G. Frazer, *Psyche's Task* [orig. 1913] (2nd ed.; London: Dawsons of Pall Mall, 1968). "Sociology" is used in

W. H. R. Rivers, "Kin, Kinship," in *Encyclopaedia of Religion and Ethics* (1915), vol. 7. See also Meyer Fortes, *Social Anthropology at Cambridge Since 1900* (Cambridge: At the University Press, 1953), pp. 3–4.

7. Edward B. Tylor, *Anthropology* [orig. 1881] (Ann Arbor Paperback ed.; Ann Arbor: University of Michigan Press, 1960), p. 275; Edward Caird, *The Evolution of Religion* (Glasgow: James Maclehose and Sons, 1893), pp. 26–27; Daniel G. Brinton, "The Aims of Anthropology," in *Proceedings of the 44th Meeting of the American Association for the Advancement of Science* (1895), pp. 13–15; John Lubbock, *The Origin of Civilisation and the Primitive Condition of Man* (London: Longmans, Green, and Co., 1875), p. 5.

8. Henry Sumner Maine, *Dissertations on Early Law and Custom* [orig. 1890] (London: John Murray, 1901), ch. 7.

9. William H. Holmes, "Use of Textiles in Pottery Making and Embellishment," *American Anthropologist* vol. 3 (1901): 397–403.

10. Karl Marx, "Preface" to *A Contribution to the Critique of Political Economy* [orig. 1859], in Karl Marx and

Frederich Engels, *Selected Works* (2 vols.; Moscow: Foreign Languages Publishing House, 1958), vol. 1.

11. W. H. R. Rivers, "Ships and Boats," in *Encyclopaedia of Religion and Ethics* (1915), vol. 11.

12. W. H. R. Rivers, "The Psychological Factor," in W. H. R. Rivers, ed., *Essays on the Depopulation of Melanesia* (Cambridge: At the University Press, 1922).

13. W. H. R. Rivers, "Report on Anthropological Research Outside America," in W. H. R. Rivers, A. E. Jenks, and S. G. Morley, *Reports upon the Present Condition and Future Needs of the Science of Anthropology* (Carnegie Institution of Washington Publication No. 200, 1913), p. 11; Marcel Mauss, *The Gift* [orig. 1925], trans. Ian Cunnison (London: Cohen and West, 1970), pp. 76–77.

14. See, for example, J. W. Powell, "Relation of Primitive Peoples to Environment, Illustrated by American Examples," in *Annual Report of the Board of Regents of the Smithsonian Institution to July, 1895* (1896). Also Wundt's folk psychology had this object; see Alexander Goldenweiser, "Wilhelm Wundt's Theories" [orig. 1922], in Alexander Goldenweiser, *History, Psychology, and Culture* (New York: Alfred A. Knopf, 1933).

15. W. H. R. Rivers, *Social Organization*, W. J. Perry, ed. (New York: Alfred A. Knopf, 1924), p. 3.

16. Edward B. Tylor, *Primitive Culture* [orig. 1871], reprinted in two volumes, each bearing a separate title: *The Origins of Culture* [Part 1 of *Primitive Culture*] (Torchbook ed.; Harper and Brothers, 1958), pp. 296–297; *Religion in Primitive Culture* [Part 2 of *Primitive Culture*] (Torchbook ed.; Harper and Brothers, 1958), pp. 285–290, 299–303, 328–329, 477. Edward B. Tylor, *Researches into the Early History of Mankind and the Development of Civilization* [orig. 1865; 3rd ed., 1878], abridged from 3rd ed. by Paul Bohannan, ed. (Phoenix Books ed.; Chicago: University of Chicago Press, 1964), pp. 100–105.

17. Marcel Mauss, *A General Theory of Magic* [orig. 1904], trans. Robert Brain (London: Routledge and Kegan Paul, 1972).

18. Gustav Klemm, "Grundideen zu einer allgemeinen Kultur-wissenschaft," in *Sitzungsberichte der kaiserlichen Akademie der Wissenschaften, philosophisch-historisches Classe* (1851), Band 7, Heft 2, pp. 167–190. "Science of Culture" is the title of the first chapter in Tylor's *Primitive Culture*, see Tylor, *Origins of Culture*, pp. 1–21.

19. The method I describe remained largely implicit, with its justification not spelled out. For a faint attempt at making it explicit see Frazer, "The Scope of Social Anthropology," pp. 164–172. In the manner of Adam Ferguson and other 18th-century philosophers, the 19th-century evolutionists were not blind to the method's shortcomings; see Tylor, *Origins of Culture*, p. 16. The note-taking used in conjunction with the method was often elaborate, as we see in Herbert Spencer, *Descriptive Sociology* (New York: D. Appleton, 1873–1933) and James G. Frazer, *The Native Races of Africa and Madagascar*, Robert Angus Downie, ed. (London: Percy Lund Humphries and Co., 1938).

20. Lewis Henry Morgan, *Systems of Consanguinity and Affinity of the Human Family* (Smithsonian Contributions to Knowledge, vol. 17, 1871), pp. 498–508.

21. Georg Gerland, *Anthropologische Beiträge* (Halle: Lippert [M. Niemeyer], 1875), pp. 461ff.

22. J. W. Powell, "Sketch of Lewis H. Morgan," *The Popular Science Monthly*, vol. 18 (1880–1881): 114–121; Bernhard J. Stern, *Lewis Henry Morgan, Social Evolutionist* (Chicago: University of Chicago Press, 1931); Leslie A. White, "Lewis Henry Morgan: Pioneer in the Theory of Social Evolution," in Harry Elmer Barnes et al., *An Introduction to the History of Sociology* (Chicago: University of Chicago Press, 1948); Carl Resek, *Lewis Henry Morgan American Scholar* (Chicago: University of Chicago Press, 1960). See also Bernhard J. Stern, "Lewis Henry Morgan:

An Appraisal of his Scientific Contributions," in Bernhard J. Stern, *Historical Sociology* (New York: Citadel Press, 1959); Leslie A. White, "Introduction," in Lewis H. Morgan, *Ancient Society* [orig. 1877], Leslie A. White, ed. (Cambridge: Belknap Press of Harvard University Press, 1964).

23. Morgan, *Systems of Consanguinity.*

24. Morgan, *Ancient Society.*

25. Frederich Engels, *The Origin of the Family, Private Property and the State; in the Light of the Researches of Lewis H. Morgan* [orig. 1884], Eleanor Burke Leacock, ed. (New York: International Publishers, 1972).

26. Frederich Engels, "Introduction to *Dialectics of Nature*" [written in 1875–1876], and "The Part Played by Labour in the Transition from Ape to Man" [written in 1876], in Marx and Engels, *Selected Works,* vol. 2, pp. 74, 80–84.

27. Karl Marx, *Selected Writings in Sociology and Social Philosophy* [orig. 1841–1880], trans. T. B. Bottomore, T. B. Bottomore and Maximilien Rubel, eds. (Pelican Books ed.; Harmondsworth: Penguin Books, 1963), pp. 67–81. Karl Marx, "The Eighteenth Brumaire of Louis Bonaparte" [orig. 1852], Frederick Engels, "Socialism, Utopian and Scientific" [written in 1877], Frederick Engels, "Ludwig Feuerbach and the End of the Classical German Philosophy" [written in 1886] and Engels's letter to Bloch, September 21–22, 1890, all in Marx and Engels, *Selected Works,* vol. 1, p. 272; vol. 2, pp. 96–98, 102–103, 136, 390–393, 488.

28. Karl Marx, "Economic and Philosophical Manuscripts" [written in 1844], trans. T. B. Bottomore, in Erich Fromm, *Marx's Concept of Man* (New York: Frederick Ungar Publishing Co., 1961), pp. 93–109; see also Fromm's discussion, pp. 43–58.

29. The sequence described here is largely from *The German Ideology* by Karl Marx and Friedrich Engels, written in 1845–1846 but not published completely until much later, and Marx's *A Contribution to Political Economy,* [orig. 1859]. I am following the summary in Stephen

Warner, "The Methodology of Marx's Comparative Analysis of Modes of Production," in Ivan Vallier, ed., *Comparative Methods in Sociology* (Berkeley: University of California Press, 1971), pp. 53–60.

30. Robert L. Carneiro, "Structure, Function, and Equilibrium in the Evolutionism of Herbert Spencer," *Journal of Anthropological Research,* vol. 29 (1973): 77–95.

31. Herbert Spencer, *An Autobiography* (2 vols.; New York: D. Appleton and Co., 1904).

32. Spencer, *An Autobiography,* p. 309.

33. Herbert Spencer, *The Principles of Sociology* [orig. 1883–1907] (Westminster [3rd] ed.; 2 vols. in 5; New York: D. Appleton and Co., 1896), vol. 1, parts 1 and 2. (By "part" I mean the divisions set up by Spencer, not the divisions into which each of the Westminster volumes is divided.) See also Carneiro, "Structure, Function, and Equilibrium."

34. R. R. Marett, *Tylor* (London: Chapman and Hall, 1936), ch. 1; Abram Kardiner and Edward Preble, *They Studied Man* (Cleveland: World Publishing Co., 1961), pp. 56–77; Godfrey Lienhardt, "Edward Tylor," in Timothy Raison, ed., *The Founding Fathers of Social Science* (Harmondsworth, Penguin Books, 1969), p. 84.

35. For the dispute with Spencer, see *Mind,* vol. 2 (1877): 415–429.

36. What follows, unless otherwise noted, is from three books by Tylor: *Early History of Mankind* and the two volumes of *Primitive Culture* reprinted as *Origins of Culture* and *Religion in Primitive Culture.*

37. Tylor, *Religion in Primitive Life.*

38. Edward B. Tylor, "On a Method of Investigating the Development of Institutions; Applied to Laws of Marriage and Descent," *Journal of the Anthropological Institute,* vol. 18 (1889): 245–272, p. 246.

39. John Wesley Powell, "From Barbarism to Civilization," *The American Anthropologist,* o.s. vol. 1 (1888): 97–123; John Wesley Powell, "Proper Training and the

Future of the Indians," *The Forum,* vol. 18 (1894–1895): 622–629.

40. Paul Meadows, *John Wesley Powell, Frontiersman of Science* (University of Nebraska Studies, n.s. No. 10, 1952); William Culp Darrah, *Powell of the Colorado* (Princeton: Princeton University Press, 1951); Don D. Fowler, Robert C. Euler, and Catherine S. Fowler, "John Wesley Powell and the Anthropology of the Canyon Country" (Geological Survey Professional Paper No. 670, 1969); John Upton Terrell, *The Man Who Rediscovered America; a Biography of John Wesley Powell* (New York: Weybright and Talley, 1969).

41. What follows is from various works by John Wesley Powell: "On Activial Similarities," in *Third Annual Report of the Bureau of American Ethnology* (1884); "Anthropology," in *Universal Cyclopaedia* (1900), vol. 1; "Competition as a Factor in Human Evolution," *The American Anthropologist,* o.s. vol. 1 (1888); "The Evolution of Religion," *The Monist,* vol. 8 (1898): 183–204; "From Barbarism to Civilization"; "The Growth of Sentiency," *The Forum,* vol. 11 (1889): 157–167; *Truth and Error or the Science of Intellection* (La Salle, Ill., Open Court Publishing Co., 1898), esp. ch. 14.

42. George Peter Murdock, "Introduction," in Julius Lippert, *The Evolution of Culture* [orig. 1886–1887], George P. Murdock, ed. and trans. (New York: Macmillan Co., 1931); Julius Lippert, "An Autobiographical Sketch," *The American Journal of Sociology,* vol. 19 (1913): 145–165.

43. Julius Lippert, *The Evolution of Culture.*

44. Wilhelm Ostwald quoted in Morris E. Opler, "Two Converging Lines of Influence in Cultural Evolutionary Theory," *American Anthropologist,* vol. 64 (1962): 524–547, pp. 526–529.

45. Morgan, *Systems of Consanguinity;* for a more succinct statement see his *Ancient Society,* part 3, chs. 1, 2, 3, and 5.

46. John Ferguson McLennan, *Primitive Marriage: An Inquiry into the Origin and Form of Capture in Marriage Ceremonies* [orig. 1865], Peter Rivière, ed. (Classics in Anthropology ed.; Chicago: University of Chicago Press, 1970).

47. John Ferguson McLennan, "The Classificatory System of Relationships" in J. F. McLennan, *Studies in Ancient History* [orig. 1876] (new ed.; London: Macmillan & Co., 1886), pp. 269–274.

48. Frazer, "Fison and Howitt," pp. 291–331.

49. A. W. Howitt, "Summary and General Conclusions," in Lorimer Fison and A. W. Howitt, *Kamilaroi and Kurnai* [orig. 1880] (Oosterhout N. B.: Anthropological Publications, 1967), p. 319.

50. Tylor, *Anthropology,* pp. 246, 249; Tylor, "Development of Institutions." The term "hologeistic method" refers to using a worldwide sample of cultures for testing, by means of mathematical statistics, theoretical generalizations about human society and culture. See Raoul Naroll, "What Have We Learned from Cross-Cultural Surveys?" *American Anthropologist,* vol. 72 (1970), 1227–1288; p. 1227.

51. G. Elliot Smith, "Introduction: Dr. Rivers and the New Vision in Ethnology," in W. H. R. Rivers, *Psychology and Ethnology,* G. Elliot Smith, ed. (New York: Harcourt, Brace and Co., 1926); J. L. Myres, "W. H. R. Rivers," *Journal of the Royal Anthropological Institute of Great Britain and Ireland,* vol. 53 (1923): 14–17; H. R. Hays, *From Ape to Angel* (New York: Alfred A. Knopf, 1958), p. 288.

52. W. H. R. Rivers, "On the Origin of the Classificatory System of Relationship," in W. H. R. Rivers et al., eds., *Anthropological Essays Presented to Edward Burnett Tylor* (Oxford: Clarendon Press, 1907); W. H. R. Rivers, *Kinship and Social Organization* [orig. 1914] (London School of Economics Monographs on Social Anthropology, no. 34, 1968); W. H. R. Rivers, "Kin, Kinship" and "Mother-Right," in *Encyclopaedia of Religion and Ethics* (1916), vols. 7, 8; W. H. R. Rivers, *Social Organization.*

184 The Development of Anthropological Ideas

53. For similar ideas see J. Kohler, "Urgeschichte der Ehe" [orig. 1897] cited in Robert H. Lowie, *Primitive Society* [orig. 1920] (Torchbook ed.; New York: Harper and Brothers, 1962), p. 61.

54. Julian H. Steward, "Alfred Lewis Kroeber, 1876–1960," *American Anthropologist,* vol. 63 (1961): 1038–1060.

55. A. L. Kroeber, "Classificatory Systems of Relationship" [orig. 1909] in A. L. Kroeber, *The Nature of Culture* (Chicago: University of Chicago Press, 1952). For Rivers's response see W. H. R. Rivers, *Kinship and Social Organization,* p. 95.

56. A. L. Kroeber, "*California Kinship Systems,*" *University of California Publications in American Archaeology and Ethnology,* vol. 12 (1917): 339–396, pp. 382–390; A. L. Kroeber, *Zuni Kin and Clan* (*Anthropological Papers of the American Museum of Natural History,* vol. 18, part 2 [1917]); A. L. Kroeber, "Kinship in the Philippines" [orig. 1919], "Kinship and History," [orig. 1936], and "Introduction" to part 2, all in A. L. Kroeber, *The Nature of Culture,* (Chicago: University of Chicago Press, 1952).

57. A. L. Kroeber, "Introduction" to part 2 in Kroeber, *The Nature of Culture,* pp. 172–173.

58. Emile Durkheim, Review of Ernst Grosse, *Die Formen der Familie und die Formen der Wirthschaft, L'Année sociologique,* (1897): 319–332; A. M. Hocart, "Kinship Systems" [orig. 1937], in J. Middleton and P. Bohannan, eds., *Kinship and Social Organization* (Garden City, N.Y.: Natural History Press, 1968).

59. Gustav Klemm, "Grundideen," p. 76. Ernst Grosse cites the evidence in *Die Formen der Familie und die Formen der Wirthschaft* (Freiburg i.B.: J. C. B. Mohr, 1896).

60. Northcote W. Thomas, *Kinship Organisations and Group Marriage in Australia* (Cambridge: At the University Press, 1906), ch. 12, but see also ch. 9; Bronislaw Malinowski, *The Family Among the Australian Aborigines* [orig. 1913] (New York: Schocken Books, 1963), pp. 113–115, 121 ff.

61. Charles Darwin, *The Descent of Man* [orig. 1871], cited in Elsie Clews Parsons, *The Family* (New York: G. P. Putnam's Sons, 1906), p. 146.

62. Carl Nicolai Starcke, *The Primitive Family* (London: Kegan Paul, Trench, and Co., 1889), pp. 229, 241–242, 256–260.

63. C. Staniland Wake, *The Development of Marriage and Kinship* [orig. 1889], Rodney Needham, ed. (Chicago: University of Chicago Press, 1967), chs. 1–4.

64. Edward Westermarck, *A Short History of Marriage* [orig. 1926; based on the 5th ed. of his *The History of Human Marriage,* orig. 1891] (New York: Macmillan Co., 1930), pp. 2–6, 18, 29, 80–96.

65. Edward Westermarck, *Memories of My Life,* trans. Anna Barwell (New York: Macaulay Co., 1929).

66. Cited in M. A. Czaplicka, *Aboriginal Siberia* (Oxford: Clarendon Press, 1914), pp. 98–99.

67. James George Frazer, *Folk-Lore in the Old Testament* (3 vols.; London: Macmillan & Co., 1919), vol. 2, pp. 193–220; for parallel cousin marriage among the Arabs, pp. 255–263.

68. Johann Jakob Bachofen, "Mother Right" [orig. 1861] and "My Life in Retrospect," in J. J. Bachofen, *Myth, Religion, and Mother Right,* trans. Ralph Manheim (Princeton: Princeton University Press, 1967), and for additional biographical material see Joseph Campbell's "Introduction" to the book.

69. Morgan, *Ancient Society,* pp. 297, 428.

70. Henry Sumner Maine, *Ancient Law* [orig. 1861] (Everyman's Library ed.; London: J. M. Dent and Sons, 1917). For anthropologists' appraisals of Maine, see Robert Redfield, "Maine's Ancient Law in the Light of Primitive Societies," *The Western Political Quarterly,* vol. 3 (1950): 574–589; Henry Orenstein, "The Ethnological Theories of Henry Sumner Maine," *American Anthropologist,* vol. 70 (1968): 264–276.

71. Kenneth E. Bock, "The Contribution of Henry Maine," *Comparative Studies in Society and History*, vol. 16 (1974); 232–262.

72. Numa Denis Fustel de Coulanges, *The Ancient City* [orig. 1864], trans. Anonymous (Garden City, N.Y.: Doubleday, 1956), pp. 56–59.

73. John R. Swanton, "The Social Organization of American Tribes," *American Anthropologist*, vol. 7 (1905): 663–673. The same conclusion minus documentation is given in Grosse, *Formen der Familie*, p. 319.

74. Thomas, *Kinship Organisations*, p. 15.

75. Rivers, "Mother-Right."

76. Robert H. Lowie, "Social Organization [orig. 1914], in Robert H. Lowie, *Selected Papers in Anthropology*, Cora Du Bois, ed. (Berkeley: University of California Press, 1960), pp. 24–31.

77. Thomas, *Kinship Organisations*, pp. 16–23.

78. Wake, *Development of Marriage*, p. 268, also Rodney Needham's introduction to the book, p. xxvi.

79. Rivers, "Mother-Right," p. 851.

80. McLennan, *Primitive Marriage*.

81. Tylor, "Development of Institutions," p. 267. One can trace the germ of Tylor's explanation back to 1878 in his *Early History of Mankind*, pp. 285–286.

82. James Jasper Atkinson, *Primal Law* (New York: Longmans, Green, and Co., 1903).

83. Morgan, *Ancient Society*, part 3, ch. 4.

84. Frazer, *Folk-Lore in the Old Testament*, pp. 231–235.

85. Starcke, *The Primitive Family*, p. 232.

86. Edward Westermarck, *The Future of Marriage in Western Civilisation* (New York: Macmillan Co., 1936), pp. 258–259. Ernest Crawley also regarded incest rules in descent groups as generalizations of incest avoidance in the nuclear family. The latter he derived from fear of pollution through any kind of strong contact with intimates. See Ernest Crawley, *The Mystic Rose* (London: Macmil-

lan & Co., 1902), pp. 214–215, 398, 443–450.

87. Frazer, *Psyche's Task*, pp. 84, 95–96.

88. Tylor, *Religion in Primitive Culture*, p. 322; Tylor, "Development of Institutions," p. 268.

89. J. F. McLennan, "Totemism," in *Chamber's Encyclopaedia* (1868), vol. 9.

90. Andrew Lang, *Social Origins* (London: Longmans, Green, and Co., 1903), ch. 8.

91. N. W. Thomas, Review of Andrew Lang, *Social Origins, Man*, vol. 3 (1903): 121–124. For a rejoinder see Andrew Lang, "Marriage Prohibitions," *Man*, vol. 3 (1903): 179–182.

92. James G. Frazer, "The Origin of Totemism" [orig. 1899] and "The Beginnings of Religion and Totemism Among the Australian Aborigines" [orig. 1905], in James G. Frazer, *Totemism and Exogamy* (4 vols.; London: Macmillan & Co., 1910), vol. 1.

93. Sigmund Freud, *Totem and Taboo* [orig. 1913], in *The Basic Writings of Sigmund Freud*, A. A. Brill, ed. and trans. (New York: Modern Library, 1938).

94. Emile Durkheim, *The Elementary Forms of the Religious Life* [orig. 1912], trans. Joseph Ward Swain (New York: Collier Books, 1961), pp. 220–234.

95. Claude Henri de Rouvroy, Comte de Saint-Simon, *The Doctrine of Saint-Simon: An Exposition; First Year, 1828–1829* [orig. 1831], trans. Georg G. Iggers (New York: Schocken Books, 1972); see also Auguste Comte, *The Positive Philosophy of Auguste Comte*, trans. Harriet Martineau (2 vols.; New York: D. Appleton and Co., 1854), vol. 2, pp. 186–225.

96. Fustel de Coulanges, *The Ancient City*.

97. Various writings of Pierre-Joseph Proudhon between 1843 and 1858 cited in Gillian Lindt Gollier, "Theories of the Good Society: Four Views on Religion and Social Change," *Journal for the Scientific*

Study of Religion, vol. 9 (1970): 1–16, pp. 8–9.

98. Friedrich Nietzsche, The Antichrist [orig. 1888] in Friedrich Nietzsche, The Portable Nietzsche, Walter Kaufmann, ed. and trans. (New York: Viking Press, 1954), sect. 16, pp. 582–583.

99. Tylor, Religion in Primitive Culture; Tylor, Early History of Mankind, p. 95.

100. Spencer, Principles of Sociology, vol. 1, part 1, chs. 9 and 10. For a summary see vol. 2, part 6, ch. 16.

101. Andrew Lang, Myth, Ritual, and Religion [orig. 1887] (new ed.; 2 vols.; New York: Longmans, Green, and Co., 1899), vol. 1, pp. 308–317; Andrew Lang, "The Supreme Being and Totems in Saráwak: A Note in Reply to Mr. McDougall," Man, vol. 2 (1902), pp. 107–108.

102. John Sutherland Black, The Life of William Robertson Smith (London: Black, 1912); James G. Frazer, "William Robertson Smith" [orig. 1894], in Frazer, The Gorgon's Head.

103. William Robertson Smith, Lectures on the Religion of the Semites [orig. 1889] (3rd ed.; New York: Macmillan Co., 1927); William Robertson Smith, "Sacrifice," in Encyclopaedia Britannica (9th ed., 1889), vol. 21.

104. Freud, Totem and Taboo, pp. 905–908, 913–918, 923–925, 927–928; Sigmund Freud, Moses and Monotheism [orig. 1937], trans. Katherine Jones (New York: Alfred A. Knopf, 1939), part 3, sects. 7–9.

105. Robert R. Holt, "Freud, Sigmund," International Encyclopedia of the Social Sciences (1968), vol. 6.

106. Durkheim, Elementary Forms. For selected passages from this and other writings on religion, see Emile Durkheim, Selected Writings, Anthony Giddens, ed. and trans. (Cambridge: At the University Press, 1972), ch. 11.

107. Henri Peyre, "Durkheim: The Man, His Time, and His Intellectual Background," in Emile Durkheim, Essays on Sociology and Philosophy,

Kurt H. Wolff, ed. (Torchbooks ed.; New York: Harper & Row, 1964).

108. Henri Hubert and Marcel Mauss, Sacrifice [orig. 1899], trans. W. D. Halls (London: Cohen and West, 1964).

109. L. Lévy-Bruhl, "In Memoriam: Marcel Mauss," L'Année sociologique, troisième série (1948–1949), (1951); 1–4; Steven Lukes, "Mauss, Marcel" International Encyclopedia of the Social Sciences (1968), vol. 10. See also Seth Leacock, "The Ethnological Theory of Marcel Mauss," American Anthropologist, vol. 56 (1954): 58–73.

110. Mauss, Gift.

111. Durkheim, Elementary Forms, pp. 488–489.

112. Arnold van Gennep, The Semischolars [orig. 1911], Rodney Needham, ed. and trans. (London: Routledge and K. Paul, 1967).

113. Arnold van Gennep, The Rites of Passage [orig. 1908], trans. Monica B. Vizedom and Gabrielle L. Caffee (Chicago: University of Chicago Press, 1960).

114. Durkheim, Elementary Forms, bk. 3, ch. 2, sect. 5; ch. 3, sect, 3; ch. 5, sect. 2.

115. ". . . whether those words and actions be sincere, or feigned: . . . they appear as signs of honouring," according to Thomas Hobbes, Leviathan (Collier Books, ed.; New York: Crowell-Collier Publishing Co., 1962), pp. 466–467.

116. Not entirely neglecting it, however, as the following references testify: Tylor, Religion in Primitive Culture, ch. 13; Robert Ranulph Marett, "Religion, Primitive Religion," in Encyclopaedia Britannica (14th ed., 1929), vol. 19; Robert Ranulph Marett, Sacraments of Simple Folk (Oxford: Clarendon Press, 1933).

117. Spencer, Principles of Sociology, vol. 2, part 4, chs. 1–12.

118. Lippert, Evolution of Culture, pp. xxiii, 92–95, 102, 112–129, 352, 378–379, 421–459, 476–503.

119. Smith, "Sacrifice."

120. Crawley, Mystic Rose; Ernest

Crawley, *The Tree of Life* (London: Hutchinson, 1905).

121. Frazer, "William Robertson Smith," pp. 286–287.

122. Robert Ranulph Marett, *The Threshold of Religion* (London: Methuen, 1909), chs. 1–2.

123. Marett, "Religion, Primitive Religion."

124. Robert Ranulph Marett, *A Jerseyman at Oxford* (London: Oxford University Press, 1941); Leonhard Adam, "In Memoriam, Robert Ranulph Marett, M. A., D. Sc., Hon. D. Litt. (Oxon.), Hon. Ll. D. (St. Andrews), F. B. A. (13th June, 1866–28th February, 1943)," *Oceania*, vol. 14 (1944): 183–190.

125. Sigmund Freud, *Civilization and Its Discontents* [orig. 1929], trans. Joan Riviere (London: Hogarth Press, 1957); Sigmund Freud, *The Future of an Illusion* [orig. 1927], trans. W. D. Robson-Scott (Doubleday Anchor Books; New York: Doubleday and Co., 1957).

126. On magic, see the following works by Edward B. Tylor: *The Origins of Culture*, p. 112 ff., where he calls it "occult science"; *Early History of Mankind*, pp. 101 ff.; *Anthropology*, p. 201, where magic is included in the chapter on science; "Magic," in *Encyclopaedia Britannica* (9th ed., 1875), vol. 15.

127. For other 19th-century views, predating or contemporary with Tylor's, see Georg Wilhelm Friedrich Hegel, *Lectures on the Philosophy of Religion* [orig. 1832], trans. E. B. Speirs and J. B. Sanderson (London: K. Paul, Trench, Trübner, 1895), vol. 1, pp. 302–303; Adolf Bastian, *Die Rechtsverhältnisse bei verschiedenen Völkern der Erde* (Berlin: Verlag von Georg Reimer, 1872), pp. 242–245; Viktor Rydberg, *The Magic of the Middle Ages* [orig. 1865], trans. August Hjalmar Edgren (New York: Henry Holt and Co., 1879), pp. 52–55.

128. Hegel, *Philosophy of Religion*, vol. 1, pp. 290–293, 297–298, 306–307. The pages I cite include the familiar distinction, popularized by Frazer, that magic seeks to control spiritual powers, whereas religion entreats favors from them, as well as the idea that magic conceives of natural phenomena as being widely interrelated, everything governing everything else.

129. James George Frazer, "Memories of My Parents," in James G. Frazer, *Creation and Evolution in Primitive Cosmogonies and Other Pieces* (London: Macmillan & Co., 1935); Stanley Edgar Hyman, *The Tangled Bank* (New York: Atheneum Publishers, 1962), pp. 187–291, 436–440.

130. James G. Frazer, "June in Cambridge," in Frazer, *The Gorgon's Head*, p. 440.

131. James G. Frazer, *The Golden Bough* [orig. 1890] (2 vols.; New York: Macmillan Co., 1894), pp. 10–12, 30–31. A second three-volume edition appeared in 1900 and a third in 12 volumes in 1911–15.

132. James George Frazer, *The Golden Bough* (one-volume abridged ed.; New York: Macmillan Co., 1942), pp. 49–51.

133. James George Frazer, "Taboo," in *Encyclopaedia Britannica* (9th ed., 1889), vol. 23.

134. Andrew Lang, *Magic and Religion* (London: Longmans, Green, and Co., 1901).

135. Freud, *Totem and Taboo*, pp. 867–879.

136. Durkheim, *Elementary Forms*, pp. 42–46, see also pp. 351–369 on "imitative rites and the principle of causality."

137. Mauss, *Theory of Magic*, esp. chs. 1, 2, 4, and 5.

138. Marett, *Threshold of Religion*, ch. 2; see also Robert Ranulph Marett, "Magic," in *Encyclopaedia of Religion and Ethics*, (1916), vol. 8, pp. 247 ff. where Mauss's influence is apparent.

139. Adolf Bastian, *Der Völkergedanke im Aufbau einer Wissenschaft vom Menschen* (Berlin: Ferd. Dümmlers Verlagsbuchhandlung, 1881); Adolf Bastian, *Ethnische Elementargedanken in der Lehre vom Menschen* (2 vols.; Berlin: Weidmannsche Buchhandlung, 1895), vol. 2, p. 16.

140. Hays, *From Ape to Angel,* ch. 25; Karl von den Steinen, "Gedächtnisrede auf Adolf Bastian," *Zeitschrift für Ethnologie,* vol. 37 (1905): 236–249.

141. Auguste Comte, *Early Essays on Social Philosophy* [orig. 1854], trans. Henry Dix Hutton (new ed.; London: George Routledge & Sons, [1911]), pp. 195ff, esp. p. 208; Emile Durkheim, *The Rules of Sociological Method* [orig. 1895], trans. Sarah A. Solovay and John J. Müller (New York: Free Press of Glencoe, 1964); Alfred Vierkandt, *Die Stetigkeit im Kulturwandel* (Leipzig: Verlag von Duncker & Humblot, 1908), p. 112.

142. Emile Durkheim and Marcel Mauss, *Primitive Classification* [orig. 1903], Rodney Needham, ed. and trans. (Chicago: University of Chicago Press, 1963); Durkheim, *Elementary Forms* pp. 141–151, 433–436.

143. Denying that social divisions form the basis of classification, van Gennep maintained that categories rest on many criteria, including sacredness, utility, external form, and sympathetic correspondence. See van Gennep, *Rites of Passage,* p. 1; also his *L'État actuel du problème totemique,* cited in Claude Lévi-Strauss, *The Savage Mind* (Chicago: University of Chicago Press, 1966), p. 162.

144. Spencer, *Principles of Sociology,* vol. 1, pp. 13–14, 73, 92–93, 759–761; Herbert Spencer, *Social Statics* [orig. 1850] (New York: Robert Schalkenbach Foundation, 1954), pp. 371–372.

145. The following sample of opinion is derived from: Henry R. Schoolcraft, *Notes on the Iroquois* (New York: Bartlett and Welford, 1846); Edward Burnett Tylor, "On Traces of the Early Mental Condition of Man," in *Smithsonian Institution, Annual Report* (1868); Tylor, *Early History of Mankind,* pp. 100–105, 107, 116; Tylor, *Origins of Culture,* vol. 1, pp. 296–297; Lang, *Myth, Ritual, and Religion,* vol. 1, pp. 3–4, 32, 48–50, 96, 104, 157; Durkheim and Mauss, *Primitive Classification,* pp. 5–6; Leo Frobenius, "Stilge-rechte Phantasie," *Internationales Archiv für Ethnographie,* vol. 9 (1896): 129–136, p. 130; John Wesley Powell, "Memorial Address for James Dwight Dana" [orig. 1896], in John Wesley Powell, *Selected Prose of John Wesley Powell,* George Crossette, ed. (Boston: David R. Godine Publisher, 1970), p. 67; Alfred Vierkandt, *Naturvölker und Kulturvölker* (Leipzig, Verlag von Duncker und Humblot, 1896), p. 246; James George Frazer, *Lectures on the Early History of the Kingship* (London: Macmillan & Co., 1905), p. 36; Edwin S. Hartland, *Primitive Paternity* (London: D. Nutt, 1909–10); Edwin S. Hartland, *Ritual and Belief* (London: Williams and Norgate, 1914), pp. 23–24.

146. Alfred Cort Haddon, ed., *Cambridge Anthropological Expedition to Torres Straits Reports,* vol. 2, *Physiology and Psychology* (6 vols. in 7; Cambridge: At the University Press, 1901). For a brief summary see John J. Honigmann, "The Study of Personality in Primitive Societies," in Edward Norbeck, Douglass Price-Williams, and William M. McCord, eds., *The Study of Personality: An Interdisciplinary Appraisal* (New York: Holt, Rinehart and Winston, 1968).

147. Jean Cazeneuve, *Lucien Lévy-Bruhl,* trans. Peter Reviére (Oxford: Basil Blackwell, 1972), pp. ix–xvi.

148. Lucien Lévy-Bruhl, *How Natives Think* [orig. 1910], trans. Lilian A. Clare (London: George Allen and Unwin, 1926), pp. 17–23, 30–37, 61, 68, 71, 77–79, 365–368; Lucien Lévy-Bruhl, *Primitive Mentality* [orig. 1922], trans. Lilian A. Clare (New York: Macmillan Co., 1923), pp. 21, 35, 91–95, 384–385.

149. Alexander Goldenweiser, "L. Lévy-Bruhl's Theories" [orig. 1925], in Goldenweiser, *History, Psychology, and Culture.*

150. W. H. R. Rivers, "The Primitive Conception of Death," in W. H. R. Rivers, *Psychology and Ethnology.*

151. Lucien Lévy-Bruhl, *Les Carnets du Lucien Lévy-Bruhl* (Paris: Presses

Universitaires de France, 1949), pp. 77–79, 135.

152. James George Frazer, *The Golden Bough*, Part 4, *Adonis, Attis, Osiris* (3rd ed.; 2 vols.; London: Macmillan & Co., 1919), vol. 2, ch. 6.

153. Freud, *Totem and Taboo*, ch. 2; Sigmund Freud, "The Taboo of Virginity" [orig. 1918], trans. Angela Richards, in *The Standard Edition of the Complete Works of Sigmund Freud*, James Strachey, ed., vol. 11, *Five Lectures on Psycho-Analysis, Leonardo da Vinci and Other Works* (London: Hogarth Press and the Institute of Psycho-Analysis, 1957).

154. Emile Durkheim, *Incest: The Nature and Origin of the Taboo* [orig. 1898], trans. Edward Sagarin (New York: Lyle Stuart, 1963), pp. 98–100. He is reinterpreting Starcke's theory.

155. Robert Hertz, *The Pre-Eminence of the Right Hand* [orig. 1907–1909] in Robert Hertz, *Death and the Right Hand*, trans. Rodney and Claudia Needham (Glencoe: Free Press, 1960), pp. 89–111, for a brief biographical sketch and appreciation see E. E. Evans-Pritchard's "Introduction."

156. Fritz Schultze, *Psychologie der Naturvölker* (Leipzig: Verlag von Veit und Comp., 1900).

157. Daniel G. Brinton, *The Basis of Social Relations*, Livingstone Farrand, ed. (New York: G. P. Putnam's Sons, 1902).

158. Truman Michelson, "Daniel Garrison Brinton," in *Dictionary of American Biography*, vol. 2 (1930), pp. 50–51.

159. Gabriel Tarde, *On Communication and Social Influence*, [orig. 1888–1903] Terry N. Clark, ed. (Chicago: University of Chicago Press, 1969), pp. 16–18. For his ideas, see Terry N. Clark, "Tarde, Gabriel," in *International Encyclopedia of the Social Sciences* (1968), vol. 15.

160. Thomas S. Kuhn, *The Structure of Scientific Revolutions* (2nd ed.; Chicago: University of Chicago Press, 1970).

161. Daniel G. Brinton, "Arrangement of Material," in Hans F. Helmolt, ed., *The History of the World* (8 vols.; New York: Dodd, Mead and Co., 1902), vol. 1, pp. 16–17.

162. Maine, *Early Law and Custom*, pp. 192, 201, 219.

163. Daniel G. Brinton, *Religions of Primitive People* (New York: Putnam and Company, 1897), p. 24.

164. K. T. Preuss, *Die geistige Kultur der Naturvölker* (Leipzig: B. C. Teubner, 1914), p. 71.

165. Marcel Mauss, Review of F. Byron Jevons, *An Introduction to the History of Religion*, *L'Année sociologique*, (1898): 160–171.

166. Arnold van Gennep, "Un Ethnographe oublié du XVIIIe siècle: J. N. Démeunier," *Revue des Idées*, vol. 7 (1910): 18–28, p. 26.

167. Leonard T. Hobhouse, G. C. Wheeler, and M. Ginsberg, *The Material Culture and Social Institutions of the Simpler Peoples* (London: Chapman and Hall, 1915).

168. Durkheim, Review of Ernst Grosse, *Die Formen der Familie*, p. 327.

169. Patrick Edward Dove, *The Theory of Human Progression* [orig. 1850], abridged by Julia A. Kellogg (New York: Isaac H. Blanchard, 1910).

170. For summaries of paleolithic archeology from this period, see Guillaume Louis Figuier, *Primitive Man* [orig. 1870], ed. (New York: Putnam and Company, 1871); Nicolas Joly, *Man Before Metals* [orig. 1879], trans. anonymous (New York: D. Appleton and Co., 1883); William Johnson Sollas, *Ancient Hunters* (London: Macmillan & Co., 1911).

171. Friedrich Ratzel, "Die afrikanischen Bögen, ihre Verbreitung und Verwandschaften, "*Abhandlungen der Königlichen Sächsische Gesellschaft der Wissenschaften. Philologisch-historichen Classe,* vol. 13 (1891): 291–346; see also his earlier paper, "Über die Stäbchenpanzer und ihre Verbreitung in nordpazifischen Gebiet," *Sitzungsberichte der philosophisch-philologischen und historischen Classe der k. b. Akademie der Wissenschaften zu München,* Heft 2 (1886): 181–216.

172. Leo Frobenius, "Der Ursprung der afrikanischen Kulturen" [orig. 1898], in Frobenius, *Ausfahrt von der Völkerkunde;* Leo Frobenius, "Die Kulturformen Ozeaniens," *Petermanns Geographische Mitteilungen,* vol. 46 (1900): 204–205, 234–238, 262–271; Leo Frobenius, *Paideuma: Umrisse einer Kultur- und Seelenlehre* (Munich: C. H. Beck'sche Verlagsbuchhandlung, 1921).

173. Helmut Straube, "Frobenius, Leo," in *International Encyclopedia of the Social Sciences,* (1968), vol. 6; Ad. E. Jensen, "Leo Frobenius, Leben und Werk," *Paideuma,* vol. 1 (1939–1940): 45–58; Eike Haberland, "Editor's Postscript," in Eike Haberland, ed., *Leo Frobenius* (Wiesbaden: Franz Steiner Verlag GMBH, 1973).

174. Frobenius, *Paideuma,* ch. 2, also pp. 107–111. Significant passages in translation are provided in Haberland, *Leo Frobenius,* pp. 19–55.

175. J. M. Ita, "Frobenius, Senghor and the Image of Africa," in Robin Horton and Ruth Finnegan, eds., *Modes of Thought: Essays on Thinking in Western and Non-Western Societies* (London: Faber and Faber, 1973).

176. Fritz Graebner, "Kulturkreise und Kulturschichten in Ozeanien," *Zeitschrift für Ethnologie,* vol. 37 (1905): 28–53; B. Ankermann, "Kulturkreise und Kulturschichten in Afrika," *Zeitschrift für Ethnologie,* vol. 37 (1905): 54–84; discussion of both papers by the audience follows on pp. 84–90. Fritz Graebner, "Die melanesische Bogenkultur und ihre Verwandten," *Anthropos,* vol. 4 (1909): 726–280, 998–1032, pp. 726–728. Paul Leser, "Fritz Graebner," *Ethnologischer Anzeiger,* vol. 3 (1934): 294–301; Hermann Baumann, "Graebner, Fritz," in *International Encyclopedia of the Social Sciences* (1968), vol. 6.

177. Fritz Graebner, *Methode der Ethnologie* (Heidelberg: Carl Winter's Universitätsbuchhandlung, 1911), pp. 78, 80–94.

178. Martin Gusinde, "Wilhelm Schmidt, S. V. D., 1868–1954," *American Anthropologist,* vol. 56 (1954): 868–870.

179. Wilhelm Schmidt, *The Culture Historical Method of Ethnology* [orig. 1937], trans. S. A. Sieber (New York: Fortuny, 1939); Wilhelm Schmidt, *The Origin and Growth of Religion* [orig. 1930], trans. H. J. Rose (London: Methuen and Co., 1931); Wilhelm Schmidt, "Position of Women with Regard to Property in Primitive Society," *American Anthropologist,* vol. 37 (1935): 244–256.

180. Grafton Elliot Smith, *The Migrations of Early Culture* [orig. 1915] (Manchester: Manchester University Press, 1929): William James Perry, *The Children of the Sun* (London: Methuen and Co., 1923); also T. Wingate Todd, "The Scientific Influence of Sir Grafton Elliot Smith," *American Anthropologist,* vol. 39 (1937): 523–526.

181. James Burnett, Lord Monboddo, *Antient Metaphysics* (6 vols.; London: T. Cadell; Edinburgh: J. Balfour and Co., 1779–1799), vol. 4, bks. 2 and 3.

182. For an early critique, see Haberlandt, M., "Zur Kritik der Lehre von den Kulturschichten und Kulturkreisen," *Petermanns Geographische Mitteilungen,* vol. 57 (1911): 113–118.

183. Robert H. Lowie, "On the Principle of Convergence in Ethnology," *Journal of American Folk-Lore,* vol. 25 (1912): 24–42, pp. 24–27.

184. Vierkandt, *Die Stetigkeit im Kulturwandel.*

185. Gabriel Tarde, *The Laws of Imitation* [orig. 1890], trans. Elsie Clews Parsons (New York: Henry Holt, 1903). For a summary of Tarde's ideas, see Terry N. Clark, "Tarde, Gabriel." Also see Tarde, *Communication and Social Influence,* parts 2 and 3; Lowie, *History of Ethnological Theory,* pp. 106–109.

186. W. H. R. Rivers, *The History of Melanesian Society* (2 vols.; Cambridge: At the University Press, 1914), vol. 2, ch. 15.

187. W. H. R. Rivers, "The Ethnological Analysis of Culture" [orig. 1911],

"Convergence in Human Culture," "The Disappearance of Useful Arts" [orig. 1912], "The Contact of Peoples" [orig. 1913], all in Rivers, *Psychology and Ethnology;* for additional principles see Rivers, *Evolution of Melanesian Society,* ch. 28.

188. My lack of punctuation copies an affectation of this self-educated American geologist who became a field-going anthropologist. W. J. McGee, "The Relation of Institutions to Environment," *Annual Report of the Board of Regents of the Smithsonian Institution to July, 1895* (1896), pp. 704–705.

189. Otis Tufton Mason, *The Origin of Invention* (New York: Charles Scribner's Sons, 1905); for his attitude to diffusion, see his "Similarities in Culture," *American Anthropologist,* vol. 8 o. s. (1895): 101–117.

190. Here I draw on Schoolcraft, *Notes on the Iroquois,* pp. 13, 63, 190; Lewis Henry Morgan, *League of the Ho-de-no sau-nee or Iroquois* [orig. 1851] (2 vols.; New Haven: Human Relations Area Files, 1954), vol. 2, pp. 108–112; James Mooney, *The Ghost-Dance Religion and the Sioux Outbreak of 1890* (14th Annual Report of the Bureau of Ethnology, Part 2, 1896); Rivers, "Psychological Factor"; Franz Boas, "Summary of the Work of the Committee in British Columbia," *Report of the British Association for the Advancement of Science, 1898* (1899), p. 682; Adolf Bastian, *Die Vorgeschichte der Ethnologie* (Berlin: Ferd. Dümmlers Verlagsbuchhandlung, 1881), pp. 64–65.

191. Otis Tufton Mason, *Woman's Share in Primitive Culture* (New York: D. Appleton and Co., 1894), pp. 274–275.

192. These ideas are chiefly found in Durkheim, *Rules of Sociological Method.* I recommend Durkheim, *Selected Writings,* chs. 1–2, which includes brief excerpts from other writings.

193. Emile Durkheim, *The Division of Labor in Society* [orig. 1893], trans. George Simpson (New York: Free Press of Glencoe, 1964), esp. pp. 256–268. For generous excerpts of the book, see Durkheim, *Selected Writings,* ch. 6.

6

The American Historical Tradition

Continuity and Change

History and Process

A tradition arises when people within a span of time take a similar approach to something, be it pottery-making, sculpting, painting pictures, or doing cultural anthropology. Once started, the approach is primarily governed from within; if external influences grow too strong, the tradition alters drastically. Members of the American Historical Tradition—Franz Boas and his contemporaries, who were frequently his students, Alfred Kroeber, Robert Louie, Leslie Spier, and others—pursued closely related interests. They communicated within a common frame of meaning. They echoed, frequently rephrasing, one another's ideas (usually without citing sources, making it hard to trace the route by which an idea attained a specific form of expression). Even their controversies possessed coherence, because the protagonists disputed over familiar assumptions and methods. The Tradition they directed matured and weakened between the two World Wars in an intellectual climate marked by unadulterated social environmentalism. Instead of emphasizing essence or being, as do concepts of instinct, race, or psychic unity, social scientists kept their eyes fixed on becoming, achievement, and change. Psychologists studied individual development as a product of inescapable social influences capable of leading to good or evil outcomes. Liberal reformers asserted the rights of workers, pupils in school, the poor, and the modal citizen against the influence of

---

Notes for this chapter begin on page 223.

big corporations and financial interests. The view that the social environment is almost all-important in its power to confer benefits and injuries waxed strongest during the New Deal.[1]

The American Historical Tradition belongs to the paradigm I have called historical ethnology, though we will see it did not agree with all the assumptions and methods of the German and British diffusionists. Like the latter, Boas and his contemporaries turned their backs on the comparative method of the evolutionists. They not only rejected the method, they were little interested in the details of long-range cultural development, although they never denied that culture had progressed from simple beginnings to stupendous complexity. The Tradition's name, coming from one of its major aims—namely, to reconstruct the histories of cultures which have left no written records—reflects its kinship with Continental historical ethnology. For Boas, the primary object in studying particular cultures or culture areas was to investigate their histories, using archeology, careful field work (in which the smallest, most commonplace detail—the pattern of a moccasin, the number of poles supporting a tipi—might be an important clue to historical relationships), and mapped geographical distributions.[2] He does not mention consulting available written documents left by literate societies that had contact with primitive contemporaries, sources ethnohistorians later found useful. Mapping culture traits and interpreting the distributions with the aid of general principles closely resembles the technique German diffusionists employed, but the Americans soon abandoned it as too deductive and unconvincing.[3] How much the Americans' orientation toward historical reconstruction owes to Continental diffusionism remains for a historian to say. The leading American historical ethnologists—Boas, Kroeber, Alexander Goldenweiser, and Lowie —felt at ease with Continental languages. Except Boas, they had not studied anthropology in Europe; but reading German presented no difficulty for them, either because they had been born in Europe or, in the case of Kroeber, grew up in a German household and neighborhood.

The American ethnologists' preoccupation with history should be kept in perspective. Behind their search for the complex relations of cultures, a more important goal initially lured Boas and a number of his followers, a goal pursued in social science since the Enlightenment. They hoped to learn the processes and causes whereby culture changes and develops, and, later, how culture mediates man's adaptation to nature, his adjustment to himself, and individuals' adjustments to one another in social relationships. Histories and customs, Boas wrote, in 1896, are not the ultimate object of research; anthropology wants to know why customs exist at all. It seeks to discover the environmental and psychological factors shaping culture. By discovering the dynamic factors operating in the histories of particular cultures, and then comparing the histories, general laws governing culture history may be found. In time, however, these inheritors of the Enlightenment disagreed on whether there could be laws of culture at all holding for every or a significant proportion of instances of a designated phenomenon.[4] Boas grew less sanguine about the discovery of such laws between 1896, when he was certain they existed, to 1931, when the general propositions anthropology had asserted struck him as vague and of only limited value in promoting understanding. By 1938, impressed by the unpredictable consequences of inventions and of forceful individuals' roles in history, he outrightly denied the possibility of finding laws of historical development. Kroeber in places acknowledges causal relationships of high probability operating in culture. He speaks of "circular causation" in social facts, exemplified in the links between population growth, specialization of labor by skill, improved technology, and increasing wealth; but he finished his mammoth *Configurations of Culture Growth* in the arts, philosophy, and sciences without having been able to find any necessities regulating the appearance of peaks and declines in those domains.[5] Lowie held firmly to lawfulness in culture, but the number of antecedents involved in every phenomenon stunned him. Almost alone, Alexander Lesser held firm to the deductive method in cross-cultural research to test the validity of suggested laws.[6]

Cultural anthropology changed methodologically and theoretically during the period of the American Historical Tradition. Use of statistics increased in archeology and ethnology. Field work, involving more women than before, intensified. From intensive field work came an enhanced appreciation of individual variability in societies, though the view that most culture traits are uniformly distributed in a tribe (except as affected by specialization) generally prevailed. In a culturally homogeneous society, Lesser thought, an ethnographer needs only a small number of informants in order to construct reliable generalizations about cultural behavior.[7] Social factors in such a group will condition individual behavior, making it conform tightly to group norms. Hence any individual selected at random can be expected to represent a complete microcosm of the group. Ethnologists insisted upon the importance of empirical data and empirical methods to test deductive propositions, and to pin down generalizations. Yet they freely employed qualitative concepts, such as style, pattern, and configuration, whose inherent subjectivity they admitted. Increasingly, they raised questions with psychological overtones: How do individual psychological processes influence culture? What is the place of the individual in culture? Out of such questions, aided by concepts borrowed from psychoanalysis, the culture and personality theory developed. Anthropology in those years became fully professionalized, and graduate school curricula for training anthropologists were set. The subject also reached audiences beyond the university through the medium of popular ethnographies and interpretative works, like Lowie's *Culture and Ethnology* (1917) and Boas's examination of race, nationalism, eugenics, and other timely matters in *Anthropology and Modern Life* (1928). Devoted as the Americans were to studying primitive culture well-nigh exclusively, they hoped the subject would be practically useful in their own society.[8] They wanted their knowledge to be applied so that people would be able to handle customs and deal with culture change as rationally as they planned diets and handled sanitation. The educational importance of anthropology for Boas lay in its power to make us understand the roots of our civilization, and to impress us with the relative value of all cultures, thereby to serve as a check on exaggerated notions of the importance of our own times. Ralph Linton saw the end of anthropology as the understanding and control of human nature and the forces at work in society. The "conquest" of society, he predicted, would exceed in significance even the conquest of interplanetary space.

A Critical Temper

Objections to Evolutionism

No anthropologists' life or work has received as much attention as that of Franz Boas, the German-born son of a prosperous businessman and a woman who founded a kindergarten.[9] In boyhood Boas was attracted to natural history, music, and travel in foreign lands, where he hoped to learn about strange customs. As a university student he specialized in physics before turning to physical and then cultural geography. After consultation with Adolf Bastian, in 1883, the young geographer—Boas was then 25—himself partially financed a scientific visit to the Baffin Island Eskimo. The experience converted him into an ethnologist. Upon returning to Imperial Germany, he worked in the Berlin ethnological museum directed by Bastian and taught geography until, two years later, in 1886, an opportunity allowed him to make the first of many field trips to the coastal Indians of British Columbia.[10] At about this time, alienated from Germany by anti-Semitism, academic intrigues, and threat of conscription, he decided to immigrate to the United States. Here his carrer prospered despite such episodes as the academic storm he promoted at Columbia University, when he spoke out against United States involvement in the European war, for which he held the Germans to be equally guilty with the French and English. Not many years later, further outspokenness caused the American Anthropological Association to rebuke him for condemning American anthropologists who, under the cover of anthropology, secretly carried out intelligence work in Latin America. His esteem rose, nevertheless, to the point where after his death the association that had rebuked him issued two memoirs reviewing his career.

Boas devoted a major part of his writing to combating misconceptions, fallacies, and weaknesses in anthropological theory or method, as well as to errors he perceived in other disciplines and in popular thought. His students joined him in this critical activity, with the result that the American Historical Tradition acquired a strongly critical temper. In the spirit of late 19th-century ethnology, Boas as early as 1896 attacked the methodological mainstay of evolutionism, its version of the comparative method.[11] No way exists, he charged, for taking traits abstracted from contemporary culture and ordering them in a verifiable developmental sequence. Nor can parallels between cultures be taken as sufficient evidence of similar causes operating everywhere; they may arise in a multitude of ways. According to psychogenic evolutionism, all branches of mankind should repeat the same steps of development in approximately the same order; for example, proceed from realistic to geometric art. Available facts deny the theory. Agreed, some cultural traits become increasingly complex with time, but not all reveal such a trend, and retrogression or stagnation can also occur. Progress in culture is most evident in the realm of technology, where advances in knowledge open up new ways of exploiting the natural environment. In social organization, does progress exist at all? Perhaps, but then it is found in changes leading to a wider concept of humanity, which diminish the importance attached to a person's ascribed status. Boas countered the evolutionists with a comparatively modest thesis: instead of civilization being determined by rational processes or psychological necessity leading to uniform development all over the world, each cultural group has its own history. Comparison of those histories reveals differentiation between cultures, as well as a leveling out of differences betwen adjacent groups, the latter being explained as due to diffusion.

Russian-born Alexander Goldenweiser, one of Boas's earliest students,[12] added another argument against the psychogenic concept employed in cultural development.[13] He charged it with exaggerating the importance of the individual, elevating his problem-solving capacity to an unrealistic level of importance. Cultural innovation is not an individual matter but a cooperative enterprise. Nor is it a purely rational process, for unconscious emotional factors also enter into the creation of new ideas.

Yet when the American ethnologists did venture into reconstructions of the state, language, housing, or tools, sometimes looking curiously at other living primates for clues to subhuman cultural beginnings,[14] they rarely referred to Darwinian selective processes at work. Their aim was still to chart the direction taken by some specific cultural feature or by culture as a whole; for example, the long-term trend from amorphousness to definiteness as culture responds to increased content, and people organize the content.[15] In other trends, cultures increasingly disengage themselves from magic, and from the obtrusion of physiological and anatomical considerations present in primitive customs like menstrual sequestration, puberty rites, and body deformations. Clark Wissler, however, shows some influence from evolutionary biology when he identifies increasing specialization in a particular culture as a factor limiting further cultural evolution.[16] Culture in general, however, manages to preserve its potential for evolutionary change thanks to the scepter of power periodically shifting from specialized, involuted groups to more generalized, wilder populations who retain initiative and originality.

Graveyard of Generalizations

Against the evolutionists Boas raised the possibility that parallel traits in different cultures may have different antecedents. Against the extreme diffusionists he maintained that similar conditions can give rise to similar traits, so that one need not resort to diffusion to explain all parallels in culture.[17] Similar innovations have arisen independently more frequently than diffusionists believe—witness their abundance in modern civilization. Applying the comparative method in a fashion different from the evolutionists, Boas's students marshaled evidence against the theory of almost indissoluble culture complexes persisting through time and spreading intact around the world.[18] Totemism, Goldenweiser showed, bears only superficial resemblances from one culture to another, and varies considerably even within a single culture area. Other studies revealed similar looseness between geometric designs and their meanings, games and their purposes, and elements making up myths. The constituents of such complexes, in fact the traits comprising entire cultures, rather than being firmly bonded together come together variously at particular times and places through a series of historical accidents. Then rationalization and other processes take over to integrate the traits and to remove almost all sign of exogenous origin. The chance element in culture history gave comfort to Robert Lowie, despite the firmness with which he held on to the lawfulness of certain cultural relationships.[19] If our civilization from the standpoint of its historical origin resembles a planless hodgepodge, a thing of shreds and patches, we can ignore Herbert Spencer's warning against tampering with the supposed iron laws of cultural evolution. We can adopt social legislation designed to improve people's lives without fear of interfering in the natural process of adaptation.

"Ethnological literature," Otis T. Mason had remarked, "is the graveyard of hasty generalization,"[20] and the American Historical Tradition sought to bury a number of popular ideas contradicted by ethnological data.[21] Criticizing geographical determinism was really reburying a corpse, but Boas thought it necessary and thereby contributed fresh insight into cultural ecology. Diverse cultures often occupy the same environment, he observed, and may avail themselves of environmental resources in many ways or indeed see no use in some. So with racial factors. Their significance for a society depends on how they are interpreted or used, and that depends on the general level of knowledge possessed by the group. How could a theory of racial determinism account for great changes in the lives of a people without demonstrating corresponding alterations in the people's biological constitution? The idea of a parental instinct could be dispensed with, for some societies had found substitutes for parental care. The nonutilitarian ends to which some people devote huge amounts of energy denies the universality of rational economic motives guiding human behavior. The idea of a universal morality deriving from nature seemed still to need correction. Most ethical conventions, anthropologists pointed out, are culturally given. The same holds true for conceptions of normality and abnormality, including the categories of modern psychiatric practice. Psychologists asserting stress to be an inevitable concomitant of adolescence, or animistic thought to occur spontaneously in all children, were proven wrong.[22] Cultural conditions can encourage or suppress those developmental phases. And culture—not biology—determines whether men and women in a society will manifest contrasting temperamental qualities, or conform to a single model of behavior.

While insisting on the autonomy of culture with respect to biology, some writers tempered cultural relativism with biological thinking.[23] Wissler thought there might be an inborn psychophysical basis for the universal features of culture, and he refers to a human drive to culture beyond man's power to arrest. Were culture destroyed, he writes, pre-echoing an ethologist's words half a century later, humans would probably rebuild it. In less novel terms, Ralph Linton explored the biological background of culture and society. He traced culture to man's biological nature, in particular his superior mental equipment, which constitutes an evolutionary adaptation of great value for it enables human beings to transmit behavior once learned, as well as to modify it as the environment changes. Another biological attribute on which all societies are based is the nonseasonal nature of human sexual activity. Together with male dominance, it underlies the family. Male physical superiority is surely the basis for allocating to men vital social tasks, like hunting and defense, and an innate need for emotional response forms the basis of group life. Linton recommended primate studies to find out more about the basic organic structures and potentialities from which culture and society developed. Discouraged by Boas from pursuing a Ph.D. in anthropology at Columbia, he did so at Harvard and graduated. In 1937, a year after Boas retired, he was invited to Columbia University, where he later became head of the department Boas had so long dominated.[24] With his eclectic theoretical outlook, he marks a big shift in the concerns of the American Historical Tradition.

The critical temper of American anthropology in this period was against taking too strong a deductive approach to exotic cultural data. With both the evolutionists and extreme diffusionists in mind, Boas feared any temptation to interpret data by deductive theories.[25] Doing so leads easily to overlooking unexpected important details, unique features of phenomena, or the multiple historical roots of events. He held a rigorously inductive view of science. For him, science meant the collection of facts even when for the moment they lacked relevance. The bias against deductive interpretation favored what came to be known in post-World War II anthropology as an emic point of view. The safest place to find the meaning of an ethnographic fact is in the society being studied. Concepts from the anthropologist's culture can rarely be applied to other ways of life without modification. What we call singing is not the same thing when songs lack words. By ignoring this rule, the evolutionists and European diffusionists committed many fallacies when they drew parallels between different cultural contexts. Boas retained his relativistic conception of meaning to the end of his life, and consequently looked skeptically at the cross-cultural use of psychological tests. Yet he encouraged students who proposed to take theories into the field for testing, perhaps because he knew they would approach the theories critically and would watch vigilantly for contrary facts. Mostly, however, the field workers tended to look for novel problems in every society they studied, and to describe every culture as if it were unique. As a result, a critic within the Tradition observed, anthropology lost opportunities to verify knowledge and to build up a body of tested propositions.[26]

Despite their unfavorable attitude toward deductive thought, but consistent with their belief that cultures do develop, Boas and his students occasionally evaluated cultures.[27] They even cited evidence of progress in the form of growing knowledge and techniques that enhanced control over nature. Lowie, however, protested, saying anthropology had passed the day of evolutionary optimism when cultures could be graded on a scale of relative progress. Kroeber ranked achievements in philosophy, science, art, and similar fields, willingly leaving it to the informed cultural outsider to judge how high a level a society had attained in those fields. More subtle evaluative criteria by Edward Sapir identified a "genuine" culture and contrasted it with a "spurious" one. Inherently harmonious, balanced, unified, consistent, and self-satisfying, a genuine culture may exist in primitive or civilized society.

Culture Theory

Trait, Style, and Pattern

Along with making frequent field trips, usually to western American Indian tribes, American anthropologists between the first and second world wars accumulated and partially systematized a body of concepts and propositions about the nature and structure of culture, relationships between culture and the geographical milieu, the individual's role in culture, and other matters. Clark Wissler's two textbooks and A. L. Kroeber's two editions of a popular textbook summarize many of these concepts.

Wissler majored in psychology while working his way through Purdue University as a schoolteacher.[28] For further professional training he went to Columbia University, obtained the Ph.D., and then deserted psychology to take courses in anthropology. In 1902, he began a long career at the American Museum of Natural History, where he organized his own field trips among the Plains Indians and the field trips of others, including Margaret Mead. Eight years later, upon joining the faculty of Yale University, he brought to Yale's newly founded interdisciplinary Institute of Human Relations a much appreciated interest in combining anthropological and psychological concepts. However, his psychological analysis of culture (given at length in the latter part of *Man and Culture*) made little impact. In contrast, his concept of culture as a temporal and spatial phenomenon gained considerable currency and was fully shared by Kroeber, the first anthropologist to receive a doctorate, in 1901, from Boas's department at Columbia University.[29] Kroeber's German-born bilingual parents educated him in their New York City home before enrolling him in a European-type preparatory school, whence he graduated to Columbia College. He majored in English until, in his senior year, a course with Boas and a chance to work with Eskimo and Chinook Indian informants visiting New York City turned him to anthropology. His professional career in the field lasted over 60 years, most of them spent on the Berkeley campus of the University of California, but with time out for many field trips.

Both Wissler and Kroeber regarded culture as a product of history, the accumulation of countless innovations made by many successive generations.[30] Some cultural innovations, those in technology and science, are rarely lost but become embodied in cumulative developments taking place in those areas. What Wissler started by analyzing culture down to its atomic components, Kroeber finished by his comprehensive conception of culture as a distinct phenomenal realm coterminous with inorganic, organic, and mental phenomena. Item, element, trait, trait-complex, form, style, and pattern are the concepts they used at the basic level.[31] Here a table with plus and minuses to indicate the presence or absence of particular elements can represent the inventory of an entire culture.[32] However, the representation would be somewhat misleading, for elements or traits do not actually exist in disjointed independence; they form part of larger units, complexes, or patterns. Some such interlocked assemblages, for example, maize farming, pottery-making, or plow agriculture, even recur from culture to culture more often than could be accounted for by chance alone. But, as we have seen, American ethnologists were wary of mistaking resemblances as identities, and Kroeber's concept of form duly noted that superficially similar traits and complexes might have different aspects even in adjacent cultures.[33] The same content can take on different meanings, assume different arrangements, or occur with different frequencies. The form that traits take in a culture or the form of an entire culture depends heavily on the volume of content there is to arrange, and on the success with which the members of the society succeed in systematizing an assemblage of traits. Kroeber employs the word "style" for the manner in which activities and human relationships achieve definite shape in a culture,[34] but he extends the word far beyond its use in the fine arts; in his hands it denotes a coherent, consistent way of doing anything: philosophy, science, governing, eating, and so on. Some styles are long-lived, while others—fashions—last only briefly. When several styles exist in a culture, they tend toward consistency; the assemblage of styles in various cultural domains influencing the culture's overall form. Styles often go through a life cycle, reaching an exhaustion point once the creators have attained the ideals they sought. Thereupon the style freezes, becomes slovenly, or deteriorates in other ways. A revolution in style may arise out of a sense of a style having exhausted its possibilities, but even then the new mode of expression may need to fight its way into being.

Patterns in Content and Process

The word "pattern" was used by the Tradition in almost as many senses as "structure" in more recent cultural anthropology. Usually, however, "pattern" refers either to the contents of culture or to the process whereby certain contents become organized.[35] In the first sense, a set of manual habits, a rule of social conduct, even an institution, a style, or a philosophic point of view, are all patterns. "Systemic patterns" is Kroeber's name for trait complexes persisting over very long periods and diffusing as units; plow agriculture and the alphabet are examples. Wisslers' generalization of a universal culture pattern,[36] although more embracive than any of the former concepts, also falls into the first category of meaning. Briefly stated, the concept, which had been recognized since the 18th century and was implicitly held in classical times, envisages a similar ground plan for all cultures, including our own. According to Wissler, the plan encompasses material traits (or technology), dress, utensils, weapons, industries, art, mythology and scientific knowledge, religious practices; family and social systems are subdivided into marriage, kinship relations, inheritance, social control, sports (or games), property, and government.

Kroeber read world culture history as a story of certain kinds of culture patterns pushing toward fulfillment and, in time, expiring.[37] Regularities in history captured his interest as fervently as they had the English evolutionists, their 18th-century predecessors, and earlier social theorists as far back as classical times. Of course, his approach envisioning a life cycle in culture patterns differs from theirs, but it is not wholly original. As he acknowledges, Velleius around the beginning of our era intimated a similar idea. In an early paper, Kroeber reports his discovery of objective trends in fashions of women's evening dress during the short span from 1844 to 1919. The trends comprise both steady tendencies, such as a constant increase in the width and depth of décolletage, and rapid oscillations in the same traits. As to the forces at work directing what is clearly more than a random pattern of change, he confesses himself to be at a loss for an explanation. *Configurations of Culture Growth*, published 25 years later, represents a much more ambitious undertaking at revealing trends in culture history. Using works by philosophers, scientists, painters, dramatists, and other writers belonging to several European and Asian civilizations, he demonstrates how frequently a pattern of endeavor in those fields reached florescence—as rated by contemporaries as well as critics of later times—and then exhausted itself and declined to a level of mere repetition. Patterns in those cultural domains develop cumulatively by a momentum he calls growth. Within a pattern, say of philosophy or painting, or within a set of such patterns—that is, within a whole culture —he demarcates cycles, the pulses within the pattern recurring after temporary lulls of activity. When a set of patterns withers, the civilization has come to an end; its highly rated productions have shrunk in volume. The culture—again in the opinion of contemporary and later critics—has deteriorated. Though Kroeber disclaims any intention to explain growth, he ventures several suggestions concerning the causes of exhaustion. The limits to which a pattern can develop may be set early by the extreme narrowness of the original pattern, thereby restricting scope for growth, since reconstituting a pattern once set or widening its scope is difficult and unlikely to happen. At other times, exhaustion follows a period of development, of saturation, after which further original elaboration seems impossible. If mere repetition, which represents a form of deterioration, is to be avoided, the philosophers, artists, or scientists must enlarge the patterns, but not by extravagance, flamboyance, or alteration simply for the sake of novelty, for those qualities also represent deterioration. While they marshall their energies and find a new direction, growth pauses. When the lull is over, development continues along new, somewhat broader lines than before.

Pattern was used with reference to culture content in another comprehensive sense to denote the overall form, organization, or quality revealed by a whole culture. Kroeber labeled this idea, which Ruth Benedict made the subject of *Patterns of Culture*, "total-culture pattern." Whatever the name, the conception shades into the second, processual, meaning of the term pattern. The total-culture pattern governs what new material a culture will accept, and shapes how new material will be reinterpreted if it is initially incompatible with the pattern. From a psychological perspective, the culture pattern was metaphorically described as an inexplicit code enabling people to recognize what is right and meaningful in behavior.[38]

The idea that cultural patterns or the total-culture pattern shapes specific cultural traits, and that it patterns covert and overt individual behavior (thereby endowing cultural systems with self-directed goal orientation, the quality that systems theorists call equifinality), has deep roots in the American Historical Tradition. In 1897, Boas refers to this idea when he explains similar meanings being attached to secret societies as well as to clans among the Kwakiutl Indians as due to a common psychical factor in the society by which both types of institutions have been molded.[39] Lowie often refers to the pattern process.[40] For example, among the Blackfoot Indians, he observes, all important bundle ceremonies include a sweat lodge performance; for every bundle, some plant is burned on an altar, etc. A Blackfoot ceremonial pattern, a norm of ceremonial routine, has given those usages a form that differs from the form given to similar usages in other tribes where different patterns operate. Ruth Benedict's early anthropological writings, predating her configurational theory, reveal the central place occupied by the pattern process in her thinking.[41] Speaking of the widely distributed vision concept among American Indians, she shows that each tribe on the plains had its own version, or pattern, to which the vision was bent. Every culture, she asserts, in *Patterns of Culture*—reiterating Lowie's thesis that, in terms of historical origins, every culture is a thing of "shreds and patches"—selects from a great range of potential interests, activities, and institutions, and in its own way elaborates those it chooses.[42] Religion, economics, or other dominant institutions toward which group life is oriented guide what a group incorporates in its culture. The society adopts traits that its members perceive to be connected with the dominant institutions, and develops them to suit the leading interests. The most heterogeneous items can be selected and consolidated to become consistent with the leading purposes toward which the culture is directed. As a result, the same institutions acquire different forms in adjacent cultures. Thus history, not individual psychology, must be studied to discover how a culture has developed, for a culture is something other than what individual members of the society have willed or created.

The configurational viewpoint appearing in the late 1920s developed from the idea of patterning. In an early example of configurational thinking, Margaret Mead characterized Samoan culture as being dominated by an emphasis on, or pattern of, formalism, which rigidly prescribes behavior to be followed by individuals in many situations.[43] Due to the selective action of the pattern, the culture never absorbed such traits as secret magical formulas, concepts of good and bad luck, and acts allowing individuals to establish personal communion with the supernatural.

The idea of a cultural configuration has taken us beyond the basic level of traits, complexes, and other units of culture to the point of considering particular cultures as wholes, the way one conceives of individual persons holistically. More comprehensively, Kroeber dealt theoretically with all culture—culture in general—regarding it as the most abstract of the four levels of phenomena with which knowledge of human beings deals.[44] The three lower levels are the somatic, psychic, and social. According to Kroeber, while culture always conforms to the human somatic endowment, serves psychological needs, and interweaves with society, it cannot be wholly explained on any of those levels. Certainly it cannot be explained in terms of individuals, for the individual—even the genius who leaves an indelible mark in history—is himself shaped by culture and acts as the product of his time. Culture is superindividual, in the sense of operating autonomously beyond the control of individuals and of persisting beyond the life of a particular individual or generation. Some of Kroeber's contemporaries much preferred to regard culture as localized in individuals, rooted in organic drives and other biological processes, interacting with geographical constraints, and influenced by population density.[45] Questioning whether anthropology needed "a superorganic," Edward Sapir accused Kroeber of having overshot the mark by eliminating all consideration of how individuals affect culture. Eight years younger than Kroeber, Sapir had been born in Germany and, as Boas's student, specialized in linguistics.[46] He is also remembered for charting the course to be followed by an individual-oriented cultural anthropology, and from that perspective he found fault with Kroeber's idea. While individuals are formed by culture, he countered Kroeber, they try always to impress themselves on their social environment, even if only to an infinitesimal degree. Culture is but a name for an arbitrary selection of phenomena, all of which can be resolved into the inorganic, organic, and mental realms.

Cultural Intensity and Environment

At the same time that Kroeber conceived of culture in superorganic terms he, together with most other American ethnologists, saw primitive cultures as firmly rooted in their natural settings. Going further, the Americans, in a pale reflection of the German diffusionists, found clues to culture history in the spatial arrangements of culture within a continental region. Wissler and Kroeber, following the example of Otis T. Mason and others, drew maps grouping North American Indian tribes into areas, each based on a combination of geographical and cultural features.[47]

Mason had delineated 18 American Indian natural environments. By correlating these with material and technical culture (including clothing, crafts, and modes of transportation), he converted the geographical blocks into "culture areas," by which name he called them. Nine years later, Livingston Farrand, the first American to receive a Ph.D. in anthropology in the United States (from Boas at Clark University), delineated six areas. Wissler raised the number to 15 for the cultures as they existed at the time of contact, and Kroeber counted as many as 80 but divided them into six main groups.

Wissler looked directly to geographical features in an area to explain population density and the presence or absence of cultural traits having to do with subsistence, clothing, shelter, and transportation. Cultures, he reasoned, become adapted to their environments, whereupon they tend to stabilize, the habitat exercising a selective influence on new technology diffusing into the area. Consequently, adoption of new items depends on whether a particular technique or artifact will work in a natural setting. He also used the culture-area concept to explain why traits unconnected with ecology tend to thin out from one region to another, as the resources supporting a particular way of life alter, and others take their place. The concept of the culture center helps him account for cultural development. Traits common to tribes inhabiting a culture area tend to cluster at the center of an area and to fade out at the boundaries, where traits of adjacent areas overlap. Life at the culture center has become adjusted to a specific mode of subsistence, made possible by climate and other environmental factors. For example, at the time of Euroamerican contact, the culture center of the Plains Indian area coincided with the point where the most favorable grass and climate occurred and bison herds clustered most thickly. Demographic factors also play an important role in cultural development at the center, whose life history parallels the rise and fall of population. Such population movement, Wissler theorizes, corresponds to how people at the center at first successfully exploit natural resources but eventually exhaust them, or are overcome by depredations inflicted by wilder, virile fighting folk who topple the thriving culture.

A center draws in new ideas compatible with the existing culture, and radiates innovations as well as individuals outward toward the area's periphery and even beyond. Hence the center concept can be employed in historical reconstruction. Assuming the center to be the major source of new cultural material and the point of dispersal, the most recently innovated traits originating in an area, the age-area hypothesis predicts, would be restricted there while older ones would be distributed more widely. The extent of the latter traits represents the time required for their diffusion from the point of origin.

Kroeber, too, recognized different degrees of cultural complexity within a culture area; and he also dealt with variation in complexity between

North American culture areas, but with no direct reference to its relationship with natural factors. Kroeber speaks of development in cultural intensity, meaning the degree of cultural growth attained in regions where cultural context is complex enough to require systematization, refinement, and specialization for its survival. Since the capacity of a culture to absorb new material increases with intensity, the high-intensity cultures are the most absorptive as well as the most productive. The absorptivity of high-intensity areas encourages climax cultures, culminations of development, to appear in an area. From those, cultural material in turn radiates. Barring fundamental changes in subsistence patterns, climax points tend to remain geographically fixed in an area, though shifts can in some cases be archeologically traced.

Without being systematically ecological, other writers occasionally generalized about correlations between types of subsistence and other aspects of culture. Class distinctions and political leadership, Robert Lowie observes, are minimally developed on the lowest plane of subsistence, i.e., among hunters and collectors.[48] With primitive farming, conditions change, and matrilineal descent sometimes appears when women do the tillage. Deploring his contemporaries' phobia against admitting environmental influences on culture, he singles out the natural setting as the source of a culture's "brick and mortar." It provides the materials not only for technology but for mythology, religion, and other subjects as well.

Acculturation studies, to which I come later, directed attention to the impact that culture makes on an indigenous group's environment.[49] As game or other resources disappear, environmental potentialities alter for the original inhabitants of a region, and survival of the society requires new forms of cultural adaptation.

Functional and Structural Relationships

Although American writers in an anti-evolutionist mood demonstrated the unreality of certain culture complexes, like totemism and kinship systems,[50] the "shreds and patches" thesis was hardly intended to deny the age-old principle of cultural integration, as it is frequently misread doing. Illustrations of integrational thinking in writings of the period are legion, and a few from Boas's writings may suffice to indicate their range. He held the principle, in 1887, when he argued against Otis T. Mason's preference for classifying museum specimens by an evolutionary Linnean scheme.[51] Mason would have grouped together objects of the same type, regardless of provenience, in a manner showing their development. Boas favored displaying many kinds of artifacts grouped by tribe or culture in order to show their relationships to one another, and to present them in spatial-temporal context. In other writings, Boas many times recognizes the interrelated nature of cultural phenomena.[52] Economic factors, he notes, determine the direction in which discoveries or inventions develop; an enhanced basis of subsistence supports art and leisure activities and encourages cultural complexity; myths in every culture possess a distinctive character corresponding to the tribe's central interests; and the systematization of myths goes hand-in-hand with greater systematization of political and social organization. Going beyond the integration of culture, he perceives cultural facts linking up with such noncultural variables as bodily form, environment, and population density. Because of those multiple connections, it is hard to find single causes for cultural features. "Functional and structural relations" between trait complexes, Wissler wrote, using new words for an old idea, might be so strong that dropping one complex from a way of life would seriously threaten the continuance of others.[53] Even as trivial a change as men ceasing to wear hats could have costly ramifications.

Recognition of cultural integration abounds in Lowie's work. With his parents, he came to New York from Vienna when he was ten.[54] He attended City College and Columbia University, where he encountered Boas. Inspiring as he found the older man's scholarship, he developed his own style of anthropology and, like other students of the cautious Boas, went far beyond the teacher in theoretical depth. He perceives integration in the mutual influence of religion and art, the impact of social institutions on kinship structure, and in cross-cultural adhesions between certain cultural traits that allow one to predict from one culture to another.[55] Kin-term systems, despite the coherence of certain logically compatible terms, he regards as only imperfectly integrated, and in modern life he notes conspicuous lags and conflicts between culture patterns, the result of culture change failing to occur harmoniously between different areas of life.

The highly original but short-lived configurational viewpoint, whose relationship to the concept of pattern as process I have already mentioned, expanded the notion of integration. Ruth Benedict, a major exponent of the viewpoint, has expressed the notion by referring to cultures as articulated wholes, with institutionalized motives, emotions, and values, in the light of which the significance of specific details of behavior must be apprehended.[56] The whole determines its parts, not only relationships between them but their very nature.

A sensitive, insightful, and imaginative woman, Benedict tried several outlets for her creativity, including poetry, before discovering anthropology.[57] Born in upper New York State, she majored in English literature at Vassar College, and later experimented briefly with a career in social work. But she balked at the task of making over the poor into middle-class people. A childless and increasingly unhappy marriage and dissatisfaction with her lot as a woman, deepened her unrest. She discovered anthropology with Alexander Goldenweiser at the New School for Social Research, followed it up at Columbia University, and in three semesters under Boas's direction earned a doctor's degree in the subject.

In *Patterns of Culture* Benedict acknowledges her awareness of configurationalism in Gestalt psychology and in Oswald Spengler's work, but she fails to mention Leo Frobenius, whose ideas about the core of culture, its paideuma, permeating a culture's carriers and giving them firm direction, closely resemble her own thesis. In *Patterns of Culture* she adopted a psychological point of view for comparing the Pueblo and Plains Indians. She contrasts the Apollonian emphasis on moderation and formality in the first with the Dionysian intensity of the latter, for whom the vision quest, mourning, shamanism, and other activities provide opportunities to transcend the ordinary limits of experience. Several years later, in a series of lectures delivered at Bryn Mawr, she relied less on a psychological vantage point as she applied configurationalism to cultures more and less synergically organized.[58] In cultures with high synergy, institutions work together, and the same act permits an individual to serve his own advantage while simultaneously serving interests of the society. Every harvest or successful hunt becomes a triumph for the village or band to share. In a system with low synergy, acts are frequently conceived of as mutually counteractive, conflict is maximized, and few possibilities allow individuals to join together for common advantages.

Individual and Culture

The relationship of the individual and the social milieu in which he grows and lives had for a long time been a part of anthropological thought. Now, as disquisitions on primitive mentality declined, and in company with psychoanalytic essays relating culture to unconscious psychodynamics, American anthropology turned enthusiastically to tracing cultural influences on personality.

Boas continued to entertain the idea of primitive culture mirroring qualitatively different ways of thinking,[59] and as late as 1938 made generalizations about primitive people's peculiar mode of cognition.[60] As if not yet aware of his pupil Mead's contrary discovery in Manus, he refers to primitives' anthropomorphic interpretation of nature. They tend to interpret events by religious ideas, and are given to extreme subjectivity in their thinking. Civilized people have developed beyond the crude, automatic categories of language dominating primitive mentality, and substitute objective, material causality compatible with scientific method for the emotional associations of primitive reasoning. In similar vein, Paul Radin claims that primitive folk appreciate giving full expression to their sensations and possess an overwhelming sense of reality.[61] They attach special significance to thought itself, thereby assigning unquestioned validity to subjective reality. Contrary to some allegations, Radin doubts whether primitive people lack self control. Rather, self-discipline is their ideal. We are misled about the primitive undisciplined self by the considerable freedom that individuals in primitive society enjoy to vent emotion, and by their readier acceptance of emotion as normal. Radin was another American-trained anthropologist who came from Europe as a small child.[62] He studied with Boas, but his books maintain a much more humanistic outlook on cultural anthropology than the works of his more austere teacher.

Numerous passages by Boas and his contemporaries—excluding Kroeber —unsystematically but consistently reiterate the individual's importance in culture, as well as on the role of individuality in culture change. The roots of culture history, according to Boas, lie in the minds of men.[63] For Goldenweiser, who criticizes Emile Durkheim for ignoring the individual's contribution to society, every cultural fact originates in the creative act of an individual mind.[64] In the last analysis, "culture is psychological," and psychology can help to explain it. An artist's fanciful image of a popular supernatural figure, Lowie points out, could alter a religious conception entertained by a whole society, and individual peculiarities in religious leaders might easily promote other innovations in religion.[65] Culture, as Wissler puts it, begins and grows with man's reflective thought.[66]

By the early 1930s Radin, in recording an Indian's life history, showed how a real, not an abstract anonymous individual manipulated cultural materials; also, a party of field workers led by Kroeber had started into the southwestern desert to collect life histories and dreams, with the object of pinpointing individual variation in a society.[67] On the basis of such studies, Ralph Linton could confidently claim that even in a homogeneous society all members do not share all elements of culture.[68] Some people practice limited cultural specialities, and a few carry out atypical or newly innovated cultural alternatives. Some peculiarities, of course, are limited to one person, but those Linton refused to class as part of culture.

No one more than Edward Sapir urged the logic of approaching culture from the standpoint of the individual.[69] Always it is an individual who thinks, acts, dreams, and revolts. The ideas and actions that constitute a society's culture originate in the minds of given individuals. Ethnographers produce culture only by abstracting behavior from its individual loci and arranging it in terms of historical antecedents. Sapir admits a high degree of regularity prevails in the performance of customs by members of a society, but he ascribes it to an implicit mental code, which guides persons to recognize and choose to do what is right or meaningful. An individual is comfortable when he adheres to the code, and experiences deviation from it as esthetically unpleasant or extremely frightening.

Kroeber, in spite of training as a psychoanalyst, virtually eliminated the individual as a significant determining factor in history.[70] Undeniably geniuses play an innovative role in society, but only when the cultural setting into which a genius is born makes it possible for a person to realize unusual capacities. Without going as far as Kroeber, but cautioning against psychological explanations for everything in culture, Lowie advises working on two levels.[71] Even when psychological explanations are available, cultural facts retain their distinctive character and can be treated ethnologically—presumably meaning historically. Although Margaret Mead was much more forthrightly psychological she, too, saw advantages in taking multiple perspectives.[72] Every social phenomenon can be regarded from an individual and a social viewpoint. The incest rule from the former position is a result of repressions induced in childhood for the purpose of controlling infantile sexuality; seen from society's side, the rule regulates conflict in the family and other groups.

Despite all the attention given to the individual's role in culture, explaining culture by reference to individuals never became important in anthropology compared to explaining individual personality traits in terms of culture. On that, everyone concurred, even Kroeber, for it was fully consistent with a major proposition in American cultural theory, the concept of patterning.

Most impressive evidence bearing on the part culture plays in patterning personality came in Margaret Mead's books reporting her South Sea researches. Her entry into anthropology predated by a decade, or less, major shifts away from American ethnology's historical orientation, and she herself was primarily responsible for one of the new directions taken: psychological anthropology. Mead grew up in eastern Pennsylvania.[73] Her professional parents permitted her early education to remain informal and for several years to be in charge of her paternal grandmother, a person whom Mead describes as the most decisive influence in her life. She studied anthropology with Boas, but was even more captivated by the ideas of Ruth Benedict. Field work in Samoa, when she was only 25 years old, and then in the Admiralty Islands, New Guinea, Bali, and, between her second and third Pacific voyages, among the Omaha Indians, provided her with data on a wide range of anthropological topics, as well as material for books and articles popularizing the subject and establishing her worldwide prominence.

Research in Samoa allowed Mead to claim that cultural factors facilitate Samoan girls' easy transition through adolescence to adulthood.[74] The casualness of island life minimizes agonizing choices, conflicts, and uncertainties such as American adolescents have to face. Field work in New Guinea provided her with facts to illustrate the variety of temperamental or psychological types produced by cultural processes in a relatively small area. The Arapesh, reared with few shocks, suckled under warmly nurturant conditions, and encouraged in passivity, grow up to be gentle, passive, warm, unacquisitive, cooperative, nurturant, and fearful of any rift in social relations. The Mundugumor, brought up through Spartan training for a world filled with harshness and danger, learn to be competitive, jealous, and ready to see insult and to avenge it.

By the late 1930s anthropologists with interest in personality were exploring a wide variety of drives, meanings, associations, and emotional evaluations underlying overt social behavior and sometimes manifested in cultural artifacts.[75] They were learning how formative experiences, especially early ones, fuse with an individual's unique constitutional qualities to form a standard personality type for each society. Ruth Benedict took a lead in considering behavioral abnormalities in relation to culture.[76] What behavior a society regards as normal or abnormal, she detected, depends on cultural norms. Trance, hysteria, homosexuality, and many other actions that our society rejects as abnormal will be valued and culturally elaborated in other societies. There, individuals who adopt those acts are able to play important social roles, unhampered by the dilemmas they would experience through their behavior amongst ourselves. From a less relativistic position, she posits abnormal behavior as being directly patterned through culture; witness such highly traditional forms as Arctic hysteria, and note the regularity with which forms of mental illness fall out of fashion.

Anthropologists pinpointed psychic stresses emanating from man-made social conditions as a cause of mental illness. Aware of a paper published in England by C. G. Seligman attributing psychosis to culture change, A. Irving Hallowell pondered the relationship between disequilibrium resulting from change and mental disorder.[77] In a few years he would be able to show a direct correlation between degree of cultural upheaval in northern North American Indian communities and signs of psychic stress revealed in responses given to Rorschach inkblots. With nonpsychiatric deviant behavior in mind, Mead gave three reasons why individuals adopt such behavior, two of them cultural: constitutional proclivities in a person may run contrary to a society's preferred patterns of conduct, the individual may have been socialized by parents or other adults who are themselves in some respects deviant, or the society lacks firm procedures for guiding socialization and for exercising control.[78]

Culture Change

Invention and Diffusion

Around the turn of the century and during the first two or three decades of the 20th century, American historical ethnology under the leadership of Boas, Kroeber, and Lowie fixed its attention on long-term relations between cultures belonging to a region. The object in research was, first, to account for the region's culture history, primarily in terms of diffusion, and beyond that to obtain greater knowledge of cultural processes. Like Fritz Graebner and W. H. R. Rivers, Boas and his followers hoped such knowledge would make up for the lack of written records in providing a sound basis for understanding how contemporary cultural distributions arose.[79] By the 1930s, however, American anthropologists were devoting a growing proportion of field research to direct observations of cultures in the process of change, and knowledge of cultural dynamics had become an end worth pursuing for itself.

In keeping with the strong psychological interest characteristic of the Americans, many anthropologists from the start approached questions of cultural dynamics from the standpoint of the individual, though at the same time looking into cultural systems, too, for characteristics influencing change. Wissler combines both points of view when he describes culture change as originating the moment an individual conceives a new idea of something.[80] Thereupon, the cultural system, directed from within, exercises selective power over what originations are to be retained. Only if a potential culture trait promises to channel or elaborate culture along established tracks will it be adopted. If the trait seems unsuited to an existing culture complex, it will be rejected regardless of its merit.

Roland B. Dixon's *Building of Cultures,* based on his lectures as professor of anthropology at Harvard, summarized the existing theory of culture change and historical growth.[81] A native of Massachusetts, he received his Ph.D. in anthropology in 1900 from Harvard, and consequently represents a branch of American historical anthropology that is cognatically rather than lineally related to Boas and his students. For the rest of his life he remained affiliated with Harvard, earning special distinction for building its anthropology program. An avid taste for outdoor life and travel complemented his scholarly interests in archeology and ethnology, interests with which he combined work in physical anthropology and linguistics. But mainly he wrote about problems of cultural and racial history. Here I present his ideas about invention and diffusion.

Dixon identifies three basic factors underlying discovery and invention: genius, need, and opportunity. Each varies from one geographical environment or cultural group to another, thereby influencing the volume of discovery and invention occurring in a given setting. Genius depends on above-average intelligence, the frequency of which is apt to differ between tribes and nations. Needs multiply as cultures grow more complex. Opportunity depends on resources present in a geographical environment, and recognized by people living there as potentially capable of solving needs arising in their lives. The more similar the three factors from one society to another, the more similar the inventions produced.

Comparing Dixon's theory of innovation with Linton's 12 years later reveals how the psychological viewpoint became increasingly influential.[82]

For Linton, culture change—including additions to and losses of knowledge, as well as new applications of the knowledge (inventions)—represents changes in the attitudes, knowledge, or habits of a society's members that result from learning or forgetting. Severe individual maladjustment produced by some culture patterns may motivate major inventions; contented people, Linton believes, produce only minor innovations apt to be designed solely for the sake of amusement or professional esteem.

Without diffusion, Dixon points out, an innovation remains a personal eccentricity. Through primary diffusion, a novelty becomes the property of other members of the innovator's group or culture area, its journey among them being speeded by its demonstrable advantages as well as by a certain amount of persuasion, and through imitation and fashion. Secondary diffusion carries the trait beyond the society of origin, the rate at which it travels depending on the extent of cultural and environmental compatibility. Abrupt cultural and environmental transitions, by reducing the utility of a new item or restricting opportunities for copying or employing it, slow down the spread. Sometimes borrowers can modify—or, to use a word of somewhat later currency, reinterpret—a trait, especially a nonmaterial item, in order to accommodate it to different cultural or environmental conditions. Like Rivers, Dixon saw an order of probability in the ease with which different kinds of traits diffuse: material items travel most readily, religious elements come next, and social traits last. When cultures of different grades meet, diffusion normally flows more strongly from the higher to the lower, but some items will also move in the reverse direction.

Again it is instructive to skip ahead and observe the psychological perspective taken on cultural diffusion by Linton, for whom the real problem in culture change is knowing why *individuals* accept new things. Acknowledging utility and compatibility to be important reasons for adoption, he ascribes the speed of diffusion to people's ability to comprehend the significance of an innovation. Hence techniques of manufacturing and foodgetting, whose value can be grasped fully without the necessity of speech, spread most readily, along with tools and other objects. Meanings attached to behavior are harder to grasp, even when they can be expressed in words, while values and attitudes lying below the threshold of consciousness don't spread at all. Sometimes modifications of meaning can be introduced into a trait to make it more comprehensible in a new cultural setting, or the tangible form of a material object can be altered to increase its compatibility. However, intrinsic qualities of tools and other objects limit such modifications, whereas nothing restricts the freedom with which new meanings can be assigned to items in diffusion. The degree of prestige conferred by an innovation, on those who accept it, strongly governs diffusion of culture and stems partly from the prestige accorded to the trait or the prestige enjoyed by the person who introduces it into a society. A group recognizing its social inferiority will borrow more extensively from those it deems superior than vice versa, though some transfer upward always occurs. Whether people will adopt a novelty depends basically on their willingness to change, and may hinge on the intensity of the discomfort and dissatisfaction they experience in their society. In culture-contact situations, the very presence of a foreign group raises individuals' consciousness of their own culture and makes them dissatisfied with existing institutions. Sapir may have been influenced by historical materialism when, in similar vein, he specified cumulative disharmony created in a society through continuous introduction of new tools, ideas, or values as a "need" favorable to further cultural change.[83]

The persistence of culture received less anthropological attention than change.[84] Emotional factors in primitive societies dominating over reason, Boas declares, imbue behavior with value and motivate profound resistance to change. Continuing in a psychological vein, he alludes to an always ready tendency to discover plausible reasons—"secondary explanations"—for continuing customary behaviors threatened with extinction. Then people persuasively advance such explanations to justify even acts for which no conscious motive existed previously. He also cites conditioning and childhood socialization as cultural conservators, especially in primitive societies where socialization is especially firm. I have mentioned the implicit code of conduct which, according to Sapir, sanctions customs as right or meaningful and thereby protects their survival. Customs will persist longest, Sapir predicts, which correspond to biological needs or are easily reinterpreted, without altering their basic form, to suit changing cultural conditions. He also ascribes cultural stability in primitive and rural societies to their small size, reasoning that change threatens social integration more in a small group than in a large one.

Acculturation

If Alfred Kroeber's description of culture patterns pushing toward fulfillment and then expiring can be applied to a field of scholarship, then in American anthropology during the latter 1930s writing about the dynamics of invention and diffusion reached a saturation point. As those topics exhausted their potential for further development, acculturation, or culture contact, pushed forward as a new pattern of thought to be elaborated.

There is no point in reviewing the varied uses to which the term "acculturation" has been put in social science. Modern usage can be traced to a paper by a German anthropologist published in the *American Anthropologist,* in 1932, where the term is applied to a sociopsychological process involving people's adaptation to new conditions of life.[85] The process includes reinterpretation of selectively borrowed new traits, the ramifying results of new cultural acquisitions, heightened cultural self-consciousness, and a reorientation of social identity. Between 1935 and 1940, American anthropologists applied the concept to situations involving close, complete contact between distinct cultural groups.[86] Some diffusion always occurs in such a situation, but without necessarily causing a merging of the cultures in contact. A group, recognizing its own social inferiority, may at first borrow extensively from the culture it admires and respects, Linton predicts, hoping thereby to overcome its inferior status and alleviate accompanying deprivations. Should the course of events kill their hope, critical and hostile attitudes may replace admiration and emulation. A nativistic movement glorifying the past may occur. Such movements frequently possess a religious aspect, though Linton's broad definition—"any [usually] conscious organized attempt . . . to revive or perpetuate selected aspects of . . . culture"—readily covers purely secular movements as well.

Writings about acculturation took two hard-to-reconcile evaluative views of the process. Prevailingly, the Americans dwelled on the unsettling effects, or maladjustments, churned up by culture contact. Sapir, for example, blames contact for having destroyed the political integration and cultural values of American Indian tribes, thereby leaving the Indian in a state of "bewildered vacuity." Paul Radin takes the other view when he dismisses reckless talk about the total disorganization of social systems undergoing acculturation. Linton, although never oblivious to the stressful concomitants of culture contact, shows faith in the enormous flexibility and adaptability of cultures. As a result of those attributes, needs blocked in acculturation will not long remain unsatisfied.

Social Structure

Sexual Dominance and Descent

American ethnologists inherited the question of when unilinear descent groups arose in society or, dismissing the possibility of obtaining a satisfactory answer in historical terms, the antecedent conditions that regularly bring them about.[87] In tackling the question "When?", the Americans, using synchronic comparison of cultures, were able to show descent groups absent among technologically very simply tribes and present in primitive societies at higher levels of cultural complexity. In time, growing political complexity and a growing amount of property were seen to promote the disappearance of descent groups; though when patrilineal descent vanishes, a patrilineal bias remains evident in many societies.

Regarding how unilinear descent comes into being, one explanation connects descent rules to the use of common terms for patrilineally or matrilineally related collateral relatives. Such usage cause a distinct group of kinsmen to take shape who treat themselves as if they were genealogically related through descent from a common ancestor. Another theory claims segregation of matrikin and patrikin, arising through customs of unilocal marital residence, produces matrisibs or patrisibs, depending upon which rule of residence is chosen. Field work suggested the importance of economic factors for unilinear descent, specifically the dominance of one or the other sex in house ownership, inheritance, and foodgetting activities. If women dominate, they are apt to stay at home after marriage, and the resultant aggregation of lineally related females leads to the rule of matrilineal descent. Male dominance, in turn, promotes patrilineal descent. Postmarital residence independent of either the wife's or husband's parents favors bilateral descent, meaning an absence of any unilinear rule and children's equal affiliation with maternal and paternal kin.

Why the Same Terms?

Two problems, classifying kin-term systems and explaining how customs of kinship nomenclature arise—both of which Lewis Henry Morgan believed he had solved—claimed much of the effort devoted to kinship terminology in the American Historical Tradition.[88] Apart from two new systems of classification devised by Robert Lowie and Leslie Spier, based on the custom of merging collateral and lineal relatives, the effort did not result in significant new insights, but it did buttress the sociological theory initiated by Morgan, which Edward B. Tylor and W. H. R. Rivers had also followed. Shorn of evolutionary assumptions, the theory singled out forms of marriage, unilinear descent groups, and other social institutions as antecedent variables governing the way given relatives will be categorized, though some anthropologists couldn't decide whether to opt for correlation or determinism when it came to linking those features with kinship terminology. An alternative theory reversing the sequence, by making features of kinship terminology the antecedent of unilinear descent groups, briefly held its ground until the lack of supporting evidence became evident. Kroeber's attempt to install a wholly different line of thought, one concerned more with meaning than cause, also quickly disappeared.

Logical demonstration citing selected ethnographic data, rather than more discriminating quasi-experimental comparative techniques using many cultures, such as later came to be employed, provided the chief means for supporting sociological explanations of kinship nomenclature. Sapir illustrates how in American Indian tribes possessing the levirate, a woman applies a common term to her husband and his brother, the man who following her husband's death will make her his wife. Consistently in such societies she calls her husband's brother's children "son" and "daughter," and they, of course, address her as "mother." Occasionally a number of cases drawn from a continental area, frequently North America, were cited to support nonstatistical correlations; for instance, between moiety organization and the terminological grouping of parallel cousins with siblings. Controlled comparison of the Hopi Indians having clans with other Shoshonean-speakers lacking them, enabled Lowie to prove that clans rather than language, as Kroeber thought, regularly link up with certain kin-term usages. A number of ethnologists struggled to penetrate the rationale of Crow- and Omaha-type kin-term systems, in which the terms applied to cross-cousins override generational distinctions. Lowie accounted for the distinctive features of those systems by influences exerted through matrilineal and patrilineal descent, respectively. The custom followed in the Crow-type system of using common terms for father's sister's children and the father's siblings recognizes those relatives as belonging to the same matrilineal descent group. Omaha-type terminology, frequent in conjunction with patrilineal descent, achieves the same result by classifying the mother's brother's children with the mother's siblings.

Behavior between relatives, anthropologists maintained, tends to correlate with nomenclature.[89] If sexual relations are prohibited with a particular related person, the prohibition will extend to other relatives categorized by the same kinship word. Ritual avoidance behavior, Lowie notes, between relatives of opposite sex tends to correlate with sexual prohibitions, while sexual license is permitted with relatives between whom marriage is potentially possible. However, he rejects James G. Frazer's functional hypothesis—holding ritual avoidance to forestall incest. Societies, Lowie claims, have stronger and more direct means of preventing illicit sexual relationships than avoidance rituals.

Types of Society

The field of nonkin social structure received little of the attention bestowed on descent groups and kinship.[90] Clark Wissler defined the primitive community as comprising a number of families living in close association; they maintain life by carrying out differentiated tasks and practicing cooperation. Heading into political anthropology, he characterized the tribe as a linguistic and territorially based political unit capable of growing by federation and of segmenting into several tribes. Communities and tribes recognize male leaders ("chiefs") whose authority generally rests on an ability to command respect by force of wisdom and personality. Social control generally remains informal among primitive people, depending heavily on sensitivity to ridicule, adverse public opinion, and dread of sorcery. This somewhat idealized view of primitive social structure becomes more pronounced in Radin, who claims that conformity normally prevails in primitive society, thanks to the network of interrelationships with which any custom is intertwined. Hence only in emergencies do customs require enforcement through the coercive power of law. Sapir may have read Henry Sumner Maine before picturing primitive societies as organized into unspecialized groups on the bases of kinship, territoriality, and status. Gradually, such organization gives way to the highly specialized groupings found in modern societies.

More popular was Robert Redfield's typological comparison of the folk society with its polar opposite, the city.[91] Some may question Redfield's affiliation with the American Historical Tradition, and undoubtedly he as well as Ralph Linton forecast a new current of anthropological thought forming under the direct influence of British social anthropology. Temporally, however, his early work falls into the period being considered. Born and reared in Chicago, he followed his father into law before a trip to Mexico and contact with the sociologist Robert Park turned him to anthropology.[92] Continued field work in Mexico after he obtained his Ph.D. from Chicago, in 1928, gave him factual material for the folk-urban continuum closely associated with his name.

In contrast to the city, the nonliterate folk society, with its tightly integrated customs dominated by religious values, possesses a high degree of homogeneity. In it the family, limited in social mobility, neighborhood, and birth strictly determine individual status. Being small and restricted from contacts with other groups, people in a folk society come to know each other intimately; they grow alike in the things they do and think, and develop a strong sense of belonging together. Behavior tends to be spontaneous, "to flow from the very nature of things"; goods are produced for use rather than trade; and division of labor rests largely on the basis of age and sex.

Other societal types were also delineated. Margaret Mead compared the competitive society, which counts heavily on individual initiative to provide the motive force for accumulation and distribution of wealth, with the cooperative society, whose highly structured forms leave little room for individual initiative.[93] And I have mentioned the distinction Benedict drew between societies of high and low synergy and the correlation of high synergy with nonaggression and cooperation.

Religion and Magic

The Extraordinary

Religion and magic, subjects highly attractive to 19th-century British anthropologists and the French sociologists, stimulated Lowie, Goldenweiser, and Radin to book-length works.[94] Lowie, remaining as he deemed proper for an anthropologist "above" partisan questions regarding the truth or falsity of supernatural beliefs, took the extraordinary, the mysterious, and the awe-inspiring to be the essential feature of every religion. Religious devotion may be lavished on the most divergent objects and experiences, sacred as well as sinister; by no means are spiritual beings always implicated in such devotion. A little-known book by Goldenweiser describes religion and craftsmanship as expressing two fundamental orientations of the human mind. In religion, with which the author merges magic, man acts to control events by projecting his mind into nature, whereas in craftsmanship he adapts his thoughts to nature, from open-minded observation learns constantly to improve his abilities. Thrill, awe, or exhilaration involved with belief in spiritual beings identify religious experience for Radin. Fear, he writes, engendered by human existence precipitates religion, which guarantees to the individual the values of success, happiness, and long life frequently threatened by economic vicissitudes. Because human beings are always traumatized, sometimes to the point of psychological unbalance, they need supernatural assistance. A small proportion of seriously unbalanced individuals, in the process of being restored to wholeness, adopt the roles of shaman and priest, thereafter employing their talents to heal others. From a developmental point of view, Radin perceives coercive magical rites to dominate the outlook of foodgatherers, among whom truly religious conceptions remain inchoate. Religion—meaning fear of spiritual beings, accompanied by offerings, propitiations, and other ritual elements directed to the beings—emerges only in societies where food production has instituted a new kind of relationship between man and nature. Elsewhere, Radin writes more originally about magic than anyone of the time.[95] He accuses anthropology of exaggerating the importance of magic in primitive society where it represents no more than an auxiliary form of coping brought into play only in company with more direct, empirical techniques. Contrary to Tylor and Frazer, Radin does not see magic declining as technology becomes more effective; rather magic increases due to the growing power of priests, medicine men, and other priviliged persons. Boas had those specialists in mind when he compared dual religious traditions in a society.[96] Like others before him who had recognized coexisting esoteric and popular versions, he describes the specialists as systematizing popular beliefs into esoteric doctrines, which in circular fashion inform the plain people's religious notions. With Mooney's *Ghost Dance Religion* (1896) as a precedent, ethnologists began to have their interest drawn to messianic religions and other religious movements arising in times of change and associated conditions of social stress.[97] Lowie, however, suspected that messianism, though apt to arise among tribes racked by acculturation, also arose under aboriginal conditions independently of cultural contact.

The ethnologists generally revealed more interest in religious belief than in ritual. Exceptions to this generalization include Wissler, who conceived of rigidity ruling ritual, though recognizing that ceremonies frequently alter in details of performance, and Lowie who studied rituals mainly as an instance of the patterning process.[98] Because of the way ceremonies conform to tribal patterns, Lowie doubts whether they are ever spontaneous outpourings of emotion. In one of those rare generalizations, which take ritual beyond the boundaries of religion into secular life, he extends the concept of ceremony to whatever people take seriously. George A. Dorsey employed conditioning theory to explain how patriotic portraits and flags at a political rally bait the trap to entice the audience to vote for a particular candidate, while Radin, like Nicholas of Cusa, apprized the symbols of chieftainship and royalty as elevating the mundane images of the persons occupying those positions and authenticating their right to office.[99]

Critical Anthropology

Complete Objectivity Impossible

Turning back on itself to examine its presuppositions, its method, and its goals, anthropology during the latter years of the American Historical Tradition developed an increasingly self-critical outlook. The earliest critical barbs, of which I have said enough, were directed against the methods and assumptions of historical reconstruction utilized by the deductive evolutionists and those historical ethnologists who outran their facts.

American anthropologists realized the construct nature of culture.[100] Confusing construct with reality, Wissler warned, is a grave mistake. Several writers frankly admitted that ethnography could never be completely objective, because the researcher's personality sifts the material he collects, gets itself projected into the people he studies, and leads him to emphasize some aspects of culture above others. Field workers also impose theoretical preconceptions on data, expecting certain phenomena to be present in certain types of society. Since those expectations are not explicitly stated in hypothesis form, Alexander Lesser complained, they cannot be successfully tested through successive field trips and advanced to the status of laws if they prove true.

Agreement on the goals of ethnological knowledge proved hard to reach; consequently dissensus reigned concerning the method to follow in analyzing cultural facts.[101] Whereas Lowie foresaw a day when ethnology, using the logic of concomitant variation and having shed its highly particularistic outlook, would reach sound conclusions about causal and functional relationships in culture, his colleague Alfred L. Kroeber remained unenthusiastic. Not only did Kroeber regard the search for laws to be extremely difficult, because of the complexity and variability of human behavior, but the growing erosion of cultural anthropology's humanistic component following from the scientific pursuit of laws dismayed him. He identified ethnology with history rather than science, history denoting for Kroeber not primarily time sequence but an attitude of mind, including an attachment to particular phenomena studied in their space and time context. Like the discipline of history itself, cultural anthropology is ideographically oriented. It tries to understand events, to integrate them, to develop the context in which they exist, and to find patterns within them. Such research takes place on a descriptive level rather than on the explanatory level, where the nomothetically oriented natural sciences pursue scientific laws by generalizing from particular phenomena, thereby stripping them of their place and time setting. But more than identifying science with the search for laws and generalization, Kroeber regarded it as reductionistic. Cultural anthropology, he agreed, could to a limited extent be scientific in organizing knowledge about cause and effect in culture, or when studying process, but he uncompromisingly held cultural phenomena to be qualitatively distinct from organic phenomena, and maintained they should not be reduced to organic factors in the process of explaining them.

A Momentous Period

Cultural Process

Each of the last two chapters covered a century or a little more; this one spans only half a century, but for the history of North American anthropology it was a momentous time. When the period began, ethnologists were almost totally occupied with culture history, employing the method of German historical ethnology, which had diffused to America. Then, as the decades went by and the number of professional anthropologists increased, ethnological interest shifted increasingly to cultural process. More and more the ethnologists asked questions like: how are culture traits invented or accommodated in a society after arriving through diffusion? How is culture learned? Why or when are culture traits dropped or exchanged for other traits during sustained culture contact? American archeology, however, could spare very little effort for studying process; it was too busy improving its ability to discover chronology, i.e., doing history.[102] The uncoordinated development of the two major divisions of cultural anthropology grew more pronounced as ethnology and what came to be called social anthropology increasingly adopted a synchronic orientation with the rise of culture and personality and following the influence exerted by Bronislaw Malinowski and A. R. Radcliffe-Brown. The period closes with archeology specializing in historical description, while ethnology has shed much of its interest in long-term history in order to study cultural process.

Reacting against the deductive thinking rampant in both classical evolutionism and German diffusionism, American ethnology became firmly inductive; particularistic; relativistic in both a heuristic and philosophical sense; and in avoiding systematic theories for explaining cultural phenomena, atheoretical. Boas and many of the anthropologists he trained were reluctant to impose—prematurely, they explained—any theoretical system on cultural forms; they were unwilling to consider almost any meaning applying to social phenomena not provided by informants, or any conclusion not based on cultural forms studied in a specific space-time context. The historical viewpoint and, increasingly with time, the integrational, configurational, and psychological perspectives were employed in ways compatible with the particularistic position adopted by members of the American Historical Tradition. In using the psychological viewpoint, the Americans did not, of course, trace culture to psychogenic causes (psychoanalysts were suggesting they do so, however); instead, with very little explicit psychological theory, they observed the role of the individual acting as innovator and as the gatekeeper who has the power to decide what new traits will enter a culture and what form they will take when they do. In the late 1920s American ethnologists also began to study the influence of culture on individuals. However, for a superorganicist like Kroeber, the idea of the individual governing culture change proved unacceptable; he saw culture moving through time in response to factors that might be hard to identify but over which, he was sure, individuals could exert little control.

Anthropologists were still humanistic enough to hope that their work would have general value for society, and they wrote books to educate the nonacademic public on race, culture, socialization, eugenics, and other subjects. But the usual problems they tackled and the discoveries they reported in books and journal articles could interest only fellow professionals who had been educated to share the same concerns. Not many members of the reading public were eager to know why the tribes of the world are different in culture and how those differences developed. Rarely did the anthropologists' professional disputes gear into political and social issues. They persisted in criticizing the method of the British developmentalists even after it ceased to be practiced, they differed over whether laws of culture could be found, and they disputed whether cultural anthropology needed the concept of the superorganic. Mostly, then, amongst themselves the anthropologists were practicing a highly specialized and sometimes recondite discipline.

The American Historical Tradition took the culture concept as Tylor defined it and extended it with additional orienting concepts, like trait, culture complex, style, and several kinds of patterns; processes, such as the patterning process, plus those old familiars, invention, diffusion, and reinterpretation; and an expanded outline of the universal culture pattern. If these ideas were not wholly new, they were now all set out together, in textbooks, for easy learning by generations of college students who had never realized how meticulously their customs could be analyzed. Acculturation fit into the list of processes, but it was also the name given to an emerging field of inquiry, the study of cultural microchange in situations of culture contact. Culture-area mapping practiced by the American ethnologists called for looking at relationships between culture and geographical environment, definitely more for ecological relationships than for geographical determinants. Growing interest in psychoanalysis and child-rearing, both in the universities and more popularly, were reflected in anthropological studies of socialization, and in the founding of a new subfield involving the relationships between culture and personality. An older set of topics—descent, kinship terms, and other aspects of domestic social structures—was energetically pursued, generally with the result of confirming extant theory rather than with any major new discoveries. In the study of religion the concept of crisis cults, inherited from Mooney, proved to be an innovation that lasted and led to productive research. Anthropologists continued to be self-critical of the discipline's methods and concepts; they recognized the construct nature of culture, and realized how chimerical it is to expect a high degree of objectivity in ethnography.

On the whole, the American Historical Tradition is more notable for the new fields it introduced, especially culture and personality and the study of cultural micro-change, and for the transition it made from primarily diachronic to increasingly synchronic research, than for any major innovations in explanatory theory or in methods. After the Second World War, such innovations would appear aplenty, the product in many cases of anthropologists who had received their training during the final decades of the Tradition.

Notes

1. Eric R. Wolf, "American Anthropologists and American Society," in Stephen A. Tyler, ed., *Concepts and Assumptions in Contemporary Anthropology* (Southern Anthropological Society Proceedings No. 3, 1969).

2. Franz Boas, "The Limitations of the Comparative Method of Anthropology" [orig. 1896] in Franz Boas,

Race, Language and Culture (Paperback ed.; New York: Free Press of Glencoe, 1966), pp. 276–280; Franz Boas, "Anthropology," in *Encyclopaedia of the Social Sciences* (1930), vol. 2, pp. 73, 106.

3. Franz Boas, *Primitive Art* [orig. 1927] (New York: Dover Publications, 1955), pp. 5–6; Leslie Spier,

"Problems Arising from the Cultural Position of the Havasupai," *American Anthropologist*, vol. 31 (1929): 213–222, pp. 218–219.

4. Boas, *Primitive Art*, p. 7; Boas, "Limitations"; Boas, "Anthropology," pp. 109–110; Franz Boas, *Anthropology and Modern Life* [orig. 1928] (New York: W. W. Norton and Co., 1962), pp. 204, 208–211, 236; Franz Boas, "Methods of Ethnology," in Boas, *Race, Language, and Culture*, pp. 267–285; A. L. Kroeber, *Anthropology* (New York: Harcourt, Brace and Co., 1923), pp. 304, 306–307, 325; A. L. Kroeber, *Configurations of Culture Growth* [orig. 1944] (Berkeley: University of California Press, 1969), p. 761; Robert H. Lowie, *Social Organization* (New York: Rinehart and Co., 1948), ch. 3.

5. Kroeber, *Configurations*, p. 843.

6. Lesser, "Research Procedure and Laws of Culture," *Philosophy of Science*, vol. 6 (1939): 345–355.

7. Lesser, "Research Procedure," pp. 348, 353.

8. Clark Wissler, *Man and Culture* (New York: Thomas Y. Crowell Co., 1923), p. 327; Franz Boas, "The History of Anthropology" [orig. 1904], in George W. Stocking, Jr., ed., *The Shaping of American Anthropology, 1883–1911* (New York: Basic Books, 1974), p. 36; Ralph Linton, *The Study of Man* (New York: D. Appleton Century Co., 1936), p. 489.

9. A. L. Kroeber et al., *Franz Boas 1858–1942* (Memoirs of the American Anthropological Association, no. 61, 1943); Walter Goldschmidt, ed., *The Anthropology of Franz Boas,* (Memoirs of the American Anthropological Association, no. 89, 1959). For critical studies see Leslie White, *The Ethnography of Franz Boas* (Texas Memorial Bulletin 6, 1963); Murray Wax, "The Limitations of Boas' Anthropology," *American Anthropologist*, vol. 58 (1956): 63–74.

10. From those trips we have letters and diaries collected in Ronald P. Rohner, ed., *The Ethnography of Franz Boas* (Chicago: University of Chicago Press, 1969).

11. Boas, "Limitations." Other criticisms in this paragraph are taken from the following works by Franz Boas: *The Mind of Primitive Man* (New York: Macmillan Co., 1911), ch. 7; "Methods of Research," in Franz Boas, ed., *General Anthropology* (New York: D. C. Heath and Co., 1938), pp. 676–677; *Primitive Art*, p. 352; *Anthropology and Modern Life*, pp. 212–21.

12. David H. French, "Goldenweiser, Alexander A.," in *International Encyclopedia of the Social Sciences* (1968), vol. 6; Wilson D. Wallis, "Alexander A. Goldenweiser," *American Anthropologist*, vol. 43 (1941): 250–255.

13. Alexander Goldenweiser, "Wilhelm Wundt's Theories" [orig. 1922], in Alexander Goldenweiser, *History, Psychology, and Culture* (New York: Alfred A. Knopf, 1933); Alexander Goldenweiser, "Diffusion and the American School of Historical Ethnology," *American Journal of Sociology*, vol. 31 (1925–1926): 19–38, p. 20.

14. See, for example, Robert H. Lowie, *The Origin of the State* (New York: Harcourt, Brace and Co., 1927); Robert H. Lowie, *An Introduction to Cultural Anthropology* (2nd ed.; New York: Rinehart and Co., 1940), pp. 98, 344; Robert H. Lowie, "Subsistence," and N. C. Nelson, "Prehistoric Archaeology," both in Boas, *General Anthropology*, p. 282 and ch. 5; A. L. Kroeber, "Sub-human Culture Beginnings," *The Quarterly Review of Biology*, vol. 3 (1928): 325–342.

15. The following works by A. L. Kroeber are referred to: *Style and Civilizations* (Paperbound ed.; Berkeley: University of California Press, 1963), pp. 149–160; *An Anthropologist Looks at History*, Theodora Kroeber, ed. (Berkeley: University of California Press, 1963), pp. 23–57, 84; *Anthropology* (new ed.; New York: Harcourt, Brace and Co., 1948), pp. 296–304; and "Evolution, History and Culture," in *Evolution after Darwin*, vol. 2, *The Evolution of Man*, Sol Tax, ed. (Chicago: University of Chicago Press, 1960), p.

15. See also Linton, *The Study of Man*, pp. 87–90.

16. Wissler, *Man and Culture*, pp. 358–359.

17. Only a small sample of references need be cited: the articles by Franz Boas, Review of Graebner *Methode der Ethnologie* [orig. 1911], and "The Methods of Ethnology" [orig. 1920], both in Boas, *Race, Language and Culture* (Paperback ed.; New York: Free Press, 1966); Goldenweiser, "Diffusionism"; Robert H. Lowie, "On the Principle of Convergence in Ethnology," *Journal of American Folk-Lore*, vol. 25 (1912): 24–42, pp. 26–27.

18. Alexander Goldenweiser, "Totemism: An Analytical Study" [orig. 1910], in Goldenweiser, *History, Psychology, and Culture;* Alexander Goldenweiser, *Anthropology* (New York: F. S. Crofts and Co., 1937), p. 326; Robert H. Lowie, "A New Conception of Totemism" [orig. 1911], in *Lowie's Selected Papers in Anthropology*, Cora Du Bois, ed. (Berkeley: University of California Press, 1960); Leslie Spier, "Historical Interrelations of Culture Traits: Franz Boas' Study of Tsimshian Mythology," in Stuart A. Rice, ed., *Methods in Social Science* (Chicago: University of Chicago Press, 1931).

19. Robert H. Lowie, *Primitive Society* [orig. 1920] (Torchbook ed.; New York: Harper and Bros., 1961), p. 441.

20. Otis T. Mason, "Similarities in Culture," *American Anthropologist*, vol. 8 o. s. (1895): 101–117, p. 114.

21. What follows is from Franz Boas, "Anthropology," pp. 98–99; Robert H. Lowie, "Psychology, Anthropology, and Race" [orig. 1923], and his "The Family as a Social Unit" [orig. 1933], both in *Lowie's Selected Papers;* Lowie, "Subsistence"; Boas, *Anthropology and Modern Life*, ch. 2; and Kroeber, *Anthropology* (1923 ed.), p. 182. The references to standards of ethics and normality are from Ruth Benedict, "Anthropology and the Abnormal" [orig. 1938], in Margaret Mead, ed., *An Anthropologist at Work* (New York: Atherton Press, 1966), p. 283. However, A. Irving

Hallowell antedates some of her ideas in his "Psychic Stresses and Culture Patterns," *American Journal of Psychiatry*, vol. 92 (1936): 1291–1310, p. 1295.

22. The rest of the paragraph is from the following works by Margaret Mead: *Coming of Age in Samoa* (New York: William Morrow and Co., 1928), ch. 13; "An Investigation of the Thought of Primitive Children with Special Reference to Animism," *Journal of the Royal Anthropological Institute*, vol. 62 (1932): 173–190; and *Sex and Temperament* (New York: William Morrow and Co., 1935), ch. 17.

23. Wissler, *Man and Culture*, pp. 260–273, 289–302; Linton, *Study of Man*, chs. 4, 5, and 9.

24. Adelin Linton and Charles Wagley, *Ralph Linton* (New York: Columbia University Press, 1971), p. 14.

25. Franz Boas, "The Aims of Anthropological Research" [orig. 1932], and Franz Boas, "Some Problems of Methodology in the Social Sciences" [orig. 1930], both in Boas, *Race, Language and Culture*, pp. 256–257, 260–269. Franz Boas, "Recent Anthropology," *Science*, vol. 98 (1943): 311–314, 334–337; pp. 314, 336, 337.

26. Lesser, "Research Procedure."

27. Boas, *Anthropology and Modern Life*, pp. 212, 214, 219–221; Kroeber, *Configurations*, pp. vii, 5; Kroeber, *Style and Civilizations*, p. 156; Lowie, *Primitive Society*, pp. 439–441; Edward Sapir, "Culture, Genuine and Spurious" [orig. 1924], in *Selected Writings of Edward Sapir in Language, Culture, and Personality*, David Mandelbaum, ed. (Berkeley: University of California Press, 1968); Kroeber, "Evolution, History, and Culture."

28. George Peter Murdock, "Clark Wissler, 1870–1947," *American Anthropologist*, vol. 50 (1948): 292–304.

29. Julian H. Steward, "Alfred Lewis Kroeber, 1876–1960," *American Anthropologist*, vol. 63 (1961): 1038–1060; Theodora Kroeber, *Alfred Kroeber* (Berkeley: University of California Press, 1970).

30. Wissler, *Man and Culture*, pp. 36–39, 41, 197–198. In the case of Kroeber,

I freely use his works and ideas that postdate the height of the Tradition but fit its interests closely and, more important, contain the mature distillate of his thinking about culture; such sources include: *Anthropology* (1948 ed.), pp. 255, 297; *Configurations*, p. 97; *Style and Civilizations*, pp. 36–37.

31. Wissler, *Man and Culture*, pp. 49–53, 63–71; Kroeber, *Anthropology* (1948 ed.), pp. 292–293.

32. Stanislaus Klimek, *Culture Element Distributions: I—The Structure of California Indian Culture* (University of California Publications in American Archaeology and Ethnology, vol. 37, no. 1, 1939), pp. 16–17.

33. A. L. Kroeber, *Cultural and Natural Areas of North America* (University of California Publications in American Archaeology and Ethnology, vol. 38, 1939); Kroeber, *Anthropology* (1948 ed.), p. 293; Kroeber, *Style and Civilizations*, p. 156.

34. Kroeber, *Anthropology* (1948 ed.), p. 329; Kroeber, *Style and Civilizations*, chs. 1–2; Kroeber, *An Anthropologist Looks at History*, pp. 14ff., 40, 67–68, 85.

35. Boas, *Primitive Art*, pp. 83, 354; Linton, *The Study of Man*, pp. 99–102; and the following works by A. L. Kroeber: *Anthropology* (1948 ed.), pp. 286–287, 311–329; "The History and Present Orientation of Cultural Anthropology," in *Nature of Culture* (Chicago: University of California Press, 1952), p. 148, and *An Anthropologist Looks at History*, p. 22, *Configurations*, pp. vii, 13, 799–800.

36. Wissler, *Man and Culture*, pp. 74–79.

37. A. L. Kroeber, "On the Principle of Order in Civilization as Exemplified by Changes of Fashion," *American Anthropologist*, vol. 21 (1919): 235–263.

38. Edward Sapir, "The Unconscious Patterning of Behavior in Society," in Ethel S. Dummer, ed., *The Unconscious* (New York: Alfred A. Knopf, 1929).

39. Boas cited in Elvin Hatch, *Theories of Man and Culture* (New York: Columbia University Press, 1973), p. 60. See also Franz Boas, "The

Growth of the Secret Societies of the Kwakiutl" [orig. 1897], in Boas, *Race, Language and Culture.*

40. R. H. Lowie, "Ceremonialism in North America" [orig. 1914], in *Lowie's Selected Papers*, pp. 354–355; Margaret Mead, "Search 1920–1930," and Edward Sapir, letter to Ruth Benedict, both in Mead, *An Anthropologist at Work*, pp. 14–15, 49.

41. Ruth Benedict, "The Vision in Plains Culture" [orig. 1922], in Mead, *An Anthropologist at Work*, pp. 19–20.

42. Ruth Benedict, *Patterns of Culture* [orig. 1934] (Sentry ed.; Cambridge: Riverside Press, 1959), pp. 23ff.

43. Margaret Mead, *Social Organization of Manua* (Bernice P. Bishop Museum Bulletin 76, 1930), pp. 80–87.

44. The following works by A. L. Kroeber: "The Superorganic" [orig. 1917], and "The Concept of Culture in Science" [orig. 1949], both in *The Nature of Culture; Anthropology* (1948 ed.), pp. 253–256.

45. Herbert J. Spinden, "The Prosaic vs. the Romantic School in Anthropology," in G. Elliott [sic] Smith et al., *Culture, The Diffusion Controversy* (New York: W. W. Norton and Co., 1927); Edward Sapir, "Do We Need a 'Superorganic'?" *American Anthropologist*, vol. 19 (1917): 441–447. Even Kroeber occasionally succumbs to this pattern of thought; see his *Anthropology* (1923 ed.), p. 238. For a contrary view, see Wissler, *Man and Culture*, pp. 252–258.

46. Ruth Benedict, "Edward Sapir," *American Anthropologist*, vol. 41 (1939): 465–477; D. G. Mandelbaum and Z. S. Harris, "Sapir, Edward," in *International Encyclopedia of the Social Sciences* (1968), vol. 14; Richard J. Preston, "Edward Sapir's Anthropology: Style, Structure, and Method," *American Anthropologist*, vol. 68 (1966): 1105–1128.

47. For North American culture-area research before and during the American Historical Tradition, see: Otis T. Mason, "Influence of Environment upon Human Industries or Arts," *Annual Reports of the Board of Regents of the Smithsonian Institution for the Year Ending June 30, 1895: 639–*

665; Livingston Farrand, *Basis of American History, 1500–1900* (New York: Harper and Bros., 1904), p. 101. Various works by Clark Wissler: "The Culture-Area Concept in Social Anthropology," *The American Journal of Sociology*, vol. 32 (1927): 881–891; *The American Indian* (3rd ed.; New York: Oxford University Press, 1938), pp. xv, 1, 200–203, 219–220, 260–261, 287, 298; *Man and Culture*, pp. 62, 139, 143, 318–319, 342–343, 350, 353, 358–359; *The Relation of Nature and Man in Aboriginal America* (New York: Oxford University Press, 1926), pp. 212–218. Kroeber, *Cultural and Natural Areas*, chs. 1, 11, 14–15; Harold E. Driver, *The Contribution of A. L. Kroeber to Culture Area Theory and Practice* (Indiana University Publications in Anthropology and Linguistics, mem. 18, 1962).

48. Lowie, "Subsistence," pp. 285, 288–289, 302, 320; Robert H. Lowie, "Cultural Anthropology: A Science" [orig. 1936], in *Lowie's Selected Papers*, pp. 398–399; Lowie, *Culture and Ethnology*, pp. 62–65.

49. Ralph Linton, "The Processes of Culture Transfer," in Ralph Linton, ed., *Acculturation in Seven American Indian Tribes* (New York: Appleton-Century-Crofts, 1940), pp. 493–494.

50. Alexander Goldenweiser, "The Origin of Totemism" [orig. 1912], in Goldenweiser, *History, Psychology, and Culture*, pp. 339ff; Lowie, *Primitive Society*, p. 441.

51. See the exchange of correspondence between Franz Boas and Otis T. Mason, joined by others, in *Science*, vol. 9 (1887): 485–486, 534–535, 587–589, 612–614.

52. Boas, "Anthropology," pp. 89, 91, 97, 98–102, 110; Boas, "Methods of Research," p. 678; Franz Boas, "Mythology and Folklore," in Boas, *General Anthropology*, pp. 618–623; Boas, "Aims of Anthropological Research," p. 256.

53. Clark Wissler, *Social Anthropology* (New York: Henry Holt and Co., 1929), p. 362; Wissler also noted close links between culture and population in *Man and Culture*, chs. 13, 16. The term "functional relations"

to express interdependence and coherence between parts of culture recurs in Kroeber, *Anthropology* (1948 ed.), p. 310.

54. Paul Radin, "Robert H. Lowie 1883–1957," *American Anthropologist*, vol. 60 (1958): 358–375; Robert F. Murphy, *Robert H. Lowie* (New York: Columbia University Press, 1972); Robert H. Lowie, *Robert H. Lowie, Ethnologist* (Berkeley: University of California, 1959).

55. The following works by Robert H. Lowie: *Primitive Religion* (London: George Routledge and Sons, 1925), p. 268; *An Introduction to Cultural Anthropology*, pp. 439, 531–532, 540; *Social Organization*, ch. 8; *A History of Ethnological Theory* (New York: Farrar and Rinehart, 1937), p. 277; Review of W. H. R. Rivers's "Kin, Kinship," *American Anthropologist*, vol. 19 (1917): 269–272, p. 269; *Culture and Ethnology* [orig. 1917] (New York: Basic Books, 1966), p. 103.

56. Benedict, *Patterns of Culture*, ch. 3 and p. 223. For other references to configurationalism see Mead, *Manua*, pp. 80–87; Boas, "Methods of Research," p. 673; Boas, "Anthropology," p. 100; Kroeber, *Anthropology* (1948 ed.), p. 294; Kroeber, *An Anthropologist Looks at History*, pp. 22–23; Linton, *Study of Man*, ch. 25.

57. Ruth Benedict, "The Story of My Life . . ." and Mead, "Search: 1920–1930," both in Mead, *An Anthropologist at Work*; Margaret Mead, "Benedict, Ruth," *International Encyclopedia of the Social Sciences* (1968), vol. 2; Victor Barnouw, "Ruth Benedict: Apollonian and Dionysian," *University of Toronto Quarterly*, vol. 18 (1949): 241–253.

58. Abraham H. Maslow and John J. Honigmann, "Synergy: Some Notes of Ruth Benedict," *American Anthropologist*, vol. 72 (1970): 320–333. In 1937 Margaret Mead also described how a social system may avoid competition by converting a desired end from an individual goal to a group goal; see her "Interpretive Statement," in Margaret Mead, ed., *Cooperation and Competition among Primitive Peoples* [orig. 1937] (re-

vised paperback ed.; Boston: Beacon Press, 1961), p. 466.

59. Franz Boas, "Introduction," in Franz Boas, ed., *Handbook of American Indian Languages* (2 vols.; New York: J. J. Augustin, 1911, 1922), vol. 1; Franz Boas, *Geographical Names of the Kwakiutl Indians,* (Columbia University Contributions to Anthropology, vol. 20, 1934), p. 9.

60. Boas, *The Mind of Primitive Man* [orig. 1911] (revised ed.; New York: Free Press, 1938), pp. 192–225, ch. 12, (the first edition of 1911 contains a chapter on "The Mental Traits of Primitive Man and of Civilized Man").

61. Paul Radin, *Primitive Man as a Philosopher* [orig. 1927] (New York: Dover Publications, 1957), chs. 5–6.

62. Stanley Diamond, "Radin, Paul," in *International Encyclopedia of the Social Sciences* (1968), vol. 13; Harry Hoijer, "Paul Radin 1883–1959," *American Anthropologist,* vol. 61 (1959): 839–843.

63. Franz Boas, "Psychological Problems in Anthropology," *American Journal of Psychology,* vol. 21 (1910): 371–384.

64. Alexander Goldenweiser, "Religion and Society" [orig. 1916] and his "Psychology and Culture" [orig. 1925], both in Goldenweiser, *History, Psychology, and Culture.*

65. Lowie, *Primitive Religion,* pp. 221, 267–272, 306; see also his "Individuum und Gesellschaft in der Religion der Naturvölker," *Zeitschrift für Ethnologie,* vol. 83 (1958): 161–169.

66. Wissler, *Man and Culture,* p. 329.

67. Robert H. Lowie, "Individual Differences in Primitive Culture," in Wilhelm Koppers, ed., *Festschrift: Publication d'homage offerte au P. W. Schmidt* (Vienna: Missionsdruckerei St. Gabriel, 1928); Paul Radin, ed., *Crashing Thunder, the Autobiography of an American Indian* (New York: Appleton-Century-Crofts, 1926); A. L. Kroeber, ed., *Walapai Ethnography* (Memoirs of the American Anthropological Association, no. 42, 1935).

68. Linton, *Study of Man,* pp. 271–274.

69. The following articles by Edward Sapir: "The Unconscious Patterning of Behavior in Society" [orig. 1927]; "Anthropology and Sociology" [orig. 1927], pp. 342–343; "Cultural Anthropology and Psychiatry" [orig. 1932]; "Personality" [orig. 1934]; "The Emergence of a Concept of Personality in the Study of Cultures" [orig. 1934]; and "Why Cultural Anthropology Needs the Psychiatrist" [orig. 1938]; all are in *Selected Writings of Edward Sapir.*

70. Kroeber, *Style and Civilizations,* pp. 58–61.

71. Lowie, *Primitive Religion,* pp. 190, 198, 203; Lowie, *Culture and Ethnology,* pp. 12–16, 25–26.

72. Margaret Mead, Review of Géza Róheim, *The Riddle of the Sphinx, Character and Personality,* vol. 4 (1935–1936): 85–90, p. 88.

73. Margaret Mead, *Blackberry Winter* (New York: William Morrow and Co., Inc., 1972); Winthrop Sargeant, "It's All Anthropology," *The New Yorker,* Dec. 30, 1961: 31–44; David Dempsey, "The Mead and Her Message," *The New York Times Magazine,* April 26, 1970: 23, 74–79, 82, 99–103.

74. Mead, *Coming of Age;* Mead, *Sex and Temperament.*

75. Linton, *Study of Man,* pp. 101, 115, 277, 292, 299, and ch. 26; Morris Opler, "Personality and Culture, a Methodological Suggestion for the Study of Interrelations," *Psychiatry,* vol. 1 (1938): 217–220, p. 218; M. Mead, "The Use of Primitive Material in the Study of Personality," *Character and Personality,* vol. 3 (1934–1935), p. 10.

76. Benedict, "Anthropology and the Abnormal"; Benedict, *Patterns of Culture,* ch. 8.

77. Hallowell, "Psychic Stresses"; C. G. Seligman, "Temperament, Conflict and Psychosis in a Stone-Age Population," *British Journal of Medical Psychology,* vol. 9 (1929): 187–202.

78. Mead, *Sex and Temperament,* ch. 18.

79. Boas, "Aims of Ethnology," p. 638. Edward Sapir wrote a manual similar to Graebner's for use in historical reconstruction, *Time Perspective in*

Aboriginal American Culture, a Study in Method (Canada, Department of Mines, Geological Survey, memoir 90, 1916).

80. Wissler, *Man and Culture*, pp. 7, 9–10.

81. Roland B. Dixon, *The Building of Cultures* (New York: Charles Scribner's Sons, 1928). For biography see A. M. Tozzer and A. L. Kroeber, "Roland Burrage Dixon," *American Anthropologist*, vol. 38 (1936): 291–300; and Robert A. McKennan, "Dixon, Roland B.," in *International Encyclopedia of the Social Sciences* (1968), vol. 4.

82. Where I compare Dixon to Linton, I am drawing from Dixon, *Building of Cultures*, chs. 2, 3, 4; Ralph Linton, "Acculturation and Processes of Culture Change," and his "The Processes of Culture Transfer," both in Linton, *Seven American Indian Tribes*.

83. Edward Sapir, "Custom" [orig. 1931], in *Selected Writings of Edward Sapir*, pp. 367–368.

84. What follows derives from Boas, *Mind of Primitive Man*, pp. 210–214, 223; Lowie, *Culture and Ethnology*, pp. 92–93; Dixon, *Building of Cultures*, pp. 61–62; Kroeber, *Anthropology* (1948 ed.), pp. 346–347; Sapir, "Unconscious Patterning of Behavior"; Sapir, "Custom," pp. 368–370; and Edward Sapir, "Fashion" [orig. 1931], in *Selected Writings of Edward Sapir*, p. 377.

85. Richard Thurnwald, "The Psychology of Acculturation," *American Anthropologist*, vol. 34 (1932): 557–569.

86. What follows is from Melville J. Herskovits, *Acculturation: The Study of Culture Contact* (New York: J. J. Augustin, 1938), pp. 10–15, 23ff, 119; Ralph Linton, "The Distinctive Aspects of Acculturation," in Linton, *Seven American Indian Tribes*, also Linton's remarks on pp. 37–38 of that book; Ralph Linton, "Nativistic Movements," *American Anthropologist*, vol. 45 (1943): 230–240; Sapir, "Culture, Genuine and Spurious," p. 318; Paul Radin, *The Method and Theory of Ethnology* [orig. 1933] (New York: Basic Books, 1966), p. 123.

87. John R. Swanton, "The Social Organization of American Tribes," *American Anthropologist*, vol. 7 (1905): 663–673: Robert H. Lowie, "Family and Sib," *American Anthropologist*, vol. 21 (1919): 28–40; Lowie, *Primitive Society*, pp. 157–160; Lowie, *Social Organization*, pp. 248–258 (here he supports his argument by citing the research of Leslie Spier and Julian Steward); Boas, "Anthropology," pp. 85–86; Ronald L. Olson, *Clan and Moiety in Native North America* (University of California Publications in American Archaeology and Ethnology, vol. 33, no. 4, 1933).

88. I draw on the following works by Robert H. Lowie: "Exogamy and Classificatory Systems of Relationship," *American Anthropologist*, vol. 17 (1915): 223–239; *Culture and Ethnology*, ch. 5; *Primitive Society*, ch. 7; "Relationship Terms," in *Encyclopaedia Britannica* (14th ed.; 1929), vol. 19; "Kinship," in *Encyclopaedia of the Social Sciences* (1932), vol. 8; *Hopi Kinship* (Anthropological Papers of the American Museum of Natural History, vol. 30, part 7, 1929). Also, Edward Sapir, "Terms of Relationship and the Levirate," *American Anthropologist*, vol. 18 (1916): 327–337; Edward Winslow Gifford, *Miwok Moieties* (University of California Publications in American Archaeology and Ethnology, vol. 12, no. 4, 1916), pp. 184–187; Leslie Spier, *The Distribution of Kinship Systems in North America* (University of Washington Publications in Anthropology, vol. 1, 1925); Leslie White, "A Problem of Kinship Terminology," *American Anthropologist*, vol. 41 (1939): 566–573. Two papers take the position that kin terms precede sibs and moieties: Alexander Lesser, "Kinship Origins in the Light of Some Distributions," *American Anthropologist*, vol. 31 (1929): 710–730, p. 728; E. W. Gifford, "A Problem in Kinship Terminology," *American Anthropologist*, vol. 42 (1940): 190–194, p. 193.

89. Lowie, *Culture and Ethnology*, pp. 98–100; Lowie, *Primitive Society*, pp. 91–105; Lowie, *Social Organization*, pp. 84–86; Gladys Reichard, "Social Life," in Boas, *General Anthropology*, p. 457.

90. Clark Wissler, *An Introduction to Social Anthropology* (New York: Henry Holt and Co., 1929), ch. 2, pp. 40–41, 123, 130–136, ch. 7; Paul Radin, *Primitive Religion* [orig. 1937] (New York: Dover Publications, 1957), p. 253; Paul Radin, *The World of Primitive Man* (New York: Henry Schuman, 1953), pp. 222–223; Sapir, "Culture, Genuine and Spurious," p. 340; Sapir, "Anthropology and Sociology."

91. Robert Redfield, *Tepoztlán, a Mexican Village* (Chicago: University of Chicago Press, 1930), pp. 1–2, 217; Robert Redfield, "Folkways and City Ways" [orig. 1935], and "The Folk Society" [orig. 1942], both in *Human Nature and the Study of Society: The Papers of Robert Redfield*, Margaret Park Redfield, ed. (Chicago: University of Chicago Press, 1962).

92. Charles M. Leslie, "Redfield, Robert," in *International Encyclopedia of the Social Sciences* (1968), vol. 13; Fay-Cooper Cole and Fred Eggan, "Robert Redfield, 1897–1958," *American Anthropologist*, vol. 61 (1959): 652–662.

93. Margaret Mead, "Interpretive Statement," p. 480.

94. Robert H. Lowie, "Ludwig Feuerbach: A Pioneer of Modern Thought," *Liberal Review*, vol. 2 (1905): 20–31, p. 30; Lowie, *Primitive Religion*, pp. xii–xvii, 324–328; Robert H. Lowie, "Religion and Human Life," *American Anthropologist*, vol. 65 (1963): 532–542; see also his *Robert H. Lowie, Ethnologist*, pp. 133–135; Alexander Goldenweiser, *Robots or Gods: An Essay on Craft and Mind* (New York: Alfred A. Knopf, 1931); Radin, *Primitive Religion*, chs. 1, 3, 4, 12; Radin, *World of Primitive Man*, pp. 72, 84–85.

95. Radin, *Primitive Man as a Philosopher*, p. 16; Radin, *World of Primitive Man*, pp. 34–35.

96. "Mythology and Folklore," pp. 620–621.

97. Wilson D. Wallis, *Messiahs: Christian and Pagan* (Boston: R. G. Badger, 1918); Lowie, *Primitive Religion*, pp. 188–204; R. H. Lowie, "Primitive Messianism and an Ethnological Problem," *Diogenes*, no. 19 (1957): 62–73; Linton, "Nativistic Movements."

98. Wissler, *Social Anthropology*, ch. 15; Lowie, *Introduction to Cultural Anthropology*, pp. 316–324.

99. George A. Dorsey, *Why We Behave Like Human Beings* (New York: Harper and Bros., 1925), p. 393; Radin, *World of Primitive Man*, p. 235.

100. The paragraph draws from Clark Wissler, *Material Culture of the Blackfoot Indians* (Anthropological Papers of the American Museum of Natural History, vol. 5, part 1, 1910); Linton, *Study of Man* pp. 299–300; Linton, *Seven American Indian Tribes*, p. 466; Ralph Linton, *Cultural Background of Personality* (New York: D. Appleton-Century Co., 1945), pp. 45–46; Cora Du Bois, "Some Psychological Objectives and Techniques in Ethnography," *Journal of Social Psychology*, vol. 8 (1937): 285–300, 287; and Lesser, "Research Procedure," pp. 348, 353.

101. Lowie, *Primitive Society*, pp. 3–4; Lowie, "Cultural Anthropology: A Science." The following works are by A. L. Kroeber: "Eighteen Professions," *American Anthropologist*, vol. 17 (1915): 283–288; "The Superorganic"; "History and Science in Anthropology" [orig. 1935], and "So-called Social Science" [orig. 1936], both in his *Nature of Culture*; "Evolution, History, and Culture"; "Concluding Remarks," in Sol Tax, et al., eds., *An Appraisal of Anthropology Today* (Chicago: University of Chicago Press, 1953); and "The Personality of Anthropology," in his *An Anthropologist Looks at History*. For the historical background of Kroeber's position, see Robert Lowie, "Reminiscences of Anthropological Currents in America Half a Century Ago," *American Anthropologist*, vol. 58 (1956): 995–1016, pp. 1007–1008. See also Radin, *Method and Theory*

of Ethnology, pp. 11, 100–102;
Ruth Benedict, "Anthropology and
the Humanities," *American Anthropologist,* vol. 50 (1948): 585–593.

102. Gordon R. Willey and Jeremy A.
Sabloff, *A History of American
Archaeology* (San Francisco: W. H.
Freeman and Co., 1973), p. 88.

7

Radcliffe-Brown and Malinowski

New Currents in Anthropological Thought

The Functionalists

By the time the American Historical Tradition culminated in the 1920s, new currents in anthropological thought destined to have a powerful effect on American and British anthropology had taken shape in England. The two men, A. R. Radcliffe-Brown and Bronislaw Malinowski, who stirred up the new currents, bypassed what had for centuries been the most important problems in cultural study, the development and history of culture. Instead of writing about invention, diffusion, and patterning, these architects of a new direction described functions, social structures, and interconnections between institutions. Malinowski practically recreated ethnography in his detailed accounts of the Trobriand Islanders, each of his books devoting itself to a central topic—kinship, trading expeditions, or magic and agriculture—and purveying synchronic analysis as freely as descriptive data.

The two innovators studied anthropology in England, the country where A. R. Radcliffe-Brown was born and to which Malinowski emigrated. Radcliffe-Brown began with historical ethnology at Cambridge University under A. C. Haddon and W. H. R. Rivers, but between 1909 and 1914, while preparing a historical thesis on the Andaman Islands, he abruptly discarded the historical approach.[1] Historical reconstruction, he

---

Notes to this chapter begin on page 245.

was convinced, being largely speculative, could rarely provide any important understanding of human society. Reading Emile Durkheim and other French sociologists spurred his thinking along other theoretical lines, in which he persisted during the next 40 years and personally carried, like a peripatetic prophet, to South Africa, Australia, China, and the United States. Oxford University appointed him to its first chair in social anthropology, in 1937, the year before Malinowski finally left England for the United States.

Bronislaw Malinowski, the son of a philologist, spent his early life in Poland when the country still belonged to the Austro-Hungarian Empire.[2] He studied mathematics and physical science, switched to psychology, and then had his interest captured both by his teacher William Wundt's ethnology by James G. Frazer's ability in *Golden Bough* to reshape ethnographic facts into dramatic narrative.[3] In 1910, he journeyed to London for instruction in anthropology and sociology. Diffusion studies disappointed him from the start. He scorned the lifeless view of cultural forms being mechanically transported in pieces and reassembled, and he branded historical reconstructions by diffusionists unverifiable. Edward Westermarck's teaching and the embracing ethnographies on the Toda and the Veddah appealed to him far more, and so did the works of Joseph Conrad, whose literary ability Malinowski resolved to emulate in anthropology. From 1924 to 1938 he lectured in social anthropology at the London School of Economics and the University of London and thereafter, still at the height of his career, in the United States where he died suddenly, in 1942.

Both men have been called "functionalists" because of heavy reliance on the term "function" in their theories, and because they themselves used the word as a self-identifying label. No one has yet documented the history of the function concept in anthropology, apart from tracing it to Durkheim who, in 1895, maintained that a complete explanation of a social event required knowing not merely its sufficient cause but also the function it fulfills.[4] In Herbert Spencer's theory of evolution, the word "function" acquires a somewhat different connotation than it possesses in Durkheim, when he conjoins it with structure and gives it primacy over structure, saying structure arises to achieve functions.[5] At about this time psychology was also calling attention to the adaptive value of psychological processes, and pragmatism in philosophy was emphasizing the importance of consequences in determining the value of a thought or act. Whether or not Durkheim was influenced by developments in those fields, clearly he did not originate the idea of functional explanations for social behavior. Writers since classical times pointed out the unintended consequences of customs, and 18th-century utilitarian philosophers who identified the value of an act with its utility were on the same track. Auguste Comte, a major influence on Durkheim, made social institutions analogous to biological structures because of the way they operate to maintain society, a social organism.[6] In 1913, Frazer viewed superstitious beliefs as helping to maintain social institutions; fear of ghosts, for example, strengthening respect for human life and thereby contributing to the security and enjoyment of life.[7] When Radcliffe-Brown and Malinowski speak of functions, they usually, but by no means invariably, have in mind a similar concept of far-reaching utility, and not, as Rivers does, simply the use, intention, or specialized application of a trait.[8]

Radcliffe-Brown's Social Anthropology

Social Systems and Their Structures

Whatever deficiencies Radcliffe-Brown found in historical reconstruction, he did not reject the idea of social evolution.[9] Following Spencer closely, he regarded social evolution as paralleling the process of organic evolution. Through a combination of accident and law, evolution over time leads to greater diversification in the forms of society as more complex structures and organizations develop from simpler ones. His interest in evolution went little further, and in his division of anthropology he relegates the subject—along with historical linguistics, archeology, and the racial or cultural classification of people—to ethnology, a branch of the discipline removed from his own active interest. He devoted himself to social anthropology, defined by Radcliffe-Brown as employing natural science methods to study social phenomena, with the aim of building valid and significant generalizations based on theoretical understanding.[10]

A social anthropologist gains data by observing the multitude of actions and interactions occurring between individuals and groups comprising a social system.[11] He makes generalizations and tests them by comparing social systems. The actions and interactions form an integral whole, and none can be understood in isolation from others. Social systems, ranging from a society—the largest—to smaller component groups, are made up of normatively guided social relationships through which members, occupying particular statuses, pursue diverse interests and express values and sentiments. For a social system to exist at all, members must in some measure share moral, aesthetic, and economic interests or values; even common fears provide a shared interest capable of linking human beings in a group. A system may be internally consistent, a harmonious ordering of interests or values, or inconsistencies and marked deviations from norms may beset it. Should the latter dysnomic conditions exist, members will try to restore the equilibrium that once existed or, failing in their attempt, will modify the existing structure, sometimes creating a wholly new one and thereby bringing a new type of social system into being.

At any given time, a social system reveals both organization and structure. Organization (to which Radcliffe-Brown devotes minimal attention) refers to the arrangement of activities; structure, to the persisting pattern according to which people relate to one another and to their external environment. An investigator abstracts the pattern of social structure from the concrete relationships and guiding norms manifested or described by members of the social system. Basically, social anthropology wants to know how social systems maintain and change their structure and protect their solidarity. Structural continuity and social solidarity, according to theory, result from the way members' behavior is fitted together and standardized through norms, shared beliefs, and rituals. But all the theory has to say about the sources of structural change is that change follows from disequilibrium.

Numerous examples in Radcliffe-Brown's writings show how norms, rituals, and other social usages contribute to structural continuity and social solidarity.[12] To preferential cross-cousin marriage he ascribes the function of maintaining a structure of intermarrying groups from one generation to another. He credits regulated opposition between groups to the structural stability and solidarity of the opposed systems. To rituals he assigns a very important role in protecting the integrity of a social system. The "objects"—God, food, chiefs, and life crises like birth and death—to which the rituals are directed possess importance in the life of the people, or they symbolize something important for the social system. Periodically affirming the importance of those objects, and expressing other sentiments associated with them, renews the sentiments on which social solidarity depends, and also maintains them at a requisite degree of intensity. The misfortune and other sanctions threatened, if rituals are not performed, indicate the great importance of rituals for society. Diverse positive and negative sanctions, applied to behavior in general, likewise function to maintain sentiments and hence promote social integration.

"Social system," "social structure," and "function," relatively novel terms in English-language anthropology, contain the gist of Radcliffe-Brown's influential conception of social anthropology. "Culture" is not among the terms he frequently employed. When he used the word after *Andaman Islanders* (1922), it was without the inclusive definition advanced by Edward B. Tylor and favored among American and German anthropologists. He restricts the term to rules, symbols, and ways of thinking or feeling that govern social usages and standardize the behavior of people in social systems.[13]

Principles of Social Life

Radcliffe-Brown's less comprehensive ideas concerning such topics as descent, marriage, totemism, and kinship were sometimes as novel as his concepts of social structure and culture, but their influence varied. Descent he regards as a jural matter concerned with rights and duties.[14] Rights normally inhere in persons who form a group by virtue of sharing common interests stemming from locality, residence, or kinship. Marriage between persons belonging to different interest groups creates problems of succession in rights which, were they to remain unsolved, would promote conflict and threaten social continuity. Hence a social need exists to formulate precisely how those rights will pass on from one generation to another. Descent rules provide a solution by answering the questions: to whom does a child belong? From which set of kin, father's or mother's, does a child acquire rights? Which persons have rights over a child? The answers vary according to whether the rules specify patrilineal, matrilineal, or cognatic descent, the latter term in Radcliffe-Brown designating descent traced through both males and females and giving rise to ego-centered kindreds.

Preferential and prohibited marriage he explains functionally by the contribution they make to social continuity or structural stability.[15] In many primitive societies preferential marriage rules, including the sororate and levirate, maintain enduring relationships between families or larger bodies of kin, as do affinal exchanges of valuables and of ritual services. Rules against certain forms of marriage he explains in Carl Nicolai Starcke's terms, saying marriage tends to be prohibited when it would disrupt established relations between the persons affected.

In 1929, Radcliffe-Brown defined totemism quite conventionally as belonging to a class of beliefs that bring nature and society into a single conceptual system.[16] Totemism does so by establishing a ritual relationship between natural entities and human beings, the entities selected tending to be species vitally important for subsistence. Far more originally, in 1951, he analyzed totemism as a symbolic system expressing the integrative opposition linking moieties in a society. The opposed groups identify themselves with a pair of animals, or other natural species, whom myths depict as both allies and antagonists. Since belief conceives of the pair as complementary yet opposed, they are ideally suited to symbolize the moieties that are likewise in some respects complementary yet sometimes act in opposition to each other.

Radcliffe-Brown took kinship terms to be means of regulating role behavior according to the rights and privileges possessed by kin, including dead kinsmen in societies with ancestor rituals.[17] Useful explanations of kin terms and the behavior they govern, he believed, should be sought in the synchronic conditions under which both are maintained, not in bygone forms of marriage. However, the conditions he pointed to differed radically from those cited by other anthropologists who were equally dissatisfied with explaining kinship by extinct social institutions. In place of tracing a direct causal connection between moieties, forms of marriage, descent, or other institutions and kinship customs, he regarded the institutions and the kinship usages as being governed by certain properties of the social system to which both belonged. A correspondence between the sororate, and calling the wife's sister by the term used for the wife, arises because both variables are affected by the same underlying principles of social life, in this instance the principle of sibling equivalence. The principle of sibling equivalence, however, is only a special instance of a larger principle, the solidary principle, according to which an individual's relationship to one member of a strong solidary group brings him into equally close relations with all members. Another rule, the generational principle, according to which members of the parental generation possess authority over ego, whereas those of the grandparent generation stand in a relationship of near equality with him, throws light on Omaha-type kinship terminology, particularly on calling a mother's brother by the same term as grandfather. Categorizing the uncle in that way, Radcliffe-Brown explains, removed him from the generation of those with authority, the parental generation, and places him in a generation where he can be joked with and treated familiarly.

But why should joking occur between mother's brother and sister's son? Radcliffe-Brown gave considerable thought to the special relationship existing in some societies between a youth and his mother's brother. In one place (1924) he identifies the maternal uncle as a kind of male mother who reveals the same tenderness for a youth as the mother herself. But because the boy and his uncle are of the same sex, and because in primitive societies much familiarity is permitted to persons belonging to the same sex, the two may joke, something a son cannot do with his mother. Some years later (1940) he advanced a functional explanation for the joking component, the explanation containing elements of what later came to be called structural thinking. In patrilineally organized societies, although a person is emotionally attached to his mother's brother and other members of the mother's lineage, the most important rights and duties are owed to patrilineally related relatives. Hence the relationship with the mother's brother comes to be uncomfortably compounded of positive emotional attachment as well as jural distance. Structurally, joking between the two expresses both friendliness and antagonism; functionally, it organizes a stable system of social behavior between the two despite the conflicting elements inherent in their relationship.

Radcliffe-Brown's principles of social life won few adherents. The more parsimonious, better testable explanations of kinship terminology along the lines taken by Lewis Henry Morgan and W. H. R. Rivers tended to be preferred, even by Radcliffe-Brown's students, and he himself occasionally reverted to them.

Malinowski's Science of Culture

An Instrumental Apparatus

Radcliffe-Brown rarely mentions culture and finds little use for the concept in his social anthropology; Malinowski, however, accepted the fact that there already was a science of culture and proposed a theory of culture to apply in it. In the theory he employs the concept comprehensively, as Tylor did, to include everything man does as a member of society, adding that culture modifies the individual's innate endowment and serves to bind individuals into organized groups.[18]

The theory regards culture as a goal-oriented instrumental apparatus, through which people satisfy the organic and learned needs on which their existence and psychological well-being depend. The needs are directly met through hundreds of learned instrumental phases harbored in the institutions comprising a society. Each institution, in addition to a charter justifying what members do, possesses a purpose, norms, personnel, material apparatus, and activities. Whatever its purpose, every institution functions to satisfy a number of organic and secondary needs, and some institutions also serve needs derived from the necessity of keeping the vital instrumental phases going. Although the derived needs reside in the culture itself, they are as stringently demanding as organic needs, for they insure that the instrumental phases will be correctly learned, mastered, and maintained. Derived needs fall into two types: instrumental imperatives (such as the demand for leadership and a system of exchange) to keep the instrumental phases operating within and between generations, and integrative imperatives (including the need for a symbolic system, a body of knowledge, and religion) to uphold the established order, thereby indirectly to protect the instrumental phases as well as the instrumental imperatives.

Although in early books, *Argonauts of the Western Pacific* (1922) and *Sexual Life of Savages* (1919), Malinowski used the term functionalism to designate the conception of culture as integrated, as a system of mutually interdependent elements, he later applied the word to his idea of culture as a need-serving instrumental apparatus. Half-mockingly he called himself the "arch-functionalist," thus upstaging Radcliffe-Brown, who took pains to publicly dissociate himself from what he called Malinowski's "biological theory of culture." Everything in culture had to make sense to Malinowski. He was determined to reveal "law and order" existing among primitive people where, as he overstates it, travelers had reported "customs none, manner beastly." Functionalism, in any of the meanings he gave the word, provided the key for discovering sense in culture. Objects, he held, cannot be correctly defined by form, only by their purpose, use, or function—three terms between which Malinowski did not systematically distinguish.[19] In fact, the forms of material objects are determined by the purpose for which they are to be used; to meet such purposes adequately, they cannot diverge widely in the forms they take. Sometimes the sense he finds in culture with the aid of his instrumental theory is obvious, or it comes so close to being a definition (the function of knowledge, he says, is to organize and integrate cultural activities) that we wonder about the power of the theory.

Against the stereotype of savage beastliness, Malinowski insisted that despite the absence of European-type legal institutions, primitive societies have means for effectively maintaining social order.[20] He struggled for a comprehensive conception of law and found it in manifold aspects of interpersonal relations, not necessarily based on forceful constraint, that cause people to fulfill their duties. Above all he emphasized reciprocity as a sanction; because people desire to remain in a network of exchange and mutual help, they are constrained to meet their obligations, knowing persistent failure to do so would deprive them of help from others.

When Radcliffe-Brown called Malinowski's theory "biological," he no doubt overlooked the fact that, like himself, Malinowski also recognized social needs underlying cultural solutions. But Radcliffe-Brown correctly perceived his contemporary's tendency to relate cultural facts to non-cultural facts of nature. Malinowski points out, for example, the biological facts of sex, maternity, pregnancy, and birth are everywhere explained or regulated through culture, and thereby acquire moral significance.[21] Culture channels human reproduction; in all societies a woman must be married before she may legitimately conceive a child. Certain institutional types—the family, marriage, courtship, unilinear descent groups, age groups, and others—are universal, Malinowski believed, because they stem from universal common biological conditions, including biological reproduction, the genealogical bonds it forms, and distinctions between individuals based on sex and age.

Means of Escape

Malinowski's application of functional thinking to magic and religion is generally more successful, in the sense of being less obvious and more insightful, than his theory of culture as a system of institutions based on needs.[22] Although his ideas about the psychological functions of supernaturalism proceeds along lines old in Western social thought, it is occasionally original not only in the Trobriand Island data, which he uses to illustrate, but in the emphasis he puts on will and emotion, together with the vivid treatment he gives the subject through his writing skill.

Like his 19th-century predecessors, he distinguishes between magic and religion; but he also perceives resemblances between the two modes of dealing with the supernatural realm. Both allow man a way out of critical situations lacking direct means of escape, and both come into action under circumstances of emotional stress, such as death, unrequited love, or unsatisfied hate. The difference chiefly lies in the pragmatic nature of magic and the consummatory nature of religion. Whereas magic serves people as a means of achieving extrinsic and utilitarian ends, religion constitutes an end in itself. Magic also rests on simpler underlying ideas than religion, and can usually be carried out more simply. Yet—here Malinowski relies too much on the Trobriand Islands for his generalization, which follows Emile Durkheim and William Robertson Smith—magic is a task for a specialist, the magician, while religion is everyone's business, being public. Finally, magic can be set in motion to produce either good or evil ends, but religion exclusively concerns morality.

However bizarre magic seems to someone not sharing its premises, and however directly ineffectual it is for accomplishing its intended ends, from an objective point of view magic may be quite effective in inspiring hope or confidence, stimulating people to effort and perseverance, marshalling energy, and, in the case of sorcery, seriously upsetting its victims. Denying the venerable intellectualistic view of magic endorsed by Frazer, which derives magic from uninformed people's incorrect notions about nature, Malinowski resorts to an emotionalist conception akin to Freud's. Magic arises when a person, confronted by a critical condition for which he lacks practical knowledge, seeks autonomously to bring about the desired end. The tension set up in the organism by the unrealized goal drives the individual to perform some, any, kind of activity related to the end he desires. The activity is the magic. Despite being directly ineffectual, magic persists in society because of the compelling aura of myth surrounding it, and because when desired ends follow its applications, people ascribe the outcomes to the magic rather than to other, more practical acts they also performed. Also, the practitioners, being impressed with the credibility of magic, are always ready to explain its failures in ways that actually reinforce belief, claiming the rite was incorrectly executed or blaming the intervention of powerful countermagic.

If in regard to the social organization of magic, Malinowski overgeneralizes from the Trobriands, with respect to the beliefs and functions of religion he, an agnostic, appears frequently to have the religion of Western societies in mind. Religious belief, he writes, predicates the existence of universal powers sympathetic to man and ready to assist him. Embodied in ritual, it expresses feelings—joy when community affairs go well, fear of the dead, bereavement, and the power inherent in tradition. Religion promises compensation for this world's pains in another existence starting after death. Functionally considered, religion promotes social conformity, provides strength, augments endurance, relieves fear and ambivalence regarding death, and reintegrates the disturbed emotions of the bereaved. Something so indispensable, he agrees with Durkheim, cannot be mere trickery or deception.

In his conception of myth, Malinowski is often original, but it, too, suffers from an inadequate data base on which to generalize.[23] Myths trace magic, religious beliefs, and ceremonies, even the social order itself, to extraordinary events in the past wherein they originated. Again he bypasses the intellectualistic tradition, which saw myths grounded in ignorance of empirical history; he refuses to discuss the truth or falsity of such narratives, saying they complement empirical knowledge rather than substitute for it. Myths vindicate belief, step up incentive, offer justification for what exists, and, by sanctioning the performance of institutions, protect the vital functions the institutions serve.

Kinship and Descent

The problem of how kin-term systems relate to marriage customs and other social institutions got little attention from Malinowski. He addressed himself to a different question in the area of kinship; namely, the meaning possessed by kin terms applied to primary relatives and simultaneously extended to other relatives. This problem is closer to the interests of Kroeber, in his 1909 paper, and to formal semantic analysis of the 1960s, than to the traditional concerns of Rivers and Robert Lowie. Although Malinowski does not acknowledge any help received from psychological theory in solving the problem of meaning, his solution to the problem as well as his analysis of extended incest rules implicitly rely on the psychological principle of generalization and are anchored in an equally inexplicit theory of individual development in what he calls a life-cycle approach.[24]

The dyadic relationship of a child with mother, father, and siblings, he maintains, provides the basic pattern of kinship attitudes, which the child later applies to consanguineally related relatives and to genealogically unrelated persons. In the "initial situation" of the family, the primary meanings of kinship terms are formed; later they are transformed as the child in a primitive society ventures into other households and discovers persons who are also identified as his "mothers" or "fathers." Although a part of the primary meaning of those words continues to inhere in their use, in fact each such term applied to a different class of persons possesses also its own specific individual meaning. Context, sound, and emotional connotation serve to distinguish the individual meanings. But the individual meanings are not haphazardly built up; "they are related to each other; they start with a main or primary reference; which then through successive extensions engenders a series of derived meanings."

Malinowski's field work taught him firsthand that the jural obligations of an individual with members of his descent group never destroy the individual's bonds to his own nuclear family. Hence in societies with unilinear descent rules, parents continue to be significant figures in a person's legal, religious, economic, and emotional life.

What Malinowski has to say about the functions of incest rules in the family and in wider social relationships had already been said. For the most part, he simply reasserts Starcke's theory, grandly declaring incest to be "incompatible with the establishment of culture."[25] Consistent with his developmental theory of kinship, he traces extensions of the incest rule back to the nuclear family, claiming that exogamy demanded between unilinear descent groups represents an elaboration of prohibitions against sexual relations between parent and child and between siblings of opposite sex.

The psychological perspective in his view of individuals initially learning kinship patterns in the nuclear family becomes much more conspicuous in *Sex and Repression,* the first substantive anthropological study of culture and personality.[26] The author asks whether the knot of ambivalent sentiments—rivalry with the father for the mother's attention, and passionate but frustrated attachment to the mother—identified by Freud as the Oedipus complex, occurs in all societies. Agreeing with the psychoanalysts that family life always hold fateful implications for human personality, he uses data from the Trobriand Islands to support the argument that the conflicts, passions, and attachments found between members of the family vary with different forms of family structure. In the matrilineal Trobriands, where sex play is allowed, where a child is permitted to cling sensuously to its mother, where a father acts as his son's friend and helper rather than as an awesome figure of authority, and where the mother's brother is the powerful figure in a child's life, children fail to develop the oedipal complications found in Europe. Instead, a different complex occurs, one involving a boy in an ambivalent relationship with his maternal uncle, and creating an illicit attraction to his sisters and other female sibmates. Significantly, the complex appears at the age when the boy must submit to the authority of his mother's brother and accept the prohibitions of sib exogamy. Evidence of the complex shows up in dreams, in myths depicting the relationship of maternal uncle and nephew as fraught with suspicion and hostility, and in other individual and cultural products.

Orthodox psychoanalysts rejected the idea of a socially influenced Oedipus complex. Nevertheless, Malinowski's venture into culture and personality accurately foreshadowed the development of sociologically oriented psychoanalytic theories emphasizing the cultural patterning of personality forces such as were constructed by Karen Horney, Erich Fromm, and to a lesser extent Abram Kardiner starting in the later 1930s.

A Dialectical Theory of Change

In his posthumously published inquiry into culture change, devoted largely to subsaharan Africa, Malinowski recognizes the ubiquity of diffusion in contemporary culture contact, but devotes most attention to the dialectical situation created by the opposition between European pressures and native resistance in those colonial lands.[27] Interaction between the two factors determines how change occurs and what new social forms will arise. Novel types of social organization cannot be predicted from a knowledge of European or African culture alone; they emerge from the clash and interplay of different ways of life. Malinowski explains resistance to change by the firm integration of native institutions with one another, and by their functional utility in satisfying essential needs. Yet he was no out-and-out cultural relativist, in the early 1940s, when he organized his conception of the dynamics of culture change in contemporary Africa. He castigates Europeans for failing to provide all the new institutions needed to satisfy the basic demands of native people. For culture change to be successful in the modern world, he implies, native communities must be helped to acquire the same range of satisfiers enjoyed by members of the dominant European societies.

Essaying into critical anthropology, he condemns the neutral stance of anthropological studies carried out in colonial territories. A true and fair presentation of native life requires the ethnographer to state very clearly, for the benefit of traders, missionaries, and other agents of the dominant society, what the natives really need and what they suffer from under the pressures of culture contact.

It was not the first time Malinowski looked at the enterprise of ethnography itself. In his first book, a study of the Australian family, done without field work from published sources, he examines how an observer's personal characteristics, role, and field relationships affect what he learns and reports.[28] Every observer, including the professional ethnographer, brings biases to what he perceives. The ethnographer's chief hazard lies in the theory guiding him when he abstracts common empirical features from a series of singular observations. He cites examples from early Australian ethnographies of instances in which theoretical presuppositions had unwittingly led reporters to substitute inference for factual generalization.

The Reorientations of Radcliffe-Brown and Malinowski

Different Routes to Functionalism

The interest North American ethnologists devoted to cultural processes after forsaking historical ethnology was paralleled in England by the attention Radcliffe-Brown and Malinowski together with their students gave to function, though that was by no means their only or even their major contribution to the development of anthropological thought.

Dissatisfied with evolutionism and historical reconstruction, Radcliffe-Brown and Malinowski contributed very little to those streams of activity. Both primarily approached society and culture synchronically, but each did so along a different conceptual route. For Radcliffe-Brown social structure, the orienting concepts he introduced, and social solidarity were the center of attention. How, he asked, do norms, rituals, and other social usages function to maintain the structural continuity and social solidarity of social systems? Malinowski focussed on culture, and brought the biological and psychological viewpoints into his instrumental perspective, asking how biological and psychological needs are satisfied through social institutions. Culture he regarded as partly a result of human biological and psychological imperatives, and partly as a solution to the universal problems encountered in maintaining society itself.

The two theorists fully acknowleged the integrated nature of society and culture, as well as the ubiquitous role of social patterning. Neither had much place for cultural relativity in his functionalism; their theories could be applied to any social system, however much social usages or customs might differ from one to another. In distinction to Malinowski, Radcliffe-Brown saw little advantage in either the psychological or biological perspective; and neither attended to the place of society in its natural environment. Both, however, tended to minimize the distinction between nature and culture, Malinowski by anchoring culture in the human organism, and Radcliffe-Brown by labeling his approach "a natural science of society."

In addition to their functionalism, Radcliffe-Brown and Malinowski brought relatively new ideas to the study of kinship, descent, religion, magic, and ritual. Compared to his British-born contemporary, Malinowski cultivated a greater variety of topics, including culture change and culture contact, and his treatment of the subjects he covered tended to be more consistent with the way they had been developed earlier in Great Britain. Radcliffe-Brown was far more original in his concepts, and closer to Durkheim and other French sociologists. He even called his approach sociological and practically dropped the culture concept as it had been defined by Edward B. Tylor. During the 1940s and early 1950s, Radcliffe-Brown's social structural theory proved widely influential in several parts of the world, including North America. Then, as we will see in the next chapter, the theory was critically reappraised from a position emphasizing the role of the individual in society, a position close to Malinowski's theoretical orientation.

Notes

1. W. C. H. Stanner, "Radcliffe-Brown, A. R.," in *International Encyclopedia of the Social Sciences* (1968), vol. 13; Fred Eggan and W. Lloyd Warner, "Alfred Reginald Radcliffe-Brown," *American Anthropologist*, vol. 58 (1956): 544–548.

2. Raymond Firth, "Introduction: Malinowski as Scientist and as Man," in Raymond Firth, ed., *Man and Culture* (London: Routledge and Kegan Paul, 1957); M. F. Ashley-Montagu, "Bronislaw Malinowski (1884–1942)," *Isis*, vol. 34 (1942): 146–150; George Peter Murdock, "Bronislaw Malinowski," *American Anthropologist*, vol. 45 (1943): 441–451; Rhoda Métraux, "Malinowski, Bronislaw," in *International Encyclopedia of the Social Sciences* (1968), vol. 9.

3. Bronislaw Malinowski, "The Paradox of Frazer's Personality and Work," in Bronislaw Malinowski, *A Scientific Theory of Culture and Other Essays* (Chapel Hill: University of North Carolina Press, 1944), p. 184.

4. Emile Durkheim, *The Rules of Sociological Method* [orig. 1895], trans. Sarah A. Solovay and John H. Mueller (New York: Free Press of Glencoe, 1964), pp. 95–97. In the same year Otis T. Mason wrote that inventions have not only an efficient cause but also a final cause, i.e., function; see his "Similarities in Culture," *American Anthropologist*, vol. 8 o.s. (1895): 101–117, p. 106.

5. Cited in Robert L. Carneiro, "Structure, Function, and Equilibrium in the Evolutionism of Herbert Spencer," *Journal of Anthropological Research*, vol. 29 (1973): 77–95, p. 82.

6. Cited in Maurice Mandelbaum, *History, Man, and Reason* (Baltimore: Johns Hopkins Press), pp. 172–173.

7. James George Frazer, *Psyche's Task* [orig. 1913] (2nd ed.; London: Dawsons of Pall Mall, 1968).

8. W. H. R. Rivers, *Kinship and Social Organization* [orig. 1914] (London School of Economics, Monographs on Social Anthropology, no. 34, 1968), pp. 45–46; W. H. R. Rivers, *Social Organization*, W. J. Perry, ed. (New York: Alfred A. Knopf, 1924), pp. 4–6.

9. A. R. Radcliffe-Brown, "Evolution: Social or Cultural?" *American Anthropologist*, vol. 49 (1947): 78–83; A. R. Radcliffe-Brown, "Social Anthropology," in A. R. Radcliffe-Brown, *Method in Social Anthropology*, M. N. Srinivas, ed. (Chicago: University of Chicago Press, 1958), pp. 159, 178–189.

10. A. R. Radcliffe-Brown defines his method in the following works: "The Meaning and Scope of Social Anthropology" [orig. 1944] and "The Methods of Ethnology and Social Anthropology [orig. 1923], both reprinted in his *Method in Social Anthropology;* "White's View of a Science of Culture," *American Anthropologist*, vol. 51 (1949): 503–512; "Historical Note on British Social Anthropology," *American Anthropologist*, vol. 54 (1952): 275–277; and the "Introduction" to the collection of his papers, *Structure and Function in Primitive Society* (London: Cohen and West, Ltd., 1952), p. 4.

11. In the following works by Radcliffe-Brown, which I have used for social system and social structure, he is sometimes inconsistent in the way he describes those basic concepts: "Introduction," to A. R. Radcliffe-Brown and Daryll Forde, eds., *African Systems of Kinship and Marriage* (London: Oxford University Press, 1950), p. 10; *Natural Science of Society* [based on oral discussions in 1937] (Chicago: University of Chicago Press, 1957); "Social Anthropology," pp. 166–177; "On Social Structure" [orig. 1940] and "Taboo" [orig. 1939], both in *Structure and Function;* "Preface," in Meyer Fortes and E. E. Evans-Pritchard, eds., *African Political Systems*, pp. xii–xiii; and *The Andaman Islanders* [orig. 1932] (Paperback ed.; New York: Free Press of Glencoe, 1964), pp. 234ff.

12. My examples derive from the following by A. R. Radcliffe-Brown: "On the Concept of Function in Social

Science" [orig. 1935], "Taboo," and "Ritual and Society" [orig. 1945], all reprinted in *Structure and Function;* "White's View," pp. 505–506; the "Introduction" to Radcliffe-Brown and Forde, *African Systems,* pp. 56–57; *Andaman Islanders,* pp. 2, 234, 275, 327–328; and "Sanction, Social," in *Encyclopaedia of the Social Sciences* (1935), vol. 13.

13. See the following works by Radcliffe-Brown: *Andaman Islanders,* pp. 400–401; *Natural Science of Society,* pp. 90–104; and "White's View," pp. 510–511.

14. A. R. Radcliffe-Brown, "Patrilineal and Matrilineal Succession" [orig. 1935] in his *Structure and Function;* also his "Introduction" to Radcliffe-Brown and Forde, *African Systems,* pp. 14ff.

15. Radcliffe-Brown, "Introduction," in Radcliffe-Brown and Forde, *African Systems,* pp. 43–72; Radcliffe-Brown, "White's View," p. 507.

16. A. R. Radcliffe-Brown, "The Sociological Theory of Totemism" [orig. 1929] in his *Structure and Function;* A. R. Radcliffe-Brown, "The Comparative Method in Social Anthropology" [orig. 1951], in his *Method in Social Anthropology.*

17. What follows concerning kinship draws from the following works by Radcliffe-Brown: "The Social Organization of Australian Tribes," *Oceania,* vol. 1 (1930–1931): 34–63, 206–246, 322–341, 426–456; "The Mother's Brother in South Africa" [orig. 1924], "The Study of Kinship Systems" [orig. 1941], and "On Joking Relationships" [orig. 1940], all reprinted in his *Structure and Function;* "Introduction," in Radcliffe-Brown and Forde, *African Systems,* pp. 23, 25, 38, 81; and "The Present Position of Anthropological Studies" [orig. 1931], reprinted in *Method in Social Anthropology,* p. 65.

18. Bronislaw Malinowski, "Culture," in *Encyclopaedia of the Social Sciences* (1931), vol. 4; Bronislaw Malinowski, "A Scientific Theory of Culture," and his "The Functional Theory," both in Malinowski, *Scientific Theory of Culture.*

19. Malinowski, "Culture," pp. 624, 626, 627, 632.

20. Bronislaw Malinowski, *Crime and Custom in Savage Society* [orig. 1926] (Paterson, N.J.: Littlefield Adams and Co., 1959).

21. Bronislaw Malinowski, "Parenthood, the Basis of Social Structure," [orig. 1930], in Bronislaw Malinowski, *Sex, Culture, and Myth* (New York: Harcourt, Brace and World, 1962); Malinowski, "Scientific Theory of Culture," pp. 62–63, 65–66.

22. For Malinowski on magic and religion, see the following works: "Magic, Science, and Religion" [orig. 1925] in his *Magic, Science and Religion and Other Essays* (Anchor Books ed.; Garden City, N.Y.: Doubleday and Co., 1954), pp. 17–92; "Culture," pp. 634–640; *Coral Gardens and Their Magic,* vol. 2, *The Language of Magic and Gardening* [orig. 1935] (Bloomington: Indiana University Press, 1965), pp. 231ff; "Foundations of Faith and Morals" [orig. 1936], in his *Sex, Culture, and Myth,* pp. 295–336.

23. Bronislaw Malinowski, "The Life of Myth" [orig. 1928], and "The Foundations of Faith and Morals" [orig. 1936], both in his *Sex, Culture, and Myth;* Bronislaw Malinowski, "Myth in Primitive Psychology" [orig. 1932], in his *Magic, Science, and Religion.*

24. Bronislaw Malinowski, "Kinship" [orig. 1929], and "The Impasse on Kinship" [orig. 1930], both in his *Sex, Culture, and Myth.*

25. Bronislaw Malinowski, *Sex and Repression in Savage Society* [orig. 1927] (New York: Meridian Books, 1959), pp. 215–216; 218–220; also his "Culture," p. 630.

26. Malinowski, *Sex and Repression,* parts 1, 2, and 3.

27. Bronislaw Malinowski, *The Dynamics of Culture Change* [orig. 1945], Phyllis M. Kaberry, ed. (New Haven: Yale University Press, 1961), especially ch. 4.

28. Bronislaw Malinowski, *The Family Among the Australian Aborigines* [orig. 1913] (Paperback ed.; New York: Schocken Books, 1963), pp. 3–5, 22–25.

8
Recent Theory

Proliferation and Diversification

Years of Change

The middle of the 1970s is still too soon to know what long-range effect A. R. Radcliffe-Brown and Bronislaw Malinowski will have on cultural anthropology. Their short-range influence, however, which arose in the 1930s and began to fade in the 1950s, is clear. The synchronic approach they illustrated in their writings and validated through their prestige during those decades transformed anthropology in Great Britain and had almost as profound an impact in North America as historical ethnology waned.

Not everything the architects of functionalism proposed exerted an equal influence; even their students, in defining their own outlooks, politely overlooked some concepts. Radcliffe-Brown's conception of social structure was widely accepted by social anthropologists, together with the importance he attached to norms, sentiments, and rituals; in short, his brand of functionalism survived. Not so his principles of social organization. Malinowski's strenuously proclaimed instrumental theory of culture, and his concept of institutions, also went largely ignored, compared to his theory of magic and, above all, the lessons for field workers displayed in his ethnographies. In the nature of diffusion, the ideas of both men were inevitably reinterpreted by others in meaning or application; as a result,

---

Notes to this chapter begin on page 336.

it is almost impossible to cite anyone's career as a perfect example of a master's influence.

After the war the aura of structural-functionalism weakened as pro-liferation of new approaches competed for attention. Some of them would undoubtedly have reached fruition sooner, were it not for the pause en-forced by the war. Though many of the new developments were more methodological than theoretical, they of course depended on underlying definitions and assumptions, some of which directly challenged concepts followed by the structure-functionalists or by the American historical tradition.

Even before the war, Great Britain and North America had become the world's active centers in the expansion of anthropological ideas. After-wards, the British and Americans continued their leadership, augmented by a few figures working in other lands, such as Fredrik Barth in Norway and Claude Lévi-Strauss in France.

What happened in anthropology during the next decades, the subjects of this and the next chapter, happened against a bellicose historical back-ground, including the cold war between Russia and the United States; the stockpiling of ever more portentous nuclear weapons; the launching of nuclear submarines; construction of intercontinental missile bases; and several hot wars fought in Korea, Africa, Vietnam, elsewhere in South Asia, and between Israel and the Arab countries. A new field, the anthro-pology of war, reflected the world's preoccupying concern with militarism; yet research into armed conflict took up only a small fraction of the dis-cipline's output compared to the many pages devoted to kinship, descent, religion, or cultural evolution. Within American society, increasing aware-ness during the 1960s of poverty as a social problem was joined by the consciousness-raising Black Revolution. But the intensity of anthropologi-cal attention to those concerns failed to match that of American society. The short-lived Youth Revolution, the environmental crisis and concern over pollution, and the Sexual Revolution inspired even less research. International assistance programs in the 1950s made a strong impression, perhaps because they provided greater direct, financial incentives to an-thropologists, than did those other movements. The women's movement definitely affected anthropological interests by more often making women the object of study and by rethinking the role of women in society.

Anthropology showed itself moderately responsive to peasant revolu-tions, and anthropologists were on hand in India, Pakistan, Latin America, and other places to observe attempts to modernize traditional cultures through planned economic change and social development. The political-ization of United States science during the postwar decades hardly touched the profession, but the enhanced political consciousness of the people that anthropologists had traditionally studied, such as the Ameri-can Indians, could hardly fail to affect it. Field workers found themselves no longer able to decide unilaterally when and where to excavate or investigate, or to set up problems solely of their own choosing regardless of the interests of the community.

In comparison to its relative imperviousness to current social history, anthropological research responded with far greater alacrity to several new, or newly refurbished, intellectual developments, including behavioral science in the 1950s, decision-making theory, communications theory, general systems theory, French structuralism, exchange theory, stress theory, developments in linguistics, new techniques for research in statistics, and computer science. I will comment on a few.

Communications theory, with its concepts of code, transmission, decoding, and noise, provided a new model whererby to represent social processes and culture itself. Systems theory struck as less novel; after all, the idea of system had been part of anthropology for a long time, having been explicitly elaborated by such theorists as Leo Frobenius, Malinowski, Radcliffe-Brown, and Ruth Benedict. However, one recent development in systems theory, control through negative feedback, attracted attention. Apparently, the discipline's increasingly positivistic temper made cybernetic control a more satisfactory concept than the idea of equifinality, that is, the concept of systems being governed through their own properties. Ruth Benedict had popularized the latter idea, and it is implicit in notions of selective borrowing, reinterpretation, and the pattern process as described by American historical ethnologists.

Exchange theory (transactionalism, as it tended to be called in anthropology) goes back to Aristotle. As formulated in sociology, psychology, and anthropology, it relied heavily on analogies with economic events. The theory reduces social interaction to exchanges of goods, services, and other values, such as prestige. Individual actors or groups are studied as they interact in complementary fashion, so that each gains some value from the transaction. Actors always face risks: the expected reward may fail, or the cost to one party may be too high for the value received. However, people are rational enough to avoid unsatisfactory encounters in the future. Consequently, as a result of accumulated experience, they mostly engage in relationships where satisfaction occurs as long as conditions remain constant. The matter becomes more complicated in situations involving several combinations of interpersonal behavior, each yielding varying amounts of satisfaction and dissatisfaction. The actors, it is assumed, will search for the maximum payoff; hence if latitude exists, alternatives will tend to be chosen yielding a combination of outcomes with maximum value. Transactionalism provided postwar anthropology with several advantages. It offered a basis for explaining institutions in nonliterate societies causally, without trying to do history or substituting functional for causal explanations. It allowed anthropologists to deal with the behavior of individuals, as they preferred to do, instead of studying only gross social patterns resulting from behavior. At the same time, the approach required no hard-to-verify motivational constructs for explaining individual behavior. Finally, transactionalism proved compatible with the important place that postwar anthropology assigned to cognition.

Extreme or chronic threatening life conditions, stress theory maintains, can severely impair the adaptive capacities of an individual or of particular organ systems. War and postwar research in the biological and social sciences on the reactions of organisms under stress resulted in a large volume of publication in which anthropology participated, especially in the United States. Under severe enduring stress, these studies documented, some people develop aberrant coping techniques in the form of physical illness, mental disease, and other types of deviant behavior. Cultural anthropologists studied the consequences of stress produced by culture change, by nutritional deficiencies, and by lack of socially approved means to attain goals socially valued in a society.

Strides made in linguistics spurred anthropologists to adapt its analytical methods to the study of meaning, which came to be seen as deriving from the contrastive relationship of symbols rather than as inherent in the symbols themselves. By working with units of analysis corresponding to the phonemes and morphemes of language, anthropologists sought to make the study of culture as rigorous as linguistics. Someday, they hoped, it would be possible to set down succinctly in cultural grammars the rules governing the indefinitely large number of things that the members of a society say, do, and think.

The hope of successfully emulating linguistics reveals how intensely postwar anthropology was concerned with devising reliable procedures for acquiring and analyzing data. Anthropologists looked with a measure of dissatisfaction at the stock of classic ethnographic monographs produced during the previous 60 or so years. Each ethnography was the effort of only one person who had collected the facts and presented their significance. Difficulties arose in comparing such personal accounts and using them for cross-cultural studies, since the topics one ethnographer emphasized in studying a culture might be largely overlooked by another covering another culture, though the topics might be equally important in both. The development and extension of rigorously objective new methods promised to remove those difficulties, and to make cultural anthropology an objective science. But some members of the profession worried lest, in devising more and more objective procedures, anthropology sacrifice in too-large measure the kind of cultural understanding and insight into human behavior provided by the classic ethnographies.[1] For some purposes, these anthropologists felt, it was worthwhile to have data from a society refracted through the sensibilities of a particular investigator, even though his report could never be perfectly replicated by anyone else. Certain other methods might insure greater reliability and verifiability;

but were they worth the effort and care they required if they produced no significant insights, ignored empathy as an avenue of understanding, and lacked human relevance?

Culture as Cognition

Five major trends appeared in anthropological thought between the second World War and the early 1970s as anthropology once again became strongly conscious of methodology—just as it had in the late 19th century, when historical ethnology overwhelmed the evolutionary paradigm.

The first trend broke with the traditional inclusive conception of culture as a realm of phenomena encompassing ideas as well as overt behavior and artifacts. "We suggest that it is more useful to define culture . . . more narrowly than has generally been the case in the American anthropological tradition, restricting its reference to transmitted and created content and patterns of values, ideas, and other symbolic-meaningful systems as factors in the shaping of human behavior. . . ."[2] With those words, in 1958, Alfred L. Kroeber, dean of American anthropologists, put his imprimatur on a new concept of culture and confined the term to symbols, values, ideas, beliefs, and rules. Culture had come to designate the ideational order of experience. Formerly, stress had been put on actions and on artifacts, ideas being regarded as essential for understanding, but not always trustworthy when reported by the actors, and hence epistemologically secondary to what empirical methods revealed. Now the emphasis was reversed. By the 1960s some of the most active theoreticians in North American anthropology—Ward Goodenough, Anthony F. C. Wallace, David Schneider, and Roger Keesing—had relegated overt culture to the secondary status of being the outcome of rules and categories of thought. Observed events hardly figured in their theorizing.

Some anthropologists who took up the study of symbols and other cognitions—especially Lévi-Strauss, but also to some extent Anthony Wallace, Victor Turner, and Roy D'Andrade—went beyond learned contents of cognition and asked whether inborn capacities of human beings might be responsible for channeling certain patterns of thought. The question reveals a striking departure from the 300-year-old tradition of empiricism in social science stemming from John Locke, a tradition from which Jean Piaget and Sigmund Freud in psychology had already departed. Rather than regarding ideas as almost wholly the product of experience, the nativists in anthropology, taking the position of Baron Gottfried von Leibnitz, saw the mind as itself supplying the categories of thought. Their position is one sign, among others, of a reaction against cultural relativism in recent anthropology.

Generally, however, American cognitive anthropologists cautiously avoided going too far in anchoring ideation to inborn structures of thought. They concentrated on the learned principles by which people in a society construe the world, code information in symbols, or decide between alternative courses of action.[3] They regarded culture as a series of preference ratings, as a means of ordering events conceptually, as a set of propositions stating how social relations and the rest of the universe are organized. Studying culture meant probing this order of experience and, like studying language, it required inferring the standards one must know, and what members of the society under investigation do know, in order to make observed events meaningful and predictable.

As I have suggested, the cognitivist program was largely written by Americans who also favored the newly coined word "emic," taken from "phonemic" and contrasting with "etic" (from "phonetic") to label their standpoint.[4] British social anthropologists who emphasized norms, while cognitively inclined, were not emicists; they did not in the manner of a linguist discovering phonemes look for criteria implicitly or explicitly recognized by the actors themselves. The etic standpoint, rashly employed, American cognitivists charged, is apt to distort meaning by interpreting events with the concepts of an alien observer, one who employs criteria of discrimination external to the cultural system being studied. The emic perspective remains within the system, though, like phonemes, the inferred criteria are not necessarily those consciously recognized by the actors. Heeding what the actors deem to be significant would eliminate many personal biases, emicists believed, and would lead to much more uniform reports than the best-trained observers could hope to write from an etic standpoint. Ward Goodenough stressed the importance of emic understanding for constructing types of culture patterns for comparative research. Comparison, he noted, tends very often to be based on behavior or things having a similar pragmatic value in different cultures: this pattern here, and that one there, are both marriage because they serve the same purpose. In order to be sure of comparing only strictly analogous patterns, it is necessary to know accurately the purpose for which a pattern is intended, i.e., how the actors themselves cognize it.

A number of American anthropologists who devoted themselves to the human being as thinker rather than doer not only emulated the psychological perspective of the phonemecist, they also substituted the formalism characteristic of linguistics for the naturalism of the older ethnography. The componential analysts and the ethnoscientists devised rigorous techniques to get at the contents of cognition through the words by which members of a society discriminate meaningful segments of experience. Frequently, the words were kinship terms. Similar rigorous methods did not arise in other countries among those studying "symbolic-meaningful systems. A Lévi-Strauss or a Mary Douglas employed far less objective procedures as they interpreted myths, caste, rituals, and other symbolic cultural forms.

In addition to following different methods, anthropologists emphasizing the ideational order disagreed on whether cultural homogeneity or organized cultural diversity characterizes a society. At the same time students of the phenomenal order were becoming more and more prepared to measure or count, expecting to find various sectors of society holding different opinions, rearing children in different ways, and so forth. Some cognitivists regarded the rules, codes, and ideational orderings of a society as generally known, and hardly troubled themselves over variations. A myth existed, whether it reposed barely intact in one old man's fragile memory or was still being vivaciously recounted by practically everyone. In Ward Goodenough's words, the ideational order belongs not to people at large, as does the phenomenal order of events; the ideational order consists of ideal forms existing in individual minds and, as such, cannot be counted like overt behaviors. And David Schneider preferred not to abstract the cultural level from the level of action but to secure it directly from informants.

Some cognitive anthropologists disagreed that one or a few informants sufficed for learning the codes of a community. Those who insisted on recognizing diversity pointed out that individuals live disparate lives, which they synchronize in order to conform to cultural codes. Heeding variations in activity, they added, may also prove a useful index to changes taking place in the guiding norms, and therefore should not be overlooked. To which the other side replied by claiming the ideational order—with its preference ratings of different forms of behavior, its prescriptions, and its definitions—to be highly stable, lacking the constant variability of the phenomenal order.

Although cognitive anthropology, especially as it came to be carried out in the United States, marked a substantial break with former modes of cultural study, for a radical departure from tradition it encountered surprisingly little negative criticism.[5] Eric Wolf objected to the analogy of culture and code because conceiving of the brain as operating, like a computer, according to the program it has been fed, reduces man to a robot. Marvin Harris called the analogy between language codes and higher-order cultural codes patently false. Language codes have very little tolerances for intrinsically objectionable features, or noise; they must be intelligible and unambiguous if they are to satisfactorily perform the important tasks to which they are constantly put. Therefore they are subject to rigorous selection, in the course of which ambiguous elements are eliminated. Invalid or useless cognitions are not as efficiently eliminated. Some beliefs continue to be accepted, even though they are ambiguous, downright obfuscating, injurious, or lack any correspondence to historical events or current empirical circumstances. The cognitivists, however, being to a great extent cultural relativists, rarely evaluate the objective validity or pragmatic efficacy of beliefs, and hence treat all as equal.

The "natives'" categorization or explanation of behavior, Harris reminds us, is not invariably preferable to an informed outsider's account. By accepting without question the actor's point of view, anthropologists limit the potential usefulness of their discipline. However valuable the information collected from the actors' perspective might be, for certain purposes it could be very worthwhile to know whether native beliefs are true or false; to know their sources, of which the actors remain unaware; or to study their consequences for the society of the actors and for other societies on which the beliefs impinge.

New Approaches in Culture History and Cultural Evolutionism

In both England and America after the war, diachronic interests, such as had dominated European historical ethnology and the American Historical Tradition, lagged behind synchronic analysis and attention devoted to short-run cultural processes. Attempts were even made to convert archeology into a search for causal relationships and other time-less propositions, though of course archeology remained committed to prehistory. Not only the paucity of objective data and the roundly criticized subjectivity of reconstructions based on synchronic distributions discouraged anthropologists from undertaking studies of diffusion. The climate of the discipline was also opposed to working with disembodied culture traits and complexes traveling in time and across space. Interest had shifted from traits to whole societies or cultures, and to dynamic processes operating in social or cultural systems.

A few ethnologists, however, persisted in unravelling relationships between culture areas of the world, including Melville J. Herskovits whose detailed study of Africanisms in New World black culture represents one of the terminal products of the American Historical Tradition.[6] At first his thesis and the method in which it was grounded failed to impress many of his colleagues, but with the black revolution, in which United States blacks reaffirmed their African heritage as part of their cultural identity, a younger generation of anthropologists returned to Herskovits's work with more positive sentiments. The prodigious memory of computers and new statistical techniques, such as factor analysis, proved tremendously helpful to a few ethnologists working on diffusion.[7] Using those means to handle large numbers of traits belonging to a region, they discovered relationships between clusters of traits from which probable migrations could be inferred. Although only probabilities, not certainties, could be claimed for the results, there is a difference between those probabilities and the conclusions of the culture-circle workers and other historical reconstructionists: the probabilities founded on statistics rest on a stronger methodological foundation, and the sheer mass of the distributional evidence on which they are based is persuasive.

For a short time it seemed as if, in the search for timeless causal, functional, and other generalizations, the historical viewpoint might entirely vanish from cultural anthropology, outside of archeology and historical linguistics, the latter now fortified by glottochronology. Several sensible voices, however, were raised to deflect some of the appetence for the synchronic orientation, warning that history could not be ignored in the search for valid scientific knowledge of cultural dynamics.[8] Necessary and sufficient causes governing events in social systems—a major goal of social anthropology—these voices said, can be discovered by comparing histories in different regions of the world. History can provide quasi-experimental controls for testing theories derived from synchronic research. Studies of culture change in particular societies also upheld the persistence of historical interests, while the new area of ethnohistory opened anthropologists' eyes to historical sources for societies without written records, including early explorers' accounts, the memories of informants, and archeological facts. Utilizing such sources, ethnohistorians were able to trace revitalization, modernization, Sanskritization, and secularization and other processes of change.[9]

The study of long-term cultural development, never wholly abandoned despite criticism by the historical ethnologists and Boasians, was much reinvigorated after the war. Sometimes it was carried out in traditional style, with emphasis primarily on the outcomes of development: greater cultural complexity, increasing specialization, greater per capita use of energy, and others. Archeological data and protohistory, of course, provided far more reliable information on which to base conclusions about long-term developmental trends than the Enlightenment and Victorian Age possessed. Increasingly, however, postwar anthropology came to stress not so much the results of cultural development as the Darwinian-like mechanisms of adaptation and extinction through environmental selection by which development occurred. Some evolutionists drew well-nigh perfect analogies between biological and cultural evolution, making invention and discovery cultural equivalents of the biological mutations on which environmental selection acts.[10]

Formalism

An increased tendency to formal analysis was the third trend to become conspicuous in cultural anthropology during the 1950s, being heralded by a 1949 article in which Joseph H. Greenberg showed how symbolic logic could be used to describe kin-term systems.[11] Applied to empirical data, the term formalism implies a high degree of abstraction from specific content leading to models, patterns, or other arrangements possessing a high degree of regularity or symmetry. A generalization comparing breakfast and dinner by saying the morning meal consists of orange juice, toast, and coffee, and the evening one comprises cooked meat, potatoes, an additional vegetable, a green salad, and dessert, remains close to the level of empirical content. An anthropologist taking the generalization and further abstracting a distinction between the two meals based on the time they are taken and on their lightness or heaviness begins to construct a formal version of the data. Formal accounts far exceed empirical generalizations in logical rigor and parsimony, but they achieve those virtues at the cost of sacrificing considerable concrete ethnographic information.

Any attempt to analyze with the aim of classifying or comparing a series of different artifacts, lexical units, sequences of behavior, myths and folktales, or even whole cultures, must to some extent be formal, since only a few crucial attributes—shape, size, distinctive features of the objects to which the lexemes refer, and so on—will be abstracted, other features unessential for the purpose being ignored. Prewar analyses of folktale motifs; archeological types of artifacts; the components, aspects, and phases of the Midwestern Taxonomic System; and the culture-element lists compiled for a number of North American Indian culture areas—all involved formal analysis. Hence the formalism appearing in the 1950s in the guise of ethnosemantics or componential analysis was not wholly new. Its major difference from what was done previously lies in the degree to which the latter methods utilized conceptual rather than perceptual attributes. Componential analysis, for example, deals not with the overt form of the words specifying different kin types, but with covert features by which the kin types are recognized. The conceptual attributes used in componential analysis and in ethnoscience were supposed to be distinctions held in the minds of the actors participating in the system being studied.

Not all recent formalism took a cognitive standpoint, nor should we identify all formal analysis with an interest in getting at reality as it is perceived by the "natives." The little-followed formal approaches put forward by Marvin Harris, Edward Hall, and George Trager are largely etic and not primarily concerned with cognition.[12]

Since explicit directions could often be provided for producing models based on formal analysis, the methods were welcomed for providing anthropology with objective, reproducible analytical procedures to replace the subjective, "impressionistic" procedures traditionally practiced. Less was said about the comparative validity of the new methods; a moment's reflection reveals there need be no necessary connection between a reproducible procedure and the truth of what it reveals. The attractiveness of formalism stemmed partly from the explicitness of the rules put forward for studying particular systems of culture, and the ease with which the rules could be learned. When critics examined the value of what the rules were revealing, formal semantic analysis could marshall few arguments in its defense.

Phenomenalism

The fourth trend constituted a reaction to regarding descent groups and other social structures as objective entities, or cultures as modular constructions containing in their ground plans some type of descent rule, a form of residence, witchcraft, and so forth. According to those traditional conceptions, people are born into an assemblage of cultural forms and fitted into the existing ground plan, normally affecting them little before death ushers them out of the society. Anthropologists with this point of view entered field work prepared to study the compartments of a culture in somewhat the way one unpacks a prefabricated house expecting to find walls, doors, window frames, and moldings. The modular conception of a culture makes no provision for individual and subgroup variations in behavior based on choice, physical disabilities, or location in the territory occupied by a society. As a number of postwar anthropologists pointed out, it ignores individual and group processes whereby culture and social structure are generated.[13] These theorists visualized cultural forms in a state of becoming, constantly emerging from, or being sustained through the actions and choices of individuals, rather than as fixed patterns governing persons.

As early as 1932 Edward Sapir had expressed discomfort with highly generalized forms of social action, thought, and feeling reported by ethnographers describing cultures. The cultures so described, he wrote, "are not and cannot be, the truly objective entities they claim to be." The true locus of culture for Sapir lay in the interactions of specific individuals and in the highly variable meanings which individuals derive from those interactions. Hence people in a society do not replicate each other's behaviors or ideas with the degree of homogeneity suggested by ethnographic descriptions. Twenty years later, Raymond Firth again called attention to the role of choice in the emergence of constantly shifting patterns of social structure. Understanding culture, he counseled, requires more than attending to persisting forms of social life and the values or rules on which the forms depend. Persisting form results from repeated social relationships and other behaviors, but repetition always occurs with variations and is never perfect, for alternatives are always available. What alternatives are chosen will affect social structure, however much their range is restricted by choices made previously and by the existence of rules governing behavior.

Whereas Sapir seems to deny the stability of culture in time or the replication of behavior from one individual or group to another, Firth admits persistence and sees it resulting from some degree of behavioral replication. Others, like Fredrik Barth and Edmund R. Leach, follow him. They also concerned themselves less with internal variation in a society—Sapir's problem—than with the manner in which cultural forms are constantly generated through personal choices made along similar lines by many individuals. The choices are not necessarily made because everyone in the society equally values the forms and consciously seeks to maintain them, though that may well be the result of the normative constraints under which choices are made. The extent to which individuals are individually inclined to achieve normative goals through their actual behavior, Barth warns, is an empirical question and should be investigated. The actual or statistical patterns revealed by people's overt behavior should be treated as independent of any ideal order existing in their minds. E. R. Leach offers similar advice when he urges treating jural norms as secondary to statistical norms, and to the patterns the latter reveal. Consequently, social structure and culture become, in Barth's words, epiphenomena, not empirical realities like the events of which they are constituted. As George P. Murdock noted, shorn of its empirical status, culture can no longer be credited with the causal efficacy formerly claimed for it, and hence cannot be used in explanations of human behavior.[14]

In the trend I call phenomenalism, then, anthropologists approached the high-order abstractions—culture and social structure—by studying more basic abstractions. Therein their approach resembles phenomenalism in philosophy, which claims our conceptual knowledge of the external forms depends fundamentally on sense data or appearances. For that reason I have borrowed the word. Anthropological phenomenalists attended to processes occurring in social interaction in order to delineate how institutions develop the forms which ethnographers conceptualize. In doing so, the phenomenalists watched for how people reach decisions and translate decisions into social behavior. A given pattern of social structure or culture, they assumed, represents the outcome, at any moment, of many similar decisions made by individuals pursuing similar ends who are subject to similar normative, ecological, and other constraints. In place of regarding family types, descent groups, social statuses, or social networks as products of history (actually, choices made in the past), the processual approach sought an explanation for the forms by examining factors operating in particular situations at a given time. New concepts and techniques came into use for studying social behavior dynamically. Families and other groups were observed as passing through cycles of development, each phase of a cycle presenting the group with different problems of adaptation. Symbols were treated as manipulatable. The concept of social strategies came into use to describe people seeking to attain or protect power, honor, prestige, or face in social relationships. Game theory proved useful for representing the dynamic aspects of social forms. Microhistory traced the course of revitalization movements, from enthusiastic inception to routinized culmination. Ethnographies of encounter, or situational analysis, revealed how legal and other norms are applied, challenged, and manipulated in pursuit of individualistic goals, and as far back as the 1930s Sapir recommended life histories to reveal culture in the locus of persons who make varying use of social institutions.

Specialized Interests and New Methods

The number of professional anthropologists working—mostly at teaching in universities—grew after the war, and so, as a fifth trend, did the number of specialties they taught and practiced. Individuals became known as specialists in cultural evolution, kinship, religion, and psychological anthropology, as well as in such newer fields as the anthropologies of law, economics, development, population, education, peasants, politics, war, medicine, and cities. Herskovits devoted himself to Black Studies many years before the Black Revolution put the subject into university curricula.[15] Specialists in proxemics examined the social uses of space; sociolinguists, language; and students of primate studies sought parallels to human culture in the social relations or foraging activities of apes and monkeys. Other specialists became authorities on cultural ecology, network theory, applied anthropology, or new methods of research, such as ethnoscience, componential analysis, mathematical anthropology, scaling, and other statistical techniques.

The new topical specialties and methods, borrowing concepts freely from other disciplines and studying problems also taken up in sociology, political science, and more academic fields, not only contributed a pronounced interdisciplinary character to cultural anthropology. They also created a crisis of disciplinary identity, especially for graduate students but also for some senior members of the profession.

Ethnography, as well as the new processual archeology, developed a more specialized cast: both became problem-centered. Details of dress, housing, religion, pottery, weapons, farming techniques, dances, games, and other parts of the complex whole that Edward B. Tylor called culture, commanded attention only if they could be brought to bear on a theoretical problem. Though field workers remained strong empiricists who placed great importance on data, ethnographic facts ceased to be significant if they simply added to knowledge about diverse ways of life. As a result, publication of "classical" comprehensive ethnographic monographs fell to a trickle. Few researchers any longer paid much attention to material culture, and for a while studies of subsistence techniques also languished. Then cultural ecologists managed to reinvigorate the study of subsistence, of course from a problem-centered point of view. Many ethnographers from that point of view devoted themselves exclusively to aspects of social relations, following in the footsteps of Radcliffe-Brown's social anthropology. But the popularity of religion and related belief systems remained high; one wonders if it wasn't because, unlike other highly distinctive customs in small-scale societies undergoing acculturation, exotic ideas held on longer in the sphere of religion, and anthropologists did after all hunger for the exotic.

One notable methodological innovation in recent anthropology began shortly before the war, as anthropology, led by Murdock and followed by his students, especially John W. M. Whiting, wholeheartedly embraced statistical analysis in cross-cultural research. With the hologeistic method, explanations for a cultural phenomenon found in one society can be tested across societies to see if the phenomenon in question results regularly from similar independent factors. Such a conclusion is warranted, provided the explanatory factor is present or strongly active in a significant proportion of societies where the phenomenon to be accounted for is also present or important, and provided the explanatory factors are absent or weak in places where the phenomenon to be explained is absent or unimportant. The new comparative method was greatly facilitated by the Human Relations Area Files, the Ethnographic Atlas, and similar coded compendia of cultural data based on hundreds of ethnographic reports.[16]

Along with adopting new specialties and interests, a number of anthropologists more or less abandoned the doctrine of the incommensurability of cultures and the impartiality associated with cultural relativity. They unabashedly evaluated other ways of life, using their own criteria of cultural fitness, and took highly critical looks at conditions allowing poverty, economic exploitation, other inequalities, and undemocratic trends. Applied and action anthropologists joined forces with administrators in foreign aid programs, or with leaders in marginal societies, to help change undesirable social conditions by introducing more effective productive techniques and new institutions. Jules Henry and Oscar Lewis were far from relativistic when they condemned flaws in the cultural fabric of the United States, and called attention to vicious man-made conditions pitting "culture against man."[17] Cultural evolutionism, ethology, cultural psychiatry, and French structuralism, you will see, in different ways also sought for common factors operating below local cultural differences, and thus countered cultural relativism.

Some anthropologists defended cultural relativity, none more vehemently than Herskovits.[18] Anthropologists, he hoped, could recognize validity in different value systems without necessarily endorsing them. The object of cultural research is to understand behavior in terms of culture, and in the light of the society's historical background out of which the behavior arose. Judging or changing the society's lifeways are not part of the anthropological mission. Herskovits regarded himself as tough-minded enough to maintain a thoroughly relativistic outlook on other cultures, and as possessing the almost superhuman ability required, as he saw it, to overcome the constraints of one's own cultural values and principles. Yet he was sufficiently tender-minded (or sensible) to admit that relativism cannot long be applied *within* a society to behavior deviating from the generally accepted ethical system or moral code.

Heuristic cultural relativity was too strongly engrained in anthropological thinking to vanish quickly. Without fanfare it continued to be a guiding value among American ethnoscientists. It also held out stubbornly under attack in economic anthropology, where "substantive" theorists insisted that the ways of allocating scarce goods in primitive societies differ fundamentally and in kind from modern, Western economic systems.[19] This view stems from Herskovits who, in 1940, claimed that economic behavior in primitive tribes is basically different from that in the industrialized world. Immediately economists retorted with a nonrelativistic counterposition. The economic principles of human actions, they held, apply to all societies. (Psychologists might well have reacted similarly, had psychological anthropologists held learning or defense mechanisms to follow special laws in small-scale societies.) Anthropologists who thought like the economists joined the debate in 1961. Known as formalists, they saw little significance in the unique forms by which exotic societies distribute goods, regarding them all as rational means of allocating scarce resources among alternative ends. True people do not always choose the absolutely cheapest or most efficient alternative for such a purpose, but they tend to look for one as good as can be found under the circumstances. Substantivists remained unconvinced. They perceived human societies following various systems of exchange, among which the market based on money and prices is only one. One substantivist, George Dalton, admitted the possibility of translating the potlatch, bride wealth, and other exotic customs into the formal, analytical concepts employed by economists. But why make such an interpretation? What of anthropological value could be learned from it? From the other side, Scott Cook questioned whether anthropology could learn more than descriptive facts following the particularistic and relativistic approach advocated by the substantivists. The objective, comparative science of economic anthropology that he endorsed would go further, and it would employ the same general theory and sophisticated model-building skills developed by economists.

End of the Discipline?

The trend I call proliferation and diversification had been with anthropology in a quiet way almost since its beginning as a discipline, but far more conspicuously than the linear development of topics. Persistence of older concepts and methods, often without modification (unless rewording be considered modification), along with newer ones further contributed to the expansive nature of development. Of course, some former ideas and interests were dropped, but not enough to make the net result anything but growth through greater diversification.

There were those who now feared that so much diversification might bring about the extinction of anthropology as a discipline.[20] Trying to do many things, it would end up being nothing clearly identifiable as an academic point of view. Anthropology, those voices warned, should adhere to a specific theoretical or methodological approach, or commit itself to a particular goal, and thereby preserve its identity and speed up advances in knowledge. I doubt that most of the ethnologists or social anthropologists in even a single country will soon agree to follow one consistent line of endeavor. The eclecticism of the field, insuring a large variety of niches, have attracted people with diverse temperaments, manifold interests, and different long-range goals. Reducing the number of niches would naturally be resisted; it would deny many of those people, who lack any other academic shelter, the right to call anthropology their disciplinary home.

British Social Anthropology

The Constraint of Norms

The approaches taken in recent anthropological thought with which the balance of the chapter will be concerned are often only analytically distinct. Those contemporary with one another frequently borrowed from one another, indicating not only their overlap but mutual compatibility. Longer established developments often flowed into new ones without major break. If I mention a particular individual under one heading, the person may also be found under another, and many names will again recur in the next chapter, where I treat conceptual developments in kinship, descent, religion, and other specific anthropological topics without paying primary attention to the approach represented. The present chapter, then, introduces the leading theoretical and, with less emphasis, methodological movements of the 1940s, 1950s, and 1960s, together with their major dramatis personae.

I start with British social anthropology, the tradition revolving around the study of social structure that was followed by a close-knit community of men and women who had either studied with A. R. Radcliffe-Brown and Bronislaw Malinowski (sometimes with both) or who had been taught by pupils of the two masters.[21] Not everyone in the community was British-born; some members came from South Africa, New Zealand, Norway, and even the United States. Two periods can be distinguished; the first, led by the students of Radcliffe-Brown and Malinowski, saw the publication of such outstanding monographs as *The Nuer* (1940), *Web of Kinship Among the Tallensi* (1949), the collected essays on *African Sys-*

tems of Kinship and Marriage (1950), *Family Herds* (1955), and *Lugbara Religion* (1960). It was a time of considerable harmony in thinking and wide agreement on how to carry out field work and analysis. The second period, on the other hand, witnessed a spate of critical writing directed against the body of structuralist assumptions and theory inherited from Radcliffe-Brown, the critics in one way or another reintroducing Malinowski's emphasis on behavior (rather than social structure) and on the individual as a manipulator of social norms.

The structuralist approach in British social anthropology concentrated on relationships between persons occupying definite positions in a society, and on links between organized groups of the society. Through those relationships, people recognize the obligations of kinship and affinity, maintain social order, carry out technical tasks and economic exchanges, and give expression to religious and other sentiments. Structural theory found its most direct expression in the classic ethnographic monographs, where it was put to work in descriptive analyses of tribal social life. Such analyses dwell heavily on the beliefs and moral or legal norms held by the society and the guiding social relationships in it. The significance of social relationships is assessed in terms of the meaning bestowed on them by norms and beliefs. The ethnographer, as the Israeli sociologist Samuel N. Eisenstadt points out,[22] places the description of social behavior performed by individuals in different social groups or situations alongside statements those individuals make about the norms that hold in those situations. He examines the groups as well as the whole society to see whether individuals uphold the norms, how different norms interrelate, and—from a functional viewpoint—how the norms influence and regulate relations between groups, or between groups and the whole society. The most engrossing theoretical problem in social anthropology stemmed from the assumption of integration between social norms, overt behavior, and groups; the question for research was: what maintains the integration? In Eisenstadt's review, the social anthropologists found integration to result, first, because the same people or groups interact in different situations, and the commitments they make in one regulate their behavior in others. Second, values and ritual symbols recurring in different situations lock those situations together with common meanings. Third, the different types of social activity—jural, ritual, economic, and political—interweave; hence each activity articulates directly with, and is upheld by, other activities practiced in most groups and situations. Obviously, the social anthropologist viewed events from a position outside of the society he studied. There could not be room for a fully emic point of view in a tradition where, as one writer put it, the natives are assumed to have only a partial and inaccurate view of the types of social relationships making up their social system, and to be incapable of analyzing the processes by which the system operates.[23]

From Radcliffe-Brown, British social anthropology acquired its central concept, social structure, generally referring to critical social relationships persisting in a social system. The frequent adjective, "structural," when used thoughtfully rather than, as tended to happen, simply habitually, denotes stability, continuity, regularity, and uniformity from one situation to another. It also implies mutually consistent values and norms from one situation to another, wherefrom persistent, or structural, relationships arise. Social anthropologists assumed a system of structured relationships to be normally in equilibrium; consequently, drastic changes in norms or overt behavior are resisted, for they threaten to disturb equilibrium or structure and replace it by disequilibrium or nonstructure.

Compared to the deep consideration given to the concept of structure, social anthropologists troubled themselves little over culture. Some identified culture with the tasks and other customs around which social relationships build up, i.e., with the content of social relations. Others applied the term to the beliefs, norms, and principles of the society, restricting culture somewhat as the cognitive anthropologists did.

Culture, in the sense of shared beliefs, norms, and values, brings social relations about, Godfrey and Monica Wilson say in *Analysis of Social Change,* a systematic synthesis of anthropological concepts.[24] People and groups enter social relationships, the Wilsons explain, because of the meaning or value they find in them. It may be material value or ultimate religious meaning, both always being present whether the relationship is primarily directed toward a practical, intellectual, or emotionally expressive purpose. Only complementary differences in meaning or value between two or more parties can induce them to enter relations, the Wilsons point out, sounding almost exactly like Aristotle. The concept of social structure they use equally dynamically to denote the bases of authority and forms of social pressure that maintain complementary diversity in social relations by checking deviant behavior. The Wilsons' brief, little-noted book, completed shortly before Godfrey Wilson's death, at the age of 35, while serving in the South African army during the Second World War, is one of the few outright theoretical works in British social anthropology, as well as being one of the earliest treatments of change in that tradition.[25] Under her maiden name of Hunter, Monica Wilson was also one of the first social anthropologists to do field work devoted to the study of change.

Organization *and* Structure

The mid-1950s heard questions raised about the nearly automatic integration of social behavior and norms in tribal societies; about social relations enduring as a consequence of governing norms and values, and about stability and regularity, those attributes of social life implied by the central concept of social anthropology—social structure. The ensuing ferment, lasting into the 1960s, marked a new period in the development of British social anthropology.

Among the most outspoken critics was Edmund R. Leach, who belonged to the third academic generation of British anthropologists.[26] Following training in mathematics and engineering, he became a pupil of Malinowski and Raymond Firth, the latter a follower of Malinowski rather than of Radcliffe-Brown. Leach thought a simpler, more empirical explanation could be found for the order in social relations than appealing to legal norms or even more "metaphysical" moral forces of society. Inspired possibly by Firth, who had acknowledged the influence of geography on culture and related moral values to technology,[27] Leach proposed material limitations, including geographical and economic factors, as the effective constraints operating on behavior in a given locality. People must perforce adapt to such limitations, because they are powerless to change them. The very layout of a village pattern gives continuity to sets of social relations. Other constraints arise as people limit one another's actions, often simply through what they do. Only after explanations by such empirical factors have been exhausted would Leach admit explanations involving norms or the moral forces of society. He also complained against the unreality present in the favorite concept of social structure; reality is far more inconsistent and imprecise than the structural models anthropologists construct. Useful as the idea of a stable social structure might sometimes be, Leach thought it cannot actually exist in a world where human beings constantly struggle for power. People in social relations are always taking advantage of opportunities to manipulate alternatives, and may do so in contradiction to the ideal patterns supposed to govern their behavior. These ideas are easily traced to Raymond Firth, who had already proposed giving thought to a process complementary to social structure—social organization. Organization, as Firth uses the word, refers to individuals modifying social structure or creating it anew as they reinterpret structural principles in the act of adapting to particular circumstances.[28]

If Leach and Firth—in their ideas about material constraints channeling social structure, and about shifts in behavior creating new structures—hint at a phenomenal approach to social structure, the Cambridge-trained Norwegian anthropologist, Fredrik Barth, shouts it plainly. Anthropologists who concentrate their attention on lineages and other structural forms of social relations, he observes, are studying only epiphenomena arising from choices constantly made by individuals and groups in allocating time and other assets to activities from which they hope to accrue prestige, money, and other rewards.[29] The choices involve them in social transactions, or interactions, through which values are exchanged for mutual benefit. Structural forms are products of the frequency with which individuals, acting under similar technical and other constraints, seek values through certain relationships rather than others.

From Structure to Process

Max Gluckman's career, in its early stage influenced indirectly by Malinowski via Isaac Schapera and later directly by Radcliffe-Brown, E. E. Evans-Pritchard, as well as by Godfrey and Monica Wilson, incorporates the shift of British social anthropology from social structure to social process.[30] In 1953, he employed Radcliffe-Brown's functionalism, analyzing conflict as helping to maintain social structure. Periodic civil wars and rebellions in African societies, he writes, although they sometimes have as their goal freeing territorial segments from the unified state, also serve to maintain the state. The claimants or rivals for the royal throne uphold the values of the state by proposing to exercise the office better, or with greater magical efficacy, than the incumbent. The goal of rebellion is less often secession than possession of the kingship itself, which means the institution is being validated and perpetuated. Around the same time, Gluckman observed in certain rituals studied by his colleagues a new way in which ritual functions to maintain social cohesion. Rites using rebellion, protest, and license symbolically exaggerate real breaks with social norms, and, in doing so, affirm the normative order as well as the enduring social arrangements which the norms protect.

Some societies in their very constitution—Gluckman is thinking of those in subsaharan Africa—contain the seeds of recurrent factionalism, intrigue, and rebellion. Yet the ensuing conflicts do not necessarily lead to revolutions against the social order. In 1958, he advanced a more general principle, holding that any social system contains a dominant cleavage, one running through all the social relationships, rooted in fundamental conflicts within the system; for example, between Africans and whites. In any part of the system, subsidiary cleavages operate similarly to the dominant cleavage. In a changing society the subsidiary cleavages all press for similar developments in different sets of social relations. Despite cleavages and accompanying conflict, cooperation remains normal, for certain purposes even being extended across the dominant lines of cleavage. Conflict, however, is equally normal in social life. Struggles over power are inevitable, being waged in any social system for the purpose of obtaining greater control over policy or more control over men and things.

By 1963 Gluckman had become dissatisfied with the model of social systems advocated by Radcliffe-Brown and to which his own ideas, despite their emphasis on conflict, conformed to a considerable extent. Social systems, he now believed, are not nearly as integrated as the organic systems to which Radcliffe-Brown compared them. Social life constitutes a field of social action comprising a series of sometimes discrepant processes operating under ecological and other influences, including technology. Sometimes the processes are set in motion by imperfect integration between traditional institutions. Gluckman did not, however, abandon the idea of social systems as fundamentally straining toward equilibrium. Oscillations in political life, he says, frequently constitute part of a stable equilibrium, the social system returning to its previous state after the disturbance has passed.

New trends in British anthropology failed to arouse his enthusiasm. A letter to a London literary weekly, in 1973, reveals his impatience with the introspection lavished on the epistemological obsession with how another society comes to be known, and on ethical concern over demeaning a people by studying them scientifically.[31] The cognitivists, Mary Douglas, E. R. Leach, and Rodney Needham, he claims, tend to concentrate exclusively on the intellectual meanings of symbols, rituals, myths, and kinship terms. In Gluckman's opinion, more significant results could be obtained by investigating the contexts in which people use symbols, myths, and rituals, or how they manipulate and change those and other social arrangements to suit their own interests.

A False Start

British social anthropology contains a partial contradiction with regard to theoretical generalization, which nearly all of Malinowski's and Radcliffe-Brown's students at one time saw to be the ultimate aim of studying primitive societies. Though generalizations were certainly forthcoming—I have cited some and will mention more in the next chapter—most of the anthropologists' efforts were devoted to understanding particular societies. Much more rarely did they engage in the comparative analysis of cases to reach or test generalizations of a wider scope. Their field reports interpret the nonobvious meanings of symbols; analyze, in painstaking detail, such topics as social roles, the structure of descent groups, and the operation of alliance ties; and, as Gluckman illustrates, explain the stability of social structures in functional terms. Generally, however, British social anthropologists did little to polish or extend the functional theory they inherited from Malinowski and Radcliffe-Brown; Americans, we will see, went much further in that respect.

Nor did the British try hard to emulate the natural science method advocated by Radcliffe-Brown, and held by him to be the primary identifying mark of social anthropology. In fact, some social anthropologists outrightly rejected the method.[32] Repudiating the aim of causal or functional analysis, Evans-Pritchard, who succeeded Radcliffe-Brown at Oxford, defined social anthropology as the search for structural connections between facts; for example, between religious practices and nonreligious concepts and values held in a society. The meaning of facts lies in their interrelationships, and the "art" of anthropology consists in revealing meaning with the more ultimate aim of making exotic and familiar societies more intelligible, whether they be taken singly or together. Leach, after adopting Claude Lévi-Strauss's structuralism, called the analogy between social anthropology and the natural sciences a "false start," blame for which falls on Radcliffe-Brown. In Leach's opinion, anthropology can be considered scientific only in the broad sense of wanting to advance the stock of knowledge. In a shrunken world of communication, the essential problem for the discipline lies in translating the "cultural language" of one society into terms understandable by another.

While their contemporaries did not all agree with Evans-Pritchard and Leach, no one loudly defended the scientific status of social anthropology in the terms Radcliffe-Brown had used.

Functionalism

Customs Serving Society and the Individual

Considering the founding role played by Malinowski and Radcliffe-Brown in anthropological functionalism while they were training a generation of British social anthropologists, it is surprising that the leading postwar functionalists did not come from the community of British anthropologists. With the exception of Malinowski's pupil Ralph Piddington,[33] who taught in Edinburgh before returning to his native New Zealand, those who most zealously developed functionalism were Americans educated in the United States. If, as has been said, functionalism belongs to an era of stability, order, and complacency, it nevertheless managed in the United States to survive the restless 1950s and 1960s. Neither the state of the world nor the criticism it drew affected its confirmed proponents, among whom none was more dedicated than Melford E. Spiro, an "unregenerate functionalist" by his own admission.

Born in Ohio, Spiro received his doctoral degree from Northwestern University, in 1950, and after holding several other teaching posts joined the University of California in San Diego. Equipped with his theory he carried out major field research in Micronesia, an Israeli kibbutz, and Burma. His work patently reveals Malinowski's approach, explaining how culture serves individual needs; but it also incorporates Radcliffe-Brown's interest in functions serving the interests of society.[34] Both types of needs are met, almost simultaneously, through rewards that motivate individuals to perform assigned roles from which both they and the social system benefit. If the role behavior serves no personal or social functions, leaving needs unmet, then the behavior may well disappear from the society.

In Spiro's theory, survival of a society depends on the operation of its social system, made up of economic, kinship, and other subsystems, each of which comprises institutions possessing reciprocal roles. Three kinds of functions emanate from the institutions where individuals play their roles: functions providing for the physical survival of members; functions contributing to the persistence of the social system, and hence to orderly social interaction; and functions promoting social solidarity, by reducing intrapersonal and interpersonal tension. These vital functions are assured by inducing members of a social system (or subsystem) to willingly carry out the roles of parent, farmer, policeman, chief, and so forth, in the institutions where they act. The 18th-century wonder of synergy reappears as Spiro describes how desirable individual goals—respect, money, prestige, power, and the like—act as incentives motivating individuals to adequately perform those roles and thereby serve their own interests, while simultaneously providing vital functions for the society.

Functional analysis, in tracing the useful consequences of behavior, can also explain the cause of the behavior, Spiro maintains, provided the functions are consciously or unconsciously intended by the actors. Here is how: achieving the sought-for functions reinforces the actors' behavior by creating an expectation that the same rewards will again be forthcoming if the custom is adequately performed again. The expectation serves as a motivational factor, a cause. If the functions are unintended, however, they cannot logically account for the cause of the behavior in question.

Other writers, amplifying Radcliffe-Brown's concept of social needs and Malinowski's list of basic human needs, specified the requirements that a social system must satisfy if it is to continue.[35] In exploring the requisites of human life and social systems they, in effect, augmented Clark Wissler's explanation of how the universal culture pattern came into existence. The "functional prerequisites" of social life, including the maintenance of biological functioning on which Malinowski bestowed most attention, demand some way of producing and distributing goods and services, of insuring the reproduction of new members, as well as their socialization, and of preserving meaning and motivation in the members of a society. The efficiency with which institutions meet the functional prerequisites constitutes one measure by which the institutions can be evaluated in other than culturally relativistic terms.

Self-Regulatory Systems in Culture

Spiro, in the manner of older functionalism, analyzed customs by their beneficial consequences—for individual physiological and psychological well-being, or for the maintenance of social order. Another functional approach, owing nothing to the arch-functionalists, Malinowski and Radcliffe-Brown, directed itself to explaining how particular systems in culture maintain themselves through negative feedback.[36] Analysis of this type depends on isolating a system—not necessarily a social system—containing a negative feedback process activated when a critical variable exceeds certain limits, thereby threatening the system with destruction. The feedback device, consisting in some form of cultural behavior, functions to return the destructive variable to within an acceptable range or, putting it differently, maintains the variable within permitted limits. If the number of domesticated animals in a community grows to exceed the capacity of the pastures, the corrective mechanism set in motion might be emigration to new pasture grounds, forceful seizure of new grazing land, redistribution of the herds, or a feast in which the excess animals are killed off and eaten. Functional analysis of this type contrasts markedly with the more rationalistic approach of the older functionalism, whose propositions are often cast in terms unsuited for testing (what, for example, are the empirical indicators of social order or societal continuity?), or that are self-evident (as when Malinowski implies that food getting and food preparation function to meet the hunger need). The older functionalism provided no means for testing the assertions it made regarding functions, whereas neofunctionalism demands the construction of models that contain testable hypotheses specifying explicitly how the system works.

Performance of Cultural Systems

Old or new, functionalists usually confined themselves to research on particular societies, thereby, as Walter Goldschmidt complains, providing no basis for generalization.[37] He proposed examining functional processes as they are variously institutionalized in different societies, with the object of seeing whether similar processes for meeting specific needs are present in all and, if they are not, account for their absence. He also proposes evaluating the satisfactoriness with which different institutionalized arrangements satisfy particular needs, universal ones as well as needs that are contingent on special circumstances, which exist only in certain types of society. All human societies share goods, he points out, but have varying institutions for doing so. Not only does the character of the particular institution depend on the type of production and other aspects of the cultural system, the efficiency with which a given institution works must also be considered in context. Illustrating with hunting and gathering cultures of comparable types, he observes that the Andamanese hunter shares his kill generously for the sake of his social standing, while in central Australia generosity doesn't count in social standing—only meeting kinship obligations through sharing does. What is the relative efficiency of one system over the other? Goldschmidt doesn't say, because the information required for comparative functional analysis was not available. If it were, Goldschmidt believes, then anthropology with such an approach would finally be able to divest itself of cultural relativity, as well as of ethnocentrism and idealized images of primitive society. Instead, we would impartially and objectively compare societies, our own among others, for the way they go about providing social stability and protecting members' physical or mental well-being.

Goldschmidt was born in Texas and trained in anthropology at the University of California in Berkeley, where he received his Ph.D., in 1942; in 1946, he became a faculty member of the University at its Los Angeles branch. His interest in evaluative functionalism reflects his long-term commitment to research of public relevance having social as well as theoretical implications.

Without identifying himself with functionalism, Cyril S. Belshaw, a New Zealander teaching in Canada with a doctorate received at the London School of Economics in 1921, also thought it important to study the performance of cultural systems.[38] Putting stress on goals, rather than human or social prerequisites, and using concepts derived from economics, he too wanted to know how successfully a particular culture meets its goals. He conceives of a culture as a stock of resources and knowledge and as a system of power and authority employed in achieving a set of material and nonmaterial goals. For evaluating cultural performance, one would have to consider the time, skill, and energy expended in meeting the goals to which a population is committed—over, say, a one-year period. The undertaking would require inventorying the stock of resources actually utilized by the social system, and weighting specific resources according to the actual use made of them. Ideas, knowledge, and skills manifested in performance would have to be accounted for, as well as significant themes or cultural orientations—toward expansion, accumulation (of things, knowledge, health, and the like), security, or innovation—affecting performance. Communication in the social system, the way people weigh and articulate goals, and specialization of individual and organizational roles, also affect cultural performance and must be taken into account. Like Goldschmidt, Belshaw did not directly study how a culture performs; he fully recognized the many problems to be faced in putting his method into operation.

Critical Scrutiny

The type of functionalism that Radcliffe-Brown and Malinowski blazoned in social science came under close critical scrutiny.[39] Charged with confusing cause and consequence when they explain why an institution arises by how it works, functionalists denied being primarily interested in why an institution arises, thereupon leaving functionalism open to criticism for being ahistorical. Critics reproved the older functionalists for not elucidating the links between customs and the useful ends they serve, for their relating cause and effect only tenuously, and for failing in their analysis to specify the steps leading, say, from the expression of sentiments in ritual to the social cohesion the ritual is supposed to bring about. Another accusation—resembling a criticism leveled against the extreme diffusionists—charged functionalists with failing to heed intention and meaning in what people did; it was heard from anthropologists like Evans-Pritchard, who advocated understanding the meaning of social forms rather than their objective consequences. Back in 1931, Robert Briffault, an unconventional social theorist alienated from the intellectual life of his era, observed the ease with which functional analyses reveal value in the most unusual customs, no matter how empirically impractical or unreasonable they might be. He recoiled from the dangerous moral relativism inherent in such unwitting justification of superstitions and fanatical institutions. For Evans-Pritchard, who grew alienated from his teachers' theoretical outlook, functionalism's pragmatic defense of any religion constituted an avowal of the irrelevancy of religious truth by anthropologists, most of whom profess no religious faith. Dorothy Lee found the concept of basic needs—that starting point of Malinowskian functionalism—inadequate to account for the world's variety of cultural forms. Valuation, she writes, not need, lies at the basis of human behavior. Value implies positive satisfaction intrinsic in the performance of a custom; need theory suggests behavior is good simply because it reduces tension or gets rid of some other kind of unpleasantness.

Instrumentalism Dominant

In addition to the anthropologists who wrote in the functionalist idiom, many others like Belshaw took a pragmatic view of culture. They regarded culture or particular cultural elements as means of adaptation, paths to achieving goals desired by the society. An instrumentalist viewpoint, I have already said, is broader than functionalism, and shows up in many things done by anthropologists who do not claim to be functionalists. It even appears when cross-cultural research compares culture patterns— subsistence techniques, child-training routines, and others—serving analogous purposes in different cultures.

If criticism robbed functionalism of some of its earlier momentum, nothing like that happened to anthropologists' tendency to treat aspects of culture and social structure in terms of the practical uses to which they are put. With the common-sense assumption, reinforced by introspection into our own conduct, that human behavior *is* purposeful, how could anyone have trouble discovering utility and purposefulness in the acts and cognitions of exotic societies? The people studied, themselves, emically, frequently justified roles, organizations, and patterns of behavior by the ends those things were supposed to accomplish. In comparison to the ubiquity of instrumental analysis, anthropological attention to the sheer expressive aspects of behavior was restricted: to a relatively few structuralists, to students of ritual, music, and mythology, and to ethnologists interested in games; and they, too, irresistibly drifted into theorizing about the pragmatics of those cultural features.

The success of the instrumental viewpoint can be largely credited to the fact that it worked successfully as a paradigm. With the exception of the critiques directed against functionalism, nobody brought forward serious instances of inconsistencies or contradictions challenging conclusions obtained by the viewpoint. More often, the expressivists' conclusions crumbled when their data were reexamined with pragmatic concepts. It is what happened when economic anthropologists and transactionalists, assuming power is a utility prized in many—if not all—societies, contradicted the conclusion that potlatchers who destroy wealth, fiesta-givers who spend hard-earned savings, and pastoralists who raise animals for the sake of numbers rather than for food, traction, or marketing were acting nonrationally or noneconomically for the sake of showing their pride, religious devotion, or love of cattle. From the standpoint of economic theory, those people were plainly maximizing their resources in rational ways with the pragmatic goal of power in mind.

Cultural Evolution

Adaptation

Mild were the strictures leveled against functionalism, compared to the raking over 19th-century evolutionism had received from the pens of German and American historical ethnologists and from Malinowski and Radcliffe-Brown. Yet, by never denying that cultures had developed over time, antievolutionists may have facilitated the renovation of evolutionary studies employing more acceptable data, methods, and theory.

Starting in the late 1930s Vere Gordon Childe, an Australian-born prehistorian, followed by a number of United States ethnologists, including Leslie A. White, Julian H. Steward, and Elman R. Service, found such acceptable resources and installed cultural evolutionism as one of the most popular subjects in postwar anthropology. A wealth of archeological, paleontological, and ethnographic data provided the evolutionists with a basis for reconstructing, less conjecturally than their predecessors, how human society had developed. Their major resource, however, for explaining cultural evolution lay in the concept of adaptation derived from Darwinian biology. According to the concept, adaptation takes place when, in response to pressures exerted on a society by factors in the natural or social environment, members employ new opportunities to optimize some aspect of their lives.[40] The new opportunities can be tools; new substances for making tools; ideas; rules, such as the rule of exogamy; or new patterns of doing things, such as waging war or cementing alliances between potentially hostile groups. The opportunities may reach them through discovery and invention, through diffusion, or by a combination of those processes. Their response to environmental pressures may simply take the route of discarding things from culture that no longer serve well. The change they make is adaptive if, in being tested against the environment, it promotes well-being or survival for at least some of the society's members over a short run of time. Since environments are constantly changing in greater or lesser degree, societies are always being confronted by new pressures. Evolution lies basically in the success with which societies meet those pressures. Whether in the long run the ensuing cultural changes promote greater cultural complexity, result in more energy being utilized, increase the differentiation of societies or groups within a society, or follow some other directional trend has nothing to do with evolution viewed as process.

Within this conception of cultural evolution as adaptation a number of unsolved questions invited debate. Did selection by the natural environment, compared to selection by social factors, grow less important in the course of history? Some anthropologists believed so, citing as causes the increasing efficiency of subsistence techniques, political organization, and other means of adaptation, as well as the growing dependence of small, formerly isolated communities on larger societies for their well-being; hence they no longer rely wholly on themselves for survival under natural conditions. Students of evolution also did not agree on clear-cut criteria or procedures for measuring adaptation, i.e., to ascertain in what respects cultural modifications have promoted well-being and survival. Asserting and logically defending the beneficial consequences of innovations like the bow, plow, or exogamy is one thing; objectively assessing the adaptive significance of a trait under given environmental conditions is more difficult and warrants a controlled comparative approach. Such an approach could not be applied by evolutionists working with the whole sweep of prehistory, or with large societies in which cultural conditions permit great laxity in adaptation. In small, relatively isolated populations, however, Alexander Alland points out, comparative studies could more readily be carried out because there failure to adopt a more efficient cultural trait or to get rid of an inefficient item would quickly show up in reduced well-being and chances of survival.[41]

Directly or by implication anthropologists have defined adaptive success with demographic and cultural indicators, including growing population (as Alland does), greater cultural complexity, new means of social integration capable of coordinating more people, a greater number of subgroups, or a larger territory. Many anthropologists have continued to be more concerned with those cultural manifestations, as well as others—including increased specialization of labor, substitution of food production for food gathering, improved agricultural and other tools indicating better control over the material environment, increased specialization of total societies, and greater cultural diversity in the world as a whole—than with the degree of biological adaptation they accompany. So much concern with outcomes of cultural development gives the impression of direction or pattern in history; for example, toward greater control over the material environment, larger social systems, greater heterogeneity, or more embracive forms of social integration. Robert L. Carneiro says so quite explicitly.[42] For him evolution consists in more than simply adaptive change. As it did for Herbert Spencer, evolution represents change from a relatively indefinite, incoherent homogeneity to increasingly definite, coherent heterogeneity.

Another view separates evolution from cultural development and sees evolution proceeding blindly in no particular direction. It is the observers who, guided by values, perceive a more or less reliable pattern when they take a long-range look at certain, selected outcomes of the process in history.[43]

Even anthropologists who emphasized evolutionary process rather than developmental trends in culture history balked at making cultural evolution as blind or purposeless as organic evolution. Human beings are different from the rest of the biological world because they are able to reach rational decisions through which they can adapt rapidly to new social and natural environmental pressures. Thus they may decide to conserve replenishable natural resources when the supply dwindles, or, through other forms of planning, apply their knowledge to practice. Similar decisions made many times in different societies living under similar conditions are responsible for creating epiphenomenal unilinear patterns of developmental change.

Although cultural evolutionism is consistent with the ideographic study of particular cultures, evolutionists emphasized generalization rather than particularism. They envisaged a single evolutionary process operating in all cultures, and looked for parallels or trends in how the process works itself out between societies. Hence cultural evolutionism constituted a setback for cultural relativity, especially in North America, where the new evolutionism possessed far more strength than in Great Britain.

Importance of Technology

Many neoevolutionists recognized a role of major evolutionary importance played by technology, while others, including Elman Service and Alexander Alland, gave less prominence to the technological factor. Two writers emphasizing the technological factor, V. Gordon Childe and

Leslie White, were unusual in England-language anthropology for using Marxist theory.

According to Childe, tools and other instruments of production, the primary means by which societies adapt to their natural and social settings, are the decisive factors in history.[44] Just as advantageous physical modifications allowed new biological species to multiply, so in human history the progressive technological improvements resulting from invention or diffusion, by increasing man's control over nature, permitted societies with new cultures to grow and survive. However, human adaptation also requires finding new means capable of meeting nonorganic, socially approved wants, fulfilling expected patterns of behavior, and dealing effectively with other social groups. Just as biological evolution promotes the diversification of life forms, so cultural evolution has led to differentiated cultures, each differently adapted to its natural and social environment. However, new instruments of production entering a society, due to resistance directed against them, do not automatically usher in new forms of adaptation. To this long-familiar idea, Childe applied dialectical thinking derived from Marxist philosophy, and describes the would-be innovators struggling against contradictory forces in the society. Not until the innovators overcome those forces can they apply the new tools or techniques. In the early empires of Southwest Asia and Egypt, contradictory forces opposed to technological progress included magical beliefs insisting on the perpetuation of established ways of doing things, cheap labor provided by slaves, the affluence some members of society derived from extant adaptations to local geographical conditions, and the attitudes of the masses fearing the new technology would only widen the gap already separating them from the wealth.

Styling himself as a materialist, Leslie A. White attached decisive importance to technology because of its life-sustaining properties.[45] Although sociological, philosophical, and emotional factors may condition or even limit the use and development of technical means of production, they exert little influence on cultural systems compared to technology's dominant role. Considering White's firm commitment to technological determinism, it is surprising to realize that he studied psychology at Columbia University before taking up anthropology and receiving his Ph.D. from Chicago, in 1927. During his many years of teaching at the University of Michigan, starting in 1930, he remained for over a decade almost alone in the United States in pursuing the study of cultural evolution.

White traces the origin of culture, its perpetuation, and its cumulative improvement through history to man's neurological ability to symbolize. But after culture began, it acquired the status of an extrasomatic phenomenon whose development followed laws independent of the laws governing its human carriers. Metaphorically, he compares culture to a temporal stream composed of systematically interrelated customs, rules, rituals, art forms, tools, and other elements. As the elements interact with one another within the stream while it flows through time, they give rise to new forms, and so the previous culture develops. Not all of the new forms are suited to more effective adaptation in the culture's natural and social environments, and only those that are will be retained, replacing less effective forms. White was one of the anthropologists who saw evolution in culture proceeding as blindly as biological evolution. Human will, purpose, or consciousness, he claimed, have little to do with the selection process whereby new cultural forms are retained or eliminated. Instead of limiting the concept of evolution to the selection of new adaptations that test out successfully against the environment, he employs it far more generally to designate the process whereby new cultural forms —axes, vehicles, writing systems, religious or political systems, or whatever—emerge over time from previous forms. Increasing energy per capita per year, captured and put to work in a society through technology controls the process. Basically, the captive energy provides the culture carriers with goods and services to satisfy their needs. $E \times T \to P$ formalizes relationships involved, E representing the energy put to work, T the technical apparatus for capturing it, and P the products resulting. As the amount of productive energy increases in a society it promotes changes in the society and its culture by influencing population growth, specialization of labor, and productivity; but White fails to go into details concerning the precise links between energy, the intervening factors of population, specialization, or productivity, and the cultural changes those factors control. Nor did he, as far as I know, ever substitute real quantities for the symbols in his formula. However, Betty Meggers, a former student of White's, applied his theory qualitatively to ethnographic data.[46] Increased energy captured and utilized as the Plains Indians adopted horses and as a Madagascar tribe changed from dry to wet rice cultivation, she found, were followed by greater cultural complexity, as the theory predicts.

Regularities deriving from technology, such as Childe, White, and Meggers found in history and prehistory, emerged even more convincingly from Julian H. Steward's qualitative comparison of the archeological and photohistorical records of Mesopotamia, Egypt, China, northern Peru, and Mesoamerica.[47] In each region, according to his analysis, substantially different cultures had independently passed through the same series of developmental stages. Instead of visualizing culture in global terms as developing toward higher levels of complexity (White's idea), Steward resembles Childe in viewing temporal processes in culture proceeding independently along parallel tracks in different regions. Of course, the end result is the same; like White, Steward, too, sees history leading toward greater sociocultural complexity every place where evolution is evident.

Aroused to an interest in anthropology in an undergraduate course taught jointly by Robert Lowie and Alfred L. Kroeber, Steward, after a sojourn at Cornell University, returned to Berkeley for his Ph.D. His later influence while teaching at Columbia University and at the University of Illinois augmented Leslie White's in reviving cultural evolutionism in the United States. Moreover, he contributed to awakening a lively interest in cultural ecology.

The two topics, evolution and ecology, are only analytically distinct in Steward's work. He defines evolution operationally as the result obtained by an investigator who starts out looking for regularities in the conjunction of cause and effect in culture change. Regularities are to be found by noting parallels in "form and function" in the development of cultures belonging to the same type, South American rubber tappers and subarctic fur trappers, for example, or agricultural societies located in dry lands.

The pat explanations of accidental discovery or fortuitous diffusion will not satisfy someone engaged in the quest for regularities, and they did not satisfy Steward. In his theory, ecological factors are primarily responsible for producing the regularities in which he is chiefly interested. The regularities—they could also be called parallels—arise when similar traits connected with subsistence and other biological imperatives (reality-facing features of culture, as Kroeber named them[48]) come into use in different societies and bring about similar forms of social structure. Cultural evolution, therefore, is rooted in technical innovations for dealing with the physical environment, i.e., in cultural ecology. Techniques of production —means for working land and extracting resources from nature—are the key factors. For Steward, however, technology always operates in conjunction with other cultural features that are causally interrelated with each other and with technology, including credit and other economic arrangements, political organization, and religious and ideological doctrines. Taken together with technology as a system, these features make up the controlling center of a culture, the culture core. The core itself is determined by the technique of production it contains. Certain noncore cultural features are closely bound to the culture core, while other features are arbitrary. The latter can change independently of the core and consequently possess great variability, even between cultures that happen to possess the same core. Cores may diffuse; but being closely linked to environment, their mobility is restricted compared to arbitrary features of culture. If a core does diffuse, the society borrowing it will reshape it to suit the problems and resources offered by its environment. Within a society, changes in the culture core, representing new adaptations to environment, can produce substantial changes in social structure as people reorganize themselves in response to their new ecological adaptations and ideologically justify the new organization. In small societies the form of ecological adaptation imposes very narrow limits on possible varieties of social structure; as a result of the possibilities being limited, regularities in structure between societies are likely to be independently produced. (George Peter Murdock, we shall see in the next chapter, offered similar reasoning to explain recurrent systems of kinship terminology.)

Through promoting secondary adaptations of social structure in response to changing culture cores, cultural evolution has brought about new levels of sociocultural integration. For example, the shift occurring in several parts of the world from food gathering to food production transformed a social structure based, Steward believed, on nuclear family bands into a multifamily folk society. Subsequent technological developments produced the state society. Man-made problems originating in social structure, especially at the higher levels of sociocultural integration, also require adaptation. Such problems are resolved through the invention or borrowing of militaristic techniques, commercial procedures, and religious ideologies capable of providing a basis for theocratic control. Each higher level of sociocultural integration is quantitatively more complex and qualitatively different from lower levels in its distinctive principles or organization. However, the structural forms and distinctive features of lower levels tend to persist into the higher; witness the ubiquity of the family as a unit of organization. Calling a level higher is not to say it is better than a lower one. Steward could find nothing in the universe making the idea of progress meaningful when applied to biological or cultural evolution. Agriculture and the state, he apparently means, are simply different forms of adaptation, in no sense superior to hunting or multifamily bands. To some degree, therefore, he remained a cultural relativist.

Steward reveals more humanism than White, for he credits individuals with power to direct the way a culture changes. People can influence evolution by exercising their potential for rational thought; by heightening their awareness, they need not drift but can deliberately order or accelerate adaptive processes.

No Prime Movers in Culture

The dominance that Childe, White, and Steward ascribe to technology in cultural evolution disappears in Elman R. Service, a member of the next anthropological generation who refused to choose any one factor in culture as the prime mover in cultural development.[49] His concept of evolution is similar to their's, however, for he defines it as an adaptive process involving the selection of new, or the adjustment of old, cultural traits whereby a society improves its chances of survival, security, and growth. Evolution continues as long as members realize new possibilities of adaptation; it ceases and involution takes over if a society becomes culturally so firmly entrenched in a given physical or social environment that it allows only changes leading to deeper entrenchment. In Service's opinion, Steward often mistakes involution for evolution.

Service studied graduate anthropology at Columbia University during the period of Steward's tenure in the anthropology department. Hence we find carry-overs of Steward's thought in the younger man's work. Even the break with exclusively technological determinism may owe something to Steward, whose core concept admitted more than tools and techniques for coping with environment. Service also recognized increasingly complex forms of social structure as outcomes of the evolutionary process. Evolution, he reasons, expanded the size and density of societies, the number of component groups in societies, the degree of task specialization, and the complexity of means for integrating subgroups and specialists. In his popular book, *Primitive Social Organization,* published in 1962, he follows vintage comparative method in arranging types of social integration—bands, chiefdoms, and states—in the order in which they supposedly developed and in illustrating them with examples from people whom he calls "our contemporary ancestors," the primitive societies described by ethnographers. In rationalistic terms he defends his revival of the 19th century's practice of ordering contemporary societies in evolutionary hierarchies, except that he admits to being unsure of whether primitive states developed prior to colonialism. The evolutionary placement of Arunta culture poses no problem. What is it, he asks, if not "a form of adaptation to a particular kind of environment made long, long ago and preserved into modern times because of isolation?" (Remember John Locke's once "all the world was America"?) It wasn't long before doubt overcame Service, after thousands of undergraduate students had used his book to learn anthropology, whereupon he simply postulated a sequence of societal types: egalitarian society, hierarchical society, the empire-state, and the classical empire of archaic civilization. He illustrated those he could with truly historical data.

One of his best-known contributions to cultural theory, the law of evolutionary potential, Service formulated at a time when American society was actively concerned with promoting economic development in underdeveloped nations. Simply stated, the law sees the greatest possibility for evolution to exist in the world's culturally backward countries, whether as a result of inventions they make or in consequence of rapid diffusion from abroad. A corollary asserts evolution to be discontinuous; cultural advances spring up in hitherto lagging societies rather than occurring in the hitherto most progressive. Historically he traces the law to

Thorstein Veblen and Leon Trotsky but not to Spencer, who advanced a similar thesis.

Where Service broke with exclusively technological determinism, another evolutionist of the new generation, Alexander Alland, gave up looking for the outcomes of cultural evolution in rising levels of social integration or cultural complexity.[50] "Cultural paleontology," he calls such efforts, and he devotes his attention strictly to the evolutionary process. Defining evolution as the process whereby systems become modified as a result of environmental pressures, he takes human populations with their cultural rules as his system, a biological system, and asks how this system becomes modified in biological factors or in cultural rules through the help of environmental action. Although Alland recognizes that both social and natural environmental pressures affect human population systems, he prefers to treat culture primarily as a response to environmental pressure, though in some cases the environment was previously altered through earlier cultural adaptations. Evolution and adaptation, he makes clear, are not identical; better adaptation is only one possible outcome of the evolutionary process. Only testing can prove whether a particular change is adaptive, nonadaptive, or neutral in regard to a specific environment. Recognizing that various and sometimes contradictory measures of adaptation have been proposed, he considers comparative population size an ultimate measure, so that between two adaptive modes of behavior operating under the same environmental conditions, the one capable of supporting a larger population is the more adaptive. Making such a test requires a competitive situation between two populations in which the population with the superior advantage will in the long run more or less completely replace, perhaps destroy, the other. Obviously, the test requires historical evidence hard to come by, and lacking such evidence cultural evolutionists are limited to explaining evolution rationalistically. One reasons, for example, that the long postpartum taboo found in some societies in tropical areas is an evolutionary adaptation selected because, by preventing frequent pregnancies and thereby leading to prolonged nursing of children, it prevents kwashiorkor, a deficiency disease found in tropical environments. Any behavioral factor affecting mortality, fertility, or disease, including social structure and medical routines for the diagnosis, treatment, or prevention of disease, may aid a population's adaptation.

The rapidity and flexibility with which human population systems can modify their behavior in response to external or internal changes—especially by borrowing already tested adaptive cultural traits from other systems—makes them extraordinarily adaptable. Alland recognizes man's capacity to control evolution in human population systems. By consciously examining the environment to discover the degree to which adaptive strategies are succeeding or failing, man is able to avoid the long, blind process of random change which other species must undergo in becoming adapted to a changing environment.

Other criteria of successful adaptation are listed by Yehudi Cohen; all purportedly represent cultural changes through which man escapes from limitations imposed by the natural habitat he occupies.[51] As criteria he offers the extent to which a society is able to subsist on essentially the same diet during the entire year, regardless of seasonal variations in the food supply; its ability to make substitutions if the usual diet becomes imperiled; the proportion of products from domesticated plants and animals in a society's total diet; the extent to which it possesses knowledge about cause and effect in nature; the degree to which social life can be controlled to reduce fortuitousness; and the society's ability to free itself generally from seasonal variations in cultural behavior. But in order to evaluate human adaptation comparatively, a critic with an eye for controlled comparison points out, the niches exploited by different groups must be comparable.[52] One cannot compare a Western industrial society's adaptive success, using as criteria the steady year-round diet free from seasonal fluctuations of the food supply, with the early variability of diet found among isolated primitive cultivators. The test would have to be between industrial systems or between different primitive cultivators. When incomparable ecologies are compared, evaluation should be in terms of the probability of long-term evolutionary success. As the law of evolutionary potential states, dominance (such as industrial societies enjoy) is not necessarily synonymous with the best chance of survival.

Capacities for Culture

Early culture, anthropologists agreed, evolved together with human abilities for learning, self-consciousness, symbolization, and other psychological capacities. In an early essay George Peter Murdock called learning one of the two major types of adaptation produced in the course of biological evolution, the other being society.[53] Neither is peculiar to human beings, but in man the combination, by making culture possible, produced a new level of complexity in natural phenomena. Compared to the amount of information in the prehistoric and historic record testifying to cultural development, the origin and early development of learning ability and the other behavioral foundations of culture are impossible to discover, having left no direct traces, and their contemporary evolution is too slow to observe in one generation. Hence scholars tackling mental development have been limited to a considerable amount of speculative reasoning based on indirect evidence.

In the absence of direct evidence from paleolithic or precultural times, A. Irving Hallowell and others interested in the psychological foundations of culture turned to studies of infrahuman primate behavior for clues to how the human foundations developed. To discover the genesis of the ego, core of the human personality and seat of man's instinct-free adaptive ability, Hallowell looked for functional equivalents of ego processes in those primates.[54] He found them in the animals' ability, under certain conditions, to defer gratification and purposefully plan their behavior. But he could find no nonhuman primate equivalent of another important ego function, the ability to symbolize privately sensed experience and thereby share the private side of oneself with others. In man's prehistory the earliest evidence of such symbolization occurs in upper paleolithic cave art.

Researchers following Hallowell vastly extended knowledge of the symboling capacities of subhuman primates, especially when they are taught by man. However, much more work remains to be done before such knowledge can illuminate the development of early man's ego processes.

Human Ethology

The Cultural Animal

Hallowell pondered the development of mind before behavioral zoology, better known as ethology, penetrated anthropology. Applied to human beings, ethology resembled the effort he made to find the roots of culture in man's behavioral capacities, in that both approaches worked backward from human behavior to analogous forms of nonhuman animal behavior.

Like certain other movements in recent anthropology, human ethology lacked appreciation of cultural relativity, and like French structuralism, it broke loose from the tight grip that social determinism had long maintained in social science. Since the classical times, explanations of social behavior tended to make the social environment a major factor shaping people's cognitions and actions. Generally speaking, social scientists demonstrated little interest in instinctive, inborn, or "natural"—including racial—bases of behavior, and at times strove to expose such explanations as overstating a partial truth or as false. Attempts periodically made to introduce nature as an explanatory factor, psychoanalysis being one such instance, met resistance. In fact, in psychoanalysis the culturalists became far more persuasive than orthodox Freudians, and their point of view predominated in anthropology. The ethologists deplored so much bias in favor of social factors to the exclusion of man's animal heritage. Robin Fox, an English anthropologist teaching at Rutgers University, complained that cultural anthropology, concentrating on the cultural heritage acquired by human beings, has taken too little interest in what human beings brought with them across the bridge from nature to culture as part of their biological heritage.[55] By calling man a cultural animal, anthropologists put stress entirely on the cultural side of human nature, relegating the animal in man to a few odd features like blinking, sucking, feeling hungry, and copulating. Even then, they usually emphasize the learned aspects of those innate proclivities.

Ethologists like Fox and his colleague Lionel Tiger made it their business to study the biological heritage for adaptation derived by man from the period before any creature had attained human status. They held culture itself to be part of the humans' biological survival equipment, for culture depends on a characteristic largely limited to our species which we acquired in the course of evolution. Instead of being a triumph of man over nature, culture represents a natural capacity rooted in human biology.

The ethologists recall other anthropologists who in less extreme terms also perceived the biological roots of culture.[56] John Gillin described culture as always limited by man's basic biological abilities, and Earl Count traced familism and other social traits to patterns of behavior man shares with other animals, especially primates. Admitting the roots of culture in biological capacities, Kroeber relativistically dwelled on the mutability of those abilities under the influence of different cultural traditions.

For Fox, the seemingly endless variety of cultural arrangements contained little of direct theoretical significance. Why be dazzled by the way man develops his abilities? Human beings are, after all, a highly developed mammal divided into a large number of populations. One would expect many local differences to appear among them. Let's not be overwhelmed by cultural variety and lose sight of the basic repertory of behavioral units which the human species possesses in common and that combine in different ways in different populations. It is one of those species-specific characteristics, our great degree of behavioral flexibility, particularly on the symbolic level, that gives us the ability to live in different cultures. But, Fox warns echoing Gillin, there are definite limits in what human animals can do and the different kinds of societies they can organize.

Male Bonding

Specific biological attributes, some with a long evolutionary history, are utilized in culture. Or—once more adopting the computer-language metaphors Fox and Tiger fancied—human beings not only acquired a general capacity for culture but through mutation and natural selection have come to be wired for some very specific cultural behaviors. Evolution has programmed them to behave in certain ways, given certain inputs of information from the environment. Should an input not be received at the point in the life cycle where the human being is ready to receive it, then the behavior either will not occur, or it will appear in a modified, perhaps distorted, form. Hence Fox did not fear, as some other anthropologists did,[57] that if a nuclear holocaust were to destroy the store of human culture, it would be difficult to reinvent it, and much of the human heritage would be lost. More likely, according to Fox, a population with no knowledge of another human culture would reproduce many of the same cultural forms we know. Cultural ethology, therefore, provided another basis for explaining at least some parts of Clark Wissler's universal culture pattern. It maintained some parts of the culture pattern to be genetically anchored, and therefore predictable, from one society to another as well as to be immutable.

To discover the behavioral potentials of a species, the ethologists resorted to comparison. They compared the behavior of closely related species in order to discover which are the common, or protobehaviors, of the total group. If comparison of nonhuman primates living in the wild state with human societies reveals a number of features common to both, it is reasonable to assume that human beings possess them because they are primates. Some features are unique to man, notably our heavy reliance on culture. Culture does for us what instincts did for our predecessors, and in the unconscious way we adopt many cultural habits and unthinkingly perform them, culture closely resembles instinctive behavior.

Great as the difference between animals with and without culture may be, man retains his animal nature. He is simply a different kind of animal, one with a specific kind of nature that brought culture into being, whose ancestors gradually became increasingly dependent on thinking and symbolization. Like Hallowell and other students of behavioral evolution, the ethologists lacked facts concerning precisely how selection for those capacities occurred. But they were confident that somewhere in the transition from ape to man, some primates came to be wired for culture.

A positive bond between males, male bonding, represents a biologically transmitted propensity to which ethological anthropologists gave considerable attention.[58] Male bonding, a relationship between two or more men in which they react differently to members within the bonding unit than to individuals outside it, generates considerable positive emotion in males, provides them with substantial gratification, and serves adaptaton. In Tiger's opinion, if bonding between men did not occur satisfactorily and the community were consequently beset by strife between males, social fission would take place. The small groups likely to result from fission would each be at a considerable disadvantage for survival.

Tiger speculates how male bonding probably arose. In small, early primate hunting groups, several advantageous biological propensities of males, including greater swiftness and greater readiness to use violence, plus the disadvantage of having females participate in hunting (sexual blandishment might distract the men from their goal), led to hunting groups being constituted on an all-male basis, with distinctly adaptive results. Such groups favored the selection of whatever genetic mutations underlie male bonding.

Conjectural as the evolutionary history of male bonding or its genetic basis must remain, the cultural forms it takes in politics, war, and other cultural domains, Tiger finds fully evident in ethnographies and in our contemporary society. Males almost exclusively participate in weighty political decision-making, dominate authority structures, mainly because they are impelled to form and maintain all-male groups, and they inspire other males to follow them. A strong anti-female bias inherent in male bonding keeps ambitious females from wedging themselves deeply into such groups, but the biological deficiencies of women are also responsible for their exclusion from all-male enterprises. Wars are primarily fought by men not only because males are prone to bond, but because maleness carries a disproportionate share of physical bravery, speed, readiness to use violence, and so on. Females being less inclined toward those traits cannot act as releasers for organized aggression; therefore, their presence would place the fighting force at a disadvantage.

The aggressive behavior to which male-bonded groups are prone offers young men opportunity to validate maleness. In turn, violent or aggressive behavior (directed, of course, against outsiders since internal aggression is prohibited) constitutes a sign that the youths possess the requisite traits for joining or remaining in all-male groups.

Generally, the ethologists sought support for the innate basis of cultural forms by looking to the universal occurrence of those activities in human society and to the widespreadness of similar behaviors among nonhuman animals. The universality or widespreadness of a trait, however, is far from being independent evidence of its innate basis or long past evolutionary origin. The ethologists, however, did not examine the possibility that the similarities between human and nonhuman species might have been produced by different causes. We detect in their reasoning the familiar attempt, going back to Herodotus, to substitute logical reasoning based on premises of unproven validity for hard-to-come-by evidence of what happened in the past.

Tiger supported the theory of male bonding largely with ethnographic evidence. Ethnography, however, simply indicates that men overwhelmingly make political decisions, create fighting groups, exclude females from certain other social activities, and so on. When he explains those facts as due to a natural proclivity of men to bond with one another in consequence of adaptations made long ago, he musters no independent evidence for the explanation. Nor does he exclude the possibility of a contradictory explanation being true. For example, might the psychological gratification accruing to men from bonding be sufficient to induce men to frequently associate together?

Even if Tiger correctly retrodicted the origin and adaptive advantages possessed by all-male groups in early human societies, he ignored the challenge that feminists directed against traditional sex roles thereby making sex a political issue. In Alland's words, "the dialectic of sex is played on the cultural stage in spite of biological differences between the sexes."[59] The exclusively biological viewpoint taken by Tiger diverted him from seriously considering the political issues in male bonding and the other masculine proclivities he defends.

Cultural ethologists thought conservatively. They knew their theory of an innate basis for male bonding, aggression, and other behaviors was unpopular with some sections of the public. Thereupon they resorted to defending their ideas with the same argument used by Herbert Spencer and favored by other conservatives defending traditional positions: they warned of dire consequences should society interfere with what nature ordains. They refused to ask under what conditions, or with what safeguards, change might be allowed, nor did they try to ascertain the fate of communities which had altered sex roles.

Cultural Ecology

Ordering the Environment

Where cultural ethologists looked for cultural universals reflecting human species characteristics, cultural ecologists observed cultural differences accompanying different ways societies have of ordering the environment.[60] Though, as anthropologists realized, the ordering process need not be considered as exclusively technological; in fact, those adaptations were the prime concern of Leslie White, Julian Steward, Marvin Harris, and other cultural ecologists.

For cultural ecologists the relationship between culture and environment is one of mutual interaction: a society's mode of ordering natural features, whether cognitively or through physical means, frequently leads to changes in the milieu, thereby confronting the society with new challenges to adaptation. While the emphasis on adaptation causes ecological theory to overlap with cultural evolutionism, it efficiently circumscribes the orbit of ecological research; otherwise, since practically everything human beings do, use, or think relates directly or indirectly to how environments are ordered, cultural ecology would be synonymous with the entire subject matter of cultural anthropology. Nevertheless, cultural ecology does give attention to a wide spectrum of cultural activities;

or, to put it in theoretical terms, adaptations to environment have consequences for other areas of life. This principle of ecological thinking can be found in early times disguised as geographical determinism, and in writers of later centuries as well. Near the start of *Ancient Society*, Lewis Henry Morgan holds improvement in mankind's technical ability to manipulate the physical environment to have been a mainspring of cultural development. In addition to "the natural logic of the human mind" having influenced the course of cultural progress, he emphasizes the importance of advances in means for procuring subsistence. The culture-area concept devised chiefly by Wissler and Kroeber maps whole cultures, or at least a range of diagnostic traits extending beyond technology, on the habitats exploited by primitive people. In culture-area theory, habitat influences human behavior as a result of the use a society makes of the resources in the natural setting.

Traces of geographical determinism occasionally still turn up in ecological writing.[61] E. E. Evans-Pritchard wrote about the Nuer partly in this vein. He credits the dead flatness of their natural setting, with its clay soils, thin and sporadic woods, the grass growing high in the rainy season, and the heavy seasonal rainfall followed by a period of severe drought, with "directly" conditioning life and influencing the social structure.[62] The country suits cattle husbandry far better than horticulture, and prohibits people from living in one locality throughout the year. He explains ecological time, the Nuer system of dating events by the rhythms of their annual migrations, as primarily reflecting significant annual changes taking place in the habitat and affecting the economy. But his reasoning is strictly ecological as he ascribes Nuer cooperation to the way the Nuer adapt to their country, specifically to the restricted ability of their technology, which can produce only a narrow margin of subsistence. Scarcity of food during much of the year causes a high degree of interdependence among members of the small villages and camps, narrowing social ties so that "the people . . . are drawn closer together, in a moral sense." The simple material culture employed in environmental adaptation narrows social ties in another way. Material objects are chains along which social relationships run; the more simple the material culture, the more concentrated the relationships expressed through it.

Ecosystems and Niches

Ecological anthropology as it developed, chiefly in the United States, generally minimized the influence of environment and stressed the practical, or instrumental, nature of culture, singling out techniques relating people to the natural environment as the critical cultural subsystem. Within the subsystem, the most important techniques for enhancing a society's welfare and ensuring survival were those through which people exploited the environment for food—subsistence activities. Technologies not directly related to subsistence but relating man to his habitat—such as road making or refuse disposal—received little notice. Subsistence techniques, cultural ecologists demonstrated, influence not only many aspects of culture but the conditions under which personality is formed and, consequently, personality itself. Techniques through which societies come face to face with the habitat also influence population variables in a society, and thereby have a further, indirect impact on culture and social structure. Finally, ecologists showed how exploitative routines may affect the physiological condition of the human organism.

Seldom did ecological anthropologists broaden the concept of environment to embrace more than the inorganic and the nonhuman organic milieu by including the surrounding social environment as well. Had they done so, they could no longer have conceived of their mission as being to study the ways societies have of ordering the "environment," for in too many cases societies are controlled by more powerful groups in their social environment whom they have little chance to order. Programmatically, Laura Thompson took up a broad ecological approach, making her basic analytical unit the ecocultural supercommunity, a human community viewed in both its biotic and social setting.[63] Within the supercommunity she saw the cultural ecosystem, conceived of as a system of goal-seeking devices operating to promote the community's biological survival. Within the limits set by the human organism and the total environment, communities as well as the persons within them strive for communal and personal self-actualization. That is, cultural and personality systems tend toward wholeness, internal consistency, and homeostatic balance. As part of the self-actualization process, all species seek out favorable ecological niches where they form local associations with a limited number of plant and animal species. The small isolated human communities that anthropologists typically study include representatives of one species, man, interacting with other species and with other effective portions of the environment, and the whole ecosystem undergoing constant evolution as the component species adapt in new ways to changing biotic and social environmental conditions.

By applying the concept of ecological niche to human beings, cultural ecologists were able to explain cultural variations between several societies occupying a single geographical region.[64] Each society selectively exploits a different ecological niche in which it perceives advantages and to which it gains access. Each niche contains resources which the group with its technological abilities can exploit, utilize, and control at that particular time in its history. Several ethnic groups may also use the same niche in succession, and sometimes they compete for niches, in which case one group may displace another previously in possession. Changes in knowledge, needs, values, or aspirations will alter the pattern of niches utilized by a society. Technical development, including improved means of transportation, may increase the number of niches exploited as well as the distance between them; witness how industrial nations derive resources from many parts of the world.

The concept of ecological niche appears in a theory holding that the natural diversification of certain world areas favored the growth of prehistoric civilizations in those places.[65] Differences in soil, climate, and vegetation in Peru, Mesopotamia, and other regions provided local societies with opportunities for regional specialization and stimulated trade to distribute the specialized products, thus providing the potential for urban growth. Where similar environmental opportunities for regional specialization were lacking, in Siberia, tropical Asia, and tropical Africa, civilizations did not develop.

Another theory directs attention to irrigation in dry regions as the critical factor promoting the rise of civilization.[66] Karl Wittfogel, a professor of Chinese history influenced by Marxist theory as well as by anthropology, correlates the complex bureaucratic structure of Oriental society with its ability to build and maintain huge waterworks on which agricultural productivity depended. Revenue from agriculture enabled prosperous cities and flourishing centers of trade, learning, and the arts to grow up around the capital city where the state coordinated the country's economic life. When war interfered with the operation of these nerve centers and disrupted the bureaucracy, collapse of the irrigation systems followed, and devastating consequences ensued for the country's economic well-being. Archeological evidence at one time also induced Julian H. Steward to trace the growth of civilization to population expansion promoted by irrigation farming in several world areas. Resultant population pressure on the land, he reasons, led to competition for resources, to the rise of militaristic states, and then to conquest. Subsequent evidence persuaded him to reject the theory, since facts indicated that irrigation had contributed little or nothing to the growth of early states in at least two of the areas he studied. Whatever the fate of Steward's theory, it calls attention to the role of population as an intervening variable in an ecological process set in motion by technology.

Steward, along with V. Gordon Childe and other cultural evolutionists, entertained similar ideas regarding the role of agricultural progress—i.e., farming with increasing efficiency—in the development of some characteristic features of protohistoric civilization. The chain of causation runs as follows: agricultural development promotes population growth, leading to increased pressure on the land, which instigates wars of expansion or conquest, bringing about the growth of empires. Recent work, reversing the first two links of the chain, regards population increase as a factor stimulating agricultural development and determining other processes in cultural evolution.[67] The violent outcome of rising populations, according to this thesis, need not have happened had societies been able to adapt to population growth by inventing more efficient means of farming.

Cultural Ecology of Disease

Departing from the ecological anthropologists' fixation on technology, Alexander Alland addressed himself to multiple relationships between cultural arrangements and disease-producing organisms in the natural environment.[68] Cultures, he points out, may facilitate the growth of those agents as well as their transmission to human hosts, but they also contain means to protect people from the disease agents. In a model treating disease as part of the environment, he shows how cultural factors in a population system affect adaptation to that environmental feature.

Practices effectively separating people from parasites—deep latrines for instance—help to control disease. On the other hand, the dense aggregation of individuals in living space, population movements, and visiting patterns help communicable disease to spread. Certain kinds of material culture, such as tailored clothing or mud walls, provide favorable breeding conditions for lice and other carriers of disease, as do pools of stagnant water and other man-made modifications of the habitat. Some parasite-bearing organisms, like rats, are practically domesticated, the cultural conditions facilitating the close relationship they have developed with people. Patterns of sleep, diet, work loads, and others that contribute to human stress also affect the resistance which people offer to disease-bearers present in the environment.

Behavioral adaptations against illness, including preventive measures as well as therapy, Alland predicts, will be most effective against those diseases which have been with a population system for a long time. Preventive measures erect barriers against infection; therapy aims to rid the body of an illness or of the symptoms it produces. While a society's ethnomedical theory of disease can be expected to guide its therapeutic measures, it is possible for people to base effective preventive techniques on grounds having nothing to do with concepts of disease. John W. M. Whiting presents an instance when he traces a relationship between kwashiorkor (a disease caused by a low protein diet) and a prolonged postpartum sex taboo between husband and wife.[69] The taboo functions preventively by prolonging the newborn infant's period of nursing, thus protecting it from nutritional deficiency and the disease; but the people do not practice the taboo with any such rationale.

Acute disease, Alland expects, will be more difficult to deal with effectively through preventive or therapeutic techniques than chronic illness, because chronic illness as well as disease endemically present in a population system allows the time needed for experimentation to discover successful means of coping. Severe illness, which raises anxiety, sharply accelerates strategies for coping; mild illness may be left alone.

Alland gives attention to the conditions under which preventive or therapeutic measures are most likely to develop. Primitive societies have been more successful in developing preventive medicine than in devising effective means of therapy, the main reason being the ability to recognize ecological factors in chronic and endemic disease. The more contagious an illness, the more likely is it that a route of infection will be discovered, though preventive measures are more difficult to apply when the route of transmission is complex than when it is simple. Compared to discovering effective preventive measures, finding effective therapies is hard, because it depends on recognizing and locating environmental specifics capable of combating the parasites lodged in the human organism. Curative materials for some diseases may be lacking in a group's environment, and hence are beyond discovery; but even if present, they may remain undetected.

From a medical anthropological point of view, cultural evolution occurs as a society devises or borrows social and technical means for adapting to disease, preventively or therapeutically. Thereby, the society becomes better adapted for surviving in its environment, although, as Alland points out, the real test lies in its ability to reproduce more successfully than a system less effectively adapted.

Limits of Ecological Explanation

Alland and other cultural ecologists revealed a pronounced tendency to treat culture as a rational and, in the long run, efficient means of coping with the environment. Given time, these anthropologists assumed, people will, within the limits of their knowledge or technical abilities, order the environment in ways which maximize advantages while simultaneously minimizing risk and cost. The 18th-century faith in human beings as basically rational was retained by those who saw the minimax principle everywhere governing human action, and as having done so since the beginning of the species.

Cultural ecology primarily directed its efforts to studying adaptation to features of the geographical environment made by relatively isolated primitive societies. Whether the ecological mode of explanation can be successfully applied to complex societies was questioned.[70] Primitive societies can be treated as systems whose steady state is maintained through negative feedback, two critics pointed out, whereas complex societies involved with surrounding nations are systems dominated by positive feedback. The outputs of the latter type of system for a time stimulate increased growth, but frequent periods of oscillation or disorder occur due to changes in what external societies expect from the system. Furthermore, ecological anthropology explains only cultural change resulting from exploitation of different natural microenvironments into which the system expands. Historical changes in complex societies remaining in the same environment are governed by political forces. These entail the local group's subjugation by and incorporation into larger groups, and from time to time demand the recombination of the group's ecological resources in new ways.

Psychoanalysis and the Psychological Approach

Libido and Ego Theories

The psychological approach captured United States anthropologists' interest while the American Historical Tradition still flourished. Commonly called culture and personality, it revealed its popularity in the titles of publications, names of college courses, the way anthropologists identified themselves, and the alarm it inspired in some quarters.[71] With controversy, popularity receded, and problems chosen for research altered. From studying the personality shared by members of primitive societies and delineating national character, psychological anthropologists turned to investigating psychological trends accompanying acculturation; to conscious motivations present in witchcraft, deviant behavior, and economic development; and in Fredrik Barth or Raymond Firth, with minimal use of explicit psychological concepts, to the individual's role in social processes. The structuralism of Claude Lévi-Strauss and the approaches taken to symbolism by David Schneider, Mary Douglas, and Victor Turner—whose work I take up later—introduced a less individual-centered psychological approach, one practically never employing clinical methods in field work. Heightened interest in cognition during the 1950s marked yet another change in the psychological approach, and tended to balance the emphasis previously put on motivation.

Early culture and personality found psychoanalysis in its several variants highly congenial in research, largely because the theory presented personality as an open system interacting with society. As developed by Freud and his associates, psychoanalysis looked to social relationships in the person's early life for antecedents of the individual's personality traits. The antecedents, however, bear little obvious resemblance to their end results. To account for the effects registered by early social experiences on personality, the theory posits mediating processes going on within the individual. Resulting from innate predispositions, these processes are the same everywhere; hence different outcomes must be due to different inputs from society.

Libido theorists and ego theorists regarded the innate predispositions in quite different ways. The former explained the intrapsychic effects of early experience as resulting from the impact of those experiences on bodily drives pressing for gratification, and they identified those drives with sexuality broadly defined. Equally drive-conscious ego theorists placed less stress on bodily drives. They stressed the individual's ego drives, his need to protect his autonomy and for mastery of his environment. Libido theorists also recognized those ego processes, but subordinated them to the drive for libidinous gratification issuing from the id.

Whether oriented to the libido or the ego, all psychoanalytic theory accepts the importance of psychological motivation, especially unconscious direction in behavior. Under the control of libido or ego processes, behavior comes to be goal-oriented. Both types of theory pay considerable attention to interpreting symbolism in individual behavior and culture, to symbols manifested in dreams, folktales or myths, and religious beliefs. Interpretation reveals the effects of social experiences on personality, and provides glimpses into innate predispositions with which social experiences interact. The symbols represent culturally defined ways of resolving dilemmas imposed on the libidinous or ego drives by social pressures. All psychoanalytic theory also views personality as originating in large part through early childhood experience. Different early experiences in different societies are held to produce distinct kinds of individual personality shared by most members of a society.

The libido theorists included Freud himself. In anthropology they were chiefly represented by the lay psychoanalyst Géza Róheim, of Hungarian origin, and by the ethnologist George Devereux, who came from a Rumanian background. Prominent ego theorists in social science include two lay analysts, Erich Fromm and Erik Erikson. Like Abram Kardiner, whose collaboration with anthropologists began about 1935 and who falls between the two psychoanalytic theories, they emigrated to the United States from German-speaking lands.

Basic Personality Structure

With the cooperation of anthropologists, Kardiner examined data from several societies to learn how innate human predispositions react to cultural practices imposed in early childhood, thereby producing different basic personality structures.[72] Knowledge gained from such research would, he hoped, provide a basis for predicting the kind of person who would be produced through given patterns of socialization.

Identifying basic personality structure with national character and related concepts, he distinguishes it from the unique character structures retained in a society by individuals who share a basic personality type. The basic personality is a structure for perceiving and dealing with biological drives, human relationships, and the supernatural. Although the structure includes many products of learning, including rules and values required for adaptation, Kardiner's interest centered on the projections to which it gives rise. In the projections, one sees the outcomes of the interaction between innate human predispositions and cultural practices. Early childhood plays a decisive role in determining those outcomes, early cultural influences persisting in the personality unless counteracted by subsequent experiences. As a rough rule, Kardiner says, one can expect a more complex projective system the greater the tensions generated by restrictions imposed through early child-rearing. Members of a society will be driven to cope with the tensions through fantasy, rationalization, and other compensatory or defensive maneuvers. The culture incorporates these devices for coping in what Kardiner calls secondary institutions, including religion and mythology. Secondary institutions reveal the projection at work. They relieve the tensions created through constrictions imposed on individuals in early life, and their forms are integrated with the kinds of constrictions imposed by particular societies. Therefore, differences in secondary institutions between various societies can be systematically related to differences in basic personality, and to differences in the socialization practices through which the basic personality was formed.

Kardiner never went far into explaining why cultures should differ in the restrictions they impose in childhood. In his early work he bypasses the problem, claiming the lack of historical material from primitive societies to account for the rise of formative institutions. In later writings he proposes looking for the origin of formative patterns in the problems of adaptation faced by the society, but doesn't develop that ecological postulate. He is far more interested in the adaptive value of the basic personality. For example, he endows religion with power to stabilize society, and ascribes the same function to other traits of basic personality that minimize social discord and promote harmony. The projective system also plays a directive role in history. Since secondary institutions relieve tension, a society will seek to retain them until new ones appear promising at least equivalent satisfaction. Radical change in secondary institutions, for instance in religion, always implies changes in basic socialization practices which alter the projective system.

They Want to Act as They Have to Act

As an ego theorist, Erich Fromm practically ignored biological needs as foundations of personality. He also minimized the significance of child-rearing, but devoted much more attention than Kardiner to the adaptive value of "social character," his term for the personality shared by most people in a society.[73]

Derived ultimately from economic, ideological, and sociological factors, including religious and philosophical ideas, the social character shapes the energies of a society's members so that they need not consciously choose whether or not to follow social expectations; their character motivates them to want to act as they have to act, and allows them to find gratification in meeting the requirements of their society. Child-rearing is one means through which the influence of economic, ideological, and other institutions reaches the individual, parents acting as models who illustrate the type of social character the child adopts.

The concept, social character, covers the way a person in the process of living orients himself to the world, to other people, and to himself. Fromm lists four basic types of orientation: the receptive type characterizes the passive person who feels all good comes from outside of himself as a result of somebody else's goodness and as his right; the exploitative orientation marks the individual who, looking for good to come from outside himself, takes it by force and cunning; the hoarding orientation identifies people who expect little from others and hold on to what they possess; and the productive orientation describes the person who draws on his own powers to work and create. An application of the social character concept in rural Mexico indicates how different classes, playing different socioeconomic roles, reveal different combinations of these four basic orientations. A productive-hoarding orientation is adaptive in the role played by the free landowner; a productive-exploitative character suits the new type of entrepreneur found in the village; and a unproductive-receptive character characterizes the landless day laborer. Individuals whose social character coincides with their class-linked role tend to be economically most successful, provided their economic situation allows the possibility of success. Where it does not, as in the landless laborers, only exceptional individuals—whose social character contains a productive orientation, and therefore differs from the character typical of their class— escape from the level of extreme poverty.

Drawing back from extreme cultural relativism, Fromm believed it was important to critically evaluate the compatibility between the social character engendered by a society and the demands of human nature. A character may function adequately, and the individuals possessing it may be socially adjusted, while at the same time the ego needs of those people may be deeply frustrated. Human beings need to feel related to one another. Yet some degree of alienation is natural, because a reasoning person possesses self-awareness and is thus disunited from the world around. People also require a degree of transcendence, the opposite of being controlled by whatever happens to them, as well as a sense of rootedness, or commitment. And each individual needs to experience himself as a distinct person. Modern industrial nations, Fromm believes, exacerbate alienation, encourage feelings of powerlessness, oppose human beings to the rest of nature, and, imposing nationalistic loyalties, prevent warm ties from developing between distant people. When social institutions frustrate the basic ego needs, a dynamic is set up, which promotes people to rebel against society in an effort to bring about a better way of life. But, as Fromm illustrates in an early psychohistorical study, *Flight from Freedom,* self-interested leaders pretending to support the effort may bring about a solution worse than the original condition.

Religion can further the development of basic human needs, or it can suppress them. Authoritarian religion emphasizes man's helplessness: his control by an external higher power entitled to obedience and demanding surrender. Such a religion impoverishes human beings and leaves them enslaved or, as David Hume, speaking of deities represented as infinitely superior to mankind, put it, they sink the human mind into passivity and submission. A humanistic religion—Fromm is thinking of Buddhism, the Judaism of Isaiah, and the Christianity of Jesus—follows a different course. By encouraging worshipers to develop their reasoning powers, relationships with fellowmen, and solidarity with all living things, it enhances human powers. Choice of one type of religion rather than another reflects the social character extant in a society. Only within societies allowing members to develop a sense of human freedom and responsibility for their own fate will a humanistic, nonauthoritarian religion prevail.

Socialization

Psychoanalysis, and other theories derived from psychology, directed anthropologists investigating the social determinants of personality and the process of acquiring culture. Prevailing opinion preferred an eclectic approach to personality formation combining features of libido and ego theory. Constitutional factors could not be wholly neglected, as they had been by some social scientists, Clyde Kluckhohn and Henry Murray pointed out.[74] But his identification of significant biological factors scarcely resembles those pointed to by Freudians. Sex and age he puts among the more striking biological determinants of personality, but he also notes the role of nature, pigmentation, and other physical traits to which the society reacts. Along with biological determinants, membership in a group, carrying with it all that an individual learns from persons surrounding him, represents a second factor operative in personality formation; it serves to explain why the members of any organized enduring group tend to manifest certain personality traits more frequently than members of other groups. Third, role determines personality by defining the tasks a person shall perform. And finally, situational determinants, events happening fortuitously to particular individuals, exert their influence. A balanced consideration of personality formation must include information about all four determinants and must consider their complex interlinkage.

Despite Kluckhohn's injunction, anthropologists, with their concept of

culture as an external environment to which individuals with few exceptions come to conform, tended to pay little attention to biological or other
individual factors in personality. Psychoanalytic theory did, however, alert
Margaret Mead to the body's importance as the medium through which
messages from the social environment reach the child in early life.[75] Cultural influences, according to her theory of socialization, occur long before
a child acquires linguistic competence. They begin with the way babies
are handled in the first few hours of life. The caretakers' cultural definition
of childhood provides a key with which they decode the meaning of the
infant's crying, grasping, or other behaviors. They respond appropriately
—that is, in terms of the culturally defined meaning of those acts—and
thereby communicate information to the child. Each such bit of information contributes to the baby's growing perception of itself and the world.
Superficially considered, swaddling, feeding, bathing the baby, and other
child-rearing routines indicate little or nothing of what caretakers are
communicating in a particular society. The same acts bear vastly different
culturally defined meanings in different societies, and anthropologists must
study those meanings to know what is being communicated or contributed
to personality formation. Societies also differ in the routines most heavily
utilized for communication; bathing babies may bear much information
in one society, but none in another. Messages are always reiterated, the
same ones passing time after time through the same and different channels, thus insuring their effective communication. No routine suffices by
itself to form any attribute of personality.

In more objective and behavioral terms, interdisciplinary-minded scholars belonging to the Institute of Human Relations at Yale University
identified socialization with psychological rewards accruing to individuals
who learned the customs of their society.[76] Behaviorism provided them
not only with a theory explaining cultural learning, it enabled them to
equate culture with habits and to ascribe cultural persistence to the
gratification those habits afford by satisfying basic biological and socially
derived secondary drives. A custom persists only as long as it brings
gratification; should lack of satisfaction eventually result, the custom will
disappear from the individual's behavioral repertory and from the inventory of cultural traits. Psychological learning theory also enabled the Yale
social scientists to interpret diffusion as copying: a person possessing
appropriate drives, including the acquired drive to copy, models his behavior on another person's conduct. In this way, habits which appear
desirable to members of a society find a place in the culture, provided
they produce manifest rewards for the copiers. If not, a brief trial will be
followed by the behavior's disappearance.

In retrospect, one catches in learning theory an evolutionary reprise
unnoticed at the time it appeared. Habits are adopted, the theory states,
if they prove rewarding—or as evolutionary language would say, if they

are adapted to the situation. According to learning theory, old habits are abandoned if new ones prove to be more satisfying—evolutionary theory would say, better adapted to changing conditions. Nobody pressed for such an evolutionary interpretation in the early 1940s when learning theory was being applied to culture, probably because many anthropologists were still downgrading cultural evolutionism.

Doubts and Other Strictures

The application of behaviorism to socialization and to other aspects of culture was an early sign of anthropologists' dissatisfaction with the hard-to-verify nature of psychoanalytical concepts. Soon more explicit strictures came to be directed against "culture and personality," and occasionally against taking any sort of psychological approach in explaining social phenomena.

Critics voiced doubt about the importance attached to early childhood in personality formation, especially since experimental attempts by psychologists to validate hypotheses deduced from psychoanalytic socialization theory gave only conflicting results.[77] Psychological anthropologists were also accused of attributing motives and reactions to young children without sound evidence that such states existed. With reference to methods for studying the personality system presumed to be shared by members of a society, anthropologists were charged with marshaling only selected facts to support the psychological patterns they reported while overlooking contradictory material. Critics questioned whether individuals uniformly share psychological traits. And they objected to the unreasonably wide gap between first- and second-order facts, between an observed custom and the unconscious or symbolic meaning assigned to the custom when it is interpreted by psychoanalytic theory.

The barrage of objections leveled against culture and personality can be compared to the way anthropologists a few decades earlier attacked the claims and methods of the extreme diffusionists, the 19th-century evolutionists, and racial theories of behavior. As a result, psychological anthropologists became wary of psychoanalytic theory and more cautious in their methods. Culture and personality also lost some momentum, though a psychological perspective applied to social phenomena did not disappear.

Complaints of other sorts were also made against how psychological concepts were being used. Melford Spiro, with socialization studies in mind, protested against the one-sided attention paid to personality as the product of culture.[78] As a confirmed functionalist, he urged making culture and the social system the prime targets of research, with the object of learning how they are maintained through personality factors.

Other writers periodically put forward social causes for social phenomena to compete with psychological causes. Rival theories of male initiation ceremonies illustrate the competition that developed between sociological and psychological explanations.[79] From a psychological perspective, initiation is an institutional means of resolving psychological conflicts in boys over dependence and female identification, traits engendered through having been reared primarily by women. The conflicts reach their height precisely at an age when male and female roles begin to diverge sharply, and successful performance of male roles requires boys to identify with men. Support for this theory of male initiation rites came from cross-cultural testing, which showed puberty rituals tending to be more elaborate in societies where, according to indirect evidence, social practices forge very strong emotional bonds between women and children. The indirect evidence consists of the custom whereby a child sleeps with its mother for some years after birth, the father being excluded from his wife's bed as a means of enforcing the postpartum taboo. The sleeping arrangement, researchers reasoned, permits the development of strong dependence and female identification for whose eradication dramatic initiation ceremonies are required

The counter-theory, also successfully tested with cross-cultural data, speaks in the idiom of sociological functionalism. It replaces the psychological need of identification with men with the social need of male solidarity. Male initiation rituals stabilize a boy's masculine role at an age when the role is especially problematic, because hitherto he has had no guidance in how to play it. The initiation ceremonies express and reinforce bonds of male solidarity, bonds on which the society's safety and survival depends.

Both explanations may be true. An eclectic position finds both useful as well as compatible.[80] However, some authors reject eclectic theories, in principle perceiving greater scientific value in adhering systematically to a single framework of explanation.

Personality as Adaptation

The studies of male initiation indicate how hologeistic research was entering psychological anthropology, largely under the aegis of John W. M. Whiting, Beatrice Whiting, and their associates or followers. Its significance lies in the use of statistics to confirm linkages between early childhood experience and adult customs.[81] Hologeistic research tended to support behavioristic concepts of learning, as well as the psychoanalytic theory attaching long-lasting determinative influence to early social experiences. More convincingly than Kardiner or Fromm, it demonstrated how psychologically formative socialization practices arise, and indicated that certain practices and resultant personality traits possess adaptive value in specific ecological contexts. In food-gathering societies, where only small amounts of food can be accumulated, socialization techniques put relatively high pressure on developing achievement, independence, and self-reliance in children. Such societies, to insure survival, require venturesome and independent adults able to take initiative in wresting food from the environment. However, in societies with animal husbandry, where large amounts of food can be accumulated, childhood socialization encourages the development of responsibility and obedience. There, responsible adults are needed who will faithfully develop, renew, and protect the herds on which life depends.

A broadly ecological factor is explicitly recognized in the Whitings' conceptual model of personality formation when child-training practices and personality are identified as dependent variables related to antecedent "maintenance systems." The latter include means of procuring subsistence as well as household structure—composition of the household being regarded as an ecological factor affecting the behavior of persons who engage in child-rearing. The Whitings conceive of child-training practices as always implying some intent on the part of parents or parental surrogates, or some culturally defined goal toward which children are explicitly directed.

Robert LeVine developed the evolutionary implications of the Whitings' ecological thinking in his "Darwinian" culture-and-personality theory.[82] He regards personality dispositions as equivalent to genetic or other biological traits, in that both are variably distributed in a population and subject to environmental selection. In the case of personality dispositions, the social system acts as the environment wherein selection takes place. Each institution in a social system makes demands of individuals and provides them with opportunities for satisfaction. Dispositions best conforming to the demands, or most suitable for obtaining satisfactions, are most likely to be implemented in socialization. The cognition of the socializers mediates between the selective pressures in the environment, as they perceive them, and the socialization process. Hence parents and other surrogates of society will tend to adopt practices that promise to duplicate socially advantageous dispositions in the next generation and to eliminate disadvantageous ones.

Anthony F. C. Wallace asked, from quite another standpoint, though without overlooking the mechanism of evolutionary selection, What are the mediating schemata, structures, or processes in the brain whence forms of organized knowledge arise?[83] His answer provided a theoretical basis for formal semantic analysis, ethnoscience, and related methods followed in cognitive anthropology.

Human thought, according to Wallace, proceeds in a limited number of ways. It works through analogy, metaphor, and metonymy, devices whereby a learned way of mapping one kind of information is extended to another kind of information. James Frazer, Lévi-Strauss, and other students of symbolism frequently called attention to evidence of those devices in magic, myths, and totemism. Thought also operates by arranging information in taxonomic systems wherein each higher level is more abstract than lower, more differentiated levels, and each level, except the highest, contains contrasting sets. People are frequently unaware of the taxonomic systems they think with, but anthropologists using eliciting techniques or componential analysis were able to infer the contrasts and hierarchies from what informants said and did. Finally, thought works by arranging information in terms of contradictions and oppositions. Psychoanalysts as well as structuralists following Lévi-Strauss have provided abundant evidence of this tendency in the human mind.

Why, Wallace wonders, do these thought structures exist? He suggests two possible explanations. First, human beings may be neurologically provided with capacities for such processes of thinking; in other words, the structures are genetically determined and have been evolutionarily selected. The second, not wholly different, possibility holds them to be different expressions of a single biologically based phenomenon, which Wallace calls autistic thought (without implying necessary pathology). Defined as a potential for going beyond the form in which information is learned, and for constantly reorganizing what has been learned, autistic thought ceaselessly recombines and differentiates learned elements into novel arrangements. Dreaming, defense mechanisms, and similar kinds of behavior, as well as creative endeavor in the fine arts and pathological autistic thinking—all reveal the operation of some such capacity in human nature.

Culture and Deviant Behavior

The postwar years witnessed considerable research by American anthropologists, often in cooperation with psychiatrists and other social scientists, on social factors contributing to mental illness and other forms of deviant behavior. Generally, the anthropologists studied aggregates of people possessing similar economic, ethnic, or other social backgrounds rather than, in clinical fashion, attending to individuals with unique life histories. Also, contrary to the position taken by Ruth Benedict, they tended to define deviance in nonrelativistic terms, and were not especially interested in whether a community found the behavior socially acceptable. According to the theory they followed, individuals in a community who, due to their location in social structure or as a result of other social conditions, experience high levels of stress will tend to adapt to stress by copying or innovating forms of behavior that are psychiatrically abnormal or that violate legal and other norms in the society where they live.[84] Social sources of stress that are mentioned include culture change and conditions frequently found in disintegrated communities, including broken homes, alienation, much experience with hostility, and exposure to models of deviant behavior. In addition to entertaining stress theory, Anthony F. C. Wallace also posited dietary and other physiological imbalances as the cause of certain types of mental illness.[85] Others followed him in developing a psychobiological approach to the relationship between culture and personality.

From sociology, anthropologists adopted the theory that delinquency, crime, and other forms of deviant conduct originate from lack of access to legitimate means for achieving goals highly valued in a society. Not economic factors alone block individuals' opportunities to achieve social values, though in modern nations poverty certainly plays a crucial role in creating powerlessness. Perceiving their weak command over the benefits going to better situated members of the society, persons unfavorably placed in the social structure are likely to use deviant means to secure similar benefits.

It seems appropriate that social scientists in an affluent society with a huge capacity for production should have indicted relative underindulgence as the culprit for social ills. Classical philosophers, it will be recalled, warned of danger in overindulgence or immoderation. While support for the modern theory was forthcoming, it did not move many social scientists to call for structural changes in society so as to bring about an equitable distribution of cultural benefits.

Cultural Morphology

Mythic World Views

Meaning, one of the most perduring interests in anthropological thought, became the main target of several theoretical approaches in recent anthropology; one of the earliest, apart from psychoanalysis, being cultural morphology.[86] Appearing in the 1930s in Germany, where it continued to be exclusively cultivated, the theory grew out of ideas about the cultural *paideuma* formulated by Leo Frobenius, one of the apical ancestors of the German culture-historical tradition. Like him, the cultural morphologists conceived of cultures as configurations governed by certain basic conceptions, and the successive cultural strata referred to by the cultural morphologists resemble, in form as well as in use, the culture circles postulated by the culture-historical ethnologists. Consequently, some reviewers were misled into regarding the two approaches as identical. Like the culture-historical method, cultural morphology also gave an impression of being developmental or evolutionary; but heavily diachronic as it is, it made no attempt to explain change by environmental selection. It looked to the past primarily to discover the current meaning of symbolic cultural forms and for clues to explain how those meanings have altered.

The world's primitive cultures fall into a small number of configurations, according to cultural morphologists, who identify each by a type of subsistence production. Yet, it is type of world view, not subsistence technology, that constitutes the nucleus of a configuration. Whenever the world view changes, a substantial cultural transformation follows involving subsistence, social organization, religion, and other significant cultural features. Revolutionary changes of this order are responsible for bringing about the configurations of primitive culture predating the advent of civilization identified by plow agriculture. Each configuration constitutes a cultural stratum varying in relative age from the others.

The world views—also called mythic perceptions or mythic realities—influencing the significant features in a cultural configuration are for the most part inferred from myths dealing with birth, death, subsistence, and other fundamental aspects of life. Myths from cultures belonging to the hunting and gathering stratum testify to a world view in which people stand in partnership with the animals they hunt; animals have not yet been hierarchically subordinated to human beings, as they are in later strata. The myths of tropical forest tuber-agriculturalists furnish evidence of people's close relationships to friendly ancestors, known as dema-gods, to whom the world order owes its creation. Myths of the cereal cultivators, who also raise large animals, reveal the conception of a creator sky god who brings mankind everything that is good. Finally, the stratum of cereal cultivators who farm with the use of fertilizer, terracing, and irrigation contains the concept of the divine king who concentrates magical power in himself and links human beings to the cosmos.

I have listed the cultural configurations in the temporal order in which cultural morphologists believe they developed, but clearly they have all continued to exist into recent times, partly because it is in the nature of a cultural configuration to maintain itself. In systems theory parlance, a configuration possesses the quality of equifinality. The force binding its elements, and its tendency to persist, originate in the mythic world view as well as, to some extent, in the temperamental, or personality, traits of people, some of which may be genetically rooted. Through these stabilizing forces a configuration is also guided and limited in what it will absorb through cultural diffusion.

Nevertheless, external and internal factors do bring about change in world views. For one thing, the myths become semantically depleted, making it impossible for ethnographers to obtain their older meaning directly from the people who still recall them. Similar degeneration of world views shows up when religion ceases to be purely expressive but comes to be pragmatic, its performance promising eternal happiness or other rewards. When that happens, ceremonies no longer make people aware of the origin of the world or the partnership linking man to animals or the cosmos; they become means to ends. Adolf Jensen, the leading representative of cultural morphology, followed Frobenius in distinguishing between two phases of religious phenomena: a creative phase wherein myth and ceremony express sacred reality, and a phase of petrified routinization in which belief ceases to be vivid. When routinization sets in, people continue to possess the same capacity for experience they revealed before, but the capacity is largely neglected. Semantic depletion and related forms of degeneration occurring in religious phenomena share something with the concept of cultural survivals, as put forward by Edward B. Tylor, and with the idea of secondary interpretation in Boasian anthropology. All these concepts recognize circumstances in which cultural forms gradually lose their former meaning and acquire altered significance. Jensen considers contemporary astrology and spiritualism senseless forms, compared to the profound meaning their component ideas formerly possessed as mythic perceptions of reality. Knowing that meaning changes puts the anthropologist on guard against adopting the distorted meanings of customs advanced by informants. The original meaning must be deductively sought by relating customs to the world view of the cultural configuration where they belong. He illustrates with pederasty and other sexual practices sometimes accompanying a youth's initiation rite. The key to the original meaning of those acts, lost to the people who perform them, resides in a world view that conceives of human life as continuous with a cosmic power incarnated in people and objects and very strongly present in the genital organs.

Below cultural morphology's superficial originality lurk some very old research problems—such as the origin of religion[87]—and long-persisting methodological difficulties. Lacking historical documentation in its search for the primal meaning of myths and other customs, it made do with deductive modes of interpretation whose validity was never proven. Although cultural morphologists purported to be methodologically critical, they never examined the validity of their own methods, nor seemed to realize that their history went beyond the reach of verification.

Materialism

An Approach Magnified

Ever since the era of early Greek philosophy, materialism sought to extend its foothold in Western thought and gradually succeeded. The influential ideas of Karl Marx and Friedrich Engels applied to history, social science, and other scholarship in eastern Europe greatly magnified the materialistic approach in the 20th century, while in the United States it gained attention through the efforts of Leslie White and Marvin Harris.

In the Soviet Union and other East European countries, historical materialism—called by Marx "the science of man"—became the fundamental law of history. It offered scholars not only an explanation of historical cultural development, but also a theory about the integration of culture, or the interdependence of technology, social relations, and ideology, including religion.[88] One aim of the theory is to explain social change objectively, in superorganic terms, without making it the product solely of individual purposes, accomplishments, or ideas. Individuals play a role in history, historical materialists believe, but their goals and accomplishments are insufficient to explain how historical change occurred.

The mode of production in society, constituting the material basis of social life, plays the dominant role in culture and in social change. Its importance lies in the fact that people can obtain goods essential for living—clothing, food, shelter, and other necessities—only by processing material objects. In contrast to functionalists, who derive institutions from basic human needs, historical materialists do not hold the needs themselves determinative but the way societies go about satisfying needs through producing food and other goods. The mode of production includes first and most importantly the physical instruments of production and the activities people perform. These forces of production influence, and are influenced by, the social relations different categories of people enter into in order to produce goods. The roles of various social categories in production in turn depend on the form of ownership present in society.

New knowledge and skills increasing a society's capacity to produce goods and to satisfy the growing body of needs of an increasing number of people represents technical progress. In turn, increased production of material goods chiefly determines other aspects of social development. For many purposes, societies with similar modes of production can be treated alike, as having developed to the same level of technical progress. Their cultural superstructures—the arrangement of political, legal, philosophical, artistic, and religious ideas and associated social relations—are similar, being based on similar modes of production. (Language and mathematics, it might be noted, belong neither to the material basis of society nor to the superstructure.)

Although historical materialism calls the mode of production dominant in history and basic in culture, it nevertheless treats it as dependent on geographical and other factors present in the situation of a society. The geographical environment by the resources it provides influences, favorably or unfavorably, how material wealth is produced, thereby affecting technical progress and social development. Population also constitutes an influential factor, since production is social and depends on a supply of human labor. Likewise, the cultural superstructure interacts with the material basis of society; ideas, for example, serving as a justification for holding on to a given mode of production, or for destroying it in favor of a different one. However, all ideas do not exercise equal influence on society.[89] Those corresponding to objective reality, the empirically derived concepts of natural and social science, are most influential because they are directly useful in furthering the society's adaptation. Ideas not corresponding to objective conditions—religious conceptions, for instance—are useless, despite giving the illusion of being serviceable. For temporary periods, in an accidental manner, they may subjectively help people to cope with problems, but sometimes at the cost of retarding progress toward objective knowledge.

Although it was brought about by the material basis of society, the superstructure nevertheless possesses a relative degree of autonomy, and may persist after the mode of production has begun to change. In time of change, when the mode of production contains contradictions—for example, between the interests of opposed social categories who vie for control of the forces of production—the superstructure reflects the diverse, contradictory interests of each group in the form of opposing philosophies, laws, styles of art, and so forth.

Psychological differences marking off one society from another, or distinguishing social categories within a society, are also created by the material forces lying at the basis of social life. Each social class in a stratified society, depending on its relationship to the mode of production, harbors distinctive sentiments leading to action capable of influencing the course of history. So much the Marxist philosopher George Plekhanov admitted back in the late 19th century.[90] Following changes in the social relations of production, he said, the sentiments of the social classes as well as the *Zeitgeist* of the society also change. Despite this precedent in materialist thought, Soviet anthropologists objected to national character and other culture-and-personality research carried out in the United States. American anthropologists, they asserted, fail to investigate personality development historically as consequences and conditions of social development. The Americans were also charged with using personality studies to promote neocolonialism through economic aid programs carried out by the United States in underdeveloped countries.

In refusing to credit individuals with much influence on the origin and historical course of ideas, historical materialists took a position similar to Emile Durkheim's and Alfred Kroeber's. A scientist or philosopher, they claimed, never makes discoveries alone, unaided by society. A particular society's interests and values, which are based on the mode of production, by the control they exercise over a scholar's thought determine what he discovers. With technical progress and social development, interests change, and so do the contents of individual cognition. On the other hand, historical materialism admits that the objective laws operating in history are manifested only through the thoughts and actions of many—but not necessarily all—individuals caught in a historical moment. People make history and bring about change. Furthermore, although historical materialism denies the great man theory of history, it leaves room for human freedom by admitting that individuals may deliberately apply their knowledge of objective laws in order to control social development. The philosopher Jean-Paul Sartre found this is too limited a degree of freedom; Marxian anthropology, he promises, will totally forget human freedom unless, adopting existentialism, it perceives man to be the very basis of social existence.[91]

Soviet anthropologists' views on the origin of totemism afford a glimpse of how they have dealt with a traditional ethnological problem.[92] Taking totemism to be a form of religious belief, a part of the cultural superstructure, they ascribe its origin to a hunting and gathering stage of development. There, conditioned by the mode of production, the germinal form of totemism arose in the group's feeling of being connected with a species of plant or animal. This primary idea then expanded into the conception of a tie between the group, its territory, and the forces of production at work in the territory. At least one Soviet theorist rejected as unlikely and "nihilistic" Franz Boas's and Alexander Goldenweiser's thesis of totemism, saying a culture complex such as totemism may vary considerably between societies but still be similar in essence from one place to another.

Cultural Materialism

Among North American anthropologists, Leslie White and Marvin Harris strongly advocated materialist concepts. According to White, everything in the cosmos can be interpreted in terms of matter and energy.[93] Culture, whether manifested in chopping wood, singing a song, or breathing a prayer, is "merely" matter in motion and therefore a form of energy.

Harris's conception of "cultural materialism" appears in his explanation of cultural determinism, where it is most explicitly developed, as well as in his epistemological theory of culture.[94] Cultural determinism, according to him, involves the concerted action of three classes of phenomena: technology, economy, and the natural environment. Techniques for coping with environment, especially those used to procure subsistence, influence such important patterns of culture as the organization of labor and the distribution of goods. Those economic factors in turn call forth other social groupings designed for other purposes, the activities of which are coordinated by rules and ideologies. Stated operationally, the principle of "techno-economic determinism," as Harris calls it, maintains that similar techniques applied to similar natural environments will be associated with similar social groupings coordinated by similar systems of values and beliefs. Julian Steward advanced a definition of cultural evolution couched in very similar words. Harris awards Steward, his teacher, the distinction of having been a cultural materialist, first, because of the way he gave priority to technically mediated interaction between human behavior and natural environment and, second, because Steward saw social structure and ideology as generally depending on material conditions rather than vice versa.

In his epistemological theory of culture, Harris not only assigns research priority to those features of society—verbal behavior, body motions, and cultural artifacts—in which competent observers are able to perceive phenomenal distinctions.[95] He goes further and strongly implies that because phenomenal events are material things capable of altering the environment they are more important to study than inferred events. Because meanings and purposes that actors attach to such occurrences cannot by themselves alter the environment, Harris, the materialist, questions the value of concentrating on cognition, as ethnoscience does.

Harris does not identify culture with particular bits of observed behavior or unique artifacts. Operationally defined, culture consists of classes of material things constructed by anthropologists on the basis of appropriate phenomenal distinctions they note in the occurrences they study. If the constructions follow clearly precribed, replicable operations they will be readily verifiable and therefore will represent objective knowledge. Nothing in this definition limits culture to phenomena enduring beyond a single generation, or restricts culture to shared behavior. Nor does it limit culture to human behavior alone. Inasmuch as the objective methods used to discriminate classes in material things do not require knowing the discriminations that actors themeslves make, it can be applied to infrahuman organisms as well as to human beings.

The Radiance of Materialism

Both historical and cultural materialism must be granted leeway in the way they define materials, since calling a mode of production "ecological relationships" and fleeting body motions "material," departs widely from the common-sense idea that material things are tangible and occupy space. Why, one wonders, do the materialists not refer to themselves and their theories by the less equivocal word, "empirical"? No doubt because the words "material" and "materialism" possess considerable positive emotional value for those who use them with philosophical commitment; and perhaps also because the users cherish the radiance conferred on their ideas by the scholarly tradition which those words symbolize.

Interaction Theory

Who Interacts With Whom?

At the outbreak of war, in 1942, a Harvard instructor, Eliot D. Chapple, and a professor at the same school, Carleton S. Coon, published a highly original 700-page book, *Principles of Anthropology*.[96] Following it, a companion volume appeared, consisting mainly of ethnographic selections collected by Coon, who graded the 19 human cultures reported on into six levels of complexity plus a zero level occupied by subhuman primates. Both books give major attention to social relationships, comparing them in terms of a systematic theory of interaction designed to insure objectivity. Chapple originally developed the theory in order to study human relations in small groups and organizations, but in *Principles* the authors with little tentativeness apply it to much larger social systems. They open the book with a chapter on scientific method, where they urge investigators to limit observations to what can be directly observed, measured, and replicated by other observers. Anthropology can be a science, they claim, only if it concentrates on phenomena possessing the property of functional dependence. Tools, rituals, social relations, and other cultural phenomena possess this property if they can be characterized by measurable variables, such as efficiency or complexity, and if the variables of one phenomenon change directly with those of another.

Principles was a tour de force, admirable for the very original perspective adapted from A. R. Radcliffe-Brown. Perhaps the perspective was too original, especially in the United States where cultural anthropology was still known by the style followed in the American Historical Tradition. At any rate, the theory was hardly noticed. Following others, I have named it interaction theory because, in primarily methodological terms, it identifies anthropology as the study of who interacts with whom, with what frequency, through the performance of what techniques, and in what contexts. Anthropologists may observe such features of behavior in any type of social system—a factory, a street-corner gang, the traditional tribal society, or even in a bloc of nations.[97] They are all social systems and therefore possess the same features of social interaction. Interaction itself, the process through which people in society survive and adjust psychologically, consists of actions manifested by individuals in propinquity. Words, other sounds, gestures, facial expressions, and ritual acts illustrate interactive behavior. Sometimes those acts are stimuli, origins, which elicit similar acts as termini. Interaction may be qualitatively described, or it can be quantitatively measured in terms of the amount involved in a technological routine or a social context. Measurement can reveal, for example, how often a person playing a given role, say a priest, originates to people acting a different role, compared to the number of times he terminates, or responds, to them.

Theoretically speaking, interactions constitute the basis of cultural sequences; for example, making beer. Completion of the sequence elicits responses from people not engaged in the sequence itself, say from kinsmen who receive the beer as part of a ceremonial exchange. A sequence may be performed by a person alone, or, in division of labor, with a number of persons organized to carry out particular steps. In the latter case, a sequence may involve many complex interactions, and all must be completed before the sequence elicits responses from other members or groups in the society. Different technological operations require different amounts of interaction in their performance; hence social systems with different technologies—hunters compared to agriculturalists, for example —vary in the frequency with which members interact. Sex or age differences and other anatomical and physiological states of individuals, as well as technical division of labor, govern who does what and guides interaction in cultural sequences. Interruptions at any point in a sequence or chain of sequences produce emotional disturbances, indicating an intimate connection existing between social interaction and the biological makeup of the persons involved. In a book *Culture and Behavior,* published in 1970, Chapple calls attention to rhythmicity in biology and culture. Circadian (approximately 24-hour) and other biological rhythms, he believes, as well as culturally imposed rhythms, also contribute to organizing human interaction and personality.

Social interaction standardizes the meaning of symbols in a particular society and governs their power to evoke responses from members who understand the meaning. Take "father"; in many societies the word refers to the man who much more frequently originates action to his children than he responds to them. The word's emotional connotation derives from the father's dominance in social interaction. Every person has a number of such status designations—mother, sister, daughter, and so on—by which people who have different relations with her address her. Verbs signify the character of the event wherein interaction is taking place; prepositions fix the relative time of the actions. Individuals are also symbolized by objects regularly present in the relationships they form: a nurse by her cap or a policeman by a badge, and when several objects regularly serve as symbols they form a configuration. The greatest evocative significance attaches to symbols referring to many emotionally intense interactional contexts—in an agricultural society the staple crop, among pastoralists the animal they raise, or a nation's flag. These evocative symbols tend to be prominent in religious and other rituals.

Almost all of an individual's interaction, throughout life, takes place in institutions, including the family, school, work group, and church.

Frequently, institutions involve interaction between more than two people, so that one person or a group tends mainly to originate while the others respond. In such "set events" every person belongs to a class, either one whose members regularly originate, one whose members regularly respond, or an intermediate class, the members of which sometimes respond and sometimes originate.

So much for interaction, the most important concept of the theory. Equilibrium is another crucial concept, and refers to the condition of a steady state maintained in individuals, institutions, or a whole society. In 1942, when Chapple and Coon used the concept, it was still relatively unfamiliar in United States cultural anthropology, though Radcliffe-Brown had introduced it. Learning in every society, the authors of interaction theory state, conditions a person's equilibrium—his internal adjustment—to his interactions with others and to the environment. Should changes in interaction or in the environment upset a person's equilibrium, he will probably have recourse to socially provided opportunities for restoring it. Such provisions usually again involve interaction, perhaps in special institutions, such as a church, where techniques bring about new patterns of interaction that restore him to equilibrium. Institutions lose equilibrium through recurrent or nonrecurrent changes impinging on them from the environment, or because individuals within them become disturbed; and when such disturbances occur, an institution employs standardized means to restore a steady set. Leaders, persons belonging to the class of individuals who primarily originate in set events, play a significant role in the measures resorted to for bringing individuals and institutions back to equilibrium. A close relationship exists between the inner adjustment of an individual, involving his biological makeup, and the steady state of the institution in which he is interacting; one affects the other, so that a person's inner adjustment can be taken as an index of his adjustment in social relations.

Reinterpreting Technology and Ritual

Chapple and Coon's *Principles* presents a number of familiar ethnological concepts, including technology, ritual, government, and war, in terms that bring out the interactional features in such activities. Using technology and ritual, I will show how the authors reinterpret to suit the demands of their theory.

A society's technology—its system of physical techniques—adjusts it to the physical environment; therefore, technologies tend to vary with environment, at least in the case of primitive societies. By virtue of the interdependence existing between the members of a society, all the techniques practiced by them are also interrelated. Cutting tools, methods of obtain-

ing food, and modes of transportation are the three basic, mutually interdependent sets of techniques dominating a technology, and they govern
the extent to which a society will be able to accumulate an economic
surplus, develop division of labor, and attain complex forms of social
structure. Thus they also regulate social interaction and affect the personal adjustment of the society's members. Technology also controls the
complexity of societies as gauged by the number of types of institutions
they contain. At the simple level, food gatherers working only with stone
tools, like the Fuegians, have no institutions except the family and small
bands of related families. Many more forms of institutions and associations
are found in more complex societies: those founded on metal cutting tools,
on food obtained through plow agriculture, and on advanced animal
transportation. Complex societies also contain special institutions for the
purpose of restoring equilibrium disturbed during social interaction in
one or another of the several institutions in which everyone participates.
That religion should be so elaborately developed in complex societies reflects the greater frequency with which peoples' adjustment is upset in
those systems, with their multiple, interconnected institutions.

Every society, however, contains religious leaders, shamans or priests,
who through their role in ritual serve to counteract periodical disturbances
in equilibrium. Rites of passage restore equilibrium in persons whose lives
have been affected by changes in interaction brought about through
marriage, death, the birth of a child, and other life-cycle events. The rites
set up new habits of interaction suitable to the altered circumstances
created by the particular event. Rites of intensification deal with recurrent crises frequently affecting not just one or a few individuals but the
community as a whole. They work through increasing the interaction rates
of all members in the group. In both types of ritual, readjustment is
brought about by people acting together in a concerted fashion, usually
but not necessarily in response to a religious leader, while exposed to the
presence of emotionally powerful symbols.

Some reinterpretations of ethnological concepts in *Principles* are much
less clear than the authors, with their confident manner of writing, suggest. For example, their claim that the ritual of grace before meals in
American society symbolizes the habitual relationships of family members
and serves to restore equilibrium in the family group needs more documentation than is furnished. The authors are more successful in supporting the idea of functional dependencies between such variables as the
efficiency of cutting tools and the complexity of subsistence or transportation techniques. The evidence they present for such interdependence consists of maps showing, for example, how metal cutting tools tend to occur
together with plow agriculture and advanced animal transportation. The
correlations are qualitative and not, as far as the reader knows, based on
statistics.

Systems of Symbols

Symbols, Norms, and Action

Although symbols for a long time attracted scholars' attention, in recent times—as meaning became a major object to anthropological inquiry and, according to a philosopher, the dominant concept of the times[98]—symbols came to be identified with culture. David Schneider and Clifford Geertz in the 1960s conceived of culture as a system of meanings, and of social relations as a trafficking in symbols. I am unsure if their theories owe anything to Robert Redfield's brief reference to symbolic systems—myths, dance forms, religion, and allegories—as representing the whole culture in both its real and ideal aspects.[99] Unlike Geertz and Schneider, who define culture exclusively as cognition, Redfield employed the culture concept in its traditional broad meaning to include what people do. The myths and other symbolic assemblages he regarded as either transformations of social structure and other aspects of culture as they exist or, especially in the case of religion, as pointing to ideal behavior for members of a society to follow.

Schneider and Geertz likewise viewed a society's shared symbols as referring to the way people conceive of things in the world they inhabit, or as stating the way things should be. In Schneider, who presents his basic concepts more explicitly than Geertz, the symbols of a society comprise systems, each system pertaining to a particular domain of life—kinship for example.[100] The symbols delineate what the domain is all about; they specify the basic units of the domain, define and differentiate between those units, and organize them into a single, coherent, interdependent whole. All the systems together make up the whole culture, culture for Schneider being a conceptual means of categorizing the various domains of the world and of stating how those domains relate to one another. The total cultural system of a society *is* the world as people conceive it, and it is distinct from the level of action.

How does an anthropologist learn the cultural systems of a society? Schneider, who is also methodologically the more explicit of the two theorists, identifies the symbols through the words people use to express them; usually, but not invariably, as single-lexeme names. It might well mislead, he warns, to infer the cultural system from what people do; far better to question informants about their ideas. Elsewhere, however, he describes his strategy as starting from concrete, observable patterns of action and abstracting the norms they reveal. The norms pertaining to a domain of behavior constitute another system, one lying between the level of action and the symbolic—the cultural—level. Whereas the cultural system cognitively defines a domain belonging to the world, the normative system gives directions, or rules, to follow for getting along in that domain. The rules mediate the influence of the cultural symbols on action. Schneider abstracts the symbols of the cultural level from this middle, normative, level in which they are embedded. The cultural level, he wants it understood, is not a psychological level; nor does it correspond to the social level on which people and groups are organized and perform functions for the society. And definitely the cultural level is not the level of action studied when one observes the frequency with which individuals perform certain kinds of action, or when one notes differences in frequency of performance between one social category and another. Information about such differences may be useful, however, for revealing variation in norms from one category of people to another, perhaps even variation in the cultural symbols, or changes underway in the norms and symbols. But even in a complex society like the United States, Schneider believes, the norms, like the cultural symbols, are highly stable and unlikely to vary between classes or other social categories.

Schneider derived his concept of culture from Talcott Parsons, a professor of sociology at Harvard University where Schneider got his degree in 1949. After teaching for a time at the University of California in Berkeley, he moved to the University of Chicago in 1960, at a time when a number of other scholars were quitting California universities in dismay at the loyalty oath which the trustees demanded from the state's teachers. From an early interest in culture-and-personality research he turned his interest to kinship, the domain for which he developed his concept of cultural systems. Although not a structuralist in the manner of Claude Lévi-Strauss, Schneider has been influenced by some of the French scholar's ideas, as well as by his manner of expressing himself. Where Lévi-Strauss declares that totemism is not concerned with animals good to eat but with those good for thinking, Schneider says a society's ideas about kinship are not about biological relationships; rather, people use biology to formulate models about kinship. He also echoes the French structuralist when, referring to the contradiction between nature and culture, he describes the American folk model of the family as transcending nature by imposing rules on natural biological processes. No doubt he would also agree with Lévi-Strauss's assertion that mental images—models —have a reality of their own and can be studied as perfectly objective facts.[101] That is what Schneider does with kinship regarded as a system of symbols.

Symbols and Norms of American Kinship

Two basic symbols define American kinship at the most general level: the family and relatives. By *the* family, Americans mean the group containing a husband, a wife, and their children. The husband and wife are united through sexual intercourse, or conjugal love, the bond through which children are produced, while parents and children are united through cognatic love. Sexual intercourse, therefore, the symbol uniting the two parents, also serves to symbolize the relationship of parents and children, and is a general symbol of the American family.

By relatives, Americans mean persons related "by blood" and persons related through marriage. Blood relatives share a common physical substance, which creates a basis of identity. No such common substance joins relatives created by marriage, who are related through sharing a common code of behavior. From the two kinds of kin relationship symbolically recognized and differentiated by Americans, Schneider, with some prompting from French structuralism, abstracts the two distinctive features of American kinship. People, Americans believe, are either related by nature or by marriage, the latter an instance of the order of law (note use of the suffix "in-law" in designating affinal kin). The order of law, therefore, contrasts with the order of nature.

On the normative level, rules—precisely stated in legislative statutes or those far more vaguely understood—define how persons related through kinship shall act; for example, to show unity through displaying signs of love. The rules are influenced not only by the general definition of kinship but contain elements from other cultural systems, especially from the one defining persons of a particular age or sex. A wife, for example, is expected to cook and keep house not because she is a wife, for women cook and clean house when they are not wives, but because she is a woman. Cooking and keeping house are parts of the definition of women in American culture.

Field work revealed to Schneider that the members of different classes in the United States hold the same cultural symbols of kinship but differ in rules governing sex-linked family roles.[102] As a result, in the lower-class most tasks are sharply divided between those the husband, and those the wife performs, whereas middle-class spouses allocate household activities according to convenience; a wife may do any task for which she feels competent, even if it is culturally defined as more suitable for men.

Templates of Behavior

Clifford Geertz also conceives of symbols as modeling physical, psychological, and social events in the world, thereby enabling a society's members to understand reality and deal with it.[103] With words more straightforwardly functional than Schneider's, Geertz describes the symbol systems of culture as sources of information about reality and as templates for behavior that make up for human beings' lack of inborn responses and enable people to carry out all kinds of purposeful action. Despite his pragmatic view, however, he remains primarily concerned with the expressive symbols of religion and related domains of culture, rather than with those resulting in directly practical, purposeful action.

Schneider acknowledges being influenced by Geertz's concept of symbol, but when we look up the latter's definition in "Religion as a Cultural System," the two men at first glance seem far apart. Geertz defines symbol to include not only ideas, feelings, and other aspects of meaning, but acts, relationships, qualities, and other concrete things embodying the meaning and from which he abstracts it. He compares the distinction between the symbolic dimension and the things embodying it to the difference between the plan of a house and building the house. He is, we gather, not really concerned with the concrete aspect of symbols but, like Schneider, with meanings themselves. What probably influenced Schneider was not Geertz's inclusive definition of symbol (derived, Geertz says, from Susanne Langer) but Geertz's concept of symbols as arranged in complexes—culture patterns, Geertz calls them.

The two men's careers run parallel in their relationship to Parsons, graduation from Harvard, teaching in California, and migration to Chicago, which Geertz left to join the Institute for Advanced Study in Princeton, New Jersey. But when Schneider wholeheartedly embraced a cognitive conception of culture, their views diverged. Geertz condemns the conception of culture as a purely symbolic system divorced from behavior and artifacts—from the embodiments of meaning. He also repudiates cognitivists who locate culture primarily in the heads of people, citing Ward Goodenough as an example. For Geertz, meaning is public; it exists outside the minds of individuals. But where? In the marketplace, in church, in the theatre, or wherever individuals traffic in symbols and impose meaning on experience. Meaning exists in the intersubjective understandings reached between members of a society. Meaning resides in such symbol complexes as initiation rites, philosophical tales, shamanistic exhibitions, communal feasts, or Javanese puppet plays. These are both models of the world and models for dealing with the world. In a Javanese puppet play, for instance, a man seeking an unattainable goal who is swallowed by a little god exactly the image of himself dramatizes an important principle. After seeing the whole world in the god's body and emerging, the man learns that ultimate reality lies within oneself in a balanced system of thought and feeling. A spiritually enlightened person, the play says, guards his stability through carefully regulating worldly involvement. Elsewhere Geertz notes the infatuation of Balinese men with their cocks—ambulatory penises—and interprets the cocks as symbolic magnifications of the male narcissistic ego as well as of animality, the direct inversion of human status. Primarily, though, Geertz interprets cockfights with their heavy betting. He presents the mates as symbolically dramatizing status concerns. Men who make big wagers lay their public self on the line through the medium of their cocks. They risk big losses, but the meaning they impose on life by betting compensates them for the economic costs involved.

From a methodological standpoint, an ethnographer practicing what Geertz calls "interpretative anthropology," after having become familiar with studies of symbolism in different cultures, learns about the meaning of cockfights, puppet shows, or rituals in the society he studies by observing the use to which those things are put. Use reveals the meaning they possess for the society. The interpretation he offers of those things is a construction, a fiction, representing the meaning he imagines people place on their experience. Intrinsically, such an interpretation can never be complete; the deeper one goes in any topic, the less complete it becomes. An interpretation, one gathers, can also never be objectively validated. The best that can happen is for an interpretation to survive when it is contested in debate. But if it does survive, Geertz says, it will also be changed as debate itself deepens the ethnographers' understanding.

Some of a society's symbol complexes bear slight resemblance to the reality to which they refer. In a paper on ideology, Geertz speaks of a complex interplay of selectivity and distortion lying between reality and the concepts—a word he uses more readily than symbols—expressing reality. However greatly ideology distorts, the metaphors, hyperboles, and other literary devices with which it is constructed enable it to be rhetorically extremely forceful and powerfully convincing, as it must be to fulfill its function of making social situations meaningful and enabling people to act purposefully. By contrast, science, another cultural system, maintains much stronger disinterest toward the reality it deals with.

Symbols of religion, according to Geertz, fuse what is known about the world with moods and motivations aroused in people, and with injunctions about the way one ought to behave; they conjoin ontology and cosmology with aesthetics and morality. Much of his treatment of religion describes the capacity of religious concepts to provide, on the one hand, a general model of the world, of the self, and of the relationship between the world and self and, on the other hand, to establish long-lasting, utterly convincing moods and motivations in individuals. From this capacity of religion, social and psychological functions flow. Religion enlightens all manner of significant particular events, ranging from dictatorial coups to illness; it endows them with meaning. Religious concepts also act as templates shaping behavior. Symbols of original sin or witches, for example, depending on their definition in a society, recommend certain attitudes toward life or toward others. Although Geertz finds societies differing in the degree to which they elaborate religious conceptions, he fails to explain why, except to deny any covariation between religious elaboration and other kinds of cultural complexity.

Meanings are widely shared in a society, Geertz believes; yet different social categories in a complex society may hold distinct cultural orientations (a term, I assume, to be equivalent to complexes of symbols), or a group may reinterpret a widely shared culture pattern to make it serve sectional purposes. In a Javanese town he discovered three major cultural orientations, each embodying different philosophical systems of morality, and each related to a different occupational category. The economic behavior of a person professing one or another of these orientations is informed by the orientation, but cannot be perfectly predicted from the orientation alone, because actions are the outcomes of many situational and ideological factors, including individualistic considerations. In Java, Geertz also saw rival interest groups manipulating religious symbols for their own ends. The traditional symbols thereby acquired new meanings, varying between the opposed factions, each of which reinterpreted the symbols to support its own position. Such fragmentation of meaning, in his opinion, creates an unhappy situation for it leads to conflicts, strain, confusion, and many outbreaks of unconventional behavior.

Strong Groups and Condensed Symbols

Other anthropologists, working in traditions as diverse as psychoanalytic anthropology and British social anthropology, and representing various theoretical and methodological positions, also wrote about symbols and symbolism. Among them were Victor Turner, whose ideas regarding symbolism in ritual will be reviewed in the next chapter with other recent work on religion, and Mary Douglas, whose book, *Natural Symbols,* I will discuss here. Her ideas are not always plainly given. Some pages of the book I have reread several times, and I agree with the reviewer who admired Douglas's originality and beautiful prose but gave up over her unconnected sentences that frequently leave intriguing ideas opaque.

Symbols, she stresses, are the only means we have of communication, the sole way of expressing value, the main instrument of thought, and the only regulator of experience.[104] Her theory, however, goes nowhere near embracing the many types of symbols required for all those tasks, but restricts itself to a set of symbols expressing cosmological ideas, religion, and morality. Such symbols are never arbitrarily selected. Their choice in any society is rooted in history and in the degree of constraint imposed by the society's current social structure. Should the structure alter in ways that increase individual freedom from group constraints and allow greater social mobility, the significance or use made of the symbols will also change. Her questions deal with the relationship of symbolism to types of social structure: with what types do we encounter a tendency to pack symbols with condensed meaning, to regard them as efficacious, and to incorporate them in ritual? With what types of social structure do symbols become diffuse repositories of general thoughts and feelings? In both primitive and civilized societies, she answers, the concern with the efficacy of condensed symbols and their presence in ritual reaches a high point when groups possess strong boundaries, making membership in the group clear and permanent and giving the group a coercive grip on the individual. Conversely, symbols are diffuse and the ritual manipulations to release the power of symbols is lacking when group boundaries are weak. Under the latter structural condition, people experience control by objects—such as a precarious food supply and uncertain weather—rather than by structural arrangements of human design. Both the Ituri Pygmies and the Londoners implicated in an impersonal industrial society experience a weak sense of group constraint, and both are little given to ritual. Among both groups symbols are diffuse, referring primarily to emotional states, and in both, external signs of religion are minimally elaborated in ritual. European religious history also exemplifies antiritualism periodically making an appearance whenever social pressure slackened and the individual was able to enlarge his sphere of autonomy.

The cardinal virtues and grievous sins of a society, being symbols, likewise vary with the tightness of group boundaries, or with group power over individuals. In most primitive societies, behavior is closely controlled by ascribed role pattern, and such cardinal virtues as piety, honor, and respect for rules affirm the social structure, while the cardinal sins consist in transgressions against the social structure. But in societies where the grip of social structure is looser, allowing the value or autonomy of the individual to come forward, the cardinal virtues and sins emphasize duties toward the self; sincerity becomes a paramount good, while hypocrisy and acceptance of frustration constitute grievous sins.

Many similar propositions enrich the pages of *Natural Symbols*. The weaker the social pressures, Douglas predicts, the freer the symbolic system. To the extent that society is impoverished or confused in its social structure, to the same extent the idea of God will be impoverished and unstable in content. In a group with clear external boundaries but no definite leadership structure, where envy and favoritism confound the expectations of members, symbols of the normal-seeming yet abnormally powerful witch will flourish. Where group boundaries are weak, people see the cosmos dominated by impersonal powers and principles; but where the group is strong relative to individual autonomy, the powers ruling the universe are beings modeled on human form. Douglas sees controversies over the relationship of mind and body as metaphorical statements of the individual's relationship to society; insisting on the superiority of spirit over matter expresses the freedom of individuals from unwelcome social control; emphasizing the unity of mind and body implies the individual is subordinated to society. The body itself, she points out, furnishes a favorite source of symbolism. Societies try to create consonance between symbols of the body and symbols of society. Thus a group preoccupied with social boundaries, escape routes, or invasions will take great interest in the bodily apertures and boundaries.

Mary Douglas obtained her Ph.D. from Oxford University, in 1951, and became a teacher at University College, London. Much of her thinking can be traced to Emile Durkheim's concept of the collective consciousness; but she also drew on the work of Basil Bernstein, a British sociolinguist who called attention to the influence of social context on speech. He identified an elaborated linguistic code, enabling speakers to select freely from a wide range of syntactic alternatives, that was used in middle-class family contexts, and a restricted code with a narrow range of syntactic alternatives employed by children in lower-class families. Douglas regards the elaborated code as corresponding the diffuse symbolism found in conjunction with weak group boundaries and minimal social constraint, while the restricted code matches the condensed symbolism found in firmly bounded groups. Lower-class families are like most primitive societies in limiting the variability of behavior by ascribing status and imposing firm rules of right and wrong. Modern middle-class European and American society, on the contrary, provides individuals with less experience in authoritarian control and does not as strongly exalt obedience to the social structure. Consequently, Douglas asserts, symbols of solidarity and hierarchy are lacking.

In addition to Durkheim and Bernstein, psychoanalytic influences are suggested by the part of Douglas's theory which ascribes consonance between symbolic forms and social structure to psychological experiences generated in individuals under particular kinds of social structure. When people experience strong group pressures, they come to associate boundaries of the group or of the body—with power and danger. Under those circumstances people will try through the ritual manipulation of efficacious symbols to control that power.

Douglas's theory of symbolization ranks with the systems advanced by Durkheim and Freud, whose ideas she developed. Many of her propositions are testable, but first the crucial variables—strong or weak group boundaries, condensed and diffuse symbols—would have to be defined more explicitly than they are in *Natural Symbols*.

Structuralism

Objectified Thought

Symbols were included in the subjects studied by the postwar structuralists, the approach appearing in folktale research and linguistics in the 1920s and recommended by Claude Lévi-Strauss as superior to solely evolutionary or historical accounts of culture, and to the inductive search for laws advocated by A. R. Radcliffe-Brown.[105] Unlike the methods followed by Schneider and Geertz, structuralism did not derive the meanings of symbols primarily from questioning the individuals using the symbols. Lévi-Strauss even advises anthropologists to ignore the thinking individual entirely and to proceed as if thinking took place in totemism, myths, and similar cultural systems; but he does not follow his own advice. He hits the same key speaking of preferential marriage when he makes it clear he is alluding not to a subjective inclination to seek marriage with a particular relative but to a tendency for marriage of a certain kind to occur; preference, like meaning, lies in rules, symbols, and other phenomena, not in personal motivation. Judging from such statements, the validity of a structuralist's conclusions in no way depends on whether the people reason as he does but on whether the conclusions provide sound knowledge about the phenomena containing objectified thought. Soundness means logical, not empirical, validity. In practice, Lévi-Strauss and other structuralists frequently write as if they believe that people do hold the meaning present in objectified thought, perhaps holding it unconsciously. Admitting that meaning is solely the artifact of a method is apparently unsatisfying when human beings are the object of study.

Structuralism of the form recognizable in Lévi-Strauss represents a method that assumes, as a crucial part of its theory, the existence of a hidden logic or disguised meaning behind the surface manifestations of the social phenomena it deals with. In this broad sense, Karl Marx and Freud as well as Lévi-Strauss are structuralists. In a somewhat less comprehensive sense, structuralism refers to a mid-20th century movement in linguistics, folktale research, literary criticism, and anthropology. Roland Barthes defines the movement as an activity whose object is, first, to break down the object being studied, and then, to reconstruct it in a way that shows the rules of functioning, the rules by which meaning is produced.[106] The result is not an impression of the world but a fabrication susceptible of verification. An anthropologist, Harold Scheffler, looking just at anthropological structuralism states as its basic principle that culture consists of "ready-made orders" or sets of models of and for experience.[107] Society provides the models for its members to cognize and act with. By Barthes's or Scheffler's definition, at least two varieties of anthropological structuralism are recognizable: Lévi-Strauss's, the subject of this section, and formal semantic analysis, the subject of the next section. Scheffler, it should be noted, contrary to what Lévi-Strauss advises, identifies the order discovered by structural method with thinking individuals. The same identification, we will see, is also made by the formal semantic analysts.

The most prominent member of the structuralist company in the 1960s and early 1970s, Lévi-Strauss, belongs among those anthropologists whose worldwide popularity equaled or even rivaled their standing in the profession. James G. Frazer, Bronislaw Malinowski, and Margaret Mead hold the same rank. Anthropology had never heard of him when he left France, in 1934, to teach sociology in Brazil.[108] Twenty-six years old, the training he had received while earning degrees in philosophy fitted him perfectly for the tradition of French scholarship, with its broad erudition, rationalism, and a strong desire for intellectual synthesis. As he started for Brazil, he made up for his lack of training in ethnology by reading Robert Lowie's *Primitive Society*. It proved to be a vivid experience. The book, he says, freed his mind "from the claustrophobic, Turkish-bath atmosphere in which it was being imprisoned" by philosophy. The work astonished him with the prospects it opened up, prospects soon within his grasp when he joined an ethnological expedition visiting jungle Indians. After the trip he abandoned philosophy and sociology for ethnology, gave up his university post to make more expeditions to central Brazilian tribes, and as Lewis Henry Morgan and Edward B. Tylor had done, self-trained himself in ethnology. In the process he wove for his use a highly original, theoretical cloth from diverse threads of ideas. He himself acknowledges having lived with three intellectual "mistresses," geology, psychoanalysis, and Marxism, but the influence of Russian formalism—a structuralist approach to folktales—and structural linguistics overshadows those. Roman Jakobson, the linguist, whom he met during wartime years of exile in New York City, may have been the initial source of Lévi-Strauss's acquaintance with both the latter subjects. Saying little about his knowledge of Russian formalism, he testifies to his appreciation of structural linguistics with its method of dealing not with sounds or words as independent entities, but with the relations between those units.[109] In structural linguistics Lévi-Strauss found a social science capable of formulating simple, elegant, invariant laws; and like Giambattista Vico and other Enlightenment philosophers, he resolved to follow the same path with regard to other aspects of culture. He began with marriage and kinship, the subject of his first book, *Elementary Structures of Kinship*, published in 1949. Although much criticized on factual grounds, the book started his fame. In 1955, he began to publish on myths, treating meaning as arising from relationships between the symbols comprising myths, and looking for general laws governing mythical thought.[110] By now cultural anthropology had for Lévi-Strauss become semiology.

Contrasts and Oppositions

Structural anthropology in the hands of Lévi-Strauss became primarily a method for learning about the nature of thought, and about the constraints imposed on thought by the human mind in producing it. In tackling the problem he looked for recurrences in patterns of thought from one time or place to another, the object being to advance or support generalizations concerning the nature of thought in general. Theory lies both in the assumptions with which Lévi-Strauss goes at his work and in the conclusions he reaches through comparative research. Myths, totemic names for social groups, and other objectified forms of thought, his fundamental theoretical stance assumes, are systems containing not only the obvious, superficial meaning associated with the individual units comprising the system, but a deeper significance based on the way the system is put together. Even the meaning of the individual units, symbols, like the meaning of individual words in an utterance, derives from relationships existing between them. These relationships constitute a structure, and knowledge about the structure is the immediate object of structuralist activity. The further object is knowledge about the structure of the mind governing the structures present in objectified thought. He employs the metaphor of a code, saying myths, totemic systems, and other symbolic cultural products can be decoded to reveal a deeper meaning than appears on the surface. The code of which they are composed uses bits of familiar sensory data—natural elements, heavenly bodies, animals, and the like—taken from the zoological, cosmic, domestic, and other realms with which people are familiar. The elements are put together according to implicit rules, whereby additional meaning is imposed upon them, corresponding to the way words acquire additional meaning from their place in an utterance or to how the colors red and green acquire specific meaning when they appear as traffic signals.

In the systems Lévi-Strauss examines, he finds relationships of contrast and opposition, for example, between fire and water, sun and moon, eaglehawks and crows, raw and cooked, with similar pairs or double pairs of mutually exclusive, yet complementary, symbols. These he relates in a causal manner to unconscious, universal processes of thinking followed by the mind. It is the nature of mental activity, he explains, to reflect on experience by means of binary oppositions.

He justifies his concentration on myths and other symbolic cultural forms by claiming that mental inventiveness has much less scope to show itself in everyday, practical activities where the mind is occupied with the necessity of adapting to reality. The freest of thought takes place in poetic language, art, myths, and other areas where practical considerations are lacking. Lévi-Strauss does not take the familiar intellectualistic position of regarding myths as explanations of natural phenomena, though he is closer to that tradition than he admits when, as we shall see, he makes myths the medium through which the mind grapples with profound philosophical problems.

Lévi-Strauss advanced a number of propositions about myths. He regards a myth as a system of communication in which the mind communes with itself, without needing to come to terms with any objects in the external world. Being determined by the nature of thought, myth operates on a twofold basis. On the one hand, it reflects on actual or supposedly historical events; they provide the incidents or the story. On the other hand mythical thought draws on internal, neuromental factors like organic rhythms, memory, and the power of attention, the same factors employed in music. Each myth is a system, and different myths also comprise a system when they revolve around the same theme, even when they belong to different societies (clear proof that Lévi-Strauss has withdrawn from the tradition of cultural relativity). The different myths belonging to the same system, though found in far-distant cultures, represent different ways of expressing the same thought pattern. The differences are not to be explained diachronically in terms of diffusion or historical events, nor are they to be accounted for synchronically as due to variations in social structure or some other independent variable. The myths all have the same source, the mind, and are to be dealt with simply as transformations, reversions, or redefinitions of a common theme.

Though myths lack practical value, the thought they objectify deals with important problems of mankind: life and death, the autochthonous origin of mankind versus the knowledge that human beings are born of sexual unions, and fundamental to all such problems, the relationship between nature and culture or, using different words, between randomness and order. For Lévi-Strauss, the relationship between nature and culture is as pivotal as the Oedipus complex is for the Freudians. The latter say people in all societies attempt to resolve the Oedipus conflict in symbolic fashion; he finds all cultures struggling with the distinction between nature and culture in mythical episodes, symbols, and in the rules they establish. Incest rules, for example, convert unregulated copulation present in nature into an orderly system of marriage characteristic of culture. Affinal ties maintained through gift exchange mediate between persons—belonging to the realm of nature—who have been converted into kinsmen through marriage, a cultural act. By these devices the opposition between nature and culture is transformed into different terms; the two realms are bridged, and the tension inherent between them is temporarily resolved.

The Primitive Mind

The mind reveals its inventiveness more freely in productions which have no practical value and are unconnected with adaptation to reality; it also shows itself more clearly in primitive societies. There symbolic cultural forms provide a much clearer insight into the fundamental structure of the mind than can be obtained elsewhere.

Primitive people think basically as we do, but they symbolize differently. They think concretely, as we see from the readiness with which they express their thoughts, often in exceedingly complex fashion, through sensory images, through symbols of food, raw and cooked, and through animals and animal attributes. Their myths and rites clearly reveal a readiness to think imaginatively on a level of sensory perception, an inclination and ability to classify phenomena by their aesthetic or sensible properties. We, too, possess the capacity to think concretely, but we fail to utilize it as consistently as primitive people do. Conversely, primitive thinkers, though capable of using more abstract terms in classifying and symbolizing, neglect that capacity. It follows that primitive myths, totemism, and similar cultural forms constitute remnants of a lost time when all men thought concretely. Current or recently studied primitive societies, Lévi-Strauss recognizes, stand as far removed from the original human society as ours; their special character resides in retaining, even elaborating, a form of wisdom and distinctive cultural style that our culture has largely abandoned.

If primitive societies use less abstract terms than scientists in making distinctions between plants and other objects of the world in which they live, they do so not because they are more actuated by economic needs. Classification among them, as in all societies, rests on a demand for order. The distinctions they draw between plants or animals don't stem solely from their edible or other economic qualities. Rather, Lévi-Strauss believes, the items are deemed useful or interesting because they are known; classifying comes first, then uses may be found for some of the recognizable phenomena.

Some Systems of Thought

Let us see how some of the ideas I have identified as characteristic of Lévi-Strauss's anthropology appear in works he has written. In his first book, *Elementary Structures of Kinship,* he views incest rules and marriage rules as representing transitions from nature to culture. Incest rules took humanity from the natural fact of free mating to the cultural fact of exogamy, and marriage rules took it from relationships based solely on consanguinity to those based also on affinity.

A large part of the book is devoted to marriage rules prescribing that a sister or daughter received as a bride must be reciprocated with a sister or daughter, a topic I will return to in the next chapter. Lévi-Strauss grounds marital exchange in three mental structures inherent in human nature, three mental tendencies that allow human beings to conceive of exchange as a form of social bonding. The first structure, the most general, recognizes the exigency of rule as rule; the second recognizes reciprocity as a means for directly bridging the separation of self from others; and the third recognizes the ability of a gift to create partners and therefore to acquire a new value. Proof of the universality of these structures is forthcoming through cultural comparison, which shows them operating in social organization everywhere. Additional evidence exists in children's thought, where the structures manifest themselves more clearly than among adults.

Another early, very difficult work analyzes split representation in art, the convention of taking a face or sometimes a whole creature and representing it in a drawing or carving by showing both profiles joined, somewhat as if the creature had been sliced through the middle and the two halves peeled back.[111] From the standpoint of structural anthropology, split representations involve an integral relationship between two components: first, the graphic representation and, second, the plastic substance on which the representation is imposed. The relationship between the two components is simultaneously one of opposition and utility; opposition arises from the fact that the substance is altered to meet the requirements of the graphic representation imposed upon it. Once the design has been imposed, the object—a painted wall or carved box—acquires utility simply by virtue of what has been done to it. With a bit greater clarity, Lévi-Strauss relates split representational art to other features in culture with which it correlates. Such art, he claims, is found in cultures having genealogies linking living persons with mythological ancestors who originated privileges wherewith people validate their social rank. The interdependence between the mythological ancestors and the social roles followed by people in validating rank corresponds to the conventionality of split representational art. The plastic and graphic components of the art, I understand him to say, are related in the same way that the social and supernatural orders are related. Furthermore, an object represented in symmetrical halves metaphorically expresses the individual's social role in such a society: the creature is literally torn asunder, just as an individual is if he is severed from his mythologically sanctioned social role.

In *Totemism* he elaborates a thesis originally advanced by A. R. Radcliffe-Brown.[112] One can follow him easily as he reveals the nonobvious meaning of totemism by first decomposing the system and then recomposing it by fabricating a model of its structure. He identifies two components in totemism. On the one hand, the system utilizes animal species and other natural phenomena that, according to native belief, resemble one another in some way, yet also differ. The Australian bat and tree creeper, for example, live in trees but one is nocturnal and the other diurnal. On the other hand, a totemic system consists of people who likewise resemble each other—they are all human or belong to the same tribe—and yet also differ by virtue of belonging to several kin groups. Totemism selects differences between similar animal species or natural phenomena to symbolize the social differences. The result is a series of totems homologous to social groups and serving as classifiers for the groups. Note how totemism fastens on contrasting sensory qualities of the phenomenal world to construct a code for communicating ideas. Lévi-Strauss puts it in an unforgettable phrase: Particular animals are chosen as totems, because they are good to think with, not as previous theorists supposed, because they are good to eat or because as supernaturals they provide a psychological source of security. In *Savage Mind*, written a few years later, he incorporates myth and exogamy into his theory of totemism. The mythical element in totemism mediates between man and nature and transcends the opposition between them, equating significant contrasts found on the different planes. Exogamy between totemic groups further resolves opposition; it bridges the manifest differences between the groups by asserting that they are also alike in being part of a single social system in which women are shared. Exchange of women, brought about by exogamy, signifies solidarity and maintains each totemic group's relationship to the whole.

Savage Mind applies structural analysis to caste with highly original results.[113] Appropriately, the author approaches the topic through a preliminary examination of taboos as systems of thought. Taboos, like myths, think with the aid of concrete symbols, namely ritual prohibitions. The value of the prohibitions stems not from any physical or mystical danger cognitively associated with the forbidden things, but lies in their ability to mark distinctions between stressed and unstressed natural objects. Prohibitions single out some things in the world as being more significant than others, as obligatory observances do, too. In both types of rules we find modes of action serving as operators of thought, devices to think with. Hence prohibitions and obligations are equivalent to the concrete images used as operators in primitive myths.

In approaching caste as a system of objectified thought, Lévi-Strauss observes that all societies draw an analogy between sexual relations and eating. At least so it seems from the frequency with which exchange of women in marriage and exchange of food are employed to symbolize the interlocking of social groups. Conversely, rules against marriage or eating with persons of certain groups signify social separation or extreme differentiation. Being operators with the same significance, marital and commensal prohibitions or obligations may reinforce each other, or they provide alternative means for stating ideas of inclusion or exclusion. Caste resembles totemism in that both systems are ways of communicating something about the nature of human differences, each providing a model for making social diversity apparent in vivid, concrete terms. Totemic groups, as we saw, depict diversity on the plane of nature. Using animal species or natural phenomena, they convey the message that human beings are diverse yet in nature also alike. Caste, by employing occupational diversity as a concrete symbol for communicating the idea of social differentiation, models diversity on the cultural plane. Marriage rules in each type of social organization communicate additional information about similarity or differentiation. In totemic systems, the rule of exogamy confirms that women of different groups are alike by nature, though, of course, culturally different by virtue of belonging to different groups. In caste systems, prohibitions against intercaste marriage state women of different castes to be culturally different, though secondarily recognizing them to be also naturally alike.

The works I have cited indicate how little Lévi-Strauss relates systems of thought to other features of culture and social structure, either causally or functionally. Occasionally he does, as when he traces split representation to genealogies linking people to mythological ancestors who originated privileges the people enjoy. In the "Story of Asdiwal" he interprets a Tsimshian myth as being a critique of the society's social structure, and the Nass River version of the same tale he connects to the economic significance attached to fishing in that group.[114] Since he presents structuralism as superior to functionalism, it is understandable that he will not look for pragmatic value in myths and other objectifications of thought, though he does, of course, reiterate their importance for resolving oppositions.

Lévi-Strauss did no better than the ethologists in supporting his claim of innate behavioral tendencies. He failed to offer independent evidence that binary thinking is innate, or that all societies are concerned with the relationship of nature and culture, disorder and order. He didn't suggest a way of independently identifying the innate nature of thought or the basic problem of thought except circularly, that is by pointing to symbolic oppositions—the thing to be explained. The universality of binary opposition in objectified thought constitutes no sound evidence for anything inherent in human nature, especially since another theory has also been presented to explain it. Oppositions in myths and other cultural forms founded on language, the rival theory maintains, derive from the universal perception of two-sided spatial relationships. Such perception is learned from experiences every human being encounters with the two sides, the two ends, and the ventral and dorsal surfaces of his own body.[115]

Structural analysis has been described by its proponents as replacing less intelligible complexity with a more intelligible complexity without impoverishing the richness of the phenomena it studies. How satisfactory were the results of Lévi-Strauss's structural activity? The answer to the question depends partly on the kind of understanding being sought. Since postwar anthropologists, especially in America, greatly valued reliability, it is not surprising that Lévi-Strauss's structuralism failed to satisfy those who sought empirically verifiable conclusions and methods operationally defined which could be replicated by others. Complaints were also heard about the density of some of Lévi-Strauss's writings, making them difficult to understand. Finally, the postwar preference, again in America, for approaching culture in terms of people's own categories or meanings did not favor his structuralism. True, he insists that anthropologists wishing to follow the logic of the concrete employed by a particular society must learn how the society conceives of the symbols it employs. Knowing that people think of a bee and carpenter as both engaged in constructing things enables one to perceive why bees resemble carpenters. But Lévi-Strauss himself is not always zealous in reporting the native cognitions underlying his interpretations, and like the psychoanalysts he rapidly outruns what is given in the facts. Meaning thereby becomes an artifact of the method he employs, as he practically admits when he recommends proceeding with analysis as if thinking took place in cultural systems rather than in individuals.

Formal Semantic Analysis

Words and Their Meanings

Ethnoscience—hailed as "the new ethnography"—together with componential analysis and similar methods of formal semantic analysis took lexemes, words with a particular meaning, as the principal object of study.[116] The analysts used a set of lexemes belonging to a semantic domain—such as kinship, plants, colors, or firewood—to reveal how a society categorizes experience and the distinctive features by which the referents of each lexeme are distinguished from other referents belonging to the same domain.

Far more methodological than theoretical, formal semantic analysis was novel when introduced to anthropology. Yet it had its predecessors, ultimately the philosophical theories of classification of Plato and Aristotle and, less remotely, biological taxonomy and work on primitive and Chinese classification published by Emile Durkheim and Marcel Mauss, in 1903. Alfred L. Kroeber more directly foreshadowed componential analysis, in 1909, when he distinguished a mere eight elements underlying kinship nomenclature in the world's hundreds of kin-term systems. Occasionally, in the decades following, anthropologists applied their own kinds of formal analyses to specific kin-term systems, but their discoveries received no special attention.[117]

Formal semantic analysis won popularity after the cognitive concept of culture became favored, cognitivists being attracted to the simplicity of getting at a society's cognitions through the words that members used. The method also assured other advantages. By remaining with the society's own views of labeled experience, anthropologists expected to be able to avoid introducing biases stemming from a foreign society. Ethnoscience and componential analysis also promised a degree of reliability and replicability far superior to the methods of analysis practiced in conventional ethnography, especially where cognition was concerned. With those methods there would be no call for gifted intuitive grasps of psychological reality; anyone able to learn the techniques would be able to reach the same, or closely similar, conclusions about cognition in particular societies. The formal methods appealed mainly to United States anthropologists; British and Continental scholars interested in meaning showed no sign of being attracted to the objectivity promised by lexical analysis, perhaps because they were put off by the limited range of meaning which such methods could explore.

Analyzing Vocabularies

Those unfamiliar with formal methods of semantic analysis will appreciate a brief description of how ethnoscience and componential analysis proceeded.

The ethnoscientists built on an old interest in folk science which led philologists and anthropologists to collect vocabularies about various subjects and sometimes even to ask informants to arrange the lexical data in contrast sets. A contrast set is made up of words referring to mutually exclusive categories of animals, plants, or whatever subject the words refer to.[118] For example, in English, mares, stallions, and geldings refer to mutually exclusive categories of horses. In ethnoscience, if informants allow, the analyst organizes the contrast sets hierarchically into taxonomies modeled after scientific taxonomies. We recognize mares, stallions, and geldings as belonging to the taxon "horse," which contrasts with the taxa cattle, sheep, and swine, each of which may contain contrast sets. Together, all those taxa fit under the larger taxon of "animals." Up to this point the ethnoscientist has shown how informants categorize experiences that possess names, without revealing the distinctive features by virtue of which horses are distinguished from cattle or mares from stallions. To learn the cognitive bases of those distinctions requires a method for discovering the criteria informants regard as significant.

Such a method for the analysis of kinship terms was announced in 1956 in two papers published by anthropologists. I will confine myself to one of those papers, "Conponential Analysis and the Study of Meaning," by Ward Goodenough.[119] Disregarding connotation, the unstable aspect of meaning, and heeding only signification, or the defining features of the persons to whom kinship terms are applied, Goodenough reveals the distinctive features underlying the kin terms employed by the people of Truk.

Genealogies provided Goodenough with a list of Trukese terms, as well as a sample of the relatives for whom each is used. *Semej*, for example, designates a father, father's brother, mother's brother, father's father, and certain other relatives. *Jinej* denotes a mother, mother's sister, father's

FIGURE 1

Componential Paradigm for American Kin Terms

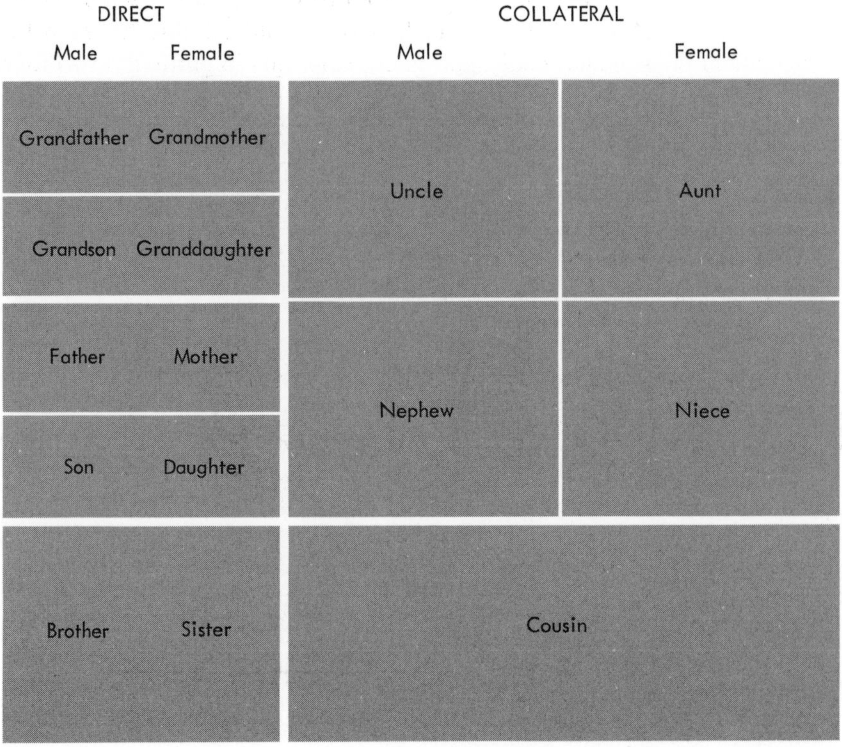

DIRECT		COLLATERAL	
Male	Female	Male	Female

Grandfather Grandmother		Uncle	Aunt
Grandson Granddaughter			
Father Mother		Nephew	Niece
Son Daughter			
Brother Sister		Cousin	

sister, mother's mother, and a limited number of additional kin. Taking each term in the list, he looked for the features it singles out in the persons it designates, and translated the term into a notational system representing those features. *Semej* becomes AB_1C_1, in which A represents a relative of the speaker; B, seniority of generation, with B_1 indicating a senior; and C, sex of relative, C_1 indicating male. *Jenej* becomes AB_1C_2, showing that *Jinej* contrasts with *Semej* only in the feature of sex. Additional terms, of course, introduced other distinctive features. Goodenough takes pains to point out that the relationship of AB_1C_1 and AB_1C_2 parallels the phonetic relationship of English "bed" and "bet"; in both cases the difference in meaning rests on one critical feature. Throughout the paper he draws attention to the resemblance between linguistic analysis and componential analysis, indicating how heavily the former method influenced the latter.

To show how terms in a system compare and contrast with each other, componential analysts since Goodenough have prepared paradigms which superficially resemble the taxonomies of ethnoscience, though the former present far more information. Figure 1 illustrates an elegantly simple componential paradigm of American kinship.[120]

Componential analysis has been little employed for semantic domains outside of kinship. In fact, it may be impossible to apply the method to lexemes without referents having distinctive features capable of being studied objectively, to domains with uncertain boundaries, or to domains whose dimensions are continuous rather than discrete. Emotion is a domain possessing all these features.[121]

Psychological Reality

With respect to theory, the basic assumption behind ethnoscience and componential analysis holds that meaningful experiences encountered by members of a society are encoded in lexemes, often in discrete lexemes. The meaning of a discrete lexeme, it is further assumed, cannot be immediately intuited from the form of the word, but derives from the relationship of the word to other words belonging to the same set (i.e., referring to the same semantic domain).

Semanticists made another assumption—one compatible with the long-standing concept of culture as shared in a society, but contradicted by a newer principle recognizing diverse subcultures in a society—namely, that members of a society by virtue of their enculturation share a common system of cognition. Cognitivists who clung to this assumption resolved the contradiction by regarding diversity as inherent in what members of a society do, in the overt manifestations of culture; the cognitions governing behavior they regarded as much more uniformly distributed.

Putting the assumption of shared cognition together with the assumption of experience being encoded in lexemes, warrants the deduction that the learned system of cognition, like meaningful experience in general, is reflected in the words the members of a society apply to events and objects. From this an important, but disputed, methodological principle follows: people's use of language provides insight into culturally patterned cognition. The contrasts, hierarchical orderings, and distinctive features found in lexemes represent the way natives conceive of the domains to which those lexemes refer. The distinctive features differentiating one kin term from another reflect the components of cognition, the criteria by which people distinguish between types of kinsmen. If analysis adheres to what competent native speakers of a language say, it has the potential for getting at psychological reality.

It took little time to uncover several problems in the assumption of psychological reality. In cases where analysts using the same set of kin terms came forth with different componential paradigms, which one reflected psychological reality?[122] Or which did so best? What evidence can be provided showing that the cognitions established by semantic analysis are not overgeneralizations produced by the method, but exist in the society? If the distinctive features obtained through componential analysis are psychologically real, why are people not aware of employing them? Those who preferred componential analysis replied, saying the components of cognition exist below the level of consciousness. They are psychologically real in the sense phonemes are. Though people remain unaware of phonemes and certain other standards, they recognize them and are troubled by ambiguities created when phonemic and other standards fail to be met in speech or other conduct. Unconvinced by these arguments, and disappointed by the restricted applicability of componential analysis solely to denotative meaning, anthropologists in the mid-1970s were searching for other, more defensible semantic approaches.[123] Second generation cognitive anthropologists were also dissatisfied, because the descriptions of cognition provided by ethnoscience failed to predict what speakers would do in specific situations, and to overcome this limitation they proposed concentrating on how people process information and reach decisions.[124]

Trends in Postwar Anthropology

A Diversified Discipline

Between the Second World War and the early 1970s, a number of cultural anthropologists parted company with Edward B. Tylor's inclusive definition of culture in favor of a much more exclusive definition, which limited the idea to the values, ideas, and symbols shaping overt behavior. Some of those who did not make this shift proposed the idea that it is more important to study the actual phenomenal events, including constraints and choices, by which cultural forms are produced and maintained, than the epiphenomenal forms themselves. Other ethnologists and social anthropologists moved toward greater abstractness in their analytical treatment of data by adopting more formal methods; for example, in regard to kinship terminology. The discipline also witnessed a renewed interest being taken in cultural evolution and culture history and, in the United States particularly, saw a rapid explosion of new topical interests and methods embodying, however, most of the familiar anthropological viewpoints, except configurationalism. All these trends point to a rapidly proliferating subject whose orienting concepts, methods, and theories were frequently incompatible with one another, leading some observers to wonder if the discipline was losing its identity. Whether it was or was not, the diversification, occurring during years when the academic market was expanding and more schools taught more courses in anthropology than ever before, allowed people possessing a wide variety of interests and talents to find in anthropology a satisfying professional career.

Since there was no longer a single culture concept, anthropologists could not even all claim they were united in studying culture, albeit following such varying approaches as functionalism, evolutionism, human ethology, cultural ecology, psychological anthropology, cultural materialism, interaction theory, formal semantic analysis, structuralism, the systems of David Schneider or Clifford Geertz, or in Germany, cultural morphology. Some approaches lacked unity within themselves. The psychological functionalism of Melford Spiro scarcely resembled the materialistic, ecological orientation Andrew P. Vayda took. Alexander Alland, eschewing direction in evolution, wrote on evolutionary processes quite differently from Elman Service, and both shared little of A. Irving Hallowell's interest in the evolution of a human capacity for culture.

Between approaches, as well as within some of them, theorists differed over explaining things primarily with reference to the individual, regarding him as the source of culture and social structure, or in terms of collective factors. Differences also appeared as some theorists stressed the role of social patterning, taking a position congenial to cultural relativity, while others inclined to nativism or, for other reasons, eschewed relativism.

One common note does join many of the approaches: far more emphasis on method than on assumptions and explanatory theory. Consequently, theory must often be inferred from the published results obtained by approaches like formal semantic analysis or French structuralism. With the strong interest in method, whose beginnings we began to mark in the 19th century after anthropology became a discipline, went an unprecedented borrowing of methodological ideas and techniques from other academic fields, such as sociology, communications science, statistics, computer science, and linguistics, as well as from contemporary intellectual movements, including French structuralism and general systems theory. The hope, expressed by some ethnologists, that anthropology would be able to achieve precision by applying the method of structural linguistics to the analysis of culture—a hope largely yet to be realized at the time I write—recalls the ethnologists who hoped to emulate historical linguistics in reconstructing the history of cultures without the benefit of written records.

A number of approaches, most definitely evolutionism, cultural ecology, human ethology, and psychological anthropology employing psychoanalytic theory, also shared a high degree of awareness concerning the extent to which culture and nature affect one another, whether it be nature in the form of the human organism or of the geographical environment. Readiness to treat the process of cultural evolution as closely akin to biological evolution, and to regard culture as an extension of biological adaptation, further overcame the earlier tendency to sunder the super-organic from lower, including biological, levels of phenomena, thereby bringing culture nearer to nature.

Although anthropologists showed themselves only moderately responsive to studying the social issues of the time, applied anthropology and research on deviant behavior and mental illness were increasingly undertaken, indicating that the discipline was relevant when it came to practical matters. Studies of factories, community development, alcoholism, and the distribution of mental illness between ethnic groups might not further any grand aims, such as the 17th- and 18th-century philosophers entertained, but they promised to further the goals of those specialized groups in society for whom the anthropologists worked.

Notes

1. Gerald D. Berreman, "Anemic and Emetic Analyses in Social Anthropology," *American Anthropologist,* vol. 68 (1966): 346–354; John J. Honigmann, "The Personal Approach in Culture-and-Personality Research," in press.

2. A. L. Kroeber and Talcott Parsons, "The Concepts of Culture and of Social System," *American Sociological Review,* vol. 23 (1958): 582–583, p. 583. See also James P. Spradley, "Foundations of Cultural Knowledge," in James P. Spradley, ed., *Culture and Cognition* (San Francisco: Chandler Publishing Co., 1972).

3. Ward H. Goodenough, "Introduction," in Ward H. Goodenough, ed., *Explorations in Cultural Anthropology* (New York: McGraw-Hill Book Co., 1964), pp. 10ff; Ward H. Goodenough, *Description and Comparison in Cultural Anthropology* (Chicago: Aldine Publishing Co., 1970), ch. 4; Charles O. Frake, "A Structural Description of Subanun 'Religious Behavior,'" in Goodenough, *Explorations in Cultural Anthropology,* p. 112; Ward H. Goodenough, "Residence Rules," *Southwestern Journal of Anthropology,* vol. 12 (1956): 22–37.

4. Kenneth L. Pike, "Etic and Emic Standpoints for the Description of Behavior," in Alfred G. Smith, ed.,

Communication and Culture (New York: Holt, Rinehart and Winston, 1966).

5. Eric Wolf, *Anthropology* (Englewood Cliffs, N.J.: Prentice-Hall, 1964), p. 40; Marvin Harris, *The Rise of Anthropological Theory* (New York: Thomas Y. Crowell Co., 1968), pp. 582–584.

6. Melville J. Herskovits, *The Myth of the Negro Past* (New York: Harper and Brothers Publishers, 1941). For the new context into which the book later fitted, see Sidney W. Mintz "Foreword" and Norman E. Whitten, Jr. and John F. Szwed, "Introduction," both in Norman E. Whitten, Jr., and John F. Szwed. eds., *Afro-American Anthropology* (New York: Free Press, 1970).

7. See Harold E. Driver and K. F. Schuessler, "Factor Analysis of Ethnographic Data," *American Anthropologist,* vol. 59 (1957): 655–661; Peter W. Hoon, "Polynesian Relationships: Initial Correlation and Factor Analyses of Cultural Data," *Ethnology,* vol. 13 (1974): 83–103.

8. E. E. Evans-Pritchard, *Social Anthropology* (London: Cohen and West, 1951), pp. 60–61; E. E. Evans-Pritchard, "Anthropology and History," in E. E. Evans-Pritchard, *Social Anthropology and Other Essays* (New York: Free Press of Glencoe, 1962), John Bennett, "The Develop-

ment of Ethnological Theory as Illustrated by Studies of the Plains Sun Dance," *American Anthropologist,* vol. 46 (1944): 162–181, pp. 167–173, 179–180; Julian Steward, "Development of Complex Societies: Cultural Causality and Law: A Trial Formulation of the Development of Early Civilizations," in Julian H. Steward, *Theory of Culture Change* (Urbana: University of Illinois Press, 1955).

9. Robert M. Carmack, "Ethnohistory: A Review of Its Development, Definitions, Methods, and Aims," *Annual Review of Anthropology,* vol. 1 (1972): 227–246.

10. Marshall D. Sahlins and Elman R. Service, eds., *Evolution and Culture* (Ann Arbor: University of Michigan Press, 1960), ch. 1.

11. Joseph H. Greenberg, "The Logical Analysis of Kinship," *Philosophy of Science,* vol. 16 (1949): 58–64.

12. Marvin Harris, *The Nature of Cultural Things* (New York: Random House, 1964); Edward T. Hall, Jr., and George L. Trager, *The Analysis of Culture* (photo offset; Washington, 1953); Irving Rouse, *Introduction to Prehistory* (New York: McGraw-Hill Book Co., 1972), ch. 5.

13. Edward Sapir, "Cultural Anthropology and Psychiatry" [orig. 1932], and "The Emergence of the Concept of Personality in a Study of Cultures" [orig. 1934], both in Edward Sapir, *Selected Writings of Edward Sapir in Language Culture, and Personality,* David Mandelbaum, ed. (Berkeley: University of California Press, 1949); Raymond Firth, *Elements of Social Organization* (London: Watts and Co., 1951), pp. 32–40; Evon Z. Vogt, "On the Concepts of Structure and Process in Cultural Anthropology," *American Anthropologist,* vol. 62 (1960): 18–33; Allan D. Coult, "The Structuring of Structure," *American Anthropologist,* vol. 68 (1966): 438–443, pp. 440–442. Fredrik Barth, *Models of Social Organization* (Royal Anthropological Institute of Great Britain and Ireland, Occasional Paper No. 23, 1966); Fredrik Barth, "On the Study of Social Change," *American Anthropologist,* vol. 69 (1967):

661–669; E. R. Leach, *Pul Eliya* (Cambridge: At the University Press, 1961), ch. 1; Norman E. Whitten, Jr. and Dorothea S. Whitten, "Social Strategies and Social Relationships," *Annual Review of Anthropology,* vol. 1 (1972): 247–270.

14. George Peter Murdock, "Anthropology's Mythology," *Proceedings of the Royal Anthropological Institute of Great Britain and Ireland for 1971:* 17–24.

15. Herskovits, *Myth of the Negro Past;* John F. Szwed, "The American Anthropological Dilemma: The Politics of Afro-American Culture," in Dell Hymes, ed., *Reinventing Anthropology* (New York: Pantheon Books, 1972).

16. For the scope of hologeistic research see James J. O'Leary, "A Preliminary Bibliography of Cross-Cultural Studies," *Behavior Science Notes,* vol. 4 (1969): 95–115, also the supplements in vol. 6 (1971): 191–203 and vol. 8 (1973): 123–134; Raoul Naroll, "What Have We Learned from Cross-Cultural Surveys?" *American Anthropologist,* vol. 72 (1970): 1227–1288.

17. Jules Henry, *Culture Against Man* (New York: Random House, 1963); Oscar Lewis, "Some of My Best Friends Are Peasants," *Human Organization,* vol. 19 (1960–1961): 179–180.

18. Melville J. Herskovits, "Tender- and Tough-Minded Anthropology and the Study of Values in Culture," *Southwestern Journal of Anthropology,* vol. 7 (1951): 22–31; Melville J. Herskovits, "Some Further Comments on Cultural Relativism," *American Anthropologist,* vol. 60 (1958): 266–273.

19. Melville J. Herskovits, *The Economic Life of Primitive Peoples* (New York: Alfred A. Knopf, 1940); George Dalton, "Theoretical Issues in Economic Anthropology," *Current Anthropology,* vol. 10 (1969): 63–102; Scott Cook, "The Obsolete 'Anti-Market' Mentality: A Critique of the Substantive Approach to Economic Anthropology," *American Anthropologist,* vol. 68 (1966): 323–345; Scott Cook, "Economic Anthropol-

ogy," in John J. Honigmann, ed., *Handbook of Social and Cultural Anthropology* (Chicago: Rand McNally and Co., 1973).

20. Conrad Arensberg, "Culture as Behavior: Structure and Emergence," *Annual Review of Anthropology*, vol. 1 (1972): 1–26, p. 1; Dell Hymes "The Uses of Anthropology: Critical, Political, Personal," in Hymes, *Reinventing Anthropology*.

21. For some primary sources see: E. E. Evans-Pritchard, *The Nuer* (Oxford: Clarendon Press, 1940), especially pp. 262ff; Evans-Pritchard, *Social Anthropology*, chs. 1 and 6; Meyer Fortes, "Analysis and Description in Social Anthropology" [orig. 1953], in Meyer Fortes, *Time and Social Structure and Other Essays* (London School of Economics, Monographs on Social Anthropology, no. 40, 1970); Meyer Fortes, *Social Anthropology at Cambridge Since 1900* (Cambridge: At the University Press, 1953); Meyer Fortes, "Social Anthropology," in A. E. Heath, ed., *Scientific Thought in the Twentieth Century* (London: Watts and Co., 1951); Firth, *Elements of Social Organization*, chs. 1 and 2. *Research in Social Anthropology*, written by a committee of the Social Science Research Council (London: Heinemann, 1968) describes recent trends, interests, and resources. For the characteristics of 142 social anthropologists see E. and S. Ardener, "A Directory Study of Social Anthropologists," *British Journal of Sociology*, vol. 16 (1965): 295–314.

22. S. N. Eisenstadt, "Anthropological Studies of Complex Societies," *Current Anthropology*, vol. 2 (1961): 201–222, pp. 201–203.

23. Max Gluckman, *Analysis of a Social Situation in Modern Zululand* (The Rhodes-Livingstone Papers, no. 28, 1958), p. 57.

24. Godfrey and Monica Wilson, *Analysis of Social Change* (Cambridge: At the University Press, 1945), pp. 45–47, 49–50.

25. Max Gluckman, "Obituary: Godfrey Baldwin Wilson," *The Rhodes-Livingstone Journal*, vol. 1 (1944): 1–3.

26. Leach, *Pul Eliya*, ch. 8; Edmund R. Leach, *Political Systems of Highland Burma* [orig. 1954] (New ed.; Boston: Beacon Press, 1965), pp. ix–xv, 285. The roman-numbered pages were written for the 1965 reprint, but the "Conclusion" contains a closely similar critique.

27. Raymond Firth, *Human Types* [orig. 1938] (Mentor ed.; New York: New American Library, 1958), ch. 2; Raymond Firth, "Structural and Moral Changes Produced in Modern Society by Scientific and Technological Advances" [orig. 1948], in Raymond Firth, *Essays on Social Organization and Values* (London: Athlone Press, 1964), ch. 7.

28. See the following by Raymond Firth: *Elements of Social Organization*, p. 35; "Social Organization and Social Change" [orig. 1954], and "Some Principles of Social Organization" [orig. 1955], both in Firth, *Essays on Social Organization*.

29. Consult the following by Fredrik Barth: "Introduction," in Fredrik Barth, ed., *The Role of the Entrepreneur in Social Change in Northern Norway* (Acta Universitatis Bergensis, series Humanorum Litterarum; Abok for Universitetit i Bergen, Humanistik Serie, no. 3, 1963); "Anthropological Models and Social Reality," *Proceedings of the Royal Society of London*, Series B, vol. 165 (1965): 20–34; *Models of Social Organization*; and "Study of Social Change."

30. Max Gluckman, "Introduction," in Max Gluckman, *Order and Rebellion in Tribal Africa* (London: Cohen and West, 1963); Gluckman, *Analysis of a Social Situation*, pp. 46ff: Max Gluckman, "The State of Anthropology," *Times Literary Supplement*, August 3, 1973: 905.

31. Max Gluckman, "State of Anthropology."

32. See the following by E. E. Evans-Pritchard: "Introduction," in Robert Hertz, *Death and the Right Hand*, trans. Rodney Needham and Claudia Needham (Glencoe, Ill.: Free Press, 1960); "Social Anthropology: Past and Present" [orig. 1950], in Evans-Pritchard, *Social Anthropology and*

Other Essays, pp. 144–148; and *Social Anthropology,* pp. 57–62. Also, Edmund R. Leach, "Ourselves and Others," *Times Literary Supplement,* July 6, 1973: 771–772.

33. Ralph Piddington, *An Introduction to Social Anthropology* (2 vols. Edinburgh: Oliver and Boyd, 1950, 1957), vol. 1, pp. 14–17 and ch. 6.

34. Melford Spiro, "Social Systems, Personality, and Functional Analysis," in Bert Kaplan, ed., *Studying Personality Cross-Culturally* (Evanston, Ill.: Row, Peterson and Co., 1961); Melford Spiro, *Burmese Supernaturalism* (Englewood Cliffs, N.J., Prentice-Hall, 1967), pp. 65–66.

35. John W. Bennett and Melvin Tumin, *Social Life: Structure and Function* (New York: Alfred A. Knopf, 1948), ch. 4; Walter Goldschmidt, *Comparative Functionalism* (Berkeley: University of California Press, 1966).

36. Francis A. Cancian, "Varieties of Functional Analysis," in *International Encyclopedia of the Social Sciences* (1968), vol. 6; Paul W. Collins and Andrew P. Vayda, "Functional Analysis and its Aims," *The Australian and New Zealand Journal of Sociology,* vol. 5 (1969): 153–156; Paul W. Collins, "Functional Analyses in the Symposium 'Man, Culture, and Animals,'" in Anthony Leeds and Andrew P. Vayda, eds., *Man, Culture, and Animals.* (American Association for the Advancement of Science, Publication No. 78, 1965); Roy A. Rappaport, *Pigs for the Ancestors* (New Haven: Yale University Press, 1967), chs. 1 and 7; Alexander Alland, Jr., *Evolution and Human Behavior* (Garden City, N.Y.: Natural History Press, 1967), pp. 218–219.

37. Goldschmidt, *Comparative Functionalism.* For his commitment to policy research, see his statement in the *Newsletter of the American Anthropological Association,* vol. 15, no. 6 (1974), pp. 21–22.

38. Cyril S. Belshaw, *The Conditions of Social Performance* (New York: Schocken Books, 1970).

39. George C. Homans and David M. Schneider, *Marriage and Final Causes* (Glencoe, Ill.: Free Press, 1955), pp. 15–18; J. C. Jarvie, *The Revolution in Anthropology* (London: Routledge and Kegan Paul, 1964), pp. 197, 222–223; Clifford Geertz, "Ritual and Social Change: A Javanese Example," *American Anthropologist,* vol. 59 (1957): 32–54; J. C. Clarke, "On the Unity and Diversity of Cultures," *American Anthropologist,* vol. 72 (1970): 545–554; Dorothy Lee, "Are Basic Needs Universal," [orig. 1948], in Dorothy Lee, *Freedom and Culture* (Englewood Cliffs, N.J.: Prentice-Hall, 1959); T. O. Beidelman, "Utani: Some Kaguru Notions of Death, Sexuality and Affinity," *Southwestern Journal of Anthropology,* vol. 22 (1966): 354–380, pp. 354–356; Robert Briffault, *Sin and Sex* (London: Allen and Unwin, 1931), pp. 144–145, 162; E. E. Evans-Pritchard, *Theories of Primitive Religion* (Oxford: Clarendon Press, 1965), p. 119; E. E. Evans-Pritchard, "Religion and the Anthropologists," in Evans-Pritchard, *Social Anthropology and Other Essays,* p. 167; Robert F. Murphy, *The Dialectics of Social Life* (New York: Basic Books, 1971), pp. 58ff.; Clifford Geertz, "Ideology as a Cultural System," in David E. Apter, ed., *Ideology and Discontent* (New York: Free Press, 1964), pp. 55–56.

40. The first section draws on several writers whose names will come up later in connection with their specific theoretical concepts. Above all I have been guided by Alland's formulation of evolutionary theory, though in this introductory section, not applying evolution to biocultural systems as he does, but only to culture. See the following by Alexander Alland, Jr.: *Evolution and Human Behavior* (Garden City, N.Y.: Natural History Press, 1967), chs. 7–10; *Adaptation in Cultural Evolution* (New York: Columbia University Press, 1970), chs. 2–3; and with Bonnie McCay, "The Concept of Adaptation in Biological and Cultural Anthropology," in John J. Honigmann, ed., *Handbook of Social and Cultural Anthropology* (Chicago: Rand McNally and Co., 1973).

41. Alland, *Evolution and Human Behavior,* pp. 213–215.

42. Robert L. Carneiro, "The Four Faces of Evolution: Unilinear, Universal, Multilinear, and Differential," in Honigmann, *Handbook of Social and Cultural Anthropology*, p. 90.

43. Robert L. Carneiro, "Scale Analysis, Evolutionary Sequences, and the Rating of Cultures," in Raoul Naroll and Ronald Cohen, ed., *A Handbook of Method in Cultural Anthropology* (Garden City, N.Y.: Natural History Press, 1970); George P. Murdock and Caterina Provost, "Measurement of Cultural Complexity," *Ethnology*, vol. 12 (1973): 379–392, pp. 387, 392.

44. See the following works by V. Gordon Childe: *Man Makes Himself* [orig. 1936] (Mentor Books ed.; New York: New American Library, 1951); *Progress and Archaeology* (London: Watts and Co., 1944); *Magic, Craftsmanship and Science* (Liverpool: University of Liverpool Press, 1949); and *Social Evolution* (London: Watts and Co., 1951). For a biographical review, see Irving Rouse, "Vere Gordon Childe," *American Antiquity*, vol. 24 (1958–1959): 82–84.

45. I have drawn on the following works by Leslie A. White: "Energy and the Evolution of Culture," in Leslie A. White, *The Science of Culture* (New York: Farrar Strauss and Cudahy Co., 1949); *The Evolution of Culture* (New York: McGraw-Hill Book Co., 1959), esp. chs. 1–3; and "Nations as Sociocultural Systems," *Ingenor*, no. 5 (1968): 5–18. In "The Energy Theory Concept of Development," in K. M. Kapadia, ed., *The Ghurye Felicitation Volume* (Bombay: Popular Book Depot, 1954), White gives a short history of the energy theory. See the biographical appreciation by Harry Elmer Barnes, "Foreword: My Personal Friendship for Leslie White," in Gertrude E. Dole and Robert L. Carneiro, eds., *Essays in the Science of Culture* (New York: Thomas Y. Crowell Co., 1960).

46. Betty J. Meggers, "The Law of Cultural Evolution as a Practical Research Tool," in Dole and Carneiro. *Science of Culture*.

47. For the parallels in these regions, see Steward's "Development of Complex Societies." I have also consulted the following by Julian H. Steward: "Multilinear Evolution: Evolution and Process," "The Concept and Method of Cultural Ecology," "Levels of Sociocultural Integration: An Operational Concept," all in Julian H. Steward, *Theory of Culture Change* (Urbana: University of Illinois Press, 1955); "Cultural Evolution," *Scientific American*, vol. 194 (1956): 69–80; "Introduction" and "Summary and Conclusions" in Julian Steward, et al., *The People of Puerto Rico* (Urbana: University of Illinois Press, 1956); "Evolutionary Principles and Social Types," in Sol Tax, ed., *Evolution after Darwin*, Volume 2, *The Evolution of Man* (Chicago: University of Chicago Press, 1960). For biography, see Robert A. Manners, "Julian Haynes Steward 1902–1972," *American Anthropologist*, vol. 75 (1972): 897–903.

48. A. L. Kroeber, *Style and Civilizations* (Paperbound ed.; Berkeley: University of California Press, 1963), pp. 36, 102; A. L. Kroeber, *A Roster of Civilizations and Culture* (Viking Fund Publications in Anthropology, no. 33, 1962), p. 9.

49. Elman R. Service, *Cultural Evolutionism* (New York: Holt, Rinehart and Winston, 1971); Elman R. Service, *Primitive Social Organization* (New York: Random House, 1962).

50. Alland, *Evolution and Human Behavior*; Alland and McCay, *Adaptation in Cultural Evolution*. For measurement of adaptation see Alland and McCay, "Concept of Adaptation," p. 151.

51. Yehudi A. Cohen, "Culture as Adaptation," in Yehudi A. Cohen, ed., *Man in Adaptation: The Cultural Present* (Chicago: Aldine Publishing Co., 1968).

52. Donald L. Hardesty, "The Human Ecological Niche," *American Anthropologist*, vol. 74 (1972): 458–466, p. 464.

53. George Peter Murdock, "The Science of Human Learning, Society, Culture, and Personality" [orig. 1949], in George Peter Murdock, *Culture and*

Society (Pittsburgh: University of Pittsburgh Press, 1965), pp. 4–6.

54. A. Irving Hallowell, "Personality, Culture, and Society in Behavioral Evolution," in Sigmund Koch, ed., *Psychology: A Study of a Science,* Volume 6, *Investigations of Man as Socius: Their Place in Psychology and Social Sciences* (New York: Mc-Graw-Hill Book Co., 1963); see also Clifford Geertz, "The Growth of Culture and the Evolution of Mind," in J. M. Scher, ed., *Theories of the Mind* (New York: Free Press of Glencoe, 1962).

55. Robin Fox, "The Cultural Animal," *Social Science Information,* vol. 9 (1970): 7–25; Lionel Tiger, *Men in Groups* (London: Nelson, 1970). Covering some of the same ground as the previous references is Lionel Tiger and Robin Fox, *The Imperial Animal* (New York: Dell Publishing Co., 1971).

56. See John Gillin, *The Ways of Men* (New York: Appleton-Century-Crofts, 1948), chs. 12–13; Earl W. Count, "A Note on Incest and the Origins of Human Familialism," *Homo,* vol. 18 (1967): 78–84; Clellan S. Ford and Frank A. Beach, *Patterns of Sexual Behavior* (New York: Harper and Brothers, 1951); A. L. Kroeber, *Anthropology* (New York: Harcourt, Brace and Co., 1948), pp. 58–71; and Clellan Ford, "Some Primitive Societies," in Georgene H. Seward and Robert C. Williamson, eds., *Sex Roles in Changing Society* (New York: Random House, 1970).

57. Margaret Mead cites the danger in *Continuities in Cultural Evolution* (New Haven: Yale University Press, 1964), p. 264.

58. Lionel Tiger, *Men in Groups.*

59. Alexander Alland, book review of *The Imperial Animal* by Lionel Tiger and Robin Fox. *American Anthropologist,* vol. 75 (1973): 1147–1148.

60. Much of this section is based on the following: June Helm, "The Ecological Approach in Anthropology," *The American Journal of Sociology,* vol. 67 (1962): 630–639; J. G. D. Clark, *Prehistoric Europe* (London: Methuen and Co., 1952), ch. 1;

Patty Jo Watson, Steven A. LeBlanc, and Charles L. Redman, *Explanation in Archaeology* (New York: Columbia University Press, 1971), ch. 4; Julian H. Steward, "Cultural Ecology," in *International Encyclopedia of the Social Sciences* (1968), vol. 4; Walter Goldschmidt, "Introduction," in Robert B. Edgerton, *The Individual in Cultural Adaptation* (Berkeley: University of California Press, 1971).

61. For example in Betty J. Meggers, "Environmental Limitation on the Development of Culture," *American Anthropologist,* vol. 56 (1954): 801–824.

62. Evans-Pritchard, *The Nuer,* ch. 2 and pp. 94–104.

63. Laura Thompson, "Steps Toward a Unified Anthropology," *Current Anthropology,* vol. 8 (1967): 67–91; Laura Thompson, *Toward a Science of Mankind* (New York: McGraw-Hill Book Co., 1961).

64. Fredrik Barth, "Ecologic Relationships of Ethnic Groups in Swat, North Pakistan," *American Anthropologist,* vol. 58 (1956): 1079–1089.

65. Robert J. Braidwood and Gordon R. Willey, "Conclusions and Afterthoughts," in Robert J. Braidwood and Gordon R. Willey, *Courses Toward Urban Life* (Viking Fund Publications in Anthropology, no. 32, 1962).

66. Karl A. Wittfogel, *Oriental Despotism* (New Haven: Yale University Press, 1957); Julian H. Steward, "Some Implications of the Symposium," in Julian H. Steward, et al., *Irrigation Civilizations: A Comparative Study* (Washington: Pan American Union, 1955); Julian H. Steward, "Causal Factors and Processes in the Evolution of Pre-farming Societies," in Richard B. Lee and Irven deVore, eds., *Man the Hunter* (Chicago: Aldine Publishing Co., 1968), p. 323. For an earlier statement of the irrigation thesis, especially its role in promoting the Urban Revolution, first published in 1936, see Childe, *Man Makes Himself,* ch. 7.

67. Ester Boserup, *The Conditions of Agricultural Growth* (Chicago: Al-

dine Publishing Co., 1965); M. J. Harner, "Population Pressure and the Social Evolution of Agriculturalists," *Southwestern Journal of Anthropology*, vol. 26 (1970): 67–86.

68. Alland, *Adaptation in Cultural Evolution*, chs. 3–4.

69. John W. M. Whiting, "Effects of Climate on Certain Cultural Practices," in Goodenough, *Explorations in Cultural Anthropology*.

70. John W. Cole and Eric W. Wolf, *The Hidden Frontier* (New York: Academic Press, 1974), pp. 284–285.

71. For alarm expressed within the anthropological community and reassurance provided see Betty Meggers, "Recent Trends in American Ethnology," *American Anthropologist*, vol. 48 (1946): 176–214; Morris E. Opler, "A Recent Trend in the Misrepresentation of the Work of American Ethnologists," *American Anthropologist*, vol. 48 (1946): 669–671.

72. Abram Kardiner, "Psychodynamics and the Social Sciences," in S. Stansfeld Sargent and Marian W. Smith, eds., *Culture and Personality* (New York: Viking Fund, 1949); Abram Kardiner, *The Psychological Frontiers of Society* (New York: Columbia University Press, 1945); Abram Kardiner and Edward Preble, *They Studied Man* (Cleveland: World Publishing Co., 1961), pp. 244–253.

73. Erich Fromm, "Psychoanalytic Characterology and Its Application to the Understanding of Culture," in Sargent and Smith, *Culture and Personality;* Erich Fromm, *Psychoanalysis and Religion* (New Haven: Yale University Press, 1950); Erich Fromm, *Beyond the Chains of Illusion* (New York: Pocket Books, 1963); Erich Fromm and Michael Maccoby, *Social Character in a Mexican Village* (Englewood Cliffs, N.J.: Prentice-Hall, 1970).

74. Clyde Kluckhohn and Henry A. Murray, "Personality Formation: The Determinants," in Clyde Kluckhohn, Henry A. Murray, and David M. Schneider, eds., *Personality in Nature, Society, and Culture* (2nd ed.; New York: Alfred A. Knopf, 1953), pp. 53–54.

75. See the following by Margaret Mead: "National Character," in A. L. Kroeber, ed., *Anthropology Today* (Chicago: University of Chicago Press, 1953); "The Swaddling Hypothesis: Its Reception," *American Anthropologist*, vol. 56 (1954): 395–409; and "Theoretical Setting–1954," in Margaret Mead and Martha Wolfenstein, eds., *Childhood in Contemporary Cultures* (Chicago: University of Chicago Press, 1955). Also see Ruth Benedict, "Child Rearing in Certain European Countries," *American Journal of Orthopsychiatry*, vol. 19 (1949): 342–350.

76. John Dollard, "Yale's Institute of Human Relations: What Was It?" *Ventures, Magazine of the Yale Graduate School*, vol. 3 (1964): 32–40; George P. Murdock, "Fundamental Characteristics of Culture" [orig. 1940], pp. 83–84, and George P. Murdock, "The Common Denominator of Cultures" [orig. 1945], both in Murdock, *Culture and Society*. See also Neal E. Miller and John Dollard, *Social Learning and Imitation* (New Haven, Yale University Press, 1941), chs. 1–4, 16; and John Gillin, *The Ways of Men* (New York: Appleton-Century-Crofts, 1948), ch. 11–15.

77. Harold Orlansky, "Infant Care and Personality," *Psychological Bulletin*, vol. 46 (1949): 1–48; Alfred R. Lindesmith and Anselm L. Strauss, "A Critique of Culture-Personality Writings," *American Sociological Review*, vol. 15 (1950): 587–600.

78. Melford E. Spiro, "An Overview and a Suggested Reorientation," in Francis L. K. Hsu, ed., *Psychological Anthropology* (new ed.; Cambridge, Mass.: Schenkman Publishing Co., 1972).

79. Psychological dynamics are used in the explanation tested in John W. M. Whiting, Richard Kluckhohn, and Albert Anthony, "The Function of Male Initiation Ceremonies at Puberty," in E. Maccoby, T. M. Newcomb, and E. L. Hartley, eds., *Readings in Social Psychology* (New York: Henry Holt and Co., 1958); social needs are the independent variables in Frank W. Young, "The Function

of Male Initiation Ceremonies: A Cross-Cultural Test of an Alternative Hypothesis," *American Journal of Sociology,* vol. 67 (1961–1962): 379–396.

80. As is demonstrated for witchcraft in Dennison Nash, "A Convergence of Psychological and Sociological Explanations of Witchcraft," *Current Anthropology,* vol. 14 (1973): 545–546.

81. John W. M. Whiting and Irvin L. Child, *Child Training and Personality* (New Haven: Yale University Press, 1953); Herbert Barry III, Irvin L. Child, and Margaret K. Bacon, "Relation of Child Training to Subsistence Economy," *American Anthropologist,* vol. 61 (1959): 51–63; Beatrice Whiting, "Introduction," in Beatrice B. Whiting, ed., *Six Cultures* (New York: John Wiley and Sons, 1963), p. 5; Charles Harrington and John W. M. Whiting, "Socialization Process and Personality," in Hsu, *Psychological Anthropology,* pp. 471–472.

82. Robert A. LeVine, *Culture, Behavior, and Personality* (Chicago: Aldine Publishing Co., 1973), ch. 7; see also Jerome H. Barkow, "Darwinian Psychological Anthropology: A Biosocial Approach," *Current Anthropology* vol. 14 (1973): 373–388.

83. Anthony F. C. Wallace, *Culture and Personality* (2nd ed.; New York: Random House, 1970), ch. 3.

84. Alexander H. Leighton, *My Name is Legion* (New York: Basic Books, 1959); Richard Jessor, et al., *Society, Personality, and Deviant Behavior* (New York: Holt, Rinehart and Winston, 1968), where Graves is the anthropologist; Anthony F. C. Wallace, "Culture Change and Mental Illness," in Wallace, *Culture and Personality,* ch. 6; Robert B. Edgerton, "On the 'Recognition' of Mental Illness," in Stanley C. Plog and Robert B. Edgerton, eds., *Changing Perspectives in Mental Illness* (New York: Holt, Rinehart and Winston, 1969).

85. Anthony F. C. Wallace, "Mental Illness, Biology, and Culture," in Hsu, *Psychological Anthropology.* Others who followed his psychobiological ap-proach include Edward F. Foulks, *The Arctic Hysterias* (Anthropological Studies, no. 10, 1972); Ralph Bolton, "Aggression and Hypoglycemia among the Qolla: A Study in Psychobiological Anthropology," *Ethnology,* vol. 12 (1973): 227–258.

86. Adolf E. Jensen, *Myth and Cult among Primitive Peoples* [orig. 1951], trans. Marianna Tax Choldin and Wolfgang Weissleder (Chicago: University of Chicago Press, 1963); Burghard Freudenfeld, ed., *Völkerkunde* (Munich: Verlag C. H. Beck, 1959); "A CA* Book Review: *Myth and Cult Among Primitive Peoples* by Adolf E. Jensen," *Current Anthropology* vol. 6 (1965): 199–215. Richard Mohr, "Wertungen und Normen im Bereiche des Geschlechtslichen," in J. Haekel, A. Hohenwart-Gerlachstein, and A. Slawik, eds., *Die Wiener Schule der Völkerkunde* (Vienna: F. Berger, 1956).

87. I am following Vittorio Lanternari's criticism directed against Adolf Jensen's book in *Current Anthropology,* vol. 6 (1965): 205–206.

88. My account of recent historical materialism is based largely on O. Kuusinen, ed., *Fundamentals of Marxism-Leninism,* trans. Clemens Dutt (Moscow: Foreign Languages Publishing House, 1961), part 2; V. Afanasyev, *Marxist Philosophy,* trans. L. Lempert (Moscow: Foreign Languages Publishing House, n. d.); and I. S. Korolev, "Some Questions of Ethno-Psychological Studies Abroad," *Soviet Anthropology and Archaeology,* vol. 5, no. 2 (1966): 3–10. I have also consulted papers presented by the Soviet Russian social scientists at the Seventh International Congress of the Anthropological and Ethnological Sciences, held in 1964, and the Sixth World Congress of Sociology of 1966. See also Bernhard J. Stern, "Some Aspects of Historical Materialism," in Roy Wood Sellars et al., *Philosophy for the Future* (New York: Macmillan Co., 1949); Stephen P. Dunn et al., "Some Preliminary Questions in International Anthropology," *Sovetskaia etnografia,* no. 6 (1965): 76–91 (mimeographed).

89. The remainder of the paragraph is based on I. A. Kryvelev, "On Gallus's Biofunctional Theory of Religion," *Current Anthropology*, vol. 15 (1974): 92–95.

90. George Plekhanov, "The Materialist Conception of History" [orig. 1897], trans. Anonymous, in George Plekhanov, *Essays in Historical Materialism* (New York: International Publishers, 1940).

91. Jean-Paul Sartre, *Search for a Method*, trans. Hazel E. Barnes (Vintage Books ed.; New York: Random House, 1968), p. 179.

92. S. A. Tokarev, "The Problem of Totemism as Seen by Soviet Scholars," *Current Anthropology*, vol. 7 (1966): 185–188.

93. Leslie A. White, "Ethnological Theory," in Sellars et al., *Philosophy for the Future*, pp. 373–375.

94. Marvin Harris, "Monistic Determinism: Anti-Service," *Southwestern Journal of Anthropology*, vol. 25 (1969): 198–206; Harris, *Rise of Anthropological Theory*, pp. 1–7, 658–660.

95. Harris, *Nature of Cultural Things;* Harris, *Rise of Anthropological Theory*, pp. 575–576.

96. Eliot D. Chapple and Carleton S. Coon, *Principles of Anthropology* (New York: Henry Holt and Co., 1942). Other sources are: Carleton S. Coon, *A Reader in General Anthropology* (New York: Henry Holt and Co., 1948); Eliot D. Chapple, *Measuring Human Relations: An Introduction to the Study of the Interaction of Individuals* (Genetic Psychology Monographs, vol. 22, 1940); and Eliot D. Chapple, *Culture and Biological Man* (New York: Holt, Rinehart and Winston, 1970). For Chapple's synopsis of the latter book, see *Current Anthropology*, vol. 15 (1974): 53–57. Arensberg, "Culture as Behavior," is a recent endorsement of the theory.

97. See F. L. W. Richardson, Jr., who did industrial research, and with James Batal wrote the chapter on "The Near East" in Ralph Linton, ed., *Most of the World* (New York: Columbia University Press, 1949).

98. The reference is to Susanne K. Langer, cited in Clifford Geertz, "Religion as a Cultural System," in Clifford Geertz, *The Interpretation of Culture* (New York: Basic Books, 1973), p. 89.

99. Robert Redfield, "Relations of Anthropology to the Social Sciences and to the Humanities," in Kroeber, *Anthropology Today*, pp. 734–735.

100. Based on the following works by David M. Schneider: *American Kinship: A Cultural Account* (Englewood Cliffs, N.J.: Prentice-Hall, 1968), ch. 1; "What is Kinship All About?" in Priscilla Reining, ed., *Kinship Studies in the Morgan Centennial Year* (Washington, D.C.: Anthropological Society of Washington, 1972), pp. 37–40; and "Kinship, Nationality and Religion in American Culture: Toward a Definition of Kinship," in Robert F. Spencer, ed., *Forms of Symbolic Action* (Proceedings of the 1969 Annual Spring Meeting of the American Ethnological Society, 1969). See also David M. Schneider and Raymond T. Smith, *Class Differences and Sex Roles in American Kinship and Family Structure* (Englewood Cliffs: Prentice-Hall, 1973), ch. 1.

101. Claude Lévi-Strauss, "The Concept of Primitiveness," in Lee and deVore, *Man the Hunter*, p. 350.

102. Schneider and Smith, *Class Differences and Sex Roles*, passim.

103. I have used the following publications of Clifford Geertz: "Religious Belief and Economic Behavior in a Central Javanese Town: Some Preliminary Considerations," *Economic Development and Cultural Change*, vol. 4 (1956): 134–158; "Thick Description: Toward an Interpretative Theory of Culture," in Geertz, *Interpretation of Culture;* "Religion as a Cultural System"; "Ideology as a Cultural System"; "The Impact of the Concept of Culture on the Concept of Man," in John R. Platt, ed., *New Views of the Nature of Man* (Chicago: University of Chicago Press, 1965); "Ethos, World-View and the Analysis of Sacred Symbols," *Antioch Review*, vol. 17 (1957): 421–437; "Deep Play:

Notes on the Balinese Cockfight," *Daedalus*, vol. 101, no. 1 (1972): 1–37; and "Ritual and Social Change."

104. Mary Douglas, *Natural Symbols* (London: Barrie and Rockliff, Cresset Press, 1970).

105. I have garnered the theoretical concepts behind Lévi-Strauss's structuralism mainly from his following works: "Introduction: History and Anthropology" [orig. 1949], in his *Structural Anthropology*, trans. Claire Jacobson and Brooke Grundfest Schoepf (New York: Basic Books, 1963); *The Elementary Structures of Kinship* [orig. 1949], trans. James Harle Bell, John Richard von Sturmer, and Rodney Needham, who also served as editor (Boston: Beacon Press, 1969), pp. xxiv, 4, 42, 57, 84–85; "The Future of Kinship Studies," *Proceedings of the Royal Anthropological Institute of Great Britain and Ireland for 1965*: 13–22; *The Savage Mind*, trans. Anonymous (Chicago: University of Chicago Press, 1966), ch. 1; *The Scope of Anthropology*, trans. Sherry Ortner Paul and Robert A. Paul (New York: Humanities Press, 1967); and "Overture," in his *The Raw and the Cooked*, trans. John Weightman and Doreen Weightman (Torchbooks ed.; New York: Harper & Row, 1969). I have found Edmund Leach, *Lévi-Strauss* (London: Fontana/Collins, 1970), chs. 2–5 helpful, as well as James A. Boon, *From Symbolism to Structuralism* (Oxford: Blackwell, 1972), chs. 3–4.

106. Roland Barthes, "The Structuralist Activity," trans. Richard Howard, in Richard T. DeGeorge and Fernande M. DeGeorge, eds., *The Structuralists from Marx to Lévi-Strauss* (Anchor Books ed.; Garden City, N.Y.: Doubleday and Co., 1972), p. 151.

107. Harold W. Scheffler, "Structuralism in Anthropology," in Jacques Ehrmann, ed., *Structuralism* (Anchor Books ed.; Garden City, N.Y.: Doubleday and Co., 1970), pp. 56–57.

108. What follows is based on Leach, *Lévi-Strauss*, ch. 1; Claude Lévi-Strauss, *Tristes tropiques*, trans. John Weightman and Doreen Weightman (New York: Atheneum, 1974), esp. p. 59; Lévi-Strauss, *Scope of Anthropology*, pp. 16–17; E. Michael Mendelson, "Some Present Trends of Social Anthropology in France," *The British Journal of Sociology*, vol. 9 (1958): 251–270; and Bob Scholte, "Epistemic Paradigms: Some Problems in Crosscultural Research on Social Anthropological History and Theory," *American Anthropologist*, vol. 68 (1966): 1192–1201.

109. Claude Lévi-Strauss, "Structural Analysis in Linguistics and in Anthropology," in Lévi-Strauss, *Structural Anthropology*.

110. Claude Lévi-Strauss, "The Structural Study of Myth," [orig. 1955], in Lévi-Strauss, *Structural Anthropology*.

111. Claude Lévi-Strauss, "Split Representation in the Art of Asia and America" [orig. 1944–1945], and Claude Lévi-Strauss, "Concept of Kinship Systems" [orig. 1945], both in Lévi-Strauss, *Structural Anthropology*.

112. Claude Lévi-Strauss, *Totemism*, trans. Rodney Needham (Boston: Beacon Press, 1963); Lévi-Strauss, *Savage Mind*, pp. 97–116. See also A. R. Radcliffe-Brown, "The Comparative Method in Social Anthropology," in A. R. Radcliffe-Brown, *Method in Social Anthropology* (Chicago: University of Chicago Press, 1958).

113. Lévi-Strauss, *Savage Mind*, ch. 4.

114. Claude Lévi-Strauss, "Story of Asdiwal," trans. Nicholas Mann, in Edmund Leach, ed., *Structural Study of Myth and Totemism* (London: Tavistock Publications, 1967).

115. C. K. Ogden, *Opposition* (Bloomington: Indiana University Press, 1967).

116. What follows draws from E. A. Hammel, "Introduction," Wallace L. Chafe, "Meaning in Language," Anthony F. C. Wallace, "The Problem of the Psychological Validity of Componential Analyses," all in E. A.

Hammel, ed., *Formal Semantic Analysis* (special publication of the *American Anthropologist,* vol. 67, no. 5, part 2, 1965); Anthony F. C. Wallace and John Atkins, "The Meaning of Kinship Terms," *American Anthropologist,* vol. 62 (1960): 54–80; Ward Goodenough, "Componential Analysis," in Spradley, *Culture and Cognition;* Brent Berlin, Dennis E. Breedlove, and Peter H. Raven, "Covert Categories and Folk Taxonomies," *American Anthropologist,* vol. 70 (1968): 290–299; Benjamin N. Colby, "Ethnographic Semantics: A Preliminary Survey," *Current Anthropology,* vol. 7 (1966): 3–32, and Paul Kay's comments to that paper, pp. 20–23; and Cecil H. Brown, "Psychological, Semantic, and Structural Aspects of American English Kinship Terms," *American Ethnologist,* vol. 1 (1974): 415–436.

117. For example, Richard Thurnwald, *Banaro Society* (Memoirs of the American Anthropological Association, vol. 3, 1916), pp. 342ff.; and Kingsley Davis and W. L. Warner, "Structural Analysis of Kinship," *American Anthropologist,* vol. 39 (1937): 291–313.

118. Charles O. Frake, "The Ethnographic Study of Cognitive Systems," in *Anthropology and Human Behavior* (Washington, D.C.: Anthropological Society of Washington, 1962); Stephen A. Tyler, "Introduction," in Stephen A. Tyler, ed., *Cognitive Anthropology* (New York: Holt, Rinehart and Winston, 1969).

119. Ward H. Goodenough, "Componential Analysis and the Study of Meaning," *Language,* vol. 32 (1956): 195–216; Wallace and Atkins, "Meaning of Kinship Terms."

120. From A. Kimball Romney and Roy G. D'Andrade, "Cognitive Aspects of American Kin Terms," in A. Kimball Romney and Roy G. D'Andrade, eds., *Transcultural Studies in Cognition* (special publication of the *American Anthropologist,* vol. 66, no. 3, part 2, 1964), p. 147. I have adopted but modified the representation prepared by Brown in "Psychological, Semantic, and Structural."

121. Wallace, *Culture and Personality,* p. 89.

122. Robbins Burling, "Cognition and Componential Analysis: God's Truth or Hocus-Pocus?" *American Anthropologist,* vol. 66 (1964): 20–28.

123. Brown, "Psychological, Semantic, and Structural," pp. 420, 423–424.

124. Naomi Quinn, "Getting Inside Our Informants' Heads. Review of William H. Geohegan, *Natural Information Processing Rules: Formal Theory and Applications to Ethnography,*" *Reviews in Anthropology,* vol. 1 (1974): 244–252. See also Naomi Quinn's review of decision theory in "Decision Models of Social Structure," *American Ethnologist,* vol. 2 (1975): 19–45.

9

Topics and Issues in Recent Anthropology

Primitive and Ethnic Groups

Many-Stranded Social Relations

From the comprehensive systems of thought and the approaches covered in the last chapter we come to topics of more delimited scope in recent anthropological thought. Among others, we will see how primitivity, cultural relativity, and other long-standing ethnological concepts fared; what happened to the classic problem of kinship terminology opened by Lewis Henry Morgan; and the issues raised in the outburst of self-criticism as anthropology reflected upon its methods and suppositions.

English-language anthropology in the postwar period was conflicted about calling any culture or people "primitive."[1] Constraints on continuing to think with the nearly 300-year-old concept may have been partly due to the disappearance of isolated cultures; but more directly, some anthropologists recoiled from the connotations of simplicity, antiquity, and even inferiority aroused by the idea and the sharp dichotomy it implied between two kinds of societies. For those anthropologists the idea lost the analytical value it once possessed. On the other hand, no one denied that a distinction existed between the traditional cultures of such groups as the Eskimo, African Pygmies, or Australian aborigines and patterns of life currently followed in India, England, or America. From different standpoints, theorists as diverse as Leslie White, Claude Lévi-Strauss, Stanley

---

Notes to this chapter are on page 397.

Diamond, and Mary Douglas insisted on substantial differences between traditional and modern societies.[2] The former, in comparison with modern civilized societies, still preserve a large measure of liberty, equality, and fraternity in their social arrangements; their economic system is communalistic; they tend to regard the self as an undifferentiated, relatively passive element in the natural environment; and in communication they tend to use symbolic codes based on concrete, sensory images. British social anthropologists pointed to the tight integration of the various aspects of social life still to be encountered in small-scale societies, more so than seen in large-scale civilizations.[3] In the former, different aspects of behavior overlap as they are carried out in a comparatively small number of social relationships and roles. Almost any given relationship combines manifold types of action as each party in interaction plays multiplex rather than segmented roles. The metaphor of a many-stranded rope served nicely to describe such relationships.

Perhaps another word, one lacking the undesirable connotations of "primitive," could be found to designate the groups and cultures around which anthropological thought resolved so steadily.[4] "Precapitalist" exuded too many ideological implications to be accepted outside of Communist countries. Robert Redfield proposed calling them "folk" societies, meaning groups small enough to allow people to know one another personally, isolated from the wider society, marked by considerable similarity in what people do and think, and strongly attached to traditional ways. Opposite the folk society, on a continuum of types, stands urban society with opposite features, and between them Redfield placed peasant society. Lacking the strong degree of isolation typical of folk systems, peasants exist in symbiosis with urban economic systems.

Many of the same features identified by Redfield with folk societies had already been ascribed to small-scale communities in a general theory of change devised by Godfrey and Monica Wilson and by other, earlier writers. Compared to the large-scale communities found in the civilized world, those small in scale are less differentiated; they possess less control over the material environment; they are more magical, meaning bound by the significance traditionally attached to things; they contain less social mobility; and relationships occur primarily between people who know one another well. These elements, like the opposite ones of a large-scale society, are mutually related, and they are correlated with the comparatively large degree of autonomy enjoyed by small-scale communities in relation to the larger society. On the other hand, the individuals or component groups making up the small-scale community enjoy only limited autonomy within the whole, compared to what individuals and groups possess in large-scale societies, where it is the community that loses its autonomy in relation to the larger society where economic and political power are concentrated.

The analytical units, culture and society, themselves came under critical examination. The continuous overlap of traits between cultures and overflow between societies due to diffusion and migration provided grounds for doubting whether discrete social and cultural units had ever actually existed. Ethnologists also questioned the logic of counting societies as equivalent when doing hologeistic research to test general theoretical propositions; should not the fact that such units vary tremendously in size be taken into account in reaching conclusions?[5]

Maintaining Social Boundaries

Since isolated groups don't exist, how do tribal and ethnic groups engulfed in larger societies preserve their identities? The identities of the Hopi Indians, Jews, American blacks, or Pakistani Pathans cannot depend primarily on substantial cultural differences marking them off from other groups in their society; diffusion has produced too high a degree of cultural homogeneity between adjacent and even distant groups to allow cultural discontinuity to function as a boundary marker. Hence cultural variation is continuous rather than discontinuous in the modern world.

Edward Spicer, Fredrik Barth, and Yehudi Cohen found ethnic identities preserved in contemporary society by the use of identity symbols and by the opposition that ethnic groups exert against pressures emanating from surrounding groups.[6] Instead of primarily attending to symbols semantically or syntagmatically as the cognitive anthropologists did, Spicer and Barth approached symbols pragmatically, observing how they are manipulated to signal incorporation or exclusion from groups. A common name, a language different from surrounding languages, and symbols referring to events in a group's past—these they found to be the major symbolic devices used to mark off ethnic or tribal boundaries and thereby to provide a sense of identity. Identity symbols further include overt cultural features, like housing, dress, music, dances, or other discrete elements of life style, as well as covert sentiments; for example, toward the land occupied by a group. Any objective differences between one group and others—the omission of certain acts, such as occur in dietary taboos, as well as the performance of others—can serve to mark off group boundaries. The intensity with which a group affiliates with identity symbols varies with the extent to which members perceive threats to ethnic identity. No organic or necessary relationship exists between the specific symbols signifying identity. As Barth says, they merely cluster statistically, and, depending on various circumstances, a group will from time to time vary in the number of symbolic features it uses or in the intensity with which it holds them.

The opposition and conflict with larger social systems, not surprisingly, frequently resolves around issues perceived as attempts to incorporate the group further into the larger system. Yehudi Cohen traced boundary-maintenance mainly to intergroup pressures, and gives little heed to identity symbols. Boundaries, he holds, result from pressure exerted both within and outside the group. Boundaries exist to the degree that pressures exclude influences from a group, or that passage rituals govern admission to it.

Ethnic boundaries, Barth says, "canalize" social life. They regulate interaction between groups or, conversely, determine degrees of insulation between them. They put constraints on the kinds of roles an individual is allowed to play in society. By virtue of such boundaries, a plural society, comprising several ethnic groups or a number of enclaved tribes, becomes divided into status categories governed by different values. The greater the value differences, the more constraints will be imposed on interethnic interaction, and the stronger will be resistance to diffusion of behavior signaling another ethnic status. Where insulation is not total, individuals in a plural society may sometimes gain advantages by manipulating their social identity, dropping one that is hard to realize successfully and assuming another that promises easier access to desirable goals.

Under conditions of culture change when an ethnic group meets an impinging society, ethnic boundaries may loosen. Members may themselves become agents of change, aiming to incorporate the group into the encompassing society. Or the group may tighten its boundaries, perhaps through adding new symbols to emphasize its distinctive identity. Political action, cult movements, missionizing zeal, occupational differentiation, and educational aspirations are among the means by which ethnic groups and enclaved tribes organize themselves culturally in relation to an impinging society. The form of organization chosen governs the symbols chosen to signal identity. Differential acculturation or biculturation, a process whereby members of an ethnic group become aware of customs practiced in the surrounding society but borrow only traits immediately relevant to their interests, may also protect ethnic identity.[7] According to Fredrik Barth, the security provided by government control in a region can affect boundary maintenance in dependent groups. Where colonial or other regimes subordinate local autonomy, thereby permitting social mobility and intergroup contact, cultural differences between groups will weaken. If ethnicity is to be maintained under such conditions, new boundary-maintaining mechanisms must be devised to regulate external interaction. Where government control is weak, and endemic violence or lack of trust characterizes intergroup relations in a region, then those conditions of themselves limit interaction between groups and preserve cultural differences with which ethnicity flourishes. Under such conditions, since the ethnic group is the primary community on which safety depends, nonconformance to its standards will be interpreted as a threat to the group's security.

Surveying considerable literature convinced an anthropologist and psychologist working together that boundaries between tribal and ethnic groups became firmer and more stable with the appearance within them of centrally controlled political organizations.[8] They regard the emergence of firmly bounded social systems—by which they mean groups in which language, social interaction, mating, and cultural homogeneity coincide— as evolutionary adaptations. Firm boundaries make for greater efficiency in processing information useful for survival, as well as in coordinating group action and administration related to survival. For those reasons, sharply bounded political groups have increased in the world and were able to displace unstable and unclearly demarcated groups. These propositions apply better to relatively independent political systems, such as modern nations, than to politically subordinated ethnic groups and tribes contained within those political systems.

Role Theory[9]

Selecting a Social Identity

In Ralph Linton's classic and widely accepted formulation, a person who adopts a different ethnic identity and assumes new standards changes his status—his position in a pattern of social relationships—and alters his role, the manner of executing the status. An individual's status, according to Linton, embraces the rights and duties bound up with a given social position in a society. Some social statuses are ascribed by virtue of a person's age, sex, skin color, and so on, while others are achieved; for example, through marriage, joining a profession, or acquiring a talent or other condition deemed relevant by the society.

Roles belong to social structure, meaning they are fixed. How then, Siegfried Nadel asked, in 1957, does it happen that the same role varies between individuals, each to some extent pursuing private purposes and following his own perceptions? Nadel's answer almost looks at roles as epiphenomena. A role is a way society has of categorizing actors; but it also serves the persons whom it labels, providing them with a blueprint for carrying out certain purposes through social relationships. Only on the cognitive level, Nadel answers, does a role exist as a total entity. In practice, it is enacted over time, phase by phase, occasion by occasion, attribute by attribute, by individuals who differ and even conflict in the purposes for which they pursue a given role or the meanings by which they interpret it. Cognitively, a role refers to a bundle of attributes demonstrated in dress, forms of address, and other acts when people engage in social relationships. Some attributes are peripheral to the role; variation in the way they are carried out, or even in their absence, does not affect the role being performed. Others are firmly entailed; their variation or omission mars the performance. Finally, some attributes are basic; a change in them means a change in the identity of the role itself.

After having taken a doctorate in psychology and philosophy in Austria, where he was born, Nadel studied anthropology in London and became a member of the British social anthropological community, though he left the British Isles for a position in Australia.[10] His association with Bronislaw Malinowski may have been an important factor enabling him to perceive that, phenomenally, roles consist of variable attributes manifested in diverse circumstances.

Less than a decade later, Ward Goodenough also adopted a phenomenal position in his approach to role theory. In rethinking the concepts of status and role, he added the idea of social identity to the theory.

Following Linton, a person who changes his ethnic identity could be said to secure a new status; according to Nadel, he combines new attributes into a novel role; and according to Goodenough, he assumes a new social identity. Everyone has at his disposal a number of social identities, which may be appropriately assumed in given forms of social interaction. Some identities, such as being an adult, a male, or a female, are very general and relevant to all social interactions. Others are appropriate only in specific situations. A person's rights and duties—or his status—depend on which identity is activated. If John Doe is both my neighbor and my employer, I must decide in which identity he is acting before I know what duties I owe him. In selecting an identity, an individual is constrained by his qualifications (though it is possible to pretend to social identities for which one is unqualified), by the occasion of interaction, and by the identity that the other party in a social relationship assumes. Any identity chosen by one party leaves only a limited number of matching identities available to the other. By matching identities, individuals enter identity relationships.

Goodenough proposes to measure identity relationships in terms of the considerations one identity owes to another: considerations like deference, cordiality, reverence, or display of affection, sexual distance, and emotional independence. Following Goodenough's instructions, an ethnographer would observe what obligations and corresponding rights exist for each identity, noting, for example, whether one must show deference to another by crawling or avoiding direct interaction, by being obliged to maintain social distance by not being seen in the other's company, and so on. By observation the field worker would gain information enabling him to sum up the aggregate of rights and duties holding for a given identity in all the identity relationships where it is selected. Goodenough's experiment with this method of meticulous analytic description confirms what perhaps needed no such vast labor: comparing all identity relationships in a society shows some identities netting fewer duties and more rights than others. In other words, identities differ in possibilities of gratification, in the freedom of choice they allow, and in the extent to which they are apt to cramp personal styles of behavior. Meticulous ethnographic methods, however, are expected with the operational definition of concepts required by a phenomenal approach.

Cultural and Social Integration

The Prevailing Assumption of Order

The idea of cultural integration, taken over by and made central to the anthropologies of A. R. Radcliffe-Brown, Malinowski, and Ruth Benedict, became a major tenet of cultural theory. Anthropologists might doubt whether whole cultures could be objectively characterized by all-pervasive qualities such as Benedict identified in the Southwestern and Great Plains Indian tribes, but they found no reason to reject the idea of interdependence between particular features of culture or social structure. Margaret Mead, after cautioning, in 1937, that not everything in a culture correlates with everything else because no group lives perfectly isolated from all foreign influence, in 1941 referred to cultures in which every detail is interdependent with every other detail.[11] Anthropologists' special contribution, she said, lies in discovering points of interdependence easily overlooked by untrained observers. Interdependence does not preclude contradictions, discrepencies, or inconsistencies existing between patterns of behavior, but when they occur, Mead believes, the discrepencies will themselves be integrated with other patterns. Thus in the United States, adolescent revolt against values upholding a tradition held by parents, while in one sense evidence of a contradiction, is at the same time linked to the deeply held value in American culture placing change and success above adherence to tradition. The integration of customs helps to maintain them, for even a desirable change will be questioned if it threatens to stir up far-reaching, unwelcome modifications in a cultural system. In applying cultural interdependence to research, Mead reverts to relativism: to be correctly understood, every item of behavior in a society must be seen in relation to the culture of which it is a part, and in terms of which it derives whatever value, positive or negative, it possesses for the society.

Following the sociologist William Graham Sumner, George Peter Murdock from a diachronic point of view expected cultural features in a society to become increasingly adjusted to each other with time, as well as more closely adjusted to the geographical environment and to adjacent other societies or their cultures.[12] John Gillin's principle of cultural compatibility also envisions cultural systems being adjusted to the cultural situation, as he called the environing conditions.[13]

Nobody dealt with the concept of cultural integration more analytically than John Gillin, who was for many years connected with the University of North Carolina and later became dean of social science at the University of Pittsburgh. Metaphorically, he describes integration as an ideal state in which all parts of a culture gear smoothly into each other, and describes how tendencies to smooth gearing come about. One way he calls "consistency," that one custom does not interfere with the performance or achievement of others; another is by relatedness, a condition whereby the performance of one custom meaningfully supports the performance of others; and a third way is functional linkage, in which the presence of one custom absolutely requires others to become operative.

The advent of cross-cultural research enabled cultural integration to be demonstrated statistically, and helped to make clear a distinction between two kinds of associations in cultural traits.[14] One results adventitiously through historical processes and can be demonstrated by comparing cultural areas in a continent. The other arises from the nature of society, culture, and personality, and is revealed by hologeistic research employed to test theories. Gillin with his theoretical bent and commitment to interdisciplinary research thought only of the second. Robert Lowie refers to the former in the "shreds and patches" thesis, and Alexander Goldenweiser had it in mind when he wrote on totemism.

The culture element distribution studies undertaken at the University of California demonstrated quantitative differences in trait assemblages between North American culture areas that resulted from accidents of invention, diffusion, and migration, the details of which can sometimes be traced through archeology and other techniques of historical research. Integration of this type lacks the theoretical interest possessed by the type called functional relationships. The latter's source lies in the nature of human personality—demonstrated, for example, between societies by positive correlations between certain modes of childhood discipline and particular concepts of disease—or in the nature of society and culture—leading, for example, to a statistical association between forms of marriage and particular types of kinship nomenclature. Hologeistic research showing correlations between patrilineal descent and patrilocal residence, between animal husbandry and political integration, and so on, never revealed invariant associations. Correlations might be statistically significant, but they never occur in all cultures belonging to a sample. In other words, the interdependencies discovered through cross-cultural research are only tendencies, precisely as Murdock had claimed for integration in particular cultures.

Although anthropologists were quite prepared for some degree of slippage between associations in cross-cultural research, discordances or inconsistencies in particular cultures struck them as puzzling and calling for elucidation. So it was when Clifford Geertz found discontinuity between culture—in his usage, the system of symbols—and social structure in an Indonesian village.[15] He discovered opposing groups using common symbols conflictingly for the purpose of furthering different and incompatible ends. To resolve the discordance, he drew a distinction between two kinds of cultural integration present in society: logical-meaningful, in which symbols cohere at the level of culture, and causal-fuctional, found on the level of social relations where the symbols are used coherently, if segmentally, to promote social cohesion within the segments of the society. Convinced that cultural order exists, Geertz like Margaret Mead found it even in the presence of manifest discrepancies.

Several writers, however, questioned the idea of cultural integration. Elman Service did so on a small scale when he took issue with the almost axiomatic view that a society's set of kin terms constitutes a system.[16] Particular terms in a set, he points out, can change without the whole set being affected. Max Gluckman abandoned the integrational thinking inherent in the theory of his teacher, Radcliffe-Brown, reasoning that because customs and social institutions are only imperfectly adjusted and frequently conflict or contradict each other, they instigate discrepant processes in a field of social interaction. In that way, change is instigated within a social system.[17] Still more comprehensively, Robert Murphy charged the concept of integration with seriously distorting social reality when applied to something as pervasive as the relationship of norms and values to action.[18] Instead of correspondence between the two realms being the rule, he finds chaos. Other anthropologists before him, he points out, had noted incongruence between normative ideals and manifest behavior, but they sought to minimize its significance. They regarded the discrepancy as merely temporary, as evidence of change occurring in the social system; soon norms would catch up with action, and integration would return. More often field workers, guided by what they had come axiomatically to expect, desperately searched for order, ignoring the inconsistencies, contradictions, paradoxes, and flux that their experience revealed. Investigators reduced the randomness they encountered to the integration they assumed must be present. Thereby anthropology falsified reality. Anthropologists are not alone in striving to produce order in the world, Murphy observes; the members of the societies being studied do, too.

Murphy was one of the few members of his discipline who adopted tenets of existential philosophy. In his view, there must always be strain between norm and action, because society and the individuals who comprise it have contradictory requirements. Individuals require order as strongly as society requires flexibility and latitude for improvisation if it is continually to adapt to changing conditions. Order is served by the norms; improvisation and change are achieved through action, which frequently outruns the norms. Only in ritual and etiquette, behaviors of essentially the same type, do norm and action regularly correspond. Sometimes called an "empty form," ritual seals the break between ideal and real when, however briefly, it orchestrates the ideal relationship of people to each other with their actual conduct.

Murphy urges taking a critical, skeptical attitude toward the stability which the mind is prone to construct as it overlooks contradictions in existence. He recommends questioning the obvious truths of culture and science and looking for paradox as much as for complementarity, for ideological opposition as well as for accommodation. By heeding the dissonance underlying the apparent order of society, he promises, we will come across a deeper order, one more faithful to reality.

Of course Murphy recognizes a degree of integration in society, not only in the deeper "order" he hoped to come across but in the relevance values always have for action, even when the two are incongruent. Nevertheless, he overstates his case in insisting so much on the inconsistencies and contradictions besetting social relations. He fails to acknowledge the constraints that norms impose on behavior and the degree to which values manage to preserve order and consistency, not merely on the cognitive level but by limiting behavioral variation. An existential point of view doesn't require denying the degree of consistency found in social life. Nor does existentialism see any point in balancing the search for complementarity and accommodation with equal attention to paradox and contradiction. It regards the order of society, including the tested propositions of science—Murphy's as much as the integrationalists'—as a successful concealment of the void that only a few people dare acknowledge.

Social Integration

Cultural integration is one thing; social integration quite another. Even Murphy probably agreed with Julian Steward and Elman Service who, more explicitly than the philosophers of preceding times, described new forms of social integration, or sociocultural complexity, developing as societies increased their populations and improved their adaptation to the natural environment.[19] Band, tribal, and folk or chiefdomship levels preceded the state level on which, according to Steward, several multifamily folk societies are brought into functional interdependence. Each level of development entails new forms of cooperation, interaction, and increasing formal organization.

African Political Systems, the book edited by Meyer Fortes and E. E. Evans-Pritchard, with which political anthropology began, dealt with social integration synchronically and, as the title indicates, from the standpoint of government.[20] The editors define government as the organization of power through which people are coordinated and social stability maintained. They distinguish three types of political systems, the simplest being coterminous with a group of kinsmen and therefore approximating the bands with which other writers frequently begin their progressive series of types. Most of the book's attention goes to the two other types of political systems, one the centralized state and the other lineage-based. No clear or consistent relationship exists between the size and density of population and either type, at least not in the societies reported on, though the authors believe a limit exists to the number of people that can be coordinated in a society without centralized government. The statelike structure of centralized political systems is also necessary if culturally diverse groups are to be coordinated in a society. Constitutionally speaking, it accomplishes the task of social integration by balancing the power of the center and other interest groups in the society. Lineage-based systems, on the other hand, comprise territorially localized lineages that are coordinated, as it were, through their own counterpoised power. Each of the lineage segments possesses many of the same interests as the others, but they are also opposed in the sense that each segment is a solidary group distinct from the others. Stability of the system depends on equilibrium between opposing loyalties and ties or, as the authors say, on a balance of forces and interests located in the homologous segments of the society.

Despite the number and variety of man-made forces recognized by anthropologists as coordinating people in society, the concept of social integration was rarely employed as axiomatically as the assumption of cultural integration. Perhaps the historical record of ceaseless revolution, civil war, and other dissidences in social life plainly indicated the fragility of social bonds, at least in complex society. Cultural integration exists—if I correctly interpret the anthropological concept—because of the nature of culture; it fluctuates independently of human volition and is not manipulable, whereas theorists implicitly conceived of social integration as consciously sought after and achieved through human ingenuity. The number and variety of forces anthropologically recognized as coordinating people are the means human beings have devised to achieve that purpose, means including—in addition to political systems—associations, networkers, brokers who bridge levels of social structure, patterns of reciprocity, symbolic devices extending from flags to ideologies, as well as less obvious processes. In one such nonobvious process, social integration in small-scale societies, results from the close linkage between the several roles every individual plays—a man in his capacity as household head is both an elder participating in the political affairs of the village, a ritual leader in relations with the ancestors, and an educator transmitting values.[21] The more roles an individual combines, the more he comes into relationships with persons playing complementary roles, and the denser the social interaction of particular persons, which in a large-scale society would be more thinly distributed. Max Gluckman attached importance to another nonobvious source of social cohesion: conflicting loyalties between lineages and other groups.[22] Conflicting loyalties, arising from affinal ties created through lineage or village exogamy, overcome tendencies toward extreme segmentalism and counteract tendencies to social fission. The interests created "abroad" restrain conflict in the wider society. Should conflict break out, people with common interests are led to press for quick settlement lest the conflict spread and spoil relations with affines or partners. Prohibiting people from creating substantial interests afield may decrease conflict of loyalties, but doing so brings about a relatively low state of cohesion in the larger society. Gluckman also pointed out the ability of civil wars and rebellions directed against particular leaders to counter fissive tendencies in centralized societies. They do so by directing attention to the values of the kingship, which the rebels hope to capture, and they encourage the formation of relatively large interest blocks wherein a sense of social cohesion is generated.

Culture Change

Equivalent to Stability

The last chapter revealed considerable, many-faceted recent interest in history and change. Cultural evolutionists, cultural ecologists, psychological anthropologists, and persons pursuing other approaches acknowledged the importance of history for rounding out cultural understanding and accepted change as inevitable. They even saw change as indispensable if a social or cultural system is to maintain equilibrium in a constantly shifting environment and therefore, paradoxically, equivalent to stability.[23] However, most writers studying change meant something considerably more restricted or more dramatic by change when, as they were prone to do, they traced it back to needs, strain, conflict, contradiction, radical opposition, or some other maladjustment in the social system. They had drastic, revolutionary, or structural changes in mind rather than the constant small changes necessary to keep a system on course. Significant change, their theory claims, never occurs unless equilibrium, consistency, congruence, adjustment, psychological satisfaction, or some similar quality has been upset either in the social system, in its component structures, in the psychological makeup of individual members, or in the relationship of the society to its external environment, natural or social.[24] Evon Z. Vogt specifies tension within society inducing cultural evolution, culture growth, pattern saturation, and similar directional movements. Taking the psychological point of view, A. Irving Hallowell and his student Melford Spiro explain that as long as members of a society expect existing cultural patterns to gratify their drives and allay their anxieties they lack incentive to change.[25] Drive frustration provides the motivational impulse necessary for change to occur. Frustration may arise through norms proscribing the satisfaction of certain drives, or through structural arrangements blocking access to opportunities for gratification.

Postwar students of change realized that heavy, drastic cultural and structural change could be accomplished within a single generation, and even in a primitive society need not cause psychological trauma or serious difficulties. What is important if such problems are to be avoided, Margaret Mead advises, is the completeness with which a people want to change rather than merely submitting to being changed by external agencies.[26] Whereas anthropologists had long thought that gradual, partial change provides a helpful bridge between old and new, permitting people slowly to learn unfamiliar lifeways, Mead's experience taught her the contrary. Heavy, rapid change is not only possible, it may even be desirable. Partial change creates conditions in which discordant and discrepant practices develop in a society, with corresponding discordancies being painfully reflected in the lives of individuals. Parts of an old culture pattern surviving tend to reinstate the rest of the pattern and so act as a drag on establishing new habits. Rapid change, however, avoids inconsistencies between old and new cultural elements. Besides, Mead believes, it can be much easier, and highly exhilarating, to learn a whole new set of habits rather than to graft a few foreign habits on a set of old ones.

Field workers were distressed at the bleak and even hostile circumstances that change had brought about in the lives of formerly primitive societies compared to their previous, comparatively autonomous life styles. Seeing what was happening among a number of American Indian tribes and elsewhere, anthropologists could hardly avoid describing culture change in negative terms, employing words like "cultural decay," "deculturation," "social disintegration," and "proletarization" to express their concern and dismay.

Uneven Change

Before Mead called attention to difficulties created by partial change, Godfrey and Monica Wilson had observed the unhappy consequences of change which occurs unevenly.[27] Basing their observations on work they had done in Central Africa, and writing in the tradition of British social anthropology where their training lay, they begin with the proposition that opposition between groups, between individuals, and between ideas or between values may be expected in any society. Sometimes opposition occurs independently in particular areas of life, where it is normally quickly settled by the effective application of law, logical reasoning, or conventional sanctions. In time of major change, however, opposition may become general, or radical; one manifestation cannot be settled by itself because all manifestations are related and reinforce each other. It cannot be controlled by law, logic, or convention because it is rooted in opposition over the authority behind those forms of social pressure. Hence radical opposition continually disturbs personal and social equilibrium.

Radical opposition is created by uneven change in a society or, more specifically, by differences which change produces in social scale and in the correlates of scale. Under conditions of culture contact, for example, some people or groups in a formerly traditional society develop relatively large-scale outlooks corresponding to the new values and ideas being introduced by administrators, teachers, missionaries, and other agents of change. Others, untouched by the new currents or rejecting them, remain traditional in their outlooks; they remain relatively small in scale. A given individual may also be personally muddled as he tries simultaneously to adhere to both large- and small-scale customs. On the one hand, the society strains to expand its scale; on the other, attitudes of the native members or restrictive policies enforced by the agents of change prevent scale from expanding evenly in all areas of life or for all groups. The dialectical situation of extreme disequilibrium thereby brought about can only be overcome through further change that reduces the unevenness, either by increasing the scale of the small-scale elements or decreasing that of the large-scale ones. In the absence of such adaptive change, unhappy persons and dissident groups may seek to quit the society, which will of itself diminish scale.

Radical opposition resembles the dialectical concept of contradiction employed by historical materialists and other Marxist scholars to explain why social progress sometimes slows down.[28] The Marxist concept traces stagnation to opposition between on the one hand economic, political, or religious institutions and on the other hand new material forces of production pressing for adoption.

Research continued to demonstrate that change may have unexpected and far-reaching repercussions in a social system. A social anthropologist, Alexander Spoehr, working out of the Field Museum of Natural History in Chicago, showed how economic change might affect even kinship terminology.[29] Among the Seminole and other Southeastern United States Indians, the sequence started with economic development through which some individuals in a formerly egalitarian society with unilinear descent groups were able to expand their wants and develop their skills, thereby becoming relatively wealthy while some of their kinsmen became poor. Their wealth constituted a direct incentive for replacing extended families with independent nuclear households, and for thinning out relations with members of the lineage, thus escaping from the need to follow traditional patterns of sharing wealth. As the extended family and lineage weakened, the kin-term system based on those structures likewise altered, giving rise to one compatible with bilateral filiation.

Conjunctions of Autonomous Culture Systems

Interest in acculturation, or culture contact as British anthropologists preferred to say, stayed high for a decade or so after the war but declined in the 1960s. Curiously, the decline came close on the heels of a Social Science Research Council (SSRC) seminar devoted to the topic where the concept was apprized as offering an excellent means for learning about culture dynamics.[30] The seminar redefined the term to limit it to those changes initiated by the conjunction of two or more autonomous culture systems, i.e., systems not requiring any other for their continued existence. By this definition the seminar eliminated from acculturation the changes induced by contacts between social classes, ethnic groups, or occupational groups within a single society. Though acculturation involves diffusion, the members pointed out, it includes more than passive cultural receiving; acculturation is frequently accompanied by creative, culture-producing activities embodied in processes like organization, reinterpretation, and syncretism. Sometimes, however, acculturation leads to cultural disintegration as groups become devested of their political and cultural autonomy, though to prevent that a social system may resort to forms of reactive adaptation, withdrawing from contact with other systems and encysting itself with its traditional values. Societies have also been known to respond to culture contact with progressive adjustment, the seminar observed, rushing into fusion with another. Arrested fusion produces stabilized pluralism, a state in which each social system in contact retains some degree of autonomy.

Within a few years of the seminar, field workers, looking at far from autonomous social systems, recognized a type of acculturation, differential acculturation or biculturation, wherein component groups belonging to an ethnically complex society borrow cultural material selectively from one another, thereby preserving their ethnic identities.[31] Members of each group come to know something about the cultural routines of the others and borrow from among the alien ways traits suiting their needs. Lifetime socialization takes place concurrently into two or more cultures.

Four years after the SSRC seminar, Alfred Kroeber was complaining about the monotony and dullness of acculturation studies published in the United States. One after another reiterated the same obvious results produced by one culture overrunning another in the manner of a bulldozer leveling soil that nature had been depositing for ages.[32] Robert F. Murphy criticized the concept more trenchantly, pointing out how very few societies are autonomous. Most have structured relationships with other societies through which they are constantly undergoing change.

Hence what need is there for a concept of acculturation? Good field work should always heed the larger social system in which a society is lodged. The phenomena to which acculturation refers belong to ordinary social processes; they are not something special.

Innovation

If acculturation theorists left room for creative, culture-producing innovations occurring in culture-contact situations, they conceived of those innovations as largely triggered by events external to the culture. Thereby they lined up with the diffusionists against the proponents of independent invention, although by now the debate between those two positions had subsided. Nevertheless, a few writers gave equal emphasis to both sources of change, as Homer Barnett was particularly fitted to do by his long, diversified career. After receiving his Ph.D. from the University of California, Berkeley, he served as ethnologist with the Bureau of American Ethnology, then became staff anthropologist in the Trust Territory of the Pacific Islands (Micronesia), and afterwards went to the University of Oregon. From his book I single out only the painstaking attention he gives to culturally endogenous sources of innovation.[33] These include the size and complexity of the cultural inventory of traits available to the innovator, facilities socially provided for funneling cultural elements to innovators, and provisions for fostering collaboration between inventors. The larger the number of cultural elements available to innovators, he finds, the greater the frequency of discovery and invention in a society, though opportunities for ideas to meet and interpenetrate must be provided. Existence of conflicting values, ideas, and customs in a culture also favors innovation, the ambiguity or stress resulting from the conflict motivating people to seek ways of escaping from their dilemma. The extent to which a society expects change or has faith in progress strongly influences the rate of innovation, the favorable attitudes toward the possibility of improvement favoring the inventive process, while resignation to things as they are has the opposite effect.

Great and Little Traditions[34]

If the concept of acculturation is restricted to contact between autonomous cultures, it will not encompass the meeting of great and little cultural traditions in a single society, a topic which Robert Redfield and other anthropologists at the University of Chicago investigated. Although Redfield defined the peasant community as part of the larger society with which peasants maintain continual contact, he recognized basic differences between rural and urban ideas, especially in the area of religion. To those variants of civilization, with which students of religion had long been familiar, he applied the terms little tradition and great tradition. In rural communities the unlettered folk work out the small tradition, while scholars in schools and temples cultivate the greater one.

Change ensues when the two traditions interact. In India, the Chicago scholars learned, materials from the little tradition have been universalized, refined, and systematized to the point where they become part of the great tradition, the city being the place where the transformations are most fully accomplished. In the reverse process, parochialization, the elements of the great tradition brought to the village are refashioned to become part of the local cult. Sanskritization, a process studied by M. N. Srinivas, an Indian anthropologist who worked with A. R. Radcliffe-Brown at Oxford, forms another aspect of the interaction between great and little traditions. As it takes place in India, a local caste collectively embarks on enhancing its moral reputation by voluntarily assuming more stringent rules formalized in the Sanskrit scriptures belonging to the great tradition. By practicing those rules the caste acquires greater ritual purity, and therefore higher standing, in the system of castes to which it belongs.

Advice for Technical Assistance

International assistance by Western countries for the purpose of furthering economic development and the modernization of agriculture, public health, or other adaptive activities in underdeveloped lands attracted a number of social scientists during the period of the cold war.[35] Most of the anthropologists who participated probably ignored the political strategy represented in technical aid, which they saw primarily as an opportunity to make practical use of their theories of culture and their ethnographic skills for a humanitarian purpose. Nevertheless problems over and beyond being useful faced the academic collaborators, not the least of which arose from the concept of modernization, which anthropologists in particular came to dislike. In it they sensed unpleasant ethnocentric overtones conflicting with the doctrine of cultural relativity, for it implied that change along Western lines is preferable to traditional ways.

Applied anthropologists who took part in technical assistance claimed that successful cultural transformation requires knowing a good deal about the cultural background of the society in which change is to be brought about, as well as about the dynamics of change. The latter the discipline already possessed, and field work provided the relevant background information, on the basis of which the technical experts were urged to base their plans.

A general theory designed to account for acceptance or rejection in programs of directed culture change pretty well sums up the bases of anthropological action and advice.[36] The authors specify three influences acting on an innovation following its deliberate introduction: first, the innovator's behavior, including his manner of communicating with the society, his role, whether he actually demonstrates the innovation and secures voluntary participation from the recipients, the timeliness of what he proposes, and his degree of flexibility; second, the motivational state of the recipients, including the need they feel for the change and what they expect from it; and finally, compatibility or incompatibility between traditional cultural elements and the innovation. A manual for an international organization, edited by Margaret Mead, recommends stripping unfamiliar practices being introduced into a society of as many extraneous cultural accretions as possible.[37] Change, the book urges, should always be implemented with the fullest possible consent of and participation by those whose lives would be affected. If much of this advice regarding directed culture change sounds somewhat familiar, it should, for it repeats in new language earlier ideas advanced by historical ethnologists who sought a set of sound principles accounting for what happens in diffusion.

Interest in technical assistance waned in the 1960s for a number of reasons, including the decline of interest in acculturation, the genera to which research on technical assistance belongs. At the same time the big nations cut down on appropriations for developmental aid. Another possible factor might have been the growing concern about environmental deterioration that moved intellectuals to ask whether unlimited development was desirable.

The Process Itself

Despite the many specific factors controlling change identified by diffusionists, ecologists, evolutionists, psychological anthropologists, and other theorists, we will never improve our analytic and predictive understanding of social change, Fredrik Barth wrote in 1967, until we give up concentrating descriptively on institutions and culture patterns, i.e., on the final outcome of change, rather than the process itself.[38] Instead of focusing solely on patterns of structure resulting from the way aggregates of people on many occasions organize their behavior, he calls for isolating the determinants of the social forms. Institutions and culture patterns result from the way people in a community, acting in behest of certain values, allocate their time, effort, and other resources as they are confronted by ecologic and other constraints. As Alexander Spoehr's report back in the middle 1940s demonstrated, if people obtain, or hope to obtain, gratifying payoffs from new ways of orienting their sentiments and allocating their wealth, new culture patterns come into being and old ones disappear.

In a discipline which had long valued tracing long-term directions in cultural change, and in which Kroeber studied configurations of growth whose fulfillment required centuries, not everyone saw a big payoff in a method of microhistorical analysis such as Barth advocated. Research on culture change continued to be pursued in many ways, thereby contributing to the diversification of postwar cultural anthropology.

Kinship

Social Equalizers and Differentials

Research into the linkage between kin-terms with other forms of social structure reached its apogee in George Peter Murdock's *Social Structure* published in 1949. Thereafter a measure of pattern exhaustion appears to have set in. I don't imply a total loss of interest in kinship, for in place of the classic problem opened up by Lewis Henry Morgan and continued by W. H. R. Rivers, Robert Lowie, and Murdock came the sematic analysis of kin terms, David Schneider's venture into kinship as a symbol system, and a reopening of a question submerged in the debate between Morgan and John Ferguson McLennan, whether kin terms refer primarily to genealogical relationships or designate categories of kinship.

There seems to have been nothing in Murdock's early training predicting his future interest in kinship. He himself speaks of having "drifted" to Harvard Law School following graduation from Yale University,[39] and the same word might describe the process whereby he entered anthropology and shaped his comprehensive theory of relationship terms and other aspects of kinship behavior. He withdrew from law school after three months and drew on a small legacy to spend a year in worldwide travel. What he saw activated a dormant interest in anthropology. His effort to become a graduate student at Columbia University was defeated by Franz Boas, who regarded him as a dilettante; so he returned to Yale for graduate study in anthropology and sociology. Here he was influenced by George Keller and the ideas of William Graham Sumner, which Keller had absorbed. Some years after taking his doctorate, he joined the newly founded Yale anthropology department where his personal association with Leslie Spier and Edward Sapir may have bent his interests toward kinship. He also absorbed the behavioristic theory of Clark Hull and other psychologists in Yale's interdisciplinary Institute of Human Relations, as well as psychoanalytic theory, both of which show up in his kinship research, but especially behaviorism. Murdock never lost sight of individual psychological processes operating under the forms of social structure and culture. Hence his endorsement, in 1971, of a strictly phenomenal interpretation of culture and social structure came as less of a surprise to those who knew him than Murdock expected. All supraindividual concepts, he said in 1971, represent illusory abstractions, "mere epi-phenomena," based on the real phenomena of individuals interacting with one another and with their environment.

In the sphere of kinship studies, Murdock's accomplishment was two-fold. He took the explanations of kinship terminology that had been accumulating since Rivers and ordered them systematically in a deductive theory based on psychological principles. Then he deduced hypotheses, which he subjected to critical testing, using the hologeistic method and the vast store of data in the Cross-Cultural Survey, later known as the Human Relations Area Files. A sample of the testing can be seen in his 1947 paper where, using data from 200 societies, he compares the pre-dictive value of competing explanations of kinship terminologies contain-ing bifurcate merging.[40]

Through bifurcate merging a kin term comes to designate both lineal and collateral relatives of the same sex and generation; a parent is terminologically identified with a parent's sibling, a sibling with a parallel cousin, a son with a nephew, and so on. Murdock used his sample to test explanations for bifurcate merging offered by Rivers, Lowie, Kroeber, Sapir, and Radcliffe-Brown. Rivers attributed the custom to unilinear moieties; Murdock's data shows the connection to be indeed valid for societies with moieties, but of limited value, because River's explanation fails to account for bifurcate merging in 173 societies lacking moieties. Lowie's theory invoked the influence of exogamy in moieties and other unilinear groups on bifurcate merging. It yields a stronger coefficient of correlation than Rivers's in Murdock's test, but not as high as Kroeber's hypothesis linking any form of unilinear descent with bifurcate merging. Compared to all three, Sapir's explanation holding preferential marriage in the form of the levirate and sororate to be the determinant is very poorly sustained, and Murdock brands as simply illogical Radcliffe-Brown's idea that a universal phenomenon, the social equivalence of siblings, can be the cause of bifurcate merging, which is not universal.

The significance of Murdock's test goes beyond finding the best among rival theories to account for a feature of kinship terminology. It provides substantial backing for the classic theory holding social structure and kinship terminology to be causally connected. While correlation doesn't prove cause, the consistently positive correlations reported by Murdock in the 1947 paper and in *Social Structure* go far to support the inference of causality, especially since they are logically buttressed by a plausible theory explaining why causality operates between the two sets of variables.

Basic to Murdock's theory is the assumption that a single kin term will be applied to two or more types of kinsmen when a society perceives the types to be in some degree similar.[41] Conversely, different kin terms indi-cate perceived dissimilarities between the kin types to which the words apply. Murdock based this assumption on the psychological process of stimulus generalization identified by Clark Hull, but it closely resembles Bronislaw Malinowski's view of emotional attitudes being extended from primary relatives to more distant kin of the same generation and sex. In *Social Structure* Murdock applies the assumption of stimulus generalization to social structural factors, like descent groups. Their presence in a society may act as a social equalizer or social differential, thereby influencing people to perceive similarities or dissimilarities, respectively, between kin types. Social equalizers include nuclear families which, by virtue of their structural similarity, allow kinship terms to be extended between kin types by analogy. Thus if children call two women "mother" who occupy a similar position in two families, the children will call each other "brother" and "sister," thereby making an analogy with their biological siblings. Forms of marriage, such as polygyny, polyandry, and monogamy, may act both as social equalizers or as differentials. Sororal polygyny from the standpoint of a given individual (Ego) creates significant similarities between a mother and her sister and between a wife and the wife's sister, for the women hold a similar position in Ego's family of orientation. Consequently, with sororal polygyny each of the women is frequently called by the same term. Nonsororal polygyny acts as a social differential with regard to the mother and mother's sister, because it stresses a difference between the collateral relative outside the polygynous family and primary relatives of the same sex and generation within. Unilinear descent acts as an equalizer by promoting what Murdock calls "participation"; it places certain collateral relatives (e.g., in patrilineal descent, a man's daughter and his brother's daughter) in the same lineage, sib, or moiety. But it also differentiates those collaterals from others (in patrilineal descent, a man's sister's daughter). Other social equalizers and differentials affecting kin terms are marital residence, forms of the family, kindreds, the levirate, and the sororate. Murdock's empirical work demonstrates that participation in descent groups ranks highest in relative efficacy among the major kin-term determinants, being followed by forms of marriage (e.g., sororal or nonsororal polygyny), and marital residence rules.

Kin Terms in Evolutionary Perspective

Forms of social structure acting as social equalizers and differentials, Murdock theorizes, are produced by other cultural factors, especially by property relations and techniques of procuring food. He particularly emphasizes the latter, thereby revealing the influence of George Keller's thesis (based on Julius Lippert) that the "maintenance mores" are basic in society.[42] Specifically, Murdock's "main sequence theory" perceives subsistence techniques influencing division of labor by sex, which in turn affects the relative social importance attached to men and women in a

society, which predisposes people to adopt forms of residence corresponding to the relative importance of the sexes. Virilocal, uxorilocal, and ambi-
local residence, in their turn, promote corresponding forms of the extended family which, in the next stage of the sequence, encourage the
formation of compatible descent groups—participation in which, remember, constitutes the most effective of the kin-term determinants—or
kindreds. The absence of descent groups, or their loss if previously
present, occurs when neolocal residence creates the nuclear family living
independently. Neolocal residence, in turn, generally results from economic factors that fail to enhance the importance of one sex over the
other.

Naturally, these theoretical sequences do not always occur in reality.
At most we can expect a tendency for the theoretically predicted outcome
to follow; we look for a strain toward consistency between antecedents
and consequents. In hologeistic research, such as Murdock carried out,
the strain toward consistency will be revealed by substantial, but not perfect, correlations between given antecedents and consequents, whereas
in the histories of particular societies we will find, as Spoehr and others
have shown, evidence that economic changes bring about new patterns of
social structure and alterations in kin-term systems.[43]

Murdock conceives of the linkages between subsistence techniques,
division of labor, other social structural variables, and kin terms in
evolutionary terms. Reasoning from contemporary primitive societies, he
demonstrates how alterations in kin terms may arise as evolutionary
adaptations to antecedent adaptations in social structure and culture.[44]
Within his sequence, rules of marital residence are particularly responsive
to changes in economy, technology, property, and other cultural factors.
Therefore, evolutionarily speaking, residence is likely to adapt very
quickly to the latter changes, whereupon the new form of residence
stimulates further adaptations in the remaining social equalizers and
differentials. Parallels in kinship terminology between cultures occur
easily, Murdock points out, since the types of residence and other social
structures acting as equalizers or differentials are restricted. By that
reasoning we understand why Morgan and later students of kinship were
able to discover only a limited number of major types of kin-term systems
in societies.

Since American anthropologists, in 1949, were still mostly holding aloof
from studying cultural evolution, George Peter Murdock's effort, although
on a restricted scale, represents one of the benchmarks in the revival of
evolutionary studies, as well as a substantial contribution explaining the
dynamics of culture change.

Elman Service, following a less Darwinian approach to cultural evolution than Murdock and with a broadened conception of kin-term systems,
found kinship terminologies varying with levels of sociocultural complex-

ity.[45] Shifting from the view that kin terms specify genealogical relationships, he regards them in more sociological or categorical fashion, somewhat as McLennan did, as status terms specifying rights and duties possessed by the individuals they designate. Status terms used in societies fall into two classes: familistic and nonfamilistic. The former status terms name social positions in a group of relatives, or else they derive from such terms; the latter, the nonfamilistic terms, refer to occupational, political, and similar positions in a system of social stratification. Some status terms are egocentric, and they specify social positions relative to an ego; others are sociocentric, naming objective categories of people in a society. "My son," "his uncle," and so on, are examples of egocentric status terms; "New Yorker," "Professor so-and-so," and "he is a noble" illustrate sociocentric status terms. (One may need to consult the context to know whether a word, e.g., "father," is used egocentrically or sociocentrically.) From an evolutionary perspective, sociocentric terms are most useful in a large-scale society among people ignorant of one another's egocentrically defined social position. Hence egocentric terms prevail in small-scale societies, and sociocentric ones become more numerous as societies grow larger and become more complexly subdivided, which is what happened in the course of cultural development. As societies become more complex and social interaction ceases to be limited primarily to kinsmen, familistic terms come to be extended, at first egocentrically, then sociocentrically. Extension continues up to a certain point of sociocultural complexity, whereupon a nonkin society comes into being that employs both egocentric and sociocentric terms.

Sociocentrically extended familistic terms, Service believes, brought Crow and Omaha kinship terminologies into existence. Following up Leslie White's suggestion that those terminologies represent products of cultural evolution fostered by maturing sibs in cultural evolution,[46] Service suggests tentatively that familistic terms began to be used sociocentrically, in lieu of certain egocentric terms, when the social and geographical distance across which interaction took place increased due to the expanded size of unilinear descent groups. However, Service, like White, fails to account for Crow and Omaha kinship terminologies in societies lacking descent groups.[47]

Since 1865 when McLennan criticized Morgan, anthropologists have debated whether extended kin terms are employed primarily to designate genealogical relationships or whether, as Service suggests, they employ words referring to genealogical relationships to denote categories of people with minimal regard for how those people are genealogically related. Primary kinship terms used for secondary and other relatives, McLennan argued, indicate no thought of blood relationship with the people whom they designate. However, his interpretation, holding the terms to be simply salutations, drew no serious followers. The ensuing debate revolved around the question whether the primary or historically prior meaning of such words as "father" and "mother" is the meaning they have in the nuclear family.[48] Regarding such an interpretation as unfounded, A. M. Hocart, in 1937, hypothesized that the Polynesian term *tama* might originally have had a categorical meaning, designating patrilineally related males of the first generation above Ego. Only later was the word applied to Ego's father specifically. Such reasoning runs contrary to the prevailing extensionist position taken by Malinowski and Murdock, according to whom recognition of kinship stems from the facts of procreation and sexual intercourse and extensions of kinship nomenclature are secondary. Recently Edmund R. Leach and David M. Schneider, in rethinking kinship, took issue with the extensionist view.[49] Each in his own way argued from the cognitivist postulate: the meaning of cultural facts should be discovered within a society and not imposed from without. Anthropologists impose their dogma of biology, Schneider maintains, when they automatically interpret kinship genealogically. Kin terms connote much more than how Ego is genealogically connected to other people; in all societies they express differences people find culturally significant, be they differences based on locality, generation, property, or whatever.

The other side in the debate, represented by Harold W. Scheffler and Floyd Lounsbury, while opting for a primarily genealogical interpretation of the words used in kinship, admitted the possibility of other meanings also being present.[50] Kin terms, they point out, like many other words, are polysemous. Extended kin terms derive a portion of their meaning from the one close, or the several equally close, relatives to whom they refer who constitute the focal members of the category covered by the words. They also carry secondary references pertaining to more distant relatives; and beyond those, some terms convey information about other referents with whom no genealogical connection is implied.

Kinship Behavior

Though Morgan's successors consistently found kin-term systems to hinge on other forms of social structure, Francis L. K. Hsu, in 1961, still had grounds to complain that kinship research failed to show that varieties of kinship connect up with diverse ways of life.[51] The recurring, limited number of kinship structures terminologically identified may be predictably related to a similarly limited number of subsistence techniques, residence rules, descent rules, and so on, but they bear no resemblance to the diverse world views found in societies.

Like his teacher Malinowski, with whom he studied at the London School of Economics after leaving China where he was born, Hsu was much more interested in kinship behavior and sentiments than in kinship terminology. And kinship behavior *had* lagged as a subject of research, though it was not wholly overlooked.[52] Murdock, for example, had picked up a theme prominent in Malinowski's theory of kinship—the weakening force of intimacy, mutual aid, and emotional attachment as kinship reaches from the family to the farthest limits to which relationship is traced. Like Malinowski, though for different theoretical reasons, Murdock believes that children first learn their earliest habits of reciprocal behavior in the nuclear family and later generalize them to a wider circle of persons, trial and error and teaching appropriate discrimination. By terminologically categorizing the vast number of potential relatives an individual may have, Murdock holds, kinship terms facilitate interaction; it would be intolerably burdensome were a person expected to adopt a distinctive type of behavior toward every particular kinsman. Persons categorized together tend to be treated in similar—but, he adds pointedly—not identical ways. Similarly, speaking of behavioral norms, Roger Keesing recognized they became less compulsive in the degree to which they are applied to comparatively distant kin. Adopting Ward Goodenough's concept of social identity, he shows that not everyone for whom Ego uses a given kinship term possesses the same social identities. The social identities tend to coalesce for focal members of a kinship category—for example, Ego's father—but do not do so for more distant persons to whom the term is also applied. Anthropologists have been trapped, he says, by the illusion of isomorphism between the social identity system and the kinship terminology because of their concentration on focal members. Having described the role of father, they imply that the same behavior patterns hold, albeit in lesser degree, for other members of the category. But evidence indicates that behavioral rules not only attenuate for more distant members of a kin category; many times they divide, so that several social identities coalescing in the father's role, for instance, are distributed among different persons variously related to Ego. To these, Ego will display different behaviors, depending on the rights and duties their identities activate.

Francis L. K. Hsu undertook to explain how behavorial attributes derived from primary social relationships are extended to more remote kin and even nonkin. In doing so, he developed ideas of Malinowski utilizing psychological assumptions taken from psychoanalysis. Any one of the nuclear family's eight basic relationships—mother-son, father-son, husband-wife, and so on—may, he claims, be dominant in a specific society. Universally, each of these relationships possesses its own typical action patterns and attitudes. The attributes typical of a relationship recur from one society to another simply because they are intrinsic—by nature, as I understand it—to the relationship. Inhering in the mother-son relationship, for instance, are the attributes of discontinuity (the attitude of being unconnected with others), inclusiveness (the act of incorporating, or wishing to be incorporated), dependence, diffuseness (the tendency to spread in all directions), and libidinality (diffuse or potential sexuality). By comparison, continuity, inclusiveness, authority, and asexuality mark the father-son tie. Attributes belonging to a dominant relationship tend to determine attitudes and action patterns displayed in other relationships, in the family as well as toward more distant relatives and with unrelated persons. Thus if the husband-wife relationship happens to be dominant in a society, the attributes of discontinuity and freedom (being able or preferring to follow one's inclinations) come into play, along with others inhering in that dyadic bond. In such a society, all social relationships become imbued with discontinuity and with a strong preference for autonomy; as a result, dealing with authority becomes an acute problem in many areas of life, including between fathers and sons. Anthropologists who applied Hsu's theory found the idea of dominant relationships useful, but they balked at accepting the universality of the attributes said to be attached to each of the dyadic relationships.[53]

Descent Groups and Kindreds

Clarifying Descent Groups

Anthropology in postwar times strove hard to clarify the distinction between kinship and descent and to explain the dynamics of descent systems. British social anthropology made the unilinear descent group one of the major bases for understanding social action, at least in subsaharan Africa, for evidence showed such groups not to possess equal significance in all societies where they are present.

Both kinship and descent systems, Harold W. Scheffler noted in a comprehensive review of several decades of research, are means of ordering social relations by reference to genealogical connection.[54] The former do so egocentrically, subdividing into a smaller number of kin types the totality of persons who are genealogically connected to an individual. In Meyer Fortes's words, kinship "define[s] and sanction[s] a personal field of social relations for each individual" in a society. On the other hand, a descent system orders social relations by categorizing individuals who are conventionally recognized as descendants of a comparatively small number of usually deceased people, ancestors. In both systems, belonging to a category—a kin type or descent group—confers social identity and roles. The two systems are complementary, and an individual may derive a status in both, assuming of course that his society in addition to recognizing kinship, as all societies do, also recognizes descent.

Meyer Fortes went so far as to claim that each system has its own characteristic type of sanction. Kinship relations are morally sanctioned by reciprocities built into the relations themselves; one fulfills duties to relatives expecting they will do likewise toward oneself. A descent group, however, being organized in relation to other descent groups and to other societies, applies jural sanctions against outsiders whenever it is necessary to insure protection of the group's rights. Fortes seems to base the latter generalization on African descent groups whose members frequently undertake concerted political action. But, as critics pointed out, descent groups do not invariably act so.

After many years of talking about rules of patrilineal and matrilineal descent, anthropologists who turned from attending only to the norms in people's minds and examined the actual membership of unilinear descent groups were forced to acknowledge theoretically that the rules of descent are not always followed. Composition sometimes fails to reflect the norm by which membership is supposed to be determined, and, in some instances, the norm may be a fiction imposed to bring the actual composition of descent groups into conformity with the ideal model.

Writings on social structure frequently took up kindreds in the context of descent, but usually with the duly noted advice that kindreds, being egocentrically organized along genealogical lines, are not descent groups at all. In contrast to the intergenerational continuity marking descent groups, kindreds as well as action groups formed from some portion of a kindred, last only as long as an individual exists to organize the members. Comparative study revealed that kindreds acquire their greatest importance in societies lacking large corporate descent groups; but wherever kindreds occur, they provide individuals with a wide range of optative relationships on which to draw as interests warrant. Although kindreds are bilaterally extended from a given Ego, they need not embrace an equal number of father's and mother's relatives. A tendency to matrilateral asymmetry has been particularly noted in cities where members of nuclear families are apt to maintain closer ties with a larger number of the wife's kin than with the husband's. One explanation, following somewhat along economic lines, traces the asymmetric tendency to common domestic interests shared by the female core of the matrilateral action group, i.e., the wife, her mother, and her sisters, and supporting their solidarity. A man in modern urban society no longer shares common economic interests with his father and brothers. Though the explanation of matrilateral asymmetry refers to common interests rather than activities performed by the female core of the kindred, it is generally consistent with Barth's phenomenally oriented theory of how social structures, including descent groups, arise.[55] He ascribes them not to the power of norms but to individuals joining together in response to constraints and incentives encountered in an ecological setting for the purpose of achieving something.

Scholarly interest in descent groups by and large took different directions in America and Britain. British social anthropologists studying African societies applied to lineages the old idea of opposition between groups contributing to a social system's stability. We came across the idea in Adam Ferguson and it underlies the balance of powers doctrine written into the U.S. Constitution in the 18th century. The lineage model adopted by British social anthropologists, first presented ethnographically by E. E. Evans-Pritchard in *The Nuer* (1940), was generalized by Meyer Fortes in 1953. Both men had studied with Malinowski but later came under Radcliffe-Brown's influence and became more structurally, less behaviorally, oriented. Each did field work in Africa, paying close heed to relationships based on kinship and descent. Each became a figure of major stature in the small community of British social anthropologists.[56] Fortes, remaining staunchly orthodox in his approach, built up social anthropology at Cambridge where W. H. R. Rivers once held sway, while Evans-Pritchard succeeded Radcliffe-Brown at Oxford and thereupon, as I have already mentioned, he defected from structural-functionalism.

The model advanced by these men regards the lineage as an internally segmented group, the segments of which unite when faced by external threat.[57] Each segment, down to the minimal unit of the children of one parent, constitutes a focus of unity whose identity derives from the ancestor differentiating it from other segments with other ancestors. As genealogical time increases, i.e., with greater depth, the segments fuse in the figures of higher ancestors until the founder of the all-embracive maximal lineage is reached. In him or her all the segments are united. Minimal segments are always undergoing further segmentation as brothers in a patrilineal system mature and become the heads of their own families and thereby start new minimal segments. Sometimes lineages fission into rival factions, thereby ceasing to exist as an entity, though as British anthropologists frequently observed, in societies where lineages are important, religious institutions and rituals function to assert and protect common interests, thereby counteracting fissive tendencies. In external relations, each lineage of whatever depth stands in opposition to all other like units within the society. When threatened by another lineage section, the maximal lineage or any subsidiary segment responds as a unified group. Such political action by lineages is vital in societies lacking centralized sources of political power. Where political centralization occurs —this is best revealed in Africa—political action by lineages tends to be attenuated.

American anthropologists contributed to lineage theory by noting the role of marital residence in the formation of lineages and other unilinear descent groups and, moving back one link in the sequence, noted the significance of ecological factors in determining residence preferences.[58] Unilocal rules of residence aggregate persons of one sex who continue to reside with linear relatives after marriage and so, in time, come to regard themselves as related by virtue of common descent. In England, Peter M. Worsley called attention to ecological and economic factors governing the creation and displacement of lineages.[59] Compared to the comparative absence of lineages among people practicing very rudimentary subsistence techniques, he pointed to the prominence of lineages in relatively homogeneous precapitalist societies, where their strength derives from their control of valuable productive resources, such as the grazing lands of pastoralists. Lineages break down, he observes, when modern economic systems with heavy occupational specialization intrude on such societies.

While unilinear descent monopolized the major share of attention devoted to descent, another way of categorizing people by ancestry drew increasing recognition. Radcliffe-Brown had named this other type of descent cognatic, and the name stuck, although some anthropologists preferred to call it nonunilinear, believing the word fit better with the variability present within the type.[60] Cognatic structures possess more flexibility than unilinear groups, as far as recruitment goes, but they lack the discreteness of unilinear descent groups, which never overlap. Each type, Robin Fox observes, possesses advantages and disadvantages, and to capitalize on both some societies organize certain relationships along unilinear descent lines and others along cognatic descent lines.

Family and Marriage

Conceptual Clarification

In a period fond of "rethinking" old ideas, Meyer Fortes's concept of filiation explicated what anthropologists mean when they insist that a society, placing great importance on unilinear descent, continues to recognize the affective, jural, and pragmatic ties everywhere associated with parenthood.[61] Anthropologists sometimes tended to overlook or minimize the twin bonds of filiation through which an individual secures rights to inheritance, succession, and other matters from parents; as well as responsibilities, for example, to care for them when they are old or to perform rituals for them after their death. In African societies with patrilineages, social anthropologists observed filial ties extending to members of both parents' corporate lineages. Matrifiliation—the relationship tending to be especially overlooked with patrilineal descent—in some African groups confers rights to property in the mother's lineage, and creates jural obligations between a person and individuals in her lineage, most notably with the mother's brother.

Reconsideration of old ideas went far and proceeded fast with the concepts of the nuclear family and marriage.[62] In 1949, Murdock defined the nuclear family as a universal human group founded through marriage and containing a man, a woman, and their offspring. Anthropologists, Goodenough asserted 20 years later—his teacher, Murdock, included—have ethnocentrically exaggerated the universality of the conjugal family, the unit consisting of husband, wife, and children. They have also mistaken the universal significance of marriage, which is only one possible response to four social needs: determining when a woman is eligible for sexual relations and to bear children (the two possibilities need not coincide); knowing when a man is eligible to engage in sexual relations and, if relevant, beget children; determining who has sexual privileges with whom; and determining where a child belongs, i.e., what adults are responsible for its protection and socialization. Marriage may suffice to meet all or most of these needs, as it does in some societies, but the needs may also be dealt with through separate transactions.

E. R. Leach advanced a larger list of rights allocated by institutions commonly classed together as marriage. The rights include establishing the legal father of a woman's children and the legal mother of a man's children; giving the wife a monopoly in the husband's sexuality and vice versa; giving the husband partial or total rights to the wife's labor and vice versa; establishing a joint fund of property; and establishing socially significant relations of affinity. In no society does marriage suffice to establish all these rights simultaneously, nor is any one right invariably secured by marriage everywhere. Kathleen Gough, in a determined effort to salvage a cross-culturally applicable and etic definition of marriage, singled out the first pair of those rights. The crucial feature of marriage, she insists, lies in ascribing to a child the same jural status accorded to other members of the society or social category to which the child belongs.

Phylogenetic Origins of the Incest Rule

Ethnologists found little new to say about the functions of the incest rule; they concentrated on how the rule in the nuclear family becomes extended to other relatives and let their imagination soar over the rule's phylogenetic origin.

Murdock summed up the familiar functions of incest regulations found in the family and larger groups:[63] first, they control sexual rivalries and jealousies, thereby curbing disruption and enhancing social solidarity. Second, by encouraging exogamy, the incest rule creates larger areas of social cooperation endowed with competitive advantages. Exogamy, he added, also fosters the exchange of cultural material in a society, thereby accelerating social progress. Adverting to previous origin theories, he finds little to support the theory that the incest rule is based on recognition of biological danger associated with close inbreeding, nor can he accept Edward Westermarck's reasoning—ascribing it to the sexual unattractiveness of relatives with whom a person has been in prolonged, intimate association.[64] Murdock explains the source of incest regulations as simply a consequence of learning. A child initially learns the incest taboo when adults in the nuclear family enjoin him from behaving to a parent or to siblings of opposite sex in ways resembling sexual responses. (The reasons Murdock advances for such discouragement resemble Ernest Hutcheson's and Carl Nicolai Starcke's functions of the incest rule.) Through generalization, the prohibition becomes extended from primary to more distant relatives, but not in perfect coincidence with nearness of genealogical relationship. Instead, extension tends to be stronger for relatives who, in some way, resemble tabooed members of the nuclear family. A mother's sister, for example, resembles the mother by belonging to the same sex, to the same family orientation, and to the same generation; perhaps she even possesses some of the same physical traits. Social structural factors in a society, such as marital residence, the sororate and levirate, and unilinear descent groups, themselves create similarities between primary and other relatives; thus matrilocal residence, where the two women are housemates, strengthens already present resemblances between mother and mother's sister. Statistical examination of data from some 200 societies provides Murdock with consistent support for his extensionist theory, especially for the postulate that structural conditions act as social equalizers in channeling directions that the incest rule follows outside the nuclear family.

In contrast to Murdock's ontogenetic explanation of incest regulations, phylogenetic theories were advanced.[65] David F. Aberle went back to precultural and early cultural times for the origin of the prohibition. Relatively stable, two generational (i.e., familial) groups of infrahuman animals, he finds, have two main ways of forestalling attempts by the young to mate within the group. One requires no external sanction; among Canada geese, for example, imprinting alone keeps mating from taking place with members of the same brood. The second mechanism takes the form of sexual competition between the parent and offspring of the same sex and, because of the parent's greater strength, results in the offspring being expelled from the group shortly after sexual maturity. Man's ancestors, Aberle suspects, used the device of intergenerational competition. But man himself—for whom expulsion from the family soon after sexual maturity would have been fatal to survival of the species—adopted a symbolic device, the incest rule, instead of relying solely on brute force. Miriam Slater also writes in an ethological framework. Many animals with a relatively short life span, she reasons, almost always mate outside the family. So must it have been with early hominids. They could hardly have mated with parents, because with the likely early death of adults the family broke up while the offspring were still sexually immature. Mating with siblings would have been rare, because of the wide discrepancy in their ages likely under the most primitive conditions, and because of the small chance (50 percent) of birth order yielding two adjacent siblings of opposite sex. Such demographic and biological factors in early mankind rendered intrafamily breeding practically impossible. Only when prehistoric living conditions substantially improved, due to better subsistence techniques, or for other reasons, did vital statistics permit people the choice of either legitimizing some form of incest or, as most societies probably did, establishing rules prohibiting it.

In a more philosophical vein, Claude Lévi-Strauss perceives the regulation of incest through marriage rules and exogamy as an instance of how culture intervenes in nature, replacing chance by organization.[66] Intervention occurs whenever a group faces a risky distribution of fundamentally important valuables. In this case, the valuable is women, who are prized because they possess erotic value in all societies and, especially great among primitives, economic importance. Lévi-Strauss minimizes the prohibitory aspect of the incest rule. What it forbids is superficial; what counts is the rule's ability to bring about the exchange of women between groups in a society. Which brings us to what in the 1960s became a hot anthropological topic—alliance through marriage.

Alliance through Women[67]

Superficially, the incest rule forbids something from taking place; looked at positively it requires something, namely, the exchange of women between families or other groups. Thereby it brings about the integration of society. Seventen years before Lévi-Strauss made these observations in *Elementary Structures of Kinship* (1949), Reo Fortune, a New Zealander who studied anthropology at Columbia University, directly correlated the vigor with which primitive societies enforce the incest taboo in the nuclear family with the importance of marital alliances for social integration.[68] His rephrasing of Saint Augustine's formulation was one of the earliest recent statements of modern alliance theory. Kings, he notes, marry further afield than their subjects in order to make international alliances. Any other type of royal marriage he sees as usually morganatic, and he draws an interesting parallel between a morganatic marriage and incestuous marriage: both fail to create alliances. He also alludes to prescribed marriage, a topic which, after Fortune, became almost inextricably enmeshed with alliance.

Compared to Fortune's matter-of-fact discussion of alliance, Lévi-Strauss is far more dramatic. He presents the incest rule as obligating a man to give his sister or daughter in marriage to another man, and in *Elementary Structures of Kinship* he examines the many ways that societies have devised to accomplish the marital exchange of women. These range from restricted exchange, found in societies containing only two moieties, which reciprocate in wife-giving, to generalized systems in which wife-givers cannot be wife-takers and women move only in one direction during a given generation. In the restricted systems, also called direct or symmetrical, a man belonging to group A (normally a unilinear descent group) marries a woman of group B, while a man of B marries a woman of A. The exchange may occur between men belonging to the same generation, or the return of a wife by group A may be delayed for a generation; then the daughter born of the woman from B will marry a man of group B. Members of the wife-taking group may have a kinship term for women eligible for marriage, the term signifying a category of potential wives. Ethnographers who approach kinship from a genealogical point of view frequently gloss such kin terms by calling the women "female cross-cousins."

In the model representing what Lévi-Strauss called "generalized exchange," and that others label asymmetrical or indirect exchange, a man from group A is expected to marry a woman of group B, but the members of B never take wives from A, only from another group, C. In turn, the members of C (imagining a three-group system) take wives from A. Although no reciprocity of women occurs in an asymmetrical marriage system between prescribed wife-givers and wife-takers, considerable bride wealth and other gifts may be forthcoming for brides. Asymmetrical wife exchange, the functional anthropologists perceived, well suits the social systems lacking centralized political organization which are fragmented into a large number of descent or other groups, for it binds the groups into larger, loosely integrated systems.

Everyone came to understand that a society prescribing "cross-cousin marriage" does not require a man to marry a real mother's brother's daughter, but an affine belonging to a descent group to which the mother's brother's daughter also belongs. This would be the group where men of Ego's group traditionally seek brides. Prescriptive cross-cousin marriage, it was pointed out, often occurs in the absence of unilinear descent and then, of course, it lacks any alliance-making function as far as descent groups are concerned. In anthropological usage, prescriptive marriage came to imply a special kind of social constraint operating in choosing a spouse—in contrast to marriage entered as a matter of individual choice. For further clarity, social anthropologists proposed a distinction between preferential and prescriptive marriage; the former designating a statistically normal form of marriage, the latter the ideal form preferred by the community, and described in the people's model of their own social structure. A marriage system is prescriptive not because people frequently follow the ideal but because they recognize the ideal to exist.

Kinship terminologies distinguishing between marriageable women and others, according to Lévi-Strauss, constitute evidence that a society possesses a positive marriage rule. In distinction to the positive rules found in conjunction with restricted and generalized exchange in primitive societies, he recognizes in the "complex" marriage system of European and American society only rules of exogamy, none of alliance. Ignoring prescription, they lay down only whom one shall not marry.

Several writers sought to explain prescriptive marriage psychologically.[69] George Peter Murdock, applying the concept of generalization, predicted that secondary marriage would frequently occur with those persons outside the nuclear family who most closely resemble the initial spouse in significant characteristics; for example, with the wife's sisters. While this reasoning accounts for the sororate and sororal polygyny, it throws no light on the kind of prescribed marriage of interest to alliance theorists. George C. Homans and David M. Schneider undertook to explain why societies more often follow matrilateral than patrilateral cross-cousin marriage. Lévi-Strauss had accounted for prescribed marriage with a mother's brother's daughter in functional terms, saying it is advantageous for a society with unlinear descent groups because, as a form of exchange, it creates organic solidarity between the intermarrying segments. Homans and Schneider objected on the ground that a function, or final cause, cannot account for the origin of a culture pattern. They discovered an efficient cause for matrilateral and patrilateral cross-cousin marriage. In their theory, cross-cousin marriage is a consequence of emotional qualities inhering in the relationship with the mother's brother and with the father's brother. Reasoning about the extension of kinship sentiments somewhat as Malinowski and Murdock did, they envisage a warm tie developing between a youth and his mother's brother in patrilineal societies as sentiments from the mother are extended to the maternal uncle. Sentiments for the father's brother, however, are ambivalent because the paternal uncle shares in the authority of the father and lineage elders. As a result, the youth regards marriage with a matrilateral cross-cousin as more congenial than with a patrilateral one. The situation is reversed in matrilineal societies where the mother's brother frequently exercises authority over his sister's children, and there marriage with the daughter of the less austere paternal uncle is more congenial. Rodney Needham vigorously combatted the reasoning. Psychological solutions, he claimed, cannot be appropriately applied to a sociological problem, such as a prescriptive unilateral cross-cousin marriage. He seems to find a final cause explanation sufficient, and so he reiterates Lévi-Strauss's functionalist argument: matrilateral alliance provides a simple means of countering fissive tendencies in a segmentary society. Patrilateral cross-cousin marriage he ignores, because he could discover no certain evidence of it occurring anywhere in prescribed form.

Alliance theorists recognized, as social thinkers from Aristotle to Mauss had, that all exchange strengthens social integration; but mostly they treated so-called exchange of women. Women may, as Lévi-Strauss claims, be the most precious of a society's possessions, but alliance theory proceeded as if women were the only valuable figuring in social exchange.[70]

Magic, Ritual, and Belief

Instrumental and Expressive

A constant outpour of works dealing with ritual, mystical, and supernatural beliefs testifies to the undiminished interest those venerable social science topics continued to hold. Yet successive writers dealing with them reveal practically none of the cumulative development that occurred in the fields of kinship terminology, descent, and marriage. In the area of religion, authors often simply repeated old ideas in different language, or in an original fashion. Two theoretical routes, both of which had been firmly established in the 18th century, were followed. One analyzed ritual, belief, and magic as aids to coping, as integrational cement for the social structure, as compensation for material deprivation, or as devices providing explanations on a mystical plane for inexplicable or threatening natural conditions. Cultural relativism, heavily blanketing this subject, prevented much critical appraisal of the efficacy with which supernaturalism served those ends. From the second point of view, anthropologists sought to unlock meanings inherent in the symbolic content of rituals and beliefs. For the most part, they did so starting with distinctions made by the people being studied, suppressing their own, alien cultural presuppositions as much as possible,[71] and increasingly avoiding extreme psychodynamic interpretations of psychoanalysis. Since the two approaches are easily combined—symbols can have functions while also being expressive —the dichotomy I have drawn cannot be used to classify individual writers, only their ideas. Both views are also compatible with developmental approaches to religion, whether they be like Leslie White's, who regarded forms of belief as outcomes of the evolutionary process, or like Anthony F. C. Wallace's.[72] The latter, treating a 19th-century Seneca Indian revitalization movement in historical context, is also evolutionary as he shows how the movement promoted the adaptation of the Indian community to its drastically altered social environment.

The sharpest break with earlier thinking occurred in the conception of magic. Even before the Enlightenment, but especially then, magic had been regarded as a set of beliefs and techniques for dealing with practical problems. Now, new interpretations proposed by Godfrey and Monica Wilson in one book, and by Mary Douglas in another, made minimal or absolutely no reference to the pragmatic use of magic, but stressed its expressive significance.[73] Europeans err in ascribing complete trust and confidence to the primitive use of magic, Mary Douglas claims; primitive people are not so foolish.

For the Wilsons, magic is a variable. It generally runs very high in small-scale societies, where it characterizes many areas of life, including politics and religion. By magic, they mean an attitude attaching unfailing significance to particular things or combinations of things, such as a sign in a rite, the rite itself, a style in art, a person who is held responsible for events affecting a community. By its very nature, magic buttresses tradition and arrests modernization. When through increasing scale new ideas and practices penetrate a society, and social mobility increases and economic life develops, then magic is apt to decline. The variety, mobility, and development promoted by increased scale induce people to loosen their adherence to traditional ways of believing and doing things.

Approaching primitive magic as a form of ritual—as expressive behavior utilizing external forms and symbols—Douglas compares it to the Christian belief in miracles. It is human to hope for something miraculous to happen, and for Christians a miracle is always possible—though it cannot be guaranteed. So it is for primitives; they hope and believe magic will bring about results, but they don't think the results must necessarily follow the magical performance. Whether magical rites are directed toward the past, purporting like confession and purification to undo evil things that have already happened, or toward the future, as in agricultural rites, they affirm the order and values that ought to prevail. In these ideas, Douglas emphasizes the symbolic or expressive aspect of magic, not its instrumental side. Occasionally, she takes the actors' perspective as when, in terms reminiscent of Mauss, she says magic allows nonmaterial power to be released in human actions in controlled form.

Need Satisfier or Tranquilizer?

The functionalist thesis concerning religious beliefs put forward by Raymond Firth, the most psychological of the British social anthropologists, regards them as attempts by individuals to secure coherence in the physical and social world.[74] Beliefs also have functions going beyond the individual, because they supply organizing principles for social structure and sanctions for the moral order. Not that religious belief always serves only positive social functions; when it fails to change as the social structure changes, rather than maintaining personal and social equilibrium, it initiates disputes and produces deep structural cleavages.

Clifford Geertz, in a symbolist idiom, found new phrasing for the functionalist conception of religion.[75] Religious belief and practice render a group's ethos emotionally convincing and intellectually reasonable, so that the religious world view is presented as an image well adapted to the actual state of affairs. Religious symbols—mythological figures, skulls of deceased householders, and the like—not only express the world as conceived by a society; they also shape it by inducing in the worshipper a distinctive set of dispositions, which bestow a lasting quality on his experience. Symbols put the worshiper into certain moods (we call them reverent, solemn, or worshipful), they induce exultation and self-confidence, sometimes melancholy and self-pity. Ritual generates the veridical nature of the religious conceptions. On the ritual plane, the world as it is lived and as it is imagined fuse under the agency of a single set of symbols,[76] transporting the worshiper, totally engulfed in the ceremony, into another mode of existence.

The intellectual or explanatory functions of religion, minimized by Geertz in favor of the emotional transformation it engenders, totally occupy Robin Horton in the striking analogy he draws between supernaturalistic and scientific concepts.[77] Like scientific ideas, religious beliefs account for events in life that need to be explained—struggle, wresting a living, illness, and others. Both sets of ideas also allow believers to foretell consequences likely to follow from certain lines of conduct. Like scientific concepts, the postulated entities of religion exist in different degrees of concreteness. At the most concrete level, particular spirits—a god of smallpox, certain ancestors, or a specific witch—are held responsible for an event. At higher levels, coordinating the specific entities, explanatory concepts of broader scope operate, the most embracive being the Supreme Being who created everything. In the manner of the explanatory concepts of science, the postulated entities of religion stretch beyond the diversity, complexity, disorder, and anomaly we experience, and provide an underlying order, unity, simplicity, and regularity. Both religion and science explain by analytically breaking up the familiar features of common-sense experience into aspects of a different kind and then placing the aspects into a wider causal context. Thus success among the Tallensi is due to having been born under a good destiny and enjoying the beneficial surveillance of the ancestors. Accidents, however, reveal the hand of displeased ancestors, who restrain a person's normally good destiny.

Using different language, Melford Spiro covers the same ground as Geertz and Horton when he examines religious beliefs for the way the beliefs serve the cognitive need to know and explain, as well as substantive and affective-integrative needs.[78] To show the substantive function of religious knowledge, Spiro adopts the view of the actor who regards his religion as capable of providing benefits like rain, crops, military victory, and cures. From an alien observer's viewpoint, these are, of course, not real functions, for they cannot be confirmed objectively. For other functions, Spiro starts with an outsider's perspective. Religion satisfies affective-integrative needs when it provides opportunities for the discharge of aggression against menacing supernatural figures, or when beneficent figures allay dependency strivings, fears, and anxieties.

Religious beliefs persist over time, Spiro says, through the useful functions they perform, as well as on account of the traditional authority they bear and the absence, in small-scale societies, of alternative beliefs that seriously challenge the religious conceptions. But he is unwilling to leave the persistence of religion totally to functional and structural factors. His strong psychological inclination naturally inclines him to consider learning as an agency of continuity. Drawing on psychoanalytic theory, he ascribes the acquisition of supernatural beliefs in a society to their consistency with early perduring perceptions laid down in the personalities of members of the society through early childhood experiences. For example, in many societies a child's encounters with powerful human beings, who punish and gratify him, and who can sometimes be induced to accede to his desires, endows the child with a conception of people corresponding to the conception of deities taught in those societies. The consistency of the two conceptions favors learning the teachings.

No doubt the functionalists paid more attention to belief than to ritual, just as was always true; but they also gave heed to the pragmatic significance of the ceremonial side of religion. To take but one example, Victor Turner—coming from the University of Manchester, where anthropologists like Max Gluckman stressed social conflict and contradiction more than integration—perceived the special value of ritual in the disharmonic society where he did field work.[79] He describes conflicts among the Ndembu arising from the conjunction of virilocality and matrilineality; but whenever conflict reaches a certain point, ritual mechanisms come into play to restate common norms and values. The rites lift the emotions and raise social values to a compelling mystical plane, thereby compensating for the society's integrational deficiencies.

Historical materialists showed dissatisfaction with the instrumentalist thesis advanced by these and other British and American anthropologists. I. A. Kryvelev, a Soviet Russian ethnologist, doubted the adjustive and adaptive functions advanced for religion.[80] The adjustments religion provides, the hope and consolation it gives, are temporary, accidental, and akin to tranquilizers that alleviate distress without affecting the objective conditions causing the trouble. Religion and magic have thereby held back the growth of a correct understanding of nature, and retarded the development of rational means for dealing with natural phenomena. Kryvelev scorns the view that religion originated from a desire to understand natural phenomena. Primitive people, he claims, were not philosophical seekers after abstract truth; they were mainly concerned with obtaining food, shelter, and other practical problems. In those matters they scarcely found help in the vague, inherently contradictory ideas of religion. Nor did science start in myth and religion. There could never have been a time when people guided their activities exclusively by mythic thinking; from the start, in order to survive, mankind had to live according to the laws of the objective world.

Projections of Hostility, Hope, and Desire

Efforts to accommodate both the interpretation of meaning and functional analysis loom particularly large in writings about witchcraft, one of the most actively pursued topics in recent inquiry, as well as one productive of original knowledge.[81] The primary feature of witchcraft, i.e., suspicion that someone in the community is exerting malevolent power, makes it easily interpretable as an expression of hostility, anxiety, and other kinds of personal strain.

In any social system, held the prevailing theory of witchcraft, strain will motivate projection of hostility against persons whose behavior is frustrating or otherwise offensive, perhaps simply because the behavior departs from traditional norms. Herein, functionalists found the key to the ability of witchcraft beliefs to maintain social control: in communities where witches are an article of faith, fear of being so accused will induce people to conform by avoiding acts likely to offend or arouse suspicion. Inasmuch as rapid social change increases opportunities to behave nontraditionally, it is understandable why witchcraft epidemics should flourish under such conditions.

Rapid social change was also held partly responsible for bringing about messianic, millenarian, and similar movements, founded—so theory suggested—on deprivation.[82] Anthropologists took the movements as imaginative projections of hopes and frustrated desires into the future, where a far more satisfying existence awaits the believer. Bringing an instrumental viewpoint to bear on the movements revealed them as encouraging some actions practically suited to bringing about a materially better future. The very enthusiasm they generate helps to marshall energies, as adherents rework their economy, personal life style, and outlook along lines adapted to the altered cultural environment. In Melanesia, the cargo cults were seen as a means of integrating a fragmented social structure, welding hostile social segments into larger entities with political potential. On the psychological level, the symbols and dogmas of new faiths function to restore the sense of cognitive coherence that had been shattered through cultural confusion and rapid cultural change. One question remained unanswered: Why do some groups listen to their prophets and create new religious movements while many others, among whom cultural confusion runs just as high and change has been as rapid or more, remain without them? Do the latter groups possess functional equivalents for messianism and millenarianism?

More conventional interpretations of religious meaning were found by studying people's conceptions of the supernatural beings in whom they believed. Psychoanalytically minded ethnologists and British social anthropologists converged in treating them as refractions of social relationships. But the social anthropologists were cautious, Firth realizing there is only an imperfect nexus connecting religion and society.[83] Religious symbols, he admits, need not be a direct reflection of social structure; the symbolization may be organizationally rather than structurally contrived, so that the symbols are interpreted to suit sectional ends and special historical circumstances. Daryll Forde went further. Rather than always reflecting particular patterns of social relations, the supernatural entities and the rites directed to them may be ecologically stimulated by values and hazards attached to material resources and techniques, by the incidence of disease, and by other ecological risks or compelling interests.

At the end of a long line of postwar writings about ritual symbolization, stands the impressive work of British-trained Victor Turner, who moved to the United States, in 1961, and eventually went to the University of Chicago. A number of Turner's conclusions are most fully worked out in his ethnographic reports on the Central African Ndembu, but I will now mostly confine myself to nomothetic ideas.[84] There is a difficulty, however. It is sometimes hard to determine whether a proposition is intended to apply universally or only to Ndembu society. When he defines dominant symbols as packed with many disparate significata and occupying central positions in ritual, he is clearly offering a general concept. Then he describes dominant symbols varying between different systems of ritual within a single society, each system containing its own nuclear constellation of dominant symbols. How much comparative data does he draw on for that proposition? Or is he still thinking only of the Ndembu?

Ritual symbols, in Turner's usage of the term, are the smallest units of ceremony. They consist of objects, activities, relationships, events, gestures, or spatial units, and their most important meaning refers to normative concepts generally held in a society. Condensation gives ritual symbols a quality of multivocality so that a single one, especially a dominant one, conveys many meanings, the symbol fusing ethical and jural norms with strong emotional stimuli. The disparate referents of a particular symbol, Turner holds, are not accumulated randomly; they are all interconnected by virtue of being found together in everyday life, or because they are linked by analogous qualities, like the analogous qualities of nourishment and dependence which the Ndembu find in the milk tree. Only a portion of a symbol's full semantic wealth may be expressed in any one ritual; hence an ethnographer cannot know the full range of meaning until he has studied the whole system of rituals of which that ritual is part.

Dominant symbols fuse two poles of meaning. At the one pole is a cluster of significata referring to the moral and social order, to principles of social structure, or to values inherent in structural relationships. At the other pole, the referents are natural and physiological phenomena. Here, meaning is closely related to the outward, sensory form of the symbol; the milk tree in Ndembu ritual symbolizes breast milk, a meaning obviously related to the milky latex the tree exudes.

In one exercise of symbolic interpretation, "Betwixt and Between," Turner extends Arnold van Gennep's analysis of passage rites. Applying himself specifically to initiation rites, for they best exemplify transition, he explores the usually protracted marginal, or liminal, phase they contain. In this phase, occurring between the periods of separation and reaggregation, the individual or group undergoing initiation remains detached from any fixed point in the social structure; the initiate stands betwixt and between. Symbols express the ambiguous state of such persons, their position of structural invisibility. Often, Turner finds, the symbols of liminality refer to biological processes possessing a culturally defined negative tone, including death, decomposition, catabolism, and menstruation. Also the symbols are modeled on the processes of gestation and parturition, thereby revealing the "not yet clarified" social character of the neophytes whose state is like that of embryos, infants, and sucklings. In societies dominantly structured by kinship where sex also possesses great importance, initiates are sometimes treated as neither male nor female, or they are simultaneously assigned the character of both sexes. Frequently, too, they possess nothing during the liminal state, not status, property, clothing, insignia, kinship position, or anything else that would place them in the social structure. The simplicity of their situation is also expressed by a scarcity of jural sanctions governing their interaction with one another or with the community. Simplicity symbolizes their interstructural state. In their own group, their comradeship, familiarity, and mutual outspokenness likewise suggest structural simplicity; so does the passivity they manifest to their instructors, their submission and reduction to a uniform condition, which Turner interprets as being ground down prior to being fashioned anew. In contrast to the symbolic simplicity of the initiates' liminal state, what is exhibited, done, or communicated to them is frequently disproportionally monstrous or mysterious. Functionally, Turner hypothesizes, the disproportion impresses the neophytes with the importance of cultural factors hitherto taken for granted, and helps stamp in the basic cultural assumptions they are now learning.

A few years after the betwixt-and-between paper, Turner showed symbolic liminality occurring in periods of structurally simplified interaction other than initiation rites. Joining colleagues who were questioning the heavy stress social anthropologists traditionally placed on structural relations, and revealing the effects of his training by Gluckman, Turner looked at carnival and other short interludes of relatively free social interaction when human beings for a brief time shed structural distinctions and, united by generalized bonds, join in communitas. Rituals of status reversal, such as carnival—blending lowliness, sacredness, homogeneity, and comradeship—give a glimpse of what a society without status distinctions would be like. Participants in those affairs experience life in a relatively unstructured, undifferentiated community of equal individuals. Sometimes religious movements, such as cargo cults and related millenarian episodes, emphasizing homogeneity, equality, lack of property, and the reduction of everyone to a common level, attempt to prolong the liminal state. But inevitably, and quite soon, the antistructural phase of the movement gives way to routinization. A system of jural norms and statuses comes into being to govern the group, or the movement collapses and society returns to its structural phase.

Liminality is an ambiguous state, an anomaly like the anomalies Mary Douglas writes about in *Purity and Danger*.[85] Every culture, her theory states, is a means of ordering experience. But every ordering system gives rise to anomalies and ambiguities, with which it must be prepared to deal. Among cultural devices for reducing ambiguity and restoring order is labeling the anomalies as impure, polluting, or otherwise dangerous. Thereby the society facilitates their riddance through destruction, banishment, or execution, or it prepares the way for containing the dangers directly or symbolically. Primitive religions are replete with techniques for dealing with persons and things regarded as impure and polluting because they have violated principles of order by crossing some forbidden line. Moral sentiments support the rules of purity. The very idea of pollution occurring through, say, eating forbidden food or associating with a mystically dangerous person, may suffice to preserve order as culturally defined.

Douglas regards pollution ideas as metaphorical statements about, for example, the status of women, death, or the relation of the sexes. They express a conception of natural and social order, and to that order people seek to return when it has been temporarily upset. By attaching efficacy or value to external signs and forms of behavior, pollution ideas, together with their accompanying avoidances and purification rites, manifest a magical attitude, one of two types of attitudes Douglas finds in religion.[86] The magical attitude is not limited to primitive societies; it also crops up in large-scale societies among people profoundly attached to liturgical forms. The second religious attitude cultivates sensitivity to the symbolic meaning of concepts and observances, such as grace or the Jews' avoidance of pork. The observances themselves possess no special efficacy.

In the manner of Evans-Pritchard,[87] with whom Douglas studied, she dreads the effect of her own discipline on the richness of meaning contained in symbols, for, by heightening self-consciousness through the scientific study of religion, anthropology may destroy their credibility. By making all symbols equally plausible, it may bring about an end to meaning.

In a talk dealing with the environmental crisis, Douglas applied a lesson from primitive religions.[88] Science, she advises, will fail to bring about reforms to arrest environmental deterioration if the proposed rules lack moral conviction or if, being stated in dispassionate scientific terms, they convey no real sense of threat. Sentiments supporting the rules of traditional societies accord with popular experience. If the environmentalists' rules are to be taken seriously they, too, must accord with everyone's experience and not be based solely on what scientists know as a result of studying ecological systems.

Critical Anthropology

Culture, Empirical and Nonempirical

As anthropology proliferated and diversified, it grew more reflective about the epistemological character of the knowledge it attained, the presuppositions embedded in its methods and concepts, and its responsibilities to society, including the people it studied. Before reflection had gone far, the value of the anthropological enterprise itself came to be questioned.

By the late 1940s it had become obvious that ethnographic statements contain a fairly even match of empirical and nonempirical elements. Plainly, some things in a cultural account correspond in no direct or demonstrable manner to phenomena independent of the anthropologist. Cornelius Osgood argued the point logically, examining the different processes involved in knowing the several aspects of culture; John W. Bennett demonstrated the thesis ostensively by examining contradictions between several anthropological reports emanating from the same culture area.

Osgood, primarily an ethnographer, worked extensively among Northern Athapaskan Indians, in China, and in Korea. He admired Edward Sapir, with whom as a Ph.D. student he studied at the University of Chicago and who later became his colleague at Yale University. It may be he derived some of his epistemological bent from Sapir, who devoted a monograph, *Time Perspective in Aboriginal American Culture* (1916), to the subject of discovering chronology from ethnological, archeological, and linguistic facts. Osgood defines culture operationally as the ideas, consciously acquired by an anthropologist, first, about the external objects resulting from human actions (material culture); second, about the human actions themselves (social culture); and third, about the ideas held by a specific aggregate of human actors (mental culture).[89] Each division of culture involves the anthropologist in a different process of knowing and demands a different way of verifying whether the ideas are true (i.e., correspond to external phenomena). Objects resulting from human actions are far more static and more sharply defined than those belonging to any other division of culture, so that data pertaining to them can be easily pictured or subjected to experimentation. They are the simplest to verify directly. Reposing in the storage bins of museums or in photographs and drawings, conclusions concerning material objects can be repeatedly checked by independent observers.

Human actions, the data of social culture, remain more elusive and less well adapted to experimentation. Words and other acts vanish soon after they have been performed (except, Osgood might have added, as their traces repose in moving picture films and audiotapes) making them harder to verify directly than solid material objects, but not impossible.

When we come to ideas held by the actors, mental culture, we confront data impossible to verify directly. An observer can, within the limits represented by human actions, verify the words people used, but he possesses no control over the ideas themselves.

It would be excessive to claim that John Bennett, who received his degree from Chicago in 1941, ten years after Cornelius Osgood, discovered the biasing role values play in ethnographic description. He did, however, open anthropological eyes to the role that personal preferences play in ethnographic reports by the explanation he offered for the sharply divergent interpretations that had been published concerning Pueblo Indian culture.[90] One interpretation—he labels it "organic"—regarded the Indians' society and culture as unusually integrated by virtue of a consistent and harmonious set of values revealed in a personality ruled by the virtues of gentleness, tranquility, cooperation, and nonaggression. The other interpretation, called "repressive," reported smoldering covert tension, suspicion, coercion, fear, anxiety, and hostility among the people. Bennett traces each view to different preferences held in American culture and shared by the ethnographers who studied Pueblo life. Field workers who reported the organic image held a generally critical attitude toward the heterogeneity of modern society, in comparison to which the integration and coherency of primitive groups seemed preferable. They found those positive qualities in Pueblo society, and in their reports stressed them to the utmost, little heeding the means by which the Indians secured consistency between norms and action. Ethnographers taking the repressive view, Bennett believes, regarded the heterogeneity and diffusiveness of modern civilization as better suited to egalitarian democracy and spontaneous individual behavior than tight integration. He, too, saw the qualities of integration and consistency in Pueblo society, but stressed the coercive means through which the society attained them, and their psychological consequences in the form of hostility, suspicion, and other tensions. With his concluding advice, to cultivate awareness of personal values likely to obtrude on selection and interpretation, Bennett takes his place in the company of Joseph-Marie Degérando, James G. Frazer, and others who warned about the role of the personal equation in field research.

Along with growing epistemological sophistication and awareness of the role of values in ethnographic reporting, anthropologists recognized the construct nature of culture and social structure, and the intricate process required in formulating cultural constructs.[91] Ralph Linton, one of the first to acknowledge the construct theory, accepted it only halfheartedly, maintaining there was also a phenomenally real culture consisting of shared and transmitted behavior and material objects. Lévi-Strauss is more thoroughgoing as he speaks of the anthropologist's models; sometimes they are mechanical models and sometimes statistical ones. The first replicate the observed phenomena, the model builder following closely what his informants say or do. Statistical models do not necessarily employ statistics; they put greater distance between the observer and the things he studies. Using many individuals or instances of behavior, the observer notes tendencies, constructs typologies, and discerns processes not always recognized by the people themselves.

Ward Goodenough found the analogy of linguistics helpful in describing the construction of cultural models. Like the linguist, the ethnographer begins by defining the minimal number of distinctive elements discriminated by the actors themselves in a bit of behavior; these are equivalent to the distinctive features describing the sounds of a language. Once these emic primitives have been defined, the field worker proceeds to account for how they are combined to make more complex social forms, this being done analogously to the way phonemes are ordered into more complex linguistic units bearing specific meaning. Analytical concepts, like "marriage" and "warfare," belonging to anthropology's metalanguage, come last. They describe behavioral forms found in the culture being studied that belong to the same class as those already so labeled in other cultures, perhaps in the anthropologist's own.

Rodney Needham also called attention to the unempirical character of the analytical concepts that anthropologists construct for categorizing data and sometimes regard as if they were inductively derived from the empirical phenomena to which they refer. The builders of concepts often assume that all events grouped under a common term—"Omaha kinship terminology," "incest," or "patrilineal descent"—must have a property in common when, in fact, the specific events may have nothing in common. Ward Goodenough intimated the same criticism in his injunction to base etics on emics; i.e., to take pains in ascertaining that analytical categories correspond to similar conceptions held in various cultures. The advice tendered by Needham and Goodenough was not wholly new; classical evolutionism and diffusionism had also been criticized for applying analytical concepts without ascertaining whether the phenomena to which they referred—pyramids in Egypt and Mexico come to mind—were truly homologous.

Related to the epistemological character of analytical constructs is the question: how many people in a society do they cover? Ethnographers had long been cognizant of variation in motivation, habits, and personalities between individuals comprising a society. Sapir had it in mind when he observed that socialization never replicates the same psychological features in two individuals. Despite their knowledge, field workers wrote their accounts as if people all acted in the same way or embodied identical norms and motives. A. F. C. Wallace picked up Sapir's call for more recognition of variability in society and related diversity to conflicting individual interests.[92] He sees culture as policy tacitly concocted by groups of people for furthering their divergent interests and organizing their strivings for maximal mutual advantage. Anthropologists preferring to study diversity rather than uniformities in a society agreed with Edmund Leach.[93] The jural rules to which people are supposed to conform, he says, tell us little unless we also observe how the rules are applied. For that we must use the techniques of counting, measurement, and statistics.

A Nonobjective Science

After Bennett's paper, anthropologists could no longer believe in the complete objectivity of their discipline. Bob Scholte realized it when he portrayed anthropological traditions as cultural artifacts belonging to specific social and historical contexts.[94] Although the cumulative manner in which traditions develop—knowledge leading the inquirer to more knowledge—gives them a certain degree of autonomy; primarily, they depend on the "contextual domains" inhabited by the theorists who guide the traditions. The life-history experiences of a theorist, sometimes dimly revealed through the edited confessions he volunteers, help him to understand the field situation. The language he writes in, the institutional organization of the discipline, and the national culture in which the discipline is institutionalized further shape anthropological knowledge. In addition, the state of the art at a given time and the philosophical premises its practitioners entertain, often unquestioningly, color the results of research. Adopting the actors' perspectives, as formal semanticists do, brings no escape from the limits imposed by social and historical contexts; it simply substitutes one set of constraints for another.[95]

Thinking along those lines carries us into perspectivism, the philosophical position maintaining that we can never know pure facts, only interpretations. Jacques Maquet, a Belgian anthropologist living in the United States, applied perspectivism when, using the image of a photographer, he visualized an ethnographer always observing and conceptualizing external objects from a specific, limited position.[96] Hence he cannot avoid injecting personal elements into the material studied. He does so in interpreting, in making factual generalizations (patterns), and in creating larger inferences, say of a causal nature. Research is objective only insofar as the objects being investigated influence perception, or to the extent an investigator enlightens others about the perspective from which he viewed his material. Fuller knowledge is possible, Maquet points out, by adding to the perspectives previously used for understanding a culture, or by combining several positions in ongoing research. Each additional perspective reveals the extent to which previous ones affected knowledge. By this theory, the two opposing viewpoints concerning Pueblo Indian culture complemented one another; together they extended our knowledge beyond what it would have been had all the ethnographers used the same perspective. Lévi-Strauss, would disagree with the conclusion, if I understand him correctly.[97] When views diverge and one does not supersede a rival one, he asserts, we are left with lasting uncertainty concerning the truth.

Critical anthropologists in the 1960s followed John Bennett's lead and identified several contrasting perspectives to cultural study, though they did not pinpoint the consequences for research in a particular culture area as he did. Scott Cook unfavorably compared the humanistically inclined, Romantic approach, with its devotion to particular societies or their histories, to the formalistic tradition, which seeks to discover general abstractions holding for all events of a given type.[98] Scholte contrasted the strongly empirical Anglo-American approach to scholarship with the more strongly rationalistic Continental tradition. The former assumes the primacy of the empirical act, prefers to apply descriptive and quantitative methods to concrete human groups or individuals acting in specific situations, and makes predictions it hopes to verify. The Continental tradition, where Lévi-Strauss fits perfectly, assumes the primacy of the human mind, poses problems answerable by logical or deductive methods, and regards counting as irrelevant; a few cases suffice to establish a generalization.

Stephen Tyler confirmed the existence of an empirical and a non-empirical-rationalistic tradition but concluded, with cognitive anthropology in mind, that since cultures are mental constructs, not physical phenomena, they can only be grasped in nonempirical terms.[99] Cognitive anthropology, he claims—sounding like Alfred Kroeber upholding ethnology as "history"—discovers the meaning of a concept in context. Unlike the physical sciences, it refrains from referring the concept to independent factors ascertained by experimentation and by other objective discovery procedures.

Scholte preferred the Continental tradition. "Scientistic anthropology," he complains, leaves unutilized the personal sensitivities of an observer, relegating them to the status of idiosyncrasies, whereas in truth they constitute a most valuable means for directly experiencing reality. The goals of predictability and lawfulness absorbed from physical science, he fears, introduce an unethical "anything goes" attitude into research involving human beings. Furthermore, scientistic anthropology, infatuated with the possibility of attaining purely objective knowledge, is incapable of perceiving its cultural limitations or philosophical underpinnings; hence it remains arrogantly indifferent to empistemological considerations. As a result, most anthropologists who follow that approach don't realize how utterly culture-bound they are.

In the United States, some of those who were malcontented with the scientific tradition in anthropology proposed adopting a more humanistic approach embodying social criticism and heading toward a new praxis. To forge such an approach they looked back to the integrated science of man cultivated by philosophers of the Enlightenment.[100] Let anthropologists drawing on their now abundant information do what the best minds of the 18th century did: construct an ideal image of man and against it assess the deplorable condition into which the human race has fallen. The malcontents thought, as Kroeber had, and Robert Redfield did, too,[101] that something valuable would be lost if anthropology persisted in a strictly scientific approach. Oddly, the Americans who advocated a stronger humanistic approach showed little awareness of the philosophical anthropology being pursued, mainly abroad; the ideas around which it revolved might have suited their plea for greater social relevance.

Abetting Imperialism[102]

Some critics charged anthropology with being socially irrelevant, even irresponsible, when it came to major public issues. They pointed to the way members of the profession seek to avoid taking stands, pleading that their role and competence as scientists were unsuited to judging controversial issues. Hence anthropologists rarely question American foreign investment and the political strings attached to it; most keep silent about U.S. intervention in popular revolutions; overlook the exploitation of the people who produce raw materials for the industrial nations; and even as professionals don't study the creative cultural act taking place in the world as dependent people liberate themselves from economic and political subordination and acquire a new consciousness of themselves. Who is in a better position to evaluate policy and suggest guidelines for political action than those who study culture? But the critics left unspecified the kinds of evaluation and policy suggestions anthropologists could offer; nor did they themselves furnish examples of such activity to guide others. The discipline's silence, those calling for an adversary role pointed out, permits the government to make decisions unchallenged and even to use anthropological knowledge as it pleases, sometimes for unscrupulous ends.

Anthropology, the politically minded critics frequently noted, had begun to flourish simultaneously with the spread of white rule over the colored world. The taint of that association still commits the profession to abet imperialism, the new imperialism in which key decisions affecting the allocation of benefits to a society are made by another cultural group, often a different ethnic group, for the benefit of the dominant group. Working among dependent people would provide ethnologists and social anthropologists with excellent opportunities to study the evil effects of neocolonialism. Instead, the mostly white anthropologists from the economically powerful nations largely ignore the problem of imperialism, refuse to agitate for its overthrow, and stay blind to the struggle of dependent people to achieve political and economic liberation. They study modernization, urbanization, and westernization, concepts contrived to conceal the evidence of force, suffering, and economic exploitation among subordinated people. They refuse to see revolutionary conflict as a factor promoting change. In fact, some researchers make it their object to discover means of avoiding violence in situations of exploitation. Starting with the dubious assumption that causation is always multiple, anthropologists working within the imperialist system on theoretical grounds eliminate revolution as a practical means of bringing about political and economic enfranchisement. The anthropological concept of primitive cultures serves neocolonialism by projecting the idea of white people's relatively high social standing versus others. Another concept, cultural relativity, implies that a good life for poor, exploited, and powerless people is possible, though it will be different than the good life in rich capitalist societies.

Few people rebutted those charges or appraised the suggestions made for reforming the discipline. One response took a severely academic stand.[103] Granting that the social context—colonialism—in which anthropology had developed determined what it studied, nevertheless the discipline was also governed by an autonomous intellectual tradition that determined the problems chosen for investigation. Criticism of anthropology based on ideology helps to expose the perspectives from which research is carried out, but says nothing about the truth or falsity of results obtained through those perspectives.

New and Old Concepts

Discovering Dynamics

In this chapter we sampled topics in recent anthropology whose earlier development in some cases—religion, incest rules, and culture change—we have been following over some 2,000 years. New ideas for enlightening those topics could still be found, while old ideas persisted with little change except for the language in which they came to be expressed, or the theoretical background against which they were viewed. Thus from Geertz came the partially original idea that religion acts by transforming the emotions, a theory similar to functional explanations of ritual going back to Durkheim and beyond him to Nicholas of Cusa. At the same time, thoroughly familiar intellectualistic and emotionalistic theories of religion remained, refined in Spiro's systematic and psychologically informed account of how religion functions. Novel phylogenetic explanations for the origin of incest avoidances appeared, joining the theory that incest rules operate to create alliances—through women, Lévi-Strauss emphasized in his contribution to that familiar theory.

Less ancient ideas also persisted into recent anthropology; some were reconceived and others had their validity challenged. The concept of scale was coined to distinguish between primitive and civilized societies, and to explain what happens when a formerly isolated, historyless society widens its social boundaries in space and time. Primitive societies were seen as possessing a comparatively small number of roles and types of social relationships through which economic, religious, legal, and other activities are carried out; as a result they are characterized by a special kind of integration which is lacking in large-scale societies. Roles were regarded as open to manipulation by individuals, and as a means for shifting social identity. How descent groups affect kin terms was explained by showing descent acting as a social equalizer or differential. The distinction between kinship and descent was further clarified, and the basis of the family was established, largely by definition, as lying in the mother-child relationship. Magic was reconceived. Mary Douglas rejected the presumption that people use magic primarily as a technique for directly influencing events. She regarded magic much like other rituals, as expressive of sentiments, specifically hope. The firm control over social structure Radcliffe-Brown credited to norms and values was doubted. Some anthropologists became convinced that personal and social unrest need not accompany rapid and heavy cultural change. Hence they abandoned the idea that gradual change was necessary to avoid cultural disruption.

The heavy emphasis on method in recent anthropology, to which I referred at the close of the last chapter, did not, of course, totally eliminate theorizing about the dynamics of culture. We find ethnologists and social anthropologists employing their several approaches and devoting considerable effort in doing so to discover causes and causal consequences of cultural phenomena. I refer not to particular historical causes but to recurrent contemporary, or near-contemporary, conditions, including early life experiences. The search for cultural dynamics was the aim pursued in the study of culture change, kinship terminology, descent groups, incest rules, religion, and other topics. To some extent, in anthropology, the validity of causal relationships was still supported only logically, or by rationalistic argument; but increasingly since the late 1940s quantitative research in particular societies, and the hologeistic method in cross-cultural research, have been regarded as necessary for establishing the empirical validity of causal connections. Murdock, using data from some 200 societies, employed quasi-experimental techniques relying on comparison and statistical correlation to demonstrate empirically the validity of the theory that marriage, descent groups, and other forms of social structure determine kinship terminology. Similar procedures provided support for the theory that accusations of witchcraft are projections of hostility directed against members of the community whose behavior is frustrating or offensive and a source of stress. In psychological anthropology, hologeistic research showed that child-rearing practices are significantly related to, and presumably determine, folk theories of illness, folk systems for treating illness, concepts of deity, and other adult beliefs and behaviors.

Anthropology, along with reevaluating, reformulating, and testing its heritage of ideas, also became increasingly reflective concerning its presuppositions, the character of its knowledge, and its hitherto taken-for-granted values. Some writers challenged the moral value of the discipline, and the morality of the auspices under which it had sometimes been carried out and financially supported. Those who questioned its reason for being, like those who feared lest the identity of the discipline evaporate due to the manifold unrelated topics and interests being pursued, wondered uncertainly what the future of the field would be. In the United States, where the subject had been generously supported by the federal government and foundations, anxiety was abetted by the financial stringency of the 1970s and by a leveling off in the number of positions for university teachers.

If it is difficult for a historian to know how in the past one person's ideas influenced another's or to determine when concepts belonging to different ages are genetically related, it is infinitely harder, in fact impossible, to predict what recent developments in anthropological ideas bode for the future. Few would challenge the maxim of the historical viewpoint, that the past precipitates the future. What the precipitate will be, whether the recent past will turn out to have been "chrysalis or coffin"[104] or, for different topics and interests, both, we must wait and see.

Notes

1. Francis L. K. Hsu, "Rethinking the Concept 'Primitive,'" *Current Anthropology*, vol. 5 (1964): 169–178.

2. Leslie A. White, *The Concept of Culture* (Minneapolis: Burgess Publishing Co., 1973), pp. 65–66; Stanley Diamond, "The Search for the Primitive," in I. Galdston, ed., *Man's Image in Medicine and Anthropology* (New York: International Univer-

sities Press, 1963); Claude Lévi-Strauss, *The Savage Mind,* trans. Anonymous (Chicago: University of Chicago Press, 1962), ch. 1; Mary Douglas, *Natural Symbols* (London: Barrie and Rockliff, Cresset Press, 1970), p. 92.

3. Max Gluckman, "Les Rites de passage," in Max Gluckman, ed., *Essays on the Ritual of Social Relations* (Manchester: At the University Press, 1962); Raymond Firth, "Social Anthropology," in *Encyclopaedia Britannica* (14th ed., 1964), vol. 20.

4. Robert Redfield, "The Folk Society," *American Journal of Sociology,* vol. 52 (1947): 293–308; Robert Redfield, "Tribe, Peasant, and City" [orig. 1953], in Robert Redfield, *Human Nature and the Study of Society,* Margaret Park Redfield, ed. (Chicago: University of Chicago Press, 1962); Godfrey Wilson and Monica Wilson, *The Analysis of Social Change* (Cambridge: At the University Press, 1945), chs. 1–2.

5. J. A. Barnes, *Three Styles of Kinship* (London: Tavistock Publications, 1971), pp. 84–95; Raoul S. Naroll, "Some Thoughts on Comparative Method in Cultural Anthropology," in H. M. and A. B. Blalock, eds., *Methodology in Social Research* (New York: McGraw-Hill Book Co., 1968).

6. What follows on ethnic boundaries comes from Edward H. Spicer, "Persistent Cultural Systems," *Science,* vol. 174 (1971): 795–800; Fredrik Barth, "Introduction," in Fredrik Barth, ed., *Ethnic Groups and Boundaries* (Boston: Little Brown and Co., 1969); and Yehudi A. Cohen, "Social Boundary Systems," *Current Anthropology,* vol. 10 (1969): 103–126. For an earlier discussion of techniques and ideologies maintaining cultural boundaries see, Social Science Research Council Summer Seminar on Acculturation, 1953, "Acculturation: An Exploratory Formulation," *American Anthropologist,* vol. 56 (1954): 973–1002.

7. Daniel J. Crawley, "Plural and Differential Acculturation in Trinidad," *American Anthropologist,* vol. 59 (1957): 817–824; Steven Polgar,

"Biculturation of Mesquakie Teenage Boys," *American Anthropologist,* vol. 62 (1960): 217–235.

8. Robert A. LeVine and Donald T. Campbell, *Ethnocentrism* (New York: John Wiley and Sons, 1972), ch. 7.

9. The section considers the following studies of status and role: Ralph Linton, *The Study of Man* (New York: D. Appleton-Century, 1936), ch. 8; Siegfried Nadel, *The Theory of Social Structure* (London: Cohen and West, 1957), ch. 2; Ward Goodenough, "Rethinking 'Status' and 'Role': Towards a General Model of the Cultural Organization of Social Relationships," in Michael Banton, ed., *The Relevance of Models for Social Anthropology* (Association of Social Anthropologists Monographs 1, 1965).

10. Raymond Firth, "Siegfried Frederick Nadel 1903–1956," *American Anthropologist,* vol. 59 (1957): 117–124; Meyer Fortes, "Siegfried Frederick Nadel, 1903–1956, A Memoir," in Nadel, *Social Structure.*

11. I refer to the following works by Margaret Mead: "Introduction," and "Interpretative Statement," both in Margaret Mead, ed., *Cooperation and Competition among Primitive Peoples* [orig. 1937] (Boston: Beacon Press, 1961), pp. 460, 482–483; "The Comparative Study of Culture and the Purposive Cultivation of Democratic Values" [orig. 1941] and "Cultural Contexts of Nutrition Patterns" [orig. 1950], both in Margaret Mead, *Anthropology: A Human Science* (New York: Van Nostrand, 1964), pp. 94, 176–186; *Cultural Patterns and Technical Change* (Paris: Unesco, 1953), pp. 9–11.

12. George Peter Murdock, "Fundamental Characteristics of Culture" [orig. 1940], in George Peter Murdock, *Culture and Society* (Pittsburgh: University of Pittsburgh Press, 1965), p. 84.

13. John Gillin, *The Ways of Men* (New York: Appleton-Century-Crofts, 1948), pp. 198, 498, and ch. 24.

14. Raoul Naroll, "Galton's Problem," in Raoul Naroll and Ronald Cohen,

eds., *A Handbook of Method in Cultural Anthropology* (Garden City, N.Y.: Natural History Press, 1970), p. 975. For the use of quantitative methods in culture-area classification, see Harold E. Driver, *The Contribution of A. L. Kroeber to Culture Area Theory and Practice* (Indiana University Publications in Anthropology and Linguistics, memoir 18 of the *International Journal of American Linguistics*, 1962), pp. 14–20.

15. Clifford Geertz, "Ritual and Social Change: A Javanese Example," in Clifford Geertz, *The Interpretation of Culture* (New York: Basic Books, 1973).

16. Elman Service, *Primitive Social Organization* (New York: Random House, 1962), p. 195.

17. Max Gluckman, "Introduction," in Max Gluckman, *Order and Rebellion in Tribal Africa* (London: Cohen and West, 1963), p. 39.

18. Robert F. Murphy, *The Dialectics of Social Life* (New York: Basic Books, 1971).

19. Service, *Primitive Social Organization;* Julian H. Steward, *Theory of Culture Change* (Urbana: University of Illinois Press, 1958), chs. 3 and 6.

20. Meyer Fortes and E. E. Evans-Pritchard, "Introduction," in Meyer Fortes and E. E. Evans-Pritchard, eds., *African Political Systems* (London: Oxford University Press, 1940).

21. Nadel, *Social Structure*, pp. 65–66.

22. Max Gluckman, *Custom and Conflict in Africa* (Oxford: Basil Blackwell, 1955), chs. 1–2.

23. Theodore Schwartz cited in Mary Catherine Bateson, *Our Own Metaphor* (New York: Alfred A. Knopf, 1972), pp. 78–79.

24. Fred Voget, "Cultural Change," *Biennial Review of Anthropology, 1963:* 228–275, pp. 266ff.; Evon Z. Vogt, "On the Concepts of Structure and Process in Cultural Anthropology," *American Anthropologist*, vol. 62 (1960): 18–33.

25. A. I. Hallowell, "Sociopsychological Aspects of Acculturation" [orig. 1945], in A. I. Hallowell, *Culture and Experience* (Philadelphia: University of Pennsylvania Press, 1955); Melford E. Spiro, "Culture and Personality," in *International Encyclopedia of the Social Sciences* (1968), vol. 3.

26. Margaret Mead, *New Lives for Old* (New York: William Morrow and Co., 1956), ch. 18.

27. Wilson and Wilson, *Social Change,* ch. 5.

28. V. Gordon Childe, *What is History?* (New York: Henry Schuman, 1953), ch. 7.

29. Alexander Spoehr, *The Florida Seminole Camp,* and Alexander Spoehr, *Changing Kinship Systems* (Field Museum of Natural History, Anthropological Series, vol. 33, nos. 3 and 4, 1944, 1947).

30. Social Science Research Council Seminar, 1953, "Acculturation."

31. Crawley, "Acculturation in Trinidad"; Polgar, "Biculturation of Mesquakie Boys."

32. A. L. Kroeber, "What Ethnography Is," in A. L. Kroeber, *Ethnographic Interpretations 1–6* (University of California Publications in American Archaeology and Ethnology, vol. 47, 1957), p. 196; Robert F. Murphy, "Social Change and Acculturation," *Transactions of the New York Academy of Sciences,* ser. 2, vol. 26 (1964): 845–854.

33. Homer G. Barnett, *Innovation* (New York: McGraw-Hill Book Co., 1953), chs. 2–3.

34. Robert Redfield, *Peasant Society and Culture* (Chicago: University of Chicago Press, 1956), ch. 3; Robert Redfield and Milton B. Singer, "The Cultural Role of Cities," *Economic Development and Cultural Change,* vol. 3 (1954): 53–73; McKim Marriott, "Little Communities in an Indigenous Civilization," in McKim Marriott, ed., *Village India* (American Anthropological Association, Memoir no. 83, 1955). For a Sanskritization, see M. N. Srinivas, "Varna and Caste," in The University of Chicago, The College, *Introduction to the Civilization of India: Changing Dimensions of Indian Society and Culture* (Chicago: Syllabus

Division, University of Chicago Press, 1957).

35. George M. Foster, *Traditional Societies and Technological Change* (2nd ed.; New York: Harper & Row, 1973); Edward H. Spicer, ed., *Human Problems in Technological Change* (New York: Russell Sage Foundation, 1952); Benjamin D. Paul, ed., *Health, Culture, and Community* (New York: Russell Sage Foundation, 1955).

36. Arthur H. Niehoff and J. Charnel Anderson, "The Process of Cross-Cultural Innovation," *International Development Review*, vol. 6 (1964): 5–11.

37. Mead, *Cultural Patterns and Technical Change*.

38. Fredrik Barth, "On the Study of Social Change," *American Anthropologist*, vol. 69 (1967): 661–669.

39. For biographical information and intellectual development see the following by George P. Murdock: "Autobiographical Sketch," in Murdock, *Culture and Society; Social Structure* (New York: Macmillan Co., 1949), pp. xi–xvii; "Anthropology's Mythology," *Proceedings of the Royal Anthropological Institute of Great Britain and Ireland for 1971*: 17–24.

40. George P. Murdock, "Bifurcate Merging: A Test of Five Theories," *American Anthropologist*, vol. 49 (1947): 56–68.

41. Murdock, *Social Structure*, chs. 6–7.

42. A. G. Keller, *Societal Evolution* [orig. 1915] (rev. ed.; New York: Macmillan Co., 1931).

43. Fred Eggan, *The American Indian* (Chicago: Aldine Publishing Co., 1966), ch. 2 and pp. 171ff.

44. Murdock, *Social Structure*, ch. 8.

45. Elman R. Service, "Kinship Terminology and Evolution" [orig. 1960], in Elman R. Service, *Cultural Evolutionism* (New York: Holt, Rinehart and Winston, 1971).

46. Leslie A. White, "A Problem in Kinship Terminology," *American Anthropologist*, vol. 41 (1939): 566–573.

47. The criticism is made by Floyd Lounsbury, who offers "A Formal Account of the Crow- and Omaha-type Kinship Terminologies," in Ward H. Goodenough, ed., *Explorations in Cultural Anthropology* (New York: McGraw-Hill Book Co., 1962).

48. For a review of the debate, see Harold W. Scheffler, "Kinship Semantics," *Annual Review of Anthropology*, vol. 1 (1972): 309–328, pp. 312ff.; and Ira R. Buchler and Henry A. Selby, *Kinship and Social Organization* (New York: Macmillan Co., 1968), pp. 4–8, 33–46.

49. E. R. Leach, "Concerning Trobriand Clans and the Kinship Category *tabu*," in J. Goody, ed., *The Developmental Cycle of Domestic Groups* (Cambridge Papers in Social Anthropology, no. 1, 1962); two papers by David M. Schneider: "Kinship and Biology," in Ansley J. Coale et al., eds., *Aspects of the Analysis of Family Structure* (Princeton: Princeton University Press, 1965), and "What Is Kinship All About?" in P. Reining, ed., *Kinship Studies in the Morgan Centennial Year* (Washington, D.C.: Anthropological Society of Washington, 1972).

50. Scheffler, "Kinship Semantics"; Floyd Lounsbury, "Another View of the Trobriand Kinship Categories," in E. A. Hammel, ed., *Formal Semantic Analysis* (special publication of the *American Anthropologist*, vol. 67, no. 5, part 2, 1965).

51. Francis L. K. Hsu, "Kinship and Ways of Life: An Exploration," in Francis L. K. Hsu, ed., *Psychological Anthropology* (Homewood, Ill.: Dorsey Press, 1961), p. 402.

52. What follows is based on Murdock, *Social Structure*, pp. 14, 92, 96–97, 107; Roger M. Keesing, "On Quibblings over Squabblings of Siblings: New Perspectives on Kin Terms and Behavior," *Southwestern Journal of Anthropology*, vol. 25 (1969), 207–227; and two works by Francis L. K. Hsu: "The Effects of Dominant Kinship Relationships on Kin and Non-Kin Behavior: A Hypothesis," *American Anthropologist*, vol. 67 (1965): 638–661, and "Kinship and Ways of Life."

53. Reported in Francis L. K. Hsu, ed., *Kinship and Culture* (Chicago: Aldine Publishing Co., 1971).

54. In what follows I have relied on Harold W. Scheffler, "Kinship, Descent, and Alliance," in John J. Honigmann, ed., *Handbook of Social and Cultural Anthropology* (Chicago: Rand McNally and Co., 1973), pp. 756–762; Meyer Fortes, "The Structure of Unilineal Descent Groups" [orig. 1953], in Meyer Fortes, *Time and Social Structure and Other Essays* (London: Athlone Press, 1970); Marshall D. Sahlins, "On the Ideology and Composition of Descent Groups," *Man*, vol. 65 (1965): 104–107; and for matrilateral asymmetry Sylvia J. Vatuk, "Trends in North Indian Urban Kinship: the Matrilateral Asymmetry Hypothesis," *Southwestern Journal of Anthropology*, vol. 27 (1971): 287–307.

55. Fredrik Barth, *Models of Social Organization* (Royal Anthropological Institute Occasional Paper no. 23, 1966); J. D. Freeman, "On the Concept of the Kindred," *Journal of the Royal Anthropological Institute*, vol. 91 (1961): 192–220.

56. Adam Kuper, *Anthropologists and Anthropology* (London: Allen Lane, 1973), pp. 117, 119–121, 157–160, 161.

57. I have drawn on the following: Fortes, "Unilineal Descent Groups"; Meyer Fortes, *Kinship and the Social Order* (London: Routledge and Kegan Paul, 1969), especially pp. 291ff. for the concept of corporateness; Jack Goody, "Descent Groups," in *International Encyclopedia of the Social Sciences* (1968), vol. 8; Peter M. Worsley, "The Kinship System of the Tallensi: A Reevaluation," *Journal of the Royal Anthropological Institute*, vol. 86 (1956): 37–76; John Middleton and David Tait, "Introduction," in John Middleton and David Tait, eds., *Tribes Without Rulers* (London: Routledge and Kegan Paul, 1958).

58. For a synthesis of the ideas of Spier, Lowie, Steward, and others, see Murdock, *Social Structure*, pp. 58–60, 201ff.; also Robert H. Lowie, *Social Organization* (New York: Rinehart and Company, 1948), pp. 251–252, 260.

59. Peter M. Worsley, "The Kinship System of the Tallensi: A Revaluation," *Journal of the Royal Anthropological Institute*, vol. 86 (1956): 37–76.

60. George P. Murdock, "Cognatic Forms of Social Organization," in George P. Murdock, ed., *Social Structure in Southeast Asia* (Viking Fund Publications in Anthropology, no. 29, 1960); Ward H. Goodenough, *Description and Comparison in Cultural Anthropology* (Chicago: Aldine, 1970), ch. 2; Robin Fox, *Kinship and Marriage* (Harmondsworth: Penguin Books, 1967), pp. 49–52.

61. Meyer Fortes, "Descent, Filiation and Affinity: A Rejoinder to Dr. Leach," *Man*, vol. 59 (1959): 193–197, 206–212; Fortes, *Kinship and the Social Order*, ch. 13.

62. What I have to say about new ideas concerning the family and marriage comes from Murdock, *Social Structure*, pp. 1–4, 11; Goodenough, *Description and Comparison*, ch. 1, whose redefinition of the nuclear family is anticipated by Richard N. Adams, "An Inquiry into the Nature of the Family," in Gertrude Dole and Robert L. Carneiro, eds., *Essays in the Science of Culture* (New York: Thomas Y. Crowell Co., 1960); Edmund R. Leach, "Polyandry, Inheritance, and the Definition of Marriage," *Man*, vol. 55 (1955): 182–186, p. 183; and E. Kathleen Gough, "The Nayars and The Definition of Marriage," *Journal of the Royal Anthropological Institute*, vol. 89 (1959): 23–34.

63. Murdock, *Social Structure*, pp. 13–14, 17–18, 59–60, 285–312; for another combination of the alliance and group disruption theories see Jack Goody, "A Comparative Approach to Incest and Adultery" [orig. 1956], in Jack Goody, *Comparative Studies in Kinship* (London: Routledge and Kegan Paul, 1969).

64. However, an ethnographer in Taiwan found empirical support for the theory: see Arthur P. Wolf, "Childhood Association, Sexual Attraction, and the Incest Taboo: A Chinese Case," *American Anthropologist*, vol. 68 (1966): 883–898.

65. David F. Aberle, et al., "The Incest Taboo and the Mating Patterns of

Animals," *American Anthropologist,* vol. 65 (1963): 253–265; Miriam Kreiselman Slater, "Ecological Factors in the Origin of Incest," *American Anthropologist,* vol. 61 (1959): 1042–1059.

66. See the following by Claude Lévi-Strauss: *The Elementary Structures of Kinship* [orig. 1949], trans. James Harle Bell, John Richard von Sturmer, and Rodney Needham who also served as editor (Boston: Beacon Press, 1969), pp. 4, 24, 30, 32, 38–39, 43, 62, 129, 135, 481; and "Postscript" to chapters 3 and 4 in Claude Lévi-Strauss, *Structural Anthropology,* trans. Claire Jacobson and Brooke Grundfest Schoepf (New York: Basic Books, 1963), p. 83.

67. For Claude Lévi-Strauss I have used his *Elementary Structures,* pp. xxiii–xlii, 32–45, 62ff.; and "The Future of Kinship Studies," in *Proceedings of the Royal Anthropological Institute of Great Britain and Ireland for 1965:* 13–22. For preferential and prescriptive marriage, see also Rodney Needham, *Structure and Sentiment* (Chicago: University of Chicago Press, 1962), pp. 8–11. For the working of restricted and generalized systems, see Fox, *Kinship and Marriage,* chs. 7–8; D. Maybury-Lewis, "Prescriptive Marriage Systems," *Southwestern Journal of Anthropology,* vol. 21 (1965): 207–230; and Scheffler, "Kinship, Descent, and Alliance," pp. 782–786.

68. Reo Fortune, "Incest," in *Encyclopaedia of the Social Sciences* (1932), vol. 7.

69. Murdock, *Social Structure,* pp. 269–270; George C. Homans and David M. Schneider, *Marriage, Authority, and Final Causes* (Glencoe: Free Press, 1955); see also Needham, *Structure and Sentiment,* and Lévi-Strauss, *Elementary Structures,* ch. 27.

70. For recognition of other exchanges, see Meyer Fortes, "Analysis and Description in Social Anthropology" [orig. 1953], in Fortes, *Time and Social Structure,* pp. 134 ff.; Claude Lévi-Strauss, "The Bear and the Barber," *The Journal of the Royal*

Anthropological Institute, vol. 58 (1963): 1–11, p. 2.

71. E. E. Evans-Pritchard, "Religion," in *The Institutions of Primitive Society* (Oxford: Basil Blackwell, 1954), pp. 8–9.

72. Leslie A. White, *The Evolution of Culture* (New York: McGraw-Hill Book Co., 1959), ch. 15; belonging to the same genre is Robert N. Bellah, "Religious Evolution," *American Sociological Review,* vol. 29 (1964): 358–374. For religion as adaptation, see Anthony F. C. Wallace, "Revitalization Movements," *American Anthropologist,* vol. 58 (1956): 264–281; Anthony F. C. Wallace "Cultural Composition of the Handsome Lake Religion," in William N. Fenton and John Gulick, eds., *Symposium on Cherokee and Iroquois Culture* (Bureau of American Ethnology Bulletin 180, 1961). A religious belief system as adaptive in a changing social environment is also the theme of Eric R. Wolf, "The Social Organization of Mecca and the Origins of Islam," *Southwestern Journal of Anthropology,* vol. 7 (1951): 329–356.

73. Wilson and Wilson, *Social Change,* pp. 88–95; Douglas, *Natural Symbols,* chs. 1–3.

74. See the following by Raymond Firth: "Religious Belief and Personal Adjustment" [orig. 1948], and Raymond Firth, "Problem and Assumption in an Anthropological Study of Religion" [orig. 1959], both in Raymond Firth, *Essays on Social Organization and Values* (London: University of London, Athlone Press, 1964).

75. Clifford Geertz, "Religion as a Cultural System," in Michael Banton, ed., *Anthropological Approaches to the Study of Religion* (London: Tavistock Publications, 1966), pp. 4, 9, 11, 28, 36.

76. Murphy, *Dialects of Social Life,* p. 243.

77. Robin Horton, "African Traditional Thought and Western Science," *Africa,* vol. 37 (1967): 50–71. For destiny and the ancestors among the Tallensi, see Meyer Fortes, *Oedipus and Job in West African Religion*

(Cambridge: At the University Press, 1959).

78. All the following titles by Melford E. Spiro are pertinent: "Social Systems, Personality, and Functional Analysis," in Bert Kaplan, ed., *Studying Personality Cross-Culturally* (Evanston: Row-Peterson Co., 1961), pp. 109–112, 120; "Religion and the Irrational," in June Helm, ed., *Symposium on New Approaches to the Study of Religion* (Proceedings of the 1964 Annual Meeting of the American Ethnological Society, 1964), pp. 105, 112–114; "Religion: Problems of Definition and Explanation," in Banton, *Study of Religion;* and "Culture and Personality," pp. 255–257.

79. Victor W. Turner, *Schism and Continuity in an African Society* (Manchester: At the University Press, 1957), pp. xxi, 122–128, and ch. 10. For similar reasoning, see Max Gluckman, *Politics, Law and Ritual in Tribal Society* (Oxford: Basil Blackwell, 1965), pp. 251ff.

80. I. A. Kryvelev, "On Gallus's Biofunctional Theory of Religion," *Current Anthropology,* vol. 15 (1974): 92–95.

81. Clyde Kluckhohn, *Navaho Witchcraft* (Papers of the Peabody Museum of Archaeology and Ethnology, Harvard University, 1944); S. F. Nadel, "Witchcraft in Four African Societies," *American Anthropologist,* vol. 54 (1952): 18–29. For an article, obviously inspired by the events of the McCarthy era in the United States, extending the theory to suspected foreign agents and traitors, see Bernard J. Siegel and Alan R. Beals, "Conflict and Factionalist Dispute," *Journal of the Royal Anthropological Institute,* vol. 90 (1960): 107–117.

82. The following by Anthony F. C. Wallace: "Revitalization Movements"; "Mazeway Resynthesis: A Biocultural Theory of Religious Inspiration," *Transactions of the New York Academy of Sciences,* ser. 2, vol. 18 (1956): 626–638; "Mazeway Disintegration: The Individual's Perception of Socio-Cultural Disorganization," *Human Organization,* vol. 16 (1957): 23–27. See also Peter Worsley, *The Trumpet Shall Sound*

(London: MacGibbon and Kee, 1957), pp. 225–250; David F. Aberle, "A Note on Relative Deprivation Theory as Applied to Millenarian and Other Cult Movements," in Sylvia L. Thrupp, ed., *Millennial Dreams in Action* (New York: Schocken Books, 1970); Fred W. Voget, "American Indian Reformations and Acculturation," in *Contributions to Anthropology 1960,* part 2 (National Museum of Canada Bulletin no. 190, 1963).

83. Firth, "Problem and Assumption," p. 252; Daryll Forde, "The Context of Belief," in Daryll Forde, *Yako Studies* (London: Oxford University Press, 1964); also Godfrey Lienhardt, "Theology, Primitive," in *International Encyclopedia of the Social Sciences* (1968), vol. 15.

84. I have used the following by Victor W. Turner: "Themes and Symbols in Ndembu Hunter's Ritual," in Mario D. Zamora et al., eds., *Themes in Culture* (Quezon City: Kayumanggi Publishers, 1971), pp. 272–273; "Symbols in Ndembu Religion," in Victor W. Turner, *The Forest of Symbols* (Leiden: E. J. Brill, 1967), pp. 19–28; "Betwixt and Between: The Liminal Period in Rites of Passage," in Helm, *Symposium on Religion;* and *The Ritual Process* (London: Routledge and Kegan Paul, 1969), chs. 3 and 5.

85. Mary Douglas, *Purity and Danger* (London: Routledge and Kegan Paul, 1966).

86. Douglas, *Natural Symbols,* chs. 1–2; cf. Wilson and Wilson, *Social Change,* pp. 93–94 where the distinction is between magical and sacramental symbolism.

87. E. E. Evans-Pritchard, "Religion and the Anthropologists," in E. E. Evans-Pritchard, *Social Anthropology and Other Essays* (New York: Free Press of Glencoe, 1962), p. 166.

88. Mary Douglas, "Environments at Risk," *Times Literary Supplement,* Oct. 30, 1970, pp. 1273–1275.

89. Cornelius Osgood, "Culture: Its Empirical and Non-Empirical Character," *Southwestern Journal of Anthropology,* vol. 7 (1951): 202–214.

90. John W. Bennett, "The Interpretation of Pueblo Culture: A Question of Values," *Southwestern Journal of Anthropology*, vol. 2 (1948): 672–689.

91. Ralph Linton, *The Cultural Background of Personality* (New York: D. Appleton-Century Company, 1945), ch. 2; Claude Lévi-Strauss, "Social Structure," in A. L. Kroeber, ed., *Anthropology Today* (Chicago: University of Chicago Press, 1953); Goodenough, *Description and Comparison*, ch. 4, Rodney Needham, "Remarks on the Analysis of Kinship and Marriage," in Rodney Needham, ed., *Rethinking Kinship and Marriage* (London: Tavistock Publications, 1971).

92. Anthony F. C. Wallace, *Culture and Personality* (2nd ed.: New York: Random House, 1970), pp. 22–24.

93. Edmund R. Leach, *Political Systems of Highland Burma* (Boston: Beacon Press, 1965), pp. ix–xi; Edmund R. Leach, *Pul Eliya* (Cambridge: At the University Press, 1961), ch. 1.

94. See the following by Bob Scholte: "Epistemic Paradigms: Some Problems in Cross-Cultural Research on Anthropological Theory and History," *American Anthropologist*, vol. 68 (1966): 1192–1201; "On Defining Anthropological Traditions: An Exercise in the Ethnology of Ethnology" (forthcoming); and "Toward a Reflexive and Critical Anthropology," in Dell Hymes, ed., *Reinventing Anthropology* (New York: Pantheon Books, 1972).

95. Jean Pouillon, "Traditions in French Anthropology," *Social Research*, vol. 38 (1971): 73–92, p. 75.

96. Jacques J. Maquet, "Objectivity in Anthropology," *Current Anthropology*, vol. 5 (1964): 47–55.

97. Claude Lévi-Strauss, "The Concept of Primitiveness," in Richard B. Lee and Irven De Vore, eds., *Man the Hunter* (Chicago: Aldine Publishing Co., 1968), p. 351.

98. Scott Cook, "The Obsolete 'Anti-Market' Mentality: A Critique of the Substantive Approach to Economic Anthropology," *American Anthropologist*, vol. 68 (1966): 323–345, p. 327.

99. Stephen A. Tyler, "A Formal Science," in Stephen A. Tyler, ed., *Concepts and Assumptions in Contemporary Anthropology* (The Southern Anthropological Society Proceedings, no. 3, 1969).

100. Ernest Becker, *The Lost Science of Man* (New York: George Braziller, 1971); Stanley Diamond, "A Revolutionary Discipline," *Current Anthropology*, vol. 5 (1964): 432–437.

101. Robert Redfield, "The Frankfurt Lectures: I. The Logic and Functions of Social Science, II. Social Science and Values" [orig. 1948], in Redfield, *Human Nature and Society*, pp. 39–41, 79–81.

102. The following works constitute a symposium on social responsibility: Gerald D. Berreman, "Is Anthropology Alive? Social Responsibility in Social Anthropology," Gutorm Gjessing, "The Social Responsibility of the Social Scientist," and on colonialism and imperialism, Kathleen Gough, "New Proposals for Anthropologists," all in *Current Anthropology*, vol. 9 (1968): 391–396, 397–402, 403–407. See also William S. Willis, Jr., "Skeletons in the Anthropological Closet," and Mina Davis Caulfield, "Culture and Imperialism: Proposing a New Dialectic," both in Hymes, *Reinventing Anthropology*.

103. David Kaplan and Robert A. Manners, "Anthropology: Some Old Themes and New Directions," *Southwestern Journal of Anthropology*, vol. 27 (1971): 19–40, 27–31. For additional rebuttals, see "Comments" appended to the articles of Berreman, Gjessing, and Gough, *Current Anthropology*, vol. 9 (1968): 407–412, and the long, critical review of *Reinventing Anthropology* by David Kaplan, "The Anthropology of Authenticity: Everyman His Own Anthropologist," *American Anthropologist*, vol. 76 (1974): 824–839.

104. Dell Hymes, "The Uses of Anthropology: Critical, Political, Personal," in Hymes, *Reinventing Anthropology*, p. 36.

Appendix:
Further Readings

Chapter 1. Anthropological Ideas

Hallowell, A. Irving. "The History of Anthropology as an Anthropological Problem," *Journal of the History of the Behavioral Sciences*, vol. 1 (1965): 24–38. The history of anthropology is seen as itself a kind of anthropological problem.

Kaplan, David, and Robert A. Manners. *Culture Theory*, ch. 2 (Englewood Cliffs, N.J.: Prentice-Hall, 1972). Four theoretical orientations—evolutionism, functionalism, history, and cultural ecology—which have characterized anthropology since it became a discipline.

Lang, Gottfried O. "Theoretical Methods and Approaches to the Understanding of Man," *Anthropological Quarterly*, vol. 32 (1959): 41–66. Examines five methodological models for categorizing social anthropological approaches.

Smith, Jonathan Z. "Adde Parvum Parvo Magnus Acervus Erit," *History of Religions*, vol. 11 (1971): 67–90. Four styles of comparison in studying religion and other cultural data.

White, Leslie A. "History, Evolutionism, and Functionalism: Three Types of Interpretation of Culture," *Southwestern Journal of Anthropology*, vol. 1 (1945): 221–248.

Chapter 2. Greek and Roman Writers

Cole, Andrew Thomas. *Democritus and the Sources of Greek Anthropology* (American Philological Association Monographs no. 25), 1967. A critical comparison of ideas about social origins held by later classical authors, including Vitruvius and Lucretius.

de Waal Malefijt, Annemarie. *Images of Man,* ch. 1 (New York: Alfred A. Knopf, 1974).

Diamond, Stanley. "Plato and the Definition of the Primitive," in Stanley Diamond, ed., *Views of the World* (New York: Columbia University Press, 1964). *The Republic* interpreted as a reaction against primitive cultural elements persisting in Greek society. Diamond expands the contrasting elements in primitive and civilized society beyond those usually used in social science.

Glacken, Clarence J. *Traces on the Rhodian Shore,* chs. 1–4 (Berkeley: University of California Press, 1967). By far the best history of thought about man and nature.

Havelock, E. A. *The Liberal Temper,* ch. 1 (New Haven: Yale University Press, 1957). Anaximander, Democritus, Xenophanes, and others on social development.

Hodgen, Margaret T. *Early Anthropology in the Sixteenth and Seventeenth Centuries,* ch. 1 (Philadelphia: University of Pennsylvania Press, 1964). Brief look at "the classical heritage" of cultural anthropology.

Kluckhohn, Clyde. *Anthropology and the Classics,* ch. 2 (Providence, R.I.: Brown University Press, 1961). Greek thought as a source of anthropology.

Levin, Harry. *The Myth of the Golden Age in the Renaissance,* ch. 3 (Bloomington: Indiana University Press, 1969). Recurrence of the myth in ethnography.

Müller, Klaus E. *Geschichte der Antiken Ethnographie und Ethnologischen Theoriebildung* (Wiesbaden: Franz Steiner Verlag, 1972). Comprehensive reviews of Greek philosophers, including some not mentioned in the present chapter, and a brief treatment of Near Eastern anthropological thought.

Myres, J. L. "Herodotus and Anthropology," in R. R. Marett, ed., *Anthropology and the Classics* (Oxford: Clarendon Press, 1908).

Nisbet, Robert A. *Social Change and History,* ch. 1 (New York: Oxford University Press, 1969). Ideas of growth and change held by Greek writers.

Plischke, Hans. *Von den Barbaren zu den Primitiven,* chs. 3–4 (Leipzig: F. A. Brockhaus, 1926). Early contacts with, and views of, people culturally marginal to the classical world.

Sikes, E. E. *The Anthropology of the Greeks* (London: David Nutt, 1914). Race, biological and cultural evolution, and theories of language are among the topics reviewed by an author who is himself a classicist.

Trüdinger, Karl. *Studien zur Geschichte der griechisch-römischen Ethnographie.* Dissertation zur Erlangung der Doktorwürde der philologische-historischen Abteilung der hohen philosophischen Fakultät der Universität Basel (Basel: Buchdruckerei Emil Birkhauser, 1918). A scholarly, philologically inclined examination of Greek ethnographic writings; contains little of theoretical interest.

Voget, Fred W. *A History of Ethnology,* pp. 3–20 (New York: Holt, Rinehart and Winston, 1975). The limitations of Greco–Roman thought as anthropology.

Vries, Jan de. *The Study of Religion,* ch. 1, trans. Kees W. Bolle (New York: Harcourt, Brace & World, 1967).

Warburton, Irene P. "Plato's Linguistic Theory," *Language Sciences,* no. 6 (1969): 1–4.

Chapter 3. From the Church Fathers to the 17th Century

Atkinson, Geoffroy. *Les Relations de voyages du XVIIe siècle et l'évolution des idées* (Paris: Librairie ancienne Edouard Champion, n. d.). Writers who anticipated 18th-century thought under the influence of travelers' reports.

Barnes, Harry Elmer. *A History of Historical Writing,* pp. 174–176 (Norman: University of Oklahoma Press, 1937). Sixteenth-century origins of the theory of progress.

Becker, Howard, II. "Early Generalisations Concerning Population Movement and Culture Contact: Prolegomena to a Study of Mental Mobility," *The Sociological Review,* vol. 25 (1933): 137–152. Takes up 16th- and 17th-century writers, including Ibn Khaldun.

Boas, George. *Essays on Primitivism and Related Ideas in the Middle Ages* (Baltimore: Johns Hopkins Press, 1948). The "related ideas" are typically scripturally grounded versions of man's original condition, the savage's nobility, and progress.

de Waal Malefijt, Annemarie. *Images of Man,* chs. 2–4 (New York: Alfred A. Knopf, 1974).

Glacken, Clarence J. *Traces on the Rhodian Shore,* parts 2 and 3 (Berkeley: University of California Press, 1967). Environmental determinism, man's ability to control nature, and other ideas regarding man's relationship to nature in the Middle Ages and early modern times.

Haddon, Alfred C. *History of Anthropology,* chs. 1, 7, 12 (London: Watts, 1910).

Hodgen, Margaret T. *Early Anthropology in the Sixteenth and Seventeenth Centuries* (Philadelphia: University of Pennsylvania Press, 1964).

Huddleston, Lee Eldridge. *Origins of the American Indians* (Austin: University of Texas Press, 1967). European concepts held between 1492 and 1729.

Métraux, Alfred. "Les Précurseurs de l'ethnologie en France du XVIe au XVIIIe siècle," *Cahiers d'Histoire Mondiale,* vol. 7 (1962–63): 721–738.

Mühlmann, Wilhelm E. *Geschichte der Anthropologie,* chs. 1–3 (2nd ed; Frankfurt am Main: Athenaeum Verlag, 1968).

Oakes, Katherine B. *Social Theory in the Early Literature of Voyages and Explorations in Africa.* (Ph.D. dissertation, University of California, Department of Social Institutions, Berkeley, 1944).

Penniman, T. K. *A Hundred Years of Anthropology,* ch. 2 (3rd ed.; London: Gerald Duckworth and Co., 1965).

Plischke, Hans. *Von den Barbaren zu den Primitiven,* chs. 3–4 (Leipzig: F. A. Brockhaus, 1926). Early views of, and contact with, barbarian people.

Rowe, John Howland. "Ethnography and Ethnology in the Sixteenth Century," *Kroeber Anthropological Society Papers,* no. 30 (1959): 1–19.

———. "Renaissance Foundations of Anthropology," *American Anthropologist,* vol. 67 (1965), pp. 1–20.

Slotkin, James Sydney, ed. *Readings in Early Anthropology*, chs. 1–3 (Viking Fund Publications in Anthropology, no. 40), 1965. Excerpts from writings by Descartes, Brerewood, Hale, Temple, and others.

Stoll, Otto. "Die Entwicklung der Völkerkunde von ihren Anfängen bis in die Neuzeit," chs. 2–3, *Mitteilungen der Geographisch-Ethnographischen Gesellschaft Zürich*, Bd. 18 (1917–18): 1–128. Deals mainly with ethnography.

Voget, Fred W. *A History of Ethnology*, pp. 20–40 (New York: Holt, Rinehart and Winston, 1975). Mostly taken up with Ibn Khaldun.

Vries, Jan de. *The Study of Religion*, chs. 3–4, trans. Kees W. Bolle (New York: Harcourt, Brace & World, 1967). Allegorical and other interpretations of gods.

Chapter 4.   Century of Enlightenment

Achelis, Thomas. *Moderne Völkerkunde, deren Entwicklung und Aufgaben*, ch. 1, parts 1–3 (Stuttgart: F. Enke, 1896).

Ackerknecht, Erwin H. "George Forster, Alexander von Humboldt, and Ethnology," *Isis*, vol. 46 (1955): 83–95.

Aldridge, A. O. "The Meaning of Incest from Hutcheson to Gibbon," *Ethics*, vol. 61 (1951): 309–313.

Barnes, Harry Elmer. "Historical Sociology," pp. 239–245, in Joseph S. Roucek, ed., *Readings in Contemporary American Sociology* (new ed.; Patterson, N. J.: Littlefield, Adams and Co., 1961).

Becker, Ernest. *The Lost Science of Man*, pp. 121–152 (New York: George Braziller, 1971). "World-shaking" significance of Rousseau's *Discourse on Inequality* and its repercussions in social science literature.

Bidney, David. "Vico's New Science of Myth," in Giorgio Tagliacozzo, ed., *Giambattista Vico: An International Symposium* (Baltimore: Johns Hopkins Press, 1969). Vico's idea of a comparative science of ethnology.

Bryson, Gladys. *Man and Society: The Scottish Inquiry of the Eighteenth Century*, chs. 7–8 (Princeton: Princeton University Press, 1945). The Scottish moralists on human history and social institutions.

Daniel, Glyn. *A Hundred Years of Archaeology*, ch. 1 (London: Gerald Duckworth and Co., Ltd., 1950). Sixteenth- to 18th-century antiquarianism.

de Waal Malefijt, Annemarie. *Images of Man*, ch. 5 and pp. 94–104 (New York: Alfred A. Knopf, 1974).

Diamond, Stanley. "A Revolutionary Discipline," *Current Anthropology*, vol. 5 (1964): 432–437. Eighteenth-century origins.

Duchet, Michèle. *Anthropologie et histoire au siècle des lumières: Buffon, Voltaire, Rousseau, Helvétius, Diderot* (Paris: F. Maspero, 1971).

Evans-Pritchard, E. E. *Social Anthropology*, pp. 21–26 (London: Cohen and West, 1951).

Feldman, Burton, and Robert D. Richardson. *The Rise of Modern Mythology 1680–1860*, pp. 3–295 (Bloomington: Indiana University Press, 1972). The authors consider the period from 1680 to 1860 to anticipate all modern approaches in mythology.

Fenton, William N. "J.–F. Lafitau (1681–1746), Precursor of Scientific Anthropology," *Southwestern Journal of Anthropology*, vol. 25 (1969): 173–188. Lafitau's ethnographic accomplishments.

Flint, Robert. *The Philosophy of History in France and Germany*, book I, chs. 3–6; book II, chs. 2–6 (Edinburgh: William Blackwood and Sons, 1874). Montesquieu, Herder, and other French and German philosophers of the 18th century.

Gennep, Arnold van. "La Méthode ethnographique en France au XVIIIe siècle," in Arnold van Gennep, *Religions, moeurs et legendes* (cinquième série; deuxième édition; Paris: Mercure de France, 1914).

Glacken, Clarence J. *Traces on the Rhodian Shore*, chs. 11–14 (Berkeley: University of California Press, 1967). Comprehensive account of 18th-century thinkers' ideas about culture and the natural environment.

Goldenweiser, Alexander. "Leading Contributions of Anthropology," pp. 435–438, in H. E. Barnes et al., eds., *Contemporary Social Theory* (New York: D. Appleton-Century Co., 1940).

Gusdorf, Georges. *Introduction aux sciènces humaines*, pp. 135–227; 242–249; 281–292; 309–334 (Publications de la Faculté des Lettres de l'Université de Strausbourg, Fascicule 140), 1960. Developments in ethnology and ethnography.

Hallowell, A. Irving. "The Beginnings of Anthropology in America," pp. 4–18, 23–26, 34–37, in Frederica de Laguna, ed., *Selected Papers from the American Anthropologist 1888–1920* (Evanston, Ill.: Row, Peterson and Co., 1960).

Harris, Marvin. *The Rise of Anthropological Theory*, ch. 2 (New York: Thomas Y. Crowell Co., 1968). Brief but comprehensive account of anthropological theory in the Enlightenment.

Heizer, Robert F. "The Background of Thomsen's Three-Age System," *Culture and Technology*, vol. 3 (1962): 259–266.

Hertz, Friedrich. "Die allgemeinen Theorien vom Nationalcharakter," *Archiv für Sozialwissenschaft und Sozialpolitik*, vol. 54 (1925):1–35, 657–715.

Hervé, Georges. "Les Débuts de l'ethnographie au XVIIIe siècle (1701–1765)," *Revue de l'école d'anthropologie*, vol. 19 (1909): 345–366, 381–401.

Hodgen, Margaret T. *Early Anthropology in the Sixteenth and Seventeenth Centuries*, ch. 12 (Philadelphia: University of Pennsylvania Press, 1964). Sees 18th century as imitative.

Hoebel, E. Adamson. "William Robertson: An 18th Century Anthropologist-Historian," *American Anthropologist*, vol. 62 (1960): 648–655.

Koppers, W. P. "Die ethnologische Wirtschaftsforschung. Eine historischkritische Studie," pp. 622–627, *Anthropos*, vol. 10–11 (1915–1916): 622–651, 971–1070.

Leach, Edmund. "Vico and Lévi-Strauss on the Origins of Humanity," in Giorgio Tagliacosso, ed., *Giambattista Vico: An International Symposium* (Baltimore: Johns Hopkins Press, 1969). Elements of structuralism in Vico.

Lehmann, William C. "Sociological and Cultural-Anthropological Elements in the Writings of Johann Gottfried von Herder," in Earl W. Count and Gordon T. Bowles, eds., *Fact and Theory in Social Science* (Syracuse, N.Y.: Syracuse University Press, 1964).

Lovejoy, Arthur O. "Monboddo and Rousseau," *Modern Philology,* vol. 30 (1932–1933): 275–296.

———. "The Supposed Primitivism in Rousseau's *Discourse on Inequality,*" *Modern Philology,* vol. 21 (1923–1924): 165–186. Rousseau's idealized stage of early culture was not the earliest, brutish one.

Manuel, Frank E. *The Eighteenth Century Confronts the Gods.* (Cambridge: Harvard University Press, 1959). Vico, Hume, Herder and other 18th-century writers on the origin of religion.

McGuire, Joseph D. "Ethnology in the Jesuit Relations," *American Anthropologist,* vol. 3 (1901): 257–269.

Mitra, Panchanana. *A History of American Anthropology,* ch. 2 and parts of 3 and 4 (Calcutta: University of Calcutta, 1933).

Mühlmann, Wilhelm. *Geschichte der Anthropologie,* ch. 3 from p. 44, and chs. 4–5 (2nd ed.; Frankfurt am Main: Athenaeum Verlag, 1948). Comprehensive survey.

———. *Methodik der Völkerkunde,* pp. 20–55 (Stuttgart: Ferdinand Enke Verlag, 1938). On Meiners; Georg Forster, and his father Johann; and Herder.

Plischke, Hans. *Von den Barbaren zu den Primitiven,* ch. 5 (Leipzig: F. A. Brockhaus, 1926). Rousseau's influence on 18th-century travel reporting.

Pocock, D. F. *Social Anthropology,* pp. 1–16 (London: Sheed and Ward, 1961). Deals mostly with Montesquieu and Hume.

Poirier, Jean. "Histoire de la pensée ethnologique," pp. 3–29, in Jean Poirier, ed., *Ethnologie générale* (Paris: Editions Gallimard, 1968). From ancient origins to the first specialized research.

Pollard, Sidney. *The Idea of Progress,* ch. 2 (London: Watts and Co., 1968). Brief but effective discussions of Hume, Millar, Turgot, and Condorcet.

Radcliffe-Brown, A. R. "Social Anthropology," pp. 143–152, in A. R. Radcliffe-Brown, *Method in Social Anthropology,* M. N. Srinivas, ed. (Chicago: University of Chicago Press, 1958).

Sapir, Edward. "Herder's 'Ursprung der Sprache,'" *Modern Philology,* vol. 5 (1907): 109–142.

Shapiro, Harry L. "The History and Development of Physical Anthropology," *American Anthropologist,* vol. 61 (1959): 371–378.

Slotkin, J. S., ed. *Readings in Early Anthropology,* chs. 5–7. (Viking Fund Publications in Anthropology No. 40), 1965. A major sourcebook though the principles governing inclusion are sometimes hard to fathom.

Voget, Fred W. "Anthropology in the Age of Enlightenment: Progress and Utopian Functionalism," *Southwestern Journal of Anthropology,* vol. 24 (1968): 321–345. Eighteenth-century "wayward anthropologists" motivated by goals of furthering social progress.

———. "Forgotten Forerunners of Anthropology," *Bucknell Review,* vol. 15 (1967): 78–96. Ideas of the Scottish moralists concerning the history of man.

———. "Progress, Science, History and Evolution in Eighteenth- and Nineteenth-Century Anthropology," *Journal of the History of the Behavioral Sciences,* vol. 3 (1967): 132–155. Similarities in the idea of progress.

———. "History of Cultural Anthropology," in John J. Honigmann, ed., *Hand-*

book of Social and Cultural Anthropology (Chicago: Rand McNally and Co., 1973).

———. *A History of Ethnology*, ch. 2 (New York: Holt, Rinehart and Winston, 1975).

Vries, Jan de. *The Study of Religion*, chs. 5–7, trans. Kees W. Bolle (New York: Harcourt, Brace & World, 1967).

Chapter 5.   Anthropology Becomes a Discipline

Achelis, Thomas. *Moderne Völkerkunde, deren Entwicklung und Aufgaben*, ch. 1, parts 4–5, and ch. 2 (Stuttgart: F. Enke, 1896).

Ackerknecht, Erwin H. "On the Comparative Method in Anthropology," in Robert F. Spencer, ed., *Method and Perspective in Anthropology* (Minneapolis: The University of Minnesota Press, 1954).

Baal, J. Van. *Symbols for Communication*, ch. 5 (Assen: Van Gorcum and Comp. N. V., 1971). Brief summaries of theories of Bastian, Graebner, and other Continental diffusionists.

Barnes, Harry Elmer. *Historical Sociology: Its Origins and Development*, chs. 2–3, pp. 57–58; chs. 6–7 (New York: Philosophical Library, 1948). Evolutionary sequences and explanations for them, including those of Kovalevsky, Brooks Adams, and others.

———. "Historical Sociology," pp. 245–267, in Joseph S. Roucek, ed., *Readings in Contemporary American Sociology* (new ed.; Patterson, N.J.: Littlefield, Adams and Co., 1961). Brief reviews and appraisals of major writers.

———. *An Introduction to the History of Sociology*, chs. 3, 9, 25–31, 33–34, 37, 40 (Chicago: University of Chicago Press, 1948).

Bastian, A. *Die Vorgeschichte der Ethnologie* (Berlin: Ferd. Dümmlers Verlagsbuchhandlung, 1881). Deals with 18th- and 19th-century anthropological and ethnological organizations and events more than with the flow of ideas.

Bender, Donald. "The Development of French Anthropology," *Journal of the History of the Behavioral Sciences*, vol. 1 (1965): 139–151. Influence of Durkheim and, even more, Mauss on the development of ethnology in France.

Bianchi, Ugo. *Storia dell' etnologia*, pp. 65–134 (2nd ed.; Rome: Edizioni Abete, 1971).

Bock, Kenneth E. "Darwin and Social Theory," *Philosophy of Science*, vol. 22 (1955): 123–134. Discounts Darwin's influence on cultural evolutionism.

Boule, Marcelin. "Fossil Men," in V. F. Calverton, ed., *The Making of Man* (New York: Modern Library, 1931). History of fossil finds.

Burrow, J. W. *Evolution and Society* (Cambridge: At the University Press, 1966). Cultural evolutionary theory interpreted in a philosophical framework.

Calverton, V. F. "Introduction: Modern Anthropology and the Theory of Cultural Compulsives," in V. F. Calverton, ed., *The Making of Man* (New York: Modern Library, 1931). The influence of social values on the fate of anthropological theories. Especially good on the rise and eventual demolition of Westermarck's theories.

Carmichael, Leonard. "Anthropology and the Smithsonian Institution," in Anthony F. C. Wallace, ed., *Selected Papers of the Fifth International Congress of Anthropological and Ethnological Sciences, Philadelphia, September 1–9, 1956* (Philadelphia: University of Pennsylvania Press, 1960). Deals with institutional history rather than theory.

Carneiro, Robert L. "Classical Evolution," in Raoul Naroll and Frada Naroll, eds., *Main Currents in Cultural Anthropology* (Englewood Cliffs, N.J., Prentice-Hall, 1973).

Clark, L. K. *Pioneers of Prehistory in England* (London: Sheed and Ward, 1961).

Daniel, Glyn, E. *A Hundred Years of Archaeology* (London: Gerald Duckworth and Co., 1950).

Darnell, Regna. "The Powell Classification of American Indian Languages," *Papers in Linguistics,* vol. 4, no. 1 (1971): 71–110.

———. "The Professionalization of American Anthropology: A Case Study in the Sociology of Knowledge," *Social Science Information,* vol. 10, no. 2 (1971): 83–103. The roles of Powell and the Bureau of American Ethnology, and Boas's influence on the organization of American anthropology.

de Laguna, Frederica, ed. *Selected Papers from the American Anthropologist 1888–1920* (Evanston, Ill.: Row, Peterson and Co., 1960).

de Waal Malefijt, Annemarie. *Images of Man,* pp. 105–115, chs. 7–9, and pp. 181–192 (New York: Alfred A. Knopf, 1974).

———. *Religion and Culture,* pp. 45–74 (New York: Macmillan Co., 1968).

Dixon, Roland B. "Anthropology, 1866–1929," in Samuel Eliot Morison, ed., *The Development of Harvard University* (Cambridge: Harvard University Press, 1930). History of anthropology at Harvard.

Evans-Pritchard, E. E. "The Comparative Method in Social Anthropology," in E. E. Evans-Pritchard, *The Position of Women in Primitive Societies and other Essays in Social Anthropology* (New York: Free Press, 1965). From McLennan's first systematic attempt at comparative research to George P. Murdock's worldwide statistical approach.

———. *Social Anthropology,* pp. 27–72 (London: Cohen and West, 1951).

———. *Theories of Primitive Religion* (Oxford: Clarendon Press, 1965).

Feldman, Burton, and Robert D. Richardson. *The Rise of Modern Mythology 1680–1860* (Bloomington: Indiana University Press, 1972). The period prior to 1860 surveyed through representative selections.

Firth, Raymond. *Symbols: Public and Private,* ch. 3 (Ithaca, N.Y.: Cornell University Press, 1973). Development of anthropological interest in symbols.

Forde, Daryll. "Anthropology—the Victorian Synthesis and Modern Relativism," in British Broadcasting Corp., *Ideas and Beliefs of the Victorians* (London: Sylvan Press, 1949). Contains little about Victorian anthropology, and that is not always to be believed.

Gölz, Friedrich. *Der Primitive Mensch und seine Religion,* chs. 1–5 (Gütersloh: Gütersloher Verlagshaus Gerd Mohn, 1963).

Goldenweiser, Alexander. "Anthropological Theories of Political Origins," in C. E. Merriam and H. E. Barnes, eds., *A History of Political Theories* (New York: Macmillan Co., 1924).

————. "Anthropology and Psychology," in W. F. Ogburn and A. Goldenweiser, eds., *The Social Sciences and Their Interrelations* (Boston:
Houghton Mifflin Co., 1927). Psychological postulates in Bastian's
ethnology, Wundt's folk psychology, evolutionism, and culture circle
diffusion; reprinted in A. Goldenweiser, *History, Psychology, and
Culture.*

————. "Cultural Anthropology," in Harry Elmer Barnes, ed., *The History and
Prospects of the Social Sciences* (New York: Alfred A. Knopf, 1925). Good
summaries of theories. Reprinted in A. Goldenweiser, *History, Psychology
and Culture.*

————. "Leading Contributions of Anthropology to Social Theory," in Harry
Elmer Barnes et al., eds., *Contemporary Social Theory* (New York: D. Appleton-Century Co., 1940).

————. *History, Psychology, and Culture,* part 1, ch. 4; part 2, chs. 1–5; part
4, chs. 1–2 (New York: Alfred A. Knopf, 1933).

Graebner, Fritz. "Ethnologie," pp. 435–447, in Paul Hinneberg, ed., *Die Kultur
der Gegenwart,* part 3, *Mathematik, Naturwissenschaften, Medizin,* sect. 5,
Anthropologie (Leipzig: B. G. Teubner, 1923). Good account of the advent of historical ethnology.

Griffin, James. "The Pursuit of Archaeology in the United States," *American
Anthropologist,* vol. 61 (1959): 379–388.

Gruber, Jacob W. "In Search of Experience," in June Helm, ed., *Pioneers of
American Anthropology* (Seattle: University of Washington Press, 1966).

————. "Ethnographic Salvage and the Shaping of Anthropology," *American
Anthropologist,* vol. 72 (1970): 1289–1299. Protecting aboriginal societies
and recording their customs before it is too late as an incentive to an
emerging anthropology.

Günther, Hans F. K. *Formen und Urgeschichte der Ehe,* chs. 12–13 (3rd ed.;
Göttingen: Musterschmidt Wissenschaftlicher Verlag, 1951). Evolutionary
theories summarized.

Gusdorf, Georges. *Introduction aux sciences humaines,* pp. 365–380 (Publications de la Faculté des Lettres de l'Université de Strausbourg, Fasicule
140, 1960). Some aspects of the thoughts of Comte, Mill, and Marx.

Haddon, Alfred C. *History of Anthropology,* chs. 9–10, 12 (London: Watts,
1910).

Haller, John S., Jr. "Race and the Concept of Progress in Nineteenth Century
American Ethnology," *American Anthropologist,* vol. 73 (1971): 710–724.

Hallowell, A. Irving. "The Beginnings of Anthropology in America," pp. 18–
23, 26–34, 37–58, in Frederica de Laguna, ed., *Selected Papers from the
American Anthropologist 1888–1920* (Evanston, Ill.: Row, Peterson and
Co., 1960).

————. "Psychology and Anthropology," in John Gillin, ed., *For a Science of
Social Man* (New York: Macmillan Co., 1954). Relations between anthropologists and psychologists in historical perspective.

Harris, Marvin. *The Rise of Anthropological Theory,* chs. 2–8; pp. 464–489,
514–516 (New York: Thomas Y. Crowell Co., 1968).

Hatch, Elvin. *Theories of Man and Culture,* pp. 13–37 and ch. 4 (New York:
Columbia University Press, 1973).

Hays, H. R. *From Ape to Angel.* chs. 1–22, 25–30 (New York: Alfred A. Knopf, 1958).

Heine-Geldern, Robert. "One Hundred Years of Ethnological Theory in the German-Speaking Countries: Some Milestones," *Current Anthropology,* vol. 5 (1964): 407–418.

Henson, Hilary. "Early British Anthropologists and Language," in Edwin Ardener, ed., *Social Anthropology and Language* (London: Tavistock Publications, 1971). Since language was regarded as but the outward form and manifestation of thought, it followed that primitive languages were inferior to European.

Hodgen, Margaret T. "The Doctrine of Survivals: The History of an Idea," *American Anthropologist,* vol. 33 (1931) 307–324.

Horton, Robin. "Lévy-Bruhl, Durkheim and the Scientific Revolution," in Robin Horton and Ruth Finnegan, eds., *Modes of Thought* (London: Faber and Faber, 1973).

House, Floyd Nelson. *The Development of Sociology,* chs. 6–17 (New York: McGraw-Hill Book Co., 1936).

Howard, George Elliott. *A History of Matrimonial Institutions,* vol. 1, chs. 1–4 (2 vols.; Chicago: University of Chicago Press, 1904). Theories on the evolution of marriage and the family.

Kardiner, Abram, and Edward Preble. *They Studied Man,* pp. 33–116, 196–209 (Mentor ed.; New York: New American Library, 1963). Includes chapters on Spencer, Tylor, Frazer, Durkheim, and Freud.

Koppers, W. P. "Die ethnologische Wirtschaftsforschung: Eine historisch-kritische Studie," *Anthropos,* vol. 10–11 (1915–1916): 622–651, 971–1070. Covers the period from 1850 to 1916.

Kroeber, A. L. "The History and Present Orientation of Cultural Anthropology," in A. L. Kroeber, ed., *The Nature of Culture* (Chicago: University of Chicago Press, 1952).

Lang, Andrew. "Family," in *Encyclopaedia Britannica,* vol. 10 (11th ed.; 1910–1911). McLennan, Morgan, Spencer and Gillen, Westermarck, and others, including Lang, on marriage, classificatory kinship, totemism, etc.

———. "Mythology," in *Encyclopaedia Britannica,* vol. 17 (9th ed.; 1878). After giving earlier theories, Lang compares his own and Müller's view of the sources of myths.

Leach, Edmund R. "Social Structure. I. The History of the Concept," in *International Encyclopedia of the Social Sciences,* vol. 14 (1968).

Leser, Paul. "Zur Geschichte des Wortes Kulturkreis," *Anthropos,* vol. 58 (1963): 1–36.

Lévi-Strauss, Claude. "French Sociology," in Georges Gurvitch, ed., *Twentieth Century Sociology* (New York: Philosophical Library, 1945). Covers Durkheim, Mauss, Lévy-Bruhl, and others.

Lowie, Robert H. *The History of Ethnological Theory,* chs. 3–8, 10–12 (New York: Rinehart and Company, 1937).

———. *Primitive Religion,* chs. 5–7 (London: George Routledge and Sons, 1925). Tylor's, Frazer's, and Durkheim's theories of religion and magic, and criticisms thereof by their contemporaries and successors.

————. "Reminiscences of Anthropological Currents in America Half a Century Ago," *American Anthropologist,* vol. 58 (1956): 995–1016. Comments on Cushing; Powell; the paradigm of late 19th-century American ethnology; and European influences on later American thought.

Lurie, Nancy Oestreich. "Women in Early American Anthropology," in June Helm, ed., *Pioneers of American Anthropology* (Seattle: University of Washington Press, 1966). The careers of Erminnie Smith, Alice Fletcher, Matilda Stevenson, and Zelia Nuttall briefly described.

Mandelbaum, Maurice. *History, Man and Reason,* ch. 6 (Baltimore: Johns Hopkins Press, 1971). Nineteenth-century views on social evolution.

Mead, Margaret, and Ruth L. Bunzel, eds. *The Golden Age of American Anthropology* (New York: George Braziller, 1960). Selections from Bachman, Catlin, Schoolcraft, and other writings of Americanists before and after Morgan.

Mercier, Paul. *Histoire de 'anthropologie,* ch. 2 (Paris: Presses Universitaires de France, 1966).

Mitchell, G. Duncan. *A Hundred Years of Sociology,* chs. 1–7 (London: Gerald Duckworth and Co., 1968).

Mitra, Panchanana. *A History of American Anthropology,* chs. 3–7, 9 (part) (Calcutta: University of Calcutta, 1933).

Mühlmann, Wilhelm. *Geschichte der Anthropologie,* chs. 6–9, 11 (part) (2nd ed.; Frankfurt am Main: Athenaeum Verlag, 1968).

Murphee, I. L. "The Evolutionary Anthropologists: The Concepts of Progress and Culture in the Thought of John Lubbock, Edward B. Tylor, and Lewis H. Morgan," *American Philosophical Society Proceedings,* vol. 101 (1961): 265–300. Relationship of prehistoric archeology and social evolutionism to Darwinian theory, and comparison of several 19th-century evolutionists' approaches.

Nisbet, Robert A. *Social Change and History,* chs. 5–7 (New York: Oxford University Press, 1969).

Opler, Morris E. "Two Converging Lines of Influence in Cultural Evolutionary Theory," *American Anthropologist,* vol. 64 (1962), 524–547. Summarizes Ostwald's theory of energy and Plekhanov's theory of art.

Penniman, P. K. *A Hundred Years of Anthropology,* chs. 3–5 (3rd ed.; London: Gerald Duckworth and Co., 1965).

Pocock, D. F. *Social Anthropology,* pp. 16–49 (London: Sheed and Ward, 1971).

Poirier, Jean. *Histoire de l'ethnologie,* ch. 2 and pp. 42–75 (Paris: Presses Universitaires de France, 1969).

Radin, Paul. *The Method and Theory of Ethnology,* ch. 3 (Classics in Anthropology ed.; New York: Basic Books, 1966). Leading European figures and brief identifications of their work.

Raison, Timothy, ed. *The Founding Fathers of Social Science* (Harmondsworth: Penguin Books, 1969). Very short essays on many 19th-century figures including Comte, Marx, Engels, and Hobhouse.

Reining, Conrad C. "A Lost Period of Applied Anthropology," *American Anthropologist,* vol. 64 (1962): 593–600. Early professional associations.

Schmidt, Wilhelm. *The Culture Historical Method of Ethnology*, pp. 23–31, trans. S. A. Sieber (New York: Fortuny, 1939). Poor translation of a sketchy narrative of the roots of Schmidt's culture-historical method.

Shapiro, Harry L. "The History and Development of Physical Anthropology," *American Anthropologist*, vol. 61 (1959): 371–379.

Sorokin, Pitirim A. *Contemporary Sociological Theories*, pp. 514–546 (Harper Torchbooks; New York: Harper & Row, 1964). Traces economic theories of society which he equates with Marx and Engels, to whom he devotes a long unfavorable critique.

Stocking, George W. "Matthew Arnold, E. B. Tylor, and the Uses of Invention," *American Anthropologist*, vol. 65 (1963): 783–799.

Stoll, Otto. "Die Entwicklung der Völkerkunde von ihren Anfängen bis in die Neuzeit," pp. 58–126, *Mitteilungen der Geographisch-Ethnographischen Gesellschaft Zürich*, Bd. 18 (1917–1918): 1–128. Racial classification and other aspects of biological anthropology, archeology, and linguistics.

Tax, Sol. "From Lafitau to Radcliffe-Brown," in Fred Eggan, ed., *The Social Anthropology of North American Indian Tribes* (Enlarged ed.; Chicago: University of Chicago Press, 1955).

———. "The Integration of Anthropology," in William L. Thomas, ed., *Yearbook of Anthropology 1955* (New York: Wenner-Gren Foundation for Anthropological Research, 1955).

Taylor, Walter W. *Study of Archaeology*, ch. 1. (Memoirs of the American Anthropological Association, No. 69), 1958. Includes pre-19th-century origins.

Thoresen, Timothy H. H. "Art, Evolution, and History: A Case Study in Paradigm Change" (Paper prepared for the symposium on "Cultural Perspectives on the History of Anthropology in North America" at the annual meeting of the American Anthropological Association, 1974).

Trimborn, Herman. "Von den Aufgaben und Verfahren der Völkerkunde," in Leonhard Adam and Hermann Trimborn, eds. *Lehrbuch der Völkerkunde* (Stuttgart: Ferdinand Enke Verlag, 1958). Good for historical ethnology.

Turner, Bryan S. "Sociological Founders and Precursors: The Theories of Religion of Emile Durkheim, Fustel de Coulanges and Ibn Khaldun," *Religion*, vol. 1 (1971): 32–48.

Usher, Jean. "Apostles and Aborigines. The Social Theory of the Church Missionary Society," *Histoire Sociale. Revue Canadienne*, vol. 7 (1971): 28–52.

Voget, Fred W. "History of Cultural Anthropology," pp. 11–28, John J. Honigmann, ed., *Handbook of Social and Cultural Anthropology* (Chicago: Rand McNally and Co., 1973).

———. *A History of Ethnology*, chs. 3–8 and pp. 339–359, 480–500 (New York: Holt, Rinehart and Winston, 1975).

Vries, Jan de. *The Study of Religion*, chs. 8–23, trans. Kees W. Bolle (New York: Harcourt, Brace & World, 1967). Critical reading of many historical approaches.

Willson, Lawrence. "Thoreau: Student of Anthropology," *American Anthropologist*, vol. 61 (1959): 279–289.

Chapter 6. The American Historical Tradition

Aberle, David F. "The Influence of Linguistics on Early Culture and Personality Theory," in Gertrude E. Dole and Robert L. Carneiro, eds., *Essays in the Science of Culture* (New York: Thomas Y. Crowell Co., 1960). Development of culture-and-personality theory.

Becker, Ernest. *The Lost Science of Man,* pp. 74–108 (New York: George Braziller, 1971). Decline of anthropology as a synthesizing discipline after it lost interest in the comparative value of different social arrangements.

Bohannan, Paul. "Introduction," in Paul Bohannan and Fred Plog, eds., *Beyond the Frontier* (Garden City, N.Y.: American History Press, 1967). Development of an interest in culture change from the mid-19th to the mid-20th centuries.

———. *Social Anthropology,* pp. 61–67 (New York: Holt, Rinehart, and Winston, 1963). Lowie's role in kin-term theory.

Darnell, Regna. "Areal Linguistic Studies in North America: A Historical Perspective," *International Journal of American Linguistics,* vol. 37 (1971): 20–28. Mainly Sapir's and Kroeber's contributions.

———. "The Revision of the Powell Classification," *Papers in Linguistics,* vol. 4 (1971): 233–258. Mainly Sapir's work but with attention to his contemporaries.

Driver, Harold E. *The Contribution of A. L. Kroeber to Culture Area Theory and Practice* (Indiana University Publications in Anthropology and Linguistics, Memoir 18, 1962). Development of culture-area classification.

Goldenweiser, Alexander. "Leading Contributions of Anthropology to Social Theory," pp. 460–470, in Harry Elmer Barnes et al., eds., *Contemporary Social Theory* (New York: D. Appleton-Century Co., 1940). The orientation Boas gave to American ethnology.

Harris, Marvin. *The Rise of Anthropological Theory,* chs. 9–11 (New York: Thomas Y. Crowell Co., 1968).

Hatch, Elvin. "The Growth of Economic, Subsistence, and Ecological Studies in American Anthropology," *Journal of Anthropological Research,* vol. 29 (1973): 221–243. Ecological interests in the American Historical Tradition.

———. *Theories of Man and Culture,* pp. 37–112 (New York: Columbia University Press, 1973).

Hays, H. R. *From Ape to Angel,* chs. 23, 24, 26 (New York: Alfred A. Knopf, 1968).

Kardiner, Abram, and Edward Preble. *They Studied Man,* pp. 117–139 (Mentor ed.; New York: New American Library, 1961).

Kroeber, A. L. "The History and Present Orientation of Cultural Anthropology," in A. L. Kroeber, *The Nature of Culture* (Chicago: University of Chicago Press, 1952).

Lowie, Robert H. *The History of Ethnological Theory,* ch. 9 (New York: Rinehart and Co., 1937).

Lurie, Nancy Oestreich. "Women in Early American Anthropology," in June Helm, ed., *Pioneers of American Anthropology* (Seattle: University of

Washington Press, 1966). Only some of the women belong to the American Historical Tradition.

Mead, Margaret. "Introduction," in Margaret Mead and Ruth L. Bunzel, eds., *The Golden Age of American Anthropology* (New York: George Braziller, 1960). American Indian studies during the Boas period.

Meggers, Betty J. "Recent Trends in American Ethnology," pp. 177–186, *American Anthropologist*, vol. 48 (1946): 176–214. Psychological anthropology, acculturation studies, and community studies in America and England.

Mercier, Paul. *Histoire de l'anthropologie,* ch. 3 (Paris: Presses Universitaires de France, 1966).

Mikesell, Marvin W. "Geographic Perspectives in Anthropology," pp. 618–622, 627–628, *Annals of the Association of American Geographers,* vol. 57 (1967): 617–634.

Mitra, Panchanana. *A History of American Anthropology,* ch. 9 (Calcutta: University of Calcutta, 1933).

Poirier, Jean. *Histoire de l'ethnologie,* pp. 75–90 (Paris: Presses Universitaires de France, 1969).

Radin, Paul. *The Method and Theory of Ethnology,* ch. 5 (Classics in Anthropology ed.; New York: Basic Books, 1966). Caustic comments on historical reconstruction.

Ray, Verne F. "Cultural Convergence" and "Cultural Parallelism," in *A Dictionary of the Social Sciences* (1964).

Redfield, Margaret Park. "Introduction," in Margaret Park Redfield, ed., *The Social Uses of Social Science* (2 vols.; Chicago: University of Chicago Press, 1962–63).

Riley, Carroll L. "American Historical Anthropology—An Appraisal," in C. L. Riley and Walter W. Taylor, eds., *American Historical Anthropology* (Carbondale: Southern Illinois University Press, 1967).

Schmidt, Wilhelm. *The Culture Historical Method,* trans. S. A. Sieber, pp. 36–69 (New York: Fortuny, 1939). Brief review of American historical ethnology, defensively written by someone often attacked by members of the Tradition.

Simpson, George Eaton. *Melville J. Herskovits,* pp. 10–103 (New York: Columbia University Press, 1973).

Stocking, George W., Jr. "Boas and the Culture Concept in Historical Perspective," *American Anthropologist,* vol. 68 (1966): 867–882.

———. "Introduction: The Basic Assumptions of Boasian Anthropology," in George W. Stocking, Jr., ed., *The Shaping of American Anthropology, 1883–1911* (New York: Basic Books, 1974).

Voget, Fred W. "The History of Cultural Anthropology," pp. 33–35, in John J. Honigmann, ed., *Handbook of Social and Cultural Anthropology* (Chicago: Rand McNally and Company, 1973).

———. *A History of Ethnology,* pp. 317–339, 360–383, 400–411 (New York: Holt, Rinehart and Winston, 1975).

———. "Man and Culture: An Essay in Changing Anthropological Interpretation," *American Anthropologist,* vol. 62 (1960): 943–965.

White, Leslie A., *The Social Organization of Ethnological Theory,* pp. 3–28

(Rice University Studies, vol. 52, no. 4, 1966). Critical appraisal of the "Boas school."

Willey, Gordon R., and Jeremy A. Sabloff, *A History of American Archaeology,* ch. 4 (San Francisco: W. H. Freeman and Co., 1973).

Chapter 7. Radcliffe-Brown and Malinowski

de Waal Malefijt, Annemarie. *Images of Man,* pp. 192–206 (New York: Alfred A. Knopf, 1974).

Gluckman, Max. *Politics, Law and Ritual in Tribal Society,* ch. 1 (Oxford: Basil Blackwell, 1965). Significance of Malinowski and Radcliffe-Brown in breaking with the past.

Goddard, David. "Limits of British Anthropology," *New Left Review,* no. 58 (1969): 79–89. Criticizes the inductive empiricism of social anthropology.

Goldenweiser, Alexander. "Leading Contributions of Anthropology to Social Theory," pp. 470–475, in Harry Elmer Barnes et al., eds., *Contemporary Social Theory* (New York: D. Appleton-Century Co., 1940).

Harris, Marvin. *The Rise of Anthropological Theory,* pp. 514–536, 547–567 (New York: Thomas Y. Crowell Co., 1968).

Hatch, Elvin. *Theories of Man and Culture,* pp. 214–239 and ch. 6 (New York: Columbia University Press, 1973).

Hays, H. R. *From Ape to Angel,* pp. 304–305 and ch. 33 (New York: Alfred A. Knopf, 1958).

Kardiner, Abram, and Edward Preble, *They Studied Man,* pp. 140–162 (Mentor ed.; New York: New American Library, 1961).

Kuper, Adam. *Anthropologists and Anthropology,* chs. 1–2 (London: Allen Lane, 1973).

Lowie, Robert H. *The History of Ethnological Theory,* pp. 221–242 (New York: Rinehart and Company, 1937).

Mandelbaum, Maurice. "Functionalism in Social Anthropology," in Sidney Morgenbesser, Patrick Suppes, and Morton White, eds., *Philosophy, Science, and Method* (New York: St. Martin's Press, 1969). Close study of the integrational and instrumental components of Malinowski's and Radcliffe-Brown's thought.

Mercier, Paul. *Histoire de l'anthropologie,* ch. 4 (Paris: Presses Universitaires de France, 1966).

Pocock, D. F. *Social Anthropology,* pp. 49–83 (London: Sheed and Ward, 1971).

Poirier, Jean. *Histoire de l'ethnologie,* pp. 91–97 (Paris: Presses Universitaires de France, 1969).

Raison, Timothy, ed., *The Founding Fathers of Social Science,* pp. 178–196 (Harmondsworth: Penguin Books, 1969).

Voget, Fred W. "The History of Cultural Anthropology," pp. 28–32, in John J. Honigmann, ed., *Handbook of Social and Cultural Anthropology* (Chicago: Rand McNally and Company, 1973).

———. *A History of Ethnology,* pp. 501–538 (New York: Holt, Rinehart and Winston, 1975).

White, Leslie A. *The Social Organization of Ethnological Theory*, pp. 28–51 (Rice University Studies, vol. 52, no. 4 1966). Critical appraisal of "the school of Radcliffe-Brown."

Chapter 8. Recent Theory

Beals, Ralph L. "Current Trends in the Development of American Ethnology," Anthony F. C. Wallace, ed., *Selected Papers of the Fifth International Congress of Anthropological and Ethnological Sciences* (Philadelphia: University of Pennsylvania Press, 1960).

Beattie, J. H. M. "Contemporary Trends in British Social Anthropology," *Sociologus*, vol. 5 (1955): 1–14. Also see Firth below.

Bianchi, Ugo. *Storia dell' ethnologia*, pp. 135–255 (2nd ed.; Rome: Edizione Abete, 1971). Includes United States developments.

Durbin, Mridula Adenwalla. "Linguistic Models in Anthropology," *Annual Review of Anthropology*, vol. 1 (1972): 383–410.

Eggan, Fred. "One Hundred Years of Ethnology and Social Anthropology," in J. O. Brew, ed., *One Hundred Years of Anthropology* (Cambridge: Harvard University Press, 1968).

Evans-Pritchard, E. E. *Social Anthropology*, chs. 1, 4 (from p. 73), 6 (London: Cohen and West, 1951).

Firth, Raymond. "Function," in William L. Thomas, Jr., ed., *Yearbook of Anthropology—1955* (New York: Wenner-Gren Foundation for Anthropological Research, 1955). Development of the concept in postwar anthropology.

———. "Contemporary British Social Anthropology," *American Anthropologist*, vol. 53 (1951): 474–489. See also Beattie above.

Fortes, Meyer. *Social Anthropology at Cambridge since 1900* (Cambridge: Cambridge University Press, 1953). Sketches the rise of social anthropology and functionalism.

Geller, Ernest. "The Soviet and the Savage," *Times Literary Supplement*, Oct. 18 (1974): 1166–1168. Soviet Russian cultural anthropology.

Gillin, John. *The Ways of Men*, ch. 28 (New York: Appleton-Century-Crofts, 1948). Cultural anthropology in the late 1940s.

Halpern, Joel M., and E. A. Hammel. "Observations on the Intellectual History of Ethnology and Other Social Sciences in Yugoslavia," *Comparative Studies in Society and History*, vol. 11 (1969): 17–26.

Harris, Marvin. *The Rise of Anthropological Theory*, chs. 12–17, 22, 23; also pp. 489–501, 536–546 (New York: Thomas Y. Crowell Co., 1968).

Hays, H. R. *From Ape to Angel*, chs. 32–38 (New York: Alfred A. Knopf, 1958).

Heine-Geldern, Robert. "Recent Developments in Ethnological Theory in Europe," in Anthony F. C. Wallace, ed., *Selected Papers of the Fifth International Congress of Anthropological and Ethnological Sciences* (Philadelphia: University of Pennsylvania Press, 1960).

Hultkrantz, Ake. "Some Remarks on Contemporary European Ethnological Thought," *Ethnologia Europaea*, vol. 1 (1967): 38–44.

Kaplan, David, and Robert J. Manners. *Culture Theory*, pp. 143–150, 181–187 (Englewood Cliffs, N.J.: Prentice-Hall, 1972).

Kardiner, Abram, and Edward Preble. *They Studied Man*, pp. 210–237 (Mentor ed.; New York: New American Library, 1963). Psychodynamics in the study of culture; Kardiner's view.

Kluckhohn, Clyde. "Developments in the Field of Anthropology in the Twentieth Century," *Cahiers d'Histoire Mondiale*, vol. 3 (1956–57): 754–777.

Kuper, Adam. *Anthropologists and Anthropology*, ch. 7 (London: Allen Lane, 1973). French structuralism enters British social anthropology.

Langness, L. L. *The Study of Culture*, chs. 4–5 (San Francisco: Chandler and Sharp Publishers, 1974). Short reviews of cultural materialism, ethnoscience, ethology, and other recent topics.

Leroy, Maurice. *Main Trends in Modern Linguistics*, pp. 49–59, 72–85, 133–140, trans. Glanville Price (Berkeley: University of California Press, 1967). Summarizes de Saussure's posthumous *Cours de linguistique générale* and reviews its influence on structuralism and semantics in linguistics.

Lowie, Robert H. "Contemporary Trends in American Cultural Anthropology," *Sociologus*, vol. 5 (1955): 113–121.

———. "Beiträge zur Völkerkunde Nordamerikas," *Mitteilungen aus dem Museum für Völkerkunde in Hamburg*, vol. 23 (1951): 7–27.

———. *The History of Ethnological Theory*, ch. 14 (New York: Rinehart and Co., 1937).

Mead, Margaret. "Changing Styles of Anthropological Work," *Annual Review of Anthropology*, vol. 2 (1973): 1–26.

Meggers, Betty J. "Recent Trends in American Ethnology," *American Anthropologist*, vol. 48 (1946): 176–214.

Mendelson, E. Michael. "Some Present Trends in Social Anthropology in France," *British Journal of Sociology*, vol. 9 (1958): 251–270.

Mercier, Paul. *Histoire de l'anthropologie*, ch. 4 (Paris: Presses Universitaires de France, 1966).

Mühlmann, Wilhelm. *Geschichte der Anthropologie*, ch. 11 (2nd ed.; Frankfurt am Main: Athenaeum Verlag, 1968).

Nakane, Chie. "Cultural Anthropology in Japan," in *Annual Review of Anthropology*, vol. 3 (1974): 57–72.

Penniman, T. K. *A Hundred Years of Anthropology*, pp. 321–369 (3rd ed.; London: Gerald Duckworth and Co., 1965).

Poirier, Jean. *Histoire de l'ethnologie*, pp. 98–118 (Paris: Presses Universitaires de France, 1969).

———. "Histoire de la pensée ethnologique," in Jean Poirier, ed., *Ethnologie générale* (Paris: Editions Gallimard, 1968). Ethnology in several countries; ideas are often neglected for organizational developments.

Richards, A. I. "African Systems of Thought: An Anglo-French Dialogue," *Man*, vol. 2 (1967): 286–298.

Selby, Henry A. "Continuities and Prospects in Anthropological Studies," pp. 35–45, in Ann Fischer, ed., *Current Directions in Anthropology* (Bulletins of the American Anthropological Association, vol. 3, no. 3, pt. 2, 1970).

Singer, Milton. "A Survey of Culture and Personality Theory and Research," in Bert Kaplan, ed., *Studying Personality Cross-Culturally* (Evanston, Ill.: Row, Peterson and Co., 1961).

Voget, Fred W. "Anthropology and Sociology," in Joseph S. Roucek, ed., *Readings in Contemporary American Sociology* (paperback ed.; Patterson, N.J.: Littlefield, Adams and Co., 1961).

————. *A History of Ethnology*, pp. 411–428, chs. 12–17 (New York: Holt, Rinehart and Winston, 1975).

Willey, Gordon R. "One Hundred Years of American Archaeology," in J. O. Brew, ed., *One Hundred Years of Anthropology* (Cambridge: Harvard University Press, 1968).

Willey, Gordon R., and Jeremy A. Sabloff. *A History of American Archaeology*, chs. 5–6 (San Francisco: W. H. Freeman and Co., 1973).

Wolf, Eric R. *Anthropology*, ch. 1 (Englewood Cliffs, N.J.: Prentice-Hall, 1964).

Chapter 9.   Topics and Issues in Recent Anthropology

Barnes, J. A. *Three Styles in the Study of Kinship* (London: Tavistock Publications, 1971). The styles of Murdock, Lévi-Strauss, and Fortes.

Black, Mary B. "Belief Systems," in John J. Honigmann, ed., *Handbook of Social and Cultural Anthropology* (Chicago: Rand McNally and Company, 1973). Approaches to ideology classified and their history briefly traced.

Brown, Robert M. *Comparative Sociology*, pp. 47–104 (New York: Harcourt, Brace & World, 1967). Theories of descent, grandparenthood, and incest rules.

Dumont, Louis. *Introduction à deux théories d'anthropologie sociale* (Paris: Mouton, 1971). Evans-Pritchard, Lévi-Strauss, and others who have written on descent groups and marital alliance.

Gadamer, Hans-Georg, and Paul Vogler, eds. *Neue Anthropologie*, Band 3, *Sozialanthropologie* (Stuttgart: Georg Thieme Verlag, 1972). Several writers review population, subsistence technology, personal identity, and urbanism as anthropological topics.

————. *Neue Anthropologie*, Band 4, *Kulturanthropologie* (Stuttgart: Georg Thieme Verlag, 1973). Several writers review aesthetics, games, history, law, and other topics in recent anthropology.

Keesing, Roger M. "Theories of Culture," *Annual Review of Anthropology*, vol. 4 (1974): 73–97. Culture conceived of as an adaptive, cognitive, and symbolic system, and as a system of competence.

Kushner, Gilbert, Mickey Gibson, John Gulick, John J. Honigmann, and Richard Nonas. *What Accounts for Sociocultural Change?* (Chapel Hill: Institute for Research in Social Science, University of North Carolina, 1962). A propositional inventory based mainly on works published in the 1950s.

Lanternari, Vittorio. "Nativistic and Socio-religious Movements: A Reconsideration," Comparative Studies in Society and History, vol. 16 (1974): 482–503. A review and an extensive bibliography.

Mead, Margaret. "Some Cultural Anthropological Responses to Technical Assistance Programs," *Social Science Information,* vol. 9 (1970): 49–59.

Mitchell, J. Clyde. "Social Networks," *Annual Review of Anthropology,* vol. 3 (1974): 279–300.

Nash, Dennison, and Ronald Wintrob. "The Emergence of Self-Consciousness in Ethnography," *Current Anthropology,* vol. 13 (1972): 527–542.

Scheffler, Harold W. "Kinship, Descent, and Alliance," in John J. Honigmann, ed., *Handbook of Social and Cultural Anthropology* (Chicago: Rand McNally and Company, 1973). Relates current concepts to earlier work.

Schneider, Harold K. *Economic Man,* ch. 1 (New York: The Free Press, 1974). Summarizes the substantivist-formalist debate and shows divergent views among the formalists.

Voget, Fred W. "The History of Cultural Anthropology," pp. 38–64, in John J. Honigmann, ed., *Handbook of Social and Cultural Anthropology* (Chicago: Rand McNally and Company, 1973).

———. *A History of Ethnology,* chs. 18–20 (New York: Holt, Rinehart and Winston, 1975).

Index

This book has been set in 10 and 9 point Caledonia, leaded 2 points. Chapter numbers are 54 point Palatino italic and chapter titles are 24 point Palatino italic. The size of the type page is 27 by 46½ picas.